ANTIQUES
SOURCE | 2001
BOOK | 2002

Edited and designed for Carlton Books by PAGEOne
Cairn House, Elgiva Lane, Chesham,
Buckinghamshire HP5 2JD

CREATIVE DIRECTOR Bob Gordon
EDITORS Charlotte Stock, Michael Spilling
DESIGNERS Tim Stansfield, Robert Law

PRODUCTION Garry Lewis

ANTIQUES

SOURCE | 2001
BOOK | 2002

The Definitive Annual Guide to Retail
Prices for Antiques and Collectables

MARTIN MILLER

CARLTON

Contents

ACKNOWLEDGEMENTS

GENERAL EDITOR
Martin Miller

EDITORS
Simon Blake
Marianne Blake
Abigail Zoe Martin
Peter Blake

EDITORIAL CO-ORDINATORS
Marianne Blake
Abigail Zoe Martin

PHOTOGRAPHIC/PRODUCTION
CO-ORDINATOR
Marianne Blake

PHOTOGRAPHERS
Abigail Zoe Martin
James Beam Van Etten
Anna Malni
Chris Smailes

How to Use This Book

by Martin Miller

This book is the second full-colour antiques retail price guide published in the United Kingdom, a distinction which possibly deserves a little explanation. I started publishing antiques price guides in 1969 – and they have always been very successful – but one criticism that I have heard is from people saying, rather wistfully, 'I loved the book, but what a pity that everything in it was already sold.' And it was perfectly true, the books were designed more as compilations of information from auction sales which had already taken place than as immediate guides; as reference books rather than handbooks.

The difference with this book is that here we have used retailers, rather than auction houses, as our sources of information. Everything in this book is actually for sale at the time of going to press and many items, certainly some of the more arcane, will remain so for the lifespan of the book. As the introduction explains, a reputable and experienced dealer's assessment of the price of an antique is at least as reliable – and usually a great deal more reasoned – than a price achieved at auction, and so even when the item you wish to purchase from the book turns out to have been sold, you have a reliable guide to the price you should pay when you happen upon another.

The book is designed for maximum visual interest and appeal. It can be treated as a 'through read' as well as a tool for dipping in and out of. The Contents and Index will tell you in which area to find anything which you are specifically seeking, but the collector, enthusiast or interior designer will profit most from reading through a section or several sections and gathering information and inspiration as they go.

Should you happen upon something that you wish to buy, simply note the dealer reference to the bottom right of the entry and look up the dealer's full name and details in the Directory of Dealers section towards the back of the book. You can telephone, fax and, in many cases, visit the dealer's website. All the dealers who have helped us with the book will be happy to assist you and, if the piece you wish to buy has already been sold, they will almost certainly be able to help you find another. Should you wish to sell an item, the relevant section and dealer reference will again be of help, but do not expect to be offered the same price at which the dealer is selling. We all have to make a living!

The price shown against an entry is per item, unless the heading and description refer only to more than one item, a set or a pair. Measurements are always given in the following order, as relevant: height or length; width or diameter; depth.

In each edition of this book, there will be areas of specialization which will carry more emphasis than others. In this issue, Cameras, Chess Sets, Guitars, Books, Maps & Atlases, Taxidermy and Telephones, among others, receive careful scrutiny, while Pewter, for instance, receives less attention, tucked in behind a large section of Silver. As the years go on, balance will be restored and, with low inflation and stabilizing prices, the in-depth information offered on these areas in previous editions will hold its currency, so start your collection.

Good luck and good hunting!

Introduction

A new approach to antiques publishing, tailored to suit the modern antiques marketplace.

The international antiques trade has its roots in the traditional arts but it is constantly growing and transforming, reflecting the current fashions and desires of the day. Buyers and sellers continue to drive the industry, and as the world markets expand, a cornucopia of fresh items of interest are being made available to prospective collectors or buyers.

One of the major influences since the 1970s has been the increase in information available on antiques; the meteoric rise of the Internet has helped to put buyers and sellers in contact with each another. The growth in picture reference books, trade magazines, newspapers, and price guides has all helped to arm the general public with the information required to make a considered purchase. The increase in sources of information is further enhanced by the advent of television programmes and quiz shows along with the explosion of antiques fairs all over the country. These events make a wide range of objects and items available, and help to spread the delight of collecting across a broader audience.

Auction houses have also grown, from the small private sale rooms of the pre-1960s to the ones we see today. As the auction houses have become international, so in turn has the dealer, therefore the antique object has achieved similar status. These objects can become celebrities in their own right as they are catalogued and followed across the world, increasing their provenance, and therefore their value. Not only are auction houses considered a forum for these star pieces, they are also a primary source of information about prices and values, both actual and historical. The price of an item is usually established at auction, and subsequently becomes a barometer for the industry.

Since the nineteenth century art magazines have been of great importance and interest to collectors. They first appeared in France and Germany during the late eighteenth century, but did not achieve any prominence until the mid-nineteenth century. It was at this point, prompted by advances in printing technology, that there emerged a rush of printed information being made available to the public.

In the last couple of decades we have witnessed tremendous development in adult education. Antiques and fine art have become so popular that one can now study history of art, collecting for the future or even the restoration of paintings and furniture. Collectors can take advantage of this development as there are so many courses to choose from –

some last a day or a week, and others are spread out over a year. They all provide an interesting forum to encourage a serious and scholarly interest in collecting.

Nowadays almost every museum, academy or institute has its "Friends". These are fundraising groups which in return for their subscription fees are afforded certain privileges, such as organising lectures and visits which can be beneficial to keen collectors. Some of the largest of these organisations in Britain belong to the Royal Academy, the Victoria and Albert Museum, the Tate Gallery and the Courtauld Institute, which boasts an extensive photographic archive.

Many of Britain's great houses and estates have been opened up by the National Trust, enabling the general public to view great works of art in their natural setting. This, in turn, has stimulated the interest of young and old alike in the world of antiques and fine art. The booklets and pamphlets that these houses supply have become another important source of information for budding collectors.

The antiques industry is a multi-million pound international business and employs many thousands of people throughout the world, from photographers and advertisers, to auction house staff. The transporters of fine works of art and antiques, either for clients, antiques fairs and international exhibitions all help to contribute to the business. The industry also indirectly supports hotels across the world, as modern-day dealers travel further afield. This increased mobility will prompt the rise of the hitherto unknown character, the antiques runner, who will be able to take advantage of the third-generation mobile phones with built-in cameras to relay the details of an item at source to prospective clients. It remains to be seen in the future what effect the Internet will have on the antiques market. It is highly probable that it will enhance the availability and increase the sales of antiques and fine art worldwide.

Antiques dealers and their shops are as varied as the items they sell, and Martin Miller wishes you great fun and success on the antiques trail.

Antiquities

The artefacts of long-dead civilizations have, for centuries, made a fascinating field of study for both the collector and the forger.

From the earliest times, the great Babylonian king Hammurabi (1792 -1750 BC) sent out collectors and spies to seek out artefacts to fill the library in the ancient city of Nebo. To this day, this age-old, universal fascination with collecting and selling pieces of art remains undiminished.

Antiquities have always been popular acquisitions, and, as with all antiques there are forgeries. The world of antiquities has had its fair share of exposure at the forger's hand, but carbon dating has helped to go some way towards combating this problem.

Compared with collectors of other types of artefact, the collector of antiquities tends in general to be far less critical of cracks or imperfections, since it is the rarity and historical importance of the piece that is most significant and contributes to the item's overall value. However, this is not to suggest that the beauty of the object is not also held in high regard.

It is amazing and encouraging to discover that even today for a relatively small sum of money, the astute buyer can still purchase antiquities that were crafted thousands of years ago.

Roman Bronze Lamp ➤
- *1st century BC*
A fine Roman bronze oil lamp with dolphin finial, stylised bird adornment and fan-tail scrolled handle.
- *length 15cm*
- £2,800 • Pars

Byzantine Oil Lamp ◄
- *7th–8th century AD*
Terracotta oil lamp from the Holy Land, with an inscription in Greek around the filling hole.
- *length 11cm*
- £1,000 • Pars

Roman Garnet Ring ➤
- *circa 1st century AD*
A Roman ring with a garnet engraved with a figure of Herakles leaning on his club, with the skin of the Nemean lion draped over his other arm. The original intaglio is set in a new band.
- *diameter 1.5cm*
- £600 • Pars

Egyptian Female Divinity ➤
- *27th Dynasty, 525–404 BC*
The hippopotamus goddess Taurt, shown standing upright on her hind legs. She was the Protectress of childbirth. The amulet is executed in black faience.
- *height 8cm*
- £500 • Pars

Egyptian Sculptured Relief ▼
- *650–30 BC*
A limestone sculptor's model of a male head which has been sculptured in raised relief, from the Late Period to the Ptolemaic Period.
- *14cm x 10.5cm x 2cm*
- £1,500 • Pars

Gold Earrings ▲
- *2nd–3rd century AD*
Gold pendulous earrings, probably Sassanium, from the Zoroastrian Persian Empire.
- *length 7cm*
- £1,000 • Pars

Roman Bronze Figure ▲
- *1st–3rd century AD*
A bronze Roman figure of Jupiter with one arm raised and a cloak draped over his shoulder, mounted on a wooden plinth.
- *height 12cm*
- £2,800 • Pars

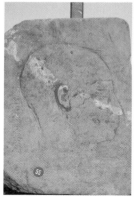

Roman Terracotta Head ◄
- *1st century BC/AD*
A Roman terracotta head of Dionysus showing the god with a full beard and mounted on a wooden plinth.
- *height 10cm*
- £700 • Pars

Anthropomorphic Janus Figure ▲
- *1000 BC*
A Luristan bronze anthropomorphic Janus tube in the form of a stylized human figure.
- *height 12cm*
- £900 • Pars

Luristan Dagger ➤
- *1000 BC*
A Luristan bronze dagger with oval pommel and a pierced hilt, in fine condition with good patination.
- *length 40cm*
- £900 • Yazdani

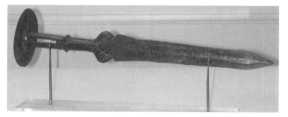

Pair of Urns ➤

- *300 BC*

A pair of urn-shaped South Italian Greek Kantharos, with large elegant handles and hand-painted red figures.
- *height 25cm*
- £4,500   • Pars

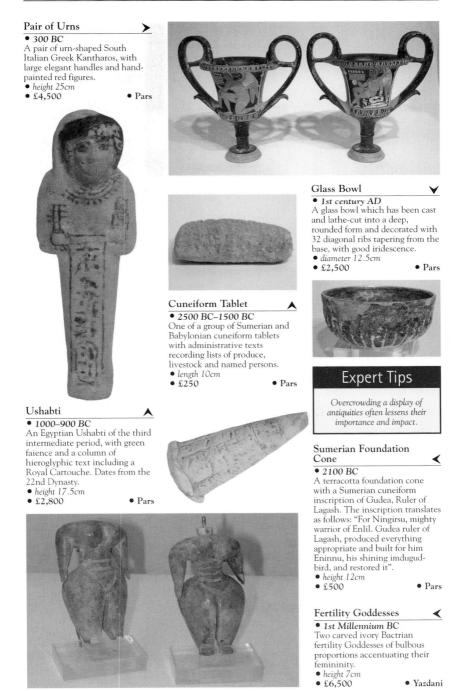

Ushabti ▲

- *1000–900 BC*

An Egyptian Ushabti of the third intermediate period, with green faience and a column of hieroglyphic text including a Royal Cartouche. Dates from the 22nd Dynasty.
- *height 17.5cm*
- £2,800   • Pars

Cuneiform Tablet ▲

- *2500 BC–1500 BC*

One of a group of Sumerian and Babylonian cuneiform tablets with administrative texts recording lists of produce, livestock and named persons.
- *length 10cm*
- £250   • Pars

Glass Bowl ▼

- *1st century AD*

A glass bowl which has been cast and lathe-cut into a deep, rounded form and decorated with 32 diagonal ribs tapering from the base, with good iridescence.
- *diameter 12.5cm*
- £2,500   • Pars

Expert Tips

Overcrowding a display of antiquities often lessens their importance and impact.

Sumerian Foundation Cone ◄

- *2100 BC*

A terracotta foundation cone with a Sumerian cuneiform inscription of Gudea, Ruler of Lagash. The inscription translates as follows: "For Ningirsu, mighty warrior of Enlil. Gudea ruler of Lagash, produced everything appropriate and built for him Eninnu, his shining imdugud-bird, and restored it".
- *height 12cm*
- £500   • Pars

Fertility Goddesses ◄

- *1st Millennium BC*

Two carved ivory Bactrian fertility Goddesses of bulbous proportions accentuating their femininity.
- *height 7cm*
- £6,500   • Yazdani

Roman Bone Doll ▲
- **6th century AD**
A Roman hollow bone doll with articulated arms showing a female figure. Late Roman, early Byzantine period.
- *height 12cm*
- £900   • Pars

Roman Glass Bowl ▲
- **5th century AD**
A pale green late Roman bowl with trailed dark blue concentric rings, and three vertical decorations.
- *8.5cm x 11cm*
- £2,000   • Pars

Glass Aryballos ▼
- **500 BC**
A Greek sand core-formed glass Aryballos with a dark blue ground, yellow line and zigzag pattern over a spherical body. Applied "Duck head" handles.
- *height 13cm*
- £3,800   • Pars

Roman Tar Bottle ▶
- **1st–3rd century AD**
Roman, ribbed-body tear bottle with handle and splaying lip. With good iridescence.
- *height 12cm*
- £680   • Shahdad

Old Babylonian Seal ▼
- **1900–1700 BC**
Cylinder seal, late Old Babylonian, with inscription, "So meeting, Beane son of Warad, Amoro servant of Amoro".
- *height 7cm*
- £700   • Pars

Sassanian Earrings ▲
- **7th century AD**
Late Roman, Sassanian earrings in the form of flat, semicircular bases with three garnets, the whole in solid gold.
- £1,500   • Pars

Amuletic Rings ▼
- **1470–750BC**
Two faience amuletic rings. The oval panels have moulded designs under a turquoise glaze.
- *length 1.5cm*
- £3,000   • Pars

Pilgrim Flask ▼
- *6th–7th century AD*

A terracotta pilgrim flask with spiral decoration to the body and double handles to the shoulders.
- *height 17cm*
- £600 • Pars

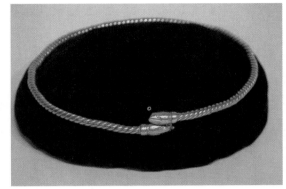

Gold Bracelet ▲
- *3rd century AD*

A Roman gold bracelet, with the terminals styled as serpents' heads mounted on a coiled hoop.
- *diameter 10cm*
- £2,800 • Pars

Byzantine Flask ◄
- *7th century AD*

Light green Byzantine hexagonal flask with iridescence, mould blown. Each side decorated with early Christian iconography.
- *height 22cm*
- £6,000 • Pars

Bull Oil Vessel ▲
- *circa 1000 BC*

Amlash Persian pottery bull oil vessel, on four legs with head upright and pronounced horns and hump.
- *height 22cm*
- £3,000 • Shiraz

Luristan Axe Head ▼
- *1000 BC*

A Luristan bronze axe head from Western Iran with good patination and in perfect condition.
- *length 18cm*
- £450 • Pars

Neolithic Stone Flint ▲
- *3600–2500BC*

A large flint arrow head from Denmark, 18cm long and a large polished flint axe.
- *length 16cm/axe*
- £750 • Pars

Cat Head ▲
- *Roman Period*
  1st Century AD

An Egyptian mummified cat head with polychrome painted features mounted on a metal shaft.
- *length 14cm*
- £5,500 • Pars

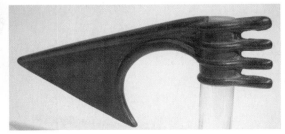

Architectural &
Garden Furniture

Television coverage and the revival of all things Victorian have led to a boom in what used to be regarded as builders' scrap.

Architectural antiques have risen greatly in value and are a must for any designer, whether in the home or the garden. Their desirability is compounded further as house owners and builders strive to upgrade older houses. From the rag and bone man of old to the modern day architectural dealer there are now specialists who will stock the contents of anything from a Victorian terraced to a Palladian villa.

In recent years the garden has gained in profile, becoming an outdoor room and with it the demand for period garden furniture, statues, urns, lead and iron works has increased to the point that it has outstripped supply. The market has responded by producing some very competent reproductions.

The level of demand has meant that many houses on the European Continent have been stripped for their finely carved doors, fireplaces, stone reliefs, floorboards and just about anything else that might enhance a country kitchen, Baroque dining hall or even a modern loft conversion in the city.

Lead Water Feature ▼
- *circa 1880*

A very fine quality Victorian lead water feature of a child holding a goose.
- *height 60cm*
- **£2,350**   • Drummonds

Stone Gargoyles ▲
- *19th century*

Pair of stone Gargoyles in excellent condition.
- *height 70cm*
- **£3,650**   • Drummonds

Stone Torso ▼
- *circa 1920*

A French stone statue of the torso and thighs of a woman, with attention to form.
- *height 1.5m*
- **£3,600**   • Drummonds

Marble Statue ▼
- *circa 1880*
Victorian marble statue of a young boy naturalistically poised on a circular base. In excellent condition.
- *height 102cm*
- **£5,400**   • Drummonds

Statue of Neptune ▼
- *circa 1765*
A finely carved standing stone figure of the god Neptune in traditional pose, with broken hand.
- *height 205cm*
- **£4,850**   • Drummonds

Pair of Urns ▶
- *1880*
An ornate pair of urns with floral garland carved out of stone.
- *height 1.5m*
- **£3,400**   • Drummonds

Expert Tips

When purchasing any terracotta objects make sure you look beyond the surface to see if there are any cracks beneath the grimey exterior. When buying second-hand roof tiles make sure you have seen the whole batch before you purchase, as often some of them may be cracked, damaged, or discoloured. Make sure your expensive or rare garden furniture is well secured or alarmed, and adequately insured.

Indian Rosewood Doors ▲
- *18th century*
A pair of rosewood grain doors from Kerala, South India. Includes a splendid ornate ironwork lock.
- *167cm x 64cm*
- **£920**   • Gordon Reece

Cast-Iron Lamp Stand ▲
- *circa 1890*
Pair of Victorian cast iron ornamental lamp posts. With pierced and moulded leaf decoration, the whole surmounted by moulded glass shades.
- *height 195cm*
- **£3,725**   • Drummonds

Terracotta Urns ▲
- *circa 1880*
One of a pair of Victorian deep red terracotta urns with carved floral swags on Corinthian columns.
- *height 180cm*
- **£3,800**   • Drummonds

Christening Font ▼

- *circa 1930*

An unusual 20th century carved stone christening font in the Fothic style with octagonal oak lid from a church in Farnham Surrey.

- *height 130cm*
- £1,950 • Drummonds

Sandstone Finials ▼

- *circa 1880*

A pair of finely carved Victorian sandstone finials with moulded decoration on a square base.

- *height 96cm*
- £1,250 • Drummonds

Cast-Iron Stove ▼

- *circa 1880*

A fine French castiiron stove, highly decorated with fan-shaped motif and scrolled decoration to legs, and "Pied Selle Noel" inscription. Original condition and fine patina.

- *58cm x 52cm*
- £340 • Drummonds

Victorian Corbels ▲

- *circa 1840*

A Victorian terracotta corbel, used in the support of a projecting ledge. With acanthus leaf and scrolled decoration to surface, and architectural mouldings to sides.

- *height 40cm*
- £85 • Drummonds

Decorated Urns ▲

- *18th century*

A pair of eighteenth century highly decorative, ornate sandstone urns with lids. Decorated with a swags of flowers and heads in excellent condition.

- *height 190cm*
- £1,475 • Drummonds

Roofing Finials ▲
- *Circa 1890*
Victorian terracotta roofing
finials, with trademark "RCR".
- *height 18cm*
- £220   • Drummonds

Fire Surround ▼
- *circa 1830*
An impressive Victorian Scottish
baronial stone fireplace, the
whole on two carved stone
pillasters.
- *190cm x 125cm*
- £9,200   • Drummonds

Marble Fire Surround ◄
- *1890*
A Victorian English fire surround
from white statutory marble with
supporting classical figures on
each side.
- *160cm x 150cm*
- £30,000   • Drummonds

Stone Angel ▼
- *19th century*
Italian statue of a cherub
embracing a pillar.
- £495   • Rainbow Antiques

French Planter ▼
- *circa 1880*
A French dual-lacquered planter
with drawer to front.
- *80cm x 50cm*
- £850   • Tredantiques

Stone Bench ◄
- *1860*
Stone bench with lead frieze,
including allegorical figures of
above average size. Formerly
belonged to Lloyd George.
- *121cm x 185cm x 61cm*
- £9,598   • Drummonds

Victorian Fire Fender ▼

- *1830*

A Victorian cast-iron fire fender in the Jacobean style with ball and finial decoration.
- *176cm x 42cm*
- £3,500   • Old World

George III Steel Fender ▲

- *1800*

A George III steel fender with brass claw feet.
- *21cm x 113cm x 26cm*
- £950   • Old World

Regency Fender ▼

- *1800*

A Regency serpentine steel fender, with urns and floral swag pierced decoration.
- *12cm x 102cm x 12cm*
- £750   • Old World

Fire Place ◄

- *1750*

Stove Carron foundry designed by Robert Adam, cast by Oldham of London for George III when he was Prince of Wales. Reputed to have come from Carlton House.
- *175cm x 40cm*
- £25,000   • Old World

Stone Window ▼

- *17th century*

An Indian Mogul window of red sandstone with a central lattice panel, and floral decoration to side panels and borders.
- *109cm x 69cm*
- £5,800   • Gordon Reece

Garden Lantern ▼

- *1920*

An oval wirework Chinoiserie garden lantern, lined with decorative parchment on a circular wooden base.
- *height 60cm*
- £210   • Myriad

Expert Tips

Check that an antique fireplace is genuine as there are many good reproductions around.

Grangemouth Terracotta Urn ▼

- *circa 1870*
A Victorian urn in biscuit terracotta from the Grangemouth Pottery in Scotland. Carved in relief with flowers and leaves.
- *height 150cm*
- £2,950
- Drummonds

Victorian Terracotta Urn ▼

- *circa 1880*
A fine Victorian terracotta urn with heavily carved floral swags.
- *height 240cm*
- £1,880
- Drummonds

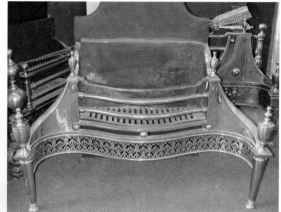

Fire Basket ▲

- *1760*
A serpentine-fronted Adam grate with pierced floral decoration and brass urn finials on conical legs.
- *90cm x 91cm x 43cm*
- £6,000
- Old World

Pair of Victorian Lions ▲

- *circa 1890*
A fine pair of Victorian fire clay lions from the Nurford fire clay works of Kilmarnock.
Produced by A. & G. Craig of Hillhead Kilmarnock, from a design by J. Neil of rare black fire clay.
- *74cm x 100cm*
- £8,250
- Drummonds

Fire Grate ◄

- *early 20th century*
Early twentieth-century fire grate after the style of Adam, originally from Reim castle in Perth, Scotland.
- *64cm x 140cm*
- £815
- Drummonds

Brass Sundial ▲

- *circa 1880*
A Victorian rustic sandstone sundial with a brass dial.
- *height 88cm*
- £285
- Tredantiques

Cast-Iron Garden Seat ▲

- *circa 1870*
An unusually attractive Victorian double-sided cast-iron seat.
Painted white with a floral design.
In original condition.
- *length 200cm*
- £1,690
- Drummonds

Copper Container ▼

• *1915*

A very unusual large copper container which was originally used as a dying vat for military uniforms and is now converted into a bath.

• £15,000 • Drummonds

Pair of Fruitwood Urns ▼

• *1770*

A pair of fine French Louis XV fruitwood urns adorned with gilt foliate and flowers, banded with ornamental gilt flowers and tassels.

• *92cm x 32cm*
• £5,500 • O.F. Wilson

Butcher's Block ➤

• *1920*

Unique French pine and beech butcher's block from the 1920s, with good patina.

• *110cm x 130cm*
• £1,625 • Drummonds

Ram's Head ▲

• *circa1850*

A pair of fine limestone Victorian wall masks, naturalistically carved, depicting a ram's head with resplendent horns. Both shown with good patina and weathering.

• *height 38cm*
• £3,950 • Drummonds

Japanese Lantern ➤

• *circa 1890*

A Victorian carved granite decorative Japanese-style lantern. Free standing.

• *height 180cm*
• £3,950 • Drummonds

Fire Basket ▲

• *1810*

A George III serpentine basket grate with urn finials on tapered legs with an apron.

• *82cm x 88cm x 38cm*
• £5,500 • Old World

Chimney Pot ▼
- *19th century*
A glazed terracotta chimney pot. With banding and fluted design around the neck tapering to a square chamfered base.
- *125cm x 30cm*
- £80 • Old School

Carved Shutters ▼
- *early 19th century*
A pair of carved shutters with Oriental paintwork.
- *74cm x 106cm*
- £425 • Gordon Reece

Coal Scuttle ▲
- *circa 1890*
English cast-iron coal scuttle with lion's head surrounded by heavily moulded edging.
- *45cm x 51xm*
- £295 • Drummonds

Park Bench ▼
- *1940s*
English garden seat with scrolled arm rests in original condition.
- *184cm x 88cm x 69cm*
- £299 • Old School

Lion Mask ◄
- *1800*
An iron lion mask with terracotta patination.
- *diameter 35cm*
- £250 • R. Conquest

Mahogany Jardinière ▼
- *1760*
A George III mahogany jardinière with carved apron.
- *length 70cm*
- £2,950 • Dial Post House

Elmwood Planter ◄
- *1850*
Elmwood planter with brass inlay.
- *length 30cm*
- £1,950 • Dial Post House

Marble Fireplace ▼

- *1887*

Victorian black marble chimney piece with double marble columns, pierced iron grate and foliate moulded decoration,
- *height 198cm*
- **£8,700**   • Drummonds

Pair of Folding Chairs ▼

- *early 19th century*

A pair of folding metal and wood green garden chairs.
- **£80**   • Old School

Wood-Burning Stove ▼

- *1910*

Cast-iron wood-burning stove with decorated top, made by G. Portway & Son of Halsted in Essex, model No. 6 Tortoise.
- *height 105cm*
- **£1,475**   • Drummonds

Road Sign ▼

- *1890*

A cast-iron road sign with the street name "Athol Road". With raised black lettering on a white background in original condition
- *112cm x 19cm*
- **£150**   • Old School

Fire Surround Picture
for Fire Back ▲

- *circa 1770*

Medieval fire surround and fire back with Fleur de Lys to the top on the right, and the cross of Lorraine. The whole surrounded by crowns of the Union of Families.
- *135cm x 140cm*
- **£1,200**   • Drummonds

French Fire Back ▲

- *circa 1780*

Louis XVI fire back with central lozenge of Fleur de Lys crowned and supported by trumpeting cherubs.
- *74cm x 67cm*
- **£970**   • Drummonds

Waywiser ▲

- *1890*

Late nineteenth century iron spoked waywiser for measuring distance.
- *height 108cm*
- **£11,000** • Langfords Marine

Panelled Door ▼

- *18th century*

A superb panelled door with imagery embracing hunting and mythology with wild and fantasy beasts. From the Gono region.
- *165cm x 95cm*
- £2,600   • Gordon Reece

Gothic Revival Niches ▲

- *1880*

One of a pair of Victorian Gothic niches, having heavily carved Bathstone, with foliate design and leaf decoration terminating to a Fleur de Lys finial.
- *height 140cm*
- £1,450   • Drummonds

Fire Grate ▲

- *1805*

A fine George III cast-iron fire grate of the Regency period. Includes pierced and moulded decoration.
- *125cm x 130 cm*
- £4,600   • Drummonds

Cast-Iron Fire Back ▲

- *circa 1880*

An impressive Victorian cast-iron fire back, depicting Neptune with mythical sea creatures and scallop shell decoration with scrolled border.
- *75cm x 60cm*
- £1,350   • Drummonds

Second Empire Spiral Flight ▼

- *1863*

A romantic French Louis Philippe Second Empire spiral flight, floor-to-floor walnut with fine cast iron decorative spinales.
- *height 620cm*
- £25,750   • Drummonds

Bronze Urns ▼

- *19th century*

Pair of large bronze ormolu tazzas on marble bases.
- *height 36cm*
- £3,950   • O.F. Wilson

Fire Surround ◄

- *1650*

A fine statutory marble fire surround from Warwick Castle depicting a classical allegorical frieze with chorus sea horses and mermaids playing with musical instruments.
- *180cm x 200cm*
- £585,000   • Drummonds

Regency Fender ◄
- *1800*
A Regency steel fender standing on claw feet.
- *22cm x 124cm x 26cm*
- £600   • Old World

Carved Heads ►
- *circa 1880*
Victorian ecclesiastical-style carved stone corbel. Designed to hold roof trusses.
- £750   • Drummonds

Bronze Statue ▲
- *1880*
A very fine bronze statue of a boy.
- *height 140cm*
- £14,250   • Drummonds

Victorian Stone Frieze ▼
- *circa 1890*
Victorian carved stone frieze surround, depicting cherubs with allegorical animals.
- *length 320cm*
- £5,800   • Drummonds

Teak Planter ▲
- *circa 1870*
A carved Burmese teak planter.
- *height 95cm*
- £685   • Tredantiques

Arms & Armour

From suits of English Civil War armour, through early firearms, edged weapons and World War II medals, the collection of militaria remains a fascination.

The art of war and its history has fascinated people throughout the ages. The weapons used often embodied the status of the warrior, from a finely chased pistol to a beautifully engraved sword or a purposeful infantryman dagger. These were later arranged into fine displays that dressed the halls of large country houses, but unfortunately these collections were all too often broken up and sold. The important factor with almost all militaria lies in the condition of the item, none more so than with Japanese weapons – the blade, as

with the lacquer must be in fine condition.

The film industry and theatre would be at a loss without the collector, dealer and museum collections along with their knowledge of military history. The history and the stories behind personal weapons, guns, swords, medals, badges and uniforms drive the interest of the collector. This interest also extends to cards, prints and oil paintings.

A love of fine craftsmanship combined with the strange beauty found in weapons of destruction ensure that militaria will be popular for many years to come.

Flintlock Pistols ➤
- *1840*

A pair of flintlock pistols heavily inlaid with chasing. Made in France in the mid-nineteenth century, specifically for export to the Middle East.
- £750   • Chelsea (OMRS)

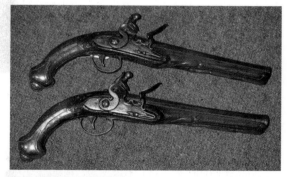

World War I Binoculars ▼
- *1917*

A pair of military binoculars dated 1917, with leather carrying case inscribed with the name of a soldier serving with the Highland Light Infantry.
- *length 18cm*
- £115   • Chelsea (OMRS)

Welsh Guards Bearskin ▲
- *1980*

An NCO's bearskin from the Welsh Guards regiment, showing plumed insignia and brass retaining strap. This headgear is current issue.
- *height 64cm*
- £585   • Chelsea (OMRS)

Paper Rack ▲
- *1940*

A paper rack from World War II, hand-crafted and scrolled in wrought iron and mounted on a splay-footed stand constructed of pieces of collected shrapnel.
- *height 46cm*
- £100   • Chelsea (OMRS)

Great War Picture Frame ▼

- **1917**

A World War I picture frame
made from the tip of a wooden
aeroplane propellor blade and
mounted on a mahogany stand,
showing the photograph of a
uniformed nurse from the period.
- **£45**   • Chelsea (OMRS)

World War II RAF Cap ▲

- **1940**

A Royal Air Force warrant
officer's uniform cap dating from
the beginning of World War II.
- **£85**   • Chelsea (OMRS)

Boer War Two Pound Shell Case ▲

- **1900**

A Boer War two-pound "Pom
Pom" artillery shell case, in brass
with projectile head in place but
powder and percussion cap
removed.
- *length 20cm*
- **£15**   • Chelsea (OMRS)

English Copper Powder Flask ▲

- *circa 1800*

An English copper powder flask,
used for the storage of powder
for guns.
- *length 12cm*
- **£180**   • Holland & Holland

Scottish Powder Flask ▲

- *circa 1800*

A Scottish powder flask,
embossed with a shell pattern.
- *length 20cm*
- **£180**   • Holland & Holland

Tin of Boer War Chocolate ▲

- **1900**

A hinged metal tin from the Boer
War, originally containing
chocolate and showing the royal
crest, the profile of Queen
Victoria, the inscription "South
Africa 1900" and a signed
message in the Queen's
handwriting wishing the
recipient, "A happy new year".
- *19cm x 11cm*
- **£145**   • Chelsea (OMRS)

Expert Tips

*Weapons must be cleaned very
carefully in order to maintain
them, and should be stored in a
dry, well-ventilated place.
Always wear cotton gloves
when handling fine weapons
and armour to prevent the
formation of rust deposits.*

World War II German Red Cross Dagger ▲

- *World War II*

A World War II German red
cross man's "heuer" dress dagger,
with serrated edge and blood
gutter.
- *length 30cm*
- **£375**   • Chelsea (OMRS)

Breech-Loading Cannon ➤
- *1880*

Rare bronze breech-loading cannon on oak stand by Astley.
- *length 120cm*
- £15,000
- Holland & Holland

Lifeguard Boots ▲
- *1950s*

A pair of post-World War II dress boots of a trooper from the Royal Regiment of Lifeguards.
- *height 43cm*
- £150 • Chelsea (OMRS)

Japanese Stirrups ▲
- *19th century*

Pair of bronze Japanese stirrups, with red leather interior from the Tokugawa period.
- *width 12cm*
- £895 • Japanese Gallery Ltd

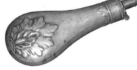

Copper Powder Flask ▲
- *circa 1800*

Copper powder flask with decoration.
- *length 38cm*
- £180 • Holland & Holland

German Sailor's Jacket ▲
- *1939*

A German naval rating's summer tunic from the beginning of World War II, with insignia.
- £100 • Chelsea (OMRS)

British Army Sword ▼
- *1920*

A post-World War I officer's dress sword belonging to an officer of the Royal Army Service Corps. The sword in steel with brass hilt and the scabbard in highly polished tan leather.
- *length 92cm*
- £185 • Chelsea (OMRS)

Great War Commemorative Frame ▲
- *circa 1918*

A World War I commemorative picture frame in bronze, modelled as a relief map of France and Belgium, with a circular glass portal displaying the photograph of a soldier.
- *height 16cm*
- £85 • Chelsea (OMRS)

WWII German Airforce Tunic ▲
- *1940*

A flight blouse of a German airforce signals section, from the Battle of Britain period, complete with insignia and collar flashes.
- £395 • Chelsea (OMRS)

29

Islamic Stirrups ▲

● *17th century*
A pair of bronze Islamic stirrups which are finely engraved with floral designs.
● *height 15cm*
● £150   ● Ghaznavid

French Fireman's Helmet ▲

● *1895*
A highly ornate late nineteenth century brass French fireman's helmet, complete with red feather plume.
● £225   ● Chelsea (OMRS)

World War II RAF Ashtray ▼

● *World War II*
An aluminum ashtray made from the piston of a Rolls Royce Merlin engine. Includes RAF emblem and Churchill dedication.
● *diameter 31cm*
● £25   ● Chelsea (OMRS)

Girl's Hitler Youth Uniform ➤

● *circa 1940*
A blouson from a girl's uniform of the Hitler Youth, dating from the beginning of World War II and emblazoned with the insignia of the National Socialist party.
● *length 34cm*
● £150   ● Chelsea (OMRS)

World War II German Paratrooper's Helmet ◄

● *1944*
A World War II paratrooper's helmet with single German airforce emblem, carrying decal camouflage painted for Normandy.
● £2,000   ● Chelsea (OMRS)

British SAS Uniform ▼

● *1990*
A British SAS sergeant's uniform and medals for the Falklands and Gulf War period (medals are replacements).
● £250   ● Chelsea (OMRS)

Expert Tips

Good period armour is very rare and complete suits are usually found in a great collection. If you see a complete suit it is likely to be nineteenth century. Never contemplate sharpening a sword as this will almost certainly render it worthless. Leave this to the specialists.

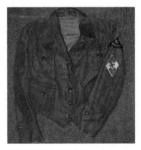

Victorian Pioneers Sword ▼

● *1890*
A late Victorian side-arm sword with sheath, the blade in steel and the hilt in brass, with the sheath mounted in brass and leather. From the Regiment of Pioneers.
● *length 58cm*
● £200   ● Chelsea (OMRS)

Commemorative Scroll ▼
- *World War II*
A World War II illuminated
memorial scroll for Driver L.S.D.
Butcher who was killed in action
during the North African
campaign.
- *38cm x 20cm*
- £25 • Chelsea (OMRS)

World War II Flying Helmet ▲
- *1944*
A World War II RAF "C" type
flying helmet with intrinsic radio
earpieces and MK VIII goggles
with webbing strap and H-type
oxygen mask for high altitude.
- £185 • Chelsea (OMRS)

German Naval Artillery Forage Cap ▲
- *1942*
A German Naval Coastal
Artillery soldier's forage cap in
field grey wool, from World War
II. With badge and insignia.
- £140 • Chelsea (OMRS)

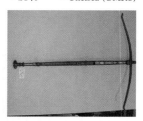

Korean War Pilot's Helmet ▼
- *1950*
A fighter pilot's helmet, Soviet-
made for a MiG fighter, used by
a North Korean pilot in the
Korean War.
- £150 • Chelsea (OMRS)

Royal Engineers Officer's Tunic ▲
- *1914*
An officer's full dress tunic of the
Royal Engineers, in scarlet,
dating from the beginning of
World War I.
- £185 • Chelsea (OMRS)

Inlaid Crossbow ▲
- *17th century*
English cross bow with bone
inlay.
- *62cm x 52cm*
- £1800 • Peter Bunting

Wall Plaque ◄
- *circa 1880*
A mahogany wall plaque of the
2nd Punjab Regiment
commemorating the service of
Lt. Col. J.F. Pear. The plaque has
a moulded edge with inlaid brass
lettering and regimental insignia.
- *27cm x 50cm*
- £65 • Chelsea (OMRS)

31

Miniature Cavalry Helmet ▲
• *1920*
A one third-sized cavalry helmet of the 2nd County of London Yeomanry, with purple horse-hair plume. Possibly made as an officer's desk ornament.
• £450   • Chelsea (OMRS)

German Navy Forage Cap ▲
• *1942*
A World War II German navy sailor's forage cap.
• £120   • Chelsea (OMRS)

Copper Powder Flask ▲
• *20th Century*
Powder flask with copper body and brass mounts.
• *length 17cm*
• £180   • Holland & Holland

Dress Busby ➤
• *1916*
A dress Busby with white plume and brass fittings and chin strap, showing insignia of the Royal Engineers and dating from World War I.
• *height 33cm*
• 275   • Chelsea (OMRS)

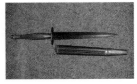

World War II Commando Knife ▲
• *1944*
A World War II British Commando fighting knife in steel and brass, complete with scabbard.
• *length 30cm*
• £85   • Chelsea (OMRS)

Victorian Naval Dirk ▼
• *1890*
A late-Victorian naval midshipman's dirk or shortsword, with ribbed brass hilt and filigreed brass sheath.
• *length 60cm*
• £325   • Chelsea (OMRS)

German Officer's Cap ◄
• *1940*
A World War II German army senior cavalry officer's peaked cap, with silver braid, badge and insignia.
• £325   • Chelsea (OMRS)

World War I Dagger ▼
• *World War I*
A World War I German fighting knife by "Ern". Has a studded wooden handle and is complete with a leather and steel sheath.
• *length 70cm*
• £70   • Chelsea (OMRS)

Sword Hilt Candlestick ▲
- *Victorian*

A Victorian infantry officer's brass sword hilt with ribbing, made into a candlestick. Mounted on a splay-legged tripod stand, also in brass.
- £150   ● Chelsea (OMRS)

World War I German Sweetheart Brooch ▲
- *1917*

A World War I German Eindekker sweetheart's brooch in the shape of a monoplane, with a German cross insignia attached by a chain. In original box with inscription in gold print.
- *length 3.8cm*
- £1,917   ● Chelsea (OMRS)

Expert Tips

When collecting firearms always ask for a proof certificate, either for black powder or modern charges. The three bywords for any collector are condition, quality and rarity.

Old Bill Mascot ▼
- *1920*

A bronze car mascot mounted on a wooden base of Bruce Bairnsfather's "Old Bill" character.
- £200   ● Chelsea (OMRS)

German Dagger ▲
- *1937*

A pre-war Third Reich Brownshirt's dress dagger, made by Friedrich Geigis. Complete with scabbard and nickel fittings; showing insignia.
- *length 30cm*
- £225   ● Chelsea (OMRS)

Silver Regimental Spoon ▲
- *World War I*

A silver regimental teaspoon showing the ornate crest of the London Rifle Brigade, topped with a crown.
- *length 9cm*
- £25   ● Chelsea (OMRS)

Grenadier Guards Cap ▲
- *circa 1940*

A World War II period Grenadier Guards peaked dress cap, with regimental cap badge insignia.
- £40   ● Chelsea (OMRS)

World War I "Brodie" Helmet ▼
- *1917*

A British army second type "Brodie" steel helmet, from the latter part of World War I, complete with adjustable leather strap.
- £75   ● Chelsea (OMRS)

Army Officer's Home Service Helmet ▲

- *Edwardian*

A Royal West Kent Regiment officer's blue cloth home service helmet, with brass insignia and embellishments including spiked finial top.

- £450   • Chelsea (OMRS)

World War I German Helmet Badge ▲

- *1914*

The helmet badge of a Prussian soldier from the beginning of World War I, with the crowned eagle of the emperor and the inscription, "Mitt Gott fur Koenig und Vaterland".

- *height 9cm*
- £50   • Chelsea (OMRS)

Cigarette Gift Tin ➤

- *1914*

An example of a gift tin sent by Queen Mary to the troops fighting in France for the first Christmas of World War I. Complete with photographs, monogrammed cigarettes and all the original contents.

- *18cm x 11cm*
- £125   • Chelsea (OMRS)

Child's Replica Guard's Uniform ▼

- *1936*

A child's replica uniform with the insignia of a lieutenant and complete with medals, brass buttons and cuffs.

- £250   • Chelsea (OMRS)

World War II German Army Helmet ▼

- *1940*

A World War II German army 1935 pattern helmet with single army decal. With evocative bullet hole sustained in battle.

- £175   • Chelsea (OMRS)

German Pilot's Log Books ▲

- *1936–1939*

Completed pilot's log books covering the years 1936 to 1939. Details the flights taken by a German pilot.

- £175   • Chelsea (OMRS)

World War I German Helmet ▲

- *1916*

A World War I camouflaged German army helmet of 1916 design, with original camouflage paint and chinstrap fittings.

- £200   • Chelsea (OMRS)

Automobilia

Motor cars are still seen as extremely romantic objects, harking back to a time when there really was an open road.

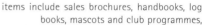

The love of the motor car has never diminished; we can still be seduced by the open road, the sound of the exhaust, the gleaming bonnet or hood, and the inspiring names of the famous makes. Driving a vintage car epitomises this feeling; it also has its perks as vintage car owners pay a lower rate of motor insurance and are exempted from paying road tax. While the cost of buying a vintage car can often be beyond our means, the memorabilia is very affordable. Collector's items include sales brochures, handbooks, log books, mascots and club programmes, and of course anything belonging to the famous drivers of the past and present.

Toy cars and the plastic model kits are still popular, and the interest in car memorabilia does not stop there, but continues as far as the factory gates, with some enthusiasts formiing collections of petrol station pumps, brands of oil, posters and even forecourt signs. In response to this interest car auctions and autojumbles are held regularly throughout the country.

Rolls Royce Pedal Car ▼
- 1980–90
A 12-volt, electric powered Sharna Rolls Royce Corniche convertible made by Tri-Ang.
- *122cm x 53cm*
- **£700** • C.A.R.S

Bugatti Pedal Car ▲
- *late 1920s*
A Bugatti Eureka made in France. Two-seater replica of the type 35 Grand Prix Sports with very fine chrome and leather detailing.
- *165cm x 56cm*
- **£3,500** • C.A.R.S

Tri-Ang Convertible ▲
- *mid 1960s*
A plastic Rolls Royce convertible with chrome detailing, made by Tri-Ang.
- *122cm x 46cm*
- **£650** • C.A.R.S

Expert Tips

Collecting brochures of new motor cars could be a wise investment for the future, since this kind of memorabilia increases in value.

Pedal Car ◄
- 1980–90
A Tri-Ang Sharna Rolls Royce Corniche convertible. Pedal-powered car in plastic.
- *122cm x 53cm*
- **£500** • C.A.R.S

Bentley Pedal Car ▲
- *mid 1960s*
A Tri-Ang Bentley continental
convertible. Plastic body with
chrome detailing.
- *122cm x 46cm*
- **£950**   • C.A.R.S

Jaguar Pedal Car ▲
- *1950s–mid 1960s*
A Jaguar XK-120 open Roadster.
Fibreglass body with chrome
detailing, pedal powered car.
- *length 150cm, width 53cm*
- **£950**   • C.A.R.S

Morgan Pedal Car ▼
- *1980*
A Morgan 4/4 Roadster with a
fibreglass body and chrome
detailing, and has working
headlights and horn.
- *122cm x 50cm*
- **£950**   • C.A.R.S

Ford Pedal Car ▼
- *Early 1960s*
A Tri-Ang Ford Zephyr-style
police car with working siren and
chrome detailing.
- *84cm x 36cm*
- **£300**   • C.A.R.S

Fire Truck Pedal Car ▼
- *1940*
An American fire truck replica
from the 1940s period. A pedal-
powered car with very fine
chrome detailing.
- *96cm x 38cm*
- **£200**   •C.A.R.S

Massiot Locomotive ▲
- *1900*
Locomotive by Radiguet Massiot.
- *39cm x 42cm*
- **£1,900**   • Langfords Marine

Speed Award Badge ▲
- *1920–1930*
A Brookland's B.A.R.C. 130mph
speed award badge. Converted to
a trophy with enamelled
decoration, showing cars banking
round the Brookland's circuit.
- *height 16cm*
- **£3,500**   • C.A.R.S

Chrysler Pedal Car ▲
- *late 1920s*
An American-made Chrysler
"Airflow" with an all-pressed
steel body and chrome detailing.
Built by Steelcraft.
- *120cm x 55cm*
- **£3,000**   • C.A.R.S

Japanese Cadillac ▲
- *1950*
A tin-plate Japanese 50s Marysan Cadillac, cream and green with working lights. Forward and reverse, very rare, in original box.
- *length 30cm*
- **£250** • Langfords Marine

Zephyr/Zodiac Pedal Car ▲
- *mid 1950s*
A Tri-Ang Zephyr/Zodiac with a pressed-steel body and chrome detailing.
- *115cm x 42cm*
- **£650** • C.A.R.S

Wolesley Pedal Car ▲
- *late 1950s*
A Tri-Ang pressed-steel bodied model of a Wolesley with chrome detailing and working headlights.
- *105cm x 43cm*
- **£450** • C.A.R.S

Moscouich Pedal Car ▲
- *early 1980s–mid 1990s*
A Moscouich pressed-steel pedal car with working lights and horn.
- *109cm x 44cm*
- **£350** • C.A.R.S

Pedal Fire Truck ▲
- *early 1920s*
An American-made fire truck with fine detailing. Wooden ladder with mascot on bonnet.
- *105cm x 52cm*
- **£3,500** • C.A.R.S

F3 Racing Pedal Car ▼
- *early 1970s*
A Tri-Ang plastic-bodied F3 racing car with dummy rear engine.
- *122cm x 63cm*
- **£150** • C.A.R.S

Brookland's Badge ▲
- *1920*
A Brookland's B.A.R.C 120mph speed award badge.
- *height 13cm*
- **£3,000** • C.A.R.S

Expert Tips
Rolls Royce's success with the Schneider Trophy led the company to offer models of the Supermarine S.6B aeroplane and an alternative to the Spirit of Ecstasy.

MG Pedal Car ▼
- *1950s*
An MG TD pedal-powered car with a fibreglass body and chrome detailing.
- *122cm x 51cm*
- **£650** • C.A.R.S

Books, Maps & Atlases

Most books are more prized for their binding than their contents. Where the contents were most prized, the print dealers have usually benefitted.

The word "book" is derived from the word "bark", and in Western Europe the bark of a beech tree was one of the first forms of writing material. By 500 AD, the pagan word had vanished from circulation, being hidden in forbidden libraries within the monastic world. It took until the second and third centuries for books to start being written again in the Christian world, albeit page by page. In some cases these books were great works of art, bound with fabulous bindings, but alas, they were only to be read by the few. During the early Middle Ages books began to circulate and by 1300 great libraries were being set up. In fact a King could receive a knock to his prestige if he possessed a poor library, even if he could not actually read. As the printing press started to churn out volumes of books, booklets and pamphlets, the demand for knowledge increased. In the seventeenth century newspapers became accessible to all. The great age of exploration helped make map-making popular. As with books, the information contained in the navigator's charts is often as important as the condition of the map.

The Great River ▼
- *1911*
The Great River by Frederick Oakes Sylvester. The book contains poetry and illustrations throughout and has an embossed and gilded leather binder.
- *15cm x 21cm*
- **£350** • Chelsea Gallery

Livingstone's Last Journals ➤
- *1874*
First edition of Livingstone's *Last Journals* including two volumes with maps.
- *23cm x 16cm*
- **£540** • Chelsea Gallery

Ornithology Volumes ▲
- *1760*
Six volumes on the subject of ornithology by Brisson. Consisting of 261 plates, leather bound and gilded.
- *20cm x 26cm*
- **£7,000** • Chelsea Gallery

Antique Globe ▼
- *1862*
Antique terrestrial globe by Malby. Brass meridian ring, horizon circle on four upright mahogany legs.
- *43cm x 48cm*
- **£6,400** • Langfords Marine

Expert Tips
Leather binding needs care and regular inspection – a wipe with a cloth smeared with Vaseline will help prevent the leather drying out.

Life of Wellington ▼
- *1914*

Life of Wellington by W.H.
Maxwell. Leather bound and
gilded and signed on the binding.
- *15cm x 22cm*
- £190   • Chelsea Gallery

Map of London ▼
- *mid 18th century*

A map of London and
surrounding environs with
vignettes covering Chelsea,
Greenwich, Kensington,
Hampton Court and Windsor,
by J.B. Homamm.
- *51cm x 60cm*
- £900   • Chelsea Gallery

The Compleat Angler ▼
- *1931*

The Compleat Angler by Izaak
Walton with fine, hand-coloured
illustrations of rural themes by
Arthur Rackham. Limited
edition.
- *27cm x 20cm*
- £750   • Chelsea Gallery

Voyages de Cook ▼
- *1774*

A first edition complete set of
thirteen volumes in French.
Illustrated throughout including
the "Death of Cook".
- *height 30cm*
- £13,000   • Chelsea Gallery

Coxe's Travels in Poland ◄
- *1784*

A two-volume set with a full calf
binding, with various illustrations
and maps. The book includes
travels to Poland, Russian,
Sweden and Denmark.
- £600   • Chelsea Gallery

Descriptions de L'Egypte ▲
- *circa 1820*

A second edition complete set,
comprising eleven volumes and
almost a thousand copper
engraved plates of various studies
of Egypt. Subjects include
architecture, natural history,
geography, views and city life.
Commissioned by Napoleon and
published by C.L.F. Panckouke.
Half Moroccan binding.
- *72cm x 55cm*
- £35,000   • Chelsea Gallery

Antichita Di Roma ▲
- *1763*

A book of the antiquities of
Rome by Ridolfino Venuti
Cortonese and published by
Bernabo & Lazzarini. This is a
first edition and consists of 96
copper engraved plates depicting
architectural views and Roman
ruins. Leather bound and gilded.
- *28cm x 22cm*
- £2,400   • Chelsea Gallery

Oscar Wilde ▲
- **1925**

A set of twelve limited edition books by Oscar Wilde, numbered from 482 to 575. Each book is bound with leather and has a marble insert.
- *height 21cm*
- £1,900   • Chelsea Gallery

Expert Tips

Rebinding can be done at a reasonable cost and helps preserve books for the long term. Always use reputable binders to ensure the job is done correctly.

The Triumph of Maximilian ▶
- **1778**

A book of woodcuts featuring the triumphs of the Holy Roman Emperor Maximilian I. This is one of the greatest series of woodcuts ever cut by Hans Burgmair.
- *56cm x 69cm*
- £18,000   • Chelsea Gallery

The British Sportsman ▲
- *circa 1790*

A book of British sports by William Augustin Osbaldiston, containing 44 copper engraved plates depicting scenes of recreation and amusement associated with riding, racing, hunting and shooting. Published by J. Stead.
- *22cm x 27cm*
- £550   • Chelsea Gallery

Mirage ▼
- **1906**

A book of various Arab stories compiled by Sliman Ben Ibrahim Bamer. It contains hand-painted illustrations throughout by E. Dinet. Decorative French binding by Rene Kieffer.
- *23cm x 17cm*
- £1,400   • Chelsea Gallery

A Display of Heraldrie ◀
- **1611**

A first edition of a single volume from the seventeenth century, written by John Guillim. Illustrated and hand coloured throughout with associated family history.
- *30cm x 20cm*
- £1,000   • Chelsea Gallery

Works of Shakespeare ▲
- **1811**

Miniature set of eight volumes, all in excellent condition, with binding and gilding by Hayday.
- *12.5cm x 8cm*
- £750   • Chelsea Gallery

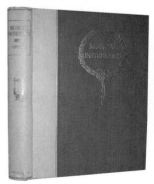

Musical Instruments ▲
- **1921**

A book by A.J. Hipkins, consisting of 48 plates covering historic, rare and unique musical instruments, bound and gilded.
- £280   • Chelsea Gallery

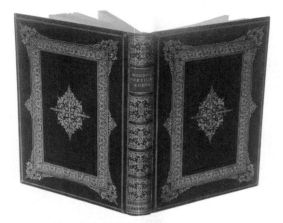

Moore's Poetical Works ◀

- *circa 1850*

A beautifully bound book of poetry entitled *Moore's Poetical Works*, containing 48 steel engraved portraits. Published by The London Printing and Publishing Company.

- *34cm x 26cm*
- £850 • Chelsea Gallery

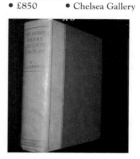

The Salmon Rivers and Locks of Scotland ▲

- 1909

The Salmon Rivers and Locks of Scotland by W.L. Calderwood with original binder and in good condition. A limited edition book, only 250 produced.

- *height 23cm*
- £550 • Chelsea Gallery

Celestial Chart ▼

- 1742

A celestial map by Doppelmayr of the northern hemisphere. It has been hand coloured and engraved by Honann, and shows the celestial sky and the heroes of mythology.

- *64cm x 55cm*
- £1,400 • Chelsea Gallery

Bartolozzi ▲

- *19th century*

Stipple engravings of the mythological characters Cupid and Psyche, in original frames.

- *diameter 40cm*
- £1,600 • Chelsea Gallery

The Children's Natural History Scrap Album ▲

- *1887*

A 55-page book of collected stickers with original binder and gilding.

- *height 42cm*
- £280 • Chelsea Gallery

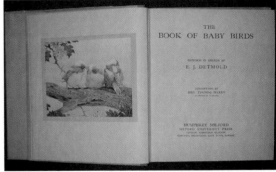

Academie de L'Epée-Fencing ◀

- **1680**

Various engraved and hand-coloured plates by Thebauld depicting the sport of fencing.
- *height 43cm*
- **£1,100** • Chelsea Gallery

Paul and Virginia ▲

- **1839**

Book by Bernardin de St. Pierre with an original memoir of the author. Illustrated throughout, leather bound and gilded.
- *height 45cm*
- **£550** • Chelsea Gallery

Green's Voyages and Travels ▼

- **1745–47**

Four-volume set of the first edition of *Green's Voyages and Travels*. Illustrated throughout with maps and views.
- *27cm x 22cm*
- **£4,000** • Chelsea Gallery

The Book of Baby Birds ▲

- **1919**

A full-colour illustrated book of baby birds by E.J. Detmold, accompanied by poetry.
- *height 35cm*
- **£300** • Chelsea Gallery

Annals of Sporting ▲

- **1822–23**

A 13-volume bound and gilded set entitled *The Annals of Sporting*, with 155 plates, 50 of which are hand coloured. Published by Sherwood, Neely & Jones.
- *23cm x 15cm*
- **£3,800** • Chelsea Gallery

Voltaire ▲

- **1930**

A unique copy of *Historie de Jenni*, with hand-coloured illustrations throughout by Lauro with original cover and gilding.
- *19cm x 24cm*
- **£1,800** • Chelsea Gallery

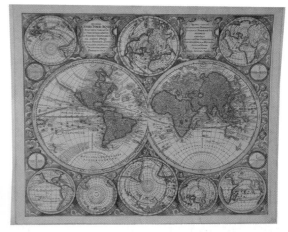

Mappe Monde ➤
- *circa 1730*

Double hemisphere world map by
M. Seutter. Hand coloured and
copper engraved.
- *63cm x 55cm*
- £3,800 • Chelsea Gallery

The Old Curiosity Shop ▼
- *1841*

First edition of Dickens novel
in good condition. Full calf
binding and gilt floral decoration
by Rowler.
- *height 16cm*
- £400 • Chelsea Gallery

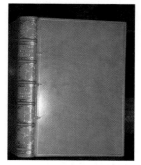

Pipes of All Nations ▼
- *1890*

Review of various pipes around
the world, by R.T. Pritchett.
Complete with 46 plates and
original binder. Slightly worn.
- *height 28cm*
- £700 • Chelsea Gallery

Journal of a Residence ➤
- *date 1824*

Account of life in nineteenth
century Chile published by John
Murray. In English, including 14
aquaintant plates. Fine condition.
- £1,200 • Paul Orssich

Gallery of the Graces ➤
- *1837*

The *Gallery of the Graces* is a
book of portraits and contains 36
copper engravings by Finden and
was published by Charles Tilt.
- *29cm x 22 cm*
- £350 • Chelsea Gallery

The Loves of the Poets ◄
- *1860*

Twelve steel plate engravings by
the most eminent artists of the
day. Published by W. Kent & Co
(Late D. Bogue).
- *30cm x 23 cm*
- £120 • Chelsea Gallery

Book of Sport ◀
- *1885*

A book of sport written by W. Bromley Davenport and illustrated throughout with various plates. Exquisitely bound and gilded by Zaehnsdorf.
- *29cm x 22cm*
- £950   • Chelsea Gallery

Expert Tips

With old books and maps look out for foxing or orange stains as these kinds of blemishes can be expensive to rectify.

Encyclopaedia Londinensis ▼
- *1808*

A collection of British heraldry containing 105 hand-coloured plates, from King George III and Queen Charlotte down to the esquires and gentleman (patrons of the work). Published by J. Wilks.
- *28cm x 22cm*
- £2,800   • Chelsea Gallery

The Spy Who Loved Me ▲
- *1962*

By Ian Fleming. Near fine first edition of James Bond caper, in dustwrapper.
- £200–250
- • Adrian Harrington

Australian Pictures ▲
- *1886*

Hand-drawn pen and pencil sketches, landscapes and portraits by Howard Willoughby.
- *34cm x 25cm*
- £125   • Bernard Shapero

Master and Commander ▲
- *1969*

By Patrick O'Brian. J.B. Lippencott Co., New York and Philadelphia. First edition, precedes the later edition published by Collins in 1970. In very good condition.
- *15cm x 22.5cm*
- £650   • Ash Books

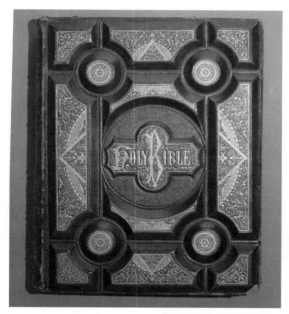

Holy Bible ◄
- **1872**
Holy Bible from Philadelphia, USA, with illustrated maps and full-page steel engravings, including coloured map of Palestine. Bound in black morrocco, ornate gilt.
- **£90–120**
- **Adrian Harrington**

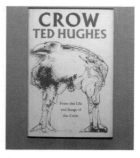

Crow ▲
- **1970**
A poem by Ted Hughes from *The Life and Songs of Crow*. Published by Faber & Faber, London. First edition.
- *22cm x 15cm*
- **£125**   • **Ash Books**

Map of New York ▼
- **1720**
Striking map of New York, New Jersey and New England, up to Maine by John Baptist Homann. J.B. Homann was the geographer to the Holy Roman Empire. Full original hand coloured.
- *48.5cm x 57cm*
- **£995**   • **Ash Books**

Stiff Upper Lip, Jeeves ►
- **1963**
Stiff Upper Lip, Jeeves, by P.G. Wodehouse. Published in New York by Simon & Schuster. This first edition precedes the London edition by five months. Very good quality.
- *14cm x 21cm*
- **£100**   • **Ash Books**

British Birds ▼
- **1915**
A book of the birds of Britain by Thorburn comprising four volumes, which contain 80 finely illustrated hand-coloured plates. Published by Longmans, Green & Co.
- *32cm x 27cm*
- **£680**   • **Chelsea Gallery**

Carpets & Rugs

Oriental carpets and rugs have been collected by Europeans for many centuries and need not be prohibitively expensive.

The invention of the loom led to the rise in importance of rugs and carpets. From the Bedouin tribe of the desert to the great moghuls of India, rugs have been seen as works of art and as tradeable commodities, and even endowed with a magical ability to fly. Some were woven with fertility and religious symbols and used as prayer mats or for decoration. No great period house could be without these rich oriental coverings, giving colour and warmth to the coldest of rooms.

During the reign of Louis XVI, tapestry and rug manufacturing began to take off with factories such as Le Brun in Paris making rugs of superb quality. This heralded the beginning of tapestry and carpet manufacture in Europe. Today, the desirability of soft furnishings and fabrics is reflected by the high prices that some rugs can command at auction, and is still at the top of the list for many looking to improve their homes.

Look out for wear and tear and repairs as this can seriously affect a rug's value.

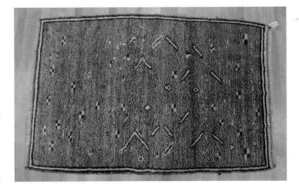

Striped Rug ▲
- *circa 1920–30*
Antique Gabbeh rug, by Luri tribe in Zagros mountains, southern Persia (code NZ00192).
- *122cm x 120cm*
- £720   • Gordon Reece

Russian Carpet ▲
- *circa 1880*
Russian Bokhra wool rug with tradtional elephant feet designed by Gul.
- *350cm x 240cm*
- £3,000   • A. Rezai Persian

Quashquai Gabbeh Rug ➤
- *20th century*
A wool carpet of striking design created without the use of dye. From the Zagros mountains, South Persia.
- *175cm x 118cm*
- £1,050   • Gordon Reece

Dhurrie ◀
- *19th century*
Cotton wool rug, the warp and
weft dyed with indigo and
turmeric. Woven by Indian
prisoners (code QT9775).
- *195cm x 116cm*
- **£695** • **Gordon Reece**

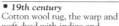

Heriz Carpet ◀
1880
A section of antique woollen
heriz with a centre medallion
design and a dragon border.
- *300cm x 400cm*
- **£6,600** • **A. Rezai Persian**

Silk Persian Carpet ▲
- *1820*
A silk Persian carpet of a
traditional Mothsham design.
- *198cm x 127cm*
- **£6,600** • **A. Rezai Persian**

Tapestry Cushions ▲
- *1880*
A selection of needlepoint
tapestry cushions.
- **£1,800** • **A. Rezai Persian**

Gabbeh Carpet ▼
- *circa 1880*
Luri Gabbeh carpet coloured
with natural dyes, showing a
strong geometric pattern on a
blue ground (code NZ00165).
- *215cm x 170cm*
- **£2,250** • **Gordon Reece**

Expert Tips

*Look out for wear and repair as
this can affect the value of the
carpet or rug, as can the cutting
or trimming of the fringe. If a
design is rare it can still fetch a
high price as it can be used as a
template by rug makers. It is
also valuable because of its
historical importance.*

Tapestry ▲
- *1880*
A beautiful tapestry with stags,
monkeys, a leopard, pheasants
and red roses. In excellent
condition.
- *180cm x 140cm*
- **£3,300** • **A. Rezai Persian**

Persian Runner ▲
- *1880*

Northwest Persian camel hair runner with paisley design on the border. The centre features an unusual diamond-shaped geometrical design.
- *550cm x 110cm*
- **£3,000** • **A. Rezai Persian**

Persian Rug ▲
- *early 20th century*

Persian Quashquai Gabbeh rug incorporating a strong central design within a geometric border on a red ground (code NZ00174).
- *165cm x 104cm*
- **£760** • **Gordon Reece**

Geometric Carpet ▲
- *1820*

An unusual carpet with a dramatic geometric design incorporating a lion, cat and scorpion with stars on the border.
- *300cm x 122cm*
- **£3,300** • **A. Rezai Persian**

Woollen Runner ▼
- *1880*

Woollen Tulish short runner of geometric design. The border design incorporating leaves.
- *240cm x 120cm*
- **£2,200** • **A. Rezai Persian**

Russian Chichi Rug ▲
- *1880*

A Russian Chichi rug with central desert flower design.
- *180cm x 120cm*
- **£3,300** • **A. Rezai Persian**

Expert Tips

Count the knots on the backside of the rug or carpet – the closer the knots the higher the quality.

Quashquai Gabbeh Rug
- **20th century**
Quashquai Gabbeh rug with classic design and lush pile. Manufactured in the Zagros mountains, southern Persia (code NZ00134).
- *215cm x 170cm*
- **£1,250**   • Gordon Reece

Dragon and Phoenix Seat Rug
- *circa 19th century*
Embroided seat cover with a stylised dragon and phoenix within floral and vine decoration on a yellow ground (code TEX0033).
- *63cm x 84cm*
- **£810**   • Gordon Reece

Expert Tips

The colour and feel of a good carpet or rug is unforgettable, but keep a sharp look out for any signs of fading colours. Good carpet runners are becoming increasingly difficult to find and are now highly sought-after items.

Ottoman Prayer Rug
- **circa 1880**
A pure silk Mihrab Ottoman design prayer rug with gold silk woven throughout. The design script are verses from the Qu'ran.
- *180cm x 120cm*

Russian Rug
- **1820**
A unique Russian wool rug being part of a cradle. The design is an old Suman brocade design.
- *109cm x 42cm*
- **£1,000**   • A. Rezai Persian

Tibetan Saddlebag
- **1500**
A Tibetan wool saddlebag, with central red panel with floral design and a cobalt border.
- *68cm x 58cm*
- **£1,500**   • A. Rezai Persian

49

Persian Rug ◄

- **early 20th century**
Luri Gabbeh rug from southwest
Persia. Includes a strong
geometric pattern in blue
and red and an alternating
zig-zag border.
- *200cm x 147cm*
- £950   • Gordon Reece

Gabbeh Carpet ▲

- **20th century**
Luri Gabbeh carpet from the
Zagros mountains, southern
Persia.
- *148cm x 121cm*
- £770   • Gordon Reece

Tibetan Rug ▼

- **1880**
Tibetan rug with an indigo
background and delicately
embroidered butterflies around a
central floral design (code
TEX0048).
- *77cm x 54cm*
- £280   • Gordon Reece

Persian Wool Carpet ►

- **1820**
A Persian wool carpet with floral
design on a rust coloured ground
with cobalt blue borders, by
Zigla Mahal.
- *120cm x 150cm*
- £3,300   • A. Rezai Persian

Expert Tips

*Cleaning should be done by
vacuum or by hand. By rotating
the rug you can avoid uneven
wear. Try to avoid direct
sunlight on the rug as this will
affect the colours.
In the seventeenth century the
fashion was to hang rugs on
walls or to cover tables with
good examples. This is
something carpet and rug
collectors could recommend as
this also helps to prolong the life
of the rug or carpet.*

Ceramics

Pottery and porcelain need to be perfect to command top prices. Conversely, great pleasure can be had by the enthusiast in finding slightly flawed bargains.

Ceramics is a term meaning "fired in the kiln". Firing clay developed from flint and the woven basket, and marks one of the first steps in advanced human endeavour. In order to achieve the highest price china and pottery must be in near perfect condition. Passable and restored pieces can be detected by holding the piece up to the light. The skilled eye or the use of ultra violet light are sure methods to detect repairs. The damaged piece is still in demand but at a much reduced price, but the lover of ceramics may overlook such misgivings to own a rare item.

From 1450 the world saw an expansion in the ceramic market due to increased sea trade. The porcelain being manufactured at this time came into Europe from China and Japan. China containers were needed in Europe to store food, spices and tea, and this helped the market to grow.

Pottery and porcelain is as collectable as it ever was and holding a fine piece in one's hands and feeling the quality of the glaze and colour is a joy that never diminishes. When buying pottery or china it is important to study the maker's marks as these can be forged or elevated in status.

English Ceramics

Royal Doulton Vase ▼
- **1890**
One of a pair of large Royal Doulton vases of bulbous form with polychrome floral decoration.
- *height 49cm*
- **£345** • A.D. Antiques

Mayer's Jug ◄
- **1850**
T.J. & J. Mayer's blue and white jug with pewter mounts and moulded decoration to the body and handle.
- *height 21cm*
- **£175** • A.D. Antiques

Pair of Spirit Barrels ▼
- **1910**
Pair of attractive salt glaze spirit barrels for brandy and whisky.
- *height 27cm*
- **£245** • A.D. Antiques

Sauce Tureen ▼
- *circa 1896*
A blue and white tureen made by the Empire Porcelain Company.
- *height 8cm*
- £65   • A.D. Antiques

Jug and Bowl ▼
- *circa 1900*
Jug and bowl, with moulded shell design.
- *height 35cm*
- £185   • A.D. Antiques

Expert Tips

Good condition is the main priority of both dealer and collector alike. With ceramics, faults and damage can affect the price severely. Missing lids or saucers can also affect the value. Perfect pieces fetch perfect prices.

Worcester Plate ▼
- *1811*
Worcester plate with hand-painted polychrome decoration.
- *diameter 22cm*
- £65   • A.D. Antiques

Water Jug ▲
- *1890*
Copeland Spode water jug with scrolled handle and painted decoration to the body and lip.
- *height 56cm*
- £75   • A.D. Antiques

Staffordshire Jug ▼
- *1860*
Mid nineteenth century moulded Staffordshire jug with pewter lid.
- *height 32cm*
- £125   • A.D. Antiques

Victorian Jug ▶
- *1880*
A Victorian lustre jug, with scrolled handle and painted decoration of a classical urn with floral sprays.
- *height 54cm*
- £65   • A.D. Antiques

Muffin Dish ▶
- *1872*
Minton muffin dish with Japanese crane design applied to the base of the cover and dish.
- *height 10cm*
- £125   • A.D. Antiques

Copeland Teapot ▲
• *1895*
Copeland teapot decorated with
Burn's design incorporating
chinoiserie scenes, with finial lid.
• *height 21cm*
• £75   • A.D. Antiques

Victorian Pail ◄
• *1890*
A Victorian Stafforshire pail and
cover, with floral transfer
decoration and two scrolled
handles.
• *height 37cm*
• £275   • A.D. Antiques

Cheese Dish ▼
• *circa 1912*
A Spode blue- and white-
transfer cheese dish and cover.
• *height 6cm*
• £90   • A.D. Antiques

Cream Jug ▲
• *1891*
A Wedgwood blue jasper cream
jug decorated with classical
figures in relief.
• *height 7cm*
• £758   • A.D. Antiques

Splayed Lip Jug ▲
• *1813*
Baker Bevin and Irvine jug of
lobed design with splayed lip and
transfer decoration.
• *height 15cm*
• £95   • A.D. Antiques

Royal Worcester Tureen ➤
• *1888*
Part of a Royal Worcester dinner
service comprising 18 dinner
plates and 3 soup tureens of oval
form, with blue and white floral
decoration and gilding.
• *35cm x 11cm*
• £2,500   • A.D. Antiques

Royal Doulton Vase ▼
- *1890*

One of a pair of nineteenth century Royal Doulton vases with enamelled floral decoration.
- *height 24cm*
- £165   • A.D. Antiques

Pair of Dalmatian Dogs ▼
- *1875*

An unusual pair of seated Staffordshire Dalmatians with an alert expression, painted with gilt collars on oval cobalt blue bases.
- *height 13cm*
- £795   • Jesse Davis

Macintyre Vases ▼
- *1900–4*

Pair of Macintyre vases in cornflower design by William Moorcroft.
- *height 17cm*
- £ 1,650   • A.D. Antiques

Sauce Tureen ▲
- *1888*

Royal Worcester soup tureen and base which is part of a dinner service. The body, cover and base are profusely decorated with floral design and gilding.
- *height 13cm*
- £ 2,500   • A.D. Antiques

Expert Tips

In the case of Delft and Majolica porcelain, chips are more acceptable on the rarer pieces as the glaze in both wares is prone to chipping.

Minton Cake Stand ▲
- *1863*

A Minton cake stand which is part of a dessert service comprising ten plates.
- *diameter 24cm*
- £125   • London Antique

Minton Bowl ▼
- *1860*

Minton bowl with polychrome floral and gilt decoration, raised on a large footpad.
- *height 15cm*
- £225   • A.D. Antiques

Chinoiserie Plate ◄
- *1780*

An English blue and white oval plate decorated with a Chinoiserie scene.
- N/A
- Ashcombe House

Pair of Perching Birds ▼
- *1865*

A pair of Staffordshire figures, showing two resplendent birds, on a stylized tree base.
- *height 32cm*
- £1,995
- Jesse Davis

Staffordshire Spaniel ▲
- *1750*

One of a pair of Staffordshire King Charles spaniels in an alert pose, splashed with iron red, and each with a gilt collar.
- *height 14cm*
- £750
- Jesse Davis

Staffordshire Pony ▲
- *1860*

An unusual moulded Staffordshire pony with cheshnut colouration and a black mane, on a moulded rock oval base with gilt banding.
- *height 8cm*
- £249
- Jesse Davis

King Charles Spaniel ▼
- *1880*

An unusual small King Charles spaniel, recumbent on a mazarin blue cushion base .
- *height 13cm*
- £498
- Jesse Davis

Pair of Spill Holders ◄
- *1850*

Pair of Staffordshire spill holders showing a ram and a ewe, with bocage and flower encrustation on rock moulded base.
- *height 13cm*
- £895
- Jesse Davis

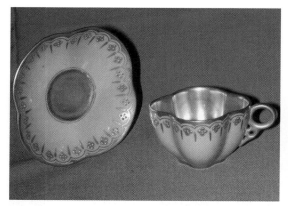

Quatrolobe Set
- *1890*

A Coalport Quatrolobe cup and saucer with pink and gold floral decoration.
- *height 2.5cm*
- £185 • London Antique

Coalport Quatrolobe Cup and Saucer ▼
- *1890*

A Coalport Quatralobe cup and saucer, heavily gilded on a green base.
- *height 2.5cm*
- £185 • London Antique

Minton Cup and Saucer ▼
- *1912–50*

A Minton cup and saucer made in New York by Cilman Collamore & Co., 5th Avenue and 30th Street, New York.
- £85 • London Antique

Coalport Gilded Cup and Saucer Set ▲
- *circa 1883*

A Coalport cup and saucer with lobed rim and gilded floral decoration on a cobalt-blue ground.
- *height 3cm*
- £175 • London Antique

Butter Dish ▼
- *1870*

Ceramic butter dish with a sitting cow on lid.
- *21cm x 14cm*
- £1,295 • Jesse Davis

Staffordshire Greyhounds ➤
1840

A pair of Staffordshire greyhounds seated upon oval bases with floral decoration.
- *height 13cm*
- £495 • Jesse

Derby Vases ➤
- *1830*

A pair of small bottle-shaped Derby vases, gilded with flower encrustation.
- *height 11cm*
- £285 • London Antique

Royal Worcester Cup and Saucer ▲
- *1936*

An English Royal Worcester cup and saucer, with interlaced scroll decoration.
- *height 9cm*
- £150 • London Antique

Staffordshire Deer with Dog ▼
- *1870*

A spill holder showing a group depicting a deer leaping through a woodland setting with a hound giving chase, on an oval base.
- *height 18cm*
- £795 • Jesse Davis

Pagoda Cup and Saucer ▼
- *circa 1785*

Cup and saucer with a pagoda pattern.
- *height 4cm*
- £135 • London Antique

Pair of Greyhounds with Prey ▲
- *1865*

A pair of Staffordshire greyhounds, each with a rabbit in its mouth. Painted in iron red, brown and gilt, and raised on a rock moulded base.
- *height 20cm*
- £258 • Jesse Davis

Poodle Group ▲
- *1860*

A Staffordshire dog group with poodles and their puppies, on blue cushion bases.
- *height 13cm*
- £595 • Jesse Davis

Staffordshire Figure ▼
- *1863*

A Staffordshire figure of Bonnie
Prince Charles in a woodland
setting.
- *height 23cm*
- £225 • Jesse Davis

Staffordshire Group ▲
- *1866*

A Staffordshire group showing
Royal children in Scottish dress
with sheep, on a naturalistically
formed oval base.
- *height 20cm*
- £695 • Jesse Davis

Minton Cup and Saucer ▲
- *1850*

A Minton cup and saucer with
polychrome floral decoration and
cobalt blue banding with gilt
meanderings.
- *height 5cm; diameter 10cm resp.*
- £139 • Jesse Davis

Polychrome Set ▼
- *1860*

A polychrome cup and saucer
with an Edward pattern,
decorated with sunflowers and
yellow ochre banding with pink
interior to the cup.
- *height 8cm; diameter 11cm resp.*
- £295 • Jesse Davis

Royal Worcester Set ▼
- *1951*

A Royal Worcester cup and
saucer with large, colourful
fruit decoration. Includes
gilding inside the cup, base
and handle.
- *height 7cm*
- £335 • London Antique

Expert Tips

*Staffordshire figures remain as
popular as ever but as they were
produced in large numbers they
were not always treated with
care, so keep a sharp eye out for
damages and repairs.
Best period for Staffordshire
figures is 1854–6.*

Minton Barometer ▽

- *1835*

A Minton barometer with a frame encrusted with flowers.

- *height 18cm*
- £235 • London Antique

Elephant Spill Holders ▽

- *1865*

A pair of Staffordshire elephant spill holders shown standing on a bocage oval base.

- *height 14cm*
- £1,095 • Jesse Davis

Pair of Staffordshire Spill Holders ▽

- *1870*

One of a pair of Staffordshire spill holders modelled as mother and calf with bocage, raised on a naturalistically moulded oval base.

- *height 28cm*
- £895 • Jesse Davis

Staffordshire Cottage ▲

- *1890*

A Staffordshire cottage with recess for a time piece, with additional floral decoration and two lead-lined windows either side of the front door.

- *height 13cm*
- £168 • Jesse Davis

English Ewer ▲

- *1810*

An English Ewer with a moulded Bacchanal face about the body, decorated with a band of vines and floral sprays. Includes a stylised handle in the form of a monkey with a splayed lip on a circular pedestal base.

- *height 18cm*
- £395 • Jesse Davis

Hunting Pair ▲

- *1865*

One of a pair of Staffordshire harlequin greyhounds with a hare on a bocage base.

- *height 29cm*
- £2,450 • Jesse Davis

Cream Ware Jug ▼
- *1790*

A Cream Ware jug for milk or beer, with a transfer print depicting a gentleman in period costume within a vine border.
- *height 25cm*
- £4,950 ● Jonathan Horne

Staffordshire Spill Holder ▼
- *1820*

A Staffordshire spill holder modelled with bocage showing a young boy and two recumbent leopards on a naturalistically formed base.
- *height 25cm*
- £4,950 ● Jonathan Horne

Minton Plate ➤
- *1863*

A Minton white plate with a turquoise rim, with a cherub depicted in the centre sitting by a tree with a bird basket.
- *diameter 24cm*
- £100 ● London Antique

Wedgwood Plate ➤
- *1860*

A tullic design Wedgwood plate showing a leaf pattern on a basket weave base with a green glaze.
- *height 23cm*
- £149 ● Jesse Davis

Bull with Dog ▼
- *1820*

A Staffordshire group showing a tethered bull with a farmer and his dog on a rectangular base.
- *23cm x 36cm*
- £6,600 ● Jonathan Horne

Cruet Set ◄
- *1865*

A most unusual English or Scottish cruet set consisting of salt and pepper. The gentleman is shown with a tri-cornered hat, a red overcoat and a wry expression.
- *height 91cm*
- £295 ● Jesse Davis

Cream Ware Plate ▼

- *1790*

English Cream Ware plate decorated in Holland with a biblical scene, surrounded by a key pattern border, with floral decoration to the rim.
- *diameter 29cms*
- £315   • Jonathan Horne

Figure of a Dog ➤

- *18th century*

A Staffordshire model of a dog with a red collar sitting attentively on a cushion base.
- *height 12cm*
- £655   • Jonathan Horne

Staffordshire Hound ▲

- *circa 1800*

A Staffordshire figure of a hound, finely modelled shown standing on a naturalistically styled base.
- *height 14cm*
- £2,200   • Jonathan Horne

Bristol Vase ▼

- *circa 1715*

A polychrome Bristol vase of bulbous proportions raised on a splayed base with scrolled and floral decoration.
- *height 19cm*
- £6,800   • Jonathan Horne

Water Jug ▼

- *1804*

A Staffordshire water jug with gilded rim and scrolled handle with an oval cartouche depicting the Duke of Leinster.
- *height 17cm*
- £1,500   • Jonathan Horne

Tea Kettle ◄

- *1770*

A Leeds tea kettle with a crossover strap handle and moulded spout with female decoration and black and white geometric design.
- *height 16cm*
- £3,650   • Jonathan Horne

Staffordshire Group ▲

- *early 19th century*

A Staffordshire Prattware figure
of a young woman and a small
boy holding a baby chicken in his hat
entitled "Spring". Both standing
on a rectangular base .
- *height 23cm*
- £780   • Jonathan Horne

Lion Figurine ▲

- *1815*

An early Staffordshire lion with
protruding tongue shown with
one paw raised on a single ball,
on a rectangular base.
- *27cm x 38cm*
- £5,580   • Jonathan Horne

Expert Tips

*Factory marks change
periodically and are a good
indicator as to the maker and
date of the item. Look out for
the potter's or painter's initials
and beware of false marks.
These can be detected by a
blurred or off-colour mark, or
by recognising that the wrong
mark has been used for the
attributed period.*

Slipware Dishes ▲

- *1791*

One of three Derbyshire slipware
dishes dated 1791. Decorated
with a cockerel.
- *length 40cm*
- £400   •Peter Bunting

Royal Doulton Figure of Clarissa ◄

- *20th century*

A Royal Doulton figure of a
young girl in flowing dress with a
wicker basket containing flowers
entitled "Clarissa".
- *height 14cm*
- £110   • London Antique

Cache Pot ▼

- *1890*

English cache pot with japanned
lacquer.
- *18.5cm x 41.5cm x 34.5cm*
- £3,250   • O.F. Wilson

Staffordshire Jar ▼

- *19th century*

A Staffordshire jar of bulbous
form with banding and floral
decoration and two applied
handles.
- *height 17cm*
- £650   • Jonathan Horne

Cream Ware Teapot ➤
- *1770*

A Staffordshire CreamWare
teapot with crossover strap
handle, moulded decorations to
the spout and finial lid. Painted
with an unusual abstract pattern.
- *height 6.5cm*
- £1,650   • Jonathan Horne

Cream Ware Jug ▲
- *circa 1790*

An English Cream Ware jug for
beer or milk, with transfer printed
scenes depicting summer and
winter applied to the body.
- *height 19cm*
- £550   • Jonathan Horne

Fortune Teller Jug ➤
- *1790*

A Cream Ware jug with transfer
printed scenes entitled "'The
Gipsy Fortune Teller". With
turned decoration to the base.
- *height 14cm*
- £365   • Jonathan Horne

Glazed Teapot ▼
- *1760*

A Staffordshire octagonal
green glazed teapot with moulded
decoration depicting chinoiserie
scenes. Scrolled handle and
finial lid.
- *height 16cm*
- £3,950   • Jonathan Horne

Toby Jug ◄
- *circa 1790*

A Staffordshire Prattware Toby
jug showing an old lady sitting,
entitled "Martha Gunn". With
painted decoration
- *height 25cm*
- £1,680   • Jonathan Horne

Ralph Wood Toby Jug ▼
- *1790*

A Ralph Wood Toby Jug
showing a seated gentleman in a
tri-cornered hat and blue
overcoat holding a pitcher of ale.
- *height 25cm*
- £1,150   • Jonathan Horne

Sailor Figurine ◄
- **18th century**
A Staffordshire Prattware model
of a sailor shown standing in a
hat and coat on a flower
encrusted base.
- *height 20cm*
- **£1,650** • Jonathan Horne

Fluted Cup and Saucer ▲
- **1755–90**
A Worcester cup and saucer with
fluted design, interlaced floral
decoration around the rim in gilt
and blue, with gilt floral sprays.
- *height 6cm*
- **£195** • London Antique

Staffordshire
Cream Ware Teapot ▼
- *circa 1770*
A Staffordshire Cream Ware
teapot with moulded decoration,
crossover strap handle and finial
lid. Painted with a chinoiserie
style design.
- *height 5.5cm*
- **£ 1,450** • Jonathan Horne

Yorkshire
Cream WareTeapot ▲
- **1790**
A Yorkshire Cream Ware teapot
with moulded basketweave design
and Dutch applied decoration of
pastoral scenes.
- *height 5.5cm*
- **£950** • Jonathan Horne

Spinner Figurine ▼
- **1790**
A Ralph Wood-style figure of a
spinner with pigeons.
- *height 20cm*
- **£3,850** • Jonathan Horne

Expert Tips

*When purchasing very
expensive ceramics it is best to
contact a specialist dealer for the
right advice and peace of mind.*

Cream Ware Teapot ▲
- **1760**
A Staffordshire Cream Ware
teapot with a cabbage spout
design, scrolled handle and
painted designs of flowers.
- *height 7cm*
- **£880** • Jonathan Horne

Susie Cooper Milk Jug ▼
- *circa 1930s*

A Susie Cooper milk jug with graduated banding and stylised bird lip. Stamped "698 83".
- *height 20cm*
- £63   • London Antique

Porcelain Set ▲
- *1773*

A Worcester porcelain cup and saucer decorated with pink roses and gilding to the rim and handle.
- *height 5.5cm*
- £295   • London Antique

Staffordshire Plate ▼
- *circa 1770*

A Staffordshire plate with a tortoiseshell lead oxide glaze and raised basket design to lip.
- *height 9.5cm*
- £365   • Jonathan Horne

Ralph Wood Spill Vase ▼
- *1790*

A Ralph Wood spill vase showing a recumbent stag with bocage in which a squirrel is perched. Painted in a green and iron red glaze.
- *height 12.5cm*
- £1,680   • Jonathan Horne

Tea Canister ▼
- *circa 1735*

An octagonal Staffordshire bottle with moulded decoration showing figures in a Chinoiserie setting.
- *height 10cm*
- £1,455   • Jonathan Horne

Staffordshire Teapot ➤
- *1765*

A Staffordshire underglazed oxide teapot with floral decoration and a finial lid.
- *height 11cm*
- £1,355   • Jonathan Horne

English Cup and Saucer ◄
- *1930*

An English cup and saucer colourfully decorated with a pastoral scene.
- £130 • London Antique

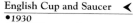

Expert Tips

If you are looking for a secure investment and are aiming to keep your risk to a minimum, it is best to try and stretch your budget by buying one good piece rather than two or three damaged or indifferent items.

Shelly Jug ➤
- *1930*

A porcelain Shelly milk jug with swallow and pastoral scene with a yellow handle.
- *height 10cm*
- £55 • London Antique

Susie Cooper Trio ▼
- *1930–40*

A Susie Cooper trio comprising a white teacup, blue saucer and plate with a moulded rim.
- *diameter 19cm/plate; 9cm/saucer*
- £75 • London Antique

Soup Bowl ◄
- *1930–40*

A Susie Cooper soup bowl with a variegated pink glaze and a central pink rose.
- *diameter 23cm*
- £85 • London Antique

Vegetable Dish ▼
- *1930–40*

A Susie Cooper vegetable dish with a graduated pale blue glaze with flower designs and banding.
- *18cm x 9cm*
- £78
- London Antique

Minton Cup and Saucer ▲
- *1950*

Cup and saucer with a Minton white and blue leaf pattern.
- £25 • London Antique

Wedgwood Plaque ◄
- *1768–80*
A Wedgwood cameo plaque
dipped in black and white,
showing four mischievous putti,
mounted in a gilt frame.
- *20cm x 8cm*
- £200   • London Antique

Shelly Regent Bowl ▲
- *1930*
An English Art Deco Shelly
Regent bowl of deep proportions
with wide splayed lip and a
swallow and foliate design.
- *height 9cm*
- £55   • London Antique

Sauce Boat ▲
- *1930–40*
A Susie Cooper sauce boat with a
crimson band around the body
and grey matt finish above.
- *height 15cm*
- £45   • London Antique

Wedgwood Teapot ▲
- *1830*
A Wedgwood white stoneware
teapot of compressed form with
moulded relief to the body, spout
and handle, and a finial formed as
a hound on the cover.
- *height 11cm*
- £275   • London Antique

Basalt Vase ◄
- *19th century*
A Wedgwood Basalt vase of
cylindrical form with palm trees
and figurative relief, below a band
of floral swags.
- *height 28cm*
- £115   • London Antique

Cameo Plaque ▲
- *1768–80*
A Wedgwood cameo plaque
dipped in black and white and
showing classical figures in relief.
Extremely popular mantle in a
gilt frame.
- *20cm x 8cm*
- £185   • London Antique

Spode Figure ▼
- *1910*

A Spode figure of a lady in courtly dress with chinoiserie design, holding an extended fan to her side.
- *height 12cm*
- **£268**   • London Antique

Stephanie ▲
- *1975*

A Royal Doulton figurine entitled "Stephanie" showing a young girl dancing in period costume.
- *height 28cm*
- **£125**   • London Antique

Reticulated Vase ▲
- *1870–89*

A Grainger Worcester reticulated oval vase and cover with pierced decoration.
- *height 21cm*
- **£485**   • London Antique

Plate and Bowl ▲
- *1930–40*

A Susie Cooper twin-handled bowl with plate with a graduated green glaze with floral design.
- *diameter 16cm*
- **£45**   • London Antique

Royal Doulton Lady ◄
- *1982*

A Royal Doulton figurine of a young lady in a yellow dress with green waistband, holding a parasol over her shoulder and gazing upwards.
- *height 20cm*
- **£100**   • London Antique

Royal Doulton Figurine ▲
- *1950*

A Royal Doulton ceramic figure of a young girl in a red and white dress and bonnet, holding a posy.
- *height 13cm*
- **£95**   • London Antique

Art Deco Plate ▼
- *1930*
An Art Deco Shelley ceramic cake plate and side plate with swallow and foliate design.
- *width 25cm*
- **£55** • London Antique

Figure in White Gown ▼
- *1983*
A Royal Doulton figurine of young girl in a flowing white gown with her hands clasped and her head tilted to one side.
- *height 20cm*
- **£120** • London Antique

Victorian Goblet ▼
- *1860*
A Victorian copper lustre goblet with floral decoration on a sandy ground.
- *height 13cm*
- **£56** • Cekay

Haddon Hall Set ▼
- *1940*
A polychrome Minton Haddon Hall cup and saucer, with profuse floral decoration.
- *height 11cm*
- **£45** • London Antique

Figure of Young Lady ▲
- *1977*
A Royal Doulton figure of a young lady standing posed in an evening dress, entitled "Harmony".
- *height 29cm*
- **£125** • London Antique

Figure of a Seated Lady ▲
- *1950*
A figure of a young girl in nineteenth century dress on a garden seat accompanied by a macaw. The whole on an oval moulded base with gilding.
- *19cm x 18cm*
- **£195** • London Antique

Shelley Cup and Saucer ▲

- *1930*

A Shelley cup and saucer with floral pattern with the handle and base painted blue.
- *height 6cm*
- **£55** • London Antique

Bone China Cup and Saucer ▲

- *1945*

A bone china cup and saucer with gilt rim interspersed with pink rose detail.
- *height 10cm*
- **£45** • London Antique

Art Deco Coffee Set ▲

- *1930*

An Art Deco Carlton Ware coffee set comprising six cups and saucers, a sugar bowl, milk jug and coffee pot. In emerald green glaze with gilt banding and gilded interiors.
- *height 27cm/pot*
- **£295** • London Antique

Mortlake Cup and Saucer ▲

- *1945*

A Mortlake cup and saucer with gilded floral designs around cartouches with floral sprays.
- *height 11cm*
- **£38** • London Antique

Expert Tips

Complete dining and tea sets are very desirable but can be very expensive. Take care to make a note of wear to the gilding as this is expensive to restore. Try to avoid strong detergents and dishwashers for the cleaning of fine china.

Minton Bowl ▲

- *20th century*

A Minton bowl with base, fluted design and twin ribboned handles. The bowl and base have interlaced flower designs and a central panel of flowers.
- *9cm x 12cm*
- **£25** • London Antique

Royal Doulton Figure ▲

- *1954*

A Royal Doulton figurine of a sixteenth century young lady in courtly dress. Entitled "Catherine Clergon Sitzendore".
- *height 14cm*
- **£110** • London Antique

Pirate Figure ◄

- *1880*

A Staffordshire figure of man in the theatrical dress of a pirate with a parrot on his shoulder.

- *height 12cm*
- £89   • Cekay

Staffordshire Cottage ▲

- *1820*

A Staffordshire pink cottage with a white flower-encrusted roof.

- *height 11cm*
- £135   • Cekay

Staffordshire Lady ▼

- *1880*

A Staffordshire figure of a lady in theatrical dress with a bird on her shoulder.

- *height 12cm*
- £89   • Cekay

Empress Eugenie ◄

- *1880*

A Staffordshire figure of Empress Eugenie of France on horseback, riding side saddle.

- *height 29cm*
- £155   • Cekay

Romantic Group ▼

- *1880*

A Staffordshire romantic group with bocage and a swan below a bridge.

- *20cm x 13cm*
- £150   • Cekay

Wedgwood Candlesticks ▶

- *circa 1768–1800*

A pair of black Wedgwood candlesticks of cylindrical form on a wide splayed base with moulded relief and "Etruria" inscribed on the base.

- *height 20cm*
- £250   • London Antique

Davenport Set ▲
- *circa 1890*

A Davenport cup and saucer decorated with an Imari pattern.
- *height 7cm/cup*
- £95   • London Antique

Victorian Spaniel Group ◄
- *1880*

A Cream Victorian Staffordshire King Charles Spaniel and two puppies.
- *height 20cm*
- £115   • Cekay

Theatrical Figures ▲
- *1845*

A Staffordshire group showing a man and a woman in theatrical costume.
- *height 22cm*
- £165   • Cekay

Aynsley Cup and Saucer ▲
- *circa 1926*

An Aynsley cup and saucer with scrolled handle and gilt banding on a cobalt blue ground.
- *height 9cm*
- £60   • London Antique

Floral Cottage ▲
- *1830*

A Staffordshire cottage encrusted with flowers.
- *height 11cm*
- £135   • Cekay

Staffordshire Spill Holder ◄
- *1845*

A Staffordshire spill holder with two women, one seated.
- *height 111cm*
- £111   • Cekay

Royal Worcester Cabaret Set ➤

- *1918–19*
A Royal Worcester cabaret set with six cups, saucers and spoons in a presentation box. Signed by Stinton, with spoons by Henry James Hulbert.
- **£2,850** • London Antique

Porcelain Figurines ➤

- *1850*
Pair of miniature porcelain figures of an English lady and gentleman.
- *height 12cm*
- **£135** • Cekay

Double-Handled Goblet ▼

- *1830*
An English double-handled silver lustre goblet.
- *height 56cm*
- **£56** • Cekay

Derby Jug ▲

- *1820–40*
A Derby water jug of oval form with flower encrusted cartouches on a blue ground, with gilding to the handle and splayed lip.
- *height 17cm*
- **£235** • London Antique

Worcester Bowl ▼

- *1755–90*
A Worcester bowl of a fluted design with gilded floral decoration and a blue and gilded pattern around the rim..
- *height 18cm*
- **£80** • London Antique

Staffordshire Castle ▼

- *1890*
Victorian Staffordshire pink castle with a red door and arched leaded light window.
- *height 24cm*
- **£111** • Cekay

Copper Goblet ▲
- *1840*

An English copper lustre goblet, decorated with a floral design around the body with turned decoration.
- *height 12cm*
- £45   Cekay

Lustre Ware Mug ▼
- *1820*

A double-handled Lustre Ware mug, with floral decoration on a pedestal base.
- *height 12cm*
- £66   • Cekay

Chamber Pot ▲
- *circa 1860*

A Victorian chamber pot, decorated with a floral design of roses, inscribed "Ridgways".
- *height 14cm*
- £56   • Cekay

Falstaff Toby Jug ▲
- *19th century*

A porcelain Toby jug of the Shakespearean character Falstaff.
- *height 24cm*
- £225   • Cekay

Royal Doulton Bulldog ◄
- *20th century*

A porcelain Royal Doulton bulldog, shown recumbent, with a patch over one eye and draped in the Union flag.
- *16cm x 23cm*
- £395   • London Antique

Expert Tips

Toby jugs have always been popular collectable items as they are great fun and are in most cases reasonably priced (as is lustre ware). Toby jugs make ideal objects for the country cottage.

Staffordshire Figure of Girl and Beehive ▼
- *1845*
A Staffordshire figure of a
young girl seated by a beehive
on a leafy mound.
- *height 12cm*
- £110   • Cekay

Seated Shepherdess ◄
- *circa 1820*
A Staffordshire figure of a
shepherdess seated on a flower
encrusted base with a goat.
- *height 135cm*
- £135   • Cekay

King Charles Spaniel ▲
- *1880*
A Victorian Staffordshire King
Charles Spaniel painted white
with green markings.
- *height 24cm*
- £115   • Cekay

Bird with Chicks ▼
- *1860*
A Staffordshire ink well showing
a bird with chicks on a nest,
encrusted with flowers.
- *height 4cm*
- £68   • Cekay

Porcelain Turk ▼
- *1830*
A porcelain figure of a Turk,
seated on a pink cushion.
- *height 12cm*
- £89   • Cekay

English Lustre Jug ▼
- *1845*
An English copper lustre jug,
with a scrolled handle and
decorated with a rose and leaf
pattern.
- *height 11cm*
- £88   • Cekay

Spill Holder ▲
- *1860*
A Staffordshire spill holder with a
figure of a shepherdess.
- *height 28cm*
- £135   • Cekay

Toby Jug ▼
- *mid 19th century*
A lady snuff taker in green coat
with candy striped underdress,
holding a snuff bag and taking a
pich to her nose.
- *height 19cm*
- £260   • Constance Stobo

Scene from Persuasion ▼
- *circa 1820*
A scene from Jane Austen's
Persuasion, made by Sharrat. An
eager male and a coy female on
a garden seat with dog; spreading
pineapple bocage behind.
- *height 20cm*
- £6,200   • Constance Stobo

Prince of Wales ▲
- *1850*
A Staffordshire figure of the
Prince of Wales mounted on
horseback on a naturally formed
base.
- *height 12cm*
- £125   • Cekay

European Ceramics

Meissen Candelabra ▼

● 1860

One of a pair of Meissen candelabra, encrusted with flowers and fruit decoration and figures depicting a shepherd and shepherdess.

● height 43cm
● £3,500 ● London Antique

Sèvres-Style Vase ▼

● 1890

One of a pair of Sèvres-style vases with ormolu mounts, gilt banding and panels showing profiles of maidens with pineapple gilt finial.

● height 31cm
● £1,550 ● London Antique

Sugar Bowl ▲

● 1765

Meissen tea set comprising sugar bowl, tea cup, saucer and milk jug, with gilded and painted decoration.

● £3,550 ● London Antique

Cup and Saucer ▲

● 1940–50

Royal Copenhagen blue and white cup and saucer, decorated with interlaced banding and floral arrangements.

● height 8cm
● £45 ● London Antique

Nymphenburg Group ▲

● 1800

Nymphenburg group in monochrome, showing a mounted huntsman directing his eager hounds on a rock moulded base.

● height 17.5cm
● £275 ● London Antique

Asparagus Dish ▲

● 1870

French asparagus dish with cradle of ceramic asparagus tips.

● height 19cm
● £495 ● Jesse Davis

Sauce Boat ▲

● circa 1890

Sèvres sauce boat, in the form of a swan with white bisque feathers and parcel gilt interior.

● height 9cm
● £295 ● London Antique

Dresden Coffee Cup ▲
- *1890*

Dresden coffee cup and saucer painted with cartouches showing a romantic scene of floral sprays on a pink ground within gilded borders.
- *height 8cm*
- £235 • London Antique

Gilded Cup and Saucer ▲
- *1890*

Porcelain cup and saucer by Sampson. Decorated with a chinoiserie-influenced design. Both the cup and saucer have gilded rims.
- *height 8cm*
- £45 • London Antique

Picasso Bowl ▲
- *1952*

A Picasso bowl with a wide rim. The centre of the bowl is hand painted in a charcoal and grey wash, with a stylised picture of a raven with stones at its feet.
- *diameter 15cm*
- £755 • London Antique

Lady's Writing Set with Candle Holders ▲
- *1880*

Lady's glazed desktop writing set with ink well and candle holders designed with an oriental theme.
- *height 15cm*
- £3,500 • London Antique

Dresden Coffee Cup and Saucer ▲
- *1880*

Dresden coffee cup and saucer with scrolled decoration and gilding. The cup has a barley twist handle and stands on three paw feet. Decorated with a central lobed cartouche showing a romantic setting.
- *height 8cm*
- £285 • London Antique

Meissen Decorative Column ➤
- *1870*

Meissen column converted for use as an electric lamp. Featuring cherub adornment and flower encrustation with scrolled asymmetric designs about the base.
- *height 50cm*
- £485 • London Antique

Royal Copenhagen Ware ▲
- *1945*

Royal Copenhagen blue and white cup and saucer, with interlaced banding and foliate designs.
- *height 10cm*
- £35 •London Antique

Floral Sugar Bowl ➤
- *1750*

Meissen sugar bowl with floral sprays to the cover and body.
- *height 8cm*
- £235   • London Antique

Meissen Cup and Saucer ▲
- *1750*

Meissen teacup and saucer with a moulded body and scrolled handle. Decorated with floral designs and gilding around rim.
- *height 9cm/cup*
- £885   • London Antique

Helena Wolfsohn Set ▲
- *1880*

Helena Wolfsohn cup and saucer of quartra-lobed form, with lobed rims. Shepherd and shepherdess are shown within gilt cartouches and floral arrangements.
- *height 5cm/cup*
- £255   • London Antique

Expert Tips

Always inspect floral sprays on Chelsea and Meissen porcelain, as they are often damaged or have been repaired.

Meissen Teapot ▼
- *1765*

Meissen teapot with a lobed cartouche of harbour scenes within gilt borders. Part of a set comprising milk jug, sugar bowl, tea cup and saucer.
- *height 14cm*
- £3,550   • London Antique

Encrusted Cup ▼
- *1814*

A flower and bird encrusted cup and saucer, decorated with flower detailing under the saucer, and a bird nestled within foliage on the cup.
- *diameter 3cm/cup*
- £885   • London Antique

Swan-Handled Cup ▲
- *1860*

Sèvres-style cylindrical cup and saucer, with a swan handle and paw feet, and decorated with floral sprays and gilding.
- *height 7cm*
- £355   • London Antique

Cherub Figure ▲
- *1880*

Meissen figure of a cherub sharpening his arrow on a grindstone. Heavily scrolled and gilded.
- *height 12cm*
- £895   •London Antique

Fluted Cup and Saucer ▲

- *1890*

Meissen cup and saucer with fluted body, with floral decoration and gilding.
- *height 8.5cm*
- £88   • London Antique

Ceramic Jug ▲

- *16th century*

Ceramic jug with handle and a central panel, showing the portrait of Cardinal Bellamine.
- *height 24.5cm*
- £2,500   • Peter Bunting

Tobacco Jar ▲

- *1800*

Delft blue and white tobacco jar with profuse floral decoration Inscribed "Straas Burger" on the outside.
- *height 25cm*
- £1,100   • Dial Post House

Stoneware Jug ▼

- *early 19th century*

German stoneware blue and white jug with handle, decorated with birds among foliage.
- *height 30cm*
- £700   • Dial Post House

Meissen Figurine ▼

- *1880*

Meissen figure of a cherub digging on a heavily scrolled and gilded base.
- *height 12cm*
- £885   • London Antique

Small Cup and Saucer ▲

- *1860–1924*

Small Meissen cup and saucer encrusted with flowers.
- *height 3cm*
- £435   • London Antique

Maricoline Cup ▲

- *circa 1780*

Meissen Maricoline cup and saucer with floral design.
- *height 6cm*
- £295   • London Antique

Meissen Cup and Saucer ▼

- *1736*

Small Meissen cup and saucer, with panels depicting romantic landscapes set within gilt borders.

- *height 2.5cm*
- £486   •London Antique

Chocolate Cup ▼

- *1890*

Dresden chocolate cup and saucer with lobed rim and scrolled double gilt handles. Decorated with cartouches showing figures in a garden setting within gilt and jewelled borders, and floral arrangements on a primrose yellow ground.

- *height 7cm*
- £285   • London Antique

Dessert Plate ▼

- *1780*

White dessert plate with blue and gold ribboning and floral design.

- *diameter 14cm*
- £100   • London Antique

Gilded Dessert Plate ▼

- *19th century*

Third Republic dessert plate, with a central panel showing a pastoral scene with a cobalt blue and gilded border.

- *diameter 14cm*
- £235   • London Antique

Albarello ➤

- *18th century*

Spanish Talavera blue and white albarello bearing a monogram beneath a crown.

- *height 22cm*
- £575   • Dial Post House

Majolica Jug ▲

- *1870*

Majolica wine jug with Bacchanal figures predominantly dispersed around the body, standing on a drum base.

- *height 35cm*
- £395   • Jesse Davis

Ceramics

Cabinet Cup and Saucer ▼
- **1890**
Luisentasse cabinet cup and saucer with a grey ground. Cup carries a biscuit profile bust of Queen Luise of Prussia on a vermiculated gilt oval medallion.
- *height 15cm*
- **£9,995** • **London Antique**

Majolica Oyster Plate ▼
- **1865**
Circular polychrome Majolica oyster plate, with six concave receptacles centred around a cobalt blue boss.
- *diameter 27cm*
- **£450** • **Jesse Davis**

Berlin Cup and Saucer ▲
- **1840–60**
Berlin cup and saucer heavily gilded around the rim and the foot of the cup.
- **£145** • **London Antique**

Pair of Inscribed Vases ▲
- **1760**
Rare pair of vases inscribed "PB 1760". One painted with a leopard the other with a horse.
- *height 25cm*
- **£4,950** • **Dial Post House**

Strawberry Plate ▼
- **1876**
Polychrome French Surrequenine strawberry plate with moulded strawberry decorations about the border, with gilding and jewelling on a light blue base.
- *diameter 21cm*
- **£245** • **Jesse Davis**

Majolica Teapot ▼
- **1820**
Majolica teapot, showing a monkey astride a coconut with his tail coiled around the twig handle, with leaf decoration.
- *height 18.5cm*
- **£1,695** • **Jesse Davis**

Expert Tips

If possible purchase your ceramic ware through a respected dealer as these items command high prices.

Fabergé Cup and Saucer ▲
- **1894**
Fabergé cup and saucer with stylised leaf decoration to the saucer, the cup heavily gilded with lattice design on green base.
- *height 8cm*
- **£85** • **London Antique**

Majolica Twin-Handled Vase ◄
- *1875*

Majolica twin-handled urn shaped vase with a central frieze showing classical figures above acanthus leaf design on a pedestal foot, by Thomes Sargent.
- *height 49cm*
- £695   • Jesse Davis

Duck Tureens ▲
- *1875*

Pair of polychrome continental soup tureens, probably French, naturalistically formed as a duck and drake in a seated pose.
- *height 11cm*
- £395   • Jesse Davis

Flemish Jug ▲
- *17th century*

Flemish stoneware jug of oval form with silver mounts.
- *height 22cm*
- £1,400 • P. Boyd-Carpenter

Pineapple Teapot ▲
- *1865*

Majolica teapot, with the body styled as a pineapple with leaf designs, and pineapple finial applied to the cover.
- *height 21cm*
- £395   • Jesse Davis

Majolica Jug ◄
- *1865*

Majolica jug of ovoid form with a pewter lid and thumb piece. Features moulded decoration depicting a forest scene under a green glaze.
- *height 9cm*
- £195   • Jesse Davis

Italian Jug ▲
- *1870*

Italian Majolica palm-leaf jug, with vertical stylised palm leaf decoration to the body of the jug, with a pinched lip and the whole on a splayed foot.
- *height 19cm*
- £295   • Jesse Davis

Writing Set and Ink Stand ◀
- 1890

Dresden writing set and ink stand with scallop-shell base and urn-shaped ink well, decorated and gilded with floral sprays.
- *height 10cm*
- £255   • London Antique

Cup and Saucer Set ▼
- 1788

Sèvres-style cylindrical cup and saucer with floral and red and white banding as decoration. The cup carries an elaborate monogram an white oval panel.
- *height 6cm*
- £355   • London Antique

Portrait Cup and Saucer Set ▼
- 1890

Sèvres cup and saucer with a portrait set within gilded borders on a dark ground with panels decorated with floral designs. Further floral decoration to the saucer with jewelling.
- *height 4cm*
- £355   • London Antique

Chocolate Cup ◀
- 1890

Augustus chocolate cup and saucer with double-scroll handles and pierced basketholder. Decorated with two large panels showing two figures in a garden setting framed by a gilded border.
- *height 9cm*
- £265   • London Antique

Helena Cup and Saucer ▼
- 1845–87

Dresden Helena cup and saucer of lobed design decorated with bird vignettes and insects and finished with gilded borders and scrolled handle.
- *height 4cm*
- £265   • London Antique

Sèvres Cup and Saucer ▼
- 1870

Sèvres-style cup and saucer with gilding to the inside of the cup and the centre of the saucer, with gilt ribbons and swags on a dark cobalt blue base.
- *height 5.5cm*
- £235   • London Antique

Gilded Cup and Saucer ◄
- *19th century*
Sèvres-style cup and saucer with profuse gilding on a blue ground with a painted panel on the side of the cup.
- *height 5.5cm*
- £365 • London Antique

Porcelain Picture ▼
- *19th century*
Finely painted porcelain plaque with a decorative gilt porcelain frame.
- *65cm x 80cm*
- £26,000 • Sinai Antiques

Meissen Cup and Saucer ▼
- *circa 1880*
Meissen cup and saucer, with flower detailing underneath saucer adnd insects inside cup.
- *8cm x 13cm*
- £650 • David Brower

Porcelain Plaques ▲
- *circa 1860*
Pair of finely painted porcelain plaques by Thevenot.
- *81cm x 59cm*
- £26,000 • Sinai Antiques

Dresden Cup and Saucer ▲
- *1880*
Dresden flower-encrusted cup, cover and saucer, with a yellow bird finial and applied yellow and pink flower decoration.
- *height 18cm*
- £885 • London Antique

KPM Porcelain ▲
- *19th century*
Tall porcelain vase decorated with scenes of the German royal family. Handcrafted by KPM, the royal porcelain manufacturers of Germany.
- *height 190cm*
- £85,000 • Sinai Antiques

Viennese Jug ▼
- *19th century*

Viennese jug with mythological representations on the inner and outer sides of the vessel, with fine silver mounts.
- *height 5cm*
- £1,200 • P. Boyd-Carpenter

Stoneware Jug ▼
- *15th century*

Seidborg Kanne stoneware drinking vessel with handle and turned decoration.
- *height 28cm*
- £650 • P. Boyd-Carpenter

Lobed Cup and Saucer ▲
- *19th century*

Meissen cup and saucer of lobed decoration with scrolled handle and painted panels.
- *height 6cm*
- £395 • London Antique

Spanish Honey Pot ▼
- *16th century*

Spanish honey pot with hand-painted decoration and two carrying handles.
- *height 15cm*
- £450 • P. Boyd-Carpenter

Pair of Drug Jars ▲
- *17th century*

Pair of Savona drug jars decorated with pastoral scenes.
- *height 18cm*
- £1,200 • P. Boyd-Carpenter

Dresden Tea Bowl ◄
- *1866*

Dresden tea bowl with two floral displays painted to the sides of the bowl by Adolph Hamann, raised on a circular foot and inscribed on the base "P223" marks.
- *height 3.5cm*
- £45 • London Antique

Sweetmeat Dish ▲
- *1880*

Meissen sweetmeat dish showing a central figure between two scalloped shape dishes.
- *17cm x 24cm*
- £165   •London Antique

Porcelain Cachepot ▲
- *1790*

Cachepot in white porcelain with gilt decoration and harbour scenes within gilt borders.
- *14cm x 24cm*
- £880   • O.F. Wilson

Ewer and Cover ▼
- *1814–60*

Meissen ewer and cover with scrolled decoration to handle and lip, decorated with flower finial and hunting scenes.
- *height 25cm*
- £1,450   • London Antique

Albarello ▼
- *late 17th century*

Italian blue and white apothecary jar of baluster form with central name band.
- *height 35cm*
- £1,100   • Dial Post House

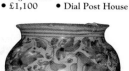

Tobacco Jar ▼
- *1800*

Dutch Delft blue and white tobacco jar from the De Bloempot factory. Inscribed "Spaanse".
- £800   • Dial Post House

Tea Cup and Saucer ◄
- *1805*

Meissen tea cup and saucer painted on grisaille. Depicting the Rhine within gilt roundel below pendant with yellow banding and gilding.
- *height 6cm*
- £295   • London Antique

Expert Tips

Some porcelain plaques can be of outstanding quality and very desirable but it is worth noting that they can suffer from chipping around the edges as a result of nails being used to secure the plaque to the frame.

Meissen Sweetmeat Dish ▲
- *circa 1880*
One of a pair of Meissen sweetmeat dishes. Modelled as a reclining shepherd and shepherdess with dishes with scrolled border.
- *20cm x 31cm*
- **£1,950** • London Antique

Meissen Coffee Pot ▲
- *1890*
Meissen coffee pot and cover with painted panels depicting harbour scenes set within enamelled and gilt decoration, with scrolled handle and finial lid.
- *height 22cm*
- **£795** • London Antique

Meissen Teapot ▲
- *1860–1924*
Large Meissen teapot and stand encrusted with flowers, with scrolled brass mounts. The scrolled base has pierced decoration and flower encrustation.
- *height 31cm*
- **£6,650** • London Antique

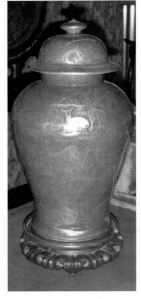

French Chinoiserie Vase ▲
- *1890*
French copy of a Chinese baluster vase with gilded chinoiserie designs on a blue ground.
- *height 48cm*
- **£425** • Mousa Antiques

Pair of Chargers ▲
- *19th century*
One of a pair of Majolica chargers with a central panel depicting grotesque scenes of battle, with floral designs to the rim.
- *height 47cm*
- **£2,400** • P. Boyd-Carpenter

Dresden Figurines ▲
- *20th century*
Dresden group of porcelain figures, modelled as a monkey band.
- *height 17cm*
- **£255** • London Antique

Porcelain Compart ▼

- *1900–20*
Continental porcelain compart
by Schashelf, embellished with
flying cupids, fruit and flowers.
The bowl pierced and
embellished with swags.
- *height 57cm*
- £585 • A.D. Antiques

Meissen Figure ▼

- *circa 1880*
Cherub in a classical pose,
piercing two hearts with an arrow.
- *height 27cm*
- £2,850 • David Brower

Model of Harvester ➤

- *1785–90*
Model of harvester reclining on
a wheatsheaf, made by the Gera
factory, Germany. The figure rests
on a base with Omega mark.
- *height 23cm*
- £1,250 • E. & H. Manners

Porcelain Busts ▲

- *20th century*
Pair of German porcelain busts of
Royal children, after models
by Kaendler.
- *height 15.5cm*
- £635 • London Antique

Vincennes Sucrier ▲

- *date 1754*
Early Vincennes sucrier painted
with birds on cartouches against
a blue lapis ground and
chrysanthemum finial gilt
decoration. With interlaced "L"
and the date letter "B".
- *height 10cm*
- £5,000 • E. & H. Manners

Wine Jug ▲

- *1630*
Wine jug from the Western
Ald, showing a religious scene of
Christ within an octagonal
border, raised on a circular foot
with pewter mounts.
- *height 23cm*
- £1,630 • Jonathan Horne

Dresden Dancing Figure ▼

- *1945*

Dresden figurine depicting a Flamenco dancer, standing on an oval moulded base with gilding.
- *height 12cm*
- £65   • London Antique

Earthenware Beer Jug ▶

- *circa 1600*

Rare German earthenware beer jug with stamped and incised decoration, together with pewter lid and thumb piece.
- *height 18cm*
- £3,750   • Jonathan Horne

German Dessert Plate ▼

- *1765*

Nymphenburg dessert plate with trellis border and birds and flower design at centre (tulips/roses) and gilt border.
- *diameter 23cm*
- £1,400   • E. & H. Manners

Alborelli Vases ▲

- *circa 1700*

Pair of Alborelli vases from Sciacca, Sicily. Predominantly blue with cartouches showing maritime scene framed with leaf design.
- *height 22cm*
- £3,000–£4,000   • Bazaart

Alberello Vase ▼

- *circa 1670*

Probably Bassano vase, of dumbbell form with floral swags from mask decoration.
- *height 27cm*
- £1,200–£1,500   • Bazaart

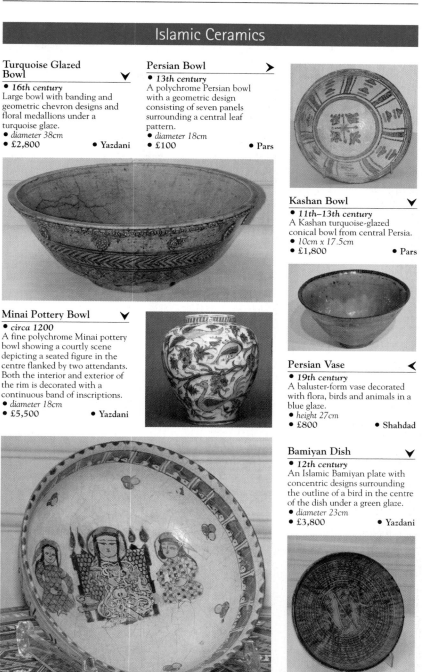

Islamic Ceramics

Turquoise Glazed Bowl ▼
- *16th century*
Large bowl with banding and geometric chevron designs and floral medallions under a turquoise glaze.
- *diameter 38cm*
- £2,800   • Yazdani

Persian Bowl ➤
- *13th century*
A polychrome Persian bowl with a geometric design consisting of seven panels surrounding a central leaf pattern.
- *diameter 18cm*
- £100   • Pars

Kashan Bowl ▼
- *11th–13th century*
A Kashan turquoise-glazed conical bowl from central Persia.
- *10cm x 17.5cm*
- £1,800   • Pars

Minai Pottery Bowl ▼
- *circa 1200*
A fine polychrome Minai pottery bowl showing a courtly scene depicting a seated figure in the centre flanked by two attendants. Both the interior and exterior of the rim is decorated with a continuous band of inscriptions.
- *diameter 18cm*
- £5,500   • Yazdani

Persian Vase ◄
- *19th century*
A baluster-form vase decorated with flora, birds and animals in a blue glaze.
- *height 27cm*
- £800   • Shahdad

Bamiyan Dish ▼
- *12th century*
An Islamic Bamiyan plate with concentric designs surrounding the outline of a bird in the centre of the dish under a green glaze.
- *diameter 23cm*
- £3,800   • Yazdani

Bamiyan Pottery Bowl ▼

- *11th–12th century*
A fine Bamiyan pottery bowl
with slightly convex flaring sides
decorated with a series of dashes
along the rim and covered with a
turquoise glaze.
- *diameter 22cm*
- £950   • Yazdani

Monochrome Bowl ▼

- *12th–13th century AD*
A Bamiyan pottery bowl with
relief surface decoration and
further dot and cross decoration
in black on the inside and rim.
- *diameter 25cm*
- £1,100   • Yazdani

Floral Leaf Bowl ▼

- *11th–12th century*
A fine Persian Bamiyan pottery
bowl. The bowl has an inverted
rim decorated under a turquoise
glaze with a floral leaf motif.
- *diameter 20cm*
- £3,000   • Yazdani

Jug with Splayed Lip ▼

- *12th century*
A water vessel with a strap
handle and splayed lip with
geometric designs under a
turquoise glaze. The vessel has
an iridescent finish and stops
to base.
- *height 20cm*
- £2,800   • Yazdani

Islamic Ceramic Jug ▼

- *12th–13th century*
Jug of globular form, glazed in
turquoise and black with stops to
base and two handles to the lip.
- *height 18cm*
- £2,500   • Aaron

Kashan Ewer ▲

- *13th century*
An earthenware Kashan
ewer with a strap handle and
banding in turquoise glaze
with stops to base.
- *length 34cm*
- £1,800   • Yazdani

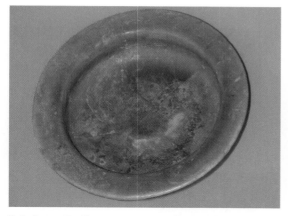

Seljuk Tray ◄
- *11th–12th century*
A turquoise glazed Seljuk tray
with iridescence.
- *diameter 15cm*
- £250 • Pars

Polychrome Bowl ▼
- *10th–11th century*
A polychrome Nishapur
bowl from northwest Iran,
with stylised palm leaf
motif.
- *diameter 24cm*
- £1,200 • Pars

Sgraffiato Dish ▼
- *11th–12th century*
A large Bamiyan Sgraffiato
pottery dish with geometric
designs to the inside of the dish,
under a green and brown glaze.
- *diameter 36cm*
- £1,500 • Pars

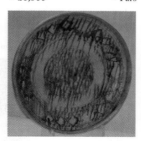

Nishapur Bowl ▲
- *11th–13th century*
An Iranian polychrome
Nishapur bowl with a central
figure of a stylized bird and
signature.
- *diameter 22.5cm*
- £800 • Pars

Cobalt Blue Jug ▲
- *12th–13th century*
A small Kushan jar with
bulbous body and a cobalt-blue
glaze on a splayed footing with a
strap handle.
- *height 13cm*
- £800 •Pars

Terracotta Pipe ◄
- *circa 1850*
A terracotta Tophane pipe with
gold and silver floral gilt design.
From Morocco.
- *height 5cm*
- £550 • Sinai

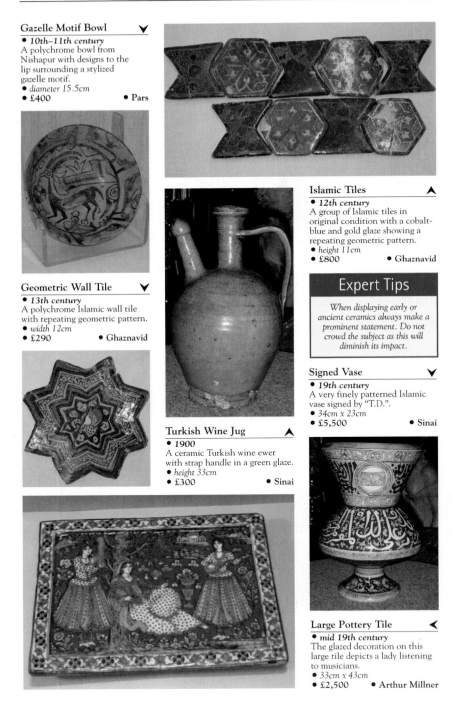

Gazelle Motif Bowl ▼
- *10th–11th century*
A polychrome bowl from
Nishapur with designs to the
lip surrounding a stylized
gazelle motif.
- *diameter 15.5cm*
- **£400**   • **Pars**

Geometric Wall Tile ▼
- *13th century*
A polychrome Islamic wall tile
with repeating geometric pattern.
- *width 12cm*
- **£290**   • **Ghaznavid**

Turkish Wine Jug ▲
- *1900*
A ceramic Turkish wine ewer
with strap handle in a green glaze.
- *height 33cm*
- **£300**   • **Sinai**

Islamic Tiles ▲
- *12th century*
A group of Islamic tiles in
original condition with a cobalt-
blue and gold glaze showing a
repeating geometric pattern.
- *height 11cm*
- **£800**   • **Ghaznavid**

Expert Tips

*When displaying early or
ancient ceramics always make a
prominent statement. Do not
crowd the subject as this will
diminish its impact.*

Signed Vase ▼
- *19th century*
A very finely patterned Islamic
vase signed by "T.D.".
- *34cm x 23cm*
- **£5,500**   • **Sinai**

Large Pottery Tile ◄
- *mid 19th century*
The glazed decoration on this
large tile depicts a lady listening
to musicians.
- *33cm x 43cm*
- **£2,500**   • **Arthur Millner**

Damascus Pottery Tile

- *17th century*

Pottery tile decorated with arabesque and iris motif.
- *20cm x 22cm*
- £400
- Arthur Millner

Kashan Jug

- *12th–13th century*

A Kashan jug of bulbous form with a splayed neck and strap handle in a turquoise and black glaze with stops to the base.
- *height 22cm*
- £1,000
- Pars

Pre-Ottoman Vase

- *12th century*

A green monochrome vase from the pre-Ottoman Empire period. Of a baluster form with a wide lip and two handles to the shoulders with extensive openwork decoration to the body. The whole is raised on a circular foot ring.
- *height 35cm*
- £400
- Pars

Nishapur Bowl

- *13th century*

A Nishapur bowl with the Kufic calligraphic inscription "healthy and long life".
- *diameter 30cm*
- £2,000
- Shiraz

Ceramic Bowl

- *circa 9th century*

A blue and white, tin-glazed ceramic bowl of the Abbasid period, the rim with blue swags.
- *diameter 21cm*
- £15,000
- Axia

Kashan Vase

- *13th century*

A small Kashan vase with balloon body and long neck with fine iridescence and stops to base.
- *height 14cm*
- £950
- Yazdani

Oriental Ceramics

Octagonal Vase ▲
- 1890

Octagonal Satsuma vase of
famille verte, with alternating
panels of stylised floral decoration
and gilding
- *height 24cm*
- £2,980 • Japanese Gallery

Imari Vases ▼
- 1890

Pair of cylindrical Imari vases
of famille verte, each with a
splayed lip.
- *height 17cm*
- £1, 890 • Japanese Gallery

Pair of Satsuma Vases ▼
- 1890

Pair of Satsuma bottle vases
in the shape of double gourds.
Each vase is decorated with two
figures at the base of the neck
embellished with profuse gilding.
- *height 24cm*
- £2,980 • Japanese Gallery

Gilded Vase ◀
- 1910

Satsuma vase of baluster form,
showing figures in a garden
setting, and decorated with
gilded and stylised floral patterns.
- *height 21cm*
- £355 • Japanese Gallery

Amari Bowl ▲
- 1880

Amari fluted bowl with famille
vert floral decoration and lattice
border, set in ormolu mounts.
- *height 20cm*
- £2,885 • Japanese Gallery

Expert Tips

*When purchasing Satsuma and
Amari ware, the general rule of
thumb is that the larger the item
the better the price. As always,
good condition is fundamental.
In the last twenty years these
oriental wares have become
so popular that it has heralded
a flood of reproductions
into the market.*

Covered Imari Pot ▲
- *late 18th century*

Imari pot and cover, with a pair
of gilded handles and ornate
dog finial.
- *height 30cm*
- £1,950 • Japanese Gallery

Arita Teapot ▼

- *1700*

Rare Arita teapot of orchid form with applied tubular handle and spout from which leaves and blossoms emerge. The cover has a similar knob in the form of one open and one closed pearlised bloom.

- *height 21cm*
- £355 • **Japanese Gallery**

Sauce Tureen ➤

- *circa 1765*

Armorial sauce tureen with cover and stand, bearing the arms of Countess Maccesfield (Parker impaling Nesbitt). Following a Leeds Cream Ware form with grisaille trellis dipper and rouge de fer rim.

- *width 18cm*
- £15,000 • **Cohen & Cohen**

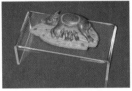

Sauce Tureen and Cover ▲

- *circa 1780*

Very rare Chinese export sauce tureen and cover of a sow suckling four piglets. Enamelled in grisaille and sepia.

- £45,000 • **Cohen & Cohen**

Pair of Tureens ▼

- *1770*

Pair of sauce tureens and covers, in the style of a European ceramic form, with floral decoration.

- £2,900 • **Cohen & Cohen**

Ribbed Coffee Pot ▲

- *1740*

Famille Rose coffee pot and cover after a Queen Anne silver form. Ribbed sides carry a painted pheasant perched on rockwork amid peony blossom.

- *height 19cm*
- £3,200 • **Cohen & Cohen**

Quianlong Vase ▲

- *1736–96*

Quinlong Chinese vase with a coral monochrome glaze. Globular body with a narrow flared neck and splayed foot.

- *height 19cm*
- £1,250 • **Guest & Grey**

Tea Bowl and Saucer ▲
- *1756*

Mythological tea bowl and saucer in famille rose, depicting the story of Leda and the Swan.
- £4,500   • Cohen & Cohen

Armorial Plate ▼
- *circa 1743*

Exceptional Chinese export armorial dinner plate with the arms of "Leake Oke Over" with an elaborate surround.
- *height 22cm*
- £11,000   • Cohen & Cohen

Salt Trencher ▲
- *1715*

Rare Chinese export salt trencher decorated in verte/mari enamels. The centre is painted with the arms of Louis XV of France.
- *3.5cm x 7cm*
- £3,850   • Cohen & Cohen

Vegetable Tureen ▲
- *1760*

Fine famille rose vegetable tureen decorated with flowers and a fence. The cover features a pomegranate-shaped knob.
- *14cm x 24cm*
- £5,650   • Cohen & Cohen

Rococo Tureen Cover ▲
- *1808*

Very rare Chinese export tureen cover and stand of bold Rococo form, with vivid colouring.
- *height 25cm*
- £60,000   • Cohen & Cohen

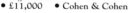

Soup Plate ▲
- *circa 1770*

Chinese export soup plate with a scalloped edge and decorated in polychrome, showing three shrews and pheasants among tobacco leaves.
- *height 14cm*
- £2,200   • Cohen & Cohen

Arita Ware Vase ▲

- **1890**
Arita ware vase in famille verte,
with a baluster form and
decorated with stylised floral
sprays on a wide splayed base.
- *height 19.5cm*
- **£1,350** • **Japanese Gallery**

Hirado Vase ▼

- **1868–1912**
Unusual Hirado vase from the
Meiji/Edo period, decorated
with the imperial "mons"
(family crest).
- *height 42cm*
- **£3,200** • **Brandt**

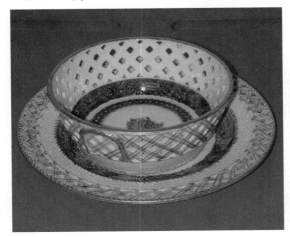

Pair of Bough Pots ◄

- *circa 1780*
Pair of bough pots and covers in
famille rose, painted with sepia
panels of a European country
house within borders of flowers.
- *height 22cm*
- **£8,500** • **Cohen & Cohen**

Expert Tips

*Chinese porcelain was made for
the imperial court. However,
you need to beware as some
pieces carrying the imperial
mark are made for export.*

Floral Coffee Pot ▼

- *circa 1780*
Coffee pot and cover of famille
rose, in a conical form, with an
S-shaped handle and tall spout
decorated with floral sprays.
- *height 20cm*
- **£2,300** • **Cohen & Cohen**

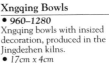

Xngqing Bowls ▼

- **960–1280**
Xngqing bowls with insized
decoration, produced in the
Jingdezhen kilns.
- *17cm x 4cm*
- **£730** • **Gordon Reece**

Lattice-Work Basket ◄

- **1780**
Unusual Chinese export basket
and stand, with moulded ring
handles. Decorated with
underglazed blue borders.
- *diameter 14cm*
- **£2,200** • **Cohen & Cohen**

Nankin Tureen ▲
- *1736–95*

Elongated, octagonal blue-and-white Nankin tureen. Decorated with tiny figures among pagodas and bridges over waterways. Well-modelled fruit as knob and handles
- *length 35cm*
- £1,200   • Anita Gray

Chinese Cloisonné Vase ➤
- *early 18th century*

Cloisonné enamel vase of yan yan form, from the Qing Dynasty period. High-shouldered tapering body with two gilt monster mask and lotus leaf handles, standing on a flared foot. Decorated in colourful enamels on a turquoise and lapis blue ground filled with scrolling lotus, dragon designs, bats, and flower heads, with gilt trim on base and rim.
- *height 67.3cm*
- £18,000 • Gerard Hawthorn

Porcelain Tureen ▼
- *17th century*

Japanese Imari porcelain tureen and underdish, featuring a bird fruit and flower decoration.
- £12,000 • Gerard Hawthorn

Swatow Dish ▼
- *early 17th century*

Circular dish painted to the centre with a circular panel of two kylins playing with a broaded ball, surrounded by symbolic objects and scrollwork
- *diameter 37cm*
- £1,600   •Anita Gray

Octagonal Bowl ▼
- *18th century*

Octagonal bowl from the Kukieman Edo period, decorated with a central design of birds with floral border.
- *5cm x 13cm*
- £1,550   • Japanese Gallery

Porcelain Punchbowl ◀
- *18th century*

Finely decorated Chinese punchbowl in famille rose, from the Quing Dynasty period. Decorated with enamel figures set in a garden landscape.
- *17cm x 40cm*
- £8,000   • Gerard Hawthorn

K'ang Hsi Teapot ▼

- *1700*

Blue and white teapot and cover
from the K'ang Hsi period,
decorated with peony branches.
- *height 12cm*
- £1,000 • Cohen & Cohen

Ceramic Pots ▼

- *circa 1930*

Three assorted ceramic pots.
- *29cm x 18cm*
- £155 • Gordon Reece

Pottery Jar and Cover ◄

- *circa 1880*

Covered jar, probably made at
the Bombay School of Arts, with
green and yellow glazed floral
decoration.
- *23cm x 12cm*
- £200 • Arthur Millner

Shallow Dish ▲

- *1700*

Large and unusual Chinese
export dish made for the Spanish
market during the K'ang Hsi
period. Features a shallow well
rising to a dome in the centre,
decorated in iron red and gilt.
- *diameter 54cm*
- £8,000 • Cohen & Cohen

Charger ◄

- *1700*

Large blue and white charger
decorated with panels of foliage
arranged in the shape of a flower
with a border of peacocks.
- *diameter 44cm*
- £5,000 • Cohen & Cohen

Grisaille Plate ▲

- *1740*

Grisaille plate, decorated with
a mythological scene depicting
Juno and Jupiter embracing
beside an eagle, peacock and
putti.
- *height 22cm*
- £4,000 • Cohen & Cohen

Famille Verte Bowl ◀
- *1662–22*

Chinese export bowl decorated on the exterior with overglaze enamels in the famille verte palette with birds flying amid prunus plants, issuing from stylised rockwork.
- *diameter 22cm*
- £980   • Anita Gray

Pair of Baluster Jars ▲
- *1740*

Important pair of baluster jars and covers of famille rose, painted with three medallions of scenes from a romance on an elaborate floral ground.
- *height 62cm*
- £55,000   • Cohen & Cohen

Chinese Teapot ▼
- *1730*

Unusual Chinese export teapot and cover in the style of a European silver shape, with loop handle and zoomorphic spout, decorated in rose/verte enamels.
- *height 14cm*
- £3,200   • Cohen & Cohen

Christening Bowl ▲
- *1750*

Massive and exceptionally rare christening bowl painted with four bands of lotus petals in green, purple, blue and rose, with four floral reserves.
- *24.5cm x 55cm*
- £43,000   • Cohen & Cohen

Oil and Vinegar Cruet ▲
- *1740*

Chinese Imari oil and vinegar cruet, comprising two lidded sparrow-beak jugs in a stand with a loop handle. All with floral decoration.
- *16cm x 14cm*
- £2,750   • Cohen & Cohen

Famille Rose Bowl ◀
- *1760*

Famille Rose punchbowl with two large panels of pagodas by a lake and surrounded by mountains on a soufflé blue and gilt ground.
- *diameter 39cm*
- £5,000   • Cohen & Cohen

Soup Plate ▼

- 1795

Polychrome soup plate decorated with tree shrews, pheasants and a tobacco leaf pattern with blue underglaze.

- *diameter 23cm*
- £2,200   • Cohen & Cohen

Imari Bowl ▼

- 1880

Imari bowl raised on a padook wood stand. Decorated with highly detailed painted swallow on the interior of the bowl.

- *diameter 9cm*
- £2,885   • Japanese Gallery

Decorated Bronze Vase ▼

- 1860

Bronze and cloisonné vase.

- *height 50cm*
- £250   • Tredantiques

Satsuma Tea Bowl ▼

- 1890

Satsuma tea bowl decorated with hundreds of birds inside and flowers and foliage.

- *height 8cm*
- £2,950   • Japanese Gallery

Pottery Figure ▼

- 1368–1644

Fine pottery model of a horse and rider of unusual quality, made in the Shanxi province during the Ming dynasty period.

- *height 35cm*
- £2,600   • Little River

Pair of K'ang Hsi Vases ▲

- 1662–1722

Pair of blue and white vases of baluster form, from the K'ang Hsi period. Bodies are painted in bright blue underglaze with a repeated pattern of meandering floral scrolls.

- *diameter 31cm*
- £1,800   • Anita Gray

Kraak Dish ➤

- *circa 1580*

Large dish from the Ming dynasty, Wanti period. Decorated with a deep cobalt underglaze and scenes of scholars, fans and scrolls
- *diameter 50cm*
- £5,500   • Cohen & Cohen

Incense Burner ◀

- *1890*

Satsuma Koro incense burner decorated with gold figures.
- £385   • Japanese Gallery

Kutani Vase ▼

- *1880*

Japanese Kutani vase of oval form, decorated with scholarly figures in garden setting.
- *height 11cm*
- £585   • Japanese Gallery

Fluted Bowls ▲

- *circa 1700*

Pair of K'ang Hsi fluted bowls, decorated with panels of flowers and mythological beasts.
- *diameter 18.5cm*
- £2,500   • Guest & Grey

Glazed Jar ▼

- *14th century*

Sawankhalon Celadon glazed tapering squat jar with short inverted neck and twin jug handles. Incised with bands of scrolling motifs above a comb pattern foot.
- *height 16.5cm*
- £585   • Japanese Gallery

Expert Tips

Cloisonné is the art of enamelling using copper, gold or brass wire. Cloisonné ware can fetch very large prices, but the cost of restoration is phenomenal and as a result damaged pieces are devalued.

Chinese Candlesticks ▲

- *18th century*

Pair of Chinese export candlesticks of early eighteenth century European silver form, brightly enamelled in famille rose of dead-leaf brown.
- *height 21cm*
- £16,000   • Cohen & Cohen

Japanese Bowl ◄

- *1890*

Japanese bowl decorated in gold with painted figures.
- *height 8cm*
- £1,250   • Japanese Gallery

Valentine Charger ▼

- *1760*

Famille Rose charger decorated with a version of the valentine pattern above which are arms of an English family.
- *diameter 25cm*
- £2250   • Cohen & Cohen

Figure of Kwanyin ▼

- *1700*

Biscuit figure in famille verte of Kwanyin seated on a throne fronted by lotus leaves. The group comprises two pieces.
- *height 44cm*
- £6,850   • Cohen & Cohen

Moon Flask Ewer ▲

- *circa 1750*

Exceptionally rare polychrome ewer and cover of moon flask form, with panels within borders of bats and cranes and cell diaper.
- *height 30cm*
- £50,000   • Cohen & Cohen

Satsuma Teapot ▼

- *1890*

Satsuma teapot, decorated with scholarly figures in a garden setting with rocks and foliage.
- *height 11cm*
- £155   • Japanese Gallery

Quenti Pot ▲

- *Mid 20th century*

Very large impressively constructed Quenti pot, with diagrammatic decoration.
- *65cm x 45cm*
- £1,800   • Gordon Reece

Yenyen Vases ►

- *1690*

One of a pair of large Chinese export blue and white Yenyen vases, decorated with panels of flowers in jardiniers between rows of floral lappets.
- *height 54cm*
- £35,000   • Cohen & Cohen

Satsuma Bowl ◀

- *19th century*

Satsuma earthenware bowl made in Japan. Decorated with goldfish on the bowl's interior.
- *height 9cm*
- £1,700 • J.A.N. Fine Art

Chinese Celadon Dish ▲

- *1276–1368*

Celadon dish from the Yang dynasty period, with barbed rim, incised decoration with repeated leaf pattern and floral central panel.
- *diameter 35cm*
- £1,950 • J.A.N. Fine Art

Pair of Soup Plates ▲

- *1735*

Pair of soup plates of famille rose style, painted with the arms of Rose of Kilvarock within a border of flowers and inner rim diaper of trellis en grisaille.
- *diameter 23cm*
- £2,600 • Cohen & Cohen

Kraak Ware Saucer Dish ◀

- *early 17th century*

Kraak Ware sauce dish painted to the centre with an eight-pointed star, with artemisia leaf. The sides decorated with eight oval panels, charged with symbolic objects, alternating with scrollwork.
- *diameter 14.5cm*
- £350 • Anita Gray

K'ang Hsi Deep Dish ▼

- *circa 1690*

Fine deep dish decorated with panels of mounted warrios in underglaze blue with six-character reign mark on the reverse and ruyi-heads on rim underside.
- *diameter 24cm*
- £1,650 • Cohen & Cohen

Snuff Box ▼

- *1760*

Snuff box unusually handpainted in famille rose and floral spray decorations.
- *height 4cm*
- £1,760 • Cohen & Cohen

Arita Ware Puppy ➤

- *19th century*
Arita ware Okimono of a
porcelain puppy scratching his
ears. Decorated with painted
polychrome ruff around its neck,
and painted eyes.
- *height 12.5cm*
- £2,000   • Gregg Baker

Figure of a Lohan with an Octopus ▲

- *circa 19th century*
Figure of a lohan in a shell boat,
talking to a caricatured octopus.
The whole set on a carved and
painted wooden base
representing the sea.
- *length 36cm*
- £850   • Gregg Baker

Junyao Tripod Censer ▲

- *960–1280*
Rare Junyao tripod censer from
the Song dynasty period, of
compressed globular form.
- *diameter 8.75cm*
- £4,800   • Guest & Grey

Expert Tips

*Chinese porcelain was made for
the imperial court. However,
you need to beware as some
pieces carrying the imperial
mark are made for export.*

Chinese Transitional Jar ▼

- *1650–60*
Blue and white jar from the
transitional period, decorated in
underglaze blue with a scene of
three figures dressed in flowing
robes. The rim features a series of
single-pointed lappets.
- *height 27.9cm*
- £2,600   • Anita Gray

Satsuma Koro ◄

- *circa 19th century*
Japanese satsuma koro with silver
cover decorated with gilt.
- *height 13cm*
- £3,600   • Gregg Baker

Clocks, Watches &
Scientific Instruments

This category includes all forms of clock from carriage to longcases, fine watches to the antiques of the future and all scientific artefacts.

Mankind's fascination with marking time dates to the earliest civilizations, with the formulation of the zodiac and the building of pyramids. By the sixteenth century mankind's desire to explore the world lead to the creation of the first scientific instruments that could accurately record time, and brought about near precise navigation. The invention of the telescope by Galileo further extended mankind's reach beyond the limitations of the human eye. The first mechanical pendulum clock

was made by Jacopo Dondi of Padua in 1344. In the fifteenth century Peter Henlein of Nurnberg was credited with the invention of coil spring driven clocks.

The seventeenth to the early nineteenth century saw the great era of English clock making. Bracket and Longcase clocks from this period can fetch record prices today but they must be complete and without alterations. In the last few years there has also been increased interest in wrist and pocket watches, which are now achieving large sums and are worth collecting.

Clocks

Longcase Clock ➤
- *circa 1830*
A small, attractive flame-mahogany coloured Scottish longcase clock with belly door and eight-day break arch dial. Painted by "Christie and Barrie" of Abroath. The words "The Cotters Saturday Night" are painted in the break arch with four seasons to the corner spandrels. The case has fully-tapered mahogany columns with wooden ringed capitals sitting on splayed feet.
The break arch includes a swan-necked hood with matching tapered mahogany columns. Eight day movement with subsidiary seconds and date.
- *205cm x 48cm x 27cm*
- **£6,500**   • **Gutlin Clocks**

Empire Clock ▼
- *circa 1815*
A French patinated bronze and Sienna marble empire clock.
- *65cm x 40cm x 13cm*
- **£2,600**   • **Tredantiques**

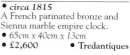

Expert Tips

The clock dealer is the best place to purchase clocks if you want good working examples as clock restoration can prove costly.

Sheraton Bracket Clock ▼

- *circa 1890–1900*

A small, late Victorian mahogany balloon-style Sheraton English bracket clock. Includes a boxwood Sheraton inlaid front panel and stringing, and flat white enamel dial with Arabic numerals within thick-cut beveled glass.
- *28cm x 18cm*
- **£1,200**   • Gutlin Clocks

Top Bracket Clock ▼

- *circa 1880*

A fine English mahogany-cased top bracket clock. Includes brass strips to the corners of the case with two inset brass-beaded mahogany panels surmounted by an original brass carrying handle. The large convex white enamel dial has no damage to the black roman numerals.
- *33cm x 23cm*
- **£1,800**   • Gutlin Clocks

French Carriage Clock ▶

- *circa 1890*

A polished brass French cornice carriage clock. The eight day movement chimes hours and half hours on a gong with original silvered English lever platform escapement. Plain white enamel dial with black roman numerals and blued spade hands.
- *19cm x 10cm x 7.5cm*
- **£1,400**   • Gutlin Clocks

Brass Carriage Clock ▲

- *circa 1890*

A polished brass cornice-cased French striking carriage clock. The eight day movement includes original silvered English lever platform escapement. Chimes hours and half hours on a gong with white enamel dial.
- *26cm x 10cm x 7.5cm*
- **£1,400**   • Gutlin Clocks

Bracket Clock ▲

- *circa 1880*

Small English mahogany, heavily inlaid bracket clock. The numbered and signed French eight day movement chimes the hours and half hours.
- *102cm x 8cm*
- **£1,200**   • Gutlin Clocks

Cornice-Cased Clock ▼

- *circa 1890*

A cornice-cased, polished brass timepiece carriage clock by "Hny Jacot" of Paris. The French eight day movement with original silvered English platform lever escapement is signed "HJ" with the parrot. White enameled dial with black roman numerals and fine blue spade hands.
- *17cm x 9cm x 7.5cm*
- **£850**   • Gutlin Clocks

Repeating Carriage Clock ▼

- *circa 1896*

A cannelée-cased, polished brass French repeating carriage clock. The French movement has hour and half hour strikes on a gong and original silvered English lever escapement. White enamel dial, black Roman numerals and outer minute markers signed "Henry Lewis & Co" to the Queen, 172 New Bond Street, with original traveling case.
- *17.5cm x 10cm x 7.5cm*
- **£2,200**   • Gutlin Clocks

Large Longcase Clock ▼

- *circa 1790*

George III flame-mahogany Moonroller longcase clock, with fan-shell satinwood inlay and cross-and-feather banding in a Gothic case. Reeded Corinthian columns with matching reeded Corinthian columns to hood. Engraved plaque reads, "Peter Fearnley of Wigan Tempest Fugit".

- *254cm x 45cm x 23cm*
- £12,500   • Gutlin Clocks

Desk Compendium ▼

- *circa 1902*

A gilt bronze and green enamel French desk compendium in an original leather travelling case. Eight day movement with original silvered English lever platform escapement. Presented to "VWL Parnett Botfield Esq" by the servants of the Hut on his coming of age, December 29, 1902.

- *15cm x 16.5cm x 6cm*
- £2,300   • Gutlin Clocks

Hopwood Clock ▼

- *circa 1800*

Country-style oak and mahogany 30 hour moonroller longcase clock sitting on ogée feet, by "Hopwood" of Rochdale. The painted dial includes scenes of two birds. The moonroller disc is painted with a galleon at sea and a fox hunt. Reeded square columns with diamond inlay to tops, with brass capitals on hood with inlayed central swan neck.

- *223cm x 52cm x 24cm*
- £3,900   • Gutlin Clocks

Mantel Clock ◄

- *circa 1875*

A French mantel clock by "J.B. Delettrez". Finely waisted green boulle case with gilt bronze ormolu mounts. Eight day French square plate movement with hour and half hour strikes on a gong. Twenty-five-piece cartouche dial with blued hands. Signed "J.B. Delettrez No.21174" with "J.B.D." stamp.

- *43cm x 23cm x 15cm*
- £4,500   • Gutlin Clocks

English Mahogany Clock ◄

- *circa 1830*

Flat-topped mahogany English longcase clock with break arch painted dial and leafy carved blind fretwork to hood. Eight day painted dial with masonic secotros to corner spandrels. Painted moonroller disc with scene of galleon at sea and country cottage scene. Made by "John P. Campbell" of Govan, Glasgow.

- *208cm x 51cm x 25cm*
- £6,500   • Gutlin Clocks

George III Clock ▲

- *circa 1790*

George III black-lacquered, pagoda-hooded, English eight day longcase clock. Chinoiserie decorated case with original hood housing a brass dial with four pillar movement. Sunburst engraving to center of dial and strike/silent in break arch.

- *238cm x 35.5cm x 18cm*
- £8,500   • Gutlin Clocks

Mahogany Bracket Clock ◄

- *circa 1839*

A flame mahogany cased, early English bracket clock. Mahogany case is very well figured. Eight day gut fusée movement with hour and half hour strikes on a large nickered bell signed and dated "D. Shaw, Leicester 1839". The engraved, silvered, one piece dial includes black roman numerals and strike/silent facility in the break arch.

- *71cm x 46cm*
- £3,900   • Gutlin Clocks

Square Dial Clock ▲

- *circa 1800*

Eight-day, maplewood and ebony English longcase clock. The brass square dial includes an engraved scene depicting two galleons at sea. Silvered date ring and subsidiary seconds. Center of dial engraved "David Rowland", Aberystwyth. Finely chiselled brass spandrels to corners. Silver chapter ring with four pillar movement. The flat topped hood is decorated with leafy fretwork to the front.

- *223cm x 47cm x 24cm*
- £5,500   • Gutlin Clocks

George II Clock ►

- *circa 1760*

George II English lacquer longcase clock with pagoda hood. Painted religious scenes to front door and base depicting scenes from the Bible. The five pillar, London-made eight day movement bears an inscription plate engraved "Andrew Moran, London". With subsidiary date and seconds ring chiming hours on a bell with strike/silent in break arch.

- *236cm x 35cm x 16.5cm*
- £9,500   • Gutlin Clocks

English Bracket Clock ◄

- *circa 1870*

A large black ebonised and gilt, ormolu-mounted, three train English bracket clock with quarter-striking triple fusée. Chimes on eight bells with hour strike on a gong. The brass dial includes engraved, silvered chapter ring and two subsidiary dials surrounded by finely cast foliate spandrels.

- *81cm x 46cm*
- £5,500   • Gutlin Clocks

Moonroller Longcase Clock ▲

- *circa 1770*

A flame mahogany, George III brass-dial moonroller longcase clock. The fine case is in its original condition, with reeded columns to trunk, surmounted by four-reeded column hood with satinwood inlaid fans in the break arch. The brass dial has trellis engraving. Four-pillar eight day movement chiming on a bell. Maker "John Joyce" of Ruthin.

- *241cm x 43cm x 22cm*
- £9,500   • Gutlin Clocks

Thomas Blakeway Clock ►

- *circa 1830*

A very fine oak and mahogany English moonroller clock with painted dial. Has reeded, tapered columns with gilded Corinthian capitals and shell inlay to door and base, and fine cross and feather banding sitting on ogee feet. Four pillar movement with hour chime on a bell, subsidiary seconds and date ring with painted moonroller disc. Maker "Thomas Blakeway" of Wellington.

- *231cm x 52cm x 25cm*
- £8,500   • Gutlin Clocks

111

Gilt Bronze Clock ▲

- *circa 1880*

A gilt bronze ormolu French mantel clock with blue porcelain panels. The fine ormolu case depicts a woman rested on a rock with her dog with original mercury gilding. The porcelain panels include pictures of flowers, eight day movement with hour and half hour strikes on a bell. White enamel dial with black roman numerals. Dial signed by the retailers "Maitrot à Dijon". movement by Vincenti and Cie.
- *45cm x 50cm x 10cm*
- **£2,900**   • **Gutlin Clocks**

French Mantel Clock ▲

- *circa 1870*

A decorative late nineteenth century French mantel clock with simulated red tortoiseshell and engraved brass boulle work. The top of the case is surmounted by a seated maiden holding a bunch of flowers with figures of children to sides of case. Eight day movement by "Hry Marc", Paris. Thirteen pieces, enamel cartouche gilt ormolu dial enclosed by a heavily chiselled front bezel with a very thick front glass.
- *63cm x 35.5cm x 16.5cm*
- **£2,500**   • **Gutlin Clocks**

George III Bracket Clock ▼

- *circa 1780*

A George III London-made bracket clock in figured mahogany case with pagoda top. Eight day movement with fully engraved backplate and original verge escapement. Unusually for an eighteenth century English clock, it strikes on the hour and half hour. Dial with centre calendar, strike/silent in the arch and signed by the maker.
- *height 58cm*
- **£8,900**   • **The Clock Clinic**

Hallmarked Clock ▼

- *1904*

Small, red leather and silver-fronted mantel clock with silver hallmark "Birmingham 1904". Eight day movement on platform escapement in very original condition, white enamel dial with roman black numerals and black spade hands.
- *20cm x 10cm x 5cm*
- **£850**   • **Gutlin Clocks**

English Moonroller Clock ▲

- *circa 1830*

An English all-mahogany moonroller longcase clock by "Carruthers" of Carlisle. Painted flower spandrels with globes below break arch. The moonroller disc includes scenes of a French galleon at sea and a country chapel. The case with canted corners, square flamed mahogany door and flame mahogany base with ebony and boxwood stringing sitting on ogée feet.
- *233cm x 53cm x 51cm*
- **£8,500**   • **Gutlin Clocks**

Lyre Clock ▲

- *circa 1900*

Attractive French lyre clock, the strings forming the moving pendulum. Paste brillants surround the floral enamel dial. *Bleu de Roi* porcelain case with gilded mounts and Medusa head in a sunray to top. Eight day movement striking the hours on a bell. The whole in excellent condition, overhauled and guaranteed.
- *height 49cm*
- **£6,600**   • **The Clock Clinic**

Grandfather Clock ▼
- *circa 1820*
Swedish birchwood Biedermeier grandfather clock signed "Beurling, Stockholm".
- *219cm x 54cm x 39cm*
- **£6,900** • **Rupert Cavendish**

Second Empire Clock ▼
- *circa 1880*
A French Second Empire ormulu and turquoise, porcelain mounted mantel clock. Finely chiselled case with original mercury gilding and adorned with an urn. Below the dial is a central plaque depicting storks in a natural foliate setting.
- *53cm x 28cm x 17cm*
- **£5,500** • **Butchoff Antiques**

Victorian Longcase Clock ▲
- *circa 1900*
A large Victorian three-train longcase clock, the mahogany case with boxwood inlaid front door, base and hood. English eight day quarter striking movement chiming on eight bells. The solid mahogany case inlaid with urns and dolphins and surmounted by an original ball and spire final. The brass chapter ring and cherub-head spandrel dial with subsidary seconds and strike/silent in the breakarch.
- *236cm x 50cm x 30.5cm*
- **£12,500** • **Gutlin Clocks**

Victorian Timepiece Clock ◄
- *circa 1830–35*
Attractive, small-sized early Victorian flame mahogany timepiece clock. Single gut, fusee eight-day English movement with original pendulum holdfast. Original white painted convex dial with carved mahogany moldings and glazed side panels showing the movement.
- *28cm x 18cm*
- **£1,800** • **Gutlin Clocks**

English Chiming Clock ▼
- *circa 1800*
Flame mahogany, English eight-day longcase clock with brass square dial and subsidiary silvered second ring. Florally engraved centre to dial bearing the inscription "John Smith, Chester". Mask-headed spandrels to corners with border engraving running around the edge of dial. Four pillar movement with hour chime on a bell.
- *223cm x 57cm x 24cm*
- **£5,900** • **Gutlin Clocks**

Large Mahogany Clock ◄
- *circa 1800*
An extremely large Liverpool mahogany moonroller longcase clock with a painted dial signed "James Cawson", depicting scenes from the battle of Trafalgar and naval anchors to the corner pieces symbolising the navy. Includes eight day moonroller movement with inside date ring. Substantial mahogany case with inlaid base. The hood with double reeded pillars and elaborate swan neck top.
- *241cm x 45cm x 20cm*
- **£11,000** • **Gutlin Clocks**

Expert Tips
English clock makers of longcase and bracket clocks are considered the best in the world for their precision and design.

English Bracket Clock ▲

- *circa 1840*
A finely figured flame mahogany English bracket clock. The twin gut fusée movement with shoulder plates and hour strike on a bell. White painted convex dial signed "Taylor of Bristol" with black spade hands within a finely figured rectangular mahogany case sitting on ball feet.
- *53cm x 30.5cm*
- **£3,500**   • Gutlin Clocks

French Mantel Clock ▲

- *circa 1900*
A good quality gilt bronze and blue porcelain panelled French mantel clock. White convex enamel dial with black roman numerals and eight day movement chiming hours and half hours on a bell signed by "Raingo Freres".
- *34cm x 24cm x 10cm*
- **£3,100**   • Gutlin Clocks

Expert Tips

Always check to see if the name of the clock maker has been engraved on the back plate – many a bargain has been found this way.

Three-Train Bracket Clock ▼

- *circa 1850*
An English three train, quarter striking, ebonized and gilt ormolu mounted bracket clock standing on its original bracket. The arch topped case has finely chiselled mounts, caryatids to sides of case and ormolu mounted side frets. The movement is of high quality with engraved back plate chiming on nine bells with hour strike on a large nickeled bell. Engraved silver chapter ring with black roman numerals and matted centre to dial with finely chiselled ormolu spandrels and two subsidiary dials in break arch.
- *55cm x 33cm*
- **£5,500**   • Gutlin Clocks

Oak Bracket Clock ▼

- *circa 1840*
A carved oak English bracket clock by the famous "Walker" of London with blue spade hands. English eight day chain fusée movement of fine quality with original pendulum holdfast.
- *43cm x 35.5cm x 20cm*
- **£1,900**   • Gutlin Clocks

Austrian Bracket Clock ▲

- *circa 1750*
A well-made oak-cased original Austrian grand sonnerie bracket clock. The very finely foliate engraved dial has Dutch-type silvered, chapter ring, date aperture and two subsidiary dials with makers name plaque signed "Augustin Heckel". The triple fusee Austrian movement is of short duration (30 hours). Chimes the hours and quarters on two original nickeled bells.
- *53cm x 27cm*
- **£3,900**   • Gutlin Clocks

Painted Dial Clock ▲

- *circa 1830*
Country-cased oak English longcase clock with readed, canted columns to case. Unusual pierced fretwork making swan neck of hood with ball and spire finiaes,a nd featuring dentistry around hood throat. The painted dial includes a scene of bird in break arch and flowers to spandrels. Subsidiary seconds and date ring chiming on a bell. Maker "W.C. Clark" of Morpeth.
- *226cm x 51cm x 25cm*
- **£5,50**   • Gutlin Clocks

Swiss Mantel Clock ▼
- *1960*

A Swiss Jaeger-le-Caultre Atmos timepiece with white chapter ring and gilt Arabic numerals. Signed "Swiss made". This clock never needs winding.
- *22cm x 17cm x 14cm*
- £1,200   • Gutlin Clocks

Ebonized Scottish Bracket Clock ▼
- *circa 1840*

A black ebonized Scottish library four glass clock by "J.&W. Mitchell", 119 New Cannon Street, Glasgow. The eight day, double-chain fusée movement of extremely high quality with hour and half hour strikes on a large original nickelled bell and pendulum holdfast. The finely engraved one-piece silver dial includes engraved and black waxed spandrels, all housed within a Bombay-style ebonized upright five glass case.
- *38cm x 23cm*
- £4,500   • Gutlin Clocks

Mappin & Webb Clock ▲

- *circa 1911*

A well-made mahogany eight day double fusée English bracket clock retailed by Mappin & Webb Ltd, Oxford Street, London W1. The finely figured mahogany case includes olive wood inlaid panel and boxwood stringing sitting on ball feet. With engraved silvered convex brass dial signed "Mappin & Webb", with blue steel counter poised moon hands.
- *37cm x 23cm*
- £2,500   • Gutlin Clocks

Porcelain Clock ▲
- *circa 1880*

A fine quality Delft porcelain clock. The eight day, two train French movement chimes the hours and half hours on a bell by a listed maker. Blue and white porcelain case surrounded by four cherubs depicting the four seasons, the white convex dial with blue roman numerals and unusually small spade hands.
- *48cm x 30cm x 18cm*
- £2,900   • Gutlin Clocks

Miniature Oak Clock ▲
- *circa 1900*

An English oak-cased miniature longcase clock with eight-day French timepiece movement, cylinder escapement and white enamel dial with black roman numerals and spade hands.
- *35cm x 10cm x 7.5cm*
- £650   • Gutlin Clocks

Victorian Bracket Clock ▲
- *circa 1870*

An English triple fusée black ebonized quarter-chiming Victorian bracket clock. The three train movement striking the quarters on eight bells with the hour strike on a gong. The brass dial with silvered and engraved chapter ring, silvered strike/silent ring and finely chiseled brass spandrels. The black ebonized case with gilt ormolu mounts sitting on gilt ormolu lion paw feet and side carrying handles.
- *38cm x 30.5cm x 20cm*
- £5,500   • Gutlin Clocks

Signed Bracket Clock ▼

- *19th century*

A fine English bracket clock, the bronzed case with gilded mounts. Engraved dial with matching steel hands, signed by the maker and numbered. Twin fusée movement striking on a bell.

- *height 35cm*
- £7,500   • The Clock Clinic

Portico Clock ▼

- *circa 1840*

A well patinated flame-mahogany French First Empire portico clock. Case with original mercury gilded ormolu mounts of rectangular form, the 14 day French movement with hour and half hour strike on a bell. White enamel convex dial with black roman numerals and black counterpoised moon-type hands.

- *51cm x 25cm x 15cm*
- £3,000   • Gutlin Clocks

Marble Clock Set ▲

- *circa 1860*

A gilt bronze and rouge marble French figural three piece drummer boy timepiece clock set. Eight day movement with original cylinder escapement, two-inch enamel dial with black roman numerals, finely chiseled gilt ormolu hands and two branch gilt ormolu and rouge marble matching candlesticks side pieces.

- *33cm x 12.5cm x 12.5cm*
- £3,500   • Gutlin Clocks

French Four-Glass Clock ▲

- *circa 1870*

A small polished brass French four glass clock with diamante bezel. Eight day movement with hour and half hour strike on a gong and mercury pendulum, the white enameled dial painted with pink music sheets.

- *25cm x 15cm x 13cm*
- £1,600   • Gutlin Clocks

French Mantel Clock ▲

- *circa 1860*

A large black French mantel clock with a gilt bronze figure of a maiden reading a book resting on a column with a lyre beside her. Eight day French movement with hour and half hour strikes on a bell.

- *61cm x 56cm x 18cm*
- £3,500   • Gutlin Clocks

Three-Piece Clock ▲

- *circa 1870*

A fine quality gilt ormolu and bronze French mantel clock in a figure of a column with a ball. Two train French movement with original English lever platform escapement. Gilt bronze arrow hands striking hours and half hours on a bell with two branch rouge marble and ormolu cherub candlesticks.

- *38cm x 15cm x 15cm*
- £5,500   • Gutlin Clocks

Marble Lyre Clock ▼

- *circa 1880*

A Carrera white marble and ormolu mounted French lyre clock, eight day French movement with knife edge suspension and swinging diamonte ring.
- *34cm x 14cm x 10cm*
- **£3,900** • Gutlin Clocks

French Lyre Clock ▼

- *circa 1860*

A highly decorative French lyre three-piece clock garniture with bronze figural side pieces. Includes four finely painted porcelain panels depicting lovers in the park. Eight day French movement chiming hours and half hours on a bell, with gilt bronze dial with 12 piece enameled cartouches.
- *51cm x 18cm x 10cm*
- **£3,800** • Gutlin Clocks

Marti et Cie Clock ➤

- *circa 1890*

French mantel clock of the Third Republic in a gilded and champleve enamel case with brilliant paste around the dial. Eight day movement, striking the fours and half hours on a gong with matching enamel pendulum. Bearing the maker's stamp of Marti et Cie.
- *height 38cm*
- **£3,900** • **The Clock Clinic**

Musical Mantel Clock ▲

- *circa 1810*

A First Empire musical gilt ormolu French mantel clock by Alibert of Paris. The timepiece movement has original verge escapement, decorated back cock signed "Alibert". The figural case features a boy carrying a bale of hay with original mercury gilding. The clock sits on a boxwood strung rosewood base, housing a fine quality music box.
- *38cm x 28cm x 14cm*
- **£2,200** • Gutlin Clocks

Pink Porcelain Clock ▲

- *circa 1860*

A gilt bronze and pink porcelain French three piece clock garniture. Features gilt bronze case with porcelain panels surmounted by a porcelain urn with gilt bronze mounts. Eight day French movement chiming hours and half hours on the bell. Jewelled porcelain dial with black roman numerals.
- *43cm x 30.5cm x 10cm*
- **£5,500** • Gutlin Clocks

Gilt Bronze and Silvered Mantel Clock ▲

- *circa 1890*

A gilt bronze and silvered French mantel clock. Eight day French movement with half hour chime on a bell. The case with silver mounts depicts Bacchus, ancient Greek god of wine. Includes engraved slate dial with gilt roman numerals.
- *39cm x 24cm x 18cm*
- **£1,700** • Gutlin Clocks

Boulle Clock ▲

- *circa 1860*

A fine quality brown tortoiseshell and cut engraved brass French boulle clock. Eight day French movement chiming hours and half hours on a bell. with original numbered pendulum. The gilt ormolu dial features 12 piece cartouches with blue roman numerals.

- *46cm x 25cm x 13cm*
- **£2,500**   • Gutlin Clocks

Walnut Bracket Clock ▲

- *circa 1850*

Burr walnut, double fusée English bracket clock by Payne & Co, 163 New Bond Street, London, numbered clock No.3234. The finely figured caddy topped walnut case features original carved walnut sound frets and inlaid brass corners. The double chain fusee eight day numbered and signed English movement is of high quality, with hour and half hour strike on a gong. Includes regulator type top cock and original pendulum holdfast.

- *43cm x 30.5cm*
- **£6,500**   • Gutlin Clocks

Thomas Pace Clock ▼

- *circa 1770*

A George III mahogany five pillar brass dial longcase clock by Thomas Pace of London. The case with long door sitting on single moulded base. Eight day brass dial movement with silver chapter ring and strike/silent subsidiary, subsidiary seconds and date with separate engraved makers name plaque signed "Thomas Pace", London. The hood with reeded columns inset with brass stringing and brass capitals.

- *223cm x 45cm x 23cm*
- **£9,500**   • Gutlin Clocks

Paris Bisque Clock ▼

- *circa 1890*

A white Paris Bisque French timepiece mantel clock with small French eight day timepiece movement. Features white convex enamel dial with roman numerals and counter poised moon hands. The white bisque case with a figure of a maiden.

- *25cm x 16.5cm x 11cm*
- **£750**   • Gutlin Clocks

Victorian Bracket Clock ▲

- *circa 1860*

A solid mahogany and brass inlaid English bracket clock retailed by Dixon of Norwich. Chimes every quarter on four bells. The nicely figured case with pierced brass side frets surmounted by a pineapple finial. The substantial eight-day triple fusée Victorian English movement features a finely engraved one piece silver dial and slow/fast subsidiary in break arch.

- *68.5cm x 39cm*
- **£4,800**   • Gutlin Clocks

French Lyre Clock ▲

- *circa 1900*

A satinwood and gilt ormolu mounted French timepiece lyre clock retailed by Howell & James, Paris. Eight day French movement with original English lever escapement, convex cream enamel dial with hand-painted swags of roses boarding black Arabic numerals.

- *26.5cm x 13cm x 9cm*
- **£1,600**   • Gutlin Clocks

Carrera Mantel Clock ▼

- *circa 1870*

A large impressive Carrera white marble and gilt bronze French mantel Clock. Carrera white marble case with two cherubs and a dolphin, ram's head to sides of case. Eight day movement with hour and half hour strikes on a bell, white enamel dial with blue enamel numerals.

- *40.5cm x 58cm x 18cm*
- £4,500   • Gutlin Clocks

American Calendar Clock ▼

- *1860*

An unusual American calendar clock by Seth Thomas, having a pine carcass, and two dials. The top dial marks the time, and the lower one is for the date.

- *107cm x 79cm*
- £2,800   • Lacquer Chest

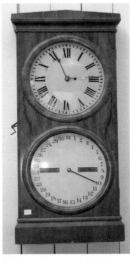

Industrial Mantel Clock ◄

- *circa 1890*

A gilt bronze French industrial mantel clock by "Hry Marc à Paris", with two week movement in the form of an open-plated bed. Strikes hours and half hours on a bell surmounted on the top of the case.

- *63.5cm x 26.5cm x 15cm*
- £3,900   • Gutlin Clocks

French Mantel Clock ◄

- *circa 1870*

A late nineteenth century French gilt bronze three-piece clock garniture. Eight day movement chiming hours and half hours on a bell. The gilt bronze and blue porcelain case with fine cloisonné enamelling and egg-shaped urn side pieces.

- *40.5cm x 23cm x 13cm*
- £3,700   • Gutlin Clocks

Victorian Desk Clock ▲

- *circa 1860*

Victorian ship's wheel eight-day desk clock of fine quality. Agate handles to the wheel. Signed "J. and M. Boyd, Greenock".

- *height 34cm*
- £925   • The Clock Clinic

Third Republic Clock ▲

- *1880*

A French Third Republic lyre-shaped ormulu and gilt clock, with a Champs-Levée platform movement by G. Jamieson. Seated at the base are two gilt cherubs holding lyres.

- *height 40cm*
- £1,400   • Barham Antiques

119

Miniature Longcase Clock

- *circa 1890–1900*

Jacobean-style oak weight-driven miniature longcase clock. Eight day duration with brass dial, flowery engraved centre to dial with separate silvered chapter ring and masked headed spandrels. Chimes hours and half hours on a gong. Oak barley twist columns and fretwork panels to sides of flat top hood.
- *152cm x 35.5cm x 24cm*
- **£3,800**   • Gutlin Clocks

Brass Dial Clock ▼

- *1730*

Eighteenth century oak 30-hour brass dial longcase clock. Made by Savage of Salop.
- *height 195cm*
- **£8,750**   • Paul Hopwell

Russian Wall Clock ▲

- *1960*

An unusual geometrically designed Russian wall clock in painted red wood, with a white dial and a raised white circular hoop. Designed by Jantaz.
- *height 40cm*
- **£45**   • Radio Days

Queen Anne Longcase Clock ▲

- *1710*

A rare Queen Anne arabesque longcase clock by John Culliford of Bristol, with excellent colour and patination. Eight day, five pillar movement with inside count wheel strike. Features 12-inch dial decorated with double cherub and crown spandrels. Typical example of clocks of the period.
- *height 264cm*
- **£25,000**   • Freshfords

Blue-Lacquered Clock ▼

- *circa 1770*

George III blue lacquer pagoda topped longcase clock. Features brass dial with chapter ring and urn and dolphin spandrels. Maker's name in round plaque in break arch appearing through aperture window, engraved "John Dewe", Made Lane, London. Subsidary seconds and date ring, with four pillar movement.
- *94cm x 33cm x 18cm*
- **£9,500**   • Gutlin Clocks

Lustre Ware Clock ▼

- *1905*

Ceramic lustre ware clock by Louis Fuler, an American who revolutionised dance in France.
- *height 27cm*
- **£350**   • Succession

George II Longcase Clock ◄

- *mid 18th century*

A George II lacquer longcase clock with calendar and unusual centre seconds hand. The dial with phases of the moon in the arch. Chinoiserie-style English lacquer case on a dark green base. Eight day movement striking on a bell.
- *height 231cm*
- **£9,200**   • The Clock Clinic

Skeleton Clock ▲
- *circa 1860*

A Victorian English striking
skeleton clock depicting the
Scott Memorial in Edinburgh,
with figures of the author and his
dog. Two-train movement with
lever escapement above the
silvered dial, rather than the
more usual pendulum, with hour
strike and repeat cord. Original
rosewood base with mother-of-
pearl inlay to the front.
- *height 37cm*
- **£5,500**   • The Clock Clinic

Carriage Clock ▲
- *circa 1880*

A striking French gilded cornice-
cased French carriage clock.
The eight-day French movement
chiming hours and half hours on
a gong with original silvered
English lever escapement.
Features white enamel dial with
black roman numerals.
- *19cm x 9cm x 7.5cm*
- **£1,300**   • Gutlin Clocks

West Country Longcase Clock ▼
- *circa 1830*

An English West Country
longcase clock with very good
faded colour and ebonised
Corinthan columns to trunk and
hood. Carved fluting to the
curved top. Painted dial signed
by the maker, "G. Stephenson".
Eight day movement striking on a
bell. Overhauled and guaranteed.
- *height 213cm*
- **£4,950**   • The Clock Clinic

French Mantel Clock ▼
- *1870*

Fine French gilded and silvered
mantel clock with original
giltwood base. The porcelain dial
and side panels with well-painted
subjects of various battle scenes.
Eight day movement striking on
a bell. Porcelain panels dated
1870. Overhauled and
guaranteed.
- *height 38cm*
- **£4,200**   • The Clock Clinic

French Carriage Clock ▲
- *circa 1900*

A gilt bronze and serpentine-
cased miniature French carriage
clock timepiece. The eight-day
French movement with original
silvered English lever platform
escapement. The gilt mask with
white convex enamel dial, black
roman numerals and blue spade
hands.
- *10cm x 5cm x 5cm*
- **£950**   • Gutlin Clocks

Mahogany Bracket Clock ▲
- *circa 1880*

An English/French flame
mahogany arched topped small-
sized chiming bracket clock.
Eight day French movement
chiming the hours and half hours
on a gong by a listed maker, the
convex white enamel dial with
black roman numerals and spade
hands. Solid mahogany case with
a flame mahogany front and
boxwood stringing.
- *25cm x 18cm*
- **£1,200**   • Gutlin Clocks

Grande Sonnerie Clock ▲

- *circa 1880*

Grande Sonnerie full one-quarter striking French carriage clock with alarm by F.A. Margaine. Substantial case, gilded and part silvered with full strike and silent lever to the base. Maker's stamp to the movement backplate, enamel dial signed by the retailer and numbered.

- *height 17cm*
- **£3,800** • The Clock Clinic

Dial and Calendar Clock ▲

- *circa 1780*

Longcase clock with figured mahogany case and quarter columns, shaped plinth and pagoda top to hood above a curved sound fret. Dial with calendar and strike/silent in the arch and signed by the maker, "Fras. Reynolds".

- *height 241cm*
- **£15,500** • The Clock Clinic

Expert Tips

Escapements come in many different kinds, including the pendulum, the verge, the lever, fusée movements and the cylinder sprung movement of the travel clock.

French Bronze Clock ▼

- *circa 1820*

A French fire-gilded bronze clock commemorating the birth of the Duke of Bordeaux in 1820. With figures of the Duchess de Berry nursing her son with her older daughter Louise kneeling. A very similar example is illustrated and described in *French Bronze Clocks* by Elke Niehuser.

- *height 50cm*
- **£6,200** • The Clock Clinic

Carved Musical Clock ▼

- *circa 1880*

A carved walnut musical automaton Swiss chalet with clock. Eight day French movement with hour and half hour strike on a bell and music box sitting in the base of the clock. Two doors opening on the hour revealing male and female musicians. The case is in carved walnut and is in a very original undamaged state.

- *48cm x 61cm x 30cm*
- **£3,500** • Gutlin Clocks

Chariot Clock ▼

- *19th century*

A good late nineteenth century chariot clock with bronze cherub driving a rather docile lion. Deep green veined marble base with gilded classical mounts. Eight day movement striking the hours and half hours on a bell.

- *32cm x 34cm*
- **£4,900** • The Clock Clinic

Lighthouse Clock ▼

- *circa 1885*

Large French Torsion pendulum lighthouse clock attributed to the best-known maker of mystery and industrial clocks, A.R. Guilmet. Case gilded and silvered, on black marble base. Eight day striking movement with brocot escapement, the torsion pendulum suspended on a long flat spring. Striking the hours and half hours on a gong.

- *height 34cm*
- **£6,200** • The Clock Clinic

Religious Table Clock ◄

- *1880*

A fine French religious table clock, the case with pewter and brass inlay and with gilt metal mounts. Velvet dial, movement striking the hours on a bell.

- *height 48cm*
- **£2,800** • The Clock Clinic

First Empire Clock ▲
- *circa 1830*
Gilt ormolu and bronze First Empire French mantel clock by Douillon. The gilt ormolu and bronze case includes two cherubs holding the face with gilt swag mounts in the center.
- *46cm x 20cm x 12.5cm*
- £2,400   • Gutlin Clocks

Cast Bronze Clock ▲
- *circa 1900*
A solidly cast gilt bronze four glass clock by Maple & Co Ltd, Paris. Beautiful convex white enamel dial with hand-painted swags of roses around blue Arabic numerals. Movement signed "Maple & Co".
- *37cm x 23cm x 18cm*
- £2,200   • Gutlin Clocks

French Four-Glass Clock ▼
- *circa 1880*
A gilt brass French four glass clock with signed miniature ivory portrait of a maiden. Eight day movement by Mougin. Features gilt dial with black Gothic Arabic numerals within a diamante paste stone bezel.
- *30.5cm x 19cm x 14cm*
- £1,500   • Gutlin Clocks

Propeller Clock ▼
- *circa 1900*
An industrial timepiece propeller blade clock with ship's capstan containing a compass, gilded lifebelt, apothec and anchor.
- *34cm x 24cm x 12.5cm*
- £1,600   • Gutlin Clocks

Louis Philippe Mantel Clock ◄
- *1824–30*
A French gilded bronze mantel clock. To the left of the clock stands a bronze figure of a male musician playing an instrument while gazing at his music sheet, which rests on a music stand to the top of the dial. To the right is a lyre placed on a small table. To the base is a raised relief depicting a classical scene with cherubs, resting on square legs.
- *height 50cm*
- £1,750   • North West 8

Mantel Clock ▲
- *circa 1893*
A Second Empire gilt ormolu and bronze French mantel clock retailed by Goldsmiths Co, 122 Regent Street, London W1. Paris-made movement by Ls Boname Seloncourt. White enamelled chapter ring with gilt watersilk center to dial and retailer's name plaque in finely handwritten script "Goldsmiths & Co, 122 Regent Street".
- *30.5cm x 20cm x 13cm*
- £1,900   • Gutlin Clocks

French Wooden Mantel Clock ▲
- *circa 1830*
A First Empire bird's-eye maple and ebony strung French wooden mantel clock. The fine quality silk suspension movement is marked "Le Paute à Fils. Hrs du Roi" (Horologer to the King). Signed silvered dial. Strikes hours and half hours on a bell.
- *35.5cm x 15cm x 13cm*
- £2,500   • Gutlin Clocks

Gilt Lacquer Clock ▲

- *circa 1970*

A gilt lacquer Atmos Jaegar-Le-Caultre mantel timepiece with the original white fitted case. Silvered dial on a gilt pierced sunburst ground with a pendulum aperture, in a rectangular black lacquer case, together with the original fitted case.

- *35.5cm x 23cm x 15cm*
- £950   • Gutlin Clocks

Porcelain Mantel Clock ▼

- *circa 1860*

Cappo do Monte porcelain three-piece garniture, the finely painted pale blue case featuring a figure of a maiden and two cherubs. The two branch figural candlesticks are of a male and maiden surmounted by flowers. Eight day French movement with hour and half hour strike on a bell.

- *43cm x 23cm x 18cm*
- £5,500   • Gutlin Clocks

Doulton Mantel Clock ▼

- *circa 1830*

An original First Empire silk suspension gilt ormolu French Louis Philippe mantel clock by Doulton. Original mercury gilding, the case with a maiden resting her arm on a lyre. watersilked silvered dial with black roman numerals and fine counterpoised moon hands.

- *56cm x 38cm x 14cm*
- £2,900   • Gutlin Clocks

Oil Lamp Mantel Clock ◄

- *circa 1870*

A First Empire-style French gilt ormolu and bronze mantel clock in the form of an oil lamp with an angel being warmed by the lamp. Eight day movement with hour and half hour strike on a bell. White enamel dial with black roman numerals and finely chiselled gilt brass hands.

- *35.5cm x 20cm x 10cm*
- £2,800   • Gutlin Clocks

Gothic Bracket Clock ▲

- *circa 1890*

A very pretty mahogany gothic English bracket clock by Webster of Cornhill, London. Fine quality double fusée English movement chiming hours and half hours on a gong with pendulum holdfast. The mahogany case with pierced wooden side frets, and a one piece silver dial with Hallibrad hands and foliate engravings.

- *25cm x 20cm*
- £2,900   • Gutlin Clocks

[Wine Barrel Clock image]

Wine Barrel Clock ▲

- *circa 1860*

Gilt ormolu French mantel clock with eight day movement chiming hours and half hours on a bell. The case in the form of a wine barrel with cherubs sitting on the barrel, supported by male figures. Twelve piece white enamel cartouche dial with fleur de lys hands and black roman numerals.

- *50cm x 35.5cm x 16.5cm*
- £2,800   • Gutlin Clocks

Scottish Longcase Clock ▲

- *circa 1780–90*

A mahogany Scottish eight day brass dial George III longcase clock. Solid mahogany case with an ebony and boxwood inlaid door depicting the Prince of Wales feathers and hearts. Break arch top with inlay to rounds, with brass 35cm chapter ring and spandrel dial signed "David Wyllie" of Saltcoats (Scotland).

- *320cm x 50cm x 25cm*
- £6,500   • Gutlin Clocks

Clocks

Gaullin Mantel Clock ▼
- *circa 1830*
A extremely large First Empire French ormolu and bronze mantel clock by Gaullin of Paris. The arched case depicts pomegranates, torches and an oil lamp, flanked by well-cast, almost naked figures of Cupid and Psyche.
- *79cm x 48cm x 18cm*
- £5,900 • Gutlin Clocks

French Mantel Clock ▲
- *circa 1830*
A gilt ormolu First Empire mantel clock by Lugrunge of Paris. Features a finely chiselled gilt bronze case with a maiden and cupid and a laurel wreath to the bottom of the case.
- *42cm x 32cm x 10cm*
- £2,300 • Gutlin Clocks

Merritt of Stroud Clock ▲
- *circa 1780–1800*
A George III, fine quality, swan automation, flame-mahogany longcase clock by Merritt of Stroud. Features a 30cm brass dial with silvered and engraved chapter ring, date, seconds and strike/silent rings and dolphin spandrels to the corners.
- *223cm x 48cm x 23cm*
- £9,500 • Gutlin Clocks

Gilt Bronze Clock ▼
- *circa 1870*
Large gilt bronze French clock. The finely chiselled case with maidens to sides surmounted by an urn with draping ormolu swags. The back door is engraved "Antony Bailly à Lyon".
- *63.5cm x 38cm 18cm*
- £4,500 • Gutlin Clocks

St Christopher Clock ◄
- *circa 1830*
A First Empire, mercury gilt bronze French mantel clock with a figure of St Christopher, the patron saint of travellers. Eight-day silk suspension movement chiming hour and half hour on a bell. Silvered water silk dial signed "Le Paute & Fils, Hrs du Roi" (Horologer to the King).
- *40cm x 18cm x 10cm*
- £1,900 • Gutlin Clocks

Scottish Regency Clock ▲
- *circa 1830*
A flame mahogany, flat-topped, weight-driven Scottish Regency longcase clock by Christopher Lawson, Edinburgh. Eight-day movement with hour strike on a bell, subsidiary seconds and date aperture.
- *216cm x 50cm x 25cm*
- £6,500 • Gutlin Clocks

Adam and Eve Clock ▲
- *18th–19th century*
An English automation mahogany and inlaid longcase clock by John Alkar of Wigan. The case with swan-neck pediment and outset square section columns. Includes painted automata figures of Adam and Eve beside a rocking tree of knowledge to the arch.
- *233cm x 45cm x 25cm*
- £12,000 • Gutlin Clocks

Expert Tips
Well maintained mantel clocks are still good value when you take into account the cost of producing these items today.

Watches

Cartier Watch ▼

- **1968**

An 18ct. gold Cartier tank watch with a square face and a white dial with roman numerals. Sapphire winding button. French marked.

- *diameter 2cm*
- **£2,250**
- **Westminster**

Rolex Pocket Watch ▼

- *circa 1930*

A Rolex sterling silver pocket watch with white enamel dial with subsidiary seconds. The 17-jewelled movement signed "Rolex". Swiss-made British import marks for the year 1930.

- **£2,250**
- **Anthony Green**

Military Pocket Watch ▲

- *circa 1939*

A rare British military issue Rolex pocket watch. The dial signed "Rolex A9172", has sub seconds and luminous numerals and hands. The nickel case signed inside "Rolex", with ordinance marks "A9172 G.S.M.K.II" on the back of the outside case and "A9172" on the outside band.

- **£975**
- **Anthony Green**

Peerless Lady's Watch ▲

- *circa 1930s*

An hexagonal, Peerless lady's watch in platinum with a light silvered dial, black Arabic numerals and hands, and an expandable gold bracelet. Swiss movement with an English case.

- *diameter 2cm*
- **£1,875**
- **Westminster**

Navigational Stop Watch ▼

- *circa 1940*

A rare Hamilton navigational stop watch with a black dial including subseconds and a minute recorder. The chrome nickel case has U.S. ordinance marks: "FCCS No.88-W-590 MERS PART NO.37297 SERIAL NO.3560-42". The movement with micrometer adjustment, adjusts to temperature with three positions. Includes original U.S. military issue box.

- **£1,200**
- **Anthony Green**

Half-Hunter Pocket Watch ▼

- *date 1880*

A high quality, English, 18ct. gold half-hunter pocket watch, with enamelled dial and enamel chapter-ring to the outer case. The movement is signed "W. Lockwood, 3 Devonshire Buildings, Victoria Lane, Huddersfield".

- **£1,950**
- **Anthony Green**

Rolex Prince Watch ▼
- *circa 1929*

Rare Prince chronometer gent's watch. Dial features original, enamelled numerals and tracks.
- £6,650 • Anthony Green

Lady's Gold Watch ▼
- *circa 1940*

A rectangular lady's Bucherer watch in 18ct. gold with a bracelet strap.
- *2.5cm x 2cm*
- £375 • Westminster

Hunter Fob ▲
- *circa 1860*

A lady's enamelled and diamond-mounted key-wound hunter Fob in 18ct. gold, with pierced cover on matching bar brooch in fitted case. Produced by Mellerio Meller, 1 Quai d'Orsay, Paris.
- £4,600 • Anthony Green

Lady's Wristwatch ▼
- *circa 1960*

An 18ct. gold Jaeger-Le-Caultre lady's wristwatch with square face and white dial with roman numerals.
- *diameter 1.5cm*
- £645 • Westminster

Vintage Lady's Watch ▶
- *circa 1925*

An hexagonal Vintage lady's 9ct. gold watch with a 9ct. gold expandable bracelet. With Arabic figures on a white porcelain face, and a second minute dial.
- *diameter 2.5cm*
- £275 • Westminster

Omega Lady's Watch ▶
- *circa 1950*

An 18ct. covered gold Omega lady's watch with a gold linked bracelet strap which, together with the lid, is encrusted with diamonds and Burma rubies.
- *diameter 3cm*
- £2,750 • Westminster

Lady's Dress Watch ▼

- *circa 1930s*

Delicate lady's dress watch in platinum with diamonds on a silk strap. Swiss movement with an English case.

- *1.5cm x 1cm*
- £1,100
- Westminster

Cocktail Watch ▼

- *circa 1930s*

A lady's platinum cocktail watch with diamonds set around the face and Arabic numerals on the dial, with a white expandable platinum bracelet.

- *diameter 3cm*
- £1,150
- Westminster

Omega Lady's Watch ▲

- *1970s*

An Omega lady's watch in 18ct. white gold with diamonds set around the bezel and a smooth 18ct. satin integral bracelet of average size. With roman numerals on an enamelled dial.

- *diameter 2.5cm*
- £1,125
- Westminster

Asprey Watch ▲

- *circa 1916*

Silver Asprey rectangular curved watch with white metal dial and Roman numerals.

- £260
- Sugar

Expert Tips

The leading makers of wristwatches include Patek Philippe, Rolex, Cartier, and Omega. The digital watch has caused a revival in interest in handmade watches and current prices are high as a consequence.

Hexagonal Rolex Watch ▼

- *1920*

A hexagonal 9ct. gold lady's Rolex watch with Arabic figures on a gold dial.

- *diameter 2.5 cm*
- £550
- AM-PM

Art Deco Watch ▼

- *circa 1940*

A lady's curved 18ct. heavy gold bracelet cocktail watch with an Art Deco design. Swiss movement.

- *width 2cm*
- £875
- Westminster

Gentleman's Manual-Wind Wrist Watch ▼
- *1925*
A gentleman's gold, manual-wind wrist watch by J.W. Benson, fetauring a white enamel face with Arabic numerals and subsidiary seconds.
- *diameter 3cm*
- £250   • **The Swan**

Bulova Gold-Plated Wrist Watch ▼
- *1940*
A gold-plated gentleman's wrist watch by Mercheaz Bulova, with a white dial and gold baton numerals.
- *3.5cm square*
- £150   • **The Swan**

Gentleman's Incaflex Wrist Watch ➤
- *1950*
A gentleman's manual wind Incaflex wrist watch by Wyler with gold batons and Arabic numerals.
- *3.2cm x 2.8cm*
- £140   • **The Swan**

Bucherer Lady's Cocktail Watch ▲
- *circa 1940*
An exquisite lady's 18ct. platinum and diamond cocktail watch designed by Bucherer, with a white dial and an original 9ct. gold flexi strap.
- *diameter 2cm*
- £2,100   • **Westminster**

Art Deco-Style Bulova Watch ▲
- *1930*
A gold-plated gentleman's manual-wind Bulova wrist watch in the Art Deco-style. With subsidiary seconds on a white enamel dial.
- *3.2cm x 2.2cm*
- £295   • **The Swan**

Chronograph ▲
- *circa 1945*
Chronograph by Eberhard & Co, showing hour/minute registers.
- £3,500   • **Anthony Green**

Expert Tips

The more expensive the watch the costlier any repairs will be. Most collectable watches are small and easily lost so make sure your watch is valued and insured.

French LIP Watch ▼

• *circa 1950*
Military-style wrist watch with stainless-steel case and subsidiary seconds. Clear digits on face.
• £140   • Sugar

Pin Set Wrist Watch ▼

• *circa 1915*
A rare gentleman's pin set wrist watch by H.Y. Moser & Cie in 14ct. pink gold with high-grade lever movement and engraved and enamelled dial. Features a very large tonneau-shaped case with hinged lugs. The case is signed "H.Y. Moser & Cie No. 635235", with Russian hallmarks.
• £2,750   • Anthony Green

Longines Cocktail Watch ▲

• *circa 1960s*
A delicate Longines lady's platinum and diamond manual wind cocktail watch, with a diamond encrusted strap. Swiss movement with an English case.
• *diameter 1.5cm*
• £3,250   • Westminster

Swiss Chronograph ▲

• *circa 1950*
A high grade Swiss-made sterling silver, hunting case "Split Seconds" chronograph with subsidiary minute recording and sweep second dials. Case number 130519. The white enamel dial signed "S.Smith & Son, 9 The Strand, London, Maker to the Admiralty, No. 142B 68, Non Magnetizable Swiss Made".
• £2,950   • Anthony Green

Constellation Watch ▲

• *1960*
A stainless steel gentleman's Omega constellation watch with digits on a silver face with a steel flip-lock bracelet.
• *diameter 3cm*
• £425   • AM-PM

Gold Pocket Watch ◄

• *1920*
A gentleman's gold pocket watch with top-wind button set by Thomas Russell.
• *diameter 4cm*
• £250   • The Swan

Hamilton Watch ▲
• **1930**
A rectangular gentleman's gold-plated manual wind watch by Hamilton with gold roman numerals on a white enamel dial with subsidiary seconds.
• *3.5cm x 2.5 cm*
• **£375**　　• The Swan

Lady's Platinum and Diamond Watch ▲
• *circa 1930s*
A lady's platinum and diamond watch by Longines, with Arabic numerals on a white face and a gold integral twin snake bracelet. Swiss movement with an English case.
• *diameter 1.5cm*
• **£895**　　• Westminster

Military Issue Watch ▲
• **1940**
A military issue pocket watch by Waltman, with white Arabic numerals on a black dial with subsidiary seconds.
• *3.5cm diameter*
• **£75**　　• The Swan

Signed Rolex Watch ▼
• **1940**
A 9ct. gold lady's Rolex watch, with a linked gold bracelet strap. Back plate signed "MA".
• *2.5cm square*
• **£275**　　• The Swan

Bulova Wrist Watch ▼
• **1930**
A gentleman's rectangular, gold plated and curved, manual wind wrist watch by Bulova. White dial with gold Arabic numerals and subsidiary seconds.
• *3.5cm x 2cm*
• **£295**　　• The Swan

Rolex Oyster Perpetual ◀
• *circa 1952*
18ct. gold Rolex Perpetual wristwatch with moon-phase calendar.
• **£35,000**　　• Somlo

131

Olympics Commemorative Watch ▲

- **1972**

A rare, limited edition commemorative wrist watch by Longines, which features a stamp from the Olympic games in Munich. With silvered baton numerals on a white dial.

- *diameter 3cm*
- **£295**   • **The Swan**

Open-Face Pocket Watch ▲

- *circa 1830*

A fine quality open-face pocket watch, the cylindrical case with turned sides. The engine-turned dial with roman chapter ring and signed "Simmons Finsbury London". English lever movement with fusée signed and numbered "778". The balance has a diamond endstone.

- **£1,500**   • **Anthony Green**

Expert Tips

Rolex is not the only sought-after make: watches made by Patek Philippe are just as keenly pursued but are not so readily found.

Lord Elgin Wrist Watch ▼

- **1950**

A rectangular, gold-plated Lord Elgin gentleman's wrist watch with subsidiary seconds by the Elgin National Watch Company.

- *width 3.5cm*
- **£275**   • **The Swan**

Longines Wrist Watch ▼

- **1980**

A rectangular lady's 9ct. gold quartz Longines wrist watch with a diamond-set linked bracelet. White dial with Arabic numerals.

- *2.5cm x 2cm*
- **£495**   • **The Swan**

Bulova Gentleman's Wrist Watch ▲

- **1940**

A rectangular, gold-plated, curved gentleman's wrist watch by Bulova. With gold baton and black Arabic numerals on a white dial, with subsidiary seconds.

- *width 3.5cm*
- **£395**   • **The Swan**

Cine Alpha Wrist Watch ▲

- **1940**

A gold-plated gentleman's Cine Alpha wrist watch, with black Arabic numerals on an orange band within a white dial.

- *diameter 3.5cm*
- **£95**   • **The Swan**

IWC Octagonal Watch ▼
- *circa 1923*

An octagonal IWC 18ct. wrist watch with Arabic numerals on a silver face.
- *width 3cm*
- £1,000
- Sugar

Vintage Lady's Watch ▼
- *circa 1930s*

Lady's 18ct. gold watch with leather strap. White porcelain dial with roman numerals and a red number 12, with black cathedral hands. Swiss lever movement and a black leather bracelet.
- *width 3cm*
- £275
- Westminster

Platinum Watch ▲
- *circa 1930*

A platinum and diamond wrist watch with a sprung platinum bracelet. A light silvered face with five numerals in black and a red number 12 with an outer chapter ring
- *1.5cm x 1cm*
- £1,275
- Westminster

Duel-Dial Wrist Watch ▼
- *late 1940s*

A Rolex Prince 9ct. gold, dual-dial, curved-back wrist watch. Features flared sides and a crocodile strap.
- *length 3.5cm*
- £2,900
- Sugar

Movado Wrist Watch ◄
- *1950s*

A gentleman's 18ct. gold Movado wrist watch, with an interesting dial arrangement with silver batons and a crocodile strap.
- *diameter 4cm*
- £650
- Sugar

German Aviator's Watch ▼
- *circa 1942*

A very rare aviator's wrist watch by A. Lange & Sohne Glashutte I Sa. model No. FI23883. German military ordinance marks to inside of case back: "Mvt #213092 Case #213092 Gerrat #127-560A-1 Werk #213092 Anforderz #FI23883".
- *diameter 5.5cm*
- **£3,500**   • **Anthony Green**

Lady's Rose Gold Watch ▼
- *circa 1940s*

A square lady's precision Rolex watch in 18ct. rose gold with an original Rolex flexi-strap.
- *diameter 1.5cm*
- **£1,800**   • **AM-PM**

IWC Automatic Watch ▼
- *circa 1950*

An automatic high grade wrist watch in steel by the International Watch Co., with waterproof screw-on back.
- **£2,000**   • **Anthony Green**

Rolex Gentleman's Dress Watch ◄
- *1933*

A rare Rolex 9ct. gold gentleman's dress watch with rectangular cut corner case. Marked "Ref#1918 Case #9817", plus British import marks for the year 1933. The movement is signed "Rolex Hairspring 15 Rubies Swiss Made". The dial is signed "Rolex & Swiss Made" with a subsidiary dial showing seconds.
- **£3,350**   • **Anthony Green**

Rolex Lady's Watch ▼
- *1920*

Rolex lady's sprung bracelet 9ct. gold watch with a Rolex-named movement and back plate. Features a white porcelain face with a red number 12, and a secondary minute dial.
- *diameter 3cm*
- **£750**   • **Westminster**

Victorian Lady's Dress Watch ▼
- *circa 1900s*

A Victorian 15ct. gold lady's dress watch with rubies and diamonds on a gate-type sprung bracelet with numerals in blue and red. With gold decoration on a white porcelain dial.
- *diameter 2.5cm*
- **£1,700**   • **Westminster**

Rolex Oyster Watch ▲
- 1970

A gentleman's Rolex Oyster watch with digits on a silver dial, with an Oyster bracelet-style band.
- *diameter 3cm*
- £650 • AM-PM

Vacheron Constantin Watch ▲
- *circa 1960s*

A rectangular white gold 18ct. Vacheron Constantin manual movement watch, with silver digits on a black dial.
- *3.5cm x 2cm*
- £1,500 • AM-PM

Lady's Rolex Watch ▼
- *circa 1957*

A 9ct. gold lady's Rolex watch with black Arabic numerals on a white enamelled dial with subsidiary seconds.
- *diameter 2.7cm*
- £525 • Sugar

Longines Watch ▼
- 1930

A rectangular Longines, stainless steel mechanical watch, with luminous green Arabic numbers on a white face.
- *2cm x 1.5cm*
- £350 • AM-PM

Rolex Prince "Brancarde" ▲
- *circa 1930*

A Rolex Prince "Brancarde" wrist watch in sterling silver, case number "0559 Ref #971", movement number "#72147". This magnificent chronometer is in its original box with the original two-part chronometer rating certificate dated 1930, the original strap and Rolex sterling silver buckle.
- £12,500 • Anthony Green

Omega Flightmaster Wrist Watch ▲
- *circa 1970*

An Omega Flightmaster aviator's multifunctional wrist watch in steel. Supplied with the original box, instructions and guarantee.
- £1,800 • Anthony Green

Rolex Earl Wrist Watch ▲
- **1930**

A gentleman's Rolex Earl manual-wind wrist watch, with a stainless steel case and a white dial with clear digits and subsidiary seconds.
- *diameter 3cm*
- **£375** • The Swan

Vintage Lady's Watch ▲
- *circa 1910*

An 18ct. gold lady's watch set with demantoid garnets and diamonds around the bezel. White porcelain face with black numerals and red number 12, decorated with gold pips with an 18ct. expandable bracelet.
- *diameter 2.2cm*
- **£1,275** • Westminster

Lady's Cocktail Watch ▼
- *circa 1940s*

A gas-tube bracelet lady's watch, inset with natural Burma rubies, with jointed finials on a circular silvered dial with black numerals. Mechanical movement.
- *width 1.2cm*
- **£2,100** • Westminster

Demi-Hunter Pocket Watch ▼
- **1905**

A 9ct. gold demi-hunter pocket watch by Wilson and Sharp of Edinburgh. With three-quarter plate movement.
- *diameter 4cm*
- **£495** • Sugar

White Gold Watch ▲
- *circa 1950s*

Lady's Rolex watch in 18ct. white gold. Integral strap with a square white dial with silvered batons and black hands. Leaver movement, Rolex case and named movement.
- *1.5cm square*
- **£875** • Westminster

Rolex Pocket Watch ▼
- *circa 1920*

A gold-plated Rolex pocket watch with luminous Arabic numerals and hands and subsidiary seconds.
- *diameter 4.2cm*
- £600   • Sugar

Omega Seamaster Wrist Watch ▼
- *circa 1950*

An Omega Seamaster automatic waterproof wrist watch in steel with early automatic bumper movement.
- £875   • Anthony Green

French Air Force Chronograph ▲
- *circa 1950*

A Breguet type XX French Air Force Pilots "Fly-Back" chronograph in steel with rotating bezel marked "1–12". The dial with subsidiary seconds and minute recording dial. The waterproof screw-on back with case mark "20645".
- £4,900   • Anthony Green

Sterling Silver Watch ▲
- *circa 1918*

A Longines sterling silver, early pin set one-button chronograph with minute recording dial and subsidiary second dial. The sweep centre seconds chronograph operating through the winding stem. The hinged lug case is marked "#2974806 Mvt#2974806". Eighteen jewels and five adjustment case dial and movement signed "Longines".
- £2,950   • Anthony Green

Aviator's Chronograph ▼
- *1968*

An aviator's Breitling "Navitimer" chronograph in steel with subsidiary dials for sweep seconds, minute and hour recording. Outer rotating bezel allowing various aviation calculations. Case marked "#1307320 Ref#806 806".
- £1,800   • Anthony Green

Longines Water-Resistant Watch ▼
- *circa 1950*

A gents Longines water-resistant two-button chronograph with minute recording dial and subsidiary seconds dial. The caseback stamped 18ct. (Swiss control marks), with the words "Shock-absorber waterproof Antimagnetic" engraved. The high grade movement dial and case signed "Longines".
- £2,450   • Anthony Green

Rolex Silver Pocket Watch ▼

- *circa 1920*

A silver Rolex pocket watch with a circular blue enamel insert to the outer casing of the watch.
- *diameter 4cm*
- £700   • Sugar

Rolex Military Pocket Watch ▼

- *circa 1940s*

A Rolex military-style pocket watch, model number "GS MK II", with a black dial with gold Arabic numerals and subsidiary seconds.
- *diameter 4.2cm*
- £650   • Sugar

Oyster Wrist Watch ▲

- *circa 1926*

A very early 9ct. pink gold Oyster waterproof wrist watch. The octagonal case signed "Rolex 20 Worlds Records", case number "#23681". The movement signed "Rolex Prima", 15 jewels timed to six positions for all climates. Swiss made. The white enamel dial signed "Rolex Oyster".
- £4,900   • Anthony Green

Lady's Rolex Watch ▼

- **1928**

A 9ct. gold lady's Rolex watch with a white enamel dial and a matching 9ct. gold expanding bracelet.
- *diameter 2cm*
- £650   • Sugar

Vacheron & Constantin Wrist Watch ◀

- **1950**

An 18ct. gold wrist watch with gold baton numerals on a white dial by Vacheron & Constantin.
- *diameter 4cm*
- £1,900   • Sugar

Movado Pocket Watch ▼

- *circa 1940*

Silver/steel pocket watch by Movado, with triple date and moon phase. Case with winding mechanism operated when opening and closing. Covered in crocodile skin.
- £1,850   • Anthony Green

Breitling Navitimer Chronograph ▼
- *1960s*

A gentleman's silver aviator's watch with the chronograph operated by two pushers on the case band. Made by Breitling Navitimer. The black dial has subsidiary seconds and minute recording dial.
- *diameter 4cm*
- £950   • Sugar

Swiss Wrist Watch ▼
- *1950s*

A Swiss-made 18ct. gold wrist watch with roman numerals and gold batons on a silvered face with subsidiary seconds.
- *diameter 3.5cm*
- £2,300   • Sugar

Oyster Submariner Diving Watch ▲
- *circa 1964*

Oyster Perpetual Submariner automatic diver's wrist watch, on a Rolex steel "flip-lock" bracelet.
- £2,950   • Anthony Green

Rolex Precision Watch ▼
- *1958*

A 9ct. gold Rolex Precision watch with an original Rolex strap.
- *diameter 3cm*
- £1,100   • Sugar

Lady's Gold Watch ▶
- *1915*

Rolex 9ct. gold watch with red numeral 12, enamel dial and expanding bracelet.
- £700   • Sugar

Expert Tips

Scratched and damaged dials can be repaired or replaced but, again, this type of work can take considerable time and expense.

Juvnenia Lady's Watch ▶
- *circa 1940s*

A rectangular 18ct. gold lady's watch by Juvnenia with an original crocodile strap.
- *1.5 x 2cm*
- £1,200   • Sugar

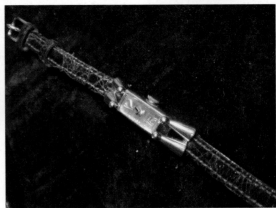

Scientific Instruments

Prismatic Compass ▼
- *late 19th century*
A dry-card prismatic compass, with polished and lacquered brass case and leather outer case.
- *7cm x 9cm*
- £299 • Langfords Marine

Medicine Cabinet ▼
- *circa 1850*
A mahogany medicine cabinet with a full set of bottles, scales, pestle and mortar, and pill boxes.
- *height 22cm*
- £1,375 • Mathias

Drawing Instruments ➤
- *early 19th century*
A set of drawing instruments in a pocket case with the trade label, "T. Blunt Optician & Co., 22 Cornhill, London". Includes a signed ivory folding sector, an ivory scale, a brass semi-circular protractor and three assorted compasses all contained in a black fish skin case.
- *20cm x 8cm*
- £649 • Langfords Marine

Equinoctical Instrument ▼
- *circa 1830*
Newman & Co. of Calcutta compass with roman numeral dial.
- *diameter 14cm*
- £1,605 • H&H

Travelling Microscope ▼
- *circa 1890*
A predominantly brass monocular microscope, with original case by Henry Grouch of London.
- *height 35cm*
- £750 • Finchley

Brass Microscope ➤
- *circa 1910*
Monocular brass microscope, with lenses of two magnifications by W. Watson and Sons, 313 High Holborn, London.
- *height 34cm*
- £650 • H&H

Victorian Barometer ▲
- *1890*
A Victorian desk barometer with silvered dial signed "Halstaf and Hannaford, 228 Regent Street". The setting hand is adjusted by the ships wheel.
- *height 32cm*
- £490 • The Clock Clinic

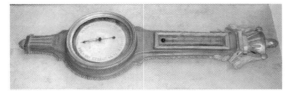

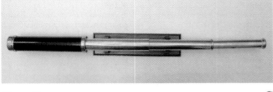

French Barometer ◄
- **19th century**
Early nineteenth century painted
wall barometer from France.
- *101cm x 30cm*
- **£1,950**   • O.F. Wilson

Three-Draw
Victorian Telescope ▲
- **1750–1817**
A three-draw Victorian telescope
signed "Dolland, London" on the
first draw. Polished and lacquered
brass with mahogany barrel, lens
slide, crisp optics.
- *73cm x 5cm*
- **£329**   • Langfords Marine

Library Telescope ►
- **early 19th century**
Single draw, 6cm diameter,
polished and lacquered brass
library telescope. Signed around
the eyepiece and end of the
barrel "I. Bradford & Sons 136
Minories, London". The long
body tube with rack and pinion
focusing and lens cap, the whole
mounted on a turned column
with three folding cabriole legs.
Original fitted mahogany box
with trade label inside the lid.
- *80cm x 46cm*
- **£1,795**   • Langfords Marine

Nautical Sextant ▲
- **late 19th century**
Nautical sextant in polished and
lacquered brass, in original
mahogany box.
- *28cm x 25cm x 13cm*
- **£1,250**   • Langfords Marine

Anemometer ►
- **1950s**
A brass and enamelled vertical
and horizontal anemometer
(wind gauge), with solid leather
case and accessories. It was used
in coal mines, flues, ventilators
and so on, to measure the lighter
currents of air.
- *8cm x 9cm*
- **£349**   • Langfords Marine

Expert Tips

*The interest in scientific
instruments has grown and
prices have increased
accordingly – in 1984, a silver
quadrant dial by Humphrey
Colle (1530–91) fetched
a phenomenal £62,000
at an auction.*

Table Telescope ►
- **circa 1880**
Brass table telescope by W. Ladd,
Chancery Lane, London, in
original wood box.
- *96cm x 41cm*
- **£2,900**   • Langfords Marine

Barometer ▲
- **1900**
Barometer by Phillips Banbury.
- *height 102cm*
- £1,900 • Langfords Marine

Oscillating Engine ▼
- **1850**
A vertical two-column oscillating engine on vertical pot boiler with safety valve. Built by Newton & Co, London.
- *height 22cm*
- £1,150 • Langfords Marine

Decorative Microscope ▲
- *Victorian*
A polished lacquered brass binocular microscope which is purely decorative.
- *36cm x 15cm*
- £79 • Langfords Marine

Military Marching Compass ▲
- *early 20th century*
A World War I hand-held prismatic military marching compass, in original anodised brass case. Dry card with mother-of-pearl dial, glass port, brass thumb ring, rotating brass bezel with clamp and two-way stopping mechanisms. Government issue, denoted by the chevron.
- *6cm x 9cm*
- £169 • Langfords Marine

Zeiss Binoculars ▲
- *circa 1940*
Cold War binoculars used on the Berlin Wall to observe Russian movements. Instrument built and design by Carl Ziess and finished in brass and aluminium. Optical magnification of 10 x 50. Standing on adjustable wooden tripod.
- *height 140cm*
- £6,250 • Simon Hatchwell

Pair of Globes ◄
- **1860**
One of a pair of globes – "Terrestrial" by Bardin, "Celestial" by Malby.
- *123cm x 62cm*
- £39,500 • Langfords Marine

Ship-Stick Barometer ▲
- *1810*

Mahogany ship-stick barometer by Lynch Dublin.
- *height 94cm*
- **£2,200** • Langfords Marine

Armillary Sphere ▲
- *late 20th century*

Large armillary sphere in polished and lacquered brass with wooden stand.
- *93cm x 59cm*
- **£2,750** • Langfords Marine

French Barograph ▶
- *19th century*

A French barograph in unusual moulded glazed brass case on turned feet. With centigrade thermometer and retailers ivory plate, marked "S. Block, Strasbourg and Mulhouse". Overhauled and guaranteed.
- *height 24cm*
- **£1,600** • The Clock Clinic

Victorian Steam Crane Engine ▲
- *1860*

A Victorian steam crane engine, Stevens model.
- *height 12cm*
- **£600** • Langfords Marine

French Barometer ▲
- *1880*

French holostenic barometer with leather case.
- *diameter 8cm*
- **£320** • Langfords Marine

Front-Stick Barometer ▲
- *circa 1850*

A mid-nineteenth century bow front-stick barometer in figured mahogany with large bore mercury tube and thermometer. The bone scales signed by maker, "Lilley & Sons".
- *height 102cm*
- **£4,800** • The Clock Clinic

Collector's Items

The important rule for the collector of 'collectables' is to take care of the ephemera of today – they may be the antiques of tomorrow.

It's an old but true saying that what one throws away today is the collectable of tomorrow. From the soap packet to the mobile phone, all have their place in the collector's market. But watch out for the fads that hit the market with a splash and are just as soon forgotten, such as the Yo-Yo. The most collectable items are those which are in some ways ground-breaking or revolutionary at the time: for example, radios, TVs or telephones. It is also worth collecting items which are gradually becoming obsolete in the new digital age, for instance records or tapes. Self-winding watches are also a good example of this as very few are currently being made and so their value is rising.

The best advice for building a collection is to start with something you have a great personal interest in; this could range from the everyday to the extremely expensive piece. The collector's market is very unpredictable but can be extremely rewarding if you are lucky enough to have chosen that forgotten item that defines the period in which it was made.

Collectables

American Handbag ▲
- *1940*
An American fabric and bamboo handbag with scrolled design.
- *24cm x 28cm*
- £150
- Linda Bee

Harlequin Glass Cocktail Set ▲
- *1950*
Harlequin glass cocktail set with brass holder, plastic feet and roped handle.
- *18cm x 35cm*
- £25
- Radio Days

Victorian Opera Glasses ▼
- *Victorian*
A pair of blue enamelled and gilded brass opera glasses with taupe leather carrying case.
- *9cm x 4cm*
- £99
- Langfords Marine

Tortoiseshell Comb ▼
- *1880*
Large tortoiseshell comb for hair.
- *height 16cm*
- **£95** • **Abacus Antiques**

Edla Fan and Humidifier ▼
- *1930s*
A French Art Deco bakelite fan and humidifier, with a central circular metal cover.
- *height 35cm*
- **£200** • **Decodence**

Hair Grip ▲
- *circa 1900*
Early twentieth century tortoiseshell hair grip.
- *height 13cm*
- **£65** • **Abacus Antiques**

Edwardian Shop Scales ▼
- *March 15th, 1906*
Early twentieth-century shop scales inscribed "London & Manchester". Made by the Automatic Scale Company of London & Manchester.
- *33cm x 60cm*
- **£125** • **Drummonds**

Alligator Skin Bag ▼
- *1920*
An English stitched alligator skin bag with leather handles.
- *55cm x 37cm*
- **£175** • **John Clay**

Eye Glass ▲
- *1920*
Tortoiseshell eye glass.
- *height 13cm*
- **£25** • **Abacus Antiques**

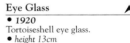

English Crocodile Skin Bag ➤
- *1920*
An English stitched, deep grained, box-shaped, brown crocodile bag with a monogrammed top.
- *42cm x 60cm*
- **£150** • **John Clay**

Stainless Steel Whistle ▲
- *1920*
A stainless steel whistle with a ring hook and "The Acme Thunderer" inscribed across the mouthpiece.
- *length 5cm*
- £16   • After Noah

American Felt Handbag ▼
- *1950*
A 1950s American handbag made out of felt. Features a poodle design fashioned from sequins with a gilt chain lead.
- *28cm x 28 cm*
- £220   • Linda Bee

Smoker's Antler Horn Compendium ◀
- *1900*
A smoker's compendium made from antler horns with a hand-stitched leather tray.
- *length 32cm/tray*
- £760   • Holland & Holland

Pair of Hair Brushes ▲
- *1921*
A pair of tortoiseshell and silver hair brushes with a silver hallmark.
- *length 27cm*
- £55   • Aurum

Meat Safe ▼
- *1910*
Fruitwood meat safe either hanging or free standing.
- *height 60cm*
- £180   • Myriad

English Lady's Powder Compact ▲
- *1940*
An English lady's powder compact with plastic dice made by Wadsworth.
- *diameter 7cm*
- £195   • Linda Bee

Bakelite Pin Box ▼
- *1930*
An English Art Deco bakelite
pin box.
- *8.5cm x 3cm*
- £12   • Radio Days

Soda Siphons ▼
- *1960*
An English soda siphon with an
emerald green metallic plastic
body and a black plastic lid.
- *height 30cm*
- £10   • Radio Days

Perspex Magazine Rack ◄
- *1960*
Magazine rack made of curved,
clear perspex, with blue, painted
steel base.
- *43cm x 38cm*
- £40   • Retro Home

English Bakelite Clock ►
- *1950*
An English brown, bakelite clock
with circular dial, free standing
on square base and feet.
Manufactured by Smith Electric
of England.
- *15cm x 12cm*
- £45   • Radio Days

Royal Doulton Mug ▼
- *20th century*
A Royal Doulton mug
naturalistically moulded as an
R.A.F. pilot from World War II.
- *height 15cm*
- £65   • London Antique

Tortoiseshell Letter Opener ►
- *1911*
Tortoiseshell letter opener with
coins inserted.
- *length 20.5cm*
- £85   • Abacus Antiques

Gillette Razor Bakelite Box ▲
- *1930*
Bakelite box inscribed "Gillette",
together with razor.
- *9cm x 6cm*
- £35   • Radio Days

Magazine Rack ▼
• *1960*
Brown plastic magazine rack.
Giotto stopping for Kartell.
• *39cm x 40cm*
• **£75**   • **Retro Home**

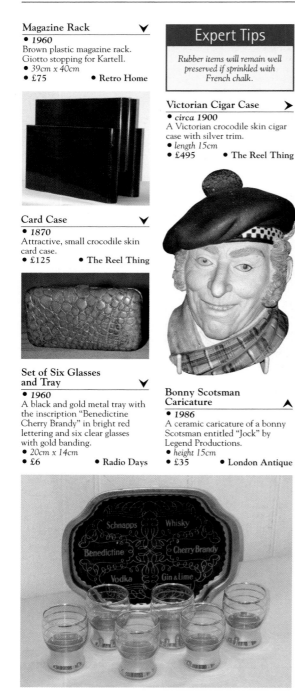

Card Case ▼
• *1870*
Attractive, small crocodile skin
card case.
• **£125**   • **The Reel Thing**

Set of Six Glasses
and Tray ▼
• *1960*
A black and gold metal tray with
the inscription "Benedictine
Cherry Brandy" in bright red
lettering and six clear glasses
with gold banding.
• *20cm x 14cm*
• **£6**   • **Radio Days**

Victorian Cigar Case ➤
• *circa 1900*
A Victorian crocodile skin cigar
case with silver trim.
• *length 15cm*
• **£495**   • **The Reel Thing**

Bonny Scotsman
Caricature ▲
• *1986*
A ceramic caricature of a bonny
Scotsman entitled "Jock" by
Legend Productions.
• *height 15cm*
• **£35**   • **London Antique**

Soda Siphon ▲
• *circa 1960*
An English 1960s reflective silver
plastic soda siphon, with a green
plastic cup to handle.
• *height 31cm*
• **£10**   • **Radio Days**

Propeller Clock ◀
- *circa 1917–18*

An Hispana Suiza working clock mounted on a mahogany propeller from a Sopworth Dolphin Scout airplane.
- *260cm x 26cm x 17cm*
- £1,780 • Henry Gregory

Bakelite Comb ◀
- *1920*

A French Art Deco bakelite hair comb.
- *length 14cm*
- £55 • Linda Bee

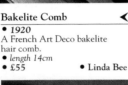

Milk Churn ▼
- *1890*

A galvanised steel milk churn of unusual shape with floral garland and swag decoration.
- *height 65cm*
- £380 • Myriad

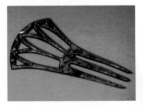

Card Case ▲
- *1880*

A pink mother-of-pearl card case decorated with birds.
- *height 9cm*
- £155 • Japanese Gallery

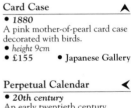

Perpetual Calendar ◀
- *20th century*

An early twentieth century English perpetual calendar.
- £85 • North West 8

Barrel Decanter ▶
- *1880*

Walnut barrel decanter.
- *20cm x 6cm*
- £825 • Langfords Marine

Art Deco Ash Tray △
- *1930*

A chrome and bakelite Art Deco
ash tray.
- *diameter 8cm*
- £45　　　　　• Linda Bee

Black Sunglasses △
- *1950*

A pair of black sunglasses from
the 1950s with diamante
decoration.
- *width 15cm*
- £20　　　　　• Linda Bee

Austrian Art Nouveau
Lady's Compact △
- *1930*

An Austrian Art Nouveau lady's
powder compact by Ledered in
the shape of a suitcase with
stickers.
- *length 8cm*
- £120　　　　　• Linda Bee

Expert Tips

*Labels should be in pristine
condition and if possible tins
should be in unscathed and
unopened in order to gain a
good price.*

French Lady's Compact ▽
- *1920*

A French Art Deco circular lady's
powder compact with a picture of
a young girl with auburn hair in a
romantic pose.
- *diameter 7cm*
- £65　　　　　• Linda Bee

Detachable Heels △
- *1920*

A pair of French black plastic
detachable heels decorated with
rhinestones.
- *height 5cm*
- £45　　　　　• Linda Bee

American Handbag △
- *1950*

An American 1950s handbag
with a handle of pink velvet,
hand-painted with pink flowers.
- *16cm x 24cm*
- £150　　　　　• Linda Bee

Model Engine ▽
- *1860*

Six pillar, brass beam stationary
engine model.
- *20cm x 30cm*
- £5,800　　• Langfords Marine

Beehive ◀
- *1890*
A most unusual English beehive.
with original basket work with
wooden finial.
- *height 70cm*
- £120   • Myriad

Crocodile Handbag ▶
- *1940*
A 1940s classically elegant
Argentinian crocodile skin
handbag with brass trim.
- *23cm x 28cm*
- £195   • Linda Bee

Pack of Cigarettes ▲
- *1940*
Original 1940s cigarettes branded
"Dandy, Special Virginia".
- £20   • Linda Bee

Poodle Handbag ▼
- *1950*
A fun American handbag in
laminated fabric with
poodles on the front.
- *19cm x 28cm*
- £125
- Linda Bee

American Handbag ▼
- *1960*
An American handbag made
from black velvet with gold metal
geometrical bands and shiny
black perspex handle and lid.
- *20cm x 17cm*
- £150   • Linda Bee

Lizard Skin Handbag ▼
- *1950*
A 1950s classic black lizard
skin bag.
- *24cm x 37cm*
- £95   • Linda Bee

World War I Truncheon ▼
- *circa 1915*
World War I reserve truncheon
with leather strap.
- *38cm x 4cm*
- £160   • Henry Gregory

Advertising and Packaging

Shop Sign ▼
• *1940s*
A wrought iron shop sign, with
scrolled decoration surrounding a
clover leaf emblem with the
hand-painted letters "Sunshine
Bakery". In original condition.
• *102cm x 65cm*
• £220   • Old School

Dresden Figurine ▼
• *1910*
A Dresden porcelain group of
figures advertising Yardley
perfumes and soaps.
• *height 17cm*
• £350   • Huxtable's

Packet of Condoms ▲
• *1950s*
An assortment of 1950s
condoms.
• *16cm x 5cm/packet*
• £10   • Huxtable's

Manufacturer's Sign ➤
• *1930s*
A sign cut from hardwood of the
figure of John Bull, advertising
John Bull Tyres.
• *height 65cm*
• £120   • Huxtable's

Ink Bottle ▼
• *1930s*
A bottle of blue black Swan ink.
• *height 8cm*
• £6   • Huxtable's

Bottle of Broseden ▲
- *1930s*

A bottle of "Broseden" made in Germany. A drink used to calm the troops during lonely times.
- *height 9cm*
- £5
- Huxtable's

Toffee Tin ▲
- *20th century*

A Macintosh's toffee tin commemorating the marriage of George VI to Elizabeth Bowes-Lyon.
- *diameter 14cm*
- £20
- Huxtable's

Brilliantine ◄
- *1930s*

A glass bottle of "Saturday Night Lotion", men's hair styling gloss.
- *height 13cm*
- £12
- Huxtable's

Bournvita Mug ▲
- *1950s*

A white Bournvita mug in the shape of a face with a blue nightcap and a red pom-pom. With large handle.
- *height 14cm*
- £40
- Huxtable's

Carton of Cigarettes ▲
- *1960s*

A carton of Senior Service cigarettes. In original white paper wrapping with navy blue lettering, unopened.
- *13cm x 5cm*
- £40
- Huxtable's

Nib Boxes ◄
- *1920s*

An assortment of unopened nib boxes.
- *width 7cm*
- £7
- Huxtable's

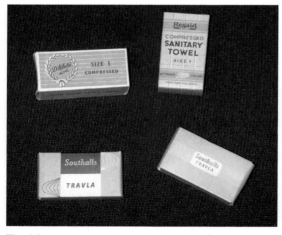

Michelin Man ▼

- *1966*

A bakelite Michelin Man used for advertising in petrol stations and shops.
- *height 150cm*
- **£85**
- **Huxtable's**

Tape Measure ▼

- *circa 1950*

A promotional tape measure with the inscription, "With compliments of A.H. Manning". Includes original box.
- *10cm x 9cm*
- **£14**
- **After Noah**

Sanitary Products ▲

- *1950s*

An assortment of female sanitary towel and tampon boxes.
- *8cm x 4cm/packet*
- **£5**
- **Huxtable's**

Expert Tips

Labels should be in pristine condition and, if possible, tins should be unscathed and unopened in order to gain a good price.

V.D. Matches ▲

- *circa 1940*

An assortment of V.D. matches from World War II.
- *5cm x 3cm*
- **£5**
- **Huxtable's**

Michelin Ashtray ◄

- *1940s*

A premium give-away Bakelite ashtray with a seated figure in the form of the Michelin Man.
- *height 18cm*
- **£150**
- **Decondence**

Babycham Glass ▼

- *circa 1960*

Babycham promotional champagne glass.
- *height 12cm*
- **£14**
- **After Noah**

Ketchup Bottle ◄
- *1950s*

A bottle of "Kraft" ketchup.
- *height 19cm*
- £15　　　　• Huxtable's

Horlicks Mug ▲
- *circa 1940*

A white porcelain Horlicks mug with blue lettering with solid handle .
- *height 11cm*
- £18　　　　• After Noah

Toffee Tin ▲
- *1930*

A "Felix the Cat" toffee tin. With Felix the cat on one side and a cartoon of Felix on the other side.
- *16cm x 16cm x 10cm*
- £500　　　　• Huxtable's

Oxo Sign ▲
- *20th century*

A red metal double-sided Oxo sign.
- *35cm x 35cm*
- £60　　　　• Huxtable's

Pottery Figure ▼
- *1950*

A painted pottery figure of a shoemaker holding a shoe, advertising Phillips Soles and Heels.
- *height 30cm*
- £200　　　　• Huxtable's

Bonzo the Dog Jug ▼
- *1930*

A water jug in the shape of Bonzo the Dog.
- *height 13cm*
- £250　　　　• Huxtable's

Commemorative Tin ◄
- *1951*

A "Festival of Britain" commemorative tin.
- *6cm x 14cm*
- £200　　　　• Huxtable's

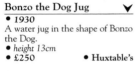

Savings Bank Tin ▼
- *1930s*

A savings bank tin issued by
various banks of the 1930s.
- £15
- Huxtable's

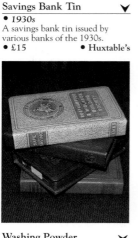

Washing Powder ▼
- *1950s*

Original unused boxes of "Surf"
and "Tide" washing powder.
- *height 17cm*
- £12
- Huxtable's

Royal Busts ▼
- *1902*

Busts of Edward VII and Queen
Alexandra made by Britains.
- *height 5cm*
- £55
- Huxtable's

Cigarette Tin ◄
- *1910*

A green cigarette tin with the
painting of a lady in red wearing
a straw hat, with the lettering
"Muratt's young ladies cigarettes"
written on the tin.
- *14cm x 9cm*
- £120
- Huxtable's

Money Tin ▲
- *1934*

A Crawfords biscuit cum money
tin fairy house by Lucie Attwell.
- *height 21cm*
- £300
- Huxtable's

Match Holder ▲
- *1910*

An Apploinaris match holder
and striker.
- *height 8cm*
- £30
- Huxtable's

Expert Tips

*Rubber items will remain well
preserved if sprinkled with
French chalk.*

Gramophone Tins ◄
- *1910–50*

Assortment of gramophone
needle tins from around the
world.
- £15
- Huxtable's

Guinness Trays ➤
- *circa 1950*

A metal drinks tray with a toucan holding the advertisement for Guinness.
- *diameter 16cm*
- £50 • Huxtable's

Guinness Toucan ▼
- *1955*

A toucan with a glass of Guinness on a stand advertising the beer with the slogan – "My goodness – my Guinness".
- *height 7cm*
- £250 • Huxtable's

Dog Food Sign ▲
- *1950*

A Spratt's wooden sign advertising dog food with the picture of a Highland terrier in the form of the word "Spratts".
- *50cm x 80cm*
- £100 • Huxtable's

Mustard Tins ▲
- *1930s*

An assortment of Coleman's mustard tins. Decorated with red writing and the Union Jack on a yellow background.
- *height 12cm*
- £7 • Huxtable's

Lollipop Man ▲
- *1960s*

A porcelain figure of a Robertson's Golly Lollipop Man.
- *height 12cm*
- £12 • Huxtable's

Guinness Tray ▲
- *circa 1950*

Circular tray advertising Guinness.
- £50 • Huxtable's

Motoring Key Rings ▲
- *1960s*

Assortment of motoring key rings.
- £10 • Huxtable's

Trumps Markers ◄
- *1930s*

Two trumps markers for use in card games.
- £20 • Huxtable's

Bottles

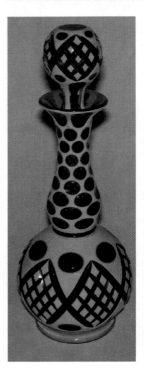

Victorian Scent Bottle ▼
- *circa 1880*
Victorian scent bottle in green glass, decorated with gold banding around the base, neck and stopper.
- *height 13.5cm*
- £110   • Trio

Pair of Scent Bottles ▼
- *circa 1880*
A pair of French scent bottles in blue glass with conical-shaped stoppers. All carrying a gold filigree design.
- *height 21cm*
- £345   • Trio

Bohemian Scent Bottle ▼
- *circa 1880*
A ruby-flashed Bohemian glass scent bottle with stopper.
- *height 19cm*
- £220   • Trio

French Perfume Bottle ▲
- *circa 1880*
A French perfume bottle in red and white decorated glass, and fitted with stopper.
- *height 11cm*
- £358   • Trio

Art Deco Scent Bottles ▼
- *1920*
A pair of English Art Deco perfume bottles in clear glass with black geometric designs.
- *height 18cm*
- £268   • Trio

Circular Scent Bottle ▼

- *1902*

A circular scent bottle painted with two Japanese ladies in traditional dress embracing each other, set against a background of green foliage.
- *diameter 7cm*
- £155
- Trio

Square Scent Bottle ▼

- *circa 1890*

A square French scent bottle in turquoise, fitted with a gold stopper and chain. Decorated with a gold floral design.
- *diameter 3cm*
- £158
- Trio

Oval Scent Bottle ▲

- *circa 1890*

An oval, Victorian scent bottle in white porcelain, with a silver stopper. Decorated with a red butterfly, pink flowers and foliage.
- *height 6cm*
- £158
- Trio

Enamel Scent Bottle ▲

- *circa 1890*

A white enamel scent bottle decorated with pink flowers and surmounted by filigree work on a gold chain.
- *diameter 3cm*
- £135
- Trio

Victorian Scent Bottle ▲

- *circa 1890*

A Victorian, oval scent bottle in clear glass, decorated with gold flowers and fitted with a pinch-back gold chain.
- *height 6cm*
- £199
- Trio

Ruby Scent Bottles ▼
- *1880*
A pair of scent bottles in ruby glass, with slender necks and floral gilt decoration.
- *height 26cm*
- £420   • Trio

English Scent Bottles ▼
- *1920*
Three English Art Deco scent bottles, in red, pink and blue glass, each carrying a long silk tassel.
- *height 9cm*
- £125   • Trio

Turquoise Scent Bottle ▲
- *circa 1910*
A turquoise scent bottle with gold foliage design and ruby glass droplets, together with a pair of decorative vases carrying a complementary design.
- *height 12cm*
- £110   • Trio

Cut-Glass Scent Bottle ▼
- *1920*
A cut-glass Art Deco scent bottle with stopper. Decorated with engraved flowers.
- *height 12cm*
- £125   • Trio

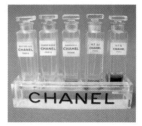

Czechoslovakian Scent Bottle ▲
- *1920*
An Art Deco smokey glass perfume bottle from the former Czechoslovakia, with a large pink silk tassel attached.
- *height 12cm*
- £58   • Trio

Chanel Tester Kit ▼
- *circa 1950*
A perfume tester kit from Chanel, comprising five tester bottles some of which hold deleted perfumes.
- £280   • Linda Bee

Bohemian Glass Bottle ▼

- *circa 1860*

Floral perfume bottle and large
cut stopper in Bohemian glass,
with enamelling.
- £300
- Trio

Red Glass Scent Bottle ▼

- *1920*

Art Deco perfume bottle in
deep red glass, with a tassel
and opaque glass stopper.
- *height 14cm*
- £168
- Trio

Jug-Shaped Scent Bottle ➤

- *1860*

A French ruby scent bottle in the
shape of a stylised jug, with ruby
stopper. Decorated with a gilt
foliage design on the bottle and
handle. The metal base carries
a gilt foliage design.
- *height 12cm*
- £210
- Trio

Square Scent Bottle ▼

- *1930*

Square glass Art Deco perfume
bottle, with a clear glass stopper
and large grey silk tassel.
Decorated with a black floral
design.
- *height 10cm*
- £138
- Trio

Heart-Shaped
Porcelain Bottle ▲

- *circa 1906*

A heart-shaped porcelain scent
bottle, with a silver stopper.
Decorated with a pair
of eighteenth century figures.
- *diameter 4cm*
- £178
- Trio

Oval Scent Bottle ◄
- *1870*
A French green oval glass bottle.
with an elaborate foliate and bird
design and a gold stopper.
- *length 6cm*
- £230   • Trio

Bohemian Scent Bottles ▲
- *circa 1880*
A pair of ruby Bohemian bottles
with foliage design with cusp and
angle rims.
- *height 18cm*
- £548   • Trio

Ruby Flashed Bottles ◄
- *circa 1880*
A pair of ruby flashed Bohemian
glass scent bottles with floral
decoration.
- *height 12cm*
- £245   • Trio

Georgian Scent Bottle ▼
- *1727–1820*
Scent bottle in purple glass with
silver stopper.
- *length 6cm*
- £240   • Trio

Opaque Glass Bottle ▲
- *19th century*
French scent bottle of opaque
glass with a cameo of a lady on
the top.
- *height 11cm*
- £238   • Trio

Art Deco Scent Bottle ▲
- *1920*
An Art Deco perfume bottle in
turquoise and silver, with stopper.
Decorated with geometric design
and inscribed "R.M.S. Homeric".
- *height 6cm*
- £68   • Trio

Venetian Glass Bottle ▼
- *1860*
Blue and white scent bottle with silver top. The blue is created by a Venetian Latticina technique.
- *length 9cm*
- £228   • Trio

Scent Bottles with Portraits ▼
- *circa 1870*
Pair of Czechoslovakian opaque and clear glass scent bottles with oval portraits of young girls, circled with grey and gold to stopper base and rim.
- *height 20cm*
- £590   • Trio

Victorian Scent Bottle ▼
- *circa 1860*
Victorian double-ended ruby scent bottle in silver with gilt stoppers, with one side for perfume and the other for smelling salts.
- *length 10cm*
- £358   • Trio

Bohemian Scent Bottle ▼
- *1880*
Victorian ruby Bohemian scent bottle and circular gold stopper. Decorated with alternating white panels with flowers and a gold floral design.
- *height 26cm*
- £288   • Trio

Turquoise Scent Bottles ➤
- *1880*
Pair of nineteenth century turquoise scent bottles with gold banding and stoppers.
- *height 18cm*
- £368   • Trio

Red Glass Scent Bottle ▼
- *circa 1860*
Cranberry glass scent bottle with gilt flower decoration and chain for holding on finger.
- *length 6cm*
- £195   • Trio

Silver Scent Bottle ▼
- *circa 1886*
English, decorative silver scent bottle with scrolls and a cut-glass stopper.
- *height 5.5cm*
- £250   • John Clay

Silver-Topped Bottle ▼
- *Georgian*
An early Georgian opaque scent bottle with silver top.
- *height 11cm*
- £178
- Trio

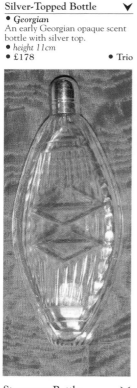

Victorian Scent Bottles ▲
- *1880*
Two Victorian cranberry and vaseline coloured scent bottles, together with their original leather carrying case.
- *height 14cm*
- £245
- Trio

Clear Glass Bottle ▼
- *circa 1870*
A clear glass scent bottle elaborately decorated with ornate pinch beck. The stopper is painted with a scene of Church Street, Magdalene.
- *height 7.5cm*
- £188
- Trio

Stoneware Bottle ▼
- *circa 1647*
Whit stoneware bottle of bulbous proportions with handle, on a splayed base, inscribed with the words, "WHIT, 1647".
- *height 6cm*
- N/A
- Jonathan Horne

English Scent Bottle ▲
- *1920*
English salmon pink Art Deco perfume bottle, styled in the shape of a sailing boat with sail.
- *height 14cm*
- £150
- Trio

Green Scent Bottle ➤
- *circa 1890*
Green simulated vaseline glass scent bottle decorated with red and gold filigree with opaque glass stopper.
- *height 12cm*
- £110
- Trio

Cameras

Rectaflex Camera ▼

• *1950s*

Rare Rota Rectaflex camera with three French-made Angenieux rotatable lenses. The lenses have three focal lengths: 50mm, 35mm and 135mm.

• *15cm x 9cm*
• **£3,000**   • Jessop Classic

Voigtlander Camera ▼

• *1958–60*

Rare Voigtlander Prominent II camera with an Ultron 50mm F2 lens. The camera has a 35mm rangefinder with interchangeable lenses and a clear viewfinder.

• *14cm x 8.5cm*
• **£699**   • Jessop Classic

Sakura Petal Camera ▲

• *1948*

Sakura Petal camera with film and case included. This is the world's smallest mass-produced camera.

• *2.5cm x 1.2cm*
• **£250**   • Jessop Classic

Kodak "Girl Guide" Camera ▲

• *1933*

Blue Kodak "Girl Guide" camera with an F6.3 Anistigmat lens. Supplied with blue case.

• *13cm x 7cm*
• **£200**   • Jessop Classic

Voigtlander Bessamatic SLR Camera ▲

• *circa 1950s*

Voigtlander Bessamatic SLR camera, with a 36–82mm F2.8 zoom lens. This was the first commercially produced zoom lens for a 35mm camera.

• *16cm x 10cm*
• **£149**   • Jessop Classic

Microtechnical Camera ◄

• *circa 1970s*

Microtechnical MK8 camera with a 150mm Symmar lens. Accompanied by a guide book.

• *18cm x 18cm*
• **£599**   • Jessop Classic

Bolex 16mm Cine Camera ➤
- **circa 1960s**

Bolex 16mm cine camera, model number H16m, with a Swiss-made body and Som Berthiot 17–85mm zoom lens.
- *33cm x 21.5cm*
- £500   • Jessop Classic

Thornton Pickard Camera ▲
- **circa 1909**

Triple extension, Thornton Pickard camera which uses ½ plate-sized negatives (glass plates used, not films). Made of wood with leather bellows.
- *21cm x 25.5cm*
- £300   • Jessop Classic

Teleca Bino Camera ▼
- **1950**

Relatively rare, subminiature 16mm Teleca Bino camera, which is built into a pair of binoculars. Fitted with standard 10mm x 14mm lenses and supplied with a brown leather case.
- *10 x 9cm*
- £299   • Photo. Gallery

C8 Cine Camera ▼
- **1954**

Bolex Standard 8 cine camera with a clockwork windup and single interchangeable lens.
- *12.5cm x 6cm*
- £50   • Jessop Classic

Widelux Super Wide Angle Camera ▲
- **circa 1970s**

Widelux super wide angle viewfinder camera with an unusual rotating lens. The camera uses 120 film.
- *23cm x 28cm*
- £1,399   • Jessop Classic

Kodak Medallist II Rangefinder Camera ▲
- **1946–253**

Rare Kodak Medallist II rangefinder camera, fitted with an F3.5 100mm Ektar lens.
- *20cm x 13cm*
- £349   • Jessop Classic

Collecting cameras is not only fun but you also have the bonus that they are usable. SLR cameras are a good future investment, especially with the onset of the digital age.

Rollei 35 Camera ▼
- **1971**

Gold Rollei 35 camera, supplied with a brown leather case and a red felt-lined wooden box. Fitted with an F3.5 Tessar lens.
- *9.5cm x 6cm*
- **£899**   • Jessop Classic

Kodak Retina II F, 35mm Camera ▼
- **1963**

Kodak Retina II F, 35mm camera with an F2.8, 45mm Xenar lens. The built-in flash bulb holder is an unusual feature for this style of camera.
- *13cm x 8.5cm*
- **£100**   • Jessop Classic

Blair Stereo Weno with Case ➤
- **1902**

Blair stereo Weno camera with case (as seen underneath), made in Rochester, New York. Supplied with a pair of Plastigmat lenses. Uses 116 Kodak film which has now been discontinued.
- *26.5cm x 11.5cm*
- **£299**   • Jessop Classic

Rollei Camera ▲
- **1966–7**

Rollei 35 standard camera fitted with an F3.5 Tessar lens.
- *9.5cm x 6cm*
- **£299**   • Jessop Classic

Houghton Ticka Camera ▲
- **1905–14**

Houghton Ticka Spy camera. This is designed to look like a pocket watch with an engraved monogram on the cover. The camera is hidden underneath the winding mechanism.
- *6.5cm x 5cm*
- **£249**   • Jessop Classic

Canon IV Camera ▲
- *circa 1950s*

Canon IV range finder camera with detachable flash unit and a 50mm 1.9 Serenar lens. Supplied with a brown leather case. This model is based on a Leica design.
- *14cm x 7cm*
- **£499**   • Jessop Classic

Kodak Suprema Camera ▲

- *circa 1950s*

Kodak Suprema camera fitted with an 8cm Xenar lens. Uses 120 standard film.
- *15cm x 10cm*
- £349   • Jessop Classic

Rolleiflex TLR Camera ▲

- *1960s*

Rolleiflex 2.8F twin lens camera (TLR), which uses standard 120 roll film.
- *15cm x 10cm*
- £649   Jessop Classic

16mm Cine Camera ▲

- *1928*

Bell and Howell 16mm cine camera with a 20mm F3.5 lens with 100ft spool, and a clockwork motor. The model is covered with grey tooled leather and is quite rare, especially outside the United States.
- *20.5cm x 3.7cm*
- £150   • Jessop Classic

Ensign Silver Midget Camera ▲

- *1935*

Ensign Silver Midget Jubilee model camera, made by Houghton, model number 22. Fitted with an Ensarlens F6.3 lens and uses E10 film which is now discontinued.
- *9cm x 4cm*
- £175   • Jessop Classic

L35 Concava Camera ▲

- *circa 1960s*

Rare miniature Tessina L35 Concava camera, designed to fit on the wrist in the style of a watch, and comes with a leather strap. It has a 25mm Tessinon lens and is supplied with 35mm film in special cassettes.
- *6.5cm x 6.5cm*
- £899   • Jessop Classic

Ashahi Pentax Camera ◄

- *1979*

Ashahi Pentax Auto 110 camera, fitted with a 24mm lens. The camera comes as part of a kit which includes a flash unit, filters and carrying bag.
- *9cm x 6cm*
- £200   • Jessop Classic

"Boy Scout" Camera ▼

- **1933**

Green Kodak "Boy Scout" camera, fitted with an F6.3 Anstigmat lens. The model is supplied with a brown leather case and uses 127 Kodak film.
- *12.5cm x 7cm*
- **£150**   • Jessop Classic

Skeky Camera ▲

- **1947**

Subminiature Skeky camera with a tele-lens. The camera uses 16mm film and comes with a brown leather case.
- *2cm x 1cm*
- **£299**   • Jessop Classic

Midget Coronet Camera ◄

- *circa 1930s*

Art-Deco style, blue bakelite, Midget Coronet camera, fitted with a Taylor Hobson F10 lens. The colour is very rare.
- *2cm x 6cm*
- **£325**   • Jessop Classic

Minox Camera ▼

- *circa 1950s*

Minox A camera which was used in the World War II as a spy camera. It takes 8 x 11mm negatives, has a brushed aluminium body and a Complan 15mm, 3.5 lens.
- *1cm x 10cm*
- **£180**   • Photo. Gallery

Leica Range Finder Camera ▲

- *circa 1930s*

Leica Range Finder camera fitted with a Summar 5cm F2 lens. This camera remains in production.
- *13cm x 7cm*
- **£299**   • Jessop Classic

8mm Cine Camera ▲

- **1927**

Extremely compact 8mm Kodak cine camera. This was the first model to use standard 8 film.
- *15cm x 11.5cm*
- **£120**   • Photo. Gallery

Expert Tips

A complete camera set in its original box or case is very desirable and should prove to be a good investment.

Chess Sets

Victorian Travelling Chess Set ◄
- *1895*
Victorian travelling chess set. with red and white pieces, made by Jakes of London. Supplied with its own original leather carrying case.
- *18cm x 18cm*
- £680　　　　• G.D. Coleman

Ivory Chess Set ▼
- *1790*
North German ivory chess set of Selenus design with white and black pieces.
- *height 8cm /king*
- £2,650　　　　• G.D. Coleman

Victorian Folding Chess Set ▼
- *1880*
Victorian folding dual-game board made from papier-mâché. Styled in the form of a two-volume book, the inside features a backgammon board and the outside features a chessboard.
- *46cm square*
- £1,250　　　• G.D. Coleman

Inlaid Chess Table ▲
- *1825*
Fine ebony and ivory inlaid penwork chess table attributed to George Merrifield of London.
- £1,825　　　　　• Freshfords

Pottery Chess Set ▲
- *1890*
German chess set in pottery, styled with a figurative theme including kneeling pawns. Figures in black and tan.
- *height 11cm/king*
- £950　　　• G.D. Coleman

Expert Tips

Always check that a chess set is complete, undamaged and in its original box. Unusual sets made in ivory bone or jade fetch the best prices.

American Chess Set ▼

- *1876*

American chess set in soft metal, signed "Le Mon" and dated 1876. Presented in its original box.
- *height 10cm/king*
- £3,500 • G.D. Coleman

Coromandel Games Compendium ▲

- *circa 1880*

Coromandel games box in wood, containing chess, backgammon, checkers, cribbage, dominoes and draughts.
- *33cm x 20cm x 22cm*
- £1,900 • Langfords Marine

French Chess Set ➤

- *1800*

French chess set with pieces carved from lion wood and bone. Figures are black or red, both colours decorated with white edging.
- *height 8cm/king*
- £1,650 • G.D. Coleman

German Chess Set ▲

- *1795*

German chess set of Selenus design, with black and white pieces in ivory.
- *height 8cm*
- £790 • G.D. Coleman

Expert Tips

The Victorian era (1837–1901) saw a great expansion in board games, and chess was no exception, and with the expansion of the British Empire pieces can be found from all over the world. The most celebrated designer of chess pieces is Jack Staunton whose work is of the Victorian era, and remains highly collectable.

Military Chess Set ◄

- *1870*

Chinese export ivory chess set based on the military theme of the Emperor Napoleon versus the Duke of Wellington.
- *height 10cm/king*
- £2,450 • G.D. Coleman

Bone Chess Set ▲
- *1840*
English chess set in carved bone, with figures in red and white.
- *height 8cm/king*
- £1,250 • G.D. Coleman

French Ivory Chess Set ▲
- *1800*
French ivory chess set, with one side in natural ivory and one side coloured in faded Shagrin green.
- *height 9cm/king*
- £1,750 • G. D. Coleman

Silver Chess Set ▼
- *1970*
English silver and silver gilt chess set of rococo design bearing a hallmark.
- *height 9cm/ king*
- £1,950 • G.D. Coleman

Expert Tips

It is possible to chart the development of board games from as far back as 5,000 years ago. These games mainly centred around themes of war, competition and chance. This is indicative of the game of chess, and even though its pieces are Medieval in character they can actually be created in any shape as it is their interaction which is important. The first chess set came from India but some have been found in Scandinavia dating back to 1,000 AD.

Backgammon and Chess Set ▼
- *1840*
Indian ivory chess and backgammon set, with black and natural ivory figures. Presented in folding ivory chessboard box.
- *45cm x 50cm x 5cm*
- £4,500 • G.D. Coleman

Staunton Chess Set ▼
- *19th century*
Ebony and boxwood chess set made by Staunton, presented in original box, by Jakes of London.
- *height 9cm/king*
- £480 • G.D. Coleman

Commemorative Ware

Bone China Jug

- *1888*

Continental bone china jug commemorating the silver wedding anniversary of Prince Edward and Princess Alexandra.
- *height 12.5cm*
- £85   • Hope & Glory

Caricature Mug

- *1991*

A caricature mug of the former Prime Minister Margaret Thatcher and her husband.
- *height 9cm*
- £33   • Hope & Glory

Queen Elizabeth II Bust

- *1953*

Bust of Queen Elizabeth II to commemorate her coronation in 1953, by Staffordshire Morloy.
- *height 18cm*
- £80   • Hope & Glory

Golden Jubilee Mug

- *1887*

Small cream and blue mug, commemorating the golden jubilee of Queen Victoria. Sold in the Isle of Wight.
- *height 6cm*
- £125   • Hope & Glory

Golden Jubilee Beaker

- *1887*

Beaker commemorating the golden jubilee of Queen Victoria, showing young and old portraits. Issued as a gift to school children in Hyde Park.
- *height 10.5cm*
- £125   • Hope & Glory

Accession Jug

- *1837*

Blue and white Accession jug inscribed "Hail Victoria". Showing a portrait of the young Queen Victoria.
- *height 29cm*
- £1,275   • Hope & Glory

Miners' Strike Plate ▲

- *1984*

Bone china plate to commemorate the great miners' strike of 1984–1985. Issued by the National Union of Mineworkers.

- *diameter 27cm*
- **£58**   • **Hope & Glory**

Loving Cup ▲

- *1987*

Bone china loving cup by Royal Crown Derby. Commemorating the third term in office of Margaret Thatcher. Limited edition of 650.

- *height 7.75cm*
- **£160**   • **Hope & Glory**

Expert Tips

The condition of any commemorative ware is just as important as the attractiveness of the item; even so, limited editions considerably enhance the desirability of a piece. Make sure that the transfers are bright and unscratched. In terms of subjects, opt for kings, queens or politicians who ruled for a short time.

Engagement Mug ▲

- *1981*

China mug depicting Prince Charles's ear. Drawn by Marc Boxer, made at the engagement of Charles and Diana.

- **£5**   • **Hope & Glory**

Victorian Cypher ▼

- *1890*

Victorian English carved wooden gesso royal cypher.

- *90cm x 65cm*
- **£2,500**   • **Lacquer Chest**

Jubilee Mug ▼

- *1935*

Ceramic mug celebrating the silver jubilee of King George V and Queen Mary.

- *height 7cm*
- **£24**   • **Magpies**

Royal Visit Teapot ▼

- *1939*

Teapot issued in commemoration of a royal visit to Canada made by George VI and Queen Elizabeth II in 1939.

- *height 13cm*
- **£85**   • **Hope & Glory**

Birthday Mug ▲
- **1991**
Bone china mug by Aynsley to commemorate the thirtieth birthday of Princess Diana.
- *height 9.5cm*
- £70   • Hope & Glory

Porcelain Mug ▲
- **1996**
Porcelain mug depicting the divorce of Prince Charles and Princess Diana.
- *height 9.5cm*
- £18   • Hope & Glory

Coronation Mug ▲
- **1902**
Copeland mug for the coronation of King Edward VII and Queen Alexandra, showing the correct date of August 9, 1902. Most items give the date as June 26, 1902, which was postponed because of the king's appendicitis.
- *height 7.5cm*
- £160   • Hope & Glory

Diamond Jubilee Bowl ▲
- **1897**
Bowl commemorating the diamond jubilee of Queen Victoria. Made by Aynsley for W. Whiteley.
- *height 8cm*
- £140   • Hope & Glory

Heraldic Plates ▲
- *circa 1780*
Set of four heraldic plates by J. Edmondson in handcrafted and gilded frames.
- *58cm x 40cm*
- £2,800   • Chelsea Gallery and Il Libro (LAPADA)

Paragon Loving Cup ▼
- **1980**
Large Paragon bone china loving cup with gold lion handles, commemorating the Queen Mother's eightieth birthday. Limited edition of 750.
- *height 13.25cm*
- £245   • Hope & Glory

Wedgwood Mug ▼
- **2000**
Black basalt mug issued by Wedgwood in commemoration of the Millennium. Designed by Richard Guyatt in a limited edition of 500.
- *height 10cm*
- £190   • Hope & Glory

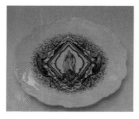

Coalport Plate ▲
- *1897*
Bone china plate issued by
Coalport to commemorate Queen
Victoria's diamond jubilee.
- *diameter 22cm*
- £140　　• Hope & Glory

Pottery Folly ▲
- *1969*
Caernarvon castle folly in
Keystone pottery, issued to
commemorate the investiture of
Prince Charles in July 1969,
- *height 21cm*
- £65　　• Hope & Glory

Coronation Cup and Saucer ▲
- *1902*
Bone china cup and saucer
commemorating the coronation
of Edward VII. Made by Foley.
- *height 5.5cm*
- £58　　• Hope & Glory

Boer War Egg Cups ▲
- *1900*
Continental bone china egg
cups depicting generals from the
Boer War.
- *height 6.5cm*
- £60 each　　• Hope & Glory

Pair of Perfume Flasks ▲
- *circa 1840*
Hand-decorated porcelain
perfume flasks by Jacob Petit,
commemorating the marriage of
Queeen Victoria and Prince
Albert.
- *height 31cm*
- £3,750　　• Hope & Glory

Bust of Wellington ◄
- *circa 1835*
Pre-Parian bust of Wellington in
Felspar porcelain. Issued by
Copeland and Garrett.
- *height 20cm*
- £290　　• Hope & Glory

Child's Plate ▲
- *1821*
Very unusual child's plate
depicting Queen Caroline.
- £325　　• Hope & Glory

Silver Jubilee Ashtray ◄
- *1935*

King George V and Queen
Mary silver jubilee ashtray in
Burleigh ware.
- *diameter 22cm*
- £55   • Chelsea (OMRS)

Bone China Mug ▼
- *1936*

Bone china mug made for the
proposed coronation of Edward
VIII with abdication details on
the reverse.
- *height 9cm*
- £170   • Hope & Glory

Coronation Mug ▲
- *1936*

Bone china mug made for the
proposed coronation of Edward
VIII.
- *height 9cm*
- £40   • Hope & Glory

Prince of Wales Plate ▲
- *1847*

Child's plate showing the young
Edward, Prince of Wales, on a
pony. Entitled "England's Hope".
- *diameter 16.5cm*
- £340   • Hope and Glory

Curtseying Cup ▲
- *1977*

Carlton Ware porcelain cup in
a curtseying pose,
commemorating the silver jubilee
of Queen Elizabeth II.
- *height 11cm*
- £50   • Hope & Glory

War Effort Teapot ◄
- *1939*

A teapot commemorating War
against Hitlerism, Liberty and
Freedom, given in exchange for
aluminium utensils. Made by
Crown Ducal.
- *height 14cm*
- £140   • Hope & Glory

Toby Jug ▼
- *1940*
A wartime Toby jug of Winston
Churchill as first Sea Lord.
- *height 17cm*
- £125   ● Hope & Glory

Expert Tips

*Include commemorative ware
by makers such as Derby,
Wedgwood and Minton when
building up a collection.*

Diamond Jubilee Jug ▲
- *1897*
A set of three Copeland/Spode
diamond jubilee jugs.
- *height 16cm/largest*
- £650   ● Hope & Glory

Four Castles Plate ▼
- *1901*
Black transfer on earthenware
plate to commemorate the death
of Queen Victoria.
- *diameter 24.5cm*
- £240   ● Hope & Glory

Coronation Mug ▼
- *1911*
Bone china mug commemorating
the coronation of George V.
- *height 8.5cm*
- £58   ● Hope & Glory

Minton Loving Cup ▼
- *1953*
Bone china loving cup by
Minton. Coronation of Queen
Elizabeth II, designed by John
Wadsworth.
- *height 10.5cm*
- £190   ● Hope & Glory

Musical Teapot ◀
- *circa 1953*
Teapot in the form of a coach,
commemorating the coronation
of Queen Elizabeth II. Plays the
national anthem.
- *height 13cm*
- £240   ● Hope & Glory

Ephemera

Scene ▲
- *1962*

Issue No. 14 of *Scene*, a theatre review magazine.
- £4   • Book & Comic

Viz ▲
- *1981*

Issue No. 7 of adult humour comic, *Viz*.
- £4   • Book & Comic

Fantastic Four ◄
- *1966*

Issue No. 48 of *Fantastic Four*, a classic silver age comic in good condition.
- £40   • Book & Comic

Cry for Dawn ▼
- *1992*

Issue No. 9 of the *Cry for Dawn* comic book.
- £8   • Book & Comic

Fantastic Four ◄
- *1966*

Issue No. 48 of *Fantastic Four*, a classic silver age comic in good condition.
- £40   • Book & Comic

Metal Men ▲
- *1962*

Issue No. 39 of *Metal Men* comic, featuring a special appearance by "The Thanker". Published by DC Comics.
- £20   • Book & Comic

Giant Superman Annual ▲
- *1963*

Edition No. 7 of the *Giant Superman* annual.
- £20   • Book & Comic

Zig Zag ◄
- *1976*

Issue No. 65 of rock music magazine, *Zig Zag*, with feature on the Beach Boys.
- £4   ● Book & Comic

The Dr Who Annual ▼
- *1979*

1979 annual based on the cult TV series *Dr Who*.
- £5   ● Book & Comic

Robotech ➤
- *1985*

The Macross Saga 7 issue, signed by the translator Frank Yonco with characteristic beard and glasses doodle. Published by Comico comics.
- £8   ● Book & Comic

The Beano ◄
- *1969*

Issue No. 1,405 of popular UK children's comic, *The Beano*.
- £1   ● Book & Comic

Continental Film Review ▼
- *August 1968*

August 1968 issue of adult film magazine.
- £3   ● Book & Comic

Mad Monsters ▼
- *1964*

Issue No. 7 of comic *Mad Monsters*.
- *height 30 cm*
- £1.50   ● Book & Comic

Dr Who Discovers ▼
- 1979

Early Man issue from a spin-off non-fiction series, *Dr Who Discovers*. Booklet with colour poster.
- £4   • Book & Comic

Amazing Stories ▼
- 1954

Issue No. 5, Volume I of sci-fi magazine featuring a story by Philip K. Dick.
- £5   • Book & Comic

True Romances ▶
- November 1938

November 1938 issue of women's magazine, *True Romances*.
- £4   • Book & Comic

Sh-Boom ▲
- 1990

American rock magazine, *Sh-Boom*, featuring Rolling Stones' vocalist Mick Jagger on the front cover.
- £2   • Book & Comic

Video Watchdog ▼
- 1990

First issue of cult underground magazine, *Video Watchdog*.
- £4   • Book & Comic

Music Star ▼
- February 1974

February 1974 issue of teenager's pop magazine, *Music Star*.
- £3   • Book & Comic

Abba International ▲
• *1981*
Issue No. 1 of Abba fan
magazine.
• £4   • Book & Comic

Second Coming ▲
• *1974*
Issue No. 3, Volume II of *Second
Coming* with a special feature on
Charles Bukowski.
• £35   • Book & Comic

The Face ▼
• *1984*
Issue No. 52 of fashion and
lifestyle magazine, *The Face*.
• £1   • Book & Comic

i-D ◄
• *1989*
Issue No. 73 of fashion and
lifestyle magazine, *i-D*.
• £3   • Book & Comic

Dr Who Annual ▲
• *1989*
Twenty-first anniversary annual
of cult TV series, *Dr Who*.
• £3   • Book & Comic

Playboy ▲
• *1969*
August 1969 issue of adult
magazine, *Playboy*, featuring
Penny Spinster and the living
theatre.
• £12   • Book & Comic

Bomp! ▲
- 1976–77
Music magazine, *Bomp!*, featuring Brian Wilson.
- £5   ● Book & Comic

Zeta ▲
- 1960s
Issue No. 5, Volume 2, of erotic photography magazine, *Zeta*.
- £10   ● Book & Comic

Rolling Stone ◄
- 1970
October 1970 issue of US rock music magazine, *Rolling Stone*, featuring the life story of Janis Joplin.
- £6   ● Book & Comic

Costume Prints ▼
- 1585
A pair of prints by Nicolo Nicolai, depicting courtly figures in Ottoman costumes, displayed in handcrafted frames.
- 39cm x 29cm
- £800   ● Chelsea Gallery

Crawdaddy ▲
- July 1973
US music magazine, *Crawdaddy*, featuring Marvin Gaye.
- £4   ● Book & Comic

Gent ▼
- 1961
Men's magazine, *Gent*, featuring interviews with Mark Russell and Klaus Rock.
- £8   ● Book & Comic

Animated Cerebus Folder ▼
- *1990s*

Book of art for cancelled film project.
- £30   ● Book & Comic

Sir! ▼
- *1962*

April 1962 issue of adult magazine, *Sir!*, featuring "Death of the Hoover" on the cover.
- £4   ● Book & Comic

Les Rendez-Vous de Sevenoaks ▼
- *1994*

Hardback edition of *Les Rendez-Vous de Sevenoaks*, featuring the first appearance of Richard Hughes.
- £5   ● Book & Comic

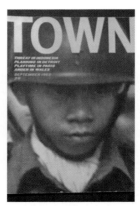

Men in Vogue ▼
- *1970*

One of the few issues of this magazine to appear, featuring B.A.L Newman on the cover. Contains features on men's fashion.
- £15   ● Book & Comic

Town ◄
- *1963*

September 1963 issue of fashion and lifestyle magazine, *Town*.
- £10   ● Book & Comic

Jamming ▲
- *1964*

Issue No. 12 of rock music magazine, *Jamming*.
- £1.50   ● Book & Comic

Music Star ▲
- **1976**
1976 annual of teenage pop
magazine, *Music Star*.
- £4 • Book & Comic

Continental Film Review ▲
- *March 1962*
March 1962 issue of *Continental
Film Review*, featuring Brigitte
Bardet on the cover.
- £4 • Book & Comic

International Times ▼
- *1974*
Issue No. 2, Volume 2, of UK
underground newspaper,
International Times.
- £1.50 • Book & Comic

Shadow Hawk ▲
- **1992**
A first copy of the comic, with
a glossy cover.
- *height 30cm*
- £2 • Book & Comic

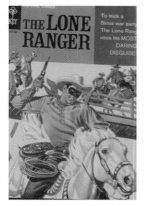

The Lone Ranger ▲
- **1958**
The Lone Ranger comic book
published by Gold Key.
- £6 • Book & Comic

Interview ➤
- **1977**
Newspaper format of Andy
Warhol's magazine, *Interview*.
- £18 • Book & Comic

The Atom ◀
- **1962**
First issue of *The Atom* comic,
published by DC Comics.
- **£40**   • Book & Comic

The Incredible Hulk ▼
- **1976**
Issue No. 202 of *The Incredible
Hulk*, feauting the Origin of
Cadavros. Published by Marvel
Comics.
- **£2**   • Book & Comic

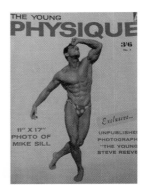

Venus Moderne ▼
- **1950s**
Issue No. 1 of digest-sized nude
photography magazine, *Venus
Moderne*.
- **£4**   • Book & Comic

Young Physique ▲
- **1960s**
Issue No. 3 of the vintage muscle
magazine, *The Young Physique*.
- **£4**   • Book & Comic

Bat Masterson ▶
- **1960**
Issue No. 3 of *Bat Masterston*,
a comic published by Dell.
- **£5**   • Book & Comic

Psychotronic ▼
- **1992**
Issue No. 13 of US film magazine,
Psychotronic.
- **£4**   • Book & Comic

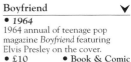

Boyfriend ▼
- **1964**
1964 annual of teenage pop
magazine *Boyfriend* featuring
Elvis Presley on the cover.
- **£10**   • Book & Comic

Fantastic Adventures ▲
- **1951**
March 1951 issue of US science-
fantasy magazine, *Fantastic
Adventures*.
- **£5**   • Book & Comic

Kitchenalia

Copper Kettle ▲
- *1860*
Victorian copper kettle with good patination.
- *height 22cm*
- £140　　　• R. Conquest

Chocolate Tin ▼
- *1890*
Dutch blue and orange chocolate tin from Weesp, the Netherlands.
- *height 19cm*
- £110　　　• R. Conquest

Tea Tins ➤
- *1920s*
Numbered and pre-painted tea tins, with oriental designs.
- *£950*　　　• North West 8

Tea Sample Tins ▼
- *circa 1880–1920*
Soldered tin containers, stamped and numbered. Originally used by tea merchants to store tea samples.
- *8cm x 5cm x 3cm*
- £550　　• After Noah (KR)

Dutch Milk Jug ▲
- *1840*
Dutch copper milk jug of baluster form and cover with handle.
- *height 45cm*
- £160　　　• R. Conquest

Coal Iron ▲
- *1880*
Dutch coal iron fitted with wooden handle.
- *height 22cm*
- £60　　　• R. Conquest

Enamelled Teapot ▲
- *1950s*
Blue-enamelled tin teapot.
- *height 23cm*
- £25　　　• Kitchen Bygones

Potato Cutter ▼

- *1940*

The New "Villa" French fried
potato cutter supplied in its
original box.
- *26cm x 12cm x 12cm*
- £14   • Radio Days

Mini-Sweeper ▲

- *1940*

Mini-sweeper presented in
its original box.
- *20cm x 14cm*
- £12   • Radio Days

Cream Maker ▼

- *1950s*

Bakelite and glass cream maker
with alloy handle.
- *height 21cm*
- £15   • Kitchen Bygones

Glass Creamer ▼

- *1940*

Jubilee model glass hand-creamer
with primrose yellow plastic cup
and handle designed by Bel.
- *height 22cm*
- £16   • After Noah (KR)

Enamelled Bread Bin ▲

- *1940s*

English enamelled bread bin with
the letters in stylised font.
- *height 50cm*
- £25   • Kitchen Bygones

Cornish Ware Mug ▼

- *1940*

Cornish ware mug decorated
with blue and white hoops.
- *height 8cm*
- £10.50   • Magpies

Measuring Jug ▼

- *1940*

Blue and white-hooped quart measuring jug.
- *height 17cm*
- £12.50 • Magpies

Tin Opener ▼

- *1920*

A cast-iron late Victorian tin-opener shaped like a bull's head. With steel blade and in good condition.
- *length 16cm*
- £14.50 • Magpies

Herb Chopper ▲

- *1910*

Victorian double-handled herb chopping knife, with wood-turned handles.
- *length 21cm*
- £22 • Magpies

Flour Jar ▲

- *1940s*

Enamelled tin flour container in flaked white and grey paint.
- *height 32cm*
- £25 • Kitchen Bygones

Pestle and Mortar ▲

- *1940*

Pestle and mortar in white stone.
- *height 11.5cm*
- £28 • Magpies

Kitchen Scales ➤

- *1940s*

Set of British-made "Popular" kitchen scales in green enamel paint, with an accompanying set of brass weights.
- *height 45cm*
- £45 • Kitchen Bygones

189

Bakelite Thermos   ▼

- *1930*

English green Bakelite thermos
with metal handle.
- *height 34cm*
- £11   ● Magpies

Squeezer   ▼

- *1950s*

Solid aluminium vegetable or
fruit squeezer made by Atlantic.
- *height 20cm*
- £15   ● Kitchen Bygones

Egg Timer   ▼

- *Victorian*

Victorian egg timer with wood-
turned column and original
glass reservoir.
- *height 14cm*
- £15   ● Kitchen Bygones

Potato Masher   ▲

- *20th century*

Wooden potato masher with
turned shaft in fruitwood on a
circular wooden base.
- *height 15cm*
- £15   ● Kitchen Bygones

Rolling Pin   ▲

- *1950s*

Good qualtiiy wooden rolling pin
with turned painted handles.
- *length 40cm*
- £10   ● Kitchen Bygones

Terracotta Bread Bin   ▲

- *20th century*

Terracotta bread bin, with lid
and carrying handles.
- *height 33cm*
- £65   ● Kitchen Bygones

Flour Jar

- *20th century*

Glossed pottery flour jar by Hunts of Liverpool.
- *height 28cm*
- £48   • Kitchen Bygones

Ceramic Coffee Jar ➤

- *1950*

Ceramic container for coffee, by Red Lamp Kitchenware.
- *height 16cm*
- £18   • Magpies

Coffee Pot ⌃

- *1950*

Coffee pot by Kleen Kitchenware, with green concentric banding.
- *height 24cm*
- £28   • Magpies

Pestle and Mortar ➤

- *1960*

Fruitwood pestle and mortar with turned decoration.
- *height 10cm*
- £12   • Magpies

Pint Milk Jug ⌃

- *1940*

Cornish ware milk jug with imperial measuring marks.
- *height 13cm*
- £40   • Magpies

Devon Coffee Pot ◄

- *1950s*

Sandygate Devon coffee pot, with white polka dots on blue.
- *height 18cm*
- £38   • Magpies

Bread Bin ▼
- *1930*
White-enamelled bread bin with green lettering.
- *height 40cm*
- **£44**   • Magpies

Hen-Shaped Dish ▼
- *1970*
Ceramic hen dish produced by Susan Wilkans Ellis, Portmeirion.
- *height 13cm*
- **£25**   • Magpies

Metal Candlestick ▼
- *1930*
Metal candlestick with green and black enamelling.
- *height 6cm*
- **£12**   • Magpies

Enamelled Kettle ▼
- *1950s*
Blue enamelled kettle.
- *height 25cm*
- **£25**   • Kitchen Bygones

Herb Storage Jar ▼
- *1950*
Herb jar and cover with red banding and the word "Marjoram" on the body. Produced by Kleen Kitchenware.
- *height 10cm*
- **£5.50**   • Magpies

Household Iron ▲
- *1940*
Small iron by J & J Siddons, West Bromwich.
- *height 8cm*
- **£14.50**   • Magpies

Expert Tips

Where would the prop finder be on period costume dramas without the collector of these everyday objects? Kitchenware items have proved to be good investments, but be careful not to pay over the odds for them as the margins for error are small. When examining items, look out for split seams, bad repairs or over-thinning of the brass or copper as this affects their collectability.

Pie Crust Funnel ▼
- *1940*
Ceramic pie crust funnel formed as a blackbird.
- *height 13cm*
- **£9.50**   • Magpies

Storage Jar ▼
- *circa 1940*
Cornish Ware jar with
characteristic blue and white
banding.
  - *height 22cm*
  - £11 • Magpies

Bean Slice ▼
- *1920*
Iron bean slice with a brass
handle, produced by Alexander
Ware.
  - £12 • Magpies

Copper Jelly Moulds ◄
- *circa 1900*
Set of three copper jelly
moulds in the shape of
oven-ready chickens. Used
for making savoury jellies
and pates.
  - £14 • Magpies

Metal Funnel ▼
- *1940*
Blue enamelled metal funnel
with handle.
  - *height 17cm*
  - £8.50 • Magpies

Ceramic Rolling Pin ▲
- *1950*
Ceramic white rolling pin with
green handles, inscribed
"Nutbrowne".
  - *length 41cm*
  - £25 • Magpies

Food Storage Flask ►
- *1930s*
A vacuum flask for food storage,
with eagle clasping the world.
  - *height 38cm*
  - £40 • Kitchen Bygones

Baker's Paddle ▼
- *1920*
A baker's folding paddle with
spatulate head.
  - *length 185cm*
  - £45 • Kitchen Bygones

Tea-Towel Holder ◄
- *1950*
French wall-mounted tea-towel
holder made from plastic,
with four metal hooks labelled
in French.
- *length 34cm*
- £15 • Magpies

Storage Jar Trio ➤
- *1930s*
Three Cornish Ware storage jars
decorated with blue and white
hoops, with covers.
- *height 16cm*
- £45 • Kitchen Bygones

Sugar Sifter ▲
- *circa 1930s*
Sugar sifter by T.G. Green, with
blue and white banding,
inscribed "Sugar"
- *height 28cm*
- £58 • Magpies

Brass Moulds ▲
- *1910*
Selection of brass aspic moulds,
comprising three shaped as roast
chickens and one as a horseshoe.
May be sold separately.
- *length 7cm*
- £60 • Magpies

Brass Weights ▼
- *1910*
Selection of English brass weights
with imperial measurements.
- £38 • Magpies

Washboard ▼
- *1895*
Victorian washboard with a
glass panel.
- *59cm x 30cm*
- £25 • Kitchen Bygones

Chamberstick ▼
- *1920*
Metal chamberstick with
green enamelled finish. Affixed
to a fluted base and fitted with a
carrying handle.
- *diameter 11cm*
- £12.50 • Magpies

Brass Ladle ▼
- *1920*
Brass ladle with long shaft.
- *length 45cm*
- £15 • Kitchen Bygones

Brass Saucepot ▲
- *1910*

Sauce pot made of brass with
iron handles and copper rivets
- *height 6cm*
- £45   • Magpies

Larder Chest ▲
- *1890*

French Provincial larder chest
consisting of four drawers and a
cupboard. The whole resting on
ogée bracket feet. With original
distressed condition.
- *120cm x 90cm*
- £880   • Myriad

Circular Mould ▼
- *1880*

Ring-shaped brass jelly mould.
- *diameter 7cm*
- £24   • Magpies

Hexagonal Mould ▶
- *1890*

Hexagonal-shaped jelly mould
in copper.
- *height 11.5cm*
- £11   • Magpies

Shirt-Sleeve Board ▲
- *1920*

Shirt-sleeve ironing board.
- *length 57cm*
- £25   • Kitchen Bygones

Cider Jar ◀
- *1940s*

Stoneware cider jar.
- *height 35cm*
- £25   • Kitchen Bygones

Weighing Scales ◀
- *1940*

Horseshoe-shaped Swedish scales
in bronze with enamelled dial
and original weighing dish.
- *height 30cm*
- £54   • Magpies

Ink Filler ▲
- *1890*

Copper ink filler fitted with a
side handle and a slender copper
funnel, used for filling inkwells.
- *height 16cm*
- £35   • Magpies

Expert Tips

*It is a marvel how items like
these can cast a spell over
kitchens, cosy restaurants or
bistros. Take care to remember
that condition and an attractive
patina is the key to success.*

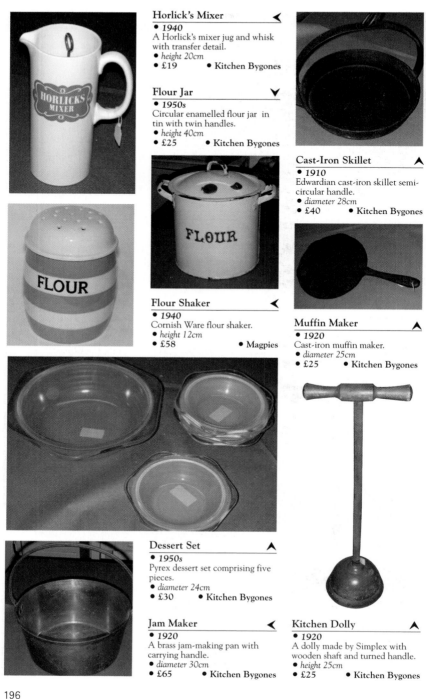

Horlick's Mixer ◄
- *1940*

A Horlick's mixer jug and whisk with transfer detail.
- *height 20cm*
- £19   • Kitchen Bygones

Flour Jar ▼
- *1950s*

Circular enamelled flour jar in tin with twin handles.
- *height 40cm*
- £25   • Kitchen Bygones

Flour Shaker ◄
- *1940*

Cornish Ware flour shaker.
- *height 12cm*
- £58   • Magpies

Cast-Iron Skillet ▲
- *1910*

Edwardian cast-iron skillet semi-circular handle.
- *diameter 28cm*
- £40   • Kitchen Bygones

Muffin Maker ▲
- *1920*

Cast-iron muffin maker.
- *diameter 25cm*
- £25   • Kitchen Bygones

Dessert Set ▲
- *1950s*

Pyrex dessert set comprising five pieces.
- *diameter 24cm*
- £30   • Kitchen Bygones

Jam Maker ◄
- *1920*

A brass jam-making pan with carrying handle.
- *diameter 30cm*
- £65   • Kitchen Bygones

Kitchen Dolly ▲
- *1920*

A dolly made by Simplex with wooden shaft and turned handle.
- *height 25cm*
- £25   • Kitchen Bygones

Luggage

English Leather Suitcase ▼
- *circa 1900*

English leather suitcase, with brass fittings and leather handle.
- *70cm x 40cm x 20cm*
- £180   • Henry Gregory

Travelling Case ▼
- *circa 1900*

English leather suitcase with brass fittings and leather straps.
- *95cm x 56cm x 30cm*
- £280   • Henry Gregory

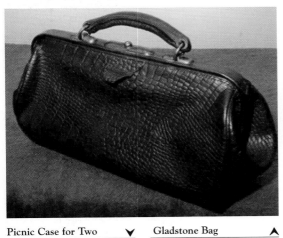

Picnic Case for Two ▼
- *circa 1910*

English leather picnic case, fully fitted with custom-made accoutrements.
- *width 28cm*
- £550   • Mia Cartwright

Gladstone Bag ▲
- *circa 1860*

Victorian crocodile Gladstone bag with leather handle and brass fittings.
- *40cm x 26cm x 15cm*
- £70   • Henry Gregory

Leather Suitcase ▼
- *circa 1900*

All-leather suitcase with brass fixtures.
- *70cm x 40cm x 25cm*
- £240   • Henry Gregory

Leather-Handled Suitcase ▼
- *circa 1900*

A small leather suitcase with brass fittings and leather handle.
- *64cm x 38cm x 15cm*
- £110   • Henry Gregory

Hat Box
- *circa 1870*
Victorian leather hat box with brass fittings and leather handle.
- *35cm x 28cm x 30cm*
- £245   • Henry Gregory

Collar Box
- *circa 1900*
Leather collar box in the shape of a horseshoe
- *18cm x 17cm x 8cm*
- £48   • Henry Gregory

Top Hat and Box
- *circa 1850*
English leather box for a top hat with brass fittings and leather strap, with red velvet lining. Complete with hat.
- *38cm x 22cm 35cm*
- £290   • Henry Gregory

Gun Case
- *circa 1900*
English leather gun case with brass fittings and leather handle, having leather straps with brass buckle.
- *84cm x 23cm x 9cm*
- £490   • Henry Gregory

Expert Tips

Old luggage carries an air of sophistication and hints at a decadent past.

Travelling Trunk
- *1850*
English leather brass studded and bound travelling trunk.
- *42cm x 91cm x 46cm*
- £400   • Tredantiques

Leather Gladstone Travelling Bag
- *circa 1870*
All-leather Gladstone bag with brass attachments, two straps and double handles.
- *length 69cm*
- £480   • Henry Gregory

Mail Bag
- *circa 1900*
Country house leather mail case with brass fixtures,
- *30cm x 25cm*
- £120   • Henry Gregory

Paperweights

Baccarat Mushroom ▲

- *circa 1850*

Baccarat Millefioni paperweight mushroom with blue tonsade and stonecut base.
- *diameter 7cm*
- £950   • G.D. Coleman

Baccarat Garland Posy ▼

- *circa 1850*

Baccarat paperweight inset with a red pansy and leaves, with stonecut base.
- *diameter 6cm*
- £1,850   • G.D. Coleman

Expert Tips

When choosing paperweights, look out for bold colours and pleasing designs, as well as items with a touch of the unusual.

St Louis Sanam-Holed ▼

- *circa 1850*

St Louis Sanam-holed, faceted paperweight with pastel jumbled cones.
- *diameter 7cm*
- £995   • G.D. Coleman

St Louis Crown Weight ◄

- *circa 1850*

St Louis Crown weight with a multicoloured canes design.
- *diameter 5.5cm*
- £1,350   • G.D. Coleman

St Louis Miniature ▲

- *circa 1855*

St Louis miniature paperweight with pink floral design.
- *diameter 4.5cm*
- £385   • G.D. Coleman

White Friars ▼

- *circa 1880*

White Friars paperweight with concentric canes.
- *diameter 8.5cm*
- £290   • G.D. Coleman

Baccarat Pansy ▼

- *circa 1850*
French Baccarat paperweight, inset with a red pansy and green foliage, on stonecut base.
- *diameter 5.5cm*
- £680 • G.D. Coleman

Bohemian Magnum ▼

- *1890*
Glass hexagonal paperweight with an etched glass coat of arms with amber faceted flank.
- *11.5cm*
- £380 • G.D. Coleman

Baccarat Sulphite ▼

- *1976*
Baccarat sulphite paperweight in facetop form, faceted with six lozenge cuts printed with a bust of Queen Elizabeth II.
- *diameter 7cm*
- £1,670 • London Antique

Floral St Louis ▲

- *1850*
St Louis paperweight with pink floral cone design.
- *diameter 6.5cm*
- £7,850 • G.D. Coleman

Wedgwood Plaque ▲

- *1977*
Glass paperweight with Wedgwood plaque of Queen Elizabeth II.
- *diameter 7cm*
- £150 • London Antique

Faceted Baccarat ▶

- *1976*
Baccarat sulphite paperweight in facetop form. Faceted with six lozenge cuts printed with a bust of Prince Charles.
- *diameter 7cm*
- £2,670 • London Antique

Sturbridge ▼

- *circa 1880*
English Sturbridge Victorian concentric paperweight with multi-coloured cane design.
- *diameter 8cm*
- £380 • G.D. Coleman

Photographs

Silver Gelatin Print ▲
- *1929*

"Solange David, Paris, 1929", by Jacques-Henri Lartique. Silver gelatin print, signed recto.
- *30.5cm x 35.5cm*
- £4,600   • Photo. Gallery

C-Type Print ▼
- *1999*

Untitled still life C-Type print taken in 1999 by Juliana Sohn. Signed verso.
- *30.5cm x 35.5cm*
- £450   • Photo. Gallery

Signed Print ▼
- *1931*

"El Ensueno" (The Daydreamer) taken in 1931 in Mexico, by Manuel Alvarez Bravo. Silver gelatin print, signed verso.
- *25.5cm x 20cm*
- £1,500   • Photo. Gallery

Untitled Print ➤
- *1999*

Untitled silver gelatin print taken in 1999 by Sheva Fruitman. Signed verso.
- *30.5cm x 35.5cm*
- £600   • Photo. Gallery

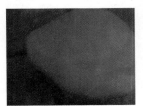

Colour Polaroid ◄
- *1999*

Untitled colour polaroid print taken by Sheva Fruitman in 1999. Signed verso.
- *12.7cm x 10.2cm*
- £300   • Photo. Gallery

Platinum Print ▼
- *1949*

"Margarita de Bonampak, Mexico, 1949" by Manuel Alvarez Bravo. Platinum print, signed verso.
- *25.5cm x 20cm*
- £2,000   • Photo. Gallery

Shirley Baker Print ▼
- *1964*

"Salford, 1964" by Shirley Baker. A silver gelatin print, signed verso.
- *30.5cm x 35.5cm*
- £200　　• Photo. Gallery

Silver Gelatin Print ▼
- *1955*

James Dean on the set of "Rebel Without a Cause" by photographer Bob Willoughby. Silver gelatin print, signed verso.
- *30.5cm x 40cm*
- £400　　• Photo. Gallery

Matthew Murray Print ▼
- *1999*

"Morris Dancers, 1999" by Matthew Murray. C-Type print, signed verso.
- *30.5cm x 35.5cm*
- £200　　• Photo. Gallery

Signed Willoughby Print ➤
- *1962*

"Billie Holliday, Tiffany Club, 1962" by Bob Willoughby. A silver gelatin print, signed verso.
- *30.5cm x 35.5cm*
- £400　　• Photo. Gallery

Signed C-Type Print ▲
- *1952*

Marilyn Monroe photographed in 1952 by Bob Willoughby. C-Type print, signed verso.
- *30.5cm x 40cm*
- £600　　• Photo. Gallery

Lartique Print ▼
- *1931*

"Cours automobile à Monthery, 1931" by Jacques-Henri Lartique. A silver gelatin print, signed verso.
- *30.5cm x 35.5cm*
- £2,800　　• Photo. Gallery

Bob Willoughby Print ◀
- *1962*

"Audrey Hepburn, 1962" by Bob Willoughby. A silver gelatin print, signed verso.
- *25.5cm x 30.5cm*
- £600　　• Photo. Gallery

Expert Tips

Pictures of famous people, from film stars to politicians, including those who have fallen from fame, often make a good investment. Fewer prints in circulation usually leads to an increase in their value.

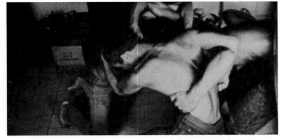

Will McBride Print ▶

- *1959*

"Stoffe, Magda and Em Eating Popcorn, Berlin, 1959" by Will McBride. Silver gelatin print, signed verso.

- *30.5cm x 40cm*
- £350 • Photo. Gallery

Signed C-Type Print ▼

- *1965*

"Hulme, 1965" by Shirley Baker. C-type print, signed recto.

- *30.5cm x 35.5cm*
- £250 • Photo. Gallery

Silver Gelatin Print ◀

- *1981*

"Flooded tree, Perwentnar, 1981" by Fay Godwin. Silver gelatin print, signed verso.

- *30.5cm x 35.5cm*
- £500 • Photo. Gallery

Signed McBride Print ◀

- *1957*

"Boys Romping at Jan's Place, 1957" by photographer Will McBride. Silver gelatin print, signed verso.

- *51cm x 35.5cm*
- £500 • Photo. Gallery

Untitled Print ▼

- *1998*

Untitled silver gelatin print by Marcus Davies from the "Footballers" series. Taken in 1998 and signed verso.

- *12.8cm x 17.9cm*
- £200 • Photo. Gallery

Signed Gelatin Print ▼

- *1982*

"What she wanted and what she got, 1982" by Graham Smith. Silver gelatin print, signed verso.

- *30.5cm x 35.5cm*
- £500 • Photo. Gallery

Silver Gelatin Print ▲
- *1987*

"North Islands in dry docks, Smith's Dock 1987" by Ian Macdonald. Silver gelatin print, signed verso.
- *51cm x 35.5cm*
- **£600** • **Photo. Gallery**

Expert Tips

Look out for prints that capture a freak or unusual moment, or that portray a familiar subject in surroundings that are out of context. Some photographs are now ranked alongside art so it is worth concentrating on collecting the work of a favourite up-and-coming photographer.

Signed C-Type Print ▼
- *2000*

"Kitchen Sink" by Nigel Shafran. C-type print, signed verso.
- *51cm x 35.5cm*
- **£750** • **Photo. Gallery**

C-Type Print ▼
- *1999*

Untitled C-type print by photographer Nigel Shafran. Signed verso.
- *25.5cm x 35.5cm*
- **£300** • **Photo. Gallery**

Ian Macdonald Print ▶
- *circa 1980*

Untitled silver gelatin print by photographer Ian Macdonald. Signed verso.
- *30.5cm x 40cm*
- **£500** • **Photo. Gallery**

Untitled Print ▲
- *circa 1950*

Untitled silver gelatin print from the 1950s, signed recto by photographer Bert Hardy.
- *12cm x 16cm*
- **£1,300** • **Photo. Gallery**

Untitled C-Type Print ▼
- *1998*

Untitled C-type print taken in 1998 by Jason Oddy, from the "Palace of Nations" series. Signed verso.
- *30.5cm x 35.5cm*
- **£500** • **Photo. Gallery**

Signed Print ➤
- *1964*

Beatles on the way to Teddington studios, 1964, by John 'Hoppy' Hopkins. Silver gelatin print, signed verso.
- *51cm x 61cm*
- £500   • Photo. Gallery

Bob Willoughby Print ⬆
- *1967*

Silver gelatin print by Bob Willoughby of Katherine Hepburn walking in the Wicklow mountains in Ireland in 1967 during the filming of "The Lion in Winter". Signed recto.
- *30.5cm x 40cm*
- £600   • Photo. Gallery

Silver Gelatin Print ➤
- *1964*

"Martin Luther King at Oxford peace conference, 1964" by John 'Hoppy' Hopkins. Signed verso.
- *25.5 x 20cm*
- £200   • Photo. Gallery

John Hopkins Print ⬇
- *circa 1964*

"The Rolling Stones, studio group" by John 'Hoppy' Hopkins. Silver gelatin print, signed verso.
- *35.5cm x 51cm*
- £350   • Photo. Gallery

Silver Gelatin Print ⬇
- *1997*

"Le Grande Arche, Paris, 1997" by Marcus Davies. With photographer's signature verso.
- *16cm x 20cm*
- £400   • Photo. Gallery

Willoughby Signed Print ◄
- *1950*

"Louis Armstrong with All Stars, 1950" by Bob Willoughby. A silver gelatin print, signed verso.
- *30.5cm x 35.5cm*
- £600   • Photo. Gallery

Bert Hardy Print ▼
- *1951*
"Maidens in waiting, Blackpool, 1951" by photographer Bert Hardy. Silver gelatin print, signed recto.
- *30.5cm x 35.5cm*
- £500   • **Photo. Gallery**

Untitled C-Type Print ▼
- *1998*
Untitled C-type print by Jason Oddy taken in 1998 as part of the "Dunroamin" series. Signed verso.
- *30.5cm x 35.5cm*
- £500   • **Photo. Gallery**

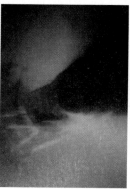

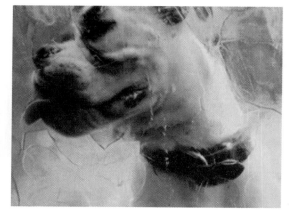

C-Type Print ▲
- *1994*
"Dog in back garden, 1994" by Matthew Murray. C-type print, signed verso.
- *30.5cm x 35.5cm*
- £200   • **Photo. Gallery**

Silver Gelatin Print ▼
- *1955*
"Locomotive 605, about to be washed, 1955" by O. Winston Link. Silver gelatin print, signed verso.
- *30.5cm x 40cm*
- £1,750   • **Photo. Gallery**

Chrystel Lebas Print ◄
- *2000*
"The Alps, 2000" from the "Moving Landscape" series by Chrystel Lebas. C-type print, signed and titled verso.
- *30.5cm x 40cm*
- £400   • **Photo. Gallery**

Signed C-Type Print ▲
- *1999*
"Kent, 1999" from the "Moving Landscape" series by Chrystel Lebas. C-type print, signed and titled verso.
- *30.5cm x 40cm*
- £400   • **Photo. Gallery**

Signed Print ▲
- *1992*
"A detective amuses colleagues" taken in Oughtraud, C. Galway, in 1992 by Leo Regan. A silver gelatin print, signed verso
- *30.5cm x 40cm*
- £300   • **Photo. Gallery**

Silver Gelatin Print ◀

- **1937**

Signed silver gelatin print by Humphrey Spender of two small children playing on a wasteland in Bolton, Lancashire. For mass observation

- *30.5cm x 40cm*
- £300   • **Photo. Gallery**

Signed Brandt Print ▼

- **1956**

"Nude, London, 1956" by Bill Brandt. A silver gelatin print, signed recto.

- *30.5cm x 40cm*
- £1,800   • **Photo. Gallery**

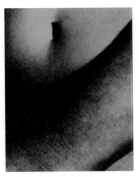

Limited Edition Print ▼

- **1965**

"Andy and Cow Wallpaper, 1965" by Nat Finkelstein. Silver gelatin print from an edition limited to 10. Signed verso.

- *30.5cm x 40cm*
- £600   • **Photo. Gallery**

Signed Silver Gelatin ➤

- **circa 1994**

'"Milton Keynes" by Leo Regan. Silver gelatin print, signed verso

- *30.5cm x 40cm*
- £300   • **Photo. Gallery**

Bill Brandt Print ▲

- **1930**

"Parlour Maid at Window, Kensington, 1930" by Bill Brandt. Silver gelatin print, signed recto.

- *30.5cm x 40cm*
- £1,300   • **Photo. Gallery**

Limited C-Type Print ▲

- **1965**

"Edie Sedgwick in Red Dress, 1965" by Nat Finkelstein. C-type print, from a limited edition of eight. Signed and numbered verso.

- *30.5cm x 40cm*
- £650   • **Photo. Gallery**

John Hopkins Print ▲
- *1964*

"Thelonius Monk" taken in 1964 by John 'Hoppy' Hopkins. Silver gelatin print, signed recto.
- *30.5cm x 40cm*
- **£350** • **Photo. Gallery**

Cornel Lucas Print ▼
- *1948*

"Yvonne de Carlo as Salome" by Cornel Lucas. A silver gelatin print, signed recto and titled verso.
- *30.5cm x 40cm*
- **£400** • **Photo. Gallery**

Silver Gelatin Print ◄
- *1948*

"Movie cameraman in the South Pacific, 1948" by Cornel Lucas. Silver gelatin print, signed recto.
- *30.5cm x 40cm*
- **£400** • **Photo. Gallery**

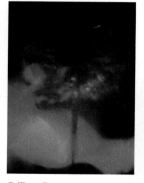

C-Type Print ▲
- *2000*

"Hot Dandelion, 2000" by photographer Delilah Dyson. C-type print, signed verso.
- *30.5cm x 40cm*
- **£250** • **Photo. Gallery**

Humphrey Spender Print ▲
- *1937*

"Bolton, 1937" by Humphrey Spender. For mass observation. Silver gelatin print, signed and titled recto.
- *30.5cm x 40cm*
- **£300** • **Photo. Gallery**

Signed Print ▼
- *2000*

"Snow Drops, 2000" by Delilah Dyson. C-type print, signed verso.
- *30.5cm x 40cm*
- **£300** • **Photo. Gallery**

Silver Gelatin Print ◄
- *1955*

"The Popes and the last passenger steam train, 1955" taken by O. Winston Link.
Silver gelatin print, signed verso by the photographer.
- *30.5 x 40cm*
- **£1,750** • **Photo. Gallery**

Posters

Moulin Rouge ▼
- *1952*

Original Polish poster, paper backed and unfolded, by Lucjan Jagodzinski.
- *84cm x 58cm*
- **£1,800** • Reel Poster Gallery

Ragtime ▼
- *1981*

Original east German poster, paper backed, featuring artwork by B. Krause.
- *81cm x 58cm*
- **£250** • Reel Poster Gallery

Othello ▲
- *1955*

Original Czech poster, linen backed, depicting Othello.
- *84cm x 58cm*
- **£500** • Reel Poster Gallery

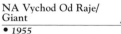

NA Vychod Od Raje/ Giant ▲
- *1955*

Original Czech poster, linen backed, for the first Czech release of "Giant" starring James Dean.
- *84cm x 58cm*
- **£750** • Reel Poster Gallery

Prazoniny V Rime/ Roman Holiday ◄
- *1953*

Original Czech poster, linen backed, promoting the film "Roman Holiday" with Audrey Hepburn.
- *84cm x 58cm*
- **£500** • Reel Poster Gallery

Gimme Shelter ▼

- **1970**
Original US poster, paper backed,
for the Rolling Stones' film
"Gimme Shelter".
- *104cm x 69cm*
- **£350** • Reel Poster Gallery

Rebellion/Bunt ➤

- **1967**
Original Polish poster, paper
backed, featuring artwork by
Rapnicki.
- *84cm x 58cm*
- **£150** • Reel Poster Gallery

Jour de Fête ◄

- **1948**
Original French poster, linen
backed, for the Jacques Tati film
"Jour de Fête", featuring artwork
by Eric.
- *160cm x 119cm*
- **£2,500** • Reel Poster Gallery

Przygoda L Avventura ▲

- **1959**
Original Polish poster, paper
backed, by Jan Lenica.
- *84cm x 58cm*
- **£250** • Reel Poster Gallery

Viaggio in Italia ▲

- **1953**
Original Italian poster, linen
backed, by Mauro Innocenti for
the film "Viaggio in Italia".
- *201cm x 140cm*
- **£1,800** • Reel Poster Gallery

Que Viva Mexiko ◄

- **1932**
Original east German poster,
paper backed, by Wenzer.
- *81cm x 58cm*
- **£180** • Reel Poster Gallery

Taxi Driver ➤
- **1976**
Original US poster, linen backed,
featuring artwork by Guy
Peelaert, Style A.
- *104cm x 69cm*
- **£500** • **Reel Poster Gallery**

A Man and a Woman ▼
- **1966**
Original US poster, paper backed,
released by Allied Artists for the
Cannes 1966 prizewinning film
"A Man and a Woman".
- *104cm x 69cm*
- **£350** • **Reel Poster Gallery**

2 Hommes Dans Manhattan ▼
- **1959**
Original French poster, linen
backed, by Georges Kerfyser, for
"2 Hommes dans Manhattan".
- *79cm x 61cm*
- **£250** • **Reel Poster Gallery**

Rosemary's Baby ➤
- **1968**
Original British poster designed
by Steve Frankfurt.
- *104cm x 69cm*
- **£350** • **Reel Poster Gallery**

Il Diritto di Uccidere/ In a Lonely Place ➤
- **1950**
Original Italian poster, linen
backed, featuring artwork by
Anselmo Ballester.
- *140cm x 99cm*
- **£3,500** • **Reel Poster Gallery**

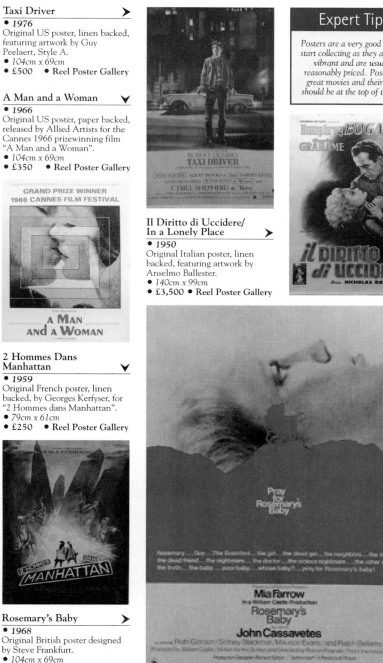

Expert Tips

*Posters are a very good way to
start collecting as they are fun,
vibrant and are usually
reasonably priced. Posters of
great movies and their stars
should be at the top of the list.*

F for Fake ▼
- 1973
Original US poster, linen backed,
designed by Donn Trethewey.
- 104cm x 69cm
- £500 • **Reel Poster Gallery**

The Graduate ▼
- 1967
Original US poster, linen backed,
designed by United Artists
Corporation.
- 206cm x 104cm
- £2,250 • **Reel Poster Gallery**

Turtle Diary ➤
- 1985
Original British poster, paper
backed, featuring artwork by
Andy Warhol, for the film
"Turtle Diary".
- 76cm x 102cm
- £225 • **Reel Poster Gallery**

Les Diaboliques ▲
- 1955
Original French poster, linen
backed, style A, with artwork by
Raymondgid.
- 160cm x 119cm
- £1,500 • **Reel Poster Gallery**

La Donna Che Visse due Volte/Vertigo ▲
- 1958
Original Italian poster featuring
art by Sandro Simeoni, for the
Hitchcock film, "Vertigo".
- 140cm x 99cm
- £1500 • **Reel Poster Gallery**

Expert Tips

*The condition and rarity of a
poster enhance its value, so
focus on these factors. Film
posters distributed and printed
in small countries have become
rare and are a good investment.*

Sueurs Froides/ Cold Sweat ◄
- 1958
Original French poster, paper
backed, art by Claude Venin.
- 79cm x 61cm
- £425 • **Reel Poster Gallery**

**Cena Strachu/
The Wages of Fear** ▲
- *1953*
Original Polish poster, paper
backed, with artwork by Jan
Lenica.
- *84cm x 58cm*
- £500 • Reel Poster Gallery

**La Mort Aux Trousses/
North by Northwest** ▼
- *1959*
Original French poster, paper
backed, for the Hitchcock film
"North by Northwest".
- *79cm x 61cm*
- £225 • Reel Poster Gallery

Diamonds Are Forever ➤
- *1971*
Original Japanese poster, paper
backed, style B.
- *76cm x 51cm*
- £350 • Reel Poster Gallery

Apocalypse Now ▲
- *1979*
Original Italian poster, linen
backed, style B, for the film
"Apocalypse Now".
- *201cm x 140cm*
- £600 • Reel Poster Gallery

**Ascenseur pour l'Echafaud/
Lift to the Scaffold** ▼
- *1957*
Original French poster, linen
backed, style B.
- *160cm x 119cm*
- £750 • Reel Poster Gallery

Zawrot Glowy/Vertigo ▼
- *1958*
Original polish poster, linen
backed, with artowrk by Roman
Cieslewicz.
- *84cm x 58cm*
- £1,200 • Reel Poster Gallery

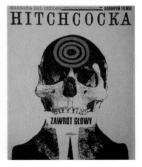

213

Radios, TV & Sound Equipment

Bendix Model 526C ▼
- *1946*
Black Bakelite American radio
with the inscription "Strong
Machine Age".
- *28cm x 35cm*
- £750   • Decodence

Fada Streamliner ▲
- *1940*
American onyx and amber
streamlined Catalin radio, with
large oval dial on the right.
- *height 19cm*
- £1,000   • Decodence

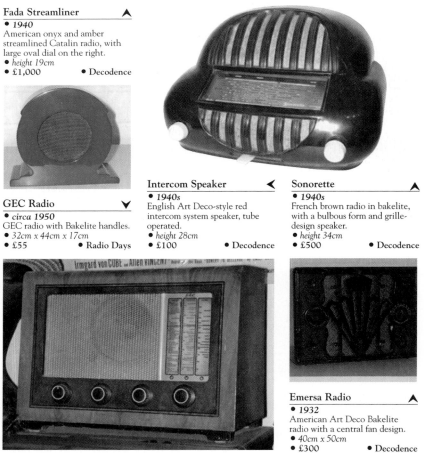

GEC Radio ▼
- *circa 1950*
GEC radio with Bakelite handles.
- *32cm x 44cm x 17cm*
- £55   • Radio Days

Intercom Speaker ◄
- *1940s*
English Art Deco-style red
intercom system speaker, tube
operated.
- *height 28cm*
- £100   • Decodence

Sonorette ▲
- *1940s*
French brown radio in bakelite,
with a bulbous form and grille-
design speaker.
- *height 34cm*
- £500   • Decodence

Emersa Radio ▲
- *1932*
American Art Deco Bakelite
radio with a central fan design.
- *40cm x 50cm*
- £300   • Decodence

Croslen Radio ◄
- *1951*

Red American Bakelite radio, styled in the shape of a speedometer.
- *height 29cm*
- N/A
- Decodence

Ekco RS3 ◄
- *1931*

Art Deco Bakelite radio standing on metal feet. This model was one of the first bakelite radios to be manufactured in the United Kingdom.
- *height 45cm*
- £800
- Decodence

Philips 930A ▲
- *1931*

Philips Art Deco radio with an unusual keel-shaped shaped body, and a stars and wavy line design, standing on a square base and legs.
- *height 48cm*
- £800
- Decodence

Roberts Radio ►
- *1970*

Roberts radio in red leather case.
- *15cm x 22cm x 8cm*
- £60
- Retro Home

Expert Tips

The design and a Bakelite casing, as well as maker and age are the key factors to consider when choosing radios. The early makers such as Logie Baird along with early combination sets currently dominate the market.

Transistor Radio ►
- *1970*

Roberts transistor radio, in wood and grey plastic.
- *14cm x 22cm*
- £60
- Retro Home

HMV TV/Radio Combination ➤

- *circa 1938*

Model No. 904 television and radio combined unit produced by HMV. This model uses the same chassis as Marconi model No. 706.
- *height 45cm*
- £1,800   • Vintage Wireless

Bush TV ▲

- *circa 1949*

Model 22 television produced by Bush. This was one of the most desired of all British Bakelite models.
- *height 39cm*
- £300   • Decodence

Wooden Radio ➤

- *circa 1930*

Valve radio housed in wooden display case.
- *30cm x 54cm*
- £85   • Radio Days

Silver Tone Bullet 6110 ◄

- *circa 1938*

Modern design push-button radio with enormous rotating turning scale. Designed by Clarence Karstacht.
- *height 17cm*
- £1,100   • Decodence

Bakelite Radio ▲

- *1930*

Brown Bakelite radio with lattice-effect front grille.
- £95   • Radio Days

Crystal Set ▲

- *circa 1910*

English Edwardian crystal set in mahogany case with brass fittings. In good condition.
- *height 30cm*
- £585   • TalkMach

Rock & Pop

Manic Street Preachers Single ▲
- **1990**
"UK Channel Boredom" flexi-disc supplied with both fanzines.
- *18cm x 18cm*
- **£120** • Music & Video

Powder Compact ▲
- *circa 1963*
Circular powder compact featuring a Dezo Hoffman black and white shot of The Beatles.
- **£475** • More Than Music

Madonna Lucky Star Single ▲
- **1983**
Full-length version of the single "Lucky Star" by Madonna.
- *30cm x 30cm*
- **£80** • Music & Video

Strawbs with Sandy Denny Album ▼
- **1969**
Strawbs music sampler No.1, issued as a limited edition of 100.
- *30cm x 30cm*
- **£675** • Music & Video

U2 Single ▼
- **1979**
U2's first single "Three", individually numbered.
- *20cm x 30cm*
- **£350** • Music & Video

U2 Helmet ▼
- **1998**
U2 helmet issued to promote the "Best of 1980–1990" album. Limited edition of 50 units.
- *30cm x 25cm x 23cm*
- **£250** • Music & Video

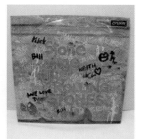

Rolling Stones Album ▲
- **1971**
Export edition of Rolling Stones "Stone Age" album.
- *30cm x 30cm*
- **£700** • Music & Video

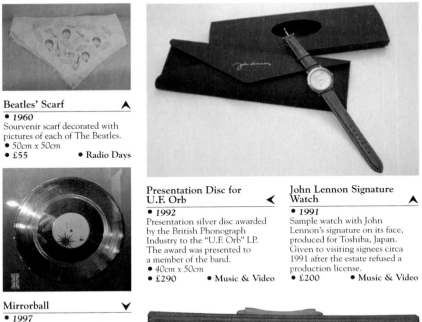

Beatles' Scarf ▲
- *1960*

Souvenir scarf decorated with pictures of each of The Beatles.
- *50cm x 50cm*
- £55
- ● Radio Days

Presentation Disc for U.F. Orb ◀
- *1992*

Presentation silver disc awarded by the British Phonograph Industry to the "U.F. Orb" LP. The award was presented to a member of the band.
- *40cm x 50cm*
- £290
- ● Music & Video

John Lennon Signature Watch ▲
- *1991*

Sample watch with John Lennon's signature on its face, produced for Toshiba, Japan. Given to visiting signees circa 1991 after the estate refused a production license.
- £200
- ● Music & Video

Mirrorball ▼
- *1997*

U2 pop mirrorball that opens up. Contains a video, poster and pen.
- *40cm x 40cm*
- N/A
- ● Music & Video

Untied Diaries Box Set ▲
- *1988*

Untied Diaries edition No. 30, with 32 cassettes individually recorded and packaged. This is different from the vinyl version.
- ●£900
- ● Music & Video

Beatles Dolls ◀
- *1966*

Set of four NEMS/King Features syndicate inflatable cartoon dolls of the Beatles.
- *35cm x 15cm*
- £120
- ● Music & Video

Beatles Poster with John Lennon Signature ▲
- *1977*

Pull-out poster from American magazine "People". Signed by band member John Lennon in 1977.
- *70cm x 45cm*
- £700   • Music & Video

Kylie Promotional Handbag ▼
- *2000*

Promotional "Puma" handbag produced for Kylie Minogue's "Light Years" album. Contains full album and interview CDs.
- *20cm x 20cm*
- £100   • Music & Video

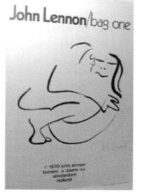

John Lennon/bag one

© 1970 john lennon
laurens a. daane n.v.
amsterdam
holland

The Verve ▲
- *circa 1992*

Mint condition copy of "Voyager 1" recorded live in New York by The Verve.
- £65   • Music & Video

Lithographs ◄
- *1970*

Packet of explicit lithographs from John Lennon's "Bag One" exhibition. Numbered edition of 1,000.
- *30cm x 50cm*
- £500   • Music & Video

Expert Tips

This market is set to explode but here again if you know your subject it really pays off. Records and record covers are a worthwhile investment as their production is now extremely limited.

Tote Bag with Five 12-inch Singles ▲
- *1985*

Duran Duran tote bag containing five maxi 12-inch singles.
- *30cm x 35cm*
- £75   • Music & Video

The Beatles: Live at the BBC ▲

- **1996**

The only existing maquette for the proposed HMV boxed set edition. Permission for the launch of this set was refused by Apple as the delayed production was considered potentially detrimental to the "Anthology" launch.

- *30cm x 30cm*
- **£4,995** • **Music & Video**

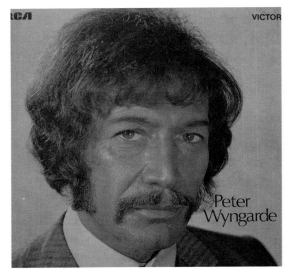

Peter Wyngarde ▲

- *circa 1970*

Music album by cult 1960s–70s television actor Peter Wyngarde's. Recorded at Olympic Sound Studios, Surrey.

- **£120** • **Music & Video**

Beatles Film Book ◄

- *Circa 1960*

Book based on the story and making of the Beatle's film "Help!", illustrated with black and white photographs.

- *25cm x 14cm*
- **£15** • **Radio Days**

Pair of Beatles Stockings ▼

- **1960**

Pair of unused Beatles stockings in original packet.

- *23cm x 17cm*
- **£55** • **Radio Days**

John and Yoko "Wedding Album" ◄

- **1969**

USA release of "Wedding Album" eight-track tape including box, slice of wedding cake, poster, photographs, postcard, bag, book, and copy of wedding certificate.

- *30cm x 30cm*
- **£175** • **Music & Video**

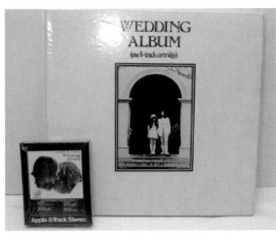

Siouxsie and The Banshees Memorabilia ➤

- *1981*
Half-page artwork for promotion of the Arabian Knights tour by Siouxsie and the Banshees.
- *40cm x 35cm*
- **£175**   • Music & Video

Bruce Springsteen Single ▲

- *1981*
"Cadillac Ranch" single by Bruce Springsteen.
- *18cm x 18cm*
- **£25**   • Music & Video

Beach Boys Album ▲

- *circa 1966*
Special disc jockey/producer copy of "The Best of the Beach Boys" album, released by EMI Records, London.
- **£184**   • Music & Video

The Police Singles Box ▲

- *1990*
Embossed wooden box containing 10 gold vinyl singles together with a picture disc by The Police.
- *18cm x 18cm*
- **£195**   • Music & Video

Manic Street Preachers Single ◄

- *1988*
Double A-side single "Suicide Alley Tennessee" containing a letter from the band.
- *18cm x 18cm*
- **£995**   • Music & Video

Album Artwork ◀
- **1984**

Unused album artwork for Jimmy the Hoover by Jamie Reid, with glass broken and damaged intentionally for the "Leaving the 21st Century" series held at the Mayfair gallery.
- *50cm x 50cm*
- **£200**   • Music & Video

4AD Calendar ▼
- **1993**

Collector's item calendar issued by record company, 4AD, and designed by 23 Envelope.
- *35cm x 55cm*
- **£25**   • Music & Video

Brute Force Album featuring John Lennon ▼
- **1970**

"Extemporaneous" album by Brute Force featuring John Lennon.
- **£395**   • Music & Video

Withdrawn Single ▼
- **1981**

"Ha ha I'm drowning" single by The Teardrop Explodes. Withdrawn issue.
- *18cm x 18cm*
- **£60**   • Music & Video

Rolling Stones Album ▼
- **1971**

Copy of the Rolling Stones album "Sticky Fingers".
- *30cm x 30cm*
- **£240**   • Music & Video

Wing's Record Sleeve ▼
- **1975**

Record sleeve for Wing's "Listen to what the man said" and "King Alfred's Rubbish", autographed by Paul and Linda McCartney.
- **£675**   • More Than Music

Scripophily & Paper Money

New Orleans Note ▲
- *circa 1860*
New Orleans $20 note issued
by Canal Bank.
- £12.50   • C. Narbeth

Military Payment Note ▼
- 1970
Military payment certificate to
the value of 10 cents.
- £6   • C. Narbeth

Colonial Note ▶
- 1773
Colonial 15 shillings note issued
in Pennsylvania. Numbered and
signed by hand.
- £48   • C. Narbeth

American Note ▲
- 1995
American note in the amount
of $2.
- £3   • C. Narbeth

National Currency
$20 Dollar Note ▼
- 1900
$20 dollar note issued by the
Citizen's Bank of Eureka, Kansas,
during the Battle of Lexington.
- £595   • C. Narbeth

Confederate States Note ▼
- 1864
Confederate States $10 note
issued in the US Civil War.
- £28   • C. Narbeth

Bank of England Note ▼
- 1972

£20 note bearing a portrait of Queen Elizabeth II.
- £1972
- C. Narbeth

Fijiian Treasury Note ▲
- 12th July 1873

Treasury note in the amount of £50, issued in Fiji.
- £495
- C. Narbeth

Railway Bond ◄
- 1911

Bond issued by the Brazil Railway Company.
- £18
- C. Narbeth

US Railway Bond ▼
- 1881

$500 dollar bond issued by the Indiana Coal and Railway Co.
- £35
- C. Narbeth

English Note ◄
- 1950

White £5 note issued by the Bank of England.
- £89.50
- C. Narbeth

Railroad Shares ▲
- 1864

Share issued by the Little Miami Railroad Company.
- £10
- C. Narbeth

English Banknote ▼
- 1987

English £50 note signed by David Somerset.
- £95
- C. Narbeth

Signed US Share ▲
- 1895

Philadelphia and Lancaster share signed "Bingham". Early US share with a vignette.
- £795
- C. Narbeth

Russian Note ▲
- 1884

Russian 10 rouble note issued in the reign of Czar Alexander III.
- £850
- C. Narbeth

Singapore Post Bill ▲
- *17th August 1860*

$50 post bill used as a banknote, issued by the Chartered Bank of India, Australia and China.
- £650   • C. Narbeth

Seychelles Note ▼
- *1972*

Government of Seychelles Rs. 50 note, carrying a portrait of Queen Elizabeth II.
- £385   • C. Narbeth

Shares Note ▲
- *1913*

Shares note issued by the Marconi Wireless Company.
- £35   • C. Narbeth

US Shares Notes ▲
- *1880*

Shares note issued by the Oregon and Transcontinental Company.
- £10   • C. Narbeth

Railroad Shares ▲
- *1860*

Shares note issued by the Cleveland and Toledo Railroad Company.
- £25   • C. Narbeth

Columbia Pictures Note ▲
- *circa 1960*

Shares note issued by Columbia Pictures Corporation.
- £9   • C. Narbeth

Expert Tips

Badly creased and stained notes, or cut and ragged edges lower the value of a note.

Chinese Bond ➤
- *1913*

Gold bond note issued by the Chinese Government.
- £25   • C. Narbeth

English Share Note ▼
- *circa 1850*
Share note issued by The Hornsey Freehold Estate Tontine Company.
- £10 • C. Narbeth

South African Note ▼
- *1864*
£25 note issued by Durban Bank, a private bank in South Africa.
- £350 • C. Narbeth

Republic Note ➤
- *1872*
£1 noted issued by the South African Republic.
- £325 • C. Narbeth

Railway Bond ▲
- *1909*
Armavir Touapse Railway Company bond in the amount of 189 roubles.
- £4 • C. Narbeth

Railroad Bond ▲
- *1866*
Bond issued by the Boston Hartford Erie Rail Road Co.
- £85 • C. Narbeth

Russian Bond ▲
- *1914*
Russian South Eastern bond to the value of 945 roubles.
- £7 • C. Narbeth

English Share Note ◀
- *1866*
Note in respect of one £20 share issued by Charles Lafitte & Co. .
- £4 • C. Narbeth

Scottish Banknote ▼
- *1915*
£1 note issued by The National Bank of Scotland
- £85 • C. Narbeth

Canadian Share Note ▼
• *1935*
Share note issued by the City of
Montreal, Canada.
• £4   • C. Narbeth

Caribbean Note ▼
• *1975*
EC$100 dollar note issued by the
East Caribbean Currency
Authority, bearing a portrait of
Queen Elizabeth II.
• £175   • C. Narbeth

Lebanese Bond ▼
• *1949*
L5,000 bond issued by the
Lebanese government.
• £8   • C. Narbeth

German Bond ►
• *1909*
DM 10,000 bond from Germany
• £15   • C. Narbeth

Scottish Pound Note ◄
• *1921*
£1 note issued by The Bank of
Scotland.
• £95   • C. Narbeth

English Banknote ▲
• *1844*
£5 note, numbered 9374, issued
by the Winchester and
Hampshire Bank, England.
• £365   • C. Narbeth

Share Warrant ►
• *1890*
Share warrant No. 1067 for one
hundred shares, issued by the
Bengal Gold and Silver Mining
Company.
• £7   • C. Narbeth

Oriental Bank Share ▲
• *1850*
Share certificate issued by the
Oriental Bank Corporation.
• £15   • C. Narbeth

Chinese Bond ➤
- *1911*

£20 bond issued by the Imperial
Chinese Government.
- £65   • C. Narbeth

Portugese Bond ⬆
- *1922*

Bond issued by the Companhia
Colonial Navegaedo.
- £7   • C. Narbeth

Iraqi Note ⬇
- *1931*

ID 1 banknote, numbered A
157545, from Iraq.
- £450   • C. Narbeth

Swiss Note ⬆
- *1952*

SFr 5 note issued by the national
bank of Switzerland.
- £38   • C. Narbeth

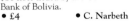

British Linen Co. Note ⬆
- *18th January 1896*

£5 note issued by the British
Linen Company.
- £325   • C. Narbeth

Expert Tips

*The first European banknote
was printed in Scandinavia in
1661. Since then a wealth of
paper money has been issued.
Keep your eyes on bank notes
as they are likely to become
a worthwhile investment.*

Irish Banknote ⬇
- *1977*

£50 note issued by The Central
Bank of Ireland.
- **£175**   • C. Narbeth

Bolivian Note ➤
- *1928*

$b1 note issued by the Central
Bank of Bolivia.
- £4   • C. Narbeth

Scottish Pound Note ⬇
- *1969*

£1 note issued by the Bank of
Scotland.
- £25   • C. Narbeth

Sewing Items

Straw-Work Sewing Box ▼
- *circa 1810–20*
Straw-work box made by
Napoleonic prisoner-of-wars,
decorated with scenes of flowers,
boats and houses.
- *width 27cm*
- £330
- Hygra

Tunbridge Ware Sewing Box ▼
- *circa 1800*
A child's early Tunbridge Ware
sewing box with pincushion and
needle envelope.
- *width 13cm*
- £280
- Hygra

Ivory Sewing Set ▼
- *1850*
French ivory sewing set with
silver gilt tools.
- *width 10cm*
- £750
- Thimble Society

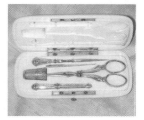

Satinwood Sewing Box ▶
- *circa 1890*
Satinwood work table with an
oval top, on square tapered legs
with splayed feet and X-shaped
stretcher.
- *78cm x 48cm x 35cm*
- £4,500
- Butchoff

Gold Thimbles ▼
- *1820–70*
Selection of continental gold
thimbles, two with stone tops and
one with foliate design, pearls
and turquoise stones.
- *height 2.5cm*
- £325
- Thimble Society

Sycamore Sewing Box ▼
- *circa 1850*
Shaped sycamore sewing box
with early transfer decoration
depicting country scenes,
standing on turned feet.
- *width 26cm*
- £550
- Hygra

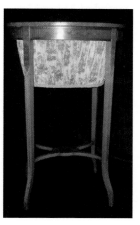

Lacquered Sewing Box ▼
- *circa 1810*
Lacquered sewing box decorated
with coloured chinoiserie scenes
on a black and gilt ground
depicting figures in a garden.
With original embossed brass
handles, standing on embossed
paw feet.
- *width 22cm*
- £1,400
- Hygra

Hardwood Sewing Box ◄

- *circa 1775*

An eighteenth century sewing box with native and imported hardwoods juxtaposed and a neo-classical central motif.

- *width 29cm*
- £720
- Hygra

Kingwood Sewing Box ▲

- *1830*

Kingwood sewing box inlaid with ivory in a diamond pattern, enclosing silver gilt needlework tools.

- *length 10cm*
- £490
- Thimble Society

Rosewood Sewing Box ▲

- *circa 1835*

Fully fitted rosewood and mother-of-pearl sewing box labelled "George Johnston Glasgow".

- *width 31cm*
- £1,800
- Hygra

Inlaid Sewing Box ▼

- *1820*

Very fine early nineteenth century anglo-Indian ivory and sadeli mosaic fitted sewing box.

- *width 32cm*
- £950
- Hygra

Expert Tips

When buying sewing machines try to look out for the smaller versions, for example a miniature Singer or the "Little Comfort", an American-made sewing machine, as these tend to be more expensive then their larger counterparts. For those who would like to collect smaller items the necessaires and thimbles, especially from the Elizabethan period are very expensive, although anything pre-eighteenth century will still command a good price.

Silver Thimbles ▲

- *mid 19th century*

A selection of three silver thimbles with intricate silver skirts set with coloured stones.

- *height 2.6cm*
- £90 each
- Thimble Society

Sycamore Sewing Box ▼

- *circa 1810*

A shaped sycamore fitted sewing box with a hand-painted design of a basket with overflowing flowers.

- *width 27cm*
- £1,800
- Hygra

Regency Sewing Box ▼

- *1835*

Regency rosewood sewing box of sarcophagus form with pewter stringing, gadroon bordering, and lozenge feet. The interior with original red velvet and silk lining. The box contains a letter dated 1843, probably from the original owner.

- *16cm x 33cm x 26cm*
- £995
- J. & T. Stone

Thimble Case ▼
- *1760*

Ormolu thimble case with hinged lid and embossed floral decoration.
- *width 3cm*
- £98   • Thimble Society

Rosewood Needlework Table ▼
- *1850*

William IV rosewood drop-leaf needlework table on six barley twist legs, two of which pull out to support the extension flaps.
- *75cm x 85cm x 54cm*
- £1,850   • Old Cinema

Italian Scissors ▼
- *circa 1770*

Steel eighteenth century Italian scissors, twith handles in the shape of peacocks.
- *length 13cm*
- £230   • Thimble Society

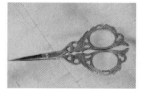

Lacquer Sewing Box ▼
- *1860*

Black lacquer sewing box on lacquered stand with horseshoe shaped stretcher. On tripod base with gilded lion paw feet.
- *92cm x 48cm*
- £1,500   • Sign of the Times

Quiver-Shaped Case ▼
- *1730*

Mother-of-pearl needle case designed in the shape of a quiver.
- *length 9cm*
- £280   • Thimble

Decorated Sewing Box ▼
- *circa 1840*

Rosewood sewing box decorated with mother of pearl.
- *width 30cm*
- £240   • Hygra

Needlework Table ▼
- *19th century*

Inlaid satinwood needlework table on tapered faux bamboo legs, with side drawer and silk fire screen.
- *75cm x 55cm x 45cm*
- £425   • C.H. Major

Octagonal Sewing Box ▼
- *circa 1820*

Shaped Chinese lacquer sewing box with very fine quality decoration depicting garden scenes, with a fully fitted interior with carved ivory tools, standing on carved dragon feet.
- *width 36cm*
- £2,100   • Hygra

Snuff Boxes & Smoking Equipment

Lady's Pipe ▲
- *1880*

Small carved Meerschaum lady's
pipe.
- *length 4cm*
- £350   • Langfords

Shoe-Shaped Snuff Box ➤
- *circa 1860*

Mahogany snuff box in the shape
of a shoe with brass inlay, the sole
inscribed "J.Dungey".
- *2.5cm x 10cm*
- £375   • Bill Chapman

Pipe Case ▲
- *1900*

An unusual silver pipe case/
tobacco box with a match box on
the inside of the lid.
- *length 11.4cm*
- £750   • N. Shaw

Cigarette Box ➤
- *1928*

A silver and enamel cigarette
box.
- *width 11cm*
- £1,150   • N. Shaw

Edwardian Vesta Case ▲
- *1909*

An Edwardian vesta case with an
Edward VII relief, made in
Birmingham
- *length 4cm*
- £295   • N. Shaw

Enamelled Vesta Case ▲
- *1912*

A George V enamel on silver
vesta case, made in Birmingham
for the Royal Yacht Club.
- *length 4cm*
- £395   • N. Shaw

Gold and Tortoiseshell Snuff Box ➤

- **1702**
Queen Anne gold and tortoiseshell snuff box made in London. The lid inset with a gold coin commemorating Queen Anne's coronation. One of 750 that were issued at the time.
- *length 8cm*
- **£4,250**   ● N. Shaw

Silver Vesta Case ➤

- **1926**
A silver George V vesta case made in London by The Goldsmith and Silversmith Company Ltd.
- *length 3cm*
- **£675**   ● N. Shaw

Novelty Vesta Case ▲

- **1888**
A silver Victorian novelty vesta case.
- *length 6cm*
- **£575**   ● N. Shaw

Austrian Snuff Box ▼

- **1924**
An Austrian snuff box with indigo enamel on a tooled silver base, with pierced floral cartouches in a neo-classical style.
- *length 8cm*
- **£480**   ● Thimble Society

Silver Gilt Snuff Box ▲

- **1855**
A Victorian silver gilt snuff box presented to Captain H. G. Kennedy of The Ship Parker. Made by Edward Smith in Birmingham
- *length 11cm*
- **£2,250**   ● N. Shaw

Mahogany Snuff Box ▲

- **1860**
Mahogany shoe inlaid with brass design and mother of pearl.
- *6cm x 9cm*
- **£525**   ● Bill Chapman

233

Cigar Box ➤
- *1920*

Unusual burr walnut cigar and cigarette box with gilded handle and decoration. Two lighter drawers with match strikers.
- *width 24cm*
- £495
- J. & T. Stone

Continental Vesta Case ▲
- *circa 1900*

A continental vesta case decorated with an enamel chestnut horse's head.
- *3cm*
- £450
- N. Shaw

George IV Snuff Box ▼
- *1822–3*

A George IV snuff box made in Birmingham by Joseph Willmore.
- *length 4cm*
- £450
- N. Shaw

Double Snuff Box ➤
- *1858*

A George IV double Regi Mari snuff box inscribed, "London 1827, Tria Juncta In Uno. Presented by Lieut Col Caulfield and the Married Officers of the mess of the 33rd Roscommon Regiment, 17 March 1858". Engraved with a four-leaf clover.
- *length 6cm*
- £3,950
- N. Shaw

Victorian Snuff Box ▲
- *1840*

A silver Victorian snuff box with an oak leaf pattern, presented to Mr William McKelvic of Redruth.
- *length 3.5cm*
- £2,750
- N. Shaw

Silver Taper ◄
- *1880*

A Victorian, silver vesta/ taper lighter made in London by Louis Dee.
- *length 11cm*
- £650
- N. Shaw

Expert Tips

Cigarette boxes are extremely collectable, especially the examples from the Art Deco period. Their value also increases if they are made from gold or silver and carry a hallmark. When purchasing these items it is important that one bears in mind the craftsmanship and style of the piece. Early cigar cutters will always command a high price, and any snuff box with a zoographical theme is always worth buying.

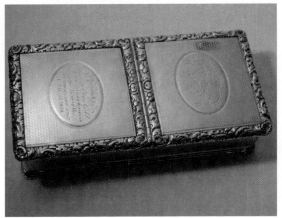

Victorian Vesta Case >

- **1893**

A silver Victorian vesta case with central oval floral decoration made in Birmingham.
- *length 3cm*
- £375　　　　• N. Shaw

George II Snuff Box ▲

- **1747**

A silver George II oval snuff box engraved with a contemporary coat of arms. Made in Dublin by Benjamin Stokes.
- *diameter 4cm*
- £2,750　　　• N. Shaw

George III Snuff Box >

- **1720**

An oval George III silver tobacco box made in London by Beesley with the inscription "Mary Annesley, Reading, 12 April".
- *length 9cm*
- £2,750　　　• N. Shaw

Victorian Snuff Box ◀

- **1843–4**

A Victorian oblong silver snuff box by Charles Rawlings and William Summers.
- *width 11cm*
- £1,430　　　• N. Shaw

Engine-Turned Snuff Box ▲

- **1854**

Victorian engine-turned silver snuff box inscribed "To Captain A. Droght, Indian Navy".
- *length 4cm*
- £1,750　　　• N. Shaw

Silver Snuff Box ▼

- **1835–6**

A silver William IV engine-turned snuff box made in Edinburgh by James Naismyth.
- *length 8cm*
- £750　　　　• N. Shaw

Chinese Snuff box ◀

- **1800–20**

Chinese tortoiseshell snuff box, deeply carved with figurative designs surrounded by a repetitive frieze.
- *length 8cm*
- £225　　　• Abacus Antiques

Telephones

English Telephone ➤
- *circa 1900s*
An English telephone with a wooden base, chrome bell and metal handset by Electric and Ordnance Accessories Ltd.
- *22.5cm x 20cm*
- **£295** • **Telephone Lines**

Candlestick Telephone ▼
- *1880*
French candlestick telephone with a chrome clip.
- *height 25cm*
- **£350** • **Telephone Lines**

Burgunder Telephone ◄
- *1912*
A Candlestick telephone by A. Burgunder, made in Paris, France.
- *height 32cm*
- **£285** • **Telephone Lines**

Western Electric Telephone ▼
- *1930*
An American candlestick telephone with original ringer box by Western Electric.
- *height 29cm*
- **£345** • **Telephone Lines**

Desk Telephone ▼
- *1908*
A desk phone with magneto handle, raised on a wooden base by Thomson-Houston, France.
- *33cm x 18cm*
- **£385** • **Telephone Lines**

Expert Tips

Coloured telephones fetch higher prices, especially the 1930s pyramid telephones. Look out for the Belgium telephones – they have a delightful ring and are not necessarily very expensive.

Chrome handset ▼
- *1900*
A French candlestick telephone with a metal base and chrome handset by Thomson-Houston.
- *height 32cm*
- £385 • Telephone Lines

Series 200 Telephone ▲
- *1930s–1940s*
An English acrylic cream coloured telephone this type of telephone did not have a bell, the bell was installed on the wall.
- *17cm x18cm*
- £420 • Decodence

Cream Telephone ▼
- *circa 1970*
An English cream plastic telephone.
- *width 20.5cm*
- £75 • After Noah (KR)

Expert Tips

You must look out for fading of bakelite telephones as this means that the telephone has been exposed to direct sunlight, and, as with all antiques sunlight is a very destructive force. Also it is very important to check that there is no cracking or chipping in the bakelite as this will decrease the value.

Pink Plastic Metallic Telephone ▼
- *circa 1965*
Pink plastic metallic telephone with black flex.
- *14cm x 14cm x 24cm*
- £55 • Radio Days

French Wooden Telephone ▲
- *1924*
French wooden candlestick telephone with metal dial and handset, and original wiring, by P. Jacquesson.
- *height 22.5cm*
- £475 • Telephone Lines

Black Telephone ▼
- *circa 1940*
Black bakelite telephone issued by G.P.O.
- £180 • After Noah (KR)

German Telephone ◄

- *1900*

A German-made magneto telephone with metal base and handset, and chrome earpiece and microphone.

- *30cm x 20cm*
- £285   • Telephone Lines

Pink Plastic Wall Telephone ▲

- *1950*

Pink plastic wall telephone with cream and silver banding to the ear and mouthpiece.

- *7cm x 13cm x 21cm*
- £75   • Radio Days

Expert Tips

Bear in mind that telephones can not be connected to a modern communications system. Make sure the wood casing is not split, maintains its original varnish and shows no sign of rot, and also displays the maker's logo.

Orange Plastic Telephone ▼

- *1970*

Orange plastic telephone with cream numerals and orange flex.

- *12cm x 10cm x 21cm*
- £20   • Radio Days

Plastic Telephone ▲

- *circa 1950*

Blue plastic telephone with cream dial and handle and silver banding.

- *14cm x 14cm x 24cm*
- £55   • Radio Days

Blue Plastic Telephone ➤

- *1960*

Blue plastic telephone with red dial, on a cream base with red flex.

- *14cm x 14cm x 24cm*
- £55   • Radio Days

Black Plastic Telephone ▲
- *1960*

Black plastic telephone with white letters and numbers, and black flex.
- *13cm x 13cm x 21cm*
- £55   • Radio Days

Ericsson Telephone ▶
- *circa 1905*

A Swedish-made, Ericsson, wooden wall-mounted phone with bell-ring display to top.
- *69cm x 26cm*
- £495   • Telephone Lines

Series 300 Telephone ▼
- *1940s–1950s*

An English acrylic golden yellow telephone with drawer for addresses and integral bell.
- *19cm x 18cm*
- £300   • Decodence

Candlestick Telephone ▲
- *1916*

French candlestick telephone with metal and chrome handset and wooden candlestick base by Grammont.
- *height 34cm*
- £415   • Telephone Lines

Desk Telephone ▲
- *1895*

A Dutch wooden desk phone with rotary dial.
- *height 15cm*
- £295   • Telephone Lines

Expert Tips

Even if a phone is termed a novelty phone this does not imply that it is of low worth. Bear in mind that these will be the collectables of the future and will increase in value as the years go by, just remember to keep the original box!

Walking Sticks

Wooden Cane ▲
- *circa 1890*
Gargoyle head on a gnarled wooden cane.
- *92cm x 6cm x 3cm*
- £240   • Henry Gregory

Snakewood Walking Cane ▲
- *circa 1900*
An elegant, rare snakewood cane with gold collar and looped handle.
- *length 89cm*
- £550   • Michael German

Whalebone Cane ▼
- *circa 1840*
A fine whalebone cane with full barley twist shaft. The whale handle loop carved with a serpent's head.
- *length 70cm*
- £1,600   • Michael German

City Walking Cane ▼
- *circa 1900*
Ebonised cane with gioche enamel ball, gold band and Austrian mark.
- *length 55cm*
- £750   • Michael German

Hoof Walking Stick ▲
- *circa 1880*
Carved horn hoof handle mounted on unusual segmented shaft formed from paper washers.
- *length 100cm/handle*
- £650   • Michael German

Japanese Walking Cane ▲
- *circa 1900*
Japanese bamboo cane inset with ivory face and silver collar.
- *length 20cm*
- £680   • Michael German

Cigar Holder Walking Stick ➤

- *circa 1880*

An unusual cane with a wood and ivory handle forming a cheroot holder mounted on an ebonised shaft.
- *length 91cm*
- £800   • Michael German

Dog Head Walking Cane ▼

- *circa 1870*

Victorian ebonised cane with silver collar and a carved ivory dog's head with open jaw.
- *length 80cm*
- £700   • Michael German

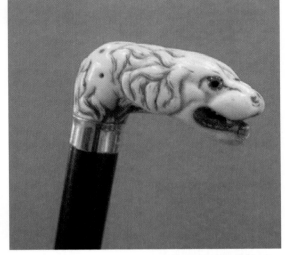

Expert Tips

Essentially there are three types of walking stick: country walking sticks, city canes and novelty walking sticks, which can have a variety of uses, from telescopes to drinking canes.

Country Walking Stick ▼

- *circa 1900*

A Scottish country walking stick with a silver-mounted snuff holder with amber inset and thistle design.
- *length 89cm*
- £550   • Michael German

Porcelain Walking Cane ▼

- *circa 1780*

Mallaca cane with porcelain Tau-shape Meissen handle with floral enamels.
- *length 100cm*
- £1,450   • Michael German

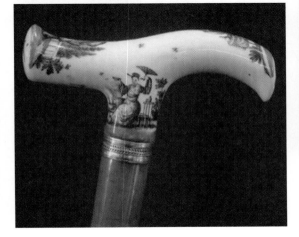

Skull Walking Stick ▲

- *circa 1880*

An unusual Victorian mallaca cane with an ivory skull.
- *length 91cm*
- £950   • Michael German

Carved Walking Stick ▼

- *circa 1860*

Folk art cane with deeply carved animals, trees and fruit, silver collar and rounded top.
- *length 92cm*
- £925 • Michael German

Russian Walking Cane ▲

- *circa 1890*

Russian ebonised cane with an elaborately decorated silver handle with overlaid enamel Tau and Russian marks
- *length 90cm*
- £1,400 • Michael German

Cricket Ball Walking Stick ▼

- *circa 1870*

Unusual folk art cane with hand holding cricket ball, carved shaft.
- *length 100cm*
- £480 • Michael German

Elephant Walking Cane ▼

- *circa 1890*

Ebonised cane with an ivory baby elephant with glass eyes, in a seated position.
- *length 78cm*
- £1,200 • Michael German

Chinese Walking Cane ◄

- *circa 1880–90*

An ornate silver cane from China with a long silver handle chased with a dragon design.
- *length 100cm*
- £680 • Michael German

Coins & Medals

Coins are probably the most collected antiques of all, existing in sufficient quantities to provide for both large and small collections.

Coins, from their earliest origins, around 1000 BC created a revolution in the marketplace and the way in which goods were traded. The stamp of an Emperor's head on the face of a coin helps to accurately record the progress of civilisation.

Coins hold the same kind of attraction to the collector as stamps. This is probably due to the fact that they are easy to index and catalogue. They are a good place start for collectors on a limited budget who can then watch their collection grow in proportion to their available funds.

Alternatively for the discerning collector there is scope to go in at the top end of the market where prices for early gold coins can reach up to four figures.

Along with coins, medals are also accurate measures of history. They are awarded to heroes both in the military field and in service to humanity. Medals for military service during the Victorian era generally command the high prices, but badges of title, for example the Star and Garter, can fetch astronomical amounts. The value of a medal is also greatly enhanced if it was awarded to someone of high status or valour.

Zulu War Medal ◄
- *1879*

A Zulu war medal, clasp inscribed "1879 to 889 Private J. Kiernan 2/3 foot".
- **£295**   • **Chelsea (OMRS)**

Gulf War Medal ►
- *1991*

Gulf War medal with clasp, awarded to Steward I. McMillan of the Royal Fleet Auxiliary.
- **£135**   • **Chelsea (OMRS)**

Boer War Medal Group ◄
- *1893–1902*

A Boer war medal group with four to a kafaking defender consists of a British South Africa Company medal "Matabeleland 1893", Queen South Africa medal with three clasps including "Defence of Making". Kings South Africa Medal with two clasps and South Africa Prison Services Long Service medal. Awarded to trooper A H Brady, South Africa Light Horse.
- **£1,800**   • **Chelsea (OMRS)**

Russian Medal ▼

- *1915*

Imperial Russian Cross of St. George IV class.
- £45 • Chelsea (OMRS)

Order of the Indian Empire ◄

- *1900*

Order of the Indian Empire Cie breast badge in case of award.
- £450 • Chelsea (OMRS)

Great War Medal ▲

- *1911–37*

A distinguished service order (George V) in Garrard & Co, in case of award.
- £450 • Chelsea (OMRS)

Miniature Medals ▼

- *1918*

A set of KCMG, CB(Gold) group of ten miniatures attributed to Major General Sir Andrew Mitchell Stuart. Royal Engineers.
- £385 • Chelsea (OMRS)

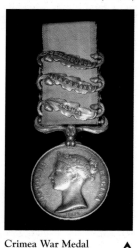

Cap Badge ▲

- *1914–18*

Royal Sussex Regiment silver and enamel officer's cap badge.
- £100 • Chelsea (OMRS)

Crimea War Medal ▲

- *1854–56*

A Crimea war medal from 1854, with three clasps, "Alma" "Inkermann" and "Sebastopol". Awarded to G. Bartlett of the 63rd Regiment.
- £350 • Chelsea (OMRS)

Expert Tips

The value of coins depends on their mint mark, design, date and condition, which is graded from FDC (fleur de coin or mint condition) to F (fair). Always have your collection photographed for insurance purposes, and store the information away from the collection.

Boer War Medal ▼

• *1893-1902*
A Boer War Queen's South Africa medal with seven clasps. Awarded to the 2688 Private G. Francis of the Welsh Regiment.
• £325   • Chelsea (OMRS)

Soviet Military Medal ◄

• *1945*
World War II U.S.S.R. Order of the Red Banner Military medal awarded for valour to members of the Soviet army.
• £30   • Chelsea (OMRS)

Military General Service Medal ▲

• *1848*
A Military General Service medal, 1848, with four clasps. Awarded to James Knowles, 5th Foot, Northumberland Fusiliers.
• £850   • Chelsea (OMRS)

Medal Group ▼

• *1914–18*
A medal group consisting of the NBE, The Military Cross, 1914 Star Trio, Defence medal, War medal and Special Constabulary medal. Awarded to Lieutenant Colonel T.L. Wall of the Fifth Lancers.
• £1,550   • Chelsea (OMRS)

Naval General Service Medal ▲

• *1847*
A Naval General Service Medal, 1847, with clasps "Martinique" and "Guadeloupe". Awarded to Private Robert Lock of the Royal Marines.
• £1,000   • Chelsea (OMRS)

German Pilot's Badge ▼

• *1940*
WWII German air force pilot's badge in silver by Bruder Schneider, Vienna.
• £350   • Chelsea (OMRS)

Russian Order of St. Stanislaus ▼

• *1900*
A Russian order of St. Stanislaus, civil type 4th class. 18ct gold.
• £275   • Chelsea(OMRS)

Belt Buckle ◀

- *1880*

A Victorian Royal Military College belt buckle in brass and silver.

- £1,880   • Chelsea (OMRS)

Officer's Cap Badge ▼

- *1914*

Irish Guards Officer's silver and enamel Great War cap badge. Attributed to Captain M. Gore-Langton MC.

- £195   • Chelsea (OMRS)

India General Service Medal ▼

- *1908*

1908 India General Service medal with clasp, "North West Frontier". Awarded to 65 Barghir Daroska of the 51st Camel Corps.

- £60   • Chelsea (OMRS)

German Assault Badge ▼

- *1942*

World War II German army/SS General Assault badge, showing eagle, Nazi insignia and combat dagger in oak-leaf and acorn surround. Mid-war plated zinc example.

- £40   • Chelsea (OMRS)

Military Medal ▼

- *1962 onwards*

Campaign Service medal with three clasps awarded to Bombardier A.J. Williams of 2/9 Commando Royal Artillery.

- £125   • Chelsea (OMRS)

RAF Flying Medal ▲

- *1939–45*

World War II RAF distinguished flying medal. For gallantry. Awarded to Sgt. G. Jones.

- £950   • Chelsea (OMRS)

Military Cigarette Case ▲

- *1943*

A Russian presentation silver cigarette case, celebrating victory over the Germans in World War II, with inscription.

- £250   • Chelsea (OMRS)

Memorial Plaque ➤

- *1914*

Great War memorial plaque dedicated to Ernest George Malyon of the 2nd/16th Battalion London Regiment and inscribed "He died for freedom and honour".

- *diameter 12cm*
- £25 • Chelsea (OMRS)

Leopold II Medal ▲

- *1915*

Order of Leopold II 2nd Class neck badge.

- £175 • Chelsea (OMRS)

Waterloo Medal ▼

- *1815*

A Waterloo medal, 1815, awarded to Joseph Porch of the 11th Light Dragons, wounded in action.

- £1,000 • Chelsea (OMRS)

Military Clasp ▲

- *1943*

World War II German Navy U-boat Clasp for Bravery. Mid-war zinc example by Peeuhaus.

- £575 • Chelsea (OMRS)

Cap Badge ▲

- *1939–45*

Royal Armoured Corps WWII plastic cap badge.

- £25 • Chelsea (OMRS)

Air Force Medal ▼

- *1945*

A European Aircrew Star, awarded to a serving member of the Royal Air Force in World War II.

- £105 • Chelsea (OMRS)

Military Medal Trio ▼

- *1918*

A trio of World War I medals, including the Victory medal, awarded to Private H. Codd of the East Yorkshire Regiment.

- £35 • Chelsea (OMRS)

WWI Medal Group △

- **WWI and later**
A WWI medal group of five medals, consisting of 1914–1915 Star Trio, 1935 Jubilee medal, RAF Long Service Good Conduct medal. Awarded to Corporal L. Thornton R.A.F.
- **£250** ● **Chelsea (OMRS)**

Iron Cross △

- **1914**
An Iron Cross 2nd Class, awarded to a German soldier at the beginning of World War I.
- **£20** ● **Chelsea (OMRS)**

Expert Tips

Avoid over cleaning of medals and coins as this can increase the wear and ruin the patina. Coins should be stored in polythene individual sachets so they can viewed without handling.

WWI Military Medal ▽

- **1914–18**
A Great War Military medal for gallantry. Awarded to Private L. Goldthorpe, 10th Battalion, Worcester Regiment. Killed in action 13/07/17.
- **£225** ● **Chelsea (OMRS)**

Military Badge ▽

- **1940**
WWII German navy U-boat badge, an early plated brass example.
- **£225** ● **Chelsea (OMRS)**

Cap Badge ▽

- **1914–18**
Leicestershire Regiment Other Ranks cap badge.
- **£10** ● **Chelsea (OMRS)**

DFC Medal ▽

- **1939–45**
Distinguished George VI Flying Cross, reverse dated 1943, in case of award.
- **£450** ● **Chelsea (OMRS)**

Medal Group ▽

- **1914–45**
WWI and WWII group of eight medals to Masters at Arms P. McArthur "H.M.S. Tamar".
- **£225** ● **Chelsea (OMRS)**

Decorative Arts

The market for decorative arts has consolidated and expanded over the last 20 years and shows no sign of easing up.

What is the meaning of the term "decorative arts"? The term in itself is ambiguous but it can be ascribed to an object that has no practical application other than as a thing to be admired and discussed.

By the late seventeenth century the term "decorative arts" could be applied to virtually the same range of objects that we use it for today, for example any objects that could not be termed "fine art" (that is, paintings, sculpture and architecture), thus leaving all other objets d'art such as ceramics, furniture and glass to be classified as decorative items.

The Victorians took the term "decorative" to new heights, applying it to even the smalles space, from architecture down to the smallest thimble, each item was lavishly embellished.

The Victorians showed no restraint when decorating their home, furnishing them with all manner of knick-knacks that their hearts and pockets could muster.

Today there are no rules when decorating your home as an eclectic interior can show off your individuality, for example a 1950s' abstract painting alongside an eighteenth century desk with an Eames chair would more than impress any guest to your home.

Figures & Busts

Figure of Young Egyptian ▼
- **1890**
Austrian terracotta group of Egyptian youth playing a stringed instrument. Gold Schneider signature on back.
- *height 5.5cm*
- **£2,650** • Gavin Douglas

Cherub Group ➤
- *circa 1870*
English Victorian plaster figures on a painted pine plinth.
- *width 205cm*
- **£1,800** • Tredantiques

Bust of Marie Antoinette ◀
- *late 18th century*
A terracotta bust of Marie Antoinette, her head inclined to dexter, raised on a splayed pedestal base.
- *65cm x 44.5cm*
- **£950** • Westland & Co

Terracotta Bust ▼
- *20th century*
An Italian terracotta bust of David after Michelangelo.
- *56cm x 14cm*
- **£850** • Westland & Co

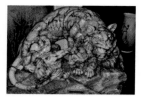

Gilt Bronze Bust ➤

- *1840*

Gilt bronze bust of a young warrior, signed on the reverse Emmanuel L. Hannsaux, with foundry stamp on a black marble base.

- *height 22cm*
- £14,750   • **Gavin Douglas**

Statue of Boy ▲

- *1920*

A naturalistically carved sandstone statue of a boy seated on a rock.

- *height 60cm*
- £220   • **R. Conquest**

Statue of Tiger Family ◄

- *19th century*

A fine marble statue of a tiger with cubs signed by La Maman-Ruggieri.

- *46cm x 70cm*
- £12,500   • **Sinai Antiques**

Marble Bust ▼

- *circa 1840*

A carved statuary marble bust of a lady in the eighteenth century manner, the head slightly turned to dexter with a full wig and two tresses of hair curling around her shoulders and drapery swathed across her dress.

- *58.5cm x 34cm*
- £3,850   • **Westland & Co**

Pair of Cherubs ◄

- *1850*

A pair of carved stone figures of cherubs on pedestal bases.

- *height 146cm*
- £5,850   • **Tredantiques**

Stone Sculpture ▼

- *14th century*

An early English stone carving depicting the head of a man, heavily rusticated.

- *height 22cm*
- £520   • **Dial Post House**

Figurine of Sarah Bernhardt ▼

- *circa 1898*

Porcelain figure of the celebrated actress Sarah Bernhardt by Joseph Mougin 1879–1955.

- *height 26cm*
- £800   • **Succession**

Pair of Marble Statues ▼
- *1885*

A fine pair of marble statues,
signed and dated, naturalistically
carved as a male and female.
- *height 83cm*
- £6,500   • Tredantiques

Figure of an Egyptian Dancer ◄
- *late 19th century*

An Italian alabaster figure of an
Egyptian dancer holding a
garland of roses and standing on
an alabaster base strewn with
flowers.
- *height 128cm*
- £15,000   • Emanouel

Gilt Figure of a Musician ▼
- *1920s*

Terracotta and gold figure of a
musician playing a flute, by the
sculptor Vigoreux.
- *46cm x 41cm x 31cm*
- £2,800   • Bizarre

Carved Figures ►
- *17th century*

A pair of carved walnut German
classical figures.
- *height 50cm*
- £1,680   • Dial Post House

Alabaster Wrestling Pair ▼
- *1840*

White alabaster statue of figures
wrestling.
- *52cm x 59cm*
- £4,200   • J. Fox

Sculpted Figure ▲
- *late 19th century*

A sculpted alabaster figure of a
lady, shown partially draped, with
African headress and seated on a
recumbent lion above a stepped
plinth.
- *height 86.4cm*
- £28,000   • Emanouel

Figure of Rebecca ▼
- *circa 1870*

A white marble figure of Rebecca
standing in biblical dress and
leaning on a vessel balanced on
the wellhead, on an oval base, by
Aristide Fontana SC Carrara.
- *height 82cm*
- £5,000
- Emanouel

Lighting

Italian Chandelier ▼

- *19th century*
Venetian Murano glass
chandelier with brass fittings.
- *height 70cm*
- £19,000   • Solaris

Ceiling Light ▼

- *1900*
A brass ceiling light with vaseline
glass and flower-shaped shades.
- *height 78cm*
- £1,200   • New Century

Bronze Candelabra ▶

- *1815*
Fine pair of French Empire
patinated bronze ormolu
candelabra.
- *height 30cm*
- £3,250   • Gavin Douglas

Chandelier ▲

- *circa 1860*
Louis XVI-style, 24-branch cut
crystal chandelier.
- *height 120cm*
- £5,500   • S. Hatchwell

Ormolu Wall Sconce ▲

- *19th century*
One of a pair of ormolu wall
sconces, with decorative foliate
scrolled branches.
- *height 30cm*
- £2,200   • Solaris

Brass Candlesticks ▼

- *late 19th century*
A pair of French brass pierced
and repressé candlesticks of very
fine quality, each raised on three
winged mono-podia.
- *height 77cm*
- £1,600   • S. Hatchwell

Gilt Candlesticks ▼
- *1890*

A pair of four-branch bronze candelabra on fluted bases.
- *height 53cm*
- £1,950   • J. Fox

Baccarrat Chandelier ▼
- *19th century*

A French glass, 12-branch chandelier signed "Baccarret".
- *75cm x 62cm*
- £6,900   • M. Luther

English Candlesticks ◀
- *1815*

Pair of English patinated bronze and ormolu three branch candelabra, with bronze figures on an oval base with gilding.
- *height 61cm*
- £5,750   • Gavin Douglas

Venetian Chandelier ▼
- *1830*

A Venetian glass chandelier in perfect condition with bronze fittings.
- *height 70cm*
- £3,000   • Solaris

Sphinx Candelabra ▼
- *1815*

Fine pair of three branch sphinx candelabra with original gilding and patination.
- *height 57cm*
- £,6950   • Gavin Douglas

Metal Lantern ▼
- *Victorian*

One of a pair of Victorian gas lanterns, with a chinoiserie influence.
- *height 90cm*
- £3,800   • S. Hatchwell

Bronze Candelabra ▼
- *1850*

A pair of bronze candelabra showing putti as caryatides holding above their heads intertwined branches with vine decoration.
- *height 54cm*
- £2,500   • C.H. Major

Victorian Chandelier ▲
- *circa 1870*
Victorian glass 10-branch
chandelier with heavily cut and
faceted crystal dishes and
droplets.
- *height 80cm*
- £1,600 • Sign of the Times

Crystal Chandelier ▼
- *1870*
French gilt bronze chandelier
consisting of 16 arms with cut
crystal glass droplets.
- *92.5cm x 50cm*
- £3,400 • Guinevere

Four-Armed Chandelier ▼
- *1890*
Small giltwood and bronzed
effect chandelier with four arms.
- *84cm x 70cm*
- £3,500 • O.F. Wilson

Wall Sconces ▲
- *1890*
Pair of Art and Crafts wall
sconces with enamel plaques.
Designed and executed by John
Fleetwood Varley.
- *19cm x 16cm*
- £1,800 • Gooday Gallery

Expert Tips

*It is important to consider
damage and incomplete objects
as these tend to be unique and
therefore expensive to repair.*

Brass Chandelier ▼
- *circa 1880s*
One of a pair of eight-branch
brass Victorian chandeliers with
gothic tracery.
- *diameter 124cm*
- £2,800 • Sign of the Times

Ormolu Candelabra ▲
- *1840*
Pair of four-branch ormolu
candelabra with acanthus leaf
detail.
- *height 60cm*
- £3,850 • O.F. Wilson

Italian Candlesticks ▼

- *mid 18th century*
Pair of carved wood and silvered candlesticks.
- *height 63cm*
- £1,900   • O.F. Wilson

Copper Candlestick ▼

- *1880*
Copper and brass Arts and Crafts candlestick designed by W.A.S Benson.
- *12cm x 26cm*
- 850   • Gooday Gallery

Bronze Lantern ◀

- *circa 1860*
A fine French bronze lantern with glass panels within floral and leaf metal frame.
- *height 90cm*
- £5,200   • S. Hatchwell

Sculpted Group ▲

- *late 19th century*
An Italian sculpted alabaster group modelled with a lady resting against a fountain, shown partially clad, the fountain with masks and dolphins and a shell dish, supporting a carved column with a bowl at the top with a light.
- *height 172.7cm*
- £28,000   • Emanouel

French Candelabra ▲

- *1880*
A pair of French, decorative seven-branch metal candelabra.
- *height 65cm*
- £450   • R. Conquest

Elm Candlesticks ▼

- *1800*
A pair of Scottish elm candlesticks of baluster form with good patina, originally from a Monastery.
- *height 58cm*
- £480   • Lacquer Chest

Floor Standing Lamp ◀

- *late 19th century*
An alabaster floor standing lamp, the bulbous dish shade carved with three adorsed winged female figures, flanked by fruit swags, with a waisted domed cover, the stem with imbricated acanthus over a tapering stop fluted shaft, descending through various further mouldings. On a circular base with three classically draped seated figures.
- *height 192cm*
- £22,000   • Emanouel

Gilt Bronze Torchéres ◄

- *1870*

One of a pair of gilt bronze torchéres with gilt candelabra for seven lights. Heavily decorated stand and base with claw feet.

- *210cm x 45cm*
- **£18,000**   • Emanouel

Gilded Chandelier ▼

- *19th century*

A decorative metal, gilded chandelier, with ornamental grapes and flowers and white ceramic roses with eight candles.

- *height 54cm*
- **£475**   • R. Conquest

Silver Gilt Candlestick ▼

- *late 17th century*

Heavily carved silver gilt candlestick, with scrolled acanthus leaf and fluted design.

- *height 126cm*
- **£1,450**   • Dial Post House

French Candelabra ▲

- *1840*

A pair of Charles X bronze ormolu candelabra with three arms, with floral meanderings on acanthus leaf bases.

- *height 60cm*
- **£4,500**   • O.F. Wilson

Oil Lamps ▼

- *1825*

A pair of oil lamps with faceted glass bowls, mounted on bronze columns.

- *height 68.5cm*
- **£3,250**   • O.F. Wilson

French Candelabra by Victor Paillard ▲

- *circa 1870*

One of a pair of French candelabra in bronze and gilt-bronze on marble pedestals. The bronze cherubs adorned with gilt-bronze garlands, embracing the four light gilt-bronze arms. Signed by Victor Paillard

- *height 152cm*
- **£75,000**   • Emanouel

Expert Tips

Bright work on lamps and electrical fittings should be without rust or dents or scratches, as these will devalue the piece. Bear this is in mind when looking at crystal chandeliers.

Italian Chandelier ▼

- *circa 1880*
Empire-style chandelier.
- £695 • Rainbow

Wooden Chandelier ▼

- *circa 1900*
An unusual wooden chandelier with a nautical theme, incorporating capston, sails, ships wheel, rigging and masts.
- *115cm x 140cm*
- £14,000 • S. Hatchwell

Italian Candlesticks ◄

- *early 19th century*
A pair of Italian gilt ormolu candlesticks with three arms on urn shaped bases.
- *61.5cm x 20cm*
- £2,850 • O.F. Wilson

Painted Lamps ▲

- *1880*
Pair of painted toile Boullotte lamps with pierced metal lamp shades.
- *51cm x 35cm*
- £2,900 • O.F. Wilson

Gothic Candlesticks ▲

- *19th century*
A pair of gothic candlesticks in brass with ecclesiastical designs.
- *height 55cm*
- £875 • N. E. McAuliffe

Sculpted Group ▲

- *late 19th century*
An Italian sculpted alabaster group. The partially draped figure shown resting against a pedestal with plinth modelled as an elephant, supporting a column to the bowl fitting. The plinth is inscribed, "Domte Zoi, Firenze".
- *height 144.8cm*
- £25,000 • Emanouel

Boullotte Lamps ▲

- *1850*
Boullotte brass table lamp with three branches on an oval base.
- *height 56cm*
- £1,500 • O.F. Wilson

Metalware

Snake-handled Coups ▼
- *1880*

A pair of marble and bronze coups with snake handles.
- *height 28cm*
- £1,150   • J. Fox

Decorative Item ◀
- *1890*

Nineteenth century English sea shells mounted on bronze dolphins.
- *height 16cm*
- £2,300   • Heytesbury

Ethiopian Cross ▲
- *circa 1750*

An Ethopian processional copper cross with a presentation inscription.
- *36cm x 27cm*
- 1850   • Iconastas

Cloisonné Vase ◀
- *1870*

Cloisonné vase with polychrome enamelled design of inverted conicle form, with stylised elephant trunk handles.
- *height 31cm*
- £1,400   • Sign of the Times

Pestle ◀
- *1820*

A bronze Chinese apothecary's pestle with ear handles and good patination.
- *9cm x 12cm*
- £300   • Sign of the Times

Bronze Eagle ▼
- *early 20th century*

A German wall-mounted bronze eagle with three enamelled crowns, red tongue and talons
- *51cm x 52cm*
- £750   • Westland & Co.

Bronze Figure ▼
- *1850*

French bronze figure of a girl holding a water jug, inscribed "La Source" by M. Moreau.
- *60cm x 15cm*
- £6,950   • David Brower

Gilt Bronze Vase ▲
- 1898

Gilt bronze vase, signed and dated by Moreau. The ceramic is by Gurin & Keller, Belgium.
- *height 31cm*
- £1,800 ● Succession

Figurine ▲
- 1895

"Nature revealing herself to science" signed Barriass.
- *height 58cm*
- £8,500 ● Succession

Chinese Figure ▲
- 1875

Chinese figure of a man riding a mythical beast.
- *height 26cm*
- £1,025 ● Sign of the Times

Bronze Retriever ▲
- *circa 1880s*

A bronze, naturalistically styled retriever, on a figured marble base.
- *23cm x 23cm*
- £1,250 ● Sign of the Times

Bust of Napoleon ▲
- 1885

A bronze bust of Napoleon with an eagle, by R Colombo, 1885.
- *height 25cm*.
- £3,800 ● David Brower

Bronze Figure ▲
- 1868–1912

A bronze figure of a Japanese girl carrying a harvest basket.
- *height 40cm*
- £1,100 ● David Brower

Bronze Urn ▲
- *circa 1860s*

One of a pair of bronze Chinese vases with shaped dragon handles.
- *height 28cm*
- £1,600 ● Sign of the Times

Queen Victoria ➤

- *1901*

Metal bust of Queen Victoria by
Elkington & Co, England.
- *height 22cm*
- £400   • Sign of the Times

Chinese Priest ▲

- *19th century*

A metal Chinese figure of a
seated holy man holding an
incense burner.
- *height 14cm*
- £500   • Sign of the Times

Reclining Figure ◄

- *late 19th century*

Bronze figure of a young woman
shown reclining with two doves
by De la Brone.
- *22cm x 29cm*
- £1,350   • Sign of the Times

Carrier de Belleuse ◄

- *1860*

Bronze bust of a woman entitled
Carrier de Belleuse by Albert
Ernest.
- *height 30cm*
- £7,500   • David Brower

Decorated Urn ▲

- *1870*

Bronze urn with goat head and
horn handles, a cherub relief and
foliate design on the base,
standing on a green marble
plinth.
- *height 33cm*
- £1,200   • Sign of the Times

Bronze Figure ▲

- *circa 1870s*

Bronze figure of an Egyptian girl
inscribed "Lykketer Jubileum
Dagen, Arne Bastholm, Alex
Conradson, F. Bohn-Willeberg.
Edwing Nerving. Edgar Hansen".
- *height 54cm*
- £2,300   • Sign of the Times

Bronze Urn ▲

- *19th century*

A bronze urn on a black marble
plinth.
- *height 21cm*
- £950   • Sign of the Times

Bronze Pony ▲

- *circa 1890*
Bronze group depicting a Russian man seated on a sleigh pulled by a pony, on a rectangular base by Fab Mophkana.
- *17cm x 14cm*
- £850 • Sign of the Times

Bronze Vase ▲

- *1868–1912*
A Japanese bronze metal vase with silver, gold and shakadu decoration, from the Meiji period.
- *height 35cm*
- £2,900 • David Brower

Bronze Samurais ▲

- *1868–1912*
A pair of Japanese bronze Samurai warriors with gold inlay on a wooden base, signed Koichi.
- *height 38.5cm*
- £13,750 • David Brower

Bronze Figure ▼

- *1868–1912*
A Japanese bronze figure of Hotei shown holding a staff, from the Meiji period.
- *height 30cm*
- £950 • David Brower

Bronze Vase ◄

- *circa 1880s*
Bronze vase of ovoid form with a splayed fluted neck, decorated with a coiled dragon.
- *height 46cm*
- £1,850 • Sign of the Times

Bronze Eagle ▲

- *1930*
A bronze eagle with spread wings on a figured marble base
- *height 34cm*
- £1,200 • Westland & Co.

Incense Burner ▲

- *1850*
Bronze incense burner with splayed lip and moulded decoration around the body, with ear shaped handles.
- *height 9cm*
- £550 • Sign of the Times

Fireplaces ▲
- *circa 1880s*

A pair of cast-iron miniature fireplaces with floral decoration.
- *22cm x 19cm*
- £400 • **Sign of the Times**

Expert Tips

Look out for reproductions and fakes as this is extensive in the field of bronzeware.

Expert Tips

If you are on a trip and considering purchasing bronze you must take into account the size and weight of the piece as handling charges can be very expensive. Try and negotiate these charges with the gallery.

Red Metal Bowl ◄
- *20th century*

Red metal bowl on a clear glass base by Haggenaur.
- *11cm x 20cm*
- £550 • **Bizarre**

Pair of Candelabra ▼
- *1900*

Highly decorative pair of bonze and gilded Regency-style candelabra with glass drops.
- *37cm x 35cm*
- £750 • **A. D. Antiques**

Bronze Wrestlers ◄
- *circa 1860*

A French classical bronze study of two wrestlers on a circular base.
- *height 140cm*
- £12,500 • **C.H. Major**

Bronze of David ▶
- *circa 1900*

Fine bronze by Mercie of David, stamped by F. Barbedienne, showing David replacing his sword after taking off the head of Goliath.
- *height 40cm*
- £3,750 • **Gavin Douglas**

Bronze Scholar ◄
- *1875*

An Italian bronze showing a classical figure dressed in a toga, in a scholarly pose on a circular base, signed "B" Boschetti, Roma.
- *height 55cm*
- £1,800 • **C.H. Major**

Silver Figurine ▲
- *1900*

R. Bruchmann & Sonne silver sculpture on onyx base.
- *height 50cm*
- £1,900 • **Succession**

Harley Davidson Jacket ▲
- *circa 1960*
A unique, American, life size bronze Harley Davidson motor cycle jacket hanging on a bronze rack, stamped "H.G.M 1/1".
- *90cm x 80cm*
- £5,000   • Pimlico

Lion Figure ▼
- *18th century*
A lead figure of a lion shown on all four legs with paw outstretched.
- *32ms x 62cm*
- £1,950   • M. Luther

Bronze Vase ◄
- *1800*
A fine bronze urn in the neo-classical style with foliate design around the rim and base.
- *38cm x 23cm*
- £2,950   • O.F. Wilson

Bronze Centaur ▲
- *1850*
Italian bronze of a centaur fighting a ram on a marble base.
- *17cm x 29cm*
- £895   • Gavin Douglas

Gaul Warrior ▲
- *1870*
Bronze figure of a Gaul warrior by E. Fremiet.
- *height 35cm*
- £2,200   • Midwinter

Mother and Infant ▲
- *1880*
A fine, patinated, cold painted and parcel gilt bronze of a mother feeding an infant while holding a sleeping toddler. Entitled "Mater Nite" by Paul Dubois, cast by F. Barbedienne foundry.
- *height 49cm*
- £4,250   • Gavin Douglas

Bronze Figure ▲
- *1860*
Unusual small Italian Grand Tour bronze of a man about to use a sling.
- £425   • Gavin Douglas

Charity Bronze ▶

- 1876

Charity is one of the large bronze allegorical figures that grace the four corners in the left transept of Nantes Cathedral, and was sculpted by P. Dubois as part of the monument to General de Lamoriciere in 1876.

- *height 60cm*
- £5,950   • David Brower

Kneeling Venus ▲

- 1860

Good patinated bronze of the kneeling Venus on a fine marble base.

- *height 51cm*
- £3,500   • Gavin Douglas

Ethiopian Cross ◀

- *circa 1800*

An Ethiopian processional brass cross.

- *10cm x 17cm*
- £1,450   • Iconastas

Bronze Figure ▼

- 1870

An Austrian bronze painted figure of an Arab riding a donkey

- *13cm x 15cm*
- £1,400   • John Clay

Expert Tips

Make a note of worn gilt as this is expensive to correct.

Mounted War Lord ◀

- 1860

Italian fine bronze model of a Renaissance war lord on a powerful horse, based on the Colleone monument, cast after the original by Verrochio.

- *height 37cm*
- £3,750   • Gavin Douglas

Bronze Andirons ▲

- *circa 1880*

A pair of bronze Andirons in the Renaissance manner, each with a central figure of winged putti looking to sinister and dexter, holding heraldic shields, standing on acanthus decorated columns flanked by two winged dragons on serpentine stepped plinths.

- *112cm x 58cm x 30.5cm*
- £18,500   • Westland & Co

Bronze Figure ▼

- 1860

A fine French cold painted bronze of an Arab Guard charging. His rifle is signed by Debut, the plaque indicating this piece had won the Prix de Roma.

- *height 35cm*
- £2,450
- Gavin Douglas

Bronze Figures ▲
- *1880*

A fine pair of bronze portrait figures of Albrecht Durer and Paul Romaine, each signed Solmson.
- *height 25.25cm*
- £2,450   • Gavin Douglas

Ethiopian Cross ▲
- *circa 1800*

An Ethiopian processional copper cross.
- *36cm x 25cm*
- £1,450   • Iconastas

Brass Tripod Incense Burner ▼
- *1860*

Unusual Renaissance-style brass tripod incense burner.
- *height 40cm*
- £575   • Gavin Douglas

Prix deRome Group ▲
- *1860*

A superb patinated bronze group of Paul and Virginia by Charles Cumberworth. He was awarded the Prix de Rome for this piece in 1849. Susse Frès foundry on marble base.
- *height 37cm*
- £4,750   • Gavin Douglas

Decorated Tazzas ▼
- *1880*

Pair of late nineteenth century leaf decorated tazzas.
- *height 28cm*
- £875   • Gavin Douglas

Pharmacy Sign ▶
- *18th century*

A French bronze pharmacy sign in the shape of a coiled serpent around a chalice.
- *height 70cm*
- £1,300   • Solaris

Tribute to Flight ▼
- *1915*

A fine bronze which celebrated the flight of the Wright brothers. Entitled "Inspiration Humaine" by Kolakowski. It was reduced by the F. Barbedienne foundry.
- *height 19.5cm*
- £1,250   • Gavin Douglas

Singer Bronze ◀
- *1898*

Superb bronze of a naked kneeling woman entitled "Helgn" signed and dated Albert Toft 29/3/98. Cast at the Singer factor as were many English bronzes. This was owned by the Singer family until 2001.
- *41cm x 39cm*
- £6,750   • Gavin Douglas

Furniture

The market for antique furniture goes from strength to strength and is spreading across the world

The traditional view about furniture is that the discerning buyer would only consider pieces made between the seventeenth and the late eighteenth century. How this view has changed today! The market is now open to all kinds of genre, from specialists in fourteenth century items right up to present day furniture. As new materials suitable for furniture-making are developed and with the advent of mass production, pieces by Conran and Philip Starck are becoming collectable, however, for the designer and cabinet-maker wood in its natural state will never lose its appeal.

In the past the appreciation of style and quality was only held by elite circles within the Royal Court. As these limitations have now been lifted the future for furniture looks extremely bright, for antiques right up to modern-day designer pieces. This can be seen by the current fashion among the discerning collector or interior designer for snapping up furniture made by art students and studios across the world.

Beds

Walnut Bed ➤
- 1860

Walnut Louis XV style bed, with elaborately carved and scrolled head and footboard, standing on scrolled splayed feet.
- width 1.8cm
- £6,250 • Sleeping Beauty

Italian Inlaid Bedheads ▼
- circa 1880

Pair of unusual Italian hand-painted iron bedheads, inlaid with mother of pearl, standing on tapered legs.
- width 90cm
- £4,500 • Sleeping Beauty

French Walnut Bedhead ▲
- 1860

French walnut, Louise Phillipe bedhead, with carved moulded arched headboard, foliate design and panelling, on bun feet.
- width 1.5m
- £5,750 • Sleeping Beauty

Louis XV Daybed ◄
- 1870

Louise XV-style daybed with painted and parcel-gilt frame and shell and leaf carving, on scrolled cabriole legs.
- length 2.42m
- £6,500 • O.F. Wilsond

Brass Bedstead ◄

- **1860**
Victorian brass bedstead with turned posts, ornate finials and scrolled decoration.
- *width 1.5m*
- **£18,000** • **Sleeping Beauty**

Expert Tips

When purchasing bedheads and ends make sure that the supporting rods fit correctly as there is nothing worse than an unsteady bed. With brass bedheads, establish whether it is solid brass or a thin leaf of brass over an iron frame as brass leaf often cracks, exposing the iron frame underneath, and looks extremely unsightly,

Louis XVI Bergère-Style Bed ▼

- *circa 1880*
A Louis XVI bergère-style bow fronted bed with carved walnut frame and central oval floral design.
- *width 1.5m*
- **£6,250** • **Sleeping Beauty**

Wrought-Iron Bed ◄

- **1860**
Unusual Victorian wrought-iron bedstead incorporating an arched design, on turned legs.
- *width 1.5m*
- **£4,000** • **Sleeping Beauty**

Carved Walnut Bed ▲

- *1885*
French walnut Louis XVI-style bed, with finely carved floral swags and garlands to the bedhead and footboard.
- *width 1.6m*
- **£6,500** • **Sleeping Beauty**

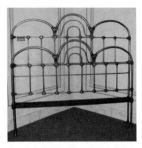

Empire Bed ◄

- **1860**
French Second Empire heavily carved and ebonised four-poster bed, with scrolled broken pediment and turned posts.
- *width 1.5m*
- **£8,500** • **Sleeping Beauty**

Bergère-Style Bed ▲

- **1885**
French bergère Louis XVI-style bed with moulded headboard and fluted posts, standing on turned feet.
- *width 1.5m*
- **£3,500** • **Sleeping Beauty**

French Second Empire Bed ▼

- *1880–90*

A French Second Empire mahogany and burr walnut bed with carved headboard and ormoulu foliate decoration, standing on tapered legs.

- *width 1.5m*
- £3,800   • Sleeping Beauty

Carved Bed ▲

- *circa 1885*

A French Louis XVI carved padded bedhead painted in off white, standing on tapered feet.

- *width 1.5m*
- £5,000   • Sleeping Beauty

Louis XVI Bed ▼

- *circa 1885*

Louis XVI flame mahogany bed with moulded arch, ormolu decoration and beading, standing on turned legs.

- *width 1.5m*
- £3,800   • Sleeping Beauty

Ormolu-Mounted Bed ◄

- *1880*

Mahogany bedstead with ormolu mounts, and inlay, standing on turned bun feet.

- *width 1.9m*
- £3,800   • Sleeping Beauty

Empire Bedheads ▼

- *1880*

Pair of flame mahogany Empire bed heads, with scalloped design on the back and front, with tapered feet.

- *width 1.5m*
- £5,500   • Sleeping Beauty

Victorian Bedstead ►

- *1860*

Early Victorian brass and iron bedstead. with turned, burnished decorative pillars.

- *width 1.5m*
- £5,500   • Sleeping Beauty

Louis XVI-Style Bed ▲
- *1880*
A French painted Louis XVI-style bed with fluted posts and finials.
- *width 1.5m*
- **£5,250** • Sleeping Beauty

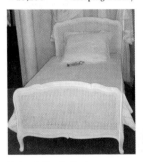

Pair of Single Beds ▲
- *1885*
Pair of single divan beds with carved headboards and swept front, standing on cabriole legs.
- *width 1m*
- **£4,500** • Sleeping Beauty

Art Deco Bed ▲
- *1920*
A painted Art Deco bed with carved headboard and gilt foliate decoration, standing on turned bun feet.
- *1.5m x 1.8m*
- **£3,200** • Sleeping Beauty

Carved Bedroom Suite ▲
- *1785*
Directoire-style heavily carved oak bedroom suite, comprising nine pieces: bed, armoire, bedside table, washstand, chest of drawers, mirror and three chairs.
- *length 2.42m*
- **£25,000** • Sleeping Beauty

Victorian Brass Bedstead ▲
- *1890*
An English Victorian brass and iron bedstead with dipped rail.
- *width 1.5m extending to 1.8m*
- **£2,450** • Sleeping Beauty

Panatière Bedhead ▼
- *1860*
A French ornately carved fruitwood bedhead with baluster decoration and carved scrolled apron front, on bulbous legs.
- *length 1.1m*
- **£1,650** • Tredantiques

Expert Tips

With wooden bed heads, check that the feet are in good repair and also that the supporting frames are intact and show no signs of worm infestation. It is unwise to retain the original mattress, especially if you are prone to allergies.

Carved Throne Bed ▼
- *18th century*
A very rare carved throne bed used by the tribal elder or chief, from the Pakistani border.
- *length 2.46m*
- **£4,200** • Gordon Reece

Bonheurs du Jour

Dutch Bonheur du Jour ▼
- **18th century**
A very rare Dutch bonheur du jour in rosewood, heightened with geometric stringing in ebony and boxwood, on castors. The upper section with two marquetry decorated cupboards, and a central tambour section above three short drawers. The lower section with push-in slide revealing lift top writing surface.
- *79cm x 88cm x 60cm*
- **£18,500** • M.W. & H.L.

Walnut Dressing Table ▼
- **19th century**
A fine Victorian walnut dressing table with brass drop handles and tilt mirror with carved, scrolled decoration.
- *150 x 58 x 180 cm*
- **£2,650** • Old Cinema

Dressing Chest ➤
- *circa 1890s*
Late Victorian burr and satin walnut dressing chest. The pediment with fine carved dolphins and foliage.
- *120cm x 130cm*
- **£1,275** • Old Cinema

Duchess Dressing Table ▲
- *circa 1850s*
Mid-Victorian light mahogany Duchess dressing table with swing mirror.
- *120cm x 165cm*
- **£1,250** • Old Cinema

Lady's Writing Desk ▲
- **1890**
A lady's writing desk with a mirror, and boxwood and ebony stringing and satinwood banding to the drawers. With original decorative brass fittings, standing on eight straight square legs on brass castors.
- *108cm x 107cm x 59cm*
- **£1,500** • Old Cinema

Victorian Dressing Table ▲
- *circa 1890s*
Victorian mahogany pedestal dressing table featuring nine, drawers, two wing tables and fitted with original brass handles.
- *130cm x 120cm*
- **£1,375** • Old Cinema

Louis XV-Style Bonheur du Jour ▲

- *late 19th century*
Kingwood and crossbanded
bonheur du jour in the Louis XV-
style, applied with gilt metal
mounts and Sèvres-style
porcelain plaques. The stepped
superstructure with a three-
quarter gallery and marble top
above a panelled door inset with
a plaque depicting courtly lovers,
and four short drawers. The
rectangular galleried top above a
frieze drawer with similar applied
decoration, on slender cabriole
legs and scroll feet with sabots.
- *117cm x 92cm x 51cm*
- £15,000   • Emanouel

Rosewood Bonheur du Jour ▼

- *circa 1820*
Regency rosewood bonheur du
jour, with satinwood inlay and
mirrored back panel, flanked by
cupboards with oval satinwood
panels, standing on straight
square tapering legs.
- *105cm x 90cm x 46cm*
- £2,995   • Harpur Deardren

Satinwood Bijouterie ▼

- *circa 1870*
Satinwood bijouterie with fine
floral design, standing on slender
tapered legs, with scrolled
stretcher.
- *height 84cm*
- £6,500   • Butchoff Antiques

Coromandel Lady's Necessaire ◄

- *1920–30*
A coromandel lady's necessaire
with fitted interior containing
original bottles and pull-out
flaps, and a stretcher below.
Standing on squared tapered legs
on splayed feet.
- *72cm x 25cm*
- £3,450   • Great Grooms

Mahogany and Satinwood Bonheur du Jour ▼

- *1850*
Mahogany and satinwood
bonheur du jour with a raised
pierced gallery, with four small
drawers and a leather writing top,
with two small drawers below,
raised on reeded tapered legs.
- *95cm x 81cm x 48cm*
- £5,950   • Ashcombe House

English Regency Bonheur du Jour ▼

- *1815*
Outstanding and rare Regency
coromandel bonheur du jour.
This is a fine and elegant
example of English Regency
furniture.
- *119cm x 70cm x 67cm/extended*
- £14,500   • Freshfords

Expert Tips

*When inspecting furniture it is
a good idea to start with the legs
as these are often the first part
to get damaged and need
replacement.*

Bookcases

Biedermeier Bookcase ▼
- *circa 1910*
Swedish birchwood bookcase in the style of Biedermeier, with ebonised pillars and details, plus a moulded top.
- *201cm x 165cm x 40cm*
- £9,800 • R. Cavendish

Pair of Bookcases ▼
- *circa 1900*
Pair of mahogany Victorian open bookcases with boxwood stringing on a plinth base.
- *110cm*
- £5,500 • Brown

Victorian Ebonised Bookcase ▶
- *circa 1870*
Ebonised Victorian bookcase with moulded pediment, two glazed doors enclosing two shelves, floral swag decoration and blue Wedgwood plaques applied to the cupboards, standing on a plinth base.
- *230cm x 137cm x 52cm*
- £2,800 • Tredantiques

Bombe Bookcase ▲
- *1720*
A walnut Dutch bombe bookcase with arched moulded cornice, inlaid with box foliate designs above three long drawers fitted with brass handles. raised on lion paw feet.
- *230cm x 184cm*
- £18,000 • J. Fox

Victorian Mahogany Bookcase ▲
- *circa 1870*
Victorian mahogany bookcase, with cavetto style moulding with two glazed doors, two longs drawers above two cupboards, by Mawer & Stevenson of London.
- *228cm x 138cm x 46cm*
- £1,850 • Tredantiques

Breakfront Bookcase ▼

- *circa 1820*

Attractive George III mahogany breakfront library bookcase with four glazed doors over a secretaire drawer, flanked by five drawers.

- *258cm x 260cm x 70cm*
- £18,000
- Tredantiques

Victorian Mahogany Bookcase ▼

- *1880*

One of a pair of Victorian flame mahogany bookcases, with fine domed tops and brass finials. The two glass cupboards with silk pleating, are raised on bun feet.

- *250 x 182cm x 42cm*
- £13,850
- Ranby Hall

George III Bookcase ➤

- *1760–1820*

A flame mahogany George III bookcase below a moulded dentil cornice and a band of blind fret carving surmounting the double astragalled doors, raised on ogée bracket feet.

- *272cm x 172cm x 38cm*
- £7,800
- Ranby Hall

Chippendale-Style Bookcase ▼

- *19th century*

A Chippendale-style mahogany bookcase cum display case, featuring a swan-neck pediment and Georgian-style glazing bars above panelled doors of flame mahogany. The whole standing on moulded bracket feet.

- *240cm x 150cm*
- £18,500
- Ranby Hall

Rosewood Bookcase ▲

- *1830*

Rosewood Regency bookcase with pierced brass gallery. Two shelves with curved supports, standing on scrolled feet.

- *95cm x 80cm*
- £2,200
- Sign of the Times

Bureau Bookcase ▼
- *circa 1785*
George III mahogany bureau
bookcase with mirrored cabinets
within serpentine mouldings.
- *190cm x 110cm*
- £10,500   • C.H. Major

Flame Mahogany Bookcase ▲
- 1870
Victorian flame mahogany
bookcase with glazed doors and
two cupboards below, with
scrolled carving at each side of
the doors, on a square base.
- *247cm x 115cm x 52cm*
- £3,395   • Old Cinema

Rosewood Bookcase ▲
- 1810
A Regency bookcase in
rosewood, of small proportions
with brass inlay, standing on
turned feet.
- *115cm x 94cm*
- £4,500   • Pimlico Antiques

Burr Walnut Bookcase ▼
- *circa 1835–40*
Early Victorian open bookcase in
burr walnut, with pierced gallery
above a single long drawer and
three open shelves.
- *150cm x 105cm*
- £4,450   • Great Grooms

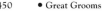

Georgian Secretaire ▲
- 18th century
Georgian mahogany Secretaire
bookcase with astragal glazed
doors above a well-fitted interior
with drawers and pigeon holes.
- *180cm x 90cm*
- £6,500   • Old Cinema

Edwardian Revolving Bookcase ▲

- *1901–10*

An Edwardian mahogany revolving bookcase of small proportions, on a stand with cabriole legs and shelf.

- *84cm x 40cm*
- **£1,450**   • **Great Grooms**

Mahogany Bookcase ▼

- *1860*

English Victorian mahogany bookcase, crowned by a broken pediment. Features three glazed doors above, with a writing slope concealed behind sliding panels, and three panelled cupboards below.

- *190cm x 150cm*
- **£3,250**   • **Old Cinema**

William IV Bookcase ▼

- *1830–1837*

William IV open-top bookcase fitted with four shelves, and four panelled doors below.

- *170cm x 210cm*
- **£9,500**   • **C.H. Major**

Victorian Bookcase ▲

- *circa 1890s*

Victorian walnut bookcase with two glazed doors above, two drawers and cupboards below, made by Shootbird & Son. Complete with with original fittings and keys.

- *150cm x 85cm*
- **£2,500**   • **Old Cinema**

Irish Bookcase ▲

- *1825*

An unusual Irish Regency mahogany carved library bookcase with good colour and patination. Formerly the property of Dr. John Shanley, one of the founders of the Irish Red Cross movement.

- *253cm x 180cm x 48cm*
- **£28,000**   • **Freshfords**

Chinese Lacquer Bureau Bookcase ▼

- *circa 1770*

Chinese lacquer bureau bookcase with broken arched pediment featuring an elaborate chinoiserie design, standing on bracket feet.
- *232cm x 91cm x 55cm*
- £90,000   • O.F. Wilson

Victorian Ebonised Bookcase ▼

- *circa 1870*

An ebonised Victorian bookcase with moulded pediment, two glazed doors enclosing two shelves, floral swag decoration and blue Wedgwood plaques applied to the cupboards, standing on a plinth base.
- *230cm x 137cm x 52cm*
- £2,800   • Tredantiques

Oak Bookcase ◄

- *19th century*

Victorian oak bookcase with two glazed doors featuring tilt top enclosing small drawers and pigeon holes, with two cupboards below, standing on a plinth base.
- *160cm x 140cm*
- £2,420   • Old Cinema

Japanned Bookcase ▲

- *1860*

A Chippendale period black and red japanned bookcase/display cabinet with swelled frieze, with gold chinoiserie designs and three panelled cupboards below.
- *232cm x 174cm x 44cm*
- £12,500   • Ranby Hall

Secretaire Bookcase ▲

- *1830–7*

A William IV mahogany secretaire bookcase with ogée moulded frieze above two glazed doors, fall front with turned handles, raised on a plinth base.
- *230cm x 110cm x 52cm*
- £4,800   • Ranby Hall

Boxes

Tortoiseshell Box ◄

- *circa 1810*

Tortoiseshell cylindrical box with silver gilt trim.

- *height 12cm*
- £178   • Abacus Antiques

Regency Tea Caddy ▲

- 1835

Late Regency walnut-based chevron strung tea caddy with two compartments.

- *12cm x 9cm x 13cm*
- £395   • J. & T. Stone

William IV Tea Caddy ▼

- 1835

Very unusual William IV rosewood sarcophagus-shaped double tea caddy, with extensive brass inlaid patterns and glass sugar bowl.

- *23cm x 37cm*
- £995   • J. & T. Stone

Medical Box ▲

- *circa 1790*

A fully fitted eighteenth century mahogany medical box with bottles, funnel, balance and weights.

- *width 15cm*
- £1,700   • Hygra

South German Table Cabinet ▲

- *circa 1700*

South German cabinet in European hardwoods. The characteristic inlay style can be seen on a portative organ at the Victoria and Albert Museum in London. The shading was created using hot sand.

- *width 36cm*
- £2,400   • Hygra

Penwork Box ▲

- 1830

Octagonal penwork box with floral designs around a central eight-sided star with silver escutcheon plate.

- *11cm x 26.5cm x 20.5cm*
- £1,250   • O.F. Wilson

American Tea Chest ▲

- 1730

Rare early American eighteenth century walnut tea chest with unusual brass decoration.

- *14.5cm x 24cm x 14cm*
- £4,950   • J. & T. Stone

Coromandel Dressing Box ◄

- *circa 1857*
Coromandel dressing box with hall marked, heavily chassed, silver topped, cut glass bottles.
- *width 36cm*
- £3,500 • Hygra

Tortoiseshell Box ▲

- *1930*
Atractive petite Art Deco tortoiseshell box.
- *length 10cm*
- £145 • Abacus Antiques

Wig Box ▲

- *late 18th century*
Lacquered wig box with painted floral decoration.
- *length 30cm*
- £950 • O.F. Wilson

Chinese Dressing Chest ▼

- *early 19th century*
A Chinese hardwood dressing chest with double hinged, mirror-lined top profusely decorated with mother of pearl.
- *width 27cm*
- £950 • Hygra

Regency Tea Caddy ▼

- *1820*
Regency tortoiseshell, double tea caddy with pagoda top, ivory facing, silver stringing, initial plate and escutcheon.
- *15cm x 18cm x 12cm*
- £3,950 • J. & T. Stone

Japanese Lacquer Box ▲

- *circa 1870*
A Japanese lacquer, fan-shaped and inspired box with multi-layered drawers and raised gold decoration.
- *height 20cm*
- £330 • Hygra

Cribbage Box ◄

- *circa 1790*
Fine anglo-Indian vizagapatnum incised ivory cribbage box.
- *width 18cm*
- £1,600 • Hygra

Leather Box ▲

- *18th century*
Rectangular carved leather casket with domed lid and pierced floral designs.
- *length 24cm*
- £450　　　• O.F. Wilson

Georgian Tea Caddy ▼

- **1790**
Georgian single apple fruitwood tea caddy of good shape and fine patination.
- *height 11cm*
- £5,950　　　• J. & T. Stone

Kashmiri Box ▲

- **mid 19th century**
Polychrome painted papier mâché octagonal box with faceted sides decorated with human figures, animals and rambling floral designs.
- *10cm x 14cm*
- £350　　　• Arthur Millner

Anglo-Indian Ebony Teapoy ▲

- *circa 1840*
Hinged carved box with finely carved serpentine lid featuring an acanthus motif, on tripod stand.
- *83cm x 36cm x 30cm*
- £2,750　　　• Arthur Millner

Italian Casket ▲

- **1760**
An Arte Povera domed casket painted and printed with courting figures in landscapes within cartouches.
- *14cm x 42cm x 25cm*
- £2,950　　　• O.F. Wilson

Merchant's Box ▲

- *18th century*
An Indian merchant's money box with heavy iron hinges and banding.
- *30cm x 38cm x 18cm*
- £260　　　• Gordon Reece

Expert Tips

It is important when collecting or purchasing a tea caddy that the container has retained its original liner.
In general, tea caddies that are styled in the form of a fruit, such as pears or apples, are extremely rare. The most affordable boxes tend to be those made from wood or papier mâché.

Belgian Box ◄

- **1830**
Box with an oil painted tavern scene on the lid.
- *13cm x 42cm x 32cm*
- £2,600　　　• O.F. Wilson

Chinese Lacquer Tea Caddy ➤

- *circa 1850*
Shaped Chinese lacquer tea caddy with boldly defined gold decoration and pewter lines, standing on claw feet.
- *width 19cm*
- £650
- Hygra

Tortoiseshell Box ▲

- *1760*
Anglo-Dutch box with ivory stringing and silver mounts on silver bun feet.
- *16cm x 28cm x 20cm*
- £3,000
- O.F. Wilson

Sycamore Box ▲

- *circa 1900*
A small sycamore box with oval pictures depicting Western Road, Littlehampton.
- *8.5cm x 7cm*
- £34
- John Clay

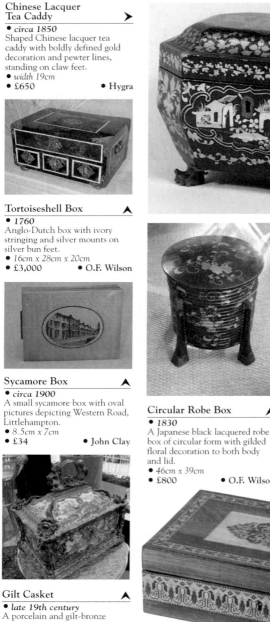

Circular Robe Box ▲

- *1830*
A Japanese black lacquered robe box of circular form with gilded floral decoration to both body and lid.
- *46cm x 39cm*
- £800
- O.F. Wilson

Gilt Casket ▲

- *late 19th century*
A porcelain and gilt-bronze casket, depicting romantic couples in pastoral settings with putti at each corner.
- *36cm x 27cm*
- £12,000
- Emanouel

Etched Sycamore Box ▼

- *circa 1900*
A sycamore box with etched scenes depicting the Isle of Wight.
- *6cm x 17cm*
- £55
- John Clay

Tunbridge Ware Box ▼

- *circa 1850*
Decorative Tunbridge ware box attributable to Alfred Talbot who worked from 1843–58.
- *width 22cm*
- £310
- Hygra

Knife Box ▼
- *circa 1770*
A George III flame mahogany knife box with satinwood inlay and brass fittings.
- *37cm x 21.7cm*
- £995 • Great Grooms

Georgian Tea Caddy ▼
- *circa 1810*
A Georgian Burr Yew Tea caddy with two compartments, standing on scrolled brass feet.
- *22cm x 30cm*
- £450 • Barham

Chinese Ivory Casket ▶
- *18th–19th century*
A fine Canton ivory casket fitted with European carrying handle, lock plate, corner reinforcement and ball and claw feet. The red silk-lined interior fitted with three Chinese pewter-lined ivory caddies, the pierced ivory panelling of the caddies decorated with geometric diapers and floral designs within ruyi-head borders. The casket decorated with low relief panels of landscapes and flowers.
- *13.6cm x 26cm*
- £8,500 • Gerard Hawthorn

Chinese Lacquer Box ▼
- *1830*
Chinese lacquer octagonal box with gilded chinoiserie and floral designs, on gilded claw feet.
- *15cm x 34cm x 23cm*
- £1,850 • O.F. Wilson

Pillow Box ▼
- *circa 1880*
Chinese pillow box made from wood with brass handles and escutcheon plate. The lid is shaped as the pillow.
- *14cm x 31cm*
- £150 • Great Grooms

Korean Lacquer Box ▲
- *17th–18th century*
Lacquer box and cover of oval form, set with a single European engraved floral design hinge and a later European lock plate. The cover and sides decorated with a free scrolling design of flowers and leaves inlaid in mother of pearl, the stem of the vine inlaid in flat silvered wire, all on a black lacquer ground.
- *9.2cm x 37.5cm*
- £6,500 • Gerard Hawthorn

Indian Dowry Box ▲
- *19th century*
A copper dowry box from the Rajasthan province, with geometric enamelled designs, standing on shaped feet.
- *39 x 28*
- £295 • Gordon Reece

Domed Box ▲
- *1820*

Small domed box with central oval panel and fruitwood stringing.
- *height 7cm*
- £850
- O.F. Wilson

Inlaid Tea Caddy ▶
- *late 18th century*

Tea caddy inlaid with fruitwood designs of floral sprays and crossbanding, surmounted with an ivory finial.
- *height 14cm*
- £600
- O.F. Wilson

Penwork Box ▲
- *1830*

An octagonal penwork box with foliate panels above basketweave patterned sides.
- *height 19cm*
- £950
- O.F. Wilson

Necessaire de Voyage ▲
- *circa 1780*

French gentleman's mahogany necessaire de voyage with original interior fittings, including porcelain cup and saucer, glass tumbler and secret compartment complete with tool pad including razors and scissors.
- *10cm x 27cm x 18.5cm*
- £7,950
- J. & T. Stone

Games Box ▼
- *circa 1860*

Extensively decorated nineteenth century Chinese export games box with unusual red figure on lid and interior.
- *width 37cm*
- £2,450
- J. & T. Stone

Sycamore Tea Caddy ▲
- *circa 1780*

An eighteenth century two-compartment tea caddy in sycamore with period decoupage decoration.
- *width 19cm*
- £490
- Hygra

Koftgari Box ▲
- *circa 1880*

Koftgari box with gold damascened floral decoration with the maker's name "Nizamoodeen Mistree Khotlee" inscribed on the lid.
- *15cm x 15cm x 28cm*
- £2,750
- Arthur Millner

Miniature Postbox ▼
- **1900**
Late Victorian oak miniature postbox with original inset rate card, brass plate inscribed "'Letters'", and carved leaf top.
- *height 38cm*
- **£2,950**   • **J. & T. Stone**

Small Lacquer Chest ▼
- **late 18th century**
A Chinese small lacquer chest with three tiers of drawers behind two doors painted with extensive chinoiserie designs.
- *height 24cm*
- **£2,250**   • **O.F. Wilson**

Chinese Tea Caddy ▼
- **circa 1840**
Shaped and lacquered Chinese tea caddy with gold decoration, on carved dragon feet.
- *width 21cm*
- **£850**   • **Hygra**

French Domed Box ▼
- **19th century**
Box with domed lid decorated with faux tortoiseshell design.
- *length 30cm*
- **£950**   • **O.F. Wilson**

Oblong Tea Caddy ▼
- **circa 1770**
Fine eighteenth century tea caddy of oblong form in native and imported hardwoods, with mother of pearl accents, having a brass handle and paw feet.
- *width 22cm*
- **£950**   • **Hygra**

Amboyna Tea Caddy ▼
- **circa 1830**
A George IV amboyna tea caddy of sarcophagus form with side handles, mother of pearl roundels, pewter stringing, and an interior with twin compartments.
- *length 30cm*
- **£1,200**   • **O.F. Wilson**

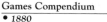

Games Compendium ▲
- **1880**
Late Victorian dome-topped and front opening coromandel wood games compendium with a comprehensive assortment of games including chess, dominoes, backgammon, tiddlywinks and numerous set of playing cards and counters all housed in a front compartment and two lift out trays.
- *18cm x 33.5cm x 23cm*
- **£4,950**   • **J. & T. Stone**

Chinese Canton Enamel Panelled Box ▲
- **18th century**
A fine canton enamel-panelled huanghuali box and cover of rectangular form and regular construction with floating panels, mitred corners and hidden dovetails, set with two bail handles at the sides and a wood lock plate.
- *18.1cm x 31.7cm*
- **£6,000**   • **Gerard Hawthorn**

Bureaux

Pine Secretaire ▲

- *20th century*
A painted pine miniature
secretaire with broken pediment
above the fall, with fitted interior,
on shaped bracket feet.
- *height 80cm*
- £675   • Solaris

William IV Secretaire ▲

- *1835*
An William IV flame mahogany
secretaire chiffonier with fall
front and heavy scrolling to the
sides of the panelled cupboards.
- *145cm x 94cm x 50cm*
- £1,750   • Tredantiques

Mahogany Bureau ▶

- *1740*
Mahogany bureau with well-fitted
walnut interior, various pigeon
holes and hidden drawers, brass
ring handles and escutcheons,
on moulded bracket feet.
- *92cm x 109cm*
- £6,500   • Pimlico Antiques

Walnut Bureau ▲

- *circa 1810*
George III walnut bureau
with cross banding, the fall
enclosing a well-fitted interior,
with four graduated drawers
with original brass fittings on
moulded bracket feet.
- *99cm x 70cm*
- £4,500   • Sign of the Times

Empire Bureau Commode ▲

- *circa 1820*
Swedish mahogany Empire
bureau commode with fitted
interior and fold down flap above
three deep drawers, flanked by
turned columns with gilt mounts.
- *94cm x 111cm x 51cm*
- £6,500   • R. Cavendish

French Empire Secretaire ▼

- *circa 1800s*
A mahogany French Empire
Secretaire àbattant with a marble
top, turned columns and pierced
ormolu mounts.
- *height 140cm x 80cm*
- £5,500   • C.H. Major

Swedish Birch Secretaire ➤
- *circa 1820*
Swedish Biedermeier secretaire, with ebony and rosewood inlays.
- *120cm x 113cm x 48cm*
- **£9,800** • R. Cavendish

Secretaire à Abbatant ◀
- *circa 1840*
An early nineteenth century flame mahogany secretaire à abbatant, with boxwood and ebony inlays and stringing. The fall front enclosing a well-fitted interior above two cupboard doors flanked by turned pillasters on bun feet.
- *154cm x 100cm x 52cm*
- **£3,200** • Great Grooms

Oak and Elm Bureau ▲
- *circa 1810*
An early Victorian oak and elm bureau with cross banding, cock beading, the whole resting on moulded bracket feet.
- *109cm x 98cm*
- **£1,750** • Great Grooms

Faux Bureau ➤
- *18th century*
A pine bureau painted to simulate oak, the fall front enclosing a fitted interior, two short and one long drawer, standing on moulded bracket feet.
- *97cm x 86cm x 50cm*
- **£5,250** • Heytesbury

Boulle Secretaire ◀
- *circa 1830*
An ebonised boulle secretaire of the Louis Philippe period, with rosewood interior, ormolu mounts and decorative ivory inlay, raised on stylised bun feet
- *136cm x 67cm*
- **£2,750** • Ranby Hall

Swedish Bureau ▼
- *late 18th century*
A Swedish late eighteenth century pine bureau with unusual patina, fold down flap with fitted interior above three tiers of drawers, with a shaped apron on bracket feet.
- *height 94cm*
- **£2,800** • Solaris

Expert Tips
Bureaux and desks, as well as chest of drawers, are prone to damage and alterations, so check the handles and escutcheons, along with the dovetailing on the drawers as these should all match up.

Dutch Mahogany Bureau ▼

- *early 18th century*

An early eighteenth century Dutch mahogany bureau with inlaid marquetry of foliage and parrots, and two short and two long drawers, standing on splayed bracket feet with brass fittings.

- *103cm x 94cm x 52cm*
- **£5,995** • Harpur Deardren

George III Mahogany Bureau ▼

- *circa 1810*

George III figured mahogany bureau with boxwood stringing, having four graduated drawers raised on splayed bracket feet.

- *height 104cm*
- **£3,650** • Ranby Hall

Oak Bureau ▲

- *18th century*

An oak bureau in three sections, the upper part with moulded cornice and a pair of arched fielded doors. The sloping fall with part ogée fielded panel, enclosing a fitted interior of pigeon holes and drawers and a part of panelled doors enclosing an interior of adjustable shelves and two side cupboards. On bracket feet.

- *height 240cm*
- **£14,995** • Great Grooms

William and Mary Bureau ▲

- *1700*

Fine English William and Mary writing bureau in veneered walnut with graduated drawers and brass fittings. The slant front with interior of shaped drawers, shelves and pigeon holes.

- *width 103cm*
- **£12,500** • M. W. & H. L.

Secretaire Chest ▲

- *circa 1810*

A secretaire chest standing on gilded lion feet with leather top writing surface. Fruitwood inlays depicting dogs, winged horses and a cherub in a chariot drawn by lions, with turned and gilded columns and ebony banding.

- *104cm x 100cm x 59cm*
- **£6,500** • Simon Hatchwell

Walnut Cabinet ▲

- *1870*

A French walnut Secretaire cabinet with arched pediment and fall front and architectural side columns, on turned bun feet.

- *194cm x 83cm*
- **£1,850** • Ranby Hall

Walnut Bureau ▼

- *1740*

A small walnut bureau with stepped interior. Boxwood and ebony line inlay on bracket feet.
- *100cm x 81cm*
- **£14,500** • Midwinter

Fiddle-Back Bureau ▼

- *circa 1900*

Edwardian fiddle-back mahogany roll-top bureau bookcase having three shelves, original glass, boxwood inlay, leather top writing desk with three drawers below.
- *207cm x 91cm x 48cm*
- **£3,950** • Simon Hatchwell

Oak Bureau ◄

- *circa 1800*

Oak bureau with well-fitted interior and swan neck handles on moulded bracket feet.
- *104cm x 91cm x 51cm*
- **£2,250** • Rod Wilson

English Walnut Chest Escritoire ▲

- *1690*

Fine English walnut William and Mary fall front escritoire with heavily moulded cornice over a cushion-moulded plan drawer. The interior having a secret drawer, with leathered writing surface. The whole on chest of two short and two long herring bone strung drawers. Raised on feet.
- *171cm x 54cm x 103cm*
- **£22,500** • M.W. & H. L.

Marble-Topped Secretaire ▼

- *circa 1840*

A flame mahogany Second Empire secretaire biblioteque with marble top, two panelled doors, with turned columns and ormolu mounts, above two cupboards on a plinth base.
- *143cm x 83cm x 50cm*
- **£6,450** • Ranby Hall

Cedarwood Bureau ▼

- *circa 1790*

An eighteenth century cedarwood bureau with superb colour and patination, the fall with fitted interior above graduated drawers the whole raised on moulded bracket feet.
- *102cm x 91cm x 48cm*
- **£3,950** • Rod Wilson

Mahogany Secretaire ▲
- *circa 1820*

Mahogany secretaire with ormolu mounts, the fall with fitted interior above two moulded cupboard doors raised on splayed bracket feet.
- *height 140cm*
- **£3,500**   ● N. E. McAuliffe

Two-Drawer Secretaire ➤
- *1830*

Secretaire in pale walnut fitted with drawer in the frieze and two drawer below the fall.
- *146cm x 96cm x 40cm*
- **£4,600**   ● O.F. Wilson

Bureau Bookcase ▲
- *1850*

Victorian figured walnut roll-top bureau with fitted interior below glazed doors with bookshelves.
- *231cm x 105cm x 60cm*
- **£9,500**   ● J. Fox

Satinwood Roll-Top Bureau ◄
- *1890*

An early nineteenth century-style bureau in satinwood. The gallery comprises three drawers above the roll-top desk and three drawers below, standing on square tapered legs.
- *100cm x 90cm x 48cm*
- **£6,000**   ● J. Fox

Gustavian Secretaire ▼
- *circa 1800*

A painted Louis XVI Swedish Gustavian secretaire, with moulded ogée cornice above two cupboard doors and pull-down writing flap with four tiers of drawers below, on bracket feet.
- *190cm x 99cm x 51cm*
- **£3,400**   ● R. Cavendish

William and Mary Oak Escritoire ➤

- *circa 1690–1700*
Unusual William and Mary oak escritoire with ogée moulding, map drawer, fall front, three long drawers with drop handles, raised on turned bun feet.
- *158cm x 93cm x 54cm*
- £11,500   • Rod Wilson

Cylinder Bureau ▲

- *circa 1870*
Fine-quality French rosewood ormolu-mounted bureau à cylindre, with galleried top and drawers, with a well-fitted interior, standing on reeded tapered legs and brass castors.
- *52cm x 51cm x 28cm*
- £18,500   • Ranby Hall

Painted Pine Bureau ▲

- *1830*
An English painted pine bureau with four drawers with brass swan neck handles, standing on moulded bracket feet.
- *108cm x 84cm x 46cm*
- £1,400   • Tredantiques

Swedish Biedermeier Secretaire ▼

- *circa 1820*
Swedish Biedermeier birchwood secretaire with moulded cornice, fold-down drawer, with fitted interior above three deep drawers.
- *136cm x 97cm x 46cm*
- £9,800   • R. Cavendish

French Secretaire ▲

- *1920*
A bombe fall-front secretaire à abattant with three small drawers, profusely decorated with foliate design, standing on splayed legs.
- *132cm x 72cm x 40cm*
- £1,150   • Tredantiques

Cabinets

Display Table ➤
- *circa 1860*

Victorian marquetry display table with floral designs and brass mounts, on cabriole legs.
- *74cm x 46cm*
- £2,650   • Great Grooms

Victorian Cabinet ▲
- *circa 1880*

A Victorian flame mahogany compactum with carved pediment, panelled doors enclosing a well-fitted interior with sliding trays and drawers, standing on a plinth base.
- *104cm x 135cm x 57cm*
- £1,865   • Ranby Hall

Chinese Cabinet ▲
- *18th century*

Chinese herbalist's cabinet with Chinese characters and painted decoration and numerous drawers.
- *118cm x 96cm*
- £2,200   • Great Grooms

French Side Cabinets ▼
- *1830*

One of a pair of French Louis Philippe flame mahogany side cabinets with figured marble top, and panelled cupboard..
- *38cm x 81cm*
- £580   • Ranby Hall

Oriental Laquer Cabinets ➤
- *1870*

One of a pair of oriental red lacquer cabinets with chinoiserie designs and gilding, above a moulded apron.
- *91cm x 59cm x 39cm*
- £1,385   • Ranby Hall

Globe Wernicke ▲
- *late 19th century*

An oak three-section Wernicke with three hinged glass flaps for housing geological items.
- *120cm x 95cm*
- £795   • Old Cinema

Empire-Style Cabinets ▲

- *1880*
One of a pair of Empire-style satinwood side cabinets, the central panelled cupboard with a lyre shaped ormolu mount, on tapered legs.
- *75cm x 42cm x 40cm*
- £1,385
- Ranby Hall

Lacquered Corner Cabinet ▲

- *1750*
A George III black lacquered corner cabinet, decorated with a chinoiserie style relief .
- *58cm x 90cm x 38cm*
- £2,950
- Mac Humble

Victorian Credenza ▲

- *circa 1860*
A Victorian ebonised credenza with oval painted porcelain panels with gilt mounts and banding .
- *110cm x 178cm x 37cm*
- £3,250
- Ranby Hall

Japanese Cabinet ▲

- **Edo period**
A mizuya dansu, or cabinet, from the late Edo period in cryptomeria. The drawer fronts in Zelkdva.
- *175cm x 170cm*
- £7,000
- Gordon Reece

Tibetan Chest ▲

- *circa 1890*
A Tibetan chest with carved and painted decoration depicting long life symbols.
- *94cm x 107cm*
- £2,300
- Great Grooms

Biedermier Cabinet ▲

- *1920*
A Biedermier light mahogany cabinet inlaid with figurative and floral designs.
- *height 130cm*
- £3,850
- Ranby Hall

Medicine Cabinet ▲

- *circa 1890*
Stripped and polished nickel plated bathroom cabinet.
- *45cm x 30cm x 15cm*
- £245
- After Noah (KR)

Regency Cabinet ➤

- *1830*

A Regency flame mahogany bedside cabinet, with black marble top, the door with moulded foliate designs on a gadrooned square plinth base.
- *79cm x 47cm*
- £2,800   • John Clay

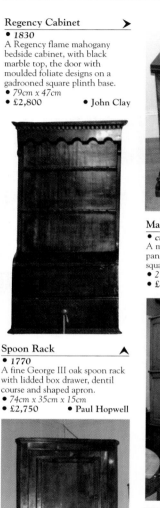

Spoon Rack ▲

- *1770*

A fine George III oak spoon rack with lidded box drawer, dentil course and shaped apron.
- *74cm x 35cm x 15cm*
- £2,750   • Paul Hopwell

Fruitwood Cupboard ▲

- *18th century*

A late eighteenth century fruitwood corner cupboard with shaped shelves.
- *92cm x 67cm*
- £1,100   • Great Grooms

Mahogany Cabinet ▼

- *circa 1900*

A mahogany cabinet with twelve panelled doors, standing on a square moulded base.
- *214cm x 135cm x 61cm*
- £3,000   • John Nicholas

Hanging Cupboard ▼

- *1620*

Oak hanging cupboard, the panels with geometric carving.
- *68cm x 63cm x 35cm*
- £6,750   • Peter Bunting

Tibetan Carved Cabinet ▼

- *18th century*

A Tibetan cabinet with carved and painted decoration showing deer in a woodland setting.
- *105cm x 106cm*
- £2,250   • Great Grooms

Walnut Cabinet ▼

- *circa 1860*

A fine light walnut cabinet with porcelain cartouches depicting romantic scenes, standing on a plinth base decorated with floral ormolu design.
- *95cm x 120cm*
- £16,500   • Butchoff

Corner Cupboard △

- *18th century*
An oak corner cupboard with
cavetto flat top.
- *105cm x 85cm*
- £1,045   • Great Grooms

Cross-Banded Cupboard ▽

- *circa 1775*
An early George III oak and
mahogany cross-banded hanging
oak cupboard.
- *42 cm x 76cm x 98 cm*
- £2,450   • Great Grooms

Display Cabinet ▽

- *18th century*
An eighteenth century Dutch
inlaid walnut display cabinet
with moulded doors.
- *77cm x 82cm x 27cm*
- £4,450   • Paul Hopwell

Expert Tips

*Highly decorative display
cabinets which contain porcelain
plaques must be completely
intact an uncracked. The break
front cabinet or credenza is
highly desirable and it is
important to remember that in
the case of ebonized cabinets the
value can be reduced.*

Breakfront Victorian Credenza ◁

- *1860*
A breakfront Victorian credenza,
with amboina wood, original
painted porcelain plaques and gilt
bronze mounts.
- *109cm x 186cm x 45cm*
- £12,000   • J. Fox

Georgian Bow-Fronted Cupboard ◁

- *circa 1810*
A Georgian glazed bow-front
corner cupboard with gothic style
glazing bars.
- *100cm x 53cm*

Regency Mahogany Side Cabinet ▷

- *circa 1800*
A Regency flame mahogany side
cabinet with oval satinwood inlay
door panels, banded in
satinwood. Raised on splayed
bracket feet.
- *105cm x 97cm x 40cm*
- £1,650   • Ranby Hall

Shrine Cabinet ▲
- *1830*

A rare Chinese black lacquer and hardwood shrine cabinet decorated in gold, red and black, with inlaid mother of pearl. With fitted interior in the shape of a pagoda and decorated panelled doors, on straight square legs.
- *183cm x 177cm x 44cm*
- £38,000   • Ranby Hall

Giltwood Vitrine ▲
- *circa 1860*

Giltwood chinoiserie vitrine with chamfered corners on cabriole legs with a carved x-frame stretcher.
- *104cm x 86cm x 45cm*
- £5,650   • Ranby Hall

Lacquer Cabinet ▼
- *circa 1880*

Black and red lacquer cabinet with brass fittings, standing on plain straight legs, from Yangtze, China .
- *78cm x 60cm x 36cm*
- £1,850   • Ranby Hall

Indian Cabinet ▼
- *circa 1880*

A fine quality Indian cabinet in the Dutch style with two bottom drawers at bottom, and a top and bottom cupboard with single shelf.
- *195cm x 122cm x 52cm*
- £3,950   • Simon Hatchwell

Pair of Pine Cabinets ➤
- *1900s*

A pair of English pine cabinets with one drawer and one panelled cupboard below, standing on bun feet.
- *75cm x 45cm*
- £250   • Old School

Hanging Cupboard ▲
- *circa 1750*

A good quality mid-eughteenth century hanging oak corner cupboard with a moulded oak panel door.
- *100cm x 70cm*
- £1,150   • Rod Wilson

Bijouterie Display Cabinet ▲
- *1837*

Louis Phillipe mahogany brass inlaid bijouterie display cabinet, with pierced brass gallery and banding, on tapered legs.
- *131 x 82cm x 47cm*
- £2,650   • Ranby Hall

Red Lacquer Chinese Cabinet ▼

- *early 1800s*
Red lacquer Chinese cabinet with long panel doors and circular brass lock.
- *92cm x 194cm*
- £11,500　● Gordon Reece

Oak Corner Cupboard ▼

- *circa 1790*
An oak corner cupboard with straight moulding, two panelled cupboards above a long cupboard with original brass fittings.
- *206cm x 105cm*
- £3,250　● Rod Wilson

Indian Apothecary's Chest ▶

- *early 1800s*
Fine antique apothecary's chest constructed in rosewood with brass handles and an ornately carved balcony.
- *38cm x 184cm*
- £3,300　● Gordon Reece

Pair of Low Cupboards ▲

- *early 1800s*
A pair of Chinese red lacquer low cupboards with brass fittings.
- *78cm x 61cm*
- £3,100　● Gordon Reece

Japanese Merchant Chest ▲

- *circa 1890*
A Japanese Choba Dansu merchant chest with a lacquered hinoki and sugi frame and secret compartments with copper and iron handles
- *90 x 95cm*
- £3,400　● Gordon Reece

Chinoiserie Cabinet ▼

- *early 18th century*
Early eighteenth century lacquer cabinet and stand with an English base and a Chinese top.
- *143cm x 72cm x 40cm*
- £11,000　● O.F. Wilson

Chest on Stand ▼

- *18th century*
An early eighteenth century Chinese coromandel lacquer cabinet, with brass hinges and lockplate, enclosing various-sized drawers. On an elaborate giltwood stand with heavily scrolled cabriole legs.
- *161cm x 87cm x 50cm*
- £28,000　● Ranby Hall

Neo-Classical Commode ▼
- *circa 1800*

Semi-circular neo-classical commode decorated with flowers and brass inlay, on turned legs.
- *45cm x 117cm*
- £26,500
- Ranby Hall

Cherrywood Armoire ▼
- *18th century*

A provincial cherrywood armoire with moulded and arched pediment and waved apron, on squat cabriole legs with brass mounts.
- *240cm x 141cm x 56cm*
- £3,800
- Tredantiques

Corner Cabinet ◄
- *1770*

Dutch black lacquer corner cupboard with chinoiserie decoration.
- *110cm x 58cm*
- £3,950
- O.F. Wilson

Indo/Portuguese Cabinet ▲
- *1840*

An Indo/Portuguese table cabinet with two doors on a square base, with pierced silver hinges.
- *72cm x 63cm x 21cm*
- £600
- Tredantiques

Apothecary Cabinet ▼
- *18th century*

A teak Chinese apothecary cabinet with carved roundels on the drawers.
- *68cm x 82cm*
- £1,100
- Gordon Reece

Expert Tips

Always take a look at the underside as well as the top of a cabinet to learn about its history. Check for joins that should not be there, as this is usually indicative of a cabinet that has been cut down to suit modern requirements.

Corner Cupboard ◄
- *circa 1760*

An attractive mid eighteenth century oak hanging corner cupboard with good patination.
- *97cm x 69cm*
- £995
- Rod Wilson

Tortoiseshell Vitrine ▼
- *circa 1880*

A miniature tortoiseshell and ormolu table top vitrine on sea scrolled cabriole legs with shell and leaf decoration.
- *25cm x 38cm*
- £2,595
- Great Grooms

French Gothic Cabinet ▼

- *1910*

A French gothic carved oak cocktail cabinet in seventeenth century-style with extensive gothic tracery.
- *182cm x 112cm x 58cm*
- £2,250 • Tredantiques

School Cupboard ➤

- *1900s*

English oak school cupboard with two interior shelves the moulded panel doors with bun handles.
- *140cm x 153cm*
- £600 • Old School

Ebonised Cabinet ▲

- *19th century*

A fine German nineteenth century ebonised cabinet with detailed Dresden porcelain plaques and figures.
- *180cm x 130cm x 52cm*
- £55,000 • Sinai Antiques

Oak Corner Cupboard ➤

- *18th century*

An oak corner cupboard with moulded dentil course.
- *98cm x 94cm*
- £1,095 • Great Grooms

Corner Cabinet ▼

- *1890*

An English oak corner cabinet with glazed door, ogée moulding, with pierced carved frieze below, on three square straight legs.
- *185cm x 103cm x 70cm*
- £1,350 • Tredantiques

Painted Sideboard ▲

- *circa 1800*

A painted Louis XVI Swedish Gustavian sideboard with moulded geometric designs.
- *98cm x 107cm x 51cm*
- £4,500 • R. Cavendish

Toy Cupboard ▲

- *1900s*

A pine cupboard with two panel doors below a moulded pediment with original brass fittings.
- *142cm x 137cm x 56cm*
- £420 • Old School

Walnut Cabinet ▲

- *circa 1840*

A Danish figured walnut cabinet with single panelled door raised on a circular plinth base.
- *142cm x 63cm*
- £4,650　　• S. Hatchwell

French Mahogany and Satinwood Cabinet ▲

- *circa 1910*

A French mahogany and satinwood cabinet with marble top over a moulded frieze drawer, the panelled doors with decorative inlay in satinwood with moulded front on cabriole legs and ormolu decoration.
- *162cm x 220cm x 42cm*
- £1,400　　• Tredantiques

Double Cabinet ▲

- *1368–1643*

Fine double cabinet of the Ming dynasty with brass fittings.
- *110cm x 121cm x 44cm*
- £3,950　　• Gordon Reece

Mahogany Etagère ▼

- *circa 1820*

Mahogany étagère, with a moulded cornice above three shelves supported by four gilt columns raised on a plinth base.
- *204cm x 77cm x 53cm*
- £8,750　　• S. Hatchwell

Tibetan Chest ◄

- *circa 1890*

A red lacquered Tibetan chest with raised carved decoration depicting dragons and long life symbols.
- *74cm x 83cm*
- £2,200　　• Great Grooms

Mahogany Cabinet ▲

- *circa 1875*

A Victorian mahogany ebonised cabinet with panelled cupboard with ivory decorative inlay.
- *77cm x 44cm x 34cm*
- £900　　• New Century

Rosewood Cabinets ▲

- *19th century*

A pair of inlaid rosewood cabinets with white marble tops.
- *79cm x 37cm x 32cm*
- £2,950　　• Brown

Canterburies

Regency Canterbury ▲
- *circa 1820*

A Regency mahogany canterbury with one drawer and four compartments and carved wreath decoration, on brass castors.
- *34cm x 65cm*
- **£2,450**   • C.H. Major

Walnut Canterbury ▼
- *1860*

A Victorian walnut Canterbury with three compartments on original porcelain castors.
- *50cm x 53cm x 38cm*
- **£1,400**   • J. Fox

Burr Walnut Canterbury ▲
- *1870*

A Victorian burr walnut canterbury with three compartments with drawer below. Standing on bulbous turned legs on original porcelain castors.
- *49cm x 57cm x 39cm*
- **£1,795**   • Harpur Deardren

Music Canterbury ◄
- *1850*

An unusual English walnut, music canterbury, bearing the maker's mark on the underside.
- *65cm x 49cm*
- **£5,350**   • Freshfords

Rosewood Canterbury ▼
- *1830*

A three-compartmented William IV rosewood canterbury with hidden drawer below, on original brass castors.
- *55cm x 56cm x 44cm*
- **£1,785**   • Harpur Deardren

Three-Compartment Canterbury ◄

- *1880*

A Victorian walnut canterbury with three compartments and drawer to front. With pierced frieze to the sides and turned legs on brass castors.
- *44cm x 59cm x 38cm*
- £1,250 • J. Fox

Sheraton Canterbury ◄

- *1860*

A Sheraton mahogany, four-division canterbury with a half shaped carrying handle, removable division slides, and a single drawer to the base, with turned legs on brass castors.
- *66cm x 49cm x 43cm*
- £4,850 • M.W. & H.L.

Victorian Canterbury with Writing Slide ▲

- *1880*

A Victorian walnut canterbury with writing slide and drawer on the base, with turned bun feet.
- *79cm x 61cm x 48cm*
- £2,500 • J. Fox

George III Canterbury ▼

- *1810*

George III mahogany canterbury with single drawer, standing on turned baluster feet on brass castors.
- *height 65cm*
- £2,850 • Mac Humble

Regency Canterbury ➤

- *1820–30*

Regency rosewood canterbury with three compartments and single draw standing on four turned legs with original castors.
- *48cm x 48cm x 38cm*
- £1,695 • Old Cinema

Chairs

French Mahogany Chairs ▼
- *1840*

One of a pair of French mahogany and gilt chairs with canework seats, standing on turned legs.
- *87cm x 38cm*
- **£970**   • John Clay

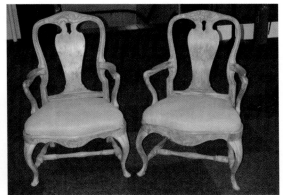

Swedish Chairs ▲
- *18th century*

Pair of late eighteenth century Swedish open armchairs, with carved back splat on cabriole legs.
- *139cm x 63cm*
- **£9,900**   • Heytesbury

Victorian Balloon Back Chair ▼
- *1870*

A Victorian green velvet, balloon back child's chair, on turned feet with castors.
- *57cm x 41cm*
- **£580**   • John Clay

Convertible Child's Chair ▲
- *early 19th century*

A bergère highchair with turned front and splayed rear legs. Easily converted to a table and chair, with a central screw to table base.
- *59cm x 42cm*
- **£1,356**   • John Clay

Hepplewhite Chair ▶
- *1780*

Hepplewhite armchair with carved shield back and painted decoration.
- *97cm x 55cm x 55cm*
- **£4,450**   • O.F. Wilson

Beechwood Child's Chair ▲
- *1880*

A child's beechwood chair with cane seat and spindle back on turned legs.
- *42cm x 22.5cm x 20cm*
- **£235**   • Lacquer Chest

Mahogany Child's Chair ▼

- *1900*

Victorian mahogany child's chair
with cane seat and back rest by
J. & J. Cone.
- *66cm x 36cm*
- £230   • John Clay

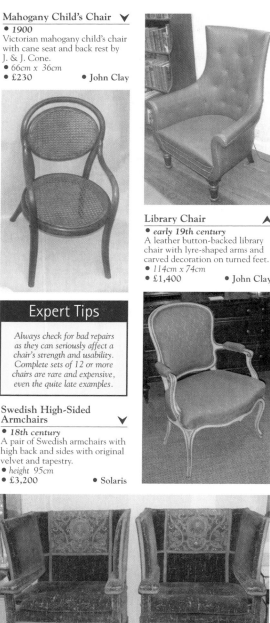

Officer's Chair ▼

- *1901–10*

Edwardian Officer's revolving
ladder back chair on brass
castors.
- *88cm x x 53cm*
- £665   • Old Cinema

Library Chair ▲

- *early 19th century*

A leather button-backed library
chair with lyre-shaped arms and
carved decoration on turned feet.
- *114cm x 74cm*
- £1,400   • John Clay

Louis XV Chair ◄

- *1770*

Louis XV period fauteuil painted
white with moulded decoration
and shaped apron on cabriole
legs.
- *height 85cm*
- £2,200   • O.F. Wilson

Expert Tips

*Always check for bad repairs
as they can seriously affect a
chair's strength and usability.
Complete sets of 12 or more
chairs are rare and expensive,
even the quite late examples.*

Swedish High-Sided Armchairs ▼

- *18th century*

A pair of Swedish armchairs with
high back and sides with original
velvet and tapestry.
- *height 95cm*
- £3,200   • Solaris

Painted Fauteuils ▲

- *1780*

One of four painted Louis XVI
French fauteuils with scrolled
back and straight arms on
turned legs.
- *86cm x 60cm x 47cm*
- £9,000   • O.F. Wilson

Windsor Chair

- 1820
An early nineteenth century
Windsor made from yew wood,
with turned legs and arm rests.
- *height* 88cm
- £695   • Red Lion

French Mahogany Chair

- 1830
French mahogany chair featuring
a carved back with scrolled top
rail, on turned legs with pad feet.
- *91cm x 49cm*
- £560   • John Clay

George II Library Chair

- 1760
George 11 carved mahogany
open library chair with back
swept arms, on cabriole legs and
scroll feet.
- *94cm x 72cm*
- £30,000   • Pimlico Antiques

Mahogany Chair

- *Early 19th century*
An English mahogany chair with
carved top rail and pierced back
splat with curved arms.
- *92.5cm x 45cm*
- £1,800   • C.H. Major

Nursing Chair

- *circa 1830*
Rosewood nursing chair with
original rose decorated
upholstery, on turned legs
with castors.
- *89cm x 52cm*
- £950   • John Clay

Ladder Back Chairs

- 1820
One of a set of six ladder back
chairs with turned decoration on
hoof feet, the carvers with
splayed arms.
- *99cm x 57cm*
- £375   • Red Lion

Spindle Back Chair

- 1820
One of a pair of spindle back
chairs with rush seats and turned
arm supports.
- *height 90cm*
- £1,820   • Red Lion

Walnut Library Chair ➤
- *circa 1830*

A Louis Phillipe directoire library chair carved from walnut with scrolled decoration and shell motifs, on cabriole legs with upturned scroll feet.
- *108cm x 57cm*
- £1,800 • Westland & Co.

Windsor Armchair ▲
- *1800*

A yew-wood Windsor armchair with back-swept arm supports,
- *height l.5 m*
- £1,275 • Rod Wilson

Desk Chair ▲
- *19th century*

Oak desk chair, with moulded back and arms and scrolled lyre-shape back, on turned legs.
- *84cm x 50cm*
- £295 • Old Cinema

Chippendale-Style Chairs ➤
- *1760*

One of a pair of Chippendale-style mahogany chairs with carved back splat and straight square legs.
- *height 94cm*
- £575 • Red Lion

Regency Chairs ◄
- *circa 1820*

One of a pair of ebonised and gilt regency chairs with cane seat, standing on sabre legs.
- *83cm x 45cm x 49cm*
- £2,750 • O.F. Wilson

Windsor Chair ▲
- *1790*

Ash and elm Windsor armchair, with back-swept arm supports.
- *height l.5 m*
- £975 • Rod Wilson

William IV Dining Chairs ➤
- *1830*
Set of six William IV mahogany dining chairs with curved backs. Re-upholstered with horsehair covers on turned legs.
- *52cm x 49cm x 55cm*
- £3,995 • Old Cinema

Child's Armchair ▲
- *circa 1830*
Nineteenth century ash and elm Windsor child's armchair.
- *92cm x 48cm x 42cm*
- £795 • Rod Wilson

Walnut Corner Chair ▲
- *1740*
A walnut corner chair with shaped backrest and carved apron, standing on pad feet.
- *125cm x 76cm x 65cm*
- £1,400 • Midwinter

Expert Tips

If a cushioned seat or stuffed back is still in possession of its original fabric or covering this can greatly enhance its value.

Bergère Chair ▼
- *1840*
Mahogany bergère chair stamped "Windsor Castle, V.R."
- *92cm x 52cm*
- £6,500 • Pimlico Antiques

Italian Carver Chairs ◀
- *circa 1820*
A spectacular pair of Italian walnut carver chairs with ornately carved mythological dog heads to arms and back, heavy leaf decoration to legs, with paw feet. The seat and back upholstered with embossed leather.
- *153cm x 81cm x 61cm*
- £22,000 • Simon Hatchwell

Ladder Back Chair ▲
- *1850*
A Lancashire elmwood ladder back chair with an unusually high back, rush seating, and turned legs.
- *123cm x 56cm x 42cm*
- £395 • Lacquer Chest

Spindle-Back Nursing Chair ▼

- *circa 1820*
Lancashire spindle back nursing chair, with rush seat on turned legs.
- *134cm x 54cm x 54cm*
- £295   • Rod Wilson

Oak Corner Chair ▼

- *circa 1750*
Oak corner chair in the Chippendale style.
- *124cm x 70cm*
- £1,250   • Rod Wilson

Expert Tips

You need to maintain the patina of a chair through regular waxing with a good quality beeswax that is non-staining. Constant polishing with a stained wax will darken the patina and compromise the attraction of the furniture.

Regency Dining Chairs ▲

- *1820*
A set of six regency chairs and two carvers, with curved back and sabre legs.
- *height 81cm*
- £12,500   • C.H. Major

Queen Anne Chair ▲

- *circa 1700*
Queen Anne oak transitional chair with good colour and patination.
- *146cm x 60cm x 51cm*
- £3,450   • Rod Wilson

Oak Country Chairs ▶

- *1840*
One of four oak country chairs, with carved top rail, pierced splayed splat, and solid seat, on square moulded legs.
- *94cm x 48cm x 41cm*
- £1,800   • Lacquer Chest

Nursing Chair ▲

- *1890*
Victorian nursing chair upholstered in calico with mahogany turned legs and original porcelain castors.
- *117cm x 70cm*
- £420   • Myriad

Wing Chair >

- *circa 1730*
Queen Anne wing chair with
padded seat and back, with
scrolled arms, on square legs.
- *176cm x 78cm*
- **£2,750**   • Rod Wilson

George III
Mahogany Chair ▲

- *1780*
A George III mahogany chair
with shaped top rail and carved
back splat with curved arms.
- *97.5cm x x 57.5cm*
- **£1,750**   • C.H. Major

Carved Hall Chair ▲

- *1890*
Mahogany hall chair with carved
top rail, slatted back, solid seat
and turned decoration.
- *109cm x 46cm*
- **£385**   • Sign of the Times

Walnut and Beechwood
Armchairs ▼

- *1760*
Pair of walnut and beechwood
fauteuils. Stamped "Rovmaion",
with continental needlework
covers.
- *167cm x 60cm*
- **£25,000**   • O.F. Wilson

Dutch Walnut
Marquetry Chairs ▼

- *1790*
One of a set of four Dutch walnut
marquetry chairs with shaped
back splat, cabriole legs, on claw
and ball feet.
- *105cm x 55cm*
- **£16,000**   • Pimlico

Scottish Carved
Dining Chairs ▼

- *1810*
A fine long set of 12 Scottish
George III mahogany dining
chairs including two armchairs.
In excellent condition, with good
colour and patination. Well
carved bearing the influence of
leading furniture maker William
Trotter.
- *height 79cm*
- **£36,000**   • Freshfords

Child's Chair ◄

- *circa 1820*
Provincial child's chair with good
colour and patination.
- *87cm x 30cm x 31cm*
- **£375**   • Rod Wilson

Regency Giltwood Armchair ▼
- *1810*

Regency giltwood armchair with painted floral decoration on tapered legs.
- *82cm x 53cm*
- £2,750
- Pimlico

Oak-Panelled Armchair ▶
- *1720*

A George I oak-panelled armchair with a recessed seat and baluster turned supports.
- *116cm x 63cm*
- £8,750
- Paul Hopwell

Leather Library Chair ▲
- *1885*

Mahogany ox-blood leather upholstered library chair, with curved arms raised on sabre back legs.
- *53cm x 65cm x 57cm*
- £995
- Old Cinema

Gilt Chairs ▶
- *1805*

A pair of gilt fauteuil chairs made for the Crutti Palace for Louise Bonaparte, King of Holland, by Jacobs Desmalter.
- *100cm x 76cm*
- £85,000
- Pimlico

Windsor Chair ▲
- *1840*

Yew wood and elm Windsor chair with crinoline stretcher and Christmas tree splat.
- *134cm x 55cm x 39cm*
- £1,350
- Rod Wilson

George I Chair ▲
- *circa 1714*

A walnut George I armchair with shaped top rail and solid vase-shaped splat, on plain cabriole legs with claw and ball feet.
- *50cm x 74cm x 56cm*
- £1,795
- Old Cinema

Carved Walnut Armchairs ▲
- *1740*

One of a pair of walnut armchairs, early Louis XV, with carved apron, raised on cabriole legs.
- *106cm x 69cm x 60cm*
- £14,000
- O.F. Wilson

Oak Wainscot Chair ▼

- *circa 1660*

An oak wainscot chair, with deep floral carved decoration, shaped arms and straight supports.
- *height 27cm*
- £3,650   • Rod Wilson

Victorian Carved Chair ▼

- *1840*

Walnut chair with shield back, carved top rail and deeply carved cabriole c-scroll legs, and stretcher.
- *116cm x 55cm*
- £1,200   • Sign of the Times

Carved Mahogany Chair ➤

- *1780*

Mahogany chair with ribbon carving to the back and top rail, on scrolled cabriole legs with hoofed feet.
- *101cm x 51cm*
- £1,550   • Sign of the Times

Victorian Tub Chair ▲

- *1870*

A small mahogany tub chair with buttoned leather padded seat, and lyre-shaped back rest, on turned legs.
- *50cm x 72cm x 72cm*
- £1,275   • Old Cinema

Yorkshire Nursing Chair ▲

- *1850*

A Yorkshire oak nursing chair with turned decoration and a rush matting seat.
- *96cm x 55cm x 39cm*
- £560   • Lacquer Chest

George III Chair ▲

- *circa 1800*

George III mahogany ladder back chair in a Chippendale style, standing on square-section legs.
- *93cm x 54cm*
- £1,200   • Sign of the Times

Venetian Armchair ▲

- *1760*

A Venetian armchair, with carved moulded back and front, scrolled padded arms and cabriole legs painted with pink foliate design.
- *108cm x 74cm x 64cm*
- £12,500   • O.F. Wilson

Expert Tips

Wickerwork on chairs can easily be repaired as there are many restorers who can offer this service. This also applies to rope or cord seats. Wickerwork may appear to be in good order, but in actuality it will not last under regular use.

Tuscan Chair ▲
- *16th century*
A late sixteenth century Tuscan walnut country chair with leafy corbel finials and carved panels of entwined branches.
- *107cm x 49cm*
- **£2,200**   • Sign of the Times

Satinwood Bergère Chair ▲
- *circa 1890*
A satinwood bergère chair with carved cane back and seat with scrolled top, standing on turned legs painted with a floral design.
- *height 73cm*
- **£2,800**   • Butchoff

Expert Tips

With winged chairs it is important to make sure that the crest of the arms and the wings of the chair are in firm condition as any movement will indicate damage.

Papier-Mâché Chair ▼
- *early 19th century*
An early nineteenth century lacquered papier-mâché chair with scrolled back, painted and heavily inlaid with mother of pearl, on cabriole legs.
- *132cm x 49cm x 42cm*
- **£1,250**   • S.Duggan

Mahogany Wing Chair ▼
- *late 19th century*
George I-style mahogany wing chair with carved legs on claw and ball feet.
- *127cm x 94cm x 81cm*
- **£3,350**   • Harpur Deardren

Irish Hall Chairs ➤
- *1830*
One of a pair of fine mahogany hall chairs with the crest of McGarrel-Hog, County Antrim Ireland.
- *90cm x 43cm x 41cm*
- **£2,700**   • Lacquer Chest

Convertible Library Chair ▲
- *19th century*
An unusual oak library chair that converts into a step ladder, with carved back and hinge within the seat.
- *87cm x 37cm*
- **£1,200**   • New Century

William IV Library Chair ▲
- *1830–7*
A William IV carved walnut library chair with button back, turned decoration and heavily carved griffins.
- *89cm x 66cm*
- **£4,950**   • Pimlico

East Anglian Reclining Chair ▼

- *18th century*
Unusual back tilting elm chair, known as an East Anglian reclining chair.
- *117cm x 68cm x 43cm*
- £3,950   • Lacquer Chest

Laburnum Wood Chair ▼

- *1700*
An extremely rare chair of Laburnum wood, having a tall back with scrolled arms and bulbous turned legs.
- *116cm x 53cm x 43cm*
- £7,850   • M.W. & H.L.

French Gilded Chairs ➤

- *circa 1890*
A pair of heavily gilded Louis XV-style bergères, with serpentine apron and l'escargot-style feet.
- *height 106cm*
- £5,850   • Ranby Hall

Flat Back Fauteuil ▲

- *circa 1780*
A French Louis XV flat back fauteuil, with serpentine drop-in seat, in moulded frame, on cabriole legs.
- *height 94cm*
- £7,500   • Butchoff

Satinwood Cane Chair ▲

- *circa 1900*
A Hepplewhite satinwood-style cane chair with painted decoration. Oval caned back and seat standing on turned legs.
- *143cm x 56cm x 52cm*
- £1,495   • John Nicholas

Shield Back Dining Chairs ▼

- *circa 1800*
A set of eight mahogany Hepplewhite-style shield back dining chairs, with two carvers.
- *height 80cm*
- £7,450   • Great Grooms

Mahogany Dining Chairs ▼

- *1835*
A set of six William IV mahogany dining chairs with finely carved back on turned legs.
- *48cm x 45cm*
- £2,450   • N.E. McAuliffe

Victorian Curved Back Ship's Chair ▼
- *circa 1880*
A Victorian walnut ship's chair, with curved back, circular padded seat on a cast iron base.
- *130cm x 57cm*
- £400   • Tredantiques

Biedermeier Armchairs ▼
- *circa 1900*
Pair of Biedermeier-style birchwood armchairs, with inlays of mother of pearl, satinwood and rosewood.
- *149cm x 60cm x 52cm*
- £5,900   • R. Cavendish

Oriental Elm Chairs ▼
- *18th century*
A pair of eighteenth century Southern Chinese elm chairs with cane seats.
- *104cm x 56cm x 48cm*
- £3,500   • Gerard Hawthorn

Child's Correction Chair ▲
- *1820*
A child's correction chair with turned ladder back and needlework seat, standing on splayed legs.
- *96cm x 33cm x 25cm*
- £1,100   • Mac Humble

Gripsholm Armchairs ▲
- *circa 1930*
Pair of Swedish Gripsholm armchairs with original paint on ball feet.
- *height78cm*
- £2,900   • R. Cavendish

Hepplewhite-Style Dining Chairs ▲
- *circa 1890*
A set of mahogany Hepplewhite-style dining chairs which include eight single chairs and two arm chairs. With splayed back, square moulded legs .
- *height 11ocm*
- £9,500   • Butchoff

William IV Nursing Chair◄
- *1830–1837*
A William IV mahogany framed nursing chair with deeply scrolled arms and arched legs.
- *100cm x 60cm*
- £2,200   • John Clay

Dutch Oak Chair ▲
- *circa 1860*
A Dutch carved oak chair. with
carved oval panels with foliate
designs, standing on cabriole legs.
- *88cm x 42cm*
- £850   • **Tredantiques**

Gilt Walnut Chairs ▲
- *1880*
A pair of gilt walnut French
Louis IX-style chairs, with high
padded back, scrolled arms and
turned baluster legs.
- *158cm x 68cm x 82cm*
- £4,500   • **J. Fox**

Child's Windsor Chair ▲
- *1820*
A child's Windsor chair made
from ash on turned legs and
arm rests, with barley twist
spindle back.
- *height 61cm*
- £635   • **Dial Post House**

French Walnut Chairs ▲
- *1880*
A pair of French Louis XV
bergères in a walnut frame,
carved with a fruit motif on
cabriole legs.
- *150cm x 70cm x 54cm*
- £2,800   • **J. Fox**

Walnut Chairs ▲
- *18th century*
A magnificent pair of early
eighteenth century walnut chairs
with original needlework and
shaped apron with x-frame
stretcher.
- *109cm x 71cm*
- £18,500   • **M.W. & H. L.**

Regency Armchair ▼
- *circa 1820*
A Regency rosewood armchair
with scrolled back and arms on
cabriole legs.
- *152cm x 60cm x 50cm*
- £2,000   • **John Nicholas**

Expert Tips

*As with all antiques, chairs
are subject to the whims of
fashion. This is worth bearing in
mind when investing in
furniture because if the chair is
currently out of vogue the price
will drop accordingly and it is
therefore a good time to invest.*

Swedish Side Chairs ▼
- *18th century*
A pair of Swedish side chairs with
original paintwork with carved
back and shaped apron on
cabriole legs.
- *92cm x 46cm x 50cm*
- £3,500   • **Heytesbury**

Walnut Padded Chair ➤
- *circa 1880*
Walnut George III-style open front, padded chair with shaped back, splayed carved scrolled legs and apron front on cabriole legs.
- *94cm x 61cm x 54cm*
- £1,870   • Ranby Hall

Swedish Empire Chairs ▼
- *circa 1820*
Pair of Swedish mahogany Empire chairs, with gilt decoration on sabre back legs.
- *height 80cm*
- £2,700   • R. Cavendish

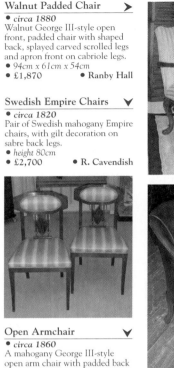

Open Armchair ▼
- *circa 1860*
A mahogany George III-style open arm chair with padded back and seat, and s-shaped arms, standing on cabriole legs with claw-and-ball feet.
- *91cm x 70cm*
- £1,880   • Ranby Hall

Mahogany Curved Back Library Chair ▲
- *circa 1890*
A George I-style mahogany library chair with curved back and studded leather seat on cabriole legs.
- *139cm x 55cm*
- £1,875   • Harpur Deardren

Pierced Back Armchair ▲
- *circa 1820*
A mahogany armchair with pierced back splat and needlepoint seat panel depicting exotic birds, standing on scrolled cabriole legs.
- *92cm x 65cm x 57cm*
- £780   • Ranby Hall

Shield Back Chair ▲
- *1780*
Mahogany shield back armchair on square tapered legs.
- *height 95cm*
- £2,950   • Ashcombe House

Regency Ebonised Chairs ➤
- *1815*
An exceptional pair of Regency ebonised and parcel gilt open armchairs on carved splayed legs.
- *33cm x 54cm*
- £5,950   • Freshfords

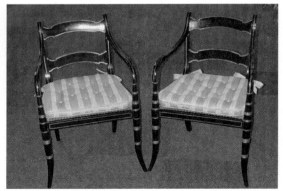

Button Back Chair ▼
- *1830*
A William IV mahogany button back armchair, with padded scroll arms, standing on cabriole legs on brass castors.
- *160cm x 70cm x 90cm*
- £2,350 • Harpur Deardren

Chinese Export Chair ▼
- *circa 1860*
A rare Chinese chair made for the European market with balloon back and apron, heavily carved, raised on cabriole legs.
- *147cm x 56cm x 40cm*
- £975 • Fay Orton

Expert Tips
Chairs with silver gilt and gilt finishes are obviously subject to damage; slight distressing is acceptable but severe wear will considerably affect the price of the item.

Carved Oak Chairs ▲
- *1870*
A set of six nineteenth century English carved oak chairs, with heavily carved back splat, padded leather seat, and turned legs, in the Flemish style.
- *160cm x 44cm*
- £850 • Tredantiques

Panelled Oak Chair ▲
- *1640*
An oak arm chair with a carved panelled back and scrolled decoration on turned legs.
- *108cm x 61cm*
- £4,950 • Peter Bunting

Open Fronted Giltwood Chairs ▲
- *1850*
A pair of giltwood open fronted bergères with carved decoration, on cabriole and knurled feet.
- *67cm x 68cm*
- £6,500 • Ranby Hall

Empire-Style Armchairs ▲
- *circa 1890*
Pair of Empire style Swedish mahogany armchairs with ormolu mounts.
- *height 83cm*
- £6,500 • R. Cavendish

Rosewood Dining Chairs ▲
- *1820*
A Regency rosewood dining chair, one of a set of six, the concave top rail with fruitwood inlay, heavily gadrooned, on turned legs.
- *48cm x 47cm*
- £3,995 • Harpur Deardren

Painted Fauteuils ➤

- *early 20th century*
A pair of French painted
fauteuils in the manner of
Louis XVI.
- *87cm x 60cm x 58cm*
- £350   • Westland & Co.

Swedish Mahogany Armchairs ▲

- *circa 1900*
Pair of Empire-style Swedish
mahogany armchairs with a lyre-
shaped front, on scrolled legs.
- *height 83cm*
- £4,500   • R. Cavendish

French Walnut Armchair ▲

- *1880*
French walnut Third Republic
armchair with padded back and
scrolled arms. on turned legs.
- *150cm x 67cm*
- £475   • Tredantiques

Balloon Back Chair ➤

- *1860*
Victorian mahogany balloon
back armchair with scrolled
decoration to arms and legs.
- *45cm x 73cm x 87cm*
- £3,200   • J. Fox

Satinwood Chair ▲

- *circa 1900*
A satinwood armchair with a
turned spindle rail back and cane
seat, standing on turned legs,
with painted floral designs.
- *131cm x 52cm x 48cm*
- £1,650   • John Nicholas

Pair of Lacquered Chairs ▲

- *1644–1911*
A pair of mid-Qing period chairs
in a wine coloured lacquer finish.
The back slat has a maise design.
- *54cm x 44cm x 95cm*
- £1,900   • Gordon Reece

Rosewood Chairs ▲

- *circa 1840*
A set of four rosewood balloon
back chairs, the carved back
decorated with floral swags, raised
on cabriole legs.
- *height 85cm*
- £1,650   • Great Grooms

Balloon Back Chairs ▼
- *circa 1850*

A set of six nineteenth century walnut balloon back dining chairs with carved scrolled oval back on cabriole legs.
- *89cm x 44cm*
- £2,995　　• Great Grooms

Painted Child's Chair ▼
- *19th century*

A child's ash painted chair with a high straight comb back, standing on turned tapered legs.
- *83cm x 30cm*
- £3,600　　• Paul Hopwell

Lacquered Elbow Chair ➤
- *19th century*

A black lacquer chair with a shaped back rest, rush seat, comb back and slender dorrick legs.
- *89cm x 52cm x 48cm*
- £498　　• Lacquer Chest

Reclining Chair ▲
- *1860*

Reclining chair with scrolled arms and turned legs on original brass castors with original leather upholstery.
- *101cm x 56cm x 65cm*
- £1,200　　• Lacquer Chest

Victorian Bedroom Chair ▲
- *1880*

A Victorian chair with cane seat painted a soft green, decorated with red autumn leaves, standing on sabre legs
- *81cm x 46cm x 38cm*
- £340　　• Lacquer Chest

Nursing Chair ▲
- *1910*

An Edwardian rosewood inlaid nursing chair with lyre back, standing on square tapered legs with a splayed foot.
- *height 74cm*
- £895　　• Great Grooms

Chippendale Elbow Chair ▲
- *1870*

A Chippendale chinoiserie-style ribbon back chair with scrolled cabriole legs on claw and ball feet.
- *107cm x 64cm x 49cm*
- £1,500　　• J. Fox

Chaises Longues & Day Beds

Cuban Chaise Longue ▲
- **1880**
A Cuban mahogany bergère
longue with serpentine back
and padded seat, on claw feet.
- *91cm x 193cm x 94cm*
- **£5,750** • Old Cinema

Mahogany Chaise Longue ▲
- *19th century*
Victorian mahogany chaise
longue with scrolled padded back
and seat, raised on turned
baluster legs.
- *43cm x 197cm x 76cm*
- **£1,995** • Old Cinema

Louis XVI Chaise Longue ▼
- *circa 1890*
Double-ended chaise longue in
Louise XVI style.
- *length 1.7m*
- **£2,700** • North West 8

French Chaise Longue ▼
- *circa 1900*
Mahogany walnut Louis XVI
style meridienne.
- *length 84cm*
- **£1,650** • French Room

Victorian Chaise Longue ▲
- *circa 1870*
Recently upholstered chaise
longue dating from the Victorian
period. Presented with original
marble castors and brass fittings.
- *length 2.13m*
- **£1,900** • Gabrielle de Giles

German Chaise Longue ▲
- *circa 1820*
German Biedermeier chaise
longue, the birchwood frame
with scrolled back, arms and legs.
- *95cm x 183cm x 70cm*
- **£9,800** • R. Cavendish

Expert Tips

*Chaise longues should
be elegant and have great
style, and can be a focal
point of any room. They can
be employed in a multitude
of ways; at the foot of a bed,
in a hall or as a daybed.
Swept feet, although attractive,
are prone to splitting or breaking
so check them carefully before
making a purchase.*

Chests of Drawers & Commodes

Medicine Chest ▼

- *1880*

A Kusuri Dansa medicine herb chest made from Hinaki and sugi woods with copper and iron hardware.
- *45cm x 57cm*
- **£1,700** • **Gordon Reece**

Burgundian Medieval-Style Chest ▼

- *1870*

An oak chest from Dijon, Burgundy. Fine chest with medieval carved panels on the front and back, standing on bracket feet.
- *72cm x 118cm x 118cm*
- **£2,750** • **Old Cinema**

George II Chest of Drawers ➤

- *circa 1760*

Georgian mahogany chest of drawers with two short drawers above three long drawers with brass swan neck handles.
- *94cm x 110cm x 55cm*
- **£2,675** • **Harpur Deardren**

Three-Panelled Indian Chest ◄

- *18th century*

An elaborately carved three panelled chest, with wrought iron strappings and brass studwork, raised on heavily carved cabriole legs.
- *96cm x 70cm x 53cm*
- **£1,100** • **Gordon Reece**

Rosewood Chest of Drawers ▲

- *circa 1880*

A French rosewood chest of drawers with marble top and carved architectural columns. Standing on turned feet.
- *167cm x 84cm x 45cm*
- **£1,900** • **Tredantiques**

Ebonised Commode ▲

- *19th century*

Ebonised bombe commode, inlaid with applied ormolu mounts and raised on cabriole legs with a scrolled foot.
- *138cm x 87cm x 62cm*
- **£3,400** • **Tredantiques**

Apothecary's Chest ▲

- *early 19th century*

An apothecary's chest with 16 small and one long drawer, and white porcelain handles, standing on bun feet.
- *73cm x 55cm x 97cm*
- **£1,350** • **Gordon Reece**

Japanese Chest ▲

- *early 18th century*
Japanese calligraphy chest with
two tiers of drawers with bun
handles and iron fittings.
- *32cm x 20cm*
- £795   • Gordon Reece

Serpentine-Fronted Chest ▲

- *19th century*
A mahogany George II style,
serpentine-fronted chest of
drawers with swan-neck brass
handles, raised on ball and
claw feet.
- *98cm x 114cm*
- £1,865   • Ranby Hall

Georgian Chest ▲

- *1727–1820*
A Georgian mahogany chest of
drawers with twelve small drawers
and turned wooden handles.
- *43cm x 68cm x 32cm*
- £1,750   • Harpur Deardren

Italian Bombe Commode ▼

- *1820*
A walnut Italian bombe
commode with serpentine front
consisting of four drawers and
brass ormolu mounts on scrolled
cabriole legs.
- *90cm x 114cm x 54cm*
- £1,250   • Ranby Hall

Empire Chest of Drawers ▼

- *1800*
An Empire commode with later
painted decoration raised on
tapered legs with circular brass
mounts.
- *88cm x 109cm x 47cm*
- £6,500   • O.F. Wilson

Oak Coffer ▼

- *circa 1700*
A small late seventeenth century
oak six-plank chest with iron
detailing, on straight legs.
- *50cm x 100cm x 33cm*
- £1,450   • Rod Wilson

African Carved Chest ▲

- *late 18th century*
Small African chest, with
eighteen carved panels from the
Morba area. The front has much
of its original paintwork intact.
- *108cm x 90cm*
- £695   • Gordon Reece

French Chest ▲

- *circa 1860*
French oak chest with 32 drawers
with brass round handles,
standing on a square base.
- *129cm x 162cm x 32cm*
- £1,400   • Tredantiques

Expert Tips

*Genuine military or campaign
chests are much sought after.
Rarer still is the navel equivalent
which has ring attachments to
secure the chest at sea.*

Spanish Oak Coffer ▼
- *circa 1680–1700*
Spanish coffer with elaborate geometric carving, standing on a square base.
- *59cm x 137cm x 52cm*
- £2,750 • Rod Wilson

Margot Fonteyn's Chest of Drawers ▼
- *1820*
An unusual decorated chest of drawers. Provenance: the Prima Ballerina, Margot Fonteyn.
- *97cm x 103cm*
- £5,250 • Pimlico Antiques

Mahogany Chest of Drawers ▼
- *circa 1800*
Mahogany chest of drawers with five long drawers with brass fittings, standing on bracket feet.
- *118cm x 107cm x 56cm*
- £1,975 • Rod Wilson

Small Carved Coffer ▲
- *circa 1680*
A well-carved late seventeenth century oak coffer in good original condition.
- *53cm x 108cm x 46cm*
- £1,400 • Rod Wilson

Heavily Carved Coffer ▲
- *circa 1680*
Oak coffer with bold carving and superb colouring and patination.
- *195cm x 144cm x 47cm*
- £1,650 • Rod Wilson

Oak Coffer ▼
- *circa 1670*
An oak coffer carved with a central rose and foliate designs. Standing on straight square legs.
- *45cm x 105cm x 75cm*
- £1,295 • Rod Wilson

Large Mahogany Chest of Drawers ▼
- *circa 1760*
A rare oversized mahogany chest of drawers with exceptional colour and patination, raised on feet.
- *119cm x 94cm x 52cm*
- £2,450 • Rod Wilson

English Oak Coffer ◀

- *circa 1760*
An English oak chest with three carved panels.
- *75cm x 118cm x 49cm*
- **£575**   • **Tredantiques**

Chest on Stand ▼

- *circa 1750*
A walnut and feather banded chest on stand. The stand has an arched apron on turned legs with serpentine stretcher on ball feet.
- *60cm x 40.7cm x 23.5cm*
- **£4,995**   • **Great Grooms**

English Mule Chest ◀

- *circa 1700*
An English oak mule chest with three carved panels above two short drawers with floral carvings.
- *80cm x 125cm x 52cm*
- **£1,000**   • **Tredantiques**

Mahogany Wellington Chest ▲

- *1860*
A fine flame mahogany Wellington chest with moulded top, having five drawers with original turned handles, on a plinth base.
- *120cm x 67cm x 40cm*
- **£2,985**   • **Old Cinema**

Oak Plank Chest ▲

- *circa 1630*
An oak plank chest of exceptional small proportions with good original carving and original iron lock.
- *50cm x 80cm x 33cm*
- **£1,850**   • **Rod Wilson**

Oak and Mahogany Chest ▶

- *1790*
Mahogany chest of drawers with oak and mahogany banding and brass mounts on bracket feet.
- *92cm x 80cm x 50cm*
- **£2,650**   • **Rod Wilson**

Chest-on-Chest ▲

- *circa 1780*
A George III mahogany chest-on-chest with moulded cornice, brass escutcheons and handles, raised on bracket feet.
- *185cm x 114cm x 53cm*
- **£6,250**   • **Rod Wilson**

Carolean Oak Chest ➤

- *1728*

A light oak chest from the Carolean/late Stuart period. The initials "G P AO 1728" carved on the finely carved panels. Standing on bracket feet.
- *76cm x 144cm x 56cm*
- £1,275   • Old Cinema

Oak Coffer ▼

- *circa 1690*

Oak coffer with three carved panels, standing on bracket feet.
- *75cm x 125cm x 60cm*
- £2,950   • Rod Wilson

Architect's Chest ▼

- *1837–1901*

Victorian mahogany architect's deskwith six drawers with original cup brass handles.
- *89cm x 116cm x 78cm*
- £980   • Old Cinema

Lacquer Commode ▼

- *late 19th century*

An Italian lacquer commode with a white marble top and five painted drawers with a chinoiserie influence, on turned bun feet.
- *86cm x 113cm x 58cm*
- £4,800   • M. Luther

Continental Commode ▼

- *19th century*

Mahogany and rosewood commode with ormolu mounts.
- *83cm x 112cm x 53cm*
- £2,850   • Harpur Deardren

Expert Tips

Chests with original bun feet are highly sought after, as they have usually been replaced.

Chest with Ebony Inlay ▼

- *19th century*

Early nineteenth century mahogany chest of drawers with ebony inlay and carved apron on swept feet.
- *100cm x 105cm*
- £1,250   • Old Cinema

Dutch Marquetry Chest ▼

- *circa 1730*

Dutch marquetry chest, inlaid with floral design, the top with shaped front and sides, the bombe front with three drawers, standing on carved paw feet.
- *70cm x 95cm x 53cm*
- £7,950   • Rod Wilson

Dutch Chest of Drawers ▲

- *mid 18th century*
Dutch mahogany chest of drawers, of serpentine form with oval brass mounts.
- *78cm x 75cm x 47cm*
- £7,800   • M. Luther

William and Mary Chest ▲

- *1690*
Rare William and Mary chest of drawers in walnut. The top, sides and drawer front decorated with reserves of floral marquetry. Raised on original bun feet.
- *94cm x 96cm x 60cm*
- £48,000   • M.W. & H.L.

Campaign Chest ▼

- *early 19th century*
A colonial rosewood chest consisting of two sections with four drawers on bracket feet.
- *93cm x 77cm x 35.5cm*
- £3,200   • M. Luther

Victorian Chest ▲

- *19th century*
Victorian mahogany chest of drawers with turned handles and four drawers resting on bun feet.
- *130cm x 120cm*
- £825   • Drummonds

Louis XVI Commode ▲

- *1790*
Louis XVI commode with brass moulding and gallery on a white marble top.
- *88cm x 110cm x 55cm*
- £10,000   • O.F. Wilson

Figured Mahogany Chest ▲

- *19th century*
Figured mahogany and pine chest with banding and graduated drawers, raised on bun feet.
- *120cm x 120cm*
- £770   • Drummonds

George III Chest of Drawers ▲

- *circa 1760*
Rare English George III oak chest of drawers with oval brass mounts, on shaped bracket feet.
- *77cm x 76cm x 44cm*
- £4,450   • M. Luther

Flame Mahogany Chest ▼

- *19th century*

Victorian mahogany chest of drawers with ogée moulded cornice and turned wooden handles, raised on bun feet.
- *140cm x 120cm*
- **£1,075**   • Drummonds

Oak Chest of Drawers ▲

- *1740*

An oak chest of drawers with brass mounts, on bracket feet.
- *height 81cm*
- **£3,850**   • Red Lion

Brass-Handled Chest ▲

- *circa 1890*

A Victorian mahogany chest of drawers with brass handles on shaped bracket feet.
- **£995**   • Old Cinema

William IV Chest ▼

- *1830–7*

Tall mahogany chest of drawers standing on plain bracket feet.
- *176cm x 88cm*
- **£2,500**   • Old Cinema

Expert Tips

Chests that contain a candle box were often given as gifts at a wedding and were packed with linen. The chest of drawers in the French or Italian style with a bombe shape is a highly desirable item among collectors.

Oak Mule Chest ◀

- *circa 1670*

Mule chest with panelled top and sides, long drawer and original chain lock on bracket feet.
- *60cm x 105cm x 48cm*
- **£1,450**   • Rod Wilson

Bow-Fronted Chest ▲

- *circa 1820*

Regency mahogany chest of drawers with shaped apron and brass handles on swept feet.
- *100cm x 70cm*
- **£1,750**   • C.H. Major

Oak Chest of Drawers ▲

- *circa 1900*

An oak chest of drawers comprising two short drawers and three long drawers on a plinth base with brass handles.
- *130cm x 95cm*
- **£595**   • Old Cinema

Queen Anne Chest of Drawers ▲

- *circa 1710*

Queen Anne veneer walnut chest of drawers on bun feet with original mounts.
- *97cm x 99cm*
- **£7,900**   • Red Lion

William IV Chest of Drawers ▲
- *1830–1837*
William IV mahogany chest with carved pilasters and turned wooden handles on bun feet
- *120cm x 110cm*
- £1,350 • Old Cinema

Tibetan Scripture Table ▲
- *circa 1890*
A red lacquered Tibetan scripture table with gilding and painted floral decoration.
- *54 cm x 80 cm x 28cm*
- £1,000 • Great Grooms

Miniature Wellington Chest ▲
- *19th century*
Miniature Wellington chest of drawers made from mahogany with turned wooden handles on a plinth base.
- *40cm x 36cm x 25cm*
- £975 • Ashcombe House

Victorian Mahogany Chest ▼
- *1890*
A flame mahogany chest of drawers with two short drawers above four long drawers, with turned handles on bun feet.
- *128cm x 118cm*
- £1,250 • Old Cinema

Victorian Chest of Drawers ▼
- *19th century*
Georgian bow fronted, mahogany chest of drawers, with four drawers and turned handles, raised on bun feet.
- *140 cm x 118 cm*
- £1,075 • Drummonds

Graduated Chest of Drawers ▶
- *1765*
A good flame mahogany Irish chest of drawers with two short drawers above six graduated drawers with brass mounts on shaped bracket feet.
- *165cm x 83cm x 44cm*
- £12,500 • M.W. & H.L.

George II Chest ◀
- *circa 1755*
George II mahogany chest of drawers with four tiers of drawers on shaped bracket feet.
- *70cm x 68cm*
- £8,750 • C.H. Major

Carved Chest-on-Chest ▲
- *circa 1770*
A George III mahogany chest-on-chest with a carved dental course, canted and fretted corners with original brass handles on bracket feet.
- *170cm x 150cm*
- £6,500 • C.H. Major

Pine Chest of Drawers ▼

- *1900s*

A pine chest having three tiers of drawers with scrolled decoration, brass fittings, standing on bun feet.
- *95cm x 58cm x 77cm*
- £400 • Old School

Blanket Box ▼

- *1899s*

Nineteenth century pine chest with scrolled apron, standing on bracket feet.
- *104cm x 49cm x 52cm*
- £220 • Old School

English Blanket Box ▲

- *1900s*

An English well-figured pine chest in restored condition on turned bun feet.
- *51cm x 99cm x 59cm*
- £225 • Old School

Biedermeier Chest of Drawers ▲

- *circa 1820*

A German Biedermeier chest of drawers made from birchwood with ebonised architectural columns.
- *78cm x 109cm x 53cm*
- £5,900 • R. Cavendish

Expert Tips

To check that the dovetailing is original on a chest of drawers, pull out all of the drawers.

Mahogany Chest-on-Chest ◀

- *1780*

Chinese Chippendale-style, mahogany chest-on-chest with blind fretwork and chamfered corners on shaped bracket feet.
- *190cm x 120cm*
- £5,900 • Midwinter

Three-Drawered Chest ▲

- *1900s*

A pine chest of drawers consisting of three deep drawers with porcelain bun handles with carved moulding to the side.
- *127cm x 102cm x 63cm*
- £495 • Old School

Rosewood Chest on Chest ▲

- *1870*

An English Victorian rosewood chest-on-chest with satinwood banding and oval brass mounts, on a plinth base.
- *194cm x 104cm x 49cm*
- £5,850 • Ranby Hall

George III Chest-on-Chest ▼

- *circa 1812*

A George III figured mahogany chest-on-chest, with chamfered corners, dental course and brass mounts on plain bracket feet.

- *71.5cm x 41cm*
- **£3,850**   • **Great Grooms**

Rosewood Commode ▼

- *18th century*

A Swedish rosewood commode with a marble top with two long drawers below, standing on tapered legs with oval brass mounts.

- *88cm x 112cm x 57cm*
- **£7,400**   • **Heytesbury**

Carved Mule Chest ➤

- *18th century*

An oak Mule Chest with three carved panels with two drawers below with original handles, on plain straight legs.

- *height 70cm*
- **£1,195**   • **Great Grooms**

Kingwood Commode ▲

- *circa 1740*

French Regency kingwood commode with ormolu mounts and rouge royale serpentine marble top.

- *85cm x 118cm x 60cm*
- **£22,000**   • **Guinevere**

Mahogany Tall Boy ▲

- *1750*

English mahogany tall boy with moulded dental cornice, seven graduated drawers with brass fittings, standing on shaped bracket feet.

- *195cm x 107cm x 55cm*
- **£11,700**   • **M.W. & H.L.**

William and Mary Chest of Drawers ▼

- *1690*

An excellent example of William and Mary period chest of drawers with two short and three long drawers on turned bun feet. The whole in oyster laburnum with broad cross banding to the sides, top and drawer fronts.

- *84cm x 91cm x 56cm*
- **£24,000**   • **M.W. & H.L.**

Swedish Bombe Commode ▼

- *circa 1890*

A Swedish Bombe commode with gilded brass mounts made from walnut raised on splayed feet.

- *82cm x 93cm x 52cm*
- **£2,250**   • **S. Hatchwell**

Davenports

George III Davenport ▲
- *1830*

A George III satinwood davenport with slide action top and leather inset writing slope on a moulded plinth base.
- *82cm x 47cm x 58cm*
- £5,250 • J. Fox

Light Oak Davenport ▲
- *1870*

A Victorian light oak davenport with unusual geometric style panelled cupboard on bracket feet, by Lamb of Manchester.
- *81cm x 56cm*
- £3,500 • New Century

Regency Davenport ▲
- *circa 1800*

Regency-style faux rosewood davenport with pen drawer to the right-hand side and fire screen.
- *75cm x 51cm x 37cm*
- £995 • Great Grooms

Piano-Top Davenport ▼
- *1860*

A piano pop-up davenport in burr-walnut with fitted interior and sliding writing surface with red leather inlay and carved supports on bun feet.
- *height 90cm*
- £4,000 • J. Fox

Expert Tips

Small and desirable, the davenport is often found in poor condition as these attractive pieces of furniture tended to be neglected.

Inlaid Davenport ▼
- *1860*

A Victorian davenport inlaid with amboyna, ebony and boxwood, with lift-up stationery compartment, four side cupboards and carved supports on bun feet.
- *86cm x 52cm*
- £2,400 • A.D. Antiques

329

Victorian Walnut Davenport ◀

- *circa 1850*

A Victorian burr walnut piano-top davenport with four side drawers and carved supports.
- *91cm x 55cm*
- **£5,600**
- **Great Grooms**

English Regency Davenport ▲

- *circa 1820*

Regency rosewood davenport stamped "Johnstone & Jeans, New Bond Street, London", with pierced gallery and leather writing slope.
- *80cm x 57cm*
- **£4,500**
- **C.H. Major**

Rosewood Davenport ▼

- *1830*

A Victorian rosewood davenport with four side drawers with turned handles, one quill drawer, with central panelled cupboard and barley twist pillars, standing on bun feet.
- *79cm x 54cm*
- **£2,600**
- **Ranby Hall**

Burr Walnut Davenport ▲

- *circa 1870*

Good quality golden burr walnut davenport with pierced gallery and carved, turned architectural supports.
- *89cm x 59cm x 57cm*
- **£4,750**
- **A.D. Antiques**

George IV Davenport ▲

- *1830*

Campherwood davenport with pull over the knee action, ebony knob handles and fruitwood stringing. The door concealing three drawers raised on turned bun feet.
- *88cm x 60cm*
- **£3,800**
- **Midwinter**

Desks

Pedestal Desk ◀
- *1800*

A late nineteenth century mahogany pedestal desk with original brass handles, raised on bun feet.
- *76cm x 135cm x 72cm*
- **£1,800**   • John Clay

Tambour Desk ▼
- *circa 1900*

A French mahogany tambour desk with Bonn retailer's label. Including sliding and rotating compartmented drawer.
- *144cm x 158cm x 90cm*
- **£14,500**   • S. Hatchwell

Kneehole Desk ▲
- *1880*

A small oak and mahogany kneehole desk with cupboard, one long drawer, and three drawers either side of the kneehole.
- *77cm x 89cm x 44cm*
- **£995**   • Great Grooms

Oak Kneehole Desk ▲
- *1727–60*

A George II-style kneehole desk made from oak with brass handles and central cupboard, resting on bracket feet.
- *height 79cm*
- **£2,650**   • Great Grooms

Biedermeier Writing Desk ▼
- *circa 1830*

A mahogany Biedermeier writing desk with galleried top and shaped kneehole on turned legs.
- *77cm x 143cm x 69cm*
- **£3,850**   • Ranby Hall

Mahogany Pedestal Desk ▲
- *1860*

A nineteenth century mahogany pedestal desk with three tiers of drawers either side of the kneehole on a moulded plinth base.
- *78cm x 120cm x 70cm*
- **£3,450**   • Brown

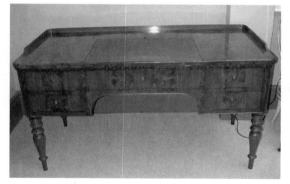

Expert Tips

The eighteenth century small kneehole desk has always been in great demand; some examples in walnut command high sums. However, some late nineteenth century copies are also valuable.

Satinwood Kidney-Shaped Desk ◄

- *circa 1900*

A good quality satinwood kidney desk having five drawers with original handles and good locks. All keys are supplied. Having a crossbanded and leather top standing on string inlaid legs with splayed feet.
- *75cm x 120cm x 65cm*
- £3,500 • S. Hatchwell

Swedish Writing Desk ▲

- *circa 1810*

Swedish Empire mahogany writing desk with drawers and brass decorated handles.
- *75cm x 94cm x 51cm*
- £3,900 • R. Cavendish

Chippendale-Style Writing Table ▼

- *circa 1900*

A Chippendale-style writing table comprising one long drawer and two side drawers on either side of the kneehole. All drawers are fitted with drop handles. The whole is raised on architectural carved legs.
- *77cm x 126cm x 60cm*
- £4,950 • Brown

Rosewood Desk ▼

- *circa 1870s*

Small Victorian rosewood desk with a writing slope concealing fitted interior and original brass handles on cabriole legs.
- *93cm x 55cm*
- £1,800 • Sign of the Times

Lacquer Kneehole Desk ▲

- *circa 1880s*

Black lacquer and gilt kneehole desk, of colonial influence.
- *103cm x 103cm*
- £1,700 • Sign of the Times

Expert Tips

The small lady's writing desk, also known as an escritoire, if well proportioned, delicate and featuring good veneers, will always be desirable and achieve a high value.
The Carlton House desk is also in demand among collectors, especially if it is in satinwood and has applied painted decoration.
When purchasing this type of desk, keep a keen eye on the elegance, lightness and quality of the overall concept of the design, taking special note of the legs.

Lady's Writing Desk   ▼
- *1825*
Rare lady's writing desk in burr ash. Stamped "Gillows of Lancaster".
- *93cm x 73cm x 53cm*
- £14,500   • Ashcombe

Victorian Oak Desk   ◀
- *1880*
An unusual oak desk with four drawers to the left of the kneehole, and a unusual filing frame with cupboard and leather writing top.
- *77cm x 153cm x 82cm*
- £1,995   • Old Cinema

Chinese Lacquered Desk ▲
- *1870*
A red lacquer Chinese desk with three drawers above ornately carved kneehole.
- *height 95cm*
- £1,585   • Ranby Hall

Satinwood Writing Table ▼
- *1870*
A nineteenth century satinwood bow-fronted writing table with three drawers and curved apron front and brass fittings on straight legs with brass castors.
- *79cm x 114 cm x 55cm*
- £1,350   • Great Grooms

Walnut Kneehole Desk   ▲
- *1870*
A walnut desk with four small drawers each side of the kneehole, and one central drawer and cupboard, with leather writing top, standing on bracket feet and moulded base.
- *78cm x 107cm x 66cm*
- £2,400   • Old Cinema

Victorian Partner's Desk

- *circa 1870*
Victorian partner's desk made from mahogany with turned wooden handles on a moulded plinth base.
- *77cm x 168cm x 120cm*
- **£6,500**   • Brown

Regency Pedestal Desk

- **1820**
Regency rosewood pedestal desk with circular inlay top, central long drawer, and five side drawers either side of the kneehole.
- *78cm x 143cm x 57cm*
- **£4,250**   • Ranby Hall

Victorian Library Desk

- **1870**
A Victorian oak library desk with one single long drawer and four drawers either side of the kneehole.
- *75cm x 170cm*
- **£4,800**   • Ranby Hall

Partner's Writing Table

- *circa 1860*
An English mahogany partner's writing table with three drawers, a black leather top and turned legs on original castors.
- *36.5cm x 150cm*
- **£4,250**   • C.H. Major

Japanese Desk

- *early 19th century*
A Japanese Tieli wood desk from the Yunnan Province with two small drawers and one long one, standing on square straight legs with a pierced broken ice stretcher.
- *82cm x 122cm x 67cm*
- **£3,200**   • Gordon Reece

Expert Tips

The exception to the small elegant, well-proportioned desk is the massive partner's desk, where the attributes to consider are completely opposite. This now becomes an object that must exude grandness, power and authority. Quality is of the utmost importance. Desks of this size with heavily carved decoration or with ormolu mounts all add to the spectacle. In fact, light colour woods such as satinwood or maple can often detract these large pieces.

Figured Walnut Desk ➤
- *1837–1901*

Continental figured walnut desk with ebonised mouldings and architectural columns with eight drawers either side of the kneehole.
- *80cm x 166cm x 85cm*
- **£6,975**   • Old Cinema

Louis XVI Bureau Plat ▲
- *circa 1780*

A Louis XVI bureau plat cross banded and veneered, in the manner of Reisener with leather lined top. The panelled frieze with three drawers, on square tapering fluted legs, mounted with chandelles.
- *98cm x 110cm*
- **£6,500**   • Butchoff

Mahogany Partner's Desk ▼
- *circa 1810*

A large George III partner's desk in figured light mahogany. Provenance: the American author Sydney Sheldon.
- *162cm x 89cm*
- **£20,000**   • Pimlico

Satinwood Desk ▼
- *1870*

A lady's satinwood writing desk wiith leather writing top on tapered legs with brass castors.
- *81cm x 72cm x 58cm*
- **£2,800**   • J. Fox

Carlton House Desk ▼
- *1890*

Mahogany Carlton House desk with a brass gallery and a horseshoe arrangement of drawers, including a raised writing slide, on tapered legs.
- *143cm x 76cm*
- **£9,000**   • J. Fox

Edwardian Desk ▼
- *1908*

Edwardian rosewood writing desk with inlaid foliate designs on the drawers, standing on tapered legs with brass castors.
- *73cm x 107cm x 57cm*
- **£3,800**   • J. Fox

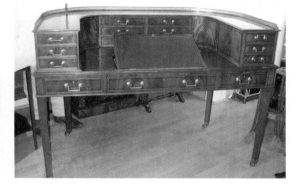

Dining Tables

Regency Dining Table ➤
- *1820*
A fine Regency mahogany
extending dining table made by
Thomas Wilkinson of London,
with a scissor-action lazy tongs
mechanism for extending the
table.
- *height 86cm*
- **£1,765**   • **Freshfords**

Expert Tips

*When looking at a dining table,
consider whether your current
set of chairs are the correct
height for the table you wish to
purchase. When considering
D- end tables, always inspect
the condition of the leaves
and their colour, as these leaves
have often been stored and
appear darker than the rest of
the table. Here again, it is
important that the patina of the
dining surface of the table is
without cracks or gauges, and
the surface should be level and
not warped or wavy.*

French Dining Table ▼
- *late 19th century*
French fruitwood provincial
farmhouse table.
- *76cm x 200cm*
- **£1,950**   • **Old Cinema**

Extendable Dining Table ▲
- *circa 1870*
A Victorian mahogany table with
baluster fluted legs, extendable to
300cm.
- *74cm x 138cm x 150cm*
- **£3,500**   • **Tredantiques**

Mahogany Three-Leaved
Dining Table ▼
- *1885*
Victorian mahogany dining table
with three leaves on turned legs
with original castors.
- *74cm x 122cm*
- **£4,250**   • **Old Cinema**

Victorian Dining Table ▲
- *1837–1901*
Victorian dining table in its
original condition, with figured
mahogany.
- *height 74cm*
- **£3,750**   • **Old Cinema**

Mahogany Table ➤

- *19th century*

A mahogany extending dining table with two inserts standing on turned legs.
- *height 225cm*
- **£4,600**　　• Drummonds

Two-Leaved Dining Table ▲

- *1830*

Early nineteenth century two-leaf mahogany draw-leaf dining table raised on turned and carved legs with original castors.
- *width 130cm*
- **£16,500**　　• Midwinter

Cuban Mahogany Table ▼

- *19th century*

A Victorian Cuban mahogany three-leaf dining table of wide proportions with heavily carved and turned legs on brass castors.
- *300cm x 105cm*
- **£4,950**　　• Old Cinema

Circular Dining Table ▼

- *early 19th century*

Irish-made circular mahogany table with three leaves, on carved and turned legs with original castors.
- *114 cm x 180cm*
- **£5,200**　　• Drummonds

Swedish Dining Table ▲

- *circa 1920*

Swedish Biedermeier-style dining table made from birchwood, with masur birch banding on a square pedestal base.
- *136cm x 196cm*
- **£10,500**　　• R. Cavendish

Extending Table ▼

- *circa 1840*

Cuban mahogany-top extending table, with tapered legs and brass tips. Supplied complete with original mahogany chairs.
- *width 180cm*
- **£3,750**　　• Abbey Green

Doors

Church Door ▲
- *18th century*
Eighteenth century moulded
panelled oak church doors after a
Tudor style, with original lock
and handle.
- *90cm x 160cm*
- **£975**   • Drummonds

Dynastic Tribal Door ▲
- *18th century*
Dynastic tribal door from central
India. Created for the chieftain of
the Gond tribe, a Dravidian
group of Primitives who are
animist believers.
- *145cm x 90cm*
- **£1,450**   • Gordon Reece

Oak Doors ▼
- *18th century*
Pair of eighteenth century oak
doors with heavily carved and
moulded panelling
- *130cm x 203cm*
- **£2,450**   • Drummonds

Curved Mahogany Doors ▼
- *19th century*
A pair of three-panelled
mahogany doors with carved
borders, and brass handles.
- *210cm x 90cm*
- **£860**   • Drummonds

White Painted Door ▲
- *circa 1930*
An English, white painted, solid
front entrance door with brass
locks and fittings.
- *210cm x 130cm*
- **£1,220**   • Drummonds

Gothic Church Doors ▲
- *19th century*
A pair of arch gothic church
entrance doors with original
iron fittings.
- *245cm x 150cm*
- **£2,420**   • Drummonds

Victorian Mahogany Door ▲

- *circa 1840s*
Early Victorian mahogany four-panelled door with original brass fittings.
- *200cm x 75cm*
- **£2,100**   • Drummonds

Gothic Oak Doors ▲

- *Late 19th century*
Oak-panelled doors with gothic tracery, original brass fittings and stained glass windows.
- *101cm x 226cm*
- **£850**   • Drummonds

Linen Fold Door ▼

- *18th century*
Light oak linen fold panelled door.
- *300cm x 120cm*
- **£1,350**   • Drummonds

Indian Panelled Doors ▼

- *18th century*
Antique panelled door with elaborate strapwork and floral decorated brass.
- *192cm x 120cm*
- **£1,250**   • Gordon Reece

Victorian Slatted Doors ▲

- *19th century*
A pair of Victorian oak-slatted doors with original scrolled iron hinges and fittings.
- *165cm x 219cm*
- **£1,475**   • Drummonds

Panelled Mahogany Door ▲

- *19th century*
Mahogany six panelled door, with no fittings and the original "PRIVATE" sign on the front.
- *200cm x 90cm*
- **£875**   • Drummonds

Expert Tips

Church doors with their elaborate iron hinges are sought after by garden designers for use within a garden scheme

Dressers

Oak Dresser ▼
- *18th century*

A fine quality English eighteenth century oak dresser with two shelves above a base with three drawers and moulded cupboard doors with turned wooden handles.
- *height 190cm*
- £8,875   • A.D. Antiques

Dresser Base ▼
- *18th century*

A provincial eighteenth century oak dresser base with three drawers with original swan neck handles on turned legs.
- *83cm x 210cm x 49.5cm*
- £4,995   • Great Grooms

Regency Sideboard ▲
- *circa 1825*

A Regency mahogany breakfront sideboard with ebony stringing on turned and fluted tapered legs.
- *95cm x 152cm x 72cm*
- £3,800   • Tredantiques

Oak Court Cupboard ▲
- *1740*

A Welsh oak court cupboard with three moulded cupboards above three drawers and two panelled cupboards on moulded bracket feet.
- *191cm x 146cm x 52cm*
- £7,500   • Peter Bunting

Painted Pine Dresser ➤
- *circa 1790*

An pine Welsh dresser with painted grain effect.
- *211cm x 159cm x 52cm*
- £5,500   • Rod Wilson

Altar Dresser ▲
- *1775*

Antique Chinese altar dresser with four drawers with a humped back stretcher beneath cylindrical legs with two cross numbers.
- *83cm x 46cm x 22cm*
- £4,500   • Gordon Reece

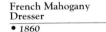

Welsh Dresser ▲

- *circa 1740*

A Welsh oak dresser with three shelves flanked by spice panelled cupboards, standing on bracket feet and brass fittings.
- *186cm x 136cm x 49cm*
- £9,500 • **Rod Wilson**

Welsh Deuddiarw ▲

- *circa 1740*

An original eighteenth century Welsh deuddiarw. The upper section with cornice above panelled cupboards.
- *177cm x 104cm x 52cm*
- £5,950 • **Rod Wilson**

Victorian Mahogany Chiffonier ➤

- *1850*

Victorian mahogany chiffonier with long drawer above two panelled cupboards, standing on small bun feet.
- *91cm x 42cm x 104cm*
- £590 • **Tredantiques**

Court Cupboard ▼

- **1691**

A Westmoreland oak court cupboard, with overhanging cornice and turned decoration with turned wood handles and good patina.
- *160cm x 133cm x 56cm*
- £7,950 • **Peter Bunting**

French Mahogany Dresser ▼

- **1860**

A fine Victorian figured mahogany dresser with two shelves, the back having a scallop design, with two drawers and panelled cupboards below, standing on bun feet.
- *169cm x 123cm x 46cm*
- £1,800 • **Tredantiques**

English Oak Dresser ◄

- *circa 1760*

An oak dresser with carved frieze above three shelves with a solid back, the dresser base with three tiers of drawers flanked by two moulded cupboard doors.
- *191cm x 181cm x 59cm*
- £5,500 • **Rod Wilson**

Pine Dresser ▲
- *1900s*

Pine dresser with original glazed doors with two interior shelves above two drawers and two cupboards, with brass fittings to the cupboards, complete with original brass key.
- *180cm x 103cm x 52cm*
- £600 • Old School

Rosewood Chiffonier ▲
- *Regency*

Regency figured rosewood chiffonier with carved back and central ormolu decoration above a glass door, standing on turned bun feet.
- *125cm x 63cm x 38cm*
- £2,150 • S. Duggan

Oak Dresser Base ◄
- *1780*

A fine mid-eighteenth century oak dresser base, with three panelled cupboards and brass swan neck handles.
- *87cm x 173cm x 49cm*
- £6,750 • Rod Wilson

William IV Sideboard ▲
- *1820*

William IV flame mahogany sideboard with carved back on double pedestal base. In the manner of Thomas Hope.
- *116cm x 180cm x 49cm*
- £4,650 • Ranby Hall

Library Cabinet ▲
- *circa 1720*

Rare George I library cabinet with excellent detail including writing slide and secret drawer.
- *205cm x 105cm x 42cm*
- £14,500 • Rod Wilson

Maplewood Chiffonier ◄
- *1885*

An early Victorian maplewood chiffonier with open shelf and back board and two glazed cupboard doors flanked by turned barley twist columns.
- *138cm x 107cm x 40cm*
- £2,950 • S. Duggan

Glazed Pine Dresser ▼

- **1900s**

Pine dresser consisting of three
glazed doors with shelving above
a pine base, with two shallow
drawers and panelled cupboard
with brass fittings.

- *128cm x 98cm x 55cm*
- **£700**   • Old School

Decorated Court Cupboard ▼

- **1760**

An oak court cupboard with
moulded cornice above a plain
frieze with drop finials, the two-
cupboard door flanking an arched
panel.

- *166cm x 146cm x 61cm*
- **£6,850**   • Rod Wilson

Buffet de Corps ▲

- **18th century**

A rare yew wood buffet de corps
with three tiers of shelves above a
base with three drawers and two
cupboard doors.

- *20cm x 137cm*
- **£5,950**   • Red Lion

Carved Oak Dresser ▲

- **late 17th century**

English oak dresser with heavily
carved sides and doors, standing
on straight square feet with iron
fittings.

- *131cm x 172cm x 56cm*
- **£2,500**   • Tredantiques

Deuddiarw Carved Cupboard ▲

- **1760**

An oak deuddiarw carved dresser
with good patina, with carved
pediment and drop finials above
two cupboards, three drawers and
panel doors.

- *167cm x 143cm*
- **£6,850**   • Red Lion

Painted French Dresser ◄

- **18th century**

French painted pine dresser with
two glass doors, and panelled
cupboards below.on a square base.

- *height 183cm*
- **£3,400**   • Solaris Antiques

Corner Cupboard ▼

- *1800*

A fine George III one-piece standing corner cupboard in faded mahogany. The upper section having 18 panel octagonal doors. The lower section with central drawer above two panelled moulded doors.
- *218cm x 110cm*
- £14,500   • M. W. & H. L.

English Oak Dresser ▼

- *1780*

An English oak dresser with moulded pediment and carved apron front, having four drawers on turned legs.
- *200cm x 206cm*
- £6,950   • Red Lion

Oak Dresser Base ▲

- *1770*

An English oak dresser with carved fretwork, two shelves above a dresser base with three drawers carved apron, raised on cabriole legs with brass fittings.
- *height 95cm*
- £8,950   • Red Lion

French Fruitwood Dresser ▲

- *18th century*

A French fruitwood dresser, with cavetto-style pediment and four shelves with carved frieze flanked by two small cupboards, with three cupboards below with decorative scrolled panelling.
- *226cm x 208cm x 54cm*
- £5,250   • Tredantiques

English Cupboard ▶

- *1700*

An English court cupboard with carved oak panels, and turned columns below a moulded pediment.
- *203cm x 150cm*
- £3,850   • Red Lion

Irish Dresser ▲

- *1780*

An Irish chestnut dresser with moulded pediment, scrolled pillasters and moulded cupboard doors.
- *200cm x 145cm*
- £3,950   • Red Lion

Dumb Waiters & Whatnots

Three-Tier Stand ▼
- *1890*
A three-tier mahogany cake stand with fruitwood banding
- *height 89cm*
- £195 • Great Grooms

Butler's Tray ▲
- *1850–70*
A Victorian mahogany butler's tray resting on a Georgian-style stand.
- *54cm x 65.5cm*
- £795 • Great Grooms

Victorian Cake Stand ▼
- *1890*
A Victorian mahogany three-tiered cake stand with fruitwood banding.
- *height 95cm*
- £280 • John Clay

Mahogany Cake Stand ▼
- *circa 1890*
A Victorian three-tier mahogany cake stand.
- *height 87cm*
- £195 • Great Grooms

Rosewood Whatnot ▼
- *1825*
A rosewood four-tier whatnot with small baluster turnings. Single drawer to the lower shelf, on original brass castors.
- *125cm x 46cm x 41cm*
- £5,250 • M. W. & H. L.

Rosewood Cake Stand ▲
- *circa 1880*
Rosewood circular cake stand with a turned base.
- *height 19cm*
- £400 • Sign of the Times

Wall Shelves ◄
- *circa 1840*
A hanging wall shelf with ormolu decorative mounts made from kingswood.
- *59cm x 39cm x 15cm*
- £1,650 • Butchoff

Victorian Whatnot ▲

- *circa 1850*

A Victorian walnut whatnot with serpentine-shaped tiers and turned supports.
- *100cm x 69.5cm*
- **£595** • **Great Grooms**

Mahogany Washstand ▲

- *1850*

A mahogany washstand having a centre section with two drawers on a tripod base with swept feet.
- *height 80cm*
- **£1,600** • **Sign of the Times**

Expert Tips

The whatnot is the ideal piece of furniture for the collector of knick knacks and it can be said that the more elaborate these are, the better.

Amboyna and Tulip Wood Etagères ▼

- *circa 1880*

One of a pair of amboyna and tulipwood bordered etagéres with pierced brass gallery raised on splayed legs and.
- *75cm x 48cm x 33 cm*
- **£5,800** • **Butchoff**

William IV Buffet ▼

- *circa 1835*

A William IV mahogany two-tier buffet by "Gillows".
- *100cm x 119cm x 51cm*
- **£3,450** • **Brown**

Mahogany Buffet ➤

- *1870*

A flame mahogany buffet with two shelves, one single long drawer and two shelves below, standing on turned legs.
- *152cm x 113cm x 44cm*
- **£2,375** • **Harpur Deardren**

Bijouterie Whatnot ▲

- *1860*

An unusual bijouterie mahogany whatnot with five shelves, standing on plain bracket feet.
- *146cm x 56cm x 47cm*
- **£1,800** • **Tredantiques**

Three-Tier Whatnot ▲

- *1840*

Three-tier mahogany whatnot standing on a tripod base.
- *height 101 cm*
- **£1,800** • **Sign of the Times**

Lowboys

Dutch Lowboy ▼
- *18th century*
Dutch marquetry walnut with lobed top above three drawers on slender cabriole legs on pad feet.
- *75cm x 86cm x 55cm*
- £9,500   • S. Duggan

Plank Top Lowboy ▼
- *18th century*
An early eighteenth century lowboy, with serpentine plank top, above three drawers, with herring bone stringing. Mounted on four cabriole legs.
- *71cm x 86cm x 51cm*
- £14,500   • M. W. & H. L.

Reproduction Lowboy ◄
- *circa 1930*
Reproduction of a four-drawer. eighteenth century, walnut lowboy, with crossbanded marquetry and raised on cabriole legs with pad feet.
- *height 75cm*
- £395   • Fulham

Expert Tips

A word of warning about lowboys, don't be taken in by the pretty little piece of furniture, it was often well copied in the 19th and 20th century.

George I Lowboy ▲
- *1720*
A George I walnut lowboy, three drawers with moulded apron front, standing on cabriole legs with a pad foot.
- *92cm x 62cm*
- £3,480   • Dial Post House

Dutch Lowboy ▲
- *circa 1750*
A fine, Dutch, eighteenth-century lowboy, with serpentine front and quarter drawers each side of the two main drawers. Original handles and fine marquetry decoration.
- *height 77cm*
- £8,250   • Chambers

Mahogany Lowboy ▼
- *circa 1740*
A Chippendale period, well-figured mahogany lowboy with three drawers, two small below one large, with original brass mounts, the whole raised on cabriole legs with pad feet. The piece has an unusually shaped kneehole and apron, reflecting its original purpose as a dressing-table.
- *height 71cm*
- £3,500   • L. & E. Kreckovic

Mirrors

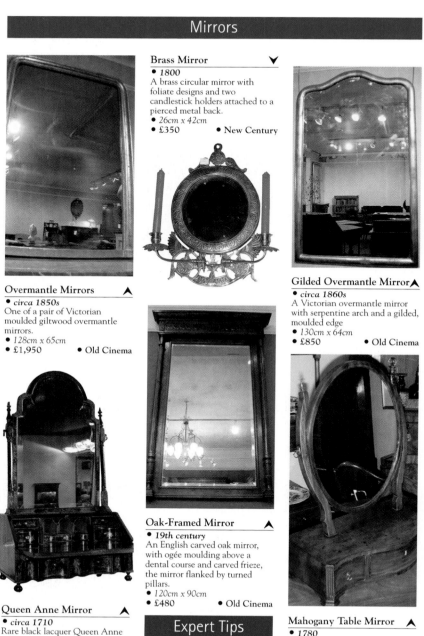

Brass Mirror ▼
- *1800*
A brass circular mirror with
foliate designs and two
candlestick holders attached to a
pierced metal back.
- *26cm x 42cm*
- £350   • New Century

Overmantle Mirrors ▲
- *circa 1850s*
One of a pair of Victorian
moulded giltwood overmantle
mirrors.
- *128cm x 65cm*
- £1,950   • Old Cinema

Queen Anne Mirror ▲
- *circa 1710*
Rare black lacquer Queen Anne
table mirror of large proportions,
retaining the original glass with
bureaux front on turned bun feet.
- *95cm x 48cm*
- £4,900   • Ashcombe House

Oak-Framed Mirror ▲
- *19th century*
An English carved oak mirror,
with ogée moulding above a
dental course and carved frieze,
the mirror flanked by turned
pillars.
- *120cm x 90cm*
- £480   • Old Cinema

Expert Tips

*The dressing table or table
mirror reached its zenith in the
Queen Anne period.*

Gilded Overmantle Mirror▲
- *circa 1860s*
A Victorian overmantle mirror
with serpentine arch and a gilded,
moulded edge
- *130cm x 64cm*
- £850   • Old Cinema

Mahogany Table Mirror ▲
- *1780*
George III mahogany serpentine
fronted mirror on ogée moulded
feet with original patination.
- *height 58cm*
- £1,550   • Ashcombe House

Dressing Table Mirror ▲
- *1760–1820*

A mahogany dressing table mirror
with ogée moulded feet and
original glass, with single drawer
with ivory handles.
- *height 50cm*
- £975 • Ashcombe House

Expert Tips

*When looking at ornamental
mirrors be sure of what you are
purchasing as many elaborate
frames are of a plaster or
composition manufacture.
Look closely to as to whether
you are purchasing a carved
wood frame or a plaster one.*

Giltwood Mirror ▲
- *circa 1880*

An English George I-style oval
carved giltwood mirror with
asymmetric C-scroll carvings.
- *128cm x 80cm*
- £3,800 • M. Luther

Painted Mirror ▲
- *1910*

A carved wood mirror with
unusual paint effect with C-scroll
border.
- *65cm x 55cm*
- £380 • Myriad

Octagonal Mirror ▲
- *1880*

French octagonal mirror with a
carved urn surrounded with leaf
designs on a moulded and beaded
edge.
- *99cm x 62cm*
- £2,100 • Looking Glass

Carved Oak Mirror ▲
- *1940*

An Italian heavily carved oak
mirror, carved with large golden
apples and pears.
- *102cm x 159cm*
- £2,800 • J. Fox

Adam-Style Mirror ▲
- *1880*

Adam-style mirror with gilt lyre
seahorse and swan designs within
the pediment and acanthus leaf
pilasters with a circular glass with
gilt borders.
- *107cm x 67cm*
- £3,400 • Looking Glass

Bevelled Glass Mirror ▲
- *1880*

Large French gilt, bevelled glass
mirror, with ribbon-moulded
designs and floral swags.
- *152cm x 145cm*
- £3,850 • Looking Glass

Silver Gilt Mirror ▲
- *1880*
French silver gilt mirror with asymmetric shell designs, with bevelled glass
- *196cm x 117cm*
- **£2,880**   • Looking Glass

Expert Tips

Over mantle mirrors have once again become extremely popular and vary considerably in style, from the Etruscan, to the Rococo, to the plain Victorian, and they all seem to be popular today.

Venetian Mirror ▼
- *1850*
Venetian etched glass oval mirror, engraved with floral and leaf designs.
- *135cm x 77cm*
- **£3,350**   • Looking Glass

Three-Panel Mirror ▼
- *1880*
Three-panel gilded mirror with architectural moulding surmounted by a frieze with classical figures.
- *89cm x 137cm*
- **£2,550**   • Looking Glass

Victorian Gilt Mirror ▼
- *1860*
English Victorian gilt mirror with scrolled floral designs and moulded edge.
- *159cm x 150cm*
- **£2,700**   • Looking Glass

Porcelain Mirror ▼
- *1890*
Late nineteenth century German mirror with flower-encrusted decoration, below two cherubs joined with a floral garland.
- *height 15cm*
- **£95**   • A.D. Antiques

Mirror and Console Table ▲
- *1830*
An Empire flame mahogany console table and mirror with swelled frieze and scrolled pilasters, on a moulded base.
- *300cm x 63cm x 35cm*
- **£3,800**   • Ranby Hall

Giltwood Mirror ▼
- **Mid-18th century**
An eighteenth century English wall mirror
- *110cm x 88cm*
- **£4,200**   • M. Luther

Lacquered Hall Mirror ◀

- *19th century*

A lacquered oak-framed hall mirror with moulded edge.
- *122cm x 48cm*
- £2,850　　　　• M. Luther

Walnut Wall Mirror ▲

- *circa 1920s*

George II-style walnut and parcel-gilt wall mirror with swan neck pediment and beaded edges.
- *112cm x 68cm*
- £1,250　　　　• M. Luther

English Regency Mirror ▼

- *circa 1810*

An English regency convex giltwood mirror, surmounted with a carved eagle.
- *112cm x 76cm*
- £5,400　　　　• M. Luther

Hour Glass Mirror ◀

- *1800*

A giltwood hour glass-shaped mirror surmounted by an urn with trailing foliage, with two candelabra, with cut glass droplets.
- *96cm x 46cm*
- £9,500　　　　• O.F. Wilson

Oval Wall Mirror ▲

- *19th century*

Nineteenth century English giltwood oval wall mirror with carved floral decoration.
- *130cm x 111cm*
- £4,950　　　　• M. Luther

Giltwood Wall Mirror ▼

- *circa 1880*

A George I-style giltwood wall mirror with a carved mask decoration.
- *122cm x 81cm*
- £3,200　　　　• M. Luther

Pier Mirrors ➤

• *circa 1860*
Graduated pair of French
giltwood pier mirrors with vines
and grapes carved into the frame.
• *160cm x 96cm*
• £18,500   • Guinevere

Dressing Table Mirror ▲

• *1780*
George III mahogany dressing
table mirror with shield back
glass and shaped drawer front
with satinwood banding.
• *height 70cm*
• £1,780 • Ashcombe House

Rococo Mirrors ▲

• *circa 1760*
One of a pair of Venetian rococo
giltwood shield mirrors with
asymmetric carved decoration.
• *65cm x 65cm*
• £11,000   • Guinevere

Venetian Mirror ▲

• *1780*
Venetian giltwood mirror with
lion and armorial cresting.
Original condition and plate.
• *84cm x 53cm*
• £3,800   • O.F. Wilson

Walnut Table Mirror ▲

• *1714–27*
A George I walnut toilet mirror
with single concave drawer to
base on bracket feet.
• *25.5 cm x 17.7cm*
• £795   • Great Grooms

Florentine Mirror ➤

• *circa 1750*
A Florentine silvered and
giltwood mirror with a carved
stylised acanthus leaf frame.
• *130cm x 75cm*
• £6,500   • Guinevere

Trumeau ▲

- *1750*

A Louis XV period giltwood and
marbled trumeau with a harbour
scene. Original glass.
- *171cm x 141.5cm*
- **£12,500** • **O.F. Wilson**

Victorian Circular Mirror ▲

- *1880*

Victorian circular mirror with a
convex glass surrounded with
gilded and beaded edge.
- *diameter 49cm*
- **£2,300** • **Looking Glass**

Carved Overmantle Mirror ▼

- *1715–74*

Carved giltwood overmantle
mirror, the frame decorated with
a basket of flowers and garden
tools.
- *117cm x 160cm*
- **£6,950** • **O.F. Wilson**

Italian Mirror ➤

- *1780*

Small Italian silvered mirror with
carved frame with swags and
original glass.
- *46cm x 38cm*
- **£2,250** • **O.F. Wilson**

German Table Mirror ▲

- *circa 1910*

German table mirror, mounted on
ivory tusks on a wooden base
with convex glass.
- *44cm x 20cm*
- **£3,000** • **Emanouel**

Walnut Wall Mirror ▲

- *1750*

A mid-eighteenth century
walnut mirror with carved
fretwork and gilding.
- *height 70cm*
- **£2,950** • **Ashcombe House**

Rectangular Mirror ➤

- *circa 1830*

A William IV giltwood
overmantle mirror with
architectural details and ebonised
slip.
- *185cm x 75cm*
- **£2,950** • **M. Luther**

Regency Mirror ▲
- *1830*

A Regency wall mirror with a carved frieze depicting shepherds and their flock within architectural details .
- *height 57cm*
- **£2,350**   • Ashcombe House

Oval Gilt Mirror ▼
- *1895*

Victorian oval gilt mirror with a carved moulded border.
- *height 125cm*
- **£1,400**   • Looking Glass

Expert Tips

The convex mirror rose to fame in the public eye when seen in the painting The Marriage *by Vermeer. The convex mirror, like a fish eye lens, has the ability to capture the whole room within its frame.*

Swedish Mirror ▲
- *circa 1860*

Nineteenth century giltwood and painted overmantle mirror with original finish, after a neo-classical style.
- *178cm x 170cm*
- **£6,900**   • M. Luther

Regency Mirror ▲
- *1820*

Regency convex gilt mirror surmounted with an eagle and decorated with carved acanthus leaf and beading.
- *117cm x 64cm*
- **£3,680**   • Looking Glass

George III Mirror ➤
- *1800*

A George III carved wood mirror with water gilding in a chinoiserie style.
- *134cm x 82cm*
- **£3,300**   • Looking Glass

Victorian Mirror ▲
- *1880*

Victorian oval gilt mirror in the Adam style with applied floral swag and ribbon detail.
- *87cm x 82cm*
- **£1,350**   • Looking Glass

Wall Mirror ▲
- *Early 18th century*

An unusual early eighteenth century wall mirror.
- *100cm x 80cm*
- **£4,800**   • M. Luther

Miscellaneous

Ebonised Pedestal ▼

- *19th century*

Nineteenth century ebonised pedestal in the form of a griffin.

- *height 111cm*
- £2,850   • S. Duggan

Chinese Hardwood Stands ▲

- *1880*

A pair of Chinese hardwood heavily carved stands, raised on claw and ball feet with inset marble tops.

- *48cm x 45cm*
- £850   • Tredantiques

Oak Plate Rack ▲

- *circa 1780*

An oak wall-mounted plate rack, with moulded cornice above three shelves.

- *104cm x 168cm x 16cm*
- £895   • Rod Wilson

Umbrella Stand ▶

- *1900*

Brass umbrella stand.

- *height 60cm*
- £950   • Mac Humble

Expert Tips

Remember that one piece of fine furniture as opposed to a number of indifferent items can really make a statement. Great care must be taken in incorporating such an item into your existing decor as they can often have a profound effect on the balance of the room.

Georgian Wash Stand ➤
- *1820*

A George III wash stand with hinged top enclosing basin above a sliding door on tapered legs.
- *height 75cm x 40cm*
- **£1,800** • C.H. Major

Rice Bucket ➤
- *1880*

Chinese rice bucket with brass fittings, central carved handle and painted Chinese characters.
- *31cm x 25cm*
- **£50** • Great Grooms

Mahogany Shaving Stand ◄
- *circa 1880*

An English mahogany shaving stand with circular mirror on a carved and turned tripod base with drop finial.
- *height 135cm*
- **£685** • Tredantiques

Indian Shrine ◄
- *late 18th century*

An Indian Hindu shrine with pink moulded dome with pierced iron rail, ornately decorated with carved pillars painted pink and green, standing on a square base.
- *153cm x 76cm x 76cm*
- **£4,700** • Gordon Reece

Oak Stand ▲
- *circa 1780*

A charming and rare eighteenth century oak stand, on tripod base with splayed feet.
- *height 72cm*
- **£1,450** • Rod Wilson

French Basin Stand ▼
- *19th century*
A French mahogany basin stand with carved lyre-shaped supports.
- *height 77cm*
- £495 • Rod Wilson

Mahogany Tray ◄
- *19th century*
A mahogany campaign butler's tray on a mahogany trestle stand.
- *70cm x 47cm*
- £2,250 • S. Duggan

Mahogany Basin Stand ▲
- *circa 1740*
Eighteenth century oak basin stand on turned supports, the draw within the stretcher, on splayed legs.
- *height 86cm*
- £1,250 • Rod Wilson

George III Bucket ►
- *circa 1790*
A mahogany brass-bound bucket of navette shape.
- *height 33cm*
- £2,350 • J. de Haan

Bamboo Umbrella Stand ▲
- *1920*
A provincial bamboo painted umbrella and stick stand with original metal liner.
- *height 80cm*
- £340 • Myriad

Expert Tips

Umbrella stands, mainly from the Victorian era, can be made in a variety of materials, including cast iron, brass and mahogany. They are attractive items to decorate the entrance to any home. All should have their original zinc liners, which are used to prevent rot from wet umbrellas and walking sticks.

Empire Birdcage ◄
- *circa 1820*
French Second Empire mahogany birdcage with pierced front and architectural pillars with gilt mounts.
- *35cm x 60cm*
- £1,500 • C.H. Major

Mahogany Cellaret ▼

- *circa 1790*
A mahogany cellaret with boxwood stringing and chequered line inlay.
- *height 66cm*
- £3,250   • J. de Haan

Artist's Portfolio and Stand ▼

- *1860*
An elaborately carved oak artist's portfolio with brushes and artists palette, with foliate design in the carving, standing on a mahogany trestle base.
- *110cm x 84cm*
- £13,500   • Ranby Hall

Painted Washstand ▲

- *circa 1800*
Green buff pine with darker green coaching lines. Larger cupboard, deep drawer and pull-out bidet.
- *height 102cm*
- £2,350   • John Clay

Regency Teapoy ▲

- *late 18th century*
A Regency lacquered tea poy with mother-of-pearl floral decoration. Standing on a tripod stand with scrolled upturned feet.
- *77cm x 42cm x 34cm*
- £3,450   • S. Duggan

English Jardinière Stand ▼

- *circa 1870*
An English mahogany jardinière stand on a turned tripod base.
- *height 85cm x 34cm*
- £390   • Tredantiques

Cast-Iron Safe ▼

- *1880*
A solid cast-iron safe with four drawers at front and combination lock, marble topped.
- *102cm x 54cm x 40cm*
- £285   • Tredantiques

Expert Tips

Jardinière stands can fetch a good price. However, wooden examples are often in poor condition as a result of plants being placed on them without draining bases. These were later replaced by cast iron or ceramic versions that did not suffer from this drawbacks.

Caste-Iron Victorian Hall Stand ◀

- *1880*
Cast-iron Victorian hall stand with gilding, marble top and gothic tracery.
- *200cm x 65cm x 30cm*
- **£1,250**   • Tredantiques

Pair of Jardinières ▼

- *circa 1840*
A pair of walnut tripod jardinières with scrolled feet and original copper lines.
- *height 107cm*
- **£14,500**   • M. W. & H. L.

Coal Box in Sarcophagus Form ◀

- *1890*
A nineteenth century mahogany coal box in sarcophagus form with lid and a brass handle.
- *54cm x 33cm*
- **£395**   • Great Grooms

Jardinière Stand ◀

- *1780*
A walnut jardinière stand on a tripod base carved as cherubs, with cloven feet.
- *height 79cm*
- **£1,400**   • Sign of the Times

Umbrella and Coat Stand ▲

- *circa 1790*
In patinated mahogany with fine shaped pegs and turned finials. With original zinc liner.
- *height 181cm*
- **£2,850**   • M. W. & H. L.

Expert Tips

In the last ten years, ornate and finely executed umbrella and coat stands have become extremely expensive, and increasingly desirable, with the finer examples employing gothic tracery and fantastical designs. The humble coat stand has established its place as a highly attractive piece of furniture that has a constant usage in our daily lives.

Screens

Ebonised Fire Screen ◄
- *1820*

A Regency ebonised fire screen, in the shape of a shield on a tapered stand with tripod base and bun feet.
- *135cm x 38cm*
- £650   • Mac Humble

Mahogany Pole Screen ▲
- *1830–7*

A William IV mahogany pole screen with a tapestry of golden pheasant in petit point.
- *height 153cm*
- £975   • Harpur Deardren

Georgian Screen ◄
- *circa 1840*

A Georgian screen with sliding side screens and turned stretchers.
- *90cm x 40cm*
- £695   • Sign of the Times

Regency Fire Screen ▲
- *1820*

Regency mahogany fire screen with brass urn finials.
- *94cm x 57cm*
- £1,200   • Sign of the Times

Chinese Screen ▼
- *1850*

One of a pair of antique Chinese filigree screens with geometric designs made of cyprus wood.
- *109cm x 51cm*
- £1,350   • Gordon Reece

Expert Tips

The pole screen was an adjustable version of the screen that could be used to protect the makeup and complexion of the sitter from the heat of the fire. Larger panelled screens were devised as a decorative means of ensuring privacy as well as a method of draft exclusion.

Victorian Fire Screen ▲
- *1900s*
A brass fire screen with
enamelled floral designs within a
brass frame.
- *61cm x 43cm*
- **£80** • Old School

Japanese Screen ▼
- *1868–1912*
A Japanese cloisonné two-fold
lacquer screen with floral
decoration.
- *167.5cm x 57.5cm*
- **£6,500** • David Brower

Leather Dutch Screen ▲
- *1800*
A four-panelled Dutch leather
screen embossed with scrolled
foliate and shell designs.
- *length 130cm*
- **£1,500** • C.H. Major

Georgian Screen ◄
- *circa 1780s*
A Georgian mahogany three
panelled screen, with original
brass hinges.
- *106cm x 106cm*
- **£665** • The Old Cinema

Needlepoint Fire Screen ▲
- *circa 1880*
A Victorian mahogany
needlepoint fire screen with a
King Charles spaniel lying on a
red cushion within a turned and
carved frame.
- *74 x 65cm*
- **£1,350** • Drummonds

Settees & Sofas

Carved Canapy Sofa ▲
- *circa 1870*

A Louis XV style sofa with painted, moulded wooden frame carved with flowers, a curved back and padded seat with small padded arm-rests, above a carved apron, on fluted cabriole legs.
- *104cm x 154cm x 60cm*
- **£2,350**   • **Ranby Hall**

Giltwood Settee ▲
- *circa 1860*

A French Louis XVI-style giltwood sofa, with carved oval padded back and seat, serpentine-fronted, elaborately carved apron, standing on cabriole legs.
- *102cm x 187cm x 65cm*
- **£2,850**   • **Ranby Hall**

Empire Sofa ▼
- *1805*

Empire sofa attributed to Ephraim Stahl, with fluted legs and painted and gilded decoration.
- *91cm x 197cm x 74cm*
- **£8,800** • **Rupert Cavendish**

Regency Settee ▲
- *1830*

A Regency mahogany classical style settee with a serpentine apron front with curved back and scroll ends, and curved cornucopaiae style legs terminating in foliate castors.
- *78cm x 200cm x 67cm*
- **£3,650**   • **Ranby Hall**

Expert Tips

Always make a point of checking the legs of newly restored pieces for signs of filler having been used on old woodworm.

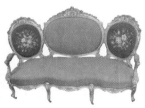

French Canapy Sofa ▲
- *circa 1860*

A French giltwood canapy with padded carved oval back and seat. With profusely carved serpentine apron, on carved cabriole legs.
- *119cm x 174cm x 62cm*
- **£2,850**   • **Ranby Hall**

George III Settee

- *circa 1890*

A George III-style mahogany settee, with shaped back and scrolled arm rests on chamfered legs.
- *78cm x 175cm x 60cm*
- £1,850 • Ranby Hall

French Restoration Sofa

- *1820*

French Restoration period sofa with a moulded wood frame painted cream with gilt banding, on stylised bun feet, designed by Julian Chichester.
- *81cm x 202cm x 78cm*
- £3,800 • Ranby Hall

Birchwood Sofa

- *circa 1890*

Swedish birchwood Biedermeier style sofa with ebonised, architecturally styled arms.
- *97cm x 211cm x 75cm*
- £4,900 • Rupert Cavendish

Double-Ended Mahogany Sofa

- *early 19th century*

An early nineteenth century mahogany double-ended sofa. Upholstered in selling fabric.
- *152cm x 205cm x 65cm*
- £3,995 • Harpur Deardren

French Giltwood Sofa

- *circa 1860*

A giltwood French Louis XV style canapy with curved, arched padded back and sides and a serpentine apron on cabriole legs.
- *120cm x 120cm x 69cm*
- £6,800 • Ranby Hall

Biedermeier Sofa

- *circa 1860*

A Biedermeier mahogany sofa with lyre back and scrolled shaped arms with carved bun feet.
- *106cm x 274cm x 64cm*
- £5,600 • Ranby Hall

Victorian Sofa ◄
- *circa 1880*
Small Victorian sofa with low button, mahogany scrolled handles and escargot feet.
- *width 1.65m*
- £2,150 • Antique Warehouse

English Painted Settee ▼
- *late 18th century*
An English painted and decorated settee with caned back and sides.
- *79cm x 170cm x 82cm*
- £11,000   • O.F. Wilson

French Sofa and Chairs ◄
- *1860*
A French Louis XVI-style sofa with curved padded back and seat with needlepoint covers, splayed arms and turned legs, together with four chairs,
- *width 125cm/settee, 65cm/chair*
- £5,500   • J. Fox

Lyre-Shaped Settee ➤
- *1860*
A mahogany lyre-shaped sofa with scrolled arms on turned legs.
- *21cm x 55cm*
- £1,500   • Great Grooms

Day-Bed Sofa ▼
- *circa 1870*
A mid Victorian satinwood day-bed sofa, in the Regency style, with gilt decoration, scrolled ends and swept feet.
- *width 2.14m*
- £1,895 • Antique Warehouse

Swedish Sofa ◄
- *circa 1820*
A Swedish sofa with covered straight back and sloping arms, with a serpentine front on cabriole legs.
- *length 200cm*
- £3,600   •Solaris

Stools

Chippendale-Style Stool ▼

- *Victorian*

Late Victorian stool in the Chippendale style on ball and claw feet.

- *40cm x 47cm x 34cm*
- £425 • Fay Orton

Louis XV Stool ➤

- *circa 1760*

A Louis XV walnut stool with a circular buttoned top, the seat rail scrolled to meet the cabriole legs standing on a whirl foot with a scrolled stretcher.

- *height 75cm*
- £1,650 • Butchoff

French Giltwood Stool ▼

- *circa 1811*

A Louis XVI giltwood stool with moulded frame and floral carving standing on cabriole legs.

- *46cm x 38cm x 86cm*
- £2,200 • O.F. Wilson

Carved Mahogany Stool ▲

- *1835*

A finely carved mahogany stool of good design and colour. Flowing X-frame legs with stretcher supports.

- *48cm x 69cm x 38cm*
- £2,950 • Mac Humble

Painted Tabourets ▼

- *1790*

Pair of late eighteenth century tabourets with painted decoration. Fluted tapered legs and carved frieze.

- *16cm x 31cm x 25cm*
- £2,600 • O.F. Wilson

Queen Anne Stool ▲

- *1710*

A rare Queen Anne period stool in walnut circular top mounted on four carved cabriole legs with turned stretcher.

- *height 47cm*
- £15,500 • M. W. & H. L.

Expert Tips

A set of two or more stools is rare and can considerably enhance the price.

Mahogany Stools ▲
- *1880*
A pair of Hepplewhite mahogany stools with scrolled arms, padded seats and standing on tapered legs.
- *73cm x 66cm*
- **£2,650**   • J. Fox

Giltwood Stools ▼
- *1880*
A pair of French Louis VXI giltwood stools with scrolled arms on cabriole legs.
- *50cm x 75cm x 52cm*
- **£2,850**   • J. Fox

Piano Stool ◀
- *1890*
Victorian piano stool with green leather seat on carved acanthus leaf legs.
- *height 51cm*
- **£400**   • J. Fox

Expert Tips

Stools come in many shapes, sizes and dimensions and remain extremely popular amongst collectors. Here again, look out for the Victorian and twentieth century copies of period pieces.

Pair of Walnut Stools ▼
- *1870*
A pair of Victorian walnut stools, on bulbous turned legs.
- *18cm x 35cm*
- **£650**   • J. Fox

Biedermeier Bench ◀
- *circa 1820*
North German Biedermeier bench. Birchwood and masur birch.
- *50cm x 94cm x 68cm*
- **£3,400**   • R. Cavendish

Expert Tips

Piano stools are always popular but their adjustment mechanisms must be studied closely, especially the cabriole leg version, as in some cases these have been exposed to extreme pressure and are weakened or damaged. Walnut versions should be closely checked for woodworm.

Oak Stool ➤
- *1880*
A small oak stool, with solid seat, and standing on four rustically turned legs.
- *19cm x 31cm x 17cm*
- £85 • Lacquer Chest

Victorian Mahogany Stool ▼
- *19th century*
Victorian mahogany stool with brass claw and ball feet.
- *height 92cm*
- £650 • Solaris Antiques

French Stool ▼
- *circa 1750*
French stool in the Louis XV style with gilded wooden legs.
- *height 46cm*
- £ 2,000 • O. F. Wilson

Charles I Stool ▼
- *17th century*
Charles I oak stool with moulded frieze on turned, baluster shaped legs.
- *51cm x 45cm x 25cm*
- £1,200 • Rod Wilson

Mahogany Stool ◄
- *19th century*
Nineteenth century mahogany stool with turned legs on brass castors by Gillars.
- *height 49cm*
- £400 • The Old Cinema

Biedermeier Stools ▼
- *circa 1825*
A pair of German birchwood stools covered in horsehair.
- *height 58cm*
- £ 4,500 • Cavendish

Tables

Mahogany Night Table ▲
- *1810*

Elegant Regency mahogany night table. With dropside standing on tapered, ring-turned legs.
- *79cm x 37cm x 31cm*
- **£2,950** • Ashcombe

Occasional Table ▲
- *1910*

Small English occasional table with a large decorative cat on the surface, with one central drawer and slender legs on pad feet.
- *74cm x 87cm x 50cm*
- **£1,200** • Lacquer Chest

Writing Table ▼
- *circa 1830*

A William IV mahogany partner's library writing table with drawers each side of a tooled leather inset. The top raised on octagonal legs and original brass castors.
- *74cm x 92cm*
- **£2,600** • Great Grooms

Walnut Lowboy ▼
- *1760*

Chippendale style lowboy made of walnut, with carved apron on straight legs.
- *70cm x 78cm x 49cm*
- **£3,850** • Mac Humble

Regency Rosewood Teapoy ▶
- *circa 1900*

A Regency rosewood brass inlay teapoy, the sarcophagus top centred with brass arabesques, lifting to reveal fitted interior. With brass ring handles, on lyre support and sabre legs with brass paw cappings.
- *72cm x 27cm*
- **£4,500** • Great Grooms

Set of Three Occasional Tables ◀
- *1900–15s*

An Edwardian set of three mahogany card tables with satinwood banding.
- *85cm x 56cm*
- **£485** • Great Grooms

Mahogany Card Table ▲
- *1740*

A superb mahogany card table on cabriole legs, with a secret drawer. Exhibited at Bradford Art Gallery in 1925.
- *74cm x 84cm x 41cm*
- **£8,900** • Dial Post House

Octagonal Work Table ▲
- *circa 1820*

Georgian octagonal mahogany work table with boxwood stringing, on square tapered legs.
- *74cm x 58cm*
- **£1,600** • Tredantiques

Hall Table and Chairs ▼
- *1850*

An oak hall suite comprising of a table on turned legs with carved back, and two hall chairs. Rigin style, marked "SP".
- *width 94cm / table*
- £3,350 • Mac Humble

Ebonised Table ▼
- *circa 1890*

Hexagonal ebonised table with green leather top, standing on four turned legs with a hoof pad foot.
- *60cm x 58cm*
- £800 • New Century

Regency Table ▼
- *1812–1830*

Regency mahogany table on an ebonised, X-framed stretcher base.
- *71cm x 107cm*
- £3,350 • The Old Cinema

Satinwood Table ▲
- *1815*

Satinwood table banded in rosewood, on a single pedestal on a tripod base with scrolled feet.
- *74cm x 52cm*
- £5,900 • Dial Post House

Standing Tray ▲
- *1780*

A satinwood tray on stand, with detachable tray with brass fittings and reeded legs.
- *48cm x 58cm*
- £1,795 • Great Grooms

Demi-Lune Card Table ▲
- *1837-1901*

Victorian burr walnut demi-lune card table with scrolled carved legs and feet.
- *74cm x 35cm x 43cm*
- £1,995 • Old Cinema

Edwardian Occasional Tables ▼
- *1910*

A nest of three Edwardian occasional tables with boxwood inlay and banding and tapered straight legs.
- *55cm x 50cm*
- £495 • Great Grooms

Inlaid Card Table ▼
- *circa 1900*

A mahogany card table with inlaid marquetry banding and medallions, on straight tapered legs.
- *72cm x 45cm*
- £2,550 • Great Grooms

Expert Tips

Occasional tables are always of interest as they have such a useful function in everyday living. They can obtain high prices, especially the ones made in rare woods and with high quality inlay.

Regency Mahogany Card Table ▼

- *circa 1800–30s*

A Regency mahogany card table with a demi-lune top, with turned feet and brass castors.

- *73cm x 58cm*
- **£6,995**   • **Great Grooms**

Lady's Work Table ▼

- *circa 1800s*

A Victorian burr walnut and quarter-sawn serpentine outline lady's work table with boxwood foliate inlays.

- *71cm x 58cm*
- **£2,495**   • **Great Grooms**

Kingwood and Porcelain Work Table ▶

- *circa 1860*

A kingwood and porcelain work table by Alphonse Giroux in Louis XV style, the shaped hinged quarter veneered top centred by a porcelain plaque with floral decoration on a bleu celeste ground, enclosing a fitted interior on cabriole legs. Headed by leaf-cast chutes joined by a platform stretcher.

- *68cm x 43cm*
- **£3,500**   • **Emanouel**

Mahogany Games Table ▲

- *circa 1880*

A mahogany Victorian work table with games compendium with a turned stretcher and having bun feet.

- *76cm x 74cm*
- **£2,650**   • **Ranby Hall**

Victorian Console Table ▲

- *circa 1860*

A carved walnut console table with a shaped marble top with carved apron, raised on scrolled cabriole legs.

- *97cm x 135cm x 54cm*
- **£4,450**   • **Brown**

Oak Cricket Table ▶

- *circa 1800*

An early nineteenth century oak cricket table with willow banding.

- *65cm x 53cm*
- **£895**   • **Rod Wilson**

Imperial Table ▼

- *19th century*

A Russian oval Imperial table with a black veined marble top, surrounded by malachite medallions with gilt ormolu mounts.

- *50cm x 70cm x 130cm*
- **£12,000**   • **Emanouel**

Kneehole Dressing Table ▼

- *1727–1820*

A mahogany Georgian dressing table with arched kneehole, satinwood banding, and brass handles, raised on square tapered legs.

- *80cm x 57cm*
- **£1,580**   • **Ranby Hall**

Expert Tips

When purchasing a console table it is wise to consider its grandness and quality as these factors contribute to its value.

George III Tripod Table ▲
- *1760*

George III small circular mahogany tripod table.
- £2,950 • Ashcombe

Rosewood Table ▲
- *1860*

A rosewood occasional table, with central long drawer, two side extensions, standing on a turned stretcher with twin scrolled supports.
- *74cm x 119cm x 65cm*
- £3,250 • Old Cinema

Austrian Work Table ▼
- *early 19th century*

An early nineteenth century olive wood work table made in Austria on stretcher base.
- *47cm x 63cm x 77cm*
- £1,150 • N. E. McAuliffe

Biedermeier Sofa Table ➤
- *circa 1820*

Swedish birchwood, Biedermeier sofa table with ebonised and gilt decoration on lion paw feet.
- *77cm x 120cm x 64cm*
- £4,500 • R. Cavendish

Italian Rosewood Table ▼
- *1900*

Italian inlaid rosewood octagonal occasional table, with circular satinwood inlay standing on eight square tapering legs.
- *72cm x 60cm*
- £900 • Tredantiques

Rosewood Games Table ◄
- *1810–1820*

A Regency rosewood games table with Moroccan leather top and brass inlay and ormolu mounts.
- *height 95cm*
- £8,500 • C.H. Major

Regency Writing Table ▲
- *1810*

An excellent Regency mahogany standard end writing table on turned stretcher base.
- *height 53cm*
- £14,500 • Ashcombe

Victorian Drinks Table ▼
- *1880*

A Victorian drinks table with an Eastern influence in light oak with ebony finials on unusual legs.
- *76cm x 58cm x 43cm*
- £460 • Myriad

Expert Tips

Snap-top or tripod tables should have good firm bases and the table top should be constructed out of a single piece of wood.

Yew Flip-Top Table ▼
- *circa 1750*
A fine original eighteenth
century yew wood tripod with
flip-top table with good
colouring and proportions.
- *67cm x 75cm*
- £2,250   • Rod Wilson

Regency Work Table ▼
- *1820*
An octagonal Regency red
lacquer work table, with gilt
foliate designs on square tapered
legs.
- *79cm x 49cm x 36cm*
- £3,200   • Ranby Hall

Chinese Side Tables ▶
- *1644–1912*
One of a pair of Chinese bamboo
and black lacquer side tables.
Featuring a straight floor
stretcher and a stylised key fret
apron.
- *84cm x 97cm x 48cm*
- £4,000   • Gerard Hawthorn

Mahogany Snap-Top Table ▲
- *1860*
An English flame mahogany
snap-top table on a tripod base
with claw feet.
- *72cm x 62cm x 49cm*
- £775   • Tredantiques

Console Table ▲
- *circa 1870*
An ornately carved giltwood
console table with heavily
scrolled legs and a marble top
with three green chinoiserie
cupboards below.
- *99cm x 197cm x 80cm*
- £18,000   • Ranby Hall

Mazarin Writing Table ▼
- *circa 1860*
A Regency Mazarin writing table
with ormolu filigre decoration to
the drawers. Standing on turned
and fluted legs. Inscribed, "V.V.E
P.Sormani and Fils, Paul
Sarmani".
- *79cm x 108cm x 76cm*
- £40,000   • Ranby Hall

Egyptian Inlaid Table ▼
- *19th century*
An Egyptian table heavily inlaid
with mother of pearl and also
inlaid with ivory.
- *82cm x 54cm*
- £5,500   • Sinai Antiques

Regency Side Table ▼
- *late 18th century*
A Regency rosewood side table
on twin carved supports with
turned stretcher, on brass castors.
- *74cm x 92cm x 50cm*
- £2,375   • Harpur Deardren

Circular Side Table ▲
- *1890*

Small circular table on tripod base, inlaid with satinwood, box and rosewood with an inlaid knight on horseback.
- *height 74cm*
- £1,400   • J. Fox

Welsh Oak Table ▲
- *circa 1740*

A Welsh country-made eighteenth century oak three drawer side table with original handles.
- *74cm x 83cm x 47cm*
- £1,850   • Rod Wilson

French Marquetry Table ▲
- *circa 1890*

A French centre table with shaped top with marquetry inlay and ormolu mounts on cabriole legs.
- *77cm x 152cm x 95cm*
- £8,500   • Tredantiques

Chinese Lacquered Table ▼
- *1800*

A pair of eighteenth century Chinese lacquer panels inset into more recent brass frames.
- *65cm x 55cm*
- £1,750   • C.H. Major

Marquetry Table ▼
- *circa 1875*

French marquetry table with hinged table top with fitted interior and carved and gilded legs.
- *74cm x 81cm*
- £2,750   • C.H. Major

Oval Hall Tables ▲
- *1860*

Victorian small oval top table with a basket base on cabriole legs with ceramic castors.
- *72cm x 116cm x 142cm*
- £4,500   • J. Fox

Mahogany Drinks Table ▲
- *1880*

A mahogany side table by Maples with silver-plated mounts and original decanters on silver plated castors.
- *97cm x 118cm x 56cm*
- £3,800   • J. Fox

Carved Writing Table ▲
- *1825*

A fine Regency rosewood table. Writing on side table attributed to Gillows of Lancaster. Made in 1825. The well figured veneers to the top are complimented by exquisite gadrooned carving to the edge and is fitted with two frieze drawers. The design for this table is included amid Gillows estimate drawerings and costings book for 1826, nos 3480 & 3496.
- *75cm x 106cm x 60cm*
- £8,950   • Freshfords

Rosewood Games Table ▲
- *1900*

A rosewood games table with roulette wheel and card table on tapered legs and brass castors.
- *74cm x 109cm x 93cm*
- **£1,200** • **J. Fox**

Painted Occasional Table ▲
- *circa 1850*

A satinwood occasional table, the top with a circular painted romantic scene on square slender tapered legs with splayed feet and finial stretcher.
- *77cm x 43cm x 29cm*
- **£2,500** • **Butchoff**

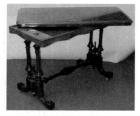

Victorian Games Table ▼
- *1870*

A Victorian walnut games table incorporating a sewing box beneath a backgammon and chess table, with turned stretcher and lion's paw castor feet.
- *74cm x 53.5cm x 41cm*
- **£2,750** • **J. Fox**

Leathertop Bureau ▼
- *circa 1900*

A very good quality Louis XV-style bureau with leather top with gut mounts. Two false drawers on the front and three drawers to the rear, with teak and mahogany inlaid marquetry.
- *79cm x 143cm x 77cm*
- **£10,500** • **Simon Hatchwell**

Inlaid Card Table ◄
- *Victorian*

Victorian card table with two-matching veneers: Beautiful burr walnut inlay with satin wood inlay. Unusual stretcher with very strong Greek key carving. Original porcelain castors.
- *75cm x 100cm x 50cm*
- **£2,995** • **Old Cinema**

French Giltwood Table ►
- *circa 1900*

A French third Republic giltwood table, with moulded pink marble top, the fluted tapering legs joined by a beaded stretcher.
- *82cm x 85cm x 53cm*
- **£1,100** • **Tredantiques**

Rosewood Sofa Table ▲
- *circa 1810*

A Rosewood sofa table, the frieze with two panelled drawers supported on centre turned column on four spayed legs.
- *73cm x 120cm x 41cm*
- **£17,000** • **Dial Post House**

Pardrouse Table ▲
- *1880*

French Pardrouse table, the serpentine top heavily inlaid in satinwood and boxwood. on tapered walnut cabriole legs with ornate gilt mounts.
- *74cm x 72.5cm x 53.5cm*
- **£2,800** • **Judy Fox Antiques**

Mahogany Side Table ▼
- *circa 1870s*

Victorian mahogany table with leather writing top and one long single drawer on tapered turned legs with original brass castors.
- *height 70cm*
- £595   • Old Cinema

Victorian Chess Table ▼
- *1860*

A Victorian mother-of-pearl chess table by Jenning and Betteridge, with pierced fan shaped decoration to top, single turned pedestal on circular base with upturned tripod feet.
- *73cm x 49cm*
- £1,250   • Tredantiques

Italian Console Table ➤
- *1830*

A Venetian giltwood console table, with pink and white marble top, serpentine carved front, with profusely carved legs and stretcher.
- *90cm x 140cm x 46cm*
- £1,950   • Tredantiques

Expert Tips

Period chess tables are always of great interest to the collector as the game of chess has a timeless appeal.

Cricket Table ▲
- *1750*

An oak oval cricket table, on a tripod base with square, straight legs.
- *62cm x 57cm*
- £3,600   • Paul Hopwell

Boulle Table ▲
- *1880*

A magnificent circular green ebonised boulle circular table with brass inlaid decoration.
- *77cm x 138cm*
- £8,500   • Old Cinema

French Circular Table ▼
- *circa 1900*

A French circular satinwood and fruitwood table standing on square tapering legs.
- *72cm x 50cm*
- £900   • Tredantiques

Spider-legged Work Table ▼
- *1800*

Mahogany work table with unusual spider legs.
- *72cm x 53cm x 40cm*
- £4,200   • O.F. Wilson

Octagonal Rosewood Table ▼

- *1800*

An octagonal rosewood table with floral satinwood inlay, on tapering cabriole legs.
- *72cm x 78cm*
- £450   • Tredantiques

Rosewood Table ▼

- *1800–30*

A Regency rosewood table, with solid trestle base on castors.
- *75cm x 153cm x 78cm*
- £3,995   • Harpur Deardren

English Regency Table ▼

- *1815*

A very fine English Regency console table with a marble top table standing on cabriole legs decorated with foliage.
- *80cm x 101cm x 55cm*
- £3,800   • Tredantiques

Expert Tips

Remember that tables should be sturdy and remain level when tested.

Rosewood Writing Table ▲

- *circa 1870*

A Parisian rosewood writing table with satinwood inlay on straight tapered legs with a turned stretcher base.
- *75cm x 85cm x 55cm*
- £12,500   • Harpur Deardren

Marble-Top Table ▲

- *circa 1860*

A high quality console table with moulded frieze draw with specimen marble top on carved stretcher base.
- *100cm x 93cm x 51cm*
- £4,800   • Fay Orton

Georgian Mahogany Table ▼

- *circa 1760*

A Georgian mahogany snap-top table, with a tripod base on plain cabriole legs on pad feet.
- *71cm x 61cm*
- £1,395   • Harpur Deardren

Art and Crafts Table ▼

- *circa 1900*

An English copper art and crafts table on square tapered and splayed legs, with circular stretcher.
- *57cm x 36cm*
- £260   • Tredantiques

Walnut Work Table ◀

- *1840–50*

An unusual walnut work table pictured open with fitted interior on a carved pedestal base.
- *74cm x 46cm x 57cm*
- £3,900   • Fay Orton

English Writing Table ▲
- *1840*

A fine English rosewood writing table. With pierced gallery above four drawers with a moulded edge. Stretcher base and casters.
- *76cm x 83cm x 50cm*
- £2,800   • Ranby Hall

Victorian Circular Table ▲
- *1840*

A Victorian mahogany occasional table, with grey and cream circular marble top with central stand and tripod base with claw feet.
- *72cm x 48cm*
- £1,500   • Tredantiques

Giltwood Console Table ▼
- *circa 1820*

A Louise XVI French carved console table with mottled green and white marble top with mythical beast supports, standing on claw feet.
- *54cm x 61cm x 48cm*
- £850   • Tredantiques

Regency Snap-Top Table ▼
- *1810*

English Regency snap-top table with brass fittings and brass acanthus leaf decoration, in the manner of Louis Le Garnier.
- *height 65cm*
- £5,000   • O.F. Wilson

Circular Occasional Table ▶
- *circa 1890*

A Regency rosewood style occasional table with circular top and brass pierced frieze, standing on splayed legs.
- *69cm x 52cm*
- £1,150   • John Nicholas

Sheraton Card Table ◀
- *1805*

George III Sheraton mahogany card table. Beautifully inlaid with rosewood.
- *76cm x 92cm x 46cm*
- £9,750   • Freshfords

Empire Mahogany Table ▲
- *1815*

Empire mahogany centre table, with green marble circular top, above a triangular base, with claw feet.
- *73cm x 82cm.*
- £5,950   • O.F. Wilson

Demi-Lune Satinwood Tables ▲
- *1790*

One of a pair of satinwood demi-lune side tables with painted floral swags.
- *72cm x 112cm x 55cm*
- £11,950   • O.F. Wilson

Expert Tips

Demi-lune tables are greatly increased in value if they come as a pair.

Louis XVI Table ▲

- *19th century*

Louis XV1-style, small mahogany table , with three tiers of drawers below a pierced brass gallery.
- *78cm x 43cm x 32cm*
- **£2,600**   • **O.F. Wilson**

Victorian Tea Table ▲

- *1860*

An English Victorian rosewood tea table, on cabriole legs with X-framed stretcher and carved finial.
- *24cm x 22cm*
- **£1,585**   • **Ranby Hall**

Games Table ▼

- *1880*

Victorian rosewood card table enclosing baize-lined interior.
- *74cm x 56cm*
- **£1,695**   • **The Old Cinema**

Lady's Sewing Table ▼

- *early 19th century*

A Regency figured mahogany inlaid lady's sewing table with a set of four drawers with ivory escutcheons, turned handles, standing on square tapered legs, with S-shaped stretcher.
- *83cm x 48cm x 37cm*
- **£1,950**   • **S. Duggan**

Granite-Top Table ➤

- *1830*

A Louise Phillipe table with a granite top, on central pedestal, with heavily carved tripod base, and scrolled paw feet.
- *77cm x 100cm*
- **£5,250**   • **Ranby Hall**

Rosewood Work Table ◄

- *1840*

Rosewood Dantas work table raised on a U-shaped pedestal base.
- *72cm x 80cm x 40cm*
- **£2,800**   • **Midwinter**

Swedish Console Table with Griffin ▲

- *18th century*

Swedish giltwood console table with central carved griffin on black-figured marble plinth.
- *82cm x 75cm x 47cm*
- **£8,500**   • **Heytesbury**

Oak Side Table ▲

- *17th century*

A seventeenth century oak side table with a single drawer on a ball-and-reel turned frame, with rich patina on ball feet.
- *68cm x 77cm x 54cm*
- **£5,600**   • **Peter. Bunting**

Wardrobes

Walnut Cupboard ▼
- *early 18th century*
A fine English walnut hall cupboard with unusual carved inlays and designs on bracket feet.
- *188cm x 121cm*
- £12,500   • M. Luther

Mahogany Linen Press ▶
- *early 19th century*
English mahogany linen press in the manner of Gillows.
- *215cm x 159cm*
- £7,800   • M. Luther

Combination Wardrobe ▼
- *19th century*
A good quality combination wardrobe with flame mahogany panelled doors, fitted interior with sliding drawers.
- *220cm x 185cm*
- £3,395   • Old Cinema

Boulle Cupboard ▲
- *19th century*
A French ebony and ebonised boulle cupboard with brass inlay raised on interlaced cross stretcher and carved legs.
- *154cm x 85cm x 43cm*
- £4,400   • M. Luther

Walnut Wardrobe ▼
- *18th century*
French walnut wardrobe with a moulded arch cornice above two shaped cupboard doors, with a serpentine apron on shaped bracket feet.
- *height 169cm*
- £1,906   • Drummonds

Mahogany Compactona ▼
- *circa 1880*
An Edwardian mahogany compactona with satinwood banding, chequered stringing, with marquetry panels and cornice.
- *170cm x 160cm*
- £2,900   • Old Cinema

Victorian Wardrobe ◀
- *circa 1890s*
A late Victorian single-door mahogany wardrobe with central mirror, flanked by circular carved panels with ribbon decoration.
- *170cm x 90cm*
- £925   • Old Cinema

Breakfront Wardrobe ▼
- *1860–80*
A Victorian breakfront mahogany wardrobe with three doors enclosing pull-out shelves.
- *210cm x 60cm x 202cm*
- **£2,250**   • Old Cinema

English Linen Press ▼
- *circa 1830*
An English light mahogany country house linen press, with panelled doors enclosing occasional slides and fittings.
- *145cm x 126cm x 54cm*
- **£3,850**   • Ranby Hall

Expert Tips

Check that the handles are matching and not broken.

Edwardian Wardrobe ◄
- *circa 1901*
An Edwardian inlaid mahogany wardrobe with central mirror and side panelling, and long drawer below.
- *180cm x 138cm*
- **£975**   • Old Cinema

Mahogany Wardrobe ▲
- *1830*
A mahogany wardrobe with unusual scrolled carving below the square pediment, two panelled doors standing on shaped bracket feet.
- *208cm x 135cm x 60cm*
- **£1,250**   • Tredantiques

Chinese Cupboard ▲
- *1930*
A Chinese red-lacquered cupboard with butterfly and floral painted decoration.
- *190cm x 103cm*
- **£1,960**   • Great Grooms

Victorian Wardrobe ▼
- *circa 1840*
A flame mahogany Victorian wardrobe with ogée moulded cornice, two panelled doors with two long drawers below, standing on a square plinth base.
- *225cm x 150cm x 55cm*
- **£7,950**   • Brown

Pine Wardrobe ▲
- **1900s**

A pine wardrobe, with arched pediment above three panelled doors with three shallow drawers below.
- *211cm x 142cm x 62cm*
- **£800** • Old School

Victorian Mahogany Wardrobe ▼
- *circa 1850s*

An early Victorian mahogany wardrobe with central mirror, flanked by panelled doors and a well-fitted interior.
- *180cm x 160cm*
- **£2,495** • Old Cinema

Oak Cupboard ▼
- **1680**

A Charles II oak-panelled cupboard with lunette carved decoration. Standing on straight square legs. Of good rich patina.
- *182cm x 110cm x 48cm*
- **£8,950** • Paul Hopwell

Mirrored Wardrobe ◄
- **1860**

An Italian mirrored wardrobe with a swan neck bonnet top and galleried pediment, with porcelain plaques either side of the mirror with gilt ormolu decoration.
- *height 240cm*
- **£7,800** • Ranby Hall

Cherrywood Armoire ▲
- *circa 1830*

A French carved cherrywood armoire Rennes with a double-dome top, from Brittany.
- *232.5cm x 140cm*
- **£7,800** • Guinevere

Triple Wardrobe ▲
- *Victorian*

Victorian burr walnut triple wardrobe with centre mirror. Wonderful matched grain and veneer. Unusual sliding removable hanging unit. Four sliding shelves and three drawers below with brass fittings.
- *203cm x 188cm x 58cm*
- **£2,895** • Old Cinema

Expert Tips

Look carefully at the feet on wardrobes, as years of wear and tear can cause them to be broken or lost.

Red Lacquer Cupboard ▼
- **late 18th century**

Chinese red lacquer hardwood cupboard with carved foliate design and two interior drawers.
- *173cm x 84cm x 43cm*
- **£9,600** • M. Luther

Georgian Linen Press ▲
- *1780*

A Georgian mahogany linen press with figured mahogany panelled doors, above three tiers of drawers with oval brass mounts.
- *110cm x 81cm*
- **£3,950**   • Old Cinema

Expert Tips

Linen presses, which are cupboards used to store linen, date from the 1600s. A Georgian linen press was usually made from mahogany or walnut, and came with panelled doors and three tiers of drawers. The doors of early oak linen presses could be constructed with six or more panels. They come in a wide range of styles, which include the breakfronted and bowfronted examples, along with a range of sizes, as some could be huge.

Breakfront Compactum ▼
- *circa 1830*

An English George IV flame mahogany breakfront compactum with central pediment, having panelled cupboards, and three long drawers below.
- *208cm x 226cm x 57cm*
- **£3,850**   • Ranby Hall

Victorian Linen Press ▼
- *circa 1860*

A fine Victorian flame mahogany linen press, with panelled doors above two short and two long drawers, enclosing an interior with sliding drawers, standing on a plinth base.
- *149cm x 129cm x 54cm*
- **£4,450**   • Ranby Hall

Housekeeper's Cupboard ◄
- *circa 1800*

An early nineteenth century housekeeper's cupboard with carved oak panelling, with four drawers below, standing on ogée bracket foot.
- *72cm x 134cm x 53cm*
- **£5,750**   • Rod Wilson

Arts and Crafts Wardrobe ▲
- *circa 1910*

Art and Crafts oak wardrobe with central mirror and one long drawer, standing on bracket feet.
- *212cm x 112cm x 55cm*
- **£975**   • Old Cinema

Bedroom Suite ▼
- *1875–80*

A French Second Empire-style wardrobe being part of a bedroom set including bed, wardrobe, and two side cabinets. The wardrobe with a moulded cornice, mirrored cupboards and ormolu foliate decoration, standing on bun feet.
- *height 240cm*
- **£35,000**   • Sleeping Beauty

Glass

Glass forms some of the most beautiful artefacts with which to create a collection – and its inherent fragility ensures ongoing rarity value.

Some of the earliest examples of glass were found in Egypt, dating from around 3,500 BC. The Egyptians used moulds, and layered one colour of glass over another. Gallé employed this technique at the turn of the last century, which is all but forgotten, although an attempt was made in the 1980s to replicate this but failed to reach the same standard.

Romans were among the first group to manipulate molten glass with pincers, and apply pillared and ribbed decoration to glass as it cooled. As this process was refined and perfected it paved the way to the creation of the fabulous glass pieces which we see in the Venetian factories today.

The Industrial Revolution saw the appearance of lead crystal and the bright cutwork which is seen in Irish and English glass and the colourful products of Bohemia, all of which are highly collectable.

Glass has proved to be a very good investment and competition is fierce for good examples. This is borne out by the fact that glass is so fragile and easily broken it will always command a premium, because unlike silver it cannot be repaired without bearing a blemish.

Georgian Rummer ◄
- *1810*
A Georgian rummer slightly waisted bowl with unusual triple banding, on a plain conical foot.
- *height 16.5cm*
- £110   • Jasmin Cameron

Engraved Rummer ◄
- *1820*
A George III Sunderland Bridge rummer engraved with pastoral scenes.
- *height 15cm*
- £850   • Templar

French Urns ▲
- *1880*
A pair of turquoise French urns with gilt mounts and a central plaque showing romantic figures.
- *height 26cm*
- £680   • Mousa

Bohemian Goblet ◄
- *1880*
A Bohemian goblet in red glass with crenellated rim, white enamelled panels and gilding.
- *height 27cm*
- £760   • Mousa

Expert Tips

Bohemian glass can suffer from chips to the enamel and worn gilding which can be extremely expensive to repair.

Bohemian Glass Dish ▲

- *1880*

Bohemian glass dish on a stand, with white enamelled panels, stylised leaf design and gilding.
- *height 24cm*
- £540
- Mousa

Cock Fighting Trophy ▲

- *1860*

Large goblet-shaped bowl standing on a knobbed pedestal stem. The body skillfully engraved with scene of fighting cocks.
- *height 22cm*
- £550
- Templar

Toddy Lifter ▼

- *1825*

Exceedingly rare toddy lifter from the early nineteenth century.
- *height 18cm*
- £350
- Jasmin Cameron

Bohemian Bottles ▲

- *1880*

Blue Bohemian faceted glass bottles with gilded decoration and lozenge-shaped stoppers.
- *height 15cm*
- £350
- Mousa

Glass Decanter ▼

- *1880*

Rose coloured glass decanter with clear glass ribbon handle and stopper.
- *height 23cm*
- £110
- Mousa

Jug and Two Beakers ◀

- *1890*

Green Bohemian glass jug and two beakers with white enamelling and gilding.
- *height 18cm*
- £126
- Mousa

Expert Tips

On decanters, check that the stopper is original and has not been ground down to fit.

Bohemian Vases ▲

• *1880*
Pair of fluted Bohemian red vases
with white panels, and gilding
around the rim and base.
• *height 21cm*
• £450   • Templar

Rock Crystal ▲

• *19th century*
Carved rock crystal lingam with
extraordinary internal figuring.
• *height 36.5cm*
• £3,600   • Zakheim

Cranberry Decanter ▶

• *1870*
A Victorian cranberry glass
decanter with pinched lip,
oversized clear glass stopper and
moulded handle.
• *height 15cm*
• £165   • Barham Antiques

Victorian Glass Epergne ◀

• *1860*
Victorian vaseline glass épergne
with four central trumpets and
green glass twists around the
stem.
• *height 44cm*
• £650   • Templar

Hock Glasses ◀

• *late 19th century*
A pair of hock glasses with green
bowls and clear stems.
• *height 11cm*
• £188   • Jasmin Cameron

Bristol Wine Glass ◀

• *1820*
A green Bristol wine glass with a
tulip bowl and baluster stem.
• *height 11cm*
• £120   • Jasmin Cameron

Glass Rummer ▼

• *1830*
Regency Sunderland Bridge
rummer, with short knobbed
stem, on a folded conical foot.
• *height 15cm*
• £850   • Templar

Mead Glass ▼

- *circa 1840*

A beaker-shaped green Bristol
mead glass.

- *height 11cm*
- **£75**   • Jasmin Cameron

Port Glasses ▼

- *1820*

A pair of Regency port glasses
engraved with the monogram
"Lac".

- *height 14cm*
- **£135**   • Jasmin Cameron

Coloured Wine Glass ▼

- *1890*

Cranberry coloured wine glass
with long stem on a domed foot.

- *height 11cm*
- **£65**   • Jasmin Cameron

Scent Bottle ➤

- *1901*

Small rose glass perfume bottle,
diamond cut and faceted with
clear stopper.

- *height 3.5cm*
- **£55**   • Mousa

Victorian Glass Epergne ◄

- *1860*

Victorian vaseline glass épergne
with four hanging flutes
stemming from a central trumpet.

- *height 52cm*
- **£690**   • Templar

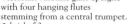

Bohemian Covered Vase ▲

- *1890*

A large Bohemian vase and
cover, the cylindrical body
tapering from a lobed base, the
whole engraved with romantic
designs.

- *height 64cm*
- **£1,680**   • Mousa

Victorian Centrepiece ▲

- *circa 1870*

A Victorian opaline and silver-plated centerpiece consisting of four conical glass vases with pinched lips, mounted on a silver stand.
- *height 28cm*
- £350   • Barham Antiques

Bohemian Vase ▲

- *1880*

Bohemian red glass vase of bottle shape on a pedestal base, with enamel and gilt foliate designs on the bowl, neck and base.
- *height 26cm*
- £480   • Mousa

Champagne Glass ▼

- *1820*

Regency champagne flute, one of a set of ten, with fluted body, knobbled stem and a cylindrical base.
- *height 16.5cm*
- £780   • Jasmin Cameron

Red Bohemian Bottles ▲

- *1880*

A pair of enamelled Bohemian bottles with onion-top stoppers, heavily cut with eastern motifs.
- *height 18cm*
- £450   • Mousa

Lemonade Jug ▼

- *1895*

Tankard-shape lemonade jug with traces of gilding around the rim and handle.
- *height 22.5cm*
- £185   • Jasmin Cameron

Scottish Gill Measure ▲

- *1810–50*

Scottish measure of one gill, a quantity of spirit to be dispensed.
- *height 12cm*
- £240   • Jasmin Cameron

Pair of Blue Ewers ▲

- *1880*

A pair of blue glass ewers with pinched lip and ribbon handle, enamelled with foliate designs.
- *height 24cm*
- £135   • Mousa

Wine Carafe ◄
- *1830*

A William IV wine carafe with fluted body and faceted neck.
- *height 27cm*
- **£265**   • **Jasmin Cameron**

Green Bohemian Goblets ▲
- *1880*

A pair of magnificent green hexagonal, cut and faceted Bohemian goblets with gilding.
- *height 15cm*
- **£550**   • **Mousa**

Bohemian Octagonal Goblet ▲
- *1880*

Blue Bohemian octagonal goblet with enamelled foliate designs and gilding.
- *height 19cm*
- **£290**   • **Mousa**

Victorian Decanter ◄
- *1890*

Bohemian clear glass decanter with profuse gilded floral decoration, and faceted glass stopper.
- *height 32.5cm*
- **£140**   • **Sharif**

Expert Tips

The technique used to cut glass is achieved by grinding wheels made of slate or fine sandstone. Glass can also be cut by cast iron discs, which are used in conjunction with an abrasive lubricant of a sand and water mixture.

Blue Bohemian Goblet ▲
- *1880*

Blue Bohemian glass goblet with a waisted bowl on a pedestal foot with white foliate design and gilt banding.
- *height 18cm*
- **£340**   • **Mousa**

Sugar Caster ►
- *1880*

A cranberry glass sugar caster with fluted sides, mounted with a silver-plated top with small finial.
- *height 7cm*
- **£110**   • **Barham Antiques**

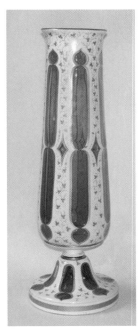

Bohemian Vase ◄
- *1880*
A large Bohemian glass vase, with white enamelled designs and gilt banding on a splayed foot.
- *height 42cm*
- £350   • Mousa

Pair of Lithayalin Beakers ▲
- *1880*
A pair of white Bohemian Lithayalin beakers, of waisted form in translucent glass, the outer surface cut with broad facets, with gilding.
- *height 12cm*
- £380   • Mousa

Cylinder Spirit Decanter ➤
- *1840*
Clear glass cylinder spirit decanter with mushroom stopper.
- *height 23cm*
- £185   • Jasmin Cameron

Turkish Hooka ▼
- *1880*
Turkish hooka used for smoking, the faceted and enamelled glass reservoir with brass apparatus.
- *height 123cm*
- £130   • Mousa

Coin Glass Goblet ➤
- *1864*
Very rare coin glass goblet, with threepenny silver piece inserted in leg.
- *height 18cm*
- £400   • Jasmin Cameron

Irish Decanter ▲
- *circa 1770*
Irish ribbed decanter in clear glass with a lozenge stopper.
- *height 21cm*
- £330   • Jasmin Cameron

Pair of Enamelled Vases ▲
- *1880*
A pair of translucent blue Bohemian vases of baluster form, enamelled with birds and foliage.
- *height 28cm*
- £550   • Mousa

Georgian Wine Glass ▲
- *1810*

Late Georgian pan-topped wine glass on a domed foot.
- *height 12cm*
- £110   • Jasmin Cameron

Wine Glass ▼
- *circa 1770*

Wine glass with multi-spiral air twist stem on a wide circular foot.
- *height 15cm*
- £580   • Jasmin Cameron

Champagne Glasses ▼
- *1880*

A Victorian set of ten hollow-stemmed champagne glasses.
- *height 12cm*
- £900   • Jasmin Cameron

Cordial Wine Glass ➤
- *circa 1750/1760*

George II cordial wine glass with an air twist stem.
- *height 10cm*
- £460   • Jasmin Cameron

Late Georgian Wine Glass ▲
- *1750–70*

A late Georgian wine glass with multi-spiral opaque twist stem on a slender foot.
- *height 12cm*
- £460   • Jasmin Cameron

Expert Tips

Expensive glass objects can be etched and engraved by scratching or gauging the glass with diamond-tipped tools. A less expensive product can be engraved by a technique known as acid etching, which uses varnish to isolate the pattern, which is subsequently submersed in acid to etch the design.

Finger Bowl ▼
- *1845*

An early Victorian green Bristol glass finger bowl.
- *height 9cm*
- £180   • Jasmin Cameron

Plain Bucket Rummer ▲

- *1890*

Plain bucket rummer signed "Val St Lambert". This maker was on a par with Baccarate & St. Louis.
- *height 21cm*
- £330 • Jasmin Cameron

Pair of Victorian Goblets ➤

- *1880*

Extremely fine pair of matching Victorian goblets of super quality. The tall funnel bowls engraved with a fern pattern on barley twist stems by W. & J. Bailey E. Lerche.
- *height 20cm*
- £380 • Jasmin Cameron

Celery Glass ▼

- *1820*

Large engraved celery glass with acid etching around the bowl, on a pedestal base.
- *height 24cm*
- £300 • Jasmin Cameron

Amber Glass Decanters ◀

- *1825*

Rare George III amber glass dessert decanters with moulded, cut and faceted designs.
- *height 22cm*
- £740 • Jasmin Cameron

Brandy Glasses ➤

- *1800*

Called "Joeys" after Joseph Hume, an eighteenth century politician from the English West Country.
- *height 5cm*
- £180 • Jasmin Cameron

Bristol Decanter ▲

- *1810*

Blue Bristol decanter with faceted stopper and gilt oval plaque with the inscription "Brandy".
- *height 27cm*
- £320 • Jasmin Cameron

Expert Tips

Engraved glasses should be looked at closely, and the age and style of the glass should be taken into account when examining the style of the engraving, as it is often the case that the original plain glasses were actually engraved at a later date.

Spirit Decanter ◄
- *1825*
An early nineteenth century
English spirit decanter, with
gilded design and fluted body.
- *height 21cm*
- £1,500 • Jasmin Cameron

Victorian Table Lustres ▲
- *1870*
Pair of Victorian blue glass table
lustres with gilding and cut-glass
crystal drops.
- *height 34cm*
- £590 • Barham Antiques

Ship's Decanter ▲
- *1810–20*
Exceedingly rare ship's decanter
cut with small diamonds and
flutes, with cut mushroom
stopper.
- *height 23cm*
- £540 • Jasmin Cameron

Georgian Finger Bowl ▲
- *1860–80*
A mid-Georgian amethyst glass
Stourbridge finger bowl.
- *height 9cm*
- £130 • Jasmin Cameron

Ship's Glass ►
- *1770–90*
Exceedingly rare ship's glass with
10-ply corkscrew and opaque
bands on a quarter inch thick
circular foot.
- *height 15cm*
- £1,500 • Jasmin Cameron

Stourbridge Finger Bowl ▼
- *1860–1880*
Stourbridge finger bowl in
green glass.
- *height 9cm*
- £141 • Jasmin Cameron

Expert Tips

*Glass pieces must be perfect but
take into account whether the
glass has suffered damage, and
if the chips have been ground or
polished out. Acid can also be
used to disguise damaged areas
of frosted glass, by recreating a
frosted effect. A restorer might
use discs or wheels made of tin
or copper, or wood and cork, in
conjunction with jeweller's
rouge, to polish out damage or
scratches to glass items.*

Glass

Bristol Dessert Plate ➤
- **1850**
Amethyst Bristol glass dessert plate, part of a set of three.
- *diameter 24cm*
- £180 • Jasmin Cameron

Green Bristol Wine Glass ➤
- **1850**
Green Bristol wine glass with scale-cut leg and domed foot.
- *height 11cm*
- £75 • Jasmin Cameron

Gilded Wine Glass ◄
- **1750**
George II wine glass, with an oxo border, gilded rim and hexagonal facet shank on a domed foot.
- *height 14.5cm*
- £560 • Jasmin Cameron

Georgian Rummer ◄
- **1809**
A late Georgian rummer, the notched bowl with terracing on a square flat foot.
- *height 14cm*
- £340 • Jasmin Cameron

Jelly Plate ▲
- **19th century**
Clear glass ice jelly plate, with crenellated rims.
- *diameter 12cm*
- £130 • Jasmin Cameron

Engraved Goblet ▼
- **circa 1800–15**
A late Georgian goblet, the bowl engraved with hunting scenes.
- *height 18.5cm*
- £700 • Jasmin Cameron

Jewellery

An incredible amount of jewellery changes hands every day in auction rooms, dealers's shops, market stalls and boot fairs. Look for quality first.

The adornment of precious metals and stones goes back to Babylonian times when lapis lazuli and gold were brought together to form the first jewellery. The wearing of amulets or the giving of jewels as presents has been part of human social interaction over millennia. Today there is hardly a high street which does not possess at least one jewellery shop. When does an object become a piece of jewellery? For example, spectacles are just spectacles until they have been exposed to the hands of a master crafsman such as Fabergé. This can be translated to all manner of objects which when adorned and encrusted with precious stones could be termed as jewellery.

When purchasing a piece of jewellery the maker is by far the most important factor, as is the quality and design. A good provenance also adds to its value, for example earrings worn by Marilyn Monroe can command stratospheric prices.

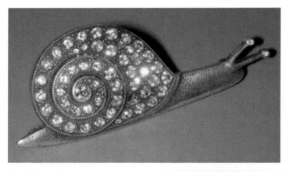

Snail Brooch ▲
- *1930*
A snail brooch in paste and silver.
- £65 • Linda Bee

Christian Dior Brooch ◄
- *1960*
Circus horse brooch by Christian Dior.
- £295 • Linda Bee

American Watch Bracelet ▼
- *1940*
Gold-plated American watch bracelet, similar to one worn by Gloria Swanson.
- £250 • Linda Bee

Cameo Brooch ◄
- *1820*
Italian cameo head of young girl with English mount.
- *height 4cm*
- £750 • RBR Group

Expert Tips

A poor setting normally reflects a poor stone and cheap manufacture. Moreover, poor settings increase the likelihood of stone loss.

Green Ring ▼
- *1960*
A fun fashion green plastic and
metal fun ring.
- *width 1cm*
- £45   ● Linda Bee

French Brooch ▼
- *1950*
A French brooch styled as a pair
of lady's legs with paste garters
and red high heeled shoes.
- *height 7cm*
- £85   ● Linda Bee

Burmese Ruby Ring ▲
- *1930*
Burmese Art Deco gold ring
with four large rubies surrounded
by diamonds.
- £2,000   ● Michele Rowan

Egyptian-Style Pendant ▲
- *1920*
An Egyptian-style hexagonal
shaped pendant with silver
sphinx and teardrop amber
stone.
- *length 2cm*
- £120   ● Linda Bee

French Art Deco
Necklace ▲
- *1930*
A French green bakelite and
silver link necklace.
- *diameter 2cm*
- £120   ● Linda Bee

Arts and Crafts Brooch ▲
- *circa 1910*
Silver and gold Arts and Crafts
brooch set with crystal and
turquoise flowers.
- *diameter 3cm*
- £650   ● RBR Group

Fun Hooped Earrings ◄
- *1960*
English green plastic hooped
earrings made in London.
- *diameter 4cm*
- £25   ● Linda Bee

Gold Earrings ▲
- *1840*
A pair of William IV gold and
foil backed earrings with
aquamarine settings and gold
tassels.
- *height 4cm*
- £750   • Michele Rowan

Pearl Ring ▲
- *circa 1890*
Victorian lozenge-shaped gold
ring set with a diamond
surrounded by pearls.
- *length 4cm*
- £750   • Michele Rowan

Masonic Gold Locket ▲
- *1900*
Masonic gold locket formed as a
ten-page book with various
engravings.
- *height 2cm*
- £500   • Michele Rowan

Padlock Brooch ◄
- *1940*
An American heart-shaped
brooch in the shape of a padlock
connected to a key, with paste
diamonds. Designed by
Castlecliff and set in sterling
silver.
- *diameter 2cm*
- £120   • Linda Bee

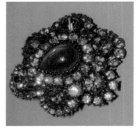

Green Lozenge-Shape Brooch ▲
- *1950*
Czechoslovakian brooch set with
a dark green lozenge stone
surrounded by bright green,
faceted stones.
- *diameter 5cm*
- £55   • Linda Bee

Navajo Ring ◄
- *circa 1970s*
Silver Navajo ring with two oval
turquoise stones set within a
feather design.
- *length 4cm*
- £169   • Wilde Ones

Expert Tips

*Prior to the Victorian age the
rose cut was the most popular
technique used for cutting gems
and stones. It was replaced by
the brilliant cut, which increases
the sparkle and desirability
of the stone.*

Schiaparelli Bracelet ▼
- *circa 1950*

Bracelet with emerald green and
sea green stones, designed by
Schiaparelli.
- *length 12cm*
- £550   • Sue Mautner

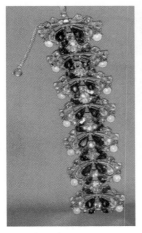

Brooch and Earrings ▼
- *circa 1950*

American brooch and earrings by
Miriam Haskell.
- £850   • Sue Mautner

Miriam Haskell Brooch ▲
- *circa 1950*

American Miriam Haskell brooch
with glass stones, set within a
stylised floral arrangement.
- *length 4cm*
- £450   • Sue Mautner

Cameo Brooch ▼
- *1820*

An Italian cameo of lady's head
within an English setting.
- *height 5cm*
- £750   • RBR Group

Bohemian Garnet Necklace ▶
- *1870*

Bohemian garnet necklace with
floral clusters and swags.
- £550   • Michele Rowan

Linked Pearl Bracelet ◀
- *circa 1950*

Miriam Haskell bracelet linked
with flowers and set with pearls.
- *length 14cm*
- £750   • Sue Mautner

Chanel Linked Brooch ▲
- *circa 1960*

Dramatic Chanel brooch
encrusted with paste diamonds
and blue, red and black stones.
- *length 12cm*
- £650   • Sue Mautner

Kokopelli Brooch ▼

- *circa 1970s*

An American Indian silver
brooch showing the fertility god
Kokopelli blowing a flute, inset
with a circular turquoise stone.

- *length 5cm*
- £129 • **Wilde Ones**

Ethiopian Pendant ▼

- *circa 1890*

An Ethiopian silver pendant
cross.

- *height 5cm*
- £48 • **Iconastas**

Brooch and Earrings ▲

- *circa 1950s*

American jewellery set consisting
of a brooch and a pair of earrings
styled as flowers by Miriam
Haskell.

- *length 5cm/brooch*
- £550 • **Sue Mautner**

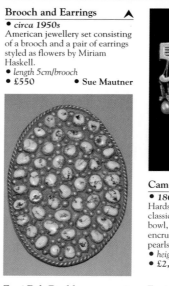

Zuni Belt Buckle ▲

- *1930*

Zuni oval belt buckle with
turquoise nuggets on a silver
setting.

- *length 8cm*
- £699 • **Wilde Ones**

Cameo Brooch ▲

- *1860*

Hardstone cameo brooch of a
classical woman with a ewer and
bowl, decorated with flowers and
encrusted with diamonds and
pearls drops.

- *height 4cm*
- £2,500 • **RBR Group**

Zuni Concha Belt ▼

- *circa 1930s*

Zuni belt with alternating
conchas of bow and lozenge form,
set with turquoise, signed "VMB".

- *length 107cm*
- £1,999 • **Wilde Ones**

Expert Tips

*The cardinal principles when
choosing jewellery are condition,
age, rarity and desirability.
Avoid pieces repaired with
solder rather than gold or
platinum. On flexible jewellery,
inspect the links and joints.*

Painted Enamel Ring ▲

- *circa 1780*
Georgian oval ring with a
painted head of a young lady
on enamel within a gold
foliate setting.
- *diameter 3cm*
- £750 • RBR Group

Rock Crystal Tiara ▲

- *1870*
Victorian silver and rock crystal
tiara in a gothic revival style.
- *diameter 17cm*
- £1,500 • Michele Rowan

Christian Dior Brooch ▲

- *1966*
Christian Dior brooch with
pearls.
- *height 8.5cm*
- £275 • Linda Bee

Enamel Swiss Brooch ▼

- *1850*
Swiss enamel brooch of madonna
and child within a pearl border.
- *height 6cm*
- £1,500 • RBR Group

Italian Cameo Brooch ▲

- *1860*
An Italian cameo brooch
depicting a Biblical scene set in
an English 15ct. gold base.
- *length 3cm*
- £1,500 • RBR Group

Shell Cameo Brooch ◄

- *1880*
Shell cameo of a lady feeding a
bird, set within 15ct. gold.
- *height 5cm*
- £850 • RBR Group

Mythological Cameo Brooch ▲

- *1890*
Shell cameo brooch of centaur
and cupid mounted in an 18ct.
gold base and set with diamonds
and natural pearls.
- *length 5cm*
- £2,000 • RBR Group

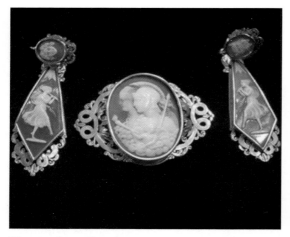

Shell Cameo Earrings and Brooch ◄

- *1840*

Shell cameo set with a mythological tone, in 18ct. gold with scrolled borders.

- £2,500
- RBR Group

Victorian Cameo Brooch ∨

- *1875*

A cameo of a pre-Raphaelite lady looking to dexter, in classical dress.

- *height 6cm*
- £950
- RBR Group

Italian Cameo Brooch ▲

- *1885*

An Italian shell cameo showing a bust of a lady set in an English 18ct. gold base.

- *length 7cm*
- £1,950
- RBR Group

French Cameo Brooch ▲

- *1870*

French cameo of lady's head set in 18ct. gold encrusted with diamonds and pearls.

- *diameter 4cm*
- £3,250
- RBR Group

Expert Tips

A good provenance accompanying a piece of jewellery, or a connection with titled persons or celebrities, can considerably enhance its value. When purchasing jewellery also bear in mind that a renowned maker or jewellery house is usually a good indicator of top quality and design. A piece of jewellery can also have its authenticity considerably enhanced if it still possesses an original presentation case.

Medusa Cameo Ring ▲

- *1880*

Ring in 18ct. gold with a cameo of Medusa.

- *diameter 1cm*
- £750
- RBR Group

Angel Cameo Brooch ◄

- *1860*

Cameo of an angel with a dove, set within a 15ct. gold base with gadrooned border.

- *height 4cm*
- £850
- RBR Group

Silver Choker ▼
- *circa 1950*

American Indian silver-beaded
necklace with an almond-shaped
turquoise pendant set in silver.
- *length 3.5cm*
- £289   • Wilde Ones

Victorian Gold Brooch ▼
- *circa 1870*

Victorian 15ct. gold brooch with
swags and tassels with a lozenge-
shaped citrine set in the centre.
- *diameter 3cm*
- £850   • RBR Group

Art Nouveau Brooch ➤
- *1900*

Art Nouveau 9ct. gold brooch set
with a turquoise and baroque
pearl drop. Marked "Liberty &
Co".
- *length 3cm*
- £480   • Gooday Gallery

Diamond Necklace ▲
- *18th century*

French rose cut diamond ribbon
necklace.
- £4,500   • Michele Rowan

Ball Pendant ▲
- *circa 1925*

Lapis ball-drop pendant with
diamonds within a star-shaped
platinum setting.
- *diameter 5cm*
- £850   • RBR Group

Hand-Painted
Enamel Locket ▼
- *circa 1850*

French hand-painted enamel
locket of a lady with three small
diamonds in her hair on an 18ct.
gold base.
- *height 5cm*
- £750   • RBR Group

Gold Brooch ▼
- *1820*

Brooch in 18ct. gold encrusted
with emeralds, rubies and pearls.
- *diameter 4cm*
- £950   • RBR Group

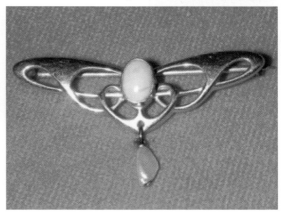

Silver Brooch ▼
- *1890*

Art and Crafts silver brooch set with Mexican fire opals and citrines.
- *diameter 3cm*
- £520   • Gooday Gallery

Victorian Star Brooch ▼
- *1880*

Victorian diamond star brooch set with a lapis centre with a further ten stones radiating from the centre.
- *diameter 4cm*
- £1,850   • RBR Group

Pendant Locket ▲
- *circa 1900*

Art Nouveau silver locket decorated with red and green enamel by Liberty & Co.
- *diameter 2cm*
- £680   • Gooday Gallery

Zuni Pendant ▲
- *circa 1940*

Zuni pin pendant showing an eagle dancer with turquoise, spiney oyster shell, jet, and mother of pearl on a silver base with beading.
- *diameter 7cm*
- £950   • Wilde Ones

Silver Necklace ▲
- *circa 1950s*

American Indian silver-beaded necklace with a silver Naga inset with coral, with fleur- de-Lys terminals.
- *diameter 5.5cm*
- £699   • Wilde Ones

Cornelian Brooch ◄
- *1890*

Arts and Crafts silver brooch of a foliate design set with cornelians, by Amy Sonheim.
- *diameter 4cm*
- £280   • Gooday Gallery

Expert Tips

Victorian jewellery has proved to be extremely collectable and ever fewer pieces are reaching the market, although jet jewellery from the 1880s, which was made to commemorate Queen Victoria's mourning of the death of Prince Albert, remains somewhat undervalued. It is always advisable when seeking a valuation, or purchasing an expensive piece of jewellery, to contact a reputable jeweller.

Art Nouveau Brooch ▲

- *circa 1900*
Art Nouveau brooch with silver
tulips with orange and green
enamel settings, designed by
Liberty & Co.
- *length 3cm*
- **£350**   ● **Gooday Gallery**

Zuni Ring ▲

- *circa 2000*
Zuni silver ring with a central sun
symbol inset with jet and
turquoise stones, surrounded by a
feather design.
- *length 3.5cm*
- **£169**   ● **Wilde Ones**

Navajo Ring ▼

- *circa 1930s*
A Navajo silver ring with a
lozenge-shaped and elongated
Kingman turquoise stone.
- *length 5.6cm*
- **£299**   ● **Wilde Ones**

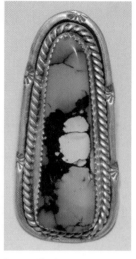

Cannetille Cross ◄

- *1820*
A gold Cannetille cross designed
as a pendant.
- **£550**   ● **Michele Rowan**

Gold Earrings ▼

- *1870*
Gold and coral Etruscan revival
hooped earrings.
- **£650**   ● **Michele Rowan**

American Indian
Bracelet ▲

- *circa 1980s*
Gentleman's channel-work silver
bracelet inset with chrysocolla
and azurite stones.
- *diameter 23.2cm*
- **£299**   ● **Wilde Ones**

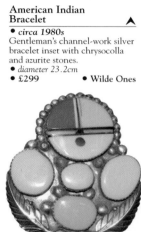

Turquoise Pendant ▲

- *circa 1970*
Zuni silver and beaded pendant
set with four lozenge-shaped
turquoise stones surmounted by a
sun symbol with red coral insert.
- *length 6cm*
- **£399**   ● **Wilde Ones**

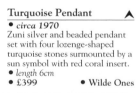

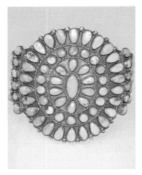

Turquoise Cuff ▲

- *circa 1920s*

American Indian silver cuff set with graduated teardrop and lozenge-shaped turquoise stones in a sunburst design.
- *diameter 8cm*
- £2,300
- Wilde Ones

Zuni Brooch ▼

- *circa 1999*

Circular silver Zuni brooch with graduated teardrop and lozenge-shaped turquoise stones set in a radiating sunburst pattern.
- *diameter 11cm*
- £899
- Wilde Ones

Enamel Brooch ◄

- *circa 1880*

Cherub brooch painted on enamel and mounted on 18ct. gold base with rope twist border set with sapphires.
- *height 5cm*
- £650
- RBR Group

French Ceramic Brooch ►

- *1950*

A green French ceramic brooch in the shape of a poodle with bronze decoration and metal clasp.
- *length 5cm*
- £45
- Linda Bee

Victorian Gold Brooch ▲

- *1880*

Victorian 18ct. gold brooch with pearl flowers set within delicate gold scrolling and a drop pendant from gold chains.
- *diameter 4cm*
- £1,500
- RBR Group

Navajo Concha Belt ◄

- *circa 1960*

Navajo silver concha engraved belt set with turquoise stones.
- *length 98cm*
- £699
- Wilde Ones

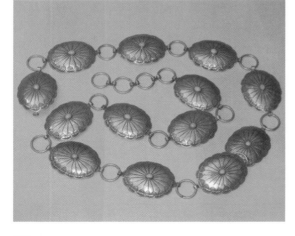

Expert Tips

When considering insuring your items it is worthwhile having an up-to-date valuation with a full description, and to have the piece photographed. These details should then be stored separately from the jewellery items.

Mosaic Brooch ➤
- *circa 1860*
Italian mosaic brooch with a
scene of doves feeding on a
black background, set within
18ct. gold.
- *length 4cm*
- £750   • RBR Group

Enamel Earrings ▲
- *circa 1840*
Enamel earrings with painted
classical landscapes within an
18ct. gold setting of acorn leaf
design.
- *length 4cm*
- £950   • RBR Group

Necklace and Bracelet ▼
- *1930*
German DRGM metal and paste
necklace and bracelet.
- £195   • Linda Bee

Painted Enamel Brooch ▼
- *circa 1840*
Painted enamel brooch of a Swiss
landscape in an 18ct. gold setting.
- *length 5cm*
- £850   • RBR Group

Fashion Ring ▲
- *1960*
Swedish ring with large
central stone surrounded by
metal band.
- £95   • Linda Bee

Zuni Silver Cuff Set ▲
- *circa 2000*
Zuni silver cuff set with jet and
turquoise stones in a geometric
pattern radiating from a stylised
eagle, signed "Benji & Shirley
Tzuni".
- *diameter 6cm*
- £899   • Wilde Ones

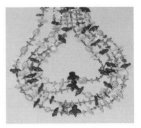

Zuni Fetish Necklace ▲
- *circa 2000*
Four-stranded Zuni fetish
necklace with a menagerie of
animals including eagles, ravens,
turtles, coyotes and crows set in
jet, turquoise, coral and other
semi-precious stones.
- *length 89cm*
- £699   • Wilde Ones

Wrist Watch ▼
- *1940*

Wrist watch by Accurist
decorated with marcasite stones.
- £120   • Linda Bee

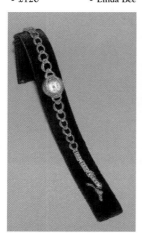

Knot Brooch ▼
- *circa 1860*

Victorian eagle's head knot
brooch 18ct. gold set with
emeralds pearls and rubies.
- *diameter 4cm*
- £1,850   • RBR Group

American Metal Bracelet ▲
- *1940*

An American metal bracelet
with bakelite plaques decorated
with flowers.
- *height 2cm*
- £120   • Linda Bee

William IV Brooch ▲
- *1830*

Gold brooch with a main central
diamond surrounded by three
others, and a pear-shaped ruby
drop.
- *length 5cm*
- £1,950   • RBR Group

Enamel Studs ▼
- *circa 1880*

Enamel 18ct. gold studs with
hand-painted cats with blue
ribbons around their necks.
- *diameter 1cm*
- £750   • RBR Group

Gold Brooch ▲
- *circa 1860*

Victorian 18ct. gold brooch with
a key pattern border and a Pietra
Dura panel of flowers.
- *height 5cm*
- £650   • RBR Group

Expert Tips

*Jewellery pieces that possess in
their design and construction the
ability to be taken apart and
transformed into separate
pieces, for example, a necklace
that can be broken down into a
brooch, a pair of earrings and a
bracelet, are rare and therefore
valuable. A purchaser of such a
special item is in fact buying
three pieces in one.*

Rose Diamond Pendant ▼
- *circa 1880*
Victorian 18ct. gold pendant with
enamel flowers set with rose
diamonds within scrolled borders.
- *length 4cm*
- £750   • RBR Group

Mosaic Brooch ▼
- *circa 1860*
Italian floral mosaic brooch
within a stylised 18ct. gold star
setting.
- *length 4cm*
- £950   • RBR Group

Victorian Pendant ▲
- *circa 1890*
Victorian pendant set in 15ct.
gold with a peridot to the centre,
surrounded by pearls.
- *height 4cm*
- £950   • RBR Group

Enamel Brooch ◀
- *circa 1840*
Victorian enamel brooch with a
painted panel of Lake Geneva,
within a blue oval frame with
gold mounts.
- *length 5cm*
- £1,150   • RBR Group

Victorian Gold Earrings ▲
- *circa 1880*
Victorian 18ct. gold hoop
earrings with pierced floral
decoration.
- *diameter 3cm*
- £1,050   • RBR Group

Regency Brooch ▲
- *1800–30*
Regency 18ct. gold filigree garnet
and turquoise brooch.
- *length 5cm*
- £650   • RBR Group

Garnet Earrings ◀
- *1820*
Drop earrings in 18ct. gold with
garnets within a flower shaped
setting.
- *length 6cm*
- £1,450   • RBR Group

Marine Items

Marine antiques, apart from being very well made, appeal to the more romantic souls of an island race.

Marine items now have worldwide appeal as interest in yachting grows every year. This fascination with the sea has been further enhanced by yacht races such as Fastnet and Round the World, and also the literature produced by the yachting and motorboat magazines. For people who love the sea it must be impossible not to collect marine items for their motorboat or yacht, and who can resist, at the end of a successful voyage, the desire to purchase something in order to remember their trip? From the small piece of scrimshaw evoking the adventures of whalers and seamen of the past, to the grand oil paintings by the great marine painters such as Turner, or Thomas Luny, we can see a range of mediums being used to describe the history and the people of the sea.

The importance of sea instruments cannot be underestimated, as the welfare of commercial seamen and the navies of the world depend on them. Chronometers or sextants, along with maps and detailed tide charts opened up the sea routes and formed the basis of the wealth of the great trading nations.

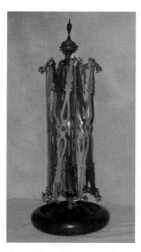

Expert Tips

In the Napoleonic Wars 60,000 French prisoners of war were billeted in England either in prisons, or in prison ships, and an industry sprung up to help the prisoners buy personal luxuries. The items made by prisoners included model ships, figures and chess sets, and guillotines.

Wooden Swift ◀
- *1880*
Antique swift made of wood.
- *height 69cm*
- **£850**   • Langfords Marine

"Faithful Freddie" Binnacle ▲
- *1930*
Brass binnacle from a submarine known as a "Faithful Freddie".
- *height 28cm*
- **£1,250**   • Langfords Marine

Sailing Ship Diorama ▶
- *1880*
Sailing ship diorama with three masts and a smaller boat in the foreground, in a mahogany glass case.
- *58cm x 82cm*
- **£1,650**   • Langfords Marine

Sea Chest ▲
- *circa 1830*
Antique sea chest Funa Dansu with original metalware.
- *35cm x 45cm x 39cm*
- **£1,600**   • Gordon Reece

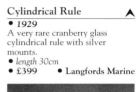

Napoleonic Model Ship ▲
- *1810*

Napoleonic prisoner-of-war ship *Defender* on a stand, made of bone. Very fine detail, good rigging, good provenance.
- *52cm x 53cm*
- £85,000 • Langfords Marine

Ivory Box ▲
- *circa 1840*

An unusual and charming ivory box, possibly originally a toothpick holder, the hinged lid with a compass inset, the base with rose gold fastener.
- *7cm x 3cm*
- £239 • Langfords Marine

Ship's Bell ▶
- *early 20th century*

Ship's brass bell made for the "Grangeburn".
- *height 31cm*
- £780 • Langfords Marine

Cylindrical Rule ▲
- *1929*

A very rare cranberry glass cylindrical rule with silver mounts.
- *length 30cm*
- £399 • Langfords Marine

Russian Chronometer ▲
- *1880*

Brass Russian chronometer with a two-day movement in a rosewood box with brass fittings.
- *19cm x 19cm*
- £1,400 • Langfords Marine

Oak-Barrelled Telescope ▲
- *19th century*

Polished brass telescope, with a lacquered oak barrel, signed on the single drawer "George Leone, Liverpool".
- *85cm x 7cm*
- £349 • Langfords Marine

Magnifying Glass ◀
- *1837–1901*

Victorian magnifying glass with ivory handle and silver decoration.
- *length 19cm*
- £69 • Langfords Marine

Ivory Baton ◄

- **1837–1901**
An ivory and ebony regimental baton or swagger stick.
- *length 53cm*
- **£149** • Langfords Marine

Brass Lamp ►

- **1912**
Polished and lacquered brass lamp, stamped on the base and lamp unit with manufacturer's details.
- *height 34cm*
- **£179** • Langfords Marine

Rolling Rule ▼

- **circa 1940**
Brass polished and lacquered parallel rolling role in original box.
- *length 42cm*
- **£149** • Langfords Marine

Ship in a Bottle ▲

- **1900**
Three-masted ship in a bottle with coastal scene in the background.
- *length 30cm*
- **£480** • Langfords Marine

Builder's Model ▼

- **circa 1910**
Builder's model of a steamer, designed by William Doxford & Sons, in a glazed mahogany case.
- *length 39cm*
- **£12,500** • Langfords Marine

Expert Tips

To identify marine furniture, look for brass handles and wheels, as well as items that can be broken down into smaller pieces as this allowed them to be removed from the cabin and fastened to the bulkheads of a ship, in order to make the deck clear and ready for action.

Air Meter ◄

- **1882**
A polished and lacquered brass air meter with a silvered dial by Elliot Bros, London.
- *diameter 28cm*
- **£699** • Langfords Marine

Half Hull ▼

- **mid-19th century**
A good example of early shipbuilder's half-hull block model of a river vessel.
- *width 56cm*
- **£799** • Langfords Marine

Model of Yacht ▼

- *late 20th century*
Scale model of Americas Cup
Yacht *Rainbow*.
- *81cm x 120cm*
- **£1,650** • **Langfords Marine**

Model Ship ▲

- *circa 1840*
Ivory model of a Dieppe brig with
fine detailed rigging, set in a glass
dome.
- *12cm x 16cm*
- **£2,600** • **Langfords Marine**

Small Pond Yacht ◄

- *circa 1930*
Mahogany model pond yacht
with full rigging, on a mahogany
stand.
- *length 82cm*
- **£510** • **Langfords Marine**

Napoleonic Ship ▼

- *circa 1800*
A Napoleonic prisoner-of-war
model of a ship, made of beef
bones, with fine detail to the
rigging and deck.
- *42cm x 36cm*
- **£3,400** • **Langfords Marine**

Shipwright's Tools ▲

- *circa 1880*
Collection of four shipwright's
tools made of wood and iron.
- *68cm x 25cm*
- **£180** • **Langfords Marine**

Pedestal Globe ▼

- *1890*
A Victorian globe circled with a
brass meridian and horizon circle,
standing on a tall mahogany
pedestal and square base.
- *height 99cm*
- **£625** • **Langfords Marine**

Expert Tips

*Among scrimshaw items it is
well worth looking out for pieces
made in the Colonies as these
fetch much higher prices,
especially pieces made
in America.*

Brass Candlestick Balance ▼

- *1840*

Victorian brass candlestick or lighthouse balance. The words, "POSTAL BALANCE" embossed with a spring scale on a circular moulded foot.

- *height 17cm*
- £299　● Langfords Marine

Brass Sextant ▶

- *1890*

Victorian brass sextant by Gebbie & Co, complete with its own mahogany box with brass handle and fittings.

- *12cm x 12cm*
- £1,400　● Langfords Marine

Model of a Ship ▼

- *1947*

Builder's model of TSMV Copeland, Clyde Shipping Co. Ltd, Glasgow.

- *length 155cm*
- £24,800　● Langfords Marine

Carved Coconut ◀

- *1880*

Victorian coconut with carving of a ship, cat, guitar, frog and foliage. These coconuts were usually carved by sailors.

- *length 6cm*
- £85　　● Langfords Marine

Expert Tips

Marine brass and copperware must be free of severe corrosion. It is worth noting that signs of corrosion cannot be accepted as a guarantee of age.

Anerold Pocket Barometer ▶

- *1890*

Victorian Anerold pocket barometer by C.W. Dixet, New Bond Street, London.

- *diameter 5cm*
- £360　　● Langfords Marine

Brass Telescope ◀

- *1910*

Brass telescope by Ladd of Chancery Lane London, in original mahogany box.

- *length 102cm*
- £2,900　● Langfords Marine

Mary Tin ◄
- *1914*

A polished and embossed brass Mary Tin, presented by Princess Mary, aged 17, to all those wearing the King's uniform at Christmas, 1914.
- *width 13cm*
- £79   • Langfords Marine

Ship in a Bottle ▼
- *1885*

Square-rigged ship in a bottle on a mahogany stand.
- *length 28cm*
- £320   • Langfords Marine

Large Brass Compass ▲
- *1880*

Brass compass with original leather case.
- *diameter 440cm*
- £440   • Langfords Marine

Dry Card Compass ▲
- *1870*

Victorian brass dry card compass encased in glass.
- *diameter 16.5cm*
- £680   • Langfords Marine

Bronze Porthole ▼
- *19th century*

A replica polished bronze or gunmetal porthole, with hinged glass port.
- *diameter 35cm*
- £119   • Langfords Marine

Pocket Sextant ◄
- *1895*

Victorian brass pocket drum sextant.
- *diameter 8cm*
- £650   • Langfords Marine

Mahogany Whaling Boat ▼
- *1800*

Rare mahogany model of a whaling boat with brass fittings on original stand.
- *100cm x 16cm*
- £5,600   • Langfords Marine

Brass Monocular ➤
- *1880*

Brass monocular with six draws.
- *height 28cm*
- £580 • Langfords Marine

First Aid Kit ▲
- *1920s*

A rare and unique piece of shipping memorabilia, "First aid outfit for lifeboats", approved by the Ministry of Transport.
- *height 30cm*
- £99 • Langfords Marine

"Faithful Freddie" Binnacle ▼
- *early 20th century*

A "Faithful Freddie" binnacle from a submarine. This one was refitted to a little ship, for the evacuation of Dunkirk.
- *height 45cm*
- £1,250 • Langfords Marine

Terrestrial Globe ◀
- *circa 1917*

Terrestrial globe by George Philip & Son Ltd, printed in colour.
- *25cm x 15cm*
- £849 • Langfords Marine

Half Sailing Boat ◀
- *1880*

Victorian mahogany half sailing boat.
- *length 97cm*
- £4,400 • Langfords Marine

Ship's Wheel ▲
- *1890*

Victorian mahogany ship's wheel, with brass banding.
- *diameter 27cm*
- £600 • Langfords Marine

Bulkhead Clock ▼
- *circa 1920*

An eight day ship's bulkhead clock marked "Smiths Empire", with a painted enamelled dial and Arabic numerals.
- *diameter 18cm*
- £240 • Langfords Marine

Mechanical Music

**Musical boxes, phonographs and gramophones
remain as popular as ever at auction**

Mechanically driven musical items have commanded a good price at auction since the 1980s. In particular, the polyphone disc musical box doubles in price to what it may have fetched twelve months previously.

The main problems to consider when purchasing musical boxes are, and always will be, the difficulty in assessing the extent of any damage, as the cost of repairing a musical box can be the same as the purchase price. Bear in mind when at auction that the cost of the damaged box

as opposed to a restored item is comparatively small, and it therefore makes sense to purchase an item that is in good working condition.

The informed collector of musical boxes listens for a good arrangement, such as the mandolin and forte piano, which can considerably raise the value of an item.

It is also worth looking out for overture boxes, as they are very collectable due to their rarity and musical quality, with most dating from the 1840s to the 1860s, which is seen as a zenith for this market.

Key-Wound Musical Box ➤
- **1825**
Early key-wound musical box in plain fruitwood case with no end flap over the controls, four airs (no tune card), 19.7cm cylinder and square head comb screws.
- *9.4cm x 31.9cm*
- **£2,400** • Keith Harding

Swiss Musical Box ➤
- **1888**
Swiss musical box in burr walnut with banding and six engraved bells by B. A. Bremond.
- *26.25cm x 48.75cm*
- **£2,750** • Keith Harding

Rocket Juke Box ◄
- **1952**
Rocket juke box, type 1434, in chrome, wood and bakelite, with 50 selections. This was the last 78 rpm player and the first 45 rpm player, by Rock Ola Manufacturing Company.
- *150cm x 76cm*
- **£5,750** • Juke Box Services

Rock Ola 1448 ▲
- **1955**
American Rock Ola 1448 juke box in chrome and bakelite, with 120 selections.
- *141cm x 76cm*
- **£5,000** • Juke Box Services

Expert Tips

Juke boxes have shown an enormous increase in value; it appears that the more outrageous the design, the greater the cost. The highest prices are generally paid for complete and working units.

Singing Bird Musical Box ➤

- *circa 1900s*

Singing bird in polished brass
cage with round embossed brass
base, probably by Bontems.

- *height 28cm*
- £1,750   • Keith Harding

Musical Banjo Player ➤

- *1890*

French Banjo player musical
automaton in orginal costume
with porcelain face, by Gustave
Vichy, Paris.

- *height 48cm*
- £4,900   • Keith Harding

Expert Tips

*Musical boxes are expensive to
restore: the more complicated
the mechanics and cylinders, the
higher the cost of restoration.*

Rock Ola Rocket ◄

- *1946*

American Rock Ola Rocket juke
box, type 1422, with 20
selections, in wood, chrome and
bakelite, with a decorated front
panel.

- *146cm x 81cm x 67cm*
- £4,000   • Juke Box Services

Coin-Operated Polyphon ◄

- *1898*

Upright coin-operated Polyphon,
Model 105, with ten discs
(62.5cm diameter), in a walnut
case with gallery.

- *height 232cm*
- £12,500   • Keith Harding

Musical Ballerina ➤

- *1880*

Musical automaton ballerina,
rotating and dancing arabesques.
Musical movement in the red
plush base by Rouillet et
Decamps.

- *height 45cm*
- £4,500   • Keith Harding

Swiss Musical Box ▲

- *circa 1890*

Swiss 12-air drums, bells and
castanets musical box with 33cm
cylinder, coloured Isle Rousseau
tune card. Popular programme
including *Patience* and *Pirates of
Penzance*. Eight stick snare drum,
six engine turned bells, and eight
beater wood block. Rosewood lid
and front, with frame of painted
leaves, the lid with marquetry in
coloured woods, with painted
foliate border under lid and round
inner glass lid.

- *62.5cm x 30cm*
- £4,950   • Keith Harding

Dog Model Gramophone ▼

- *1910*

Early dog model HMV Junior
Monarch gramophone in
laminated wood with fully
functional original brass horn and
concert soundbox. Model No 3.

- *70cm x 65cm*
- £1,950   • Keith Harding

Spanish Dancer ▼
- *circa 1890*

A Spanish dancer musical automaton, probably by Lambert, Paris. Porcelain head by Simon & Halbig, mould no. 1039. She turns her head from side to side, flicks her tambourine and stamps her foot in time to the music. With red plush base and original shoes and stockings.
- *height 52.5cm*
- £2,800   • Keith Harding

Six-Air Musical Box ➤
- *1870*

Six-air Swiss musical box in marquetry rosewood with 22cm cylinder, by Ami Rivenc, Geneva.
- *13.75cm x 43.75cm*
- £2,900   • Keith Harding

Key-Wound Musical Box ◄
- *1830*

Swiss rosewood musical box with end flap over the controls, key wind and 20cm cylinder. Plays four airs, by Henriot.
- *10.75cm x 36cm x 15cm*
- £2,900   • Keith Harding

Seeburg Wall-O-Matic ▲
- *1955*

Chrome Seeburg Wall-O-Matic, also known as an American Diner Box. Type 3WA, with 200 selections. It has a hide-away player and is wall mounted.
- *38cm x 31cm*
- £1,200   • Juke Box Services

Expert Tips

Automatons are expensive items to buy and much depends on their working order and condition. Genuine examples are proving increasingly difficult to find.

Musical Mandoline Player ▲
- *circa 1890*

Two-air musical automaton by Lambert in the form of a white-faced Pierrot playing a mandoline, swaying from side to side and plucking the strings, in original costume and hat. Key pierced "LB". Porcelain head marked "TBJ, 222, Paris". Plays "Valencia" and "On the Riviera".
- *height 50cm*
- £3,900   • Keith Harding

Carillon Musical Box ▲
- *circa 1900*

Carillon musical box by L'Epée, the nine individually played bells surmounted with doves. Eight listed airs are pinned on a 33cm cylinder. Rosewood inlaid lid with marquetry design of pipes, harp and flute.
- *22.5cm x 56.25cm*
- £4,900   • Keith Harding

Disc Table Polyphon ◄
- *1900*

Rare German 50cm disc table Polyphon with two combs, 118 notes. Carved mouldings to the case, shaped figured walnut panels and marquetry panel on the lid. Comes with original table with four turned legs at the corners supporting shelves for the discs.
- *112.5cm x 68.5cm*
- £8,500   • Keith Harding

Trashcan Juke Box ➤
- *1948*
Trashcan juke box made from bakelite and WWII scrap airplane aluminium, the whole in a wood grain finish. With 20 selections of 78 rpms, made by Seeburg.
- *144cm x 100cm*
- **£5,550** • Juke Box Services

Musical Box ▼
- *1875*
Nicole Frères musical box playing eight airs, with 33cm cylinder and rosewood marquetry lid.
- *14.5cm x 56.3cm*
- **£3,500** • Keith Harding

Six-Air Musical Box ◄
- *1865*
Swiss six-air musical box in marquetry rosewood by Ducommun Girod.
- *20.5cm x 42.5cm*
- **£3,300** • Keith Harding

Continental 2 ◄
- *1962*
Continental 2 chrome juke box in red, with 200 selections. This was the first stereo juke box by AMI and has 100 records, with or without big centres (dinked/undinked).
- *155cm x 72cm*
- **£7,500** • Juke Box Services

Mystic 478 ➤
- *1978–9*
Rock Ola Mystic 478 juke box in wood and chrome, with a digital microcomputer music system and 200 selections.
- *136cm x 104cm*
- **£1,500** • Juke Box Services

Seeburg V 200 ▲
- *circa 1960*
Chrome, wood and glass Seeburg V 200 in stereo, with a rotating title card drum and 200 plays.
- *height 125cm*
- **£8,000** • Juke Box Services

Eight-Air Musical Box ▲
- *circa 1895*
Eight-air box with 28cm x 6.5cm cylinder, coloured card listing eight dance and popular tunes, tune indicator. Walnut case with gilt carrying handles and large ornamental escutcheon, the rosewood lid with design of marquetry flowers in coloured woods, by Ami Rivenc/ Dawkins, Geneva.
- *18.75cm x 57.5cm*
- **£3,900** • Keith Harding

Musical Instruments

Some musical instruments are also beautiful pieces of furniture, and some have been played by the famous. Only the musically excellent are worth real money.

When we look at the world of musical instruments and consider collecting them we must be aware that different rules apply. Beware of the older instrument, as there are many copies on the market and do not rely on the grand maker's label as being a guarantee of authenticity. For example, a piece of antique furniture from the seventeenth century will be valued completely differently to a Stradivari violin, whose value is based not only on its historical interest, but also on the fact that it can greatly enhance the quality of a performance by a musician. With such renowned instruments, where the sound that can be achieved is of the highest quality, the prices can reach astronomical levels, as the virtuoso's future could be held back without the right violin or viola. Obviously one can also purchase good working violins at a relatively reasonable sum. After all, it is not just the maker of the instrument that is important; it is also the dedication of the player.

The market today now includes many instruments from the rock era, with guitars attracting the main interest, for example, those belonging to stars such as Jimmy Hendrix. Lately we have seen Elton John's grand piano being auctioned off to frantic bidding.

Sphere Speaker ▼
- 1970

Metal sphere enclosing 12 speakers, with a chrome stand, by Grundig of Germany.
- *height 87.5cm*
- £900   • Zoom

Casino Guitar ▲
- 1967

Epiphone Casino guitar in sunburst.
- *110cm x 41cm*
- £2,500   • V & R Guitars

Gibson Guitar ▼
- 1963

Custom-made Gibson guitar in sunburst with block markers and ebony fingerboard (left handed), serial no. ES335.
- £8,500   • Vintage Guitar

Fender Jaguar Guitar ▲
- 1968

Fender Jaguar guitar with matching headstock in factory black custom colour.
- *103cm x 37cm*
- £2,250   • V & R Guitars

Expert Tips

Musical instruments formerly played by pop stars or great musicians will always fetch the highest price.

Lap Steel Guitar ▼
- 1933

EH150 Lap Steel Gibson Guitar with a Charlie Christian pick-up, in sunburst finish, with original case.
- *68cm x 28cm*
- £850   • V & R Guitars

Plexi Bass Guitar ▶
- 1969

Dan Armstrong Plexi Bass model Dan in excellent condition, with instructions and OHSC.
- *110cm x 34cm*
- £1,150   • V & R Guitars

Les Paul Guitar ▲
- 1954

Gibson Les Paul guitar with gold top. Provenance: Richie Sanbora of American rock band *Bon Jovi*.
- £7,000   • Vintage Guitar

Cherry Red Guitar ◀
- 1962

Gibson guitar in cherry red with block markers. Serial no: ES 335.
- £4,950   • Vintage Guitar

Gibson Guitar ▼
- 1961

ES 335 TD model made by Gibson. Dot marker 335. PAFs. Highly desirable.
- *107cm x 42cm*
- N/A   • V & R Guitars

Framus Starbass ▼

- *1960*

Cherry sunburst Framus
Starbass guitar, as used by the
Rolling Stones.
- £1,960   • Zoom

Fender Jazzmaster ▲

- *1966*

Left-handed Fender Jazzmaster in
fiesta red finish. It is very rare to
find this type of left-handed
custom coloured Fender.
- *109cm x 32cm*
- £3,000   • V & R Guitars

Sunburst Gibson Guitar ▼

- *1959*

Gibson guitar in sunburst with
dot neck. Serial No. ES 335.
- £7,560   • Vintage Guitar

Epiphone Guitar ▼

- *1962*

Al Ciaola Cherry guitar made by
Epiphone. Early 1960s' Epiphones
are rare and this is in exceptional
condition.
- *109cm x 41cm*
- £1,895   • V & R Guitars

Gretsch Guitar ▲

- *1959*

Gretsch Anniversary model 6125
with F holes and cream finish.
- *107cm x 41cm*
- £1,895   • V & R Guitars

Fender Stratocaster ▼

- *1960*

Rare custom-ordered metallic
blue sparkle Stratocaster with
slab rosewood fingerboard.
Believed to be one of only five
ever made.
- £18,500   • Vintage Guitar

Fender Broadcaster ➤
- *1950*

Fender Broadcaster with maple neck and black pick-guard and the first electric solid body guitar. Previously owned by John Entwhistle of the rock band, *The Who*.
- £18,000   • Vintage Guitar

Gretsch Guitar ▲
- *1953*

Model 35 made by Gretsch with DeArmond rhythm Chief floating pick-up.
- *110cm x 41cm*
- £1,295   • V & R Guitars

Stratocaster Guitar ▲
- *1957*

Fender Stratocaster guitar, with tobacco sunburst finish. Completely original guitar with tweed case.
- *95cm x 32cm*
- £1,085   • V & R Guitars

Gibson Les Paul Guitar ▲
- *1960*

Gibson Les Paul special model with original TV yellow finish.
- *98cm x 34cm*
- £3,500   • V & R Guitars

Gibson Flying Vee ◄
- *1958*

Korina wood Gibson Flying Vee, the Holy Grail of vintage solid body guitars. Only 100 were ever made.
- £55,000   • Vintage Guitar

Acoustic Guitar ➤
- *1929*

Model No. 00045 with Brazilian rosewood back and sides, and pearl inlay, by Martin.
- £26,000   • Vintage Guitar

Expert Tips

Because of their rarity, left-handed guitars are keenly sought after and fetch a premium.

French Erard Harp ▼

- *circa 1890*

French double pedal harp in maple and gold with decorated pillar, made in Paris by Erard.

- *108cm x 183cm*
- **£23,000**   ● **Clive Morley**

Irish Harp ▲

- *circa 1880*

Green Irish harp by Harkness with gilt edging 36 strings and 18 semi-tone levers.

- *102cm x 69cm*
- **£2,500**   ● **Clive Morley**

Gibson L-5 Guitar ▼

- *1935*

Gibson L-5 1935 guitar with F holes, scratch plate and mother-of-pearl inlaid fret board.

- *length 108cm*
- **£3,500**   ● **V & R Guitars**

Fender Stratocaster ▲

- *1964*

Fiesta red Stratocaster with rosewood neck, formerly owned by Richie Sanbora of *Bon Jovi*.

- **£9,500**   ● **Vintage Guitar**

Martin Guitar ➤

- *1960*

Brazilian rosewood Martin D-28 guitar.

- **£8,500**   ● **Vintage Guitar**

Gretsch Country Club ▲

- *1959*

Chet Atkins 6119 Gretsch in western orange with single PAF filtertron pick-up.

- **£2,600**   ● **Vintage Guitar**

Epiphone Coronet ▲

- *1958*

Epiphone Coronet guitar with re-lacquered dark red body.

- *98cm x 33cm*
- **£1,850**   ● **V & R Guitars**

423

Fender Vibro Champ ▲
- *1966*
Fender Vibro Champ with black face.
- *height 42.5cm*
- £495   • Vintage Guitar

Marshall Amp ▲
- *1969*
A Marshall 100-watt valve amp with superlead red tolex, and small metal logo.
- *height 72.5cm*
- £1,500   • Vintage Guitar

Grecian-Style Harp ▲
- *circa 1840*
The Grecian-style harp decoration is one of the strongest images in decorative arts. These are practical musical instruments and can be restored to performance standard.
- *height 173cm*
- £7,000   • Clive Morley

Fender Deluxe ▲
- *1966*
Fender Deluxe Reverb amplifier with 12-inch speaker and black face.
- £1,500   • Vintage Guitar

Erard Gothic Harp ◄
- *circa 1860*
Maplewood harp with gilded column in a gothic style, made in Paris by Erard Harps. This style would have been used in London and Paris society and country houses.
- *height 176cm*
- £16,000   • Clive Morley

Thunderbird Bass ▲
- *1968*
Gibson Thunderbird bass with forward body, in sunburst finish.
- £2,500   • Vintage Guitar

Gibson Guitar ▲
- *1960*
Gibson ES-355 TDC model with PAF Humbuckers pick-ups.
- *109cm x 43cm*
- £6,000   • V & R Guitars

Expert Tips

Pianos and grand pianos vary greatly in price according to the maker and construction date.

Gibson ES-5 ▼
- *1952*
Natural body finish Gibson ES-5 with three P90s. Provenance: Gary Moore.
- £8,500   • Vintage Guitar

Silverjet Gretsch ◄
- *1955*
American Gretsch guitar in silverjet finish.
- £5,500   • Vintage Guitar

Gretsch White Falcon ▲
- *1962*
Gretsch White Falcon double cut away guitar with black paint.
- £4,950   • Vintage Guitar

Grand Piano ▲
- *circa 1850–60*
A superb example of a burr walnut grand piano with lyre-shaped peddle board raised on turned and carved legs.
- *95cm x 143cm x 240cm*
- £10,500   • Brown

Gibson Les Paul Junior ►
- *1959*
Gibson Les Paul Junior in TV yellow with double cut away.
- £4,250   • Vintage Guitar

Jazz Bass ▼
- *1972*
Fender jazz bass with maple neck, black binding and black markers with a natural body finish.
- £1,500   • Vintage Guitar

Ampeg Guitar ▲
- *1962*
AEB-1 scroll base Ampeg guitar
in cherry with white pick-guard.
- £1,580   • Vintage Guitar

Lead Amplifier ▼
- *circa 1970s*
A British Park 100-watt lead
amplifier.
- £950   • Vintage Guitar

Expert Tips

*Amplifiers and speakers are
increasing in interest and value
as the musician strives for an
authentic sound that can only be
truly heard or expressed by
using vintage equipment of the
rock era. This market still has
great potential for growth.*

Epiphone Frontier ▼
- *1960*
Epiphone Frontier guitar in
sunburst finish.
- £2,500   • Vintage Guitar

Music Box ▲
- *1820*
A French oval maplewood music
box, finely painted with birds and
flowers.
- *diameter 16cm*
- £1,200   • John Clay

Gibson Trini Lopez ▲
- *1967*
Gibson Trini Lopez in cherry red
finish with diamond inlay and
sound holes.
- £2,500   • Vintage Guitar

Precision Bass ◀
- *1963*
Fender Precision bass in metallic
turquoise with rosewood
fingerboard, custom ordered.
- £3,995   • Vintage Guitar

Silver & Pewter

Cream jugs, sugar bowls, salt cellars and tea pots are sensible items to begin with when collecting silver. Utility is always worth extra value.

Silver has been made into objects of beauty since the time of the Ancient Greeks and its status as a desirable and coveted possession is still held today. Silver is a wonderful material; it is a durable and reflective metal and can be hammered and moulded into a variety of forms, from the massive wine cooler to the smallest pepper pot.

Silver really comes alive in the hands of the master silversmith and it is the work of these great masters that fetches the highest prices. Irish, Scottish and French period silver seems to be the rarest, but pre-Restoration English silver is also scarce, as so much was melted down for coinage to finance the war during Oliver Cromwell's reign. Although later English silver is more readily available this has not diminished its value or the demand for the work of great English silversmiths such as Paul Storr and Peter and Ann Bateman.

American silversmithing started quite early, from around 1650, and the silver was usually stamped by the maker's mark, with the silver coming from dollar coins.

Art Nouveau Pewter Tureen ▼
- 1900
Art Nouveau pewter tureen finial top with twin handles on a splayed foot.
- 9.5cm x 24cm
- £280 • Gooday Gallery

Pewter Dish ▼
- 1905
Art Nouveau pewter dish with three lobed sections decorated with an organic design of stylised leaves by Gallia.
- 20cm x 31cm
- £250 • Gooday Gallery

Art Nouveau Pewter Tray ▲
- 1900
Art Nouveau pewter and mahogany tray designed by Orivit.
- length 45cm
- £650 • Gooday Gallery

Half-Pint Tankard ▲
- 1840
A half-pint tankard with scroll thumb piece and banding on a splayed base.
- height 10cm
- £45 • Jane Stewart

Late Georgian Jug ▼
- 1800
A baluster-shaped measuring jug of typical form, with excise marks, splayed lip and curved handle, on a moulded base.
- height 10cm
- £40 • Jane Stewart

Expert Tips

Art Nouveau design is allied to the Pre-Raphaelite movement from the 1880s. Many of the Art Nouveau designs were made into exciting pieces of silver and pewter, mirrors and photographic frames being two good examples.

William IV Tankard ▲
- *1840*
A pewter waisted tankard with banding and ear-shaped handle, handcrafted by James Yates.
- *height 21cm*
- £80   • Jane Stewart

Sheffield Teapot ➤
- *1840*
A pewter teapot of circular form with finial decoration by Shaw & Fisher of Sheffield.
- *height 13cm*
- £60   • Jane Stewart

Victorian Cream Jug ▼
- *1860*
A Victorian pewter jug with scrolled handle.
- *height 7cm*
- £15   • Jane Stewart

Early Georgian Tankard ▼
- *1740*
A pewter tankard of quart capacity with straight sides, banded waist and curved handle.
- *height 16cm*
- £85   • Jane Stewart

Art Nouveau Pewter Vase ◄
- *1903*
Art Nouveau pewter vase with green glass liner designed by Archibald Knox for Liberty & Co.
- *height 18cm*
- £950   • Gooday Gallery

Charles II Tankard ▲
- *1677*
A silver Charles II tankard and cover with pierced thumb piece, floral engraving and maker's mark.
- *height 16cm*
- £12,500   • B. Silverman

Pewter Candlesticks ▲
- *1800*
A pair of pewter candlesticks of plain form on circular bases with push-up ejectors.
- *height 20cm*
- £220   • Jane Stewart

Victorian Sauce Boat ▼
- *1850*

A pewter sauce boat with large splayed lip and curved handle, on three claw feet.
- *length 12cm*
- £30   • Jane Stewart

Silver Casters ▼
- *1759*

A set of George II silver casters with decorative piercing and engraving, on a tall foot with good unrestored finial.
- *height 19cm*
- £2,900   • B. Silverman

Engraved Teapot ▲
- *1850*

An Adam-style pewter teapot, finely engraved with floral decoration.
- *height 12cm*
- £55   • Jane Stewart

Pewter Fruit Bowl ▲
- *1905*

Art Nouveau pewter fruit bowl with green glass liner and pewter mounts incorporating organic designs, by Orivit.
- *11cm x 16.5cm*
- £380   • Gooday Gallery

Knox Pewter Dish ▼
- *1903*

Art Nouveau pewter fruit bowl with green glass liner raised on three legs reserved on a circular base, designed by Archibald Knox for Liberty & Co.
- *13cm x 13cm*
- £650   • Gooday Gallery

Tobacco Box ▼
- *19th century*

A pewter oriental-style tobacco box with engraved floral designs.
- *height 8cm*
- £55   • Jane Stewart

Set of Pewter Goblets ◄
- *20th century*

A set of five, half-pint capacity, pewter goblets of typical form, in fine condition on a circular base. Handcrafted by Aquineas Locke of London.
- *height 15cm*
- £100   • Jane Stewart

Bronze Cauldron ▼
- **1800**
A solid bronze cauldron of typical West Country form, raised on three moulded feet.
- *height 18cm*
- **£150**
- **Jane Stewart**

Pewter Flagon ▼
- **19th century**
A pewter flagon and cover with a curving fish tail thumb piece and C-scroll handle, made by Walker & Hall of Sheffield.
- *height 29cm*
- **£120**
- **Jane Stewart**

Pewter Syringe ▲
- **1800**
A late Georgian pewter syringe.
- *length 19cm*
- **£60**
- **Jane Stewart**

Knife Set ▼
- **1843–7**
Sixteen table knives with pistol grip handles with foliate designs, and additional four-piece carving set, by Robert Garrard of London.
- *length 17cm*
- **£3,500**
- **B. Silverman**

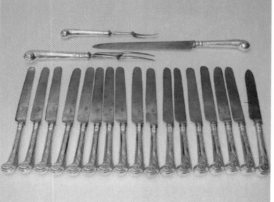

French Pewter Plate ▼
- **early 19th century**
French pewter plate with an embossed central design depicting Joan of Arc, with cartouche moulded border.
- *diameter 24cm*
- **£65**
- **Jane Stewart**

Water Jug ◄
- **1930**
A pewter water jug of bulbous proportions with unusual splayed lip and curved handle.
- *height 24cm*
- **£60**
- **Jane Stewart**

Dutch Charger ▲
- **1700**
A pewter charger with single reeded rim with wriggled work decoration.
- *diameter 42cm*
- **£400**
- **Jane Stewart**

Expert Tips

Irregular black blotches and stains on pewter items, caused by oxidisation, can be safely removed by soaking them in paraffin. Damage to pewter due to its softness and malleability is quite common, and repairs, such as the hammering out of small dents, have to be looked at closely. Damage can also occur as a result of poor design: for example, small raised feet supporting a large heavy vessel, which over time will cause the feet to break through their base.

Horn Beaker ▼

- *circa 1783*

A horn beaker with silver rim and maker's mark repeated three times. Made by John Ollivant of Manchester.
- *height 13cm*
- £590 • B. Silverman

Pilgrim's Badge ▼

- *15th century*

An early pewter pilgrim's badge.
- *height 5cm*
- £20 • Jane Stewart

George II Tankard ▲

- *1764*

A fine silver George III tankard, made by Francis Crump with lobed cover, scrolled handle and shaped thumb piece.
- *height 21cm*
- £3,500
- B. Silverman (BADA)

Pewter Goblet ▲

- *19th century*

A pewter goblet with engraved decoration on a pedestal base.
- *height 18cm*
- £75 • Jane Stewart

Tea Pot ▲

- *1930*

A pewter Chinese tea pot with Hadite spout, handle and finial.
- *height 15cm*
- £85 • Jane Stewart

Pewter Tankard ▲

- *1850*

A pewter tankard of quart capacity with banding and scrolled handle, handcrafted by James Yates.
- *height 21cm*
- £85 • Jane Stewart

Silver Toast Rack ▲

- *1815*

A silver George III toast rack with six bays and shaped handle, raised on scrolled feet, by Paul Storr.
- *height 12cm, width 19cm*
- £5,550
- B. Silverman (BADA)

Gilded Fruit Bowl ◄
- *1910*
Silver-plated fruit bowl with gilded interior and a glass liner on a pedestal foot with geometric designs and gadrooned border, engraved "W.M.F".
- *12cm x 24cm*
- £650   • Gooday Gallery

Silver Wine Funnel ▲
- *1834*
A detailed silver wine funnel made by Joseph & Albert of London.
- *height 14cm*
- £1,750   • B. Silverman

George III Candlesticks ▼
- *1760*
A pair of fine George III loaded candlesticks in the style of a Corinthian column, handcrafted by Dennis Wilks.
- *height 32cm*
- £6,500   • B. Silverman

George III Wine Funnel ▲
- *1804*
A fine George III silver wine funnel by R & D Flennell.
- *height 15cm*
- £1,500   • B. Silverman

Victorian Blotter ▼
- *1899*
A fine silver blotter made in Birmingham with engraved floral designs on the back with thistle-shaped handle.
- *width 9cm*
- £375   • Stephen Kalms

Straight-Sided Tankard ▲
- *1850*
A silver and pewter half-pint tankard of straight-sided form, with banded decoration to the base.
- *height 10cm*
- £40   • Jane Stewart

French Pewter Plate ◄
- *1900*
A French pewter plate from Orleans with embossed designs to the rim and centre.
- *diameter 24cm*
- £65   • Jane Stewart

Expert Tips

The earliest silver table candlesticks date back to the first half of the seventeenth century, during the reign of Charles I, and are now very rare. American candlesticks of this period are also extremely rare.

Dublin Dish Ring ▼
- *1913*

A Irish dish ring, made in Dublin, highly decorated with gadrooned borders, and pierced floral designs centered with oval cartouches.
- *10cm x 19cm*
- £3,500
- B. Silverman

Dessert Suite ▼
- *1862*

A Victorian solid silver épergne dessert suite, highly decorated with embossed foliate designs, raised on a serpentine base.
- *height 54cm*
- £16,000
- B. Silverman

Wine Coaster ▼
- *1845*

A finely detailed wine coaster, with pierced designs depicting flowers and birds, surmounted by a serpentine rim.
- *diameter 14cm*
- £1,800
- B. Silverman

Silver Serving Tray ▲
- *1836*

A fine William IV silver serving tray, with lavish foliate and shell design to the rim and handle, made by Robert Garrard.
- *59cm x 44cm*
- £9,000
- B. Silverman

Knife Set ▲
- *circa 1800*

Twelve pairs of George III knives with mother-of-pearl handles with unmarked silver terminals.
- *length 19cm*
- £1,500
- B. Silverman

Silver Dessert Set ▲
- *1800*

Silver dessert set, designed by Pitts & Preedy, consisting of five pieces with solid silver bases and cut glass bowls.
- *diameter 18cm/largest*
- £15,000 • B. Silverman

Cream Pail ▼
- *1764*

A finely detailed George III silver cream pail with hinged lattice handle.
- *diameter 8cm*
- £850
- B. Silverman

Entrée Dishes ▲

- *circa 1810*

A pair of old Sheffield silver entrée dishes, with gadrooned borders and handles, designed by Matthew Bolton.
- *width 29cm*
- £1,200　　　• B. Silverman

Victorian Silver Urn ▲

- *1874*

Victorian silver urn, of ovoid shape, on a pedestal base with two handles, and foliate chasing, by Robert Hannell III.
- *27cm x 16cm*
- £1,400　　　• B. Silverman

Expert Tips

In 1742 Thomas Bolsolver invented silver plate. He discovered that melted silver would adhere to the surface of copper, which consequently led to the birth of Sheffield plate. The makers of silver plate were known as cutlers and they originated from the City of Sheffield.

Silver Baskets ▲

- *1892*

A pair of Victorian silver baskets with fine pierced decoration, interlaced with floral and foliate designs on oval bases.
- *12cm x 24cm*
- £3,500　　　• B. Silverman

Glass Claret Jug ▲

- *1886*

A silver and glass claret jug with foliate etchings, made by J. Gilbert & Sons of Birmingham.
- *height 22cm*
- £900　　　• Linden & Co.

Silver Fruit Basket ▼

- *circa 1790*

Silver fruit basket of oval form with a plain hinged handle, pierced with geometric designs, and raised on an oval moulded base.
- *height 11cm*
- £550　　　• B. Silverman

Wager Cup ▼

- *1831*

A silver gilt wager cup, in the style of a Turkish King holding an embossed cup within a wreath above his head, by Reilly and Storer.
- *height 22cm*
- £12,000　　　• B. Silverman

Stuffing Spoon ◀

- *1769*

A large George III, onslow pattern, silver stuffing spoon.
- *length 33cm*
- £750　　　• B. Silverman

Silver Champagne Cup ▼
- *1902*

A silver champagne cup with saucer-shaped bowl, made by William Adams Ltd, Birmingham.
- *height 14cm*
- £1,160   • Linden & Co.

Edwardian Centrepiece ▼
- *1902*

A silver centrepiece with pierced and moulded floral designs on a raised foot, made by C.S. Morris of London.
- *14cm x 23cm*
- £990   • Stephen Kalms

Coffee Pot ▲
- *1767*

A fine silver coffee pot of simple design with high domed lid and finial, and reeded scroll handle, by T. Jones of London.
- *height 26cm*
- £1,750   • Stephen Kalms

George III Argyle ▲
- *1783*

A fine George III argyle with finial lid, thumb piece, reeded side handle and gadrooned base, made in London.
- *height 11cm*
- £6,250   • Stephen Kalms

Victorian Centrepiece ▼
- *circa 1850*

An ornate silver-plated centrepiece with four branches set with engraved cut glass bowls, surmounted by a large fifth bowl to the centre.
- *height 65cm*
- £6,500   • Butchoff

Sheffield Caster ▼
- *1911*

A fine caster of conical form with fluted designs, finial top and serpentine moulded base. Made in Sheffield.
- *height 13cm*
- £600   • Stephen Kalms

Pierced Silver Dish ◀
- *1893*

A Victorian silver dish with a wide pierced border on scrolled feet, made by W. Hutton of London.
- *width 19cm*
- £450   • Stephen Kalms

Victorian Silver Basket ▶

- *1897*
A silver cake basket with pierced designs and ribbon handle on shaped feet, made in Sheffield.
- *7cm x 30cm*
- £900 • Stephen Kalms

Edwardian Silver Card Box ▼

- *1900*
A silver card box profusely engraved with floral meanderings, including two original sets of cards from Vienna. Made in Birmingham.
- *height 6cm*
- £475 • Stephen Kalms

Double-Handled Chalice ▼

- *1937*
A simply designed silver bowl with double scrolled handles and moulded rim on a splayed shaped foot, made in Birmingham.
- *8cm x 21cm*
- £1,100 • Stephen Kalms

Silver Bell with Ivory Handle ▲

- *1884*
A small silver tea-bell with an ivory handle made by C. & T. Fox.
- *height 10cm*
- £1,250 • B. Silverman

Silver Oval Basket ▼

- *1918*
An oval silver basket with a pierced diamond lattice design and plain splayed rim, made in London.
- *length 33cm*
- £600 • Stephen Kalms

Victorian Silver Dish ▼

- *1896*
A silver dish of oval form with leaf and scroll design and serpentine border, made in London.
- *length 30cm*
- £495 • Stephen Kalms

Cutlery Set ◀

- *1840–1905*
A silver cutlery set of shell and fiddle design comprising 173 pieces including: table spoons, table knives and forks, dessert spoons, forks and knives, teaspoons, one butter knife, two stuffing spoons and two sauce ladles.
- £21,000 • B. Silverman

Fish Slice ▲
- *1820*

A George III fish slice, with king's husk patterning, by Paul Storr.
- *length 30cm*
- £2,950   • B. Silverman

Sheffield Plate Candlesticks ▲
- *1765*

Pair of Sheffield plate candlesticks in the classical style, the column stem with floral and mask decoration, on a shaped base.
- *height 34cm*
- £1,150   • Ashcombe House

Charles II Porringer ▶
- *1676*

A Charles II silver porringer with double-scrolled handles, engraved foliate designs, and centred with an armorial cartouche.
- *16cm x 12cm*
- £6,500   • B. Silverman

Irish Card Tray ▲
- *1779*

A fine Irish silver card tray, raised on three small feet with asymmetric gadrooned borders, made in Dublin.
- *diameter 15cm*
- £1,400   • B. Silverman

Silver Chamber Stick ▲
- *1800*

A fine George III silver chamber stick with snuffer, by Samuel Whitford.
- *diameter 11cm*
- £1,650   • B. Silverman

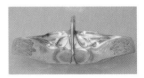

Osiris Fruit Basket ▲
- *1905*

Art Nouveau pewter fruit basket, with a handle engraved with cherries, by Osiris.
- *34cm x 18cm*
- £250   • Gooday Gallery

Salt Boats ▼
- *1794*

A pair of George III silver salts with ribbon handles on pedestal base, handcrafted by Henry Chawner.
- *width 12cm*
- £975   • B. Silverman

Miniature Porringer ▲
- *1716*

A fine George I miniature silver porringer with fluted body and scrolled double handles by John Cole.
- *diameter 5cm*
- £1,200   • B. Silverman

Four Lanterns ▲
- *circa 1900*

A set of four electro-plated lanterns with original glass on square plain bases.
- *height 47cm*
- £2,500   • B. Silverman

Silver Spoon Tray ➤
- *1733*

A very fine George II silver spoon tray with armorial cartouche within shaped borders by Francis Spilsbury.
- *length 15cm*
- £1,733   • B. Silverman

Expert Tips

The Frenchman L.Morel Ladeuil invented electrotyping.

Miniature Brazier ▲
- *1700*

A finely detailed William III silver miniature brazier, handcrafted by George Manjoy.
- *diameter 4cm*
- £1,600   • B. Silverman

Cream Jug ▼
- *1734*

A silver George II cream jug with a sparrow beak and scrolled ribbon handle, raised on a splayed base, by Thomas Rush.
- *height 9cm*
- £2,200   • B. Silverman

Silver Corkscrew ▼
- *1789*

A very fine George III silver corkscrew inlaid with mother of pearl.
- *length 8cm*
- £1,400   • B. Silverman

Silver Vinaigrette ◀
- *1830*

A fine small William IV silver vinaigrette.
- *width 3.5cm*
- £750   • B. Silverman

Adams Cutlery Set ▼

- *1857–8*

A fine quality cutlery set of Grecian style by George Adams comprising: 24 table spoons, table forks, dessert spoons, dessert forks, teaspoons, 1 soup ladle, 1 stuffing spoon, 1 salt spoon, 1 mustard spoon, and 1 sugar tong.
- **£17,500**　　• **B. Silverman**

Asparagus Tongs ▼

- *1870*

A finely detailed pair of Victorian silver tongs, with gadrooned borders and engraved foliate designs.
- *length 23cm*
- **£1,100**　　• **B. Silverman**

Snuffer Tray ▼

- *1734*

A fine George II silver snuffer tray, by Augustus Courtauld with moulded shaped rim and thumb piece.
- *width 17cm*
- **£3,750**　　• **B. Silverman**

Set of Pewter Plates ▲

- *1750*

A set of four pewter plates with plain moulded borders, made in London.
- *diameter 15cm*
- **£60**　　• **Jane Stewart**

Silver Cutlery Set ▲

- *1840*

A magnificent silver cutlery set incorporating a rare design. Comprising of 12 table spoons, table forks, dessert spoons, dessert forks, teaspoons, 2 sauce ladles, 1 soup ladle, 1 sugar sifter spoon, and 1 butter spreader.
- **£18,500**　　• **B. Silverman**

Claret Jug ▲

- *1872*

A Victorian silver mounted wine jug, the glass engraved with chariots and floral garlands, by W. & G. Sissons.
- *height 26cm*
- **£6,000**　　• **B. Silverman**

Pair of Candelabras ▲

- *1911*

A finely detailed pair of silver, five branch candelabras, with four removable branches, transforming to a single candlestick on square gadrooned bases.
- *45cm x 38cm*
- **£15,000**　　• **B. Silverman**

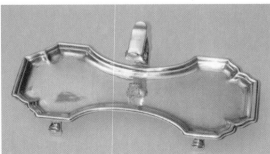

Silver Egg Cruet ▼
- *1788*
A George III silver egg cruet by
Matthew Boulton, with six silver
egg cups within a lightly designed
base and finial handle.
- *width 21cm*
- £1,500   • B. Silverman

Silver Cream Jug ▼
- *1897*
A silver jug by Wakely &
Wheeler, with a scrolled handle,
wide splayed lip, raised on three
lion paw feet from lion mask
decoration.
- *height 20cm*
- £1,800   • B. Silverman

George III Goblets ▲
- *1810*
A pair of George III urn-shaped
goblets with half-fluted bodies
engraved with grape and vine
designs, raised on pedestal bases,
by J.X. Story & W.M. Elliot.
- *height 17cm*
- £6,000   • B. Silverman

Four Silver Salts ▼
- *1841–56*
A set of four silver salts with blue
glass liners, pierced decoration
and gadrooned rim, raised on
three pad feet.
- *5cm x 8cm*
- £1,900   • B. Silverman

Pair of Sauce Boats ▲
- *1771*
A fine pair of George III silver
sauce boats with splayed lip and
scrolled handles, on three splayed
feet, made by John Irvine.
- *17cm x 6cm*
- £2,900   • B. Silverman

Early Georgian Salts ▲
- *1744*
A pair of circular silver salts with
gilt interiors made in London,
raised on animal feet from mask
decoration.
- *diameter 7cm*
- £475   • Percy's Ltd

Victorian Montieth ▲
- *1900*
Victorian montieth by Goldsmith
& Silversmith, based on a
seventeenth century design with
shaped collar and ring handles
from mask decoration.
- *26cm x 41cm*
- £9,000   • B. Silverman

Wine Coolers ▼
- **1905**
A pair of silver urn-shaped wine coolers raised on pedestal feet on a plain square base, by Walker and Hall Sheffield of London.
- *27cm x 25cm*
- **£12,750** ● Percy's Ltd

Engraved Coffee Pot ▲
- **1765**
A silver coffee pot with engraved scroll designs, C-scroll handle and ornate finial, made by William Cripps of London.
- *height 25cm*
- **£1,765** ● Percy's Ltd

Large Victorian Caster ▲
- **1898**
A fine silver sugar caster of large proportions with gadrooned and engraved decoration and bird finial, made in Sheffield.
- *height 22cm*
- **£1,100** ● Stephen Kalms

Silver Goblet ◄
- **1874**
A single silver engraved goblet with gilded interior knop stem raised on a splayed base, made by Mappin and Webb of London.
- *height 13cm*
- **£300** ● Stephen Kalms

Silver Argyle ▲
- **1788**
A fine silver Argyle with scrolled horn handle, made by Benjamin Cartwright of Sheffield.
- *height 21cm*
- **£4,650** ● Percy's Ltd

English Dish Cross ▼
- **1767**
A finely detailed adjustable dish cross made by Samuel Herbert of London.
- *length 29cm*
- **£2,475** ● Percy's Ltd

Wine Funnel ▲
- **1798**
A silver wine funnel made by Robert and David Hennell of London.
- *height 15cm*
- **£2,250** ● Percy's Ltd

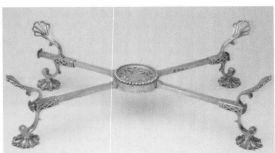

Expert Tips

Bright-cutting of silver was popular at the end of the eighteenth century. It used the same method as engraving, but a burnished steel tool cut the metal, which polished the silver as it worked, producing a sharp design which reflected the light.

Brandy Saucepan ▲

- *1250*

A silver brandy saucepan made by Samuel Meriton of London with a turned wooden side handle.
- *height 8cm*
- **£1,250** • Percy's Ltd

Late Georgian Basket ▲

- *1763*

A fine silver circular cake basket with pierced floral decoration, with a hinged handle and chased designs, on a circular splayed base, made by Richard Aldridge of London.
- *10cm x 42cm x 33cm*
- **£4,350** • Percy's Ltd

Regency Candlesticks ▲

- *1816*

A pair of silver candlesticks with a French influence, made by John and Thomas settle of Sheffield.
- *height 30cm*
- **£5,250** • Percy's Ltd

English Sugar Basket ◄

- *1796*

A silver sugar basket with hinged handle, raised on a central pedestal foot on a moulded oval base, made by Thomas Wallis of London.
- *height 10cm*
- **£750** • Percy's Ltd

Late Georgian Chamberstick ▲

- *1820*

A silver chamberstick made by William Frisbee of London with gadrooned borders and fluted pan.
- *height 10cm*
- **£1,675** • Percy's Ltd

Armenian Cross ▲

- *circa 1800*

A silver Armenian reliquary cross with a lozenge-shaped river pearl and coral stones.
- **£350** • Iconastas

Gilded Silver Salts ◄

- *1799*

A pair of elegant silver salts with gilded interior and shaped end grips, made by William Adby of London.
- *height 7cm*
- **£765** • Percy's Ltd

Expert Tips

The surface of silver is rarely plain, except for early eighteenth century English and American silver.

Frosted Sugar Basket ▼
- *1913*

A fine silver sugar basket made by
Charles Stuart Harris of London,
with a frosted glass liner.
- *height 14cm*
- £675   • Percy's Ltd

Ethiopian Cross ▼
- *circa 1850*

Silver Ethiopian processional
cross with presentation
inscription.
- *49cm x 35cm*
- £2,500   • Iconastas

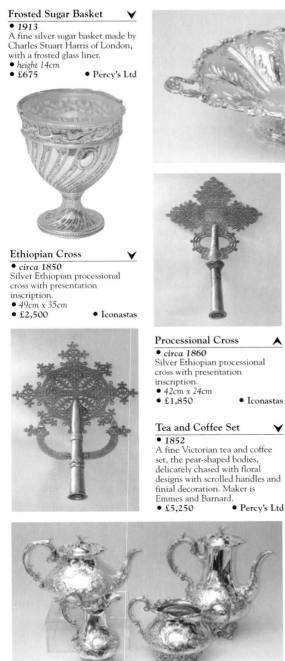

Processional Cross ▲
- *circa 1860*

Silver Ethiopian processional
cross with presentation
inscription.
- *42cm x 24cm*
- £1,850   • Iconastas

Tea and Coffee Set ▼
- *1852*

A fine Victorian tea and coffee
set, the pear-shaped bodies,
delicately chased with floral
designs with scrolled handles and
finial decoration. Maker is
Emmes and Barnard.
- £5,250   • Percy's Ltd

Silver Cake Basket ▲
- *circa 1839*

A pierced cake basket of unusual
design with chased acanthus
decoration, and double handles,
raised on a pedestal foot.
- *9cm x 4cm*
- £1,675   • Percy's Ltd

English Casters ▲
- *1759*

A pair of fine silver casters with
pierced and chased decoration
with original finials, made by
Samuel Wood of London.
- *height 16cm*
- £3,250   • Percy's Ltd

Silver Candlesticks ▲
- *1910*

A set of four silver candlesticks
made by E. J. Greenberg of
London.
- *height 29cm*
- £6,750   • Percy's Ltd

Glass-Lined Sugar Basket ▼

- *1845*

A fine silver sugar basket made by
John Foligno of London, with
pierced floral designs and with a
hinged handle and a shaped clear
blue glass liner.
- *height 10cm*
- £875   • Percy's Ltd

Victorian Cruet Set ▼

- *1860*

A fine silver cruet with original
glass bottles made by Emmes and
Barnard of London.
- *height 22cm*
- £2,650   • Percy's Ltd

Expert Tips

*Silver cruet sets should be
inspected for weak handles, and
the necks of the glass bottles
should not be chipped or
cracked. Do check the feet, as
these are often delicate and are
prone to weakness and damage.*

Shell-Motif Baskets ➤

- *1887*

A pair of fine silver baskets
chased with scrolled shell motifs,
made by Charles Stuart Harris of
London.
- *height 15cm*
- £1,885   • Percy's Ltd

Richard Hood Candlesticks ▲

- *1875*

A set of four candlesticks on
gadrooned square bases, made by
Richard Hood of London.
- *height 12cm*
- £2,450   • Percy's Ltd

Six-Bottle Cruet Set ▲

- *1862*

A six-bottle cruet with finely cut
original glass bottles on a
serpentine moulded base with
shell scrolled feet.
- *height 25cm*
- £2,650   • Percy's Ltd

English Sauce Boats ▲

- *1928*

A pair of George III-style sauce
boats made by Thomas Bradbury
of London.
- *height 6cm*
- £6,775   • Percy's Ltd

Georgian Candelabra ▲

- *1801*

A late Georgian pair of three-
branch candelabra with
interlaced branches on a shaped
square base.
- *height 36cm*
- £9,350   • Percy's Ltd

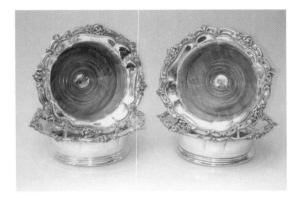

Victorian Silver Goblet ▼

- 1896

A fine silver goblet of conical form on a pedestal base made in Sheffield.

- *height 19cm*
- £225   • Stephen Kalms

Lattice-Work Sugar Bowl ▼

- 1863

A silver sugar bowl with pierced lattice decoration and hinged handle with clear blue glass liner. Made in Birmingham.

- *10cm x 11cm*
- £650   • Stephen Kalms

Glass Scent Bottle ▲

- 1886

A silver-mounted glass scent bottle with swirled moulded design, made in Birmingham.

- *height 10cm*
- £385   • Stephen Kalms

Silver Drinking Set ▼

- 1874

A silver three-piece drinking set with gilded interiors. Made by J. Elkington in Birmingham.

- £6,750   • Stephen Kalms

William IV Coasters ◄

- 1835

A set of four coasters made by Barnards of London with heavily scrolled borders and sides.

- *diameter 18cm*
- £6,750   • Percy's Ltd

Christening Cup ▲

- 1856

A silver christening cup of baluster form with scrolled handle, floral engraving and gilded interior made in London.

- *height 12cm*
- £425   • Stephen Kalms

Pair of Silver Goblets ▲

- 1881

A pair of fine silver goblets with gilded interiors on long stems with wide splayed foot. Made in London.

- *height 13cm*
- £1,200   • Stephen Kalms

Set of Four Dishes ▲

• *1736*
An unusual set of four George II silver chalice-shaped dishes, by John Le Sage.
• *5cm x 9cm*
• £11,500   • B. Silverman

Biscuit Box ▲

• *1896*
A Victorian silver biscuit box with scrolled designs centered with cartouches, the cover with ivory finial, made in Birmingham.
• *18cm x 23cm*
• £3,950   • Stephen Kalms

Sheffield Coffee Pot ▲

• *1898*
A coffee pot of baluster form with domed lid and scrolled bone handle made by Mappin & Webb of Sheffield.
• *height 25cm*
• £1,475   • Stephen Kalms

Chalice-Shaped Dishes ▼

• *1862*
A Victorian pair of silver chalice shaped dishes with fluted design on a pedestal base made in Birmingham by Elkington.
• *16cm x 22cm*
• £4,350   • Stephen Kalms

Silver-Mounted Claret Jug ▼

• *1879*
A fine silver-mounted glass claret jug with engraved stars on the glass. Made by Jenner & Knewstub of London.
• *height 32cm*
• £2,900   • Stephen Kalms

Silver Ink Stand ▼

• *1997*
A silver ink tray with reservoir of simple design, made in Birmingham.
• *width 24cm*
• £490   • Stephen Kalms

Goldsmiths Vases ▼

• *1912*
A set of three vases made by Goldsmiths of London with tapered conical necks on a splayed foot.
• £1,450   • Stephen Kalms

Silver Planter ▼
- *1892*

A Victorian silver planter made
in Sheffield with scrolled designs
on a lattice ground.
- *height 11cm*
- £650 • Stephen Kalms

Scallop-Shaped Dishes ▲
- *1884*

A pair of Victorian silver dishes,
naturalistically formed as scallop
shells.
- *width 12cm*
- £325 • Stephen Kalms

Boxed Set of Salt Dishes ▲
- *1880*

A set of small, fine salt dishes in a
fitted box made in London.
- *diameter 6cm*
- £1,100 • Stephen Kalms

Boxed Dish Set ▼
- *circa 1900*

A fitted oak case with three
dishes made by Elkington & Co.
of Birmingham.
- *length 60cm*
- £2,400 • Stephen Kalms

Double-Handled
Trophy Cup ▲
- *1861*

A silver urn-shaped cup and
cover with C-scrolled handles on
fluted pedestal base, made by H.
Wilkinson of Sheffield.
- *height 29cm*
- £1,950 • Stephen Kalms

Three-Handled Cup ▲
- *1914*

A silver cup on a raised splayed
foot with three ribbon handles,
made in Birmingham.
- *height 15cm*
- £700 • Stephen Kalms

Expert Tips

*Silver dressing table mirrors are
keenly sought after, because of
their rarity. Look out for
examples by makers such as
William Comyns, as some of his
best work is caste and chased,
and is far better than other
examples from that time.*

Covered Serving Dish ➤
- *1900*

A silver covered serving dish with
gadrooned borders and
asymmetric scrolled designs made
by Hatkins of Sheffield.
- *diameter 22cm*
- £1,200 • Stephen Kalms

Sheffield Silver Basket ➤

- *1916*
A silver basket with shaped borders hand crafted by J. Dickson of Sheffield.
- *14cm x 39cm x 29cm*
- £6,000   • Stephen Kalms

Christening Mug ▼

- *1878*
A fine silver christening mug with gilded interior and floral engraving, made in Sheffield.
- *height 10cm*
- £350   • Stephen Kalms

Silver Pierced Basket ▼

- *1907*
A pierced silver basket with floral designs, gadrooned borders and cartouche on four ball feet. Made by C.S. Hennell of London.
- *14cm x 27cm*
- £2,450   • Stephen Kalms

Condiment and Caster Set ▼

- *1895*
A fine boxed set incorporating salt, pepper, sugar and mustard condiments highly decorated with scrolled meanderings. Made in Birmingham.
- *height 20cm*
- £1,200   • Stephen Kalms

Raised Silver Dish ➤

- *1932*
A silver shallow dish on a raised splayed foot with scrolled border, made by Walker & Hall of Sheffield.
- *10cm x 23cm*
- £525   • Stephen Kalms

Goldsmiths Scent Bottle ▲

- *1902*
A silver and glass scent bottle with profuse foliate designs to the body and stopper, made by Goldsmiths of London.
- *height 14cm*
- £1,275   • Stephen Kalms

Expert Tips

When cleaning pierced silver frames or mounts with a leather or velvet backing, it is possible to remove the silver, as they are generally pinned in place.

Edwardian Monteith ➤

- *1906*
A fine silver bowl in the style of an eighteenth century monteith with scalloped collar and floral designs on a raised foot. Made in Birmingham.
- *20cm x 37cm*
- £2,450   • Stephen Kalms

Regency Cruet Set ▼

- *1820*

A silver cruet set consisting of
four cut glass bottles held within
a frame by a central handle on a
tray with gadrooned borders and
scrolled feet, made in London.
- *height 15cm*
- **£1,200**   • **Stephen Kalms**

Victorian Silver Salver ▼

- *1869*

A silver salver with shell
gadrooned borders on paw feet,
made in Sheffield.
- *diameter 22cm*
- **£600**   • **Stephen Kalms**

Ornate Claret Jug ▲

- *1874*

A highly decorative Victorian
silver mounted cut glass claret jug
made in Birmingham by J.
Grinsall.
- *height 31cm*
- **£4,700**   • **Stephen Kalms**

Edwardian Ink Stand ▼

- *1904*

A fine ink stand with two silver
mounted cut glass ink bottles on
a tray with ball feet, made in
London.
- *20cm x 15cm*
- **£1,950**   • **Stephen Kalms**

Double-Handled Dish ◀

- *1905*

A silver double-handled chalice-
shaped dish, raised on a pedestal
foot, made in London.
- *23cm x 38cm*
- **£2,750**   • **Stephen Kalms**

Claret Jug ▲

- *1880*

Late nineteenth century claret
jug, with silver mounts and
domed lid with finial and scrolled
handle.
- *height 24cm*
- **£250**   • **North West 8**

Pair of Claret Jugs ▲

- *1895*

A good pair of urn-shaped silver-
mounted glass claret jugs, hand
crafted by William Hutton of
London.
- *height 33cm*
- **£9,500**   • **Stephen Kalms**

Sporting Items

The constantly ascending value of sporting artefacts and memorabilia provides a fascinating study – and an object lesson in not throwing anything away.

The collection of sporting memorabilia has grown considerably over the past couple of decades. Sporting memorabilia is now a lucrative business and a good revenue earner for football and rugby clubs around the world.

Sport remains one of the greatest expressions of men and women all over the world, and, as we can see from major sports events such as the Olympics, all the elements of life are at work here, from the joy felt in the triumph of winning to the despair of failure. The love of sport is truly international, which is reflected by business sponsorship of sporting heroes and clubs, as these corporate companies recognise that being associated with sporting success reflects well on their own performance. Items of sporting history adorn the walls of clubhouses, restaurants and sports clubs; the most popular being those items connected with golf, football, cricket, tennis and skiing.

The media has also changed the way sport is viewed, for example, darts, which was formerly regarded as a pub game, has now been transformed into a sport with mass appeal.

Any items that have an authentic signed autograph by a sports personality will always attract keen interest among fans and collectors.

General

Black Rugby Boots ➤
- *1930*
Pair of black leather rugby boots with white laces and leather studs.
- *length 29cm*
- **£165**   • Sean Arnold

Riding Boots ▼
- *circa 1900*
Brown leather riding boots together with wooden trees and brass trim.
- *height 54cm*
- **£225**   • Sean Arnold

Football Player ▲
- *circa 1930*
Spelter figure of a football player poised and about to kick a ball.
- *height 25cm*
- **£425**   • Sean Arnold

Hotspur Football Boots ▼
- *1920*
Pair of brown leather football boots with leather studs and cream laces, from a Hotspur footballer.
- *length 30cm*
- **£225**   • Sean Arnold

Tennis Racquets ▲

- *circa 1900*
Three English lawn tennis racquets all with fishtail handles and convex wedges and thick gut stringing.
- *height 60cm*
- £245
- Sean Arnold

Rugby Player ▼

- *circa 1890*
English bronze figure of a rugby player holding a ball.
- *height 46cm*
- £1,750
- Sean Arnold

Croquet Set ▼

- *1930*
Portable croquet set on mahogany stand with brass handle and feet, containing four mallets, hoops and red, black, yellow and blue balls.
- £495
- Sean Arnold

Steel Pick Axe ▼

- *circa 1920*
A steel pick axe with a mahogany handle and leather strap.
- *length 58cm*
- £68
- Henry Gregory

Ice Axes ▶

- *1930*
Continental ice axes with wood handles and metal axe head, of various sizes. Hickory shafted.
- *length 84cm*
- £60
- Sean Arnold

Hand-Stitched Football ▲

- *circa 1890*
Original hand-stitched leather football with laces and unusual panelling.
- *diameter 25cm*
- £680
- Sean Arnold

Pond Yacht ▲

- *circa 1960*
Model Gaff rigged pond yacht on a brass stand.
- *height 98cm*
- £325
- Sean Arnold

Victorian Hip Flask ➤

- *1880*

A Victorian, clear glass hip flask with silver top and case.

- *height 16cm*
- £375   • Reel Thing

Leather Sandwich Case ▲

- *1910*

Leather sandwich case with brass clasp and a leather shoulder strap, inscribed: "J.S.W".

- *19cm square*
- £295   • Reel Thing

Sporting Magazines ▲

- *1930*

Two tennis magazines signed by Fred Perry and a selection of lawn tennis books.

- *30cm x 25cm*
- £125-145   • Sean Arnold

Crocodile Hip Flask   ◄

- *circa 1900*

Crocodile hip flask with hinged silver top and case.

- *height 16cm*
- £275   • Reel Thing

Riding Boots ▼

- *circa 1915*

Gentleman's leather riding boots, with wooden trees with brass handles.

- *height 58 cm*
- £200   • Henry Gregory

Hunting Crop ➤

- *1940*

Hunting whip with braided leather strap, ivory handle and brass collar.

- *length 120cm*
- £145   • Reel Thing

Silver-Topped Flask ▲

- *1890*

Crocodile skin hip flask, with a hinged silver top and case.

- *height 15cm*
- £345   • Reel Thing

Expert Tips

Sporting magazines and signed photographs of sports personalities should all be in good condition and come with a certificate of authenticity. Sporting programmes should also be in fine condition as damaged or dog-eared examples have little value.

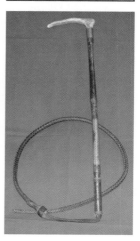

Polo Player on Pony ▲

- 1970

Bronze figure of a polo player on a galloping pony, one of a limited edition of ten, signed the artist.
- height 40cm
- £4,950   • Sean Arnold

Willow Cricket Bat ▼

- 1900

Leather cricket bag with leather handle and straps, and willow cricket bat.
- length 75cm
- £120   • Sean Arnold

Polo Helmet and Knee Pads ▶

- circa 1930

White Polo helmet with red ribbon trim, and leather knee pads.
- diameter 28cm
- helmet £65, knee pads £35
- Sean Arnold

Football Trophy ▲

- 1900

Silver-plated football trophy in the form of early football with a silver foliate tripod stand on a circular base.
- height 45cm
- £775   • Sean Arnold

Original Racquets ▶

- circa 1880

Original racquet for playing the game of Racquets with original stringing and leather press.
- height 58cm
- £475   • Sean Arnold

Cricket Cap, Shield and Trophy ▲

- 1895–1931

Silver-plated cricket shield on a mahogany base depicting an early cricketer. Blue velvet cricket cap with metallic embroidery. I.C.C. Cricket trophy decorated with a cricket ball and bearing three engraved silver shields and details of "Hat Trick" base in the form of cricket stumps.
- cricket shield £375, cricket cap £135, trophy £225
- Sean Arnold

Expert Tips

Skis, tennis rackets and cricket bats are becoming popular for decorating sporting clubs.

Rugby Ball ▼
- *circa 1900*
Original hand-stitched, four panel leather rugby ball with laces.
- *30cm*
- £680　　　• Sean Arnold

Brass Dinner Gong ▼
- *circa 1930*
Brass dinner gong flanked by two brass tennis racquets, supported on an oval mahogany stand.
- *30cm x 24cm*
- £695　　　• Sean Arnold

Football Trophy ▼
- *1900*
Continental red football trophy with silver metal finial and circular base.
- *height 44cm*
- £645　　　• Sean Arnold

Leather Punchball ◄
- *1920*
Leather punchball with leather strap used to suspend from the ceiling.
- *diameter 30cm*
- £185　　　• Sean Arnold

Boxing Gloves ▲
- *1920*
Pair of large leather boxing gloves stuffed with horsehair.
- *30cm*
- large boxing gloves £145, small gloves £95
- Sean Arnold

Shuttlecock Racquets ▲
- *1895*
Three Victorian shuttlecock and ping pong racquets, made of vellum with leather-bound handles.
- £5　　　• Sean Arnold

Bowling Balls ▼
- *circa 1910*
Lignum Vitie bowling balls with bone monogram panels.
- *diameter 16cm*
- £60　　　• Henry Gregory

Nickel-Plated Binoculars ▼
- *circa 1930*
Nickel-plated binoculars with leather grips.
- *length 6cm*
- £125   • Reel Thing

Leather Binocular Case ▼
- *1910*
Leather binocular case with leather carrying handle and shoulder strap.
- *5.5cm x 4cm*
- £95   • Reel Thing

Ivory Binoculars ▲
- *1920*
Elliott Bros ivory binoculars with brass trim.
- *4cm x 3.5cm*
- £145   • Reel Thing

Pottery Stick Stand ▼
- *1870*
A pottery stick stand in the form of riding boots by Dimmock & Co.
- *55cm x 27cm*
- £3,000   • Pimlico

Crocodile Skin Hip Flask ▶
- *1880*
A large crocodile skin, silver plated hip flask, with the inscription "F.M.P.M".
- *height 16cm*
- £445   • Reel Thing

Photograph and Tennis Racquet ▲
- *1932*
Photograph of Bunny Dusten and Hazell Streamline, together with a Hazell Streamline Blue Star lawn tennis racquet.
- £795   • Sean Arnold

Riding Crop ▲
- *1930*
A leather riding crop with notched ivory handle and silver collar.
- *length 55cm*
- £85   • Reel Thing

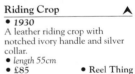

Fishing

Victorian Trout Rod ➤

- *circa 1900*
Victorian split cane trout rod
with silver banding, by Hardy
Bros.
- *length 250cm*
- £600   • Reel Thing

Expert Tips

*When purchasing split cane
fishing rods one should inspect
them for corroded metal eyes
and depleted lacquer to the
cane. This problem can easily
be rectified by re-lacquering the
cane and replacing the eyes.
This also applies to split cane
sea rods, which suffer more
from corrosion than their fresh
water counterparts.*

Reel by Hardy ▼

- *circa 1900*
Hardy fishing reel, with a unique
Duplication Mark II inscription.
- *diameter 10cm*
- £245   • Reel Thing

Milward Fishing Reel ▲

- *circa 1900*
Milward brass fishing reel with
iron arm. Trade marked.
- *diameter 10cm*
- £245   • Reel Thing

Leather Card Case ▲

- *1910*
Leather card case with a diamond-
shaped design on the cover.
- *length 8cm*
- £25   • Reel Thing

Landing Net ▼

- *1930*
Landing net with cane handle.
- *length 150cm*
- £175   • Reel Thing

Fly Wallet ◄

- *circa 1900*
Pigskin fly wallet with various
compartments made by Hardy
Bros.
- *length 20cm*
- £250   • Reel Thing

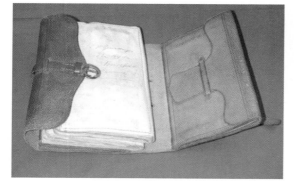

Starback Reel ▼
- *1910*

Starback wooden sea fishing reel, with star-shaped brass mounts.
- *diameter 10cm*
- £115　　　　　　　　• Reel Thing

Trout Rod ▼
- *circa 1975*

A split cane trout rod with a Hardy's cork end, by the Harris and Sheldon Group.
- *length 150cm*
- £700　　　　　　　　• Reel Thing

Fishing Nets ◄
- *1900*

Fishing net with bamboo shafts. The net on the right is patent collapsible.
- *length 78cm/left; 130cm/right*
- £90　　　　　　　　• Sean Arnold

Wicker Creel ▲
- *1900*

Wicker-weave pot-bellied creel with sloping lid and fish slot, and webbing handle.
- *22cm x 22cm*
- £125　　　　　　　　• Sean Arnold

Fishing Flies ▲
- *1920*

Alloy cases containing trout and salmon flies.
- *5cm x 9 cm/small*
15cm x 9 cm/large
- £90　　　　　　　　• Sean Arnold

Murdoch Rod ▲
- *circa 1920*

The Murdoch split cane fishing rod made by Hardy.
- *length 395cm*
- £295　　　　　　　• Reel Thing

Fishing Basket ▼
- *circa 1900*

Large English wicker-weave creel with fish slot, and leather strap.
- *38cm x 32cm*
- £125　　　　　　　• Sean Arnold

Scottish Reel ▲
- *circa 1900*
Brass salmon reel, with ivory handle, by Turnbull Princess of Edinburgh.
- *diameter 11cm*
- £275 • Reel Thing

Leather Fly Wallet ▲
- *circa 1900*
Hardy leather fly wallet with a good fly selection, and leather strap.
- *length 17cm*
- £275 • Reel Thing

Expert Tips

Antique reels have become extremely collectable. They should retain a good original patina and clearly display their maker's mark.

Fishing Gaff ➤
- *1890*
A Hardy fishing gaff with leather handle and steel and brass hook.
- *length 45cm*
- £295 • Reel Thing

Salmon Reel ▼
- *1890*
A Scottish, solid brass salmon reel, made by Anderson & Son, with bone handle.
- *diameter 10cm*
- £145 • Reel Thing

Brass Fishing Reel ◄
- *circa 1900*
A Hardy brass fishing reel in original condition, with ivory handle.
- *diameter 11cm*
- £895 • Reel Thing

Spinning Reel ▲
- *circa 1800*
Brass Mallock spinning reel.
- *diameter 10cm*
- £245 • Reel Thing

English Line Dry ▼
- *1990*
An English mahogany Line Dry with bone handle.
- *height 32cm*
- £288 • Reel Thing

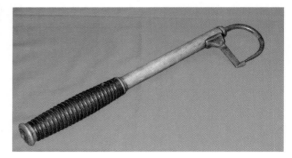

Brass Salmon Reel ▲
- *circa 1910*
Solid brass salmon fly fishing reel
with bone handle and original
leather case, by C. Farlow.
- *diameter 11cm*
- **£ 450** • Reel Thing

Platewind Reel ▲
- *1885–94*
Brass platewind reel by Chas.
Farlow & Co, with ivory handle.
- *diameter 12cm*
- £195 • Reel Thing

Leather Reel Case ▲
- *circa 1900*
Leather reel case with fitted
interior, leather strap and buckle.
- *height 17cm*
- £145 • Reel Thing

Winch Reel ➤
- *circa 1880*
Solid brass winch reel, with
turned wooden handle.
- *diameter 10cm*
- £200 • Reel Thing

John Macpherson Reel ▲
- *1930*
John Macpherson bakelite reel
with original box, by Allcock &
Co.
- *diameter 9cm*
- £95 • Reel Thing

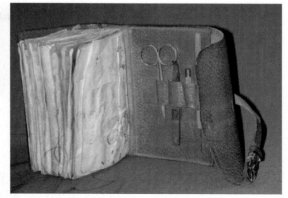

Fly Wallet with Tools ▲
- *circa 1900*
An unusual pigskin fly wallet,
with original fitted tool set.
- *length 15cm*
- £235 • Reel Thing

Fly Wallet ▲
- *1930*
Pigskin fly wallet with leather
strap, in excellent original
condition.
- *length 18cm*
- £280 • Reel Thing

Shooting

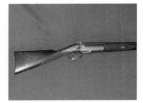

Holland & Holland Shotgun ▲
- *1896*
A pair of Royal Holland & Holland 12-bore side by side shotguns with figured walnut furniture.
- *length 71cm/barrel*
- £28,000 • Holland & Holland

Royal Deluxe Shotgun ▲
- *1956*
Holland & Holland Royal Deluxe, 12-bore side by side shotgun, with figured walnut furniture.
- *length 71cm*
- £24,000 • Holland & Holland

Badminton Shotgun ▲
- *1937*
Holland & Holland Badminton model 12-bore side by side shotgun.
- *length 71cm*
- £14,000 • Holland & Holland

Single Barrel Shotgun ▲
- *circa 1875*
A black powder, Holland & Holland single barrel, four-bore shotgun.
- *length 71cm/barrel*
- £5,500 • Holland & Holland

Expert Tips

When purchasing firearms it is important to make sure that they come with a proofing certificate of fire worthiness.

Cartridge Case ◄
- *circa 1880*
Leather cartridge magazine case for 250 cartridges with strap and key. R.B Rodda & Co gun makers and Armourers, 7-8 Dalhouse Square, Calcutta.
- £795 • Reel Thing

Holland & Holland Royal ▲
- *1908*
Holland & Holland 12-bore, Royal, side by side shotgun.
- *height 76cm*
- £10,500 • Holland & Holland

Spoon Warmer ◄
- *circa 1880*
A Victorian Scottish Britannia metal spoon warmer, with a removable brass screw handle resting on a stylised rock base.
- *29cm x 14cm*
- £510 • Holland & Holland

Leg-of-Mutton Gun Case ➤
- *1930*
Holland & Holland leather leg-of-mutton gun case.
- *length 79cm*
- £550 • Holland & Holland

Holland & Holland Shotgun ▼
- *2000*
Holland & Holland deluxe 28-bore sporting model, over and under shotgun, with figured walnut furniture.
- *length 71cm*
- £30,300 • Holland & Holland

Allcock Fishing Rod ➤
- *circa 1920*
A light caster, split cane spinning rod with cork handle by Allcock.
- *length 250cm*
- £275 • Reel Thing

Canochy Cartridge Loader ▲
- *1930*
Canochy cartridge loader encased in leather with a leather strap.
- *diameter 15cm*
- £1,500 • Holland & Holland

Gun Case ▼
- *1930*
Holland & Holland leather leg-of-mutton gun case.
- *length 79cm*
- £250 • Holland & Holland

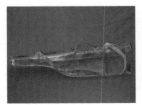

Magazine Case ◄
- *circa 1880*
Holland & Holland magazine cotton-lined leather case with leather pull thongs and dividers, and a brass lock and keys in perfect condition.
- *width 28cm*
- £950 • Holland & Holland

Leather Gun Case ▼
- *circa 1860*
A leg-of-mutton leather gun case, with brass fittings and a leather shoulder strap.
- *80cm x 26cm x 6cm*
- £260 • Henry Gregory

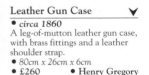

Cartridge Bag ▲
- *1930*

Leather cartridge bag with webbing shoulder strap and the monogram "M.G.F." on the buckle.
- *length 38cm*
- **£145** • **Reel Thing**

Double Barrel Hunting Rifle ▼
- *1949*

A 300 calibre Flanged Dominion double barrel hunting rifle, made by Holland and Holland
- *length 71cm*
- **£19,750** • **Holland & Holland**

Magazine Rifle ▲
- *1975*

Excellent quality Holland & Holland 7mm calibre magazine rifle, with telescopic sight.
- *length 64cm*
- **£7,000** • **Holland & Holland**

Oak Gun Case ▼
- *circa 1929*

Holland & Holland oak and leather fitted gun case, with red base lining.
- *length 70cm*
- **£2,200** • **Holland & Holland**

Double Barrel Rifle ◄
- *1945*

A 300 calibre Holland & Holland Royal, double barrelled rifle, belted and rimless.
- *length 61cm*
- **£32,000** • **Holland & Holland**

Shooting Stick ◄
- *1940s*

Leather-bound shooting stick, with metal spike.
- *length 90cm*
- **£144** • **Henry Gregory**

Canochy Loader ▼
- *circa 1930*

Leather canochy loader, with carrying strap.
- *diameter 15cm*
- **£2,250** • **Holland & Holland**

Expert Tips

Without doubt, shotguns, rifles or handguns that retain their original boxes or travelling cases and are intact command the best prices and attract the serious collector.

Taxidermy

The demand for taxidermy has declined since the Victorian period, when no drawing room was complete without the glassy stare of a furry mammal.

The earliest records of taxidermy date back to the Ancient Egyptians, who were experts in preserving flesh and bones, an art known as mummification. It is a little known fact that some Victorian and Edwardian painters actually painted with the pigment from ground mummies, which produced a sepia-toned brown, which became known as "Mummy Brown".

The use of taxidermy as a technique for keeping animals and birds, as well insects, in a preserved, real-life state, is of great importance to academic researchers, naturalists, nature lovers and sportsmen alike.

Considering the amount of time needed, along with the great skill of the taxidermist, many specimens remain somewhat undervalued. Where would the Natural History Museum in London be without its taxidermy collection?

Taxidermy reached its heyday during the Victorian and Edwardian periods. Since the late 1960s it has witnessed a revival, both as a decorative item, and as an important record of the natural world.

Tarantula and Stick Insect ◄
- **20th century**
A South American tarantula and stick insect, mounted in a display case.
- *length 40cm*
- **£55**　　　● **Get Stuffed**

Eagle Owl ◄
- **20th century**
Eagle owl mounted on a tree stump on an oval wood base.
- *height 59cm*
- **£260**　　　● **Get Stuffed**

American Teal ▼
- **20th century**
American teal perched on a branch on an oval polished wood base.
- *22cm x 26cm*
- **£95**　　　● **Get Stuffed**

Welsh Raven ◄
- **20th century**
Welsh raven perched on a stump on a square wood base.
- *height 67cm*
- **£275**　　　● **Get Stuffed**

Red Fox Cub ▲
- *20th century*
British Red fox cub shown
reclining, mounted on wooden
base.
- *height 24cm*
- £225   • Get Stuffed

Sparrow Hawk ▼
- *20th century*
Sparrow hawk with wings spread,
mounted on a branch set on a
polished wood base.
- *height 61cm*
- £195   • Get Stuffed

Baboon ▲
- *20th century*
Baboon shown on all fours baring
his teeth in an aggressive stance.
- *71cm x 81cm*
- £450   • Get Stuffed

Prevost's Squirrel ▶
- *20th century*
Prevost's squirrel posed on a
branch on an oval wood base.
- £195   • Get Stuffed

Snowy Owl ▲
- *20th century*
Snowy owl shown on a snow
covered wooden stump on a
circular wood base.
- *height 57cm*
- £590   • Get Stuffed

Pelican ▶
- *20th century*
Pelican shown standing with
open beak.
- *95cm x 63cm*
- £75   • Get Stuffed

Mongrel Dog ◀

- **20th century**
Naturalistically seated mongrel
dog shown in an alert pose.
- *height 62cm*
- £295　　　● Get Stuffed

Polar Bear Skin Rug ▼

- *circa 1920*
A Canadian polar bear skin rug,
well preserved, with a fearsome
expression.
- *285cm*
- £2,500　　　● John Clay

Armadillo ▼

- **20th century**
Adult armadillo on all fours.
- *length 65cm*
- £240　　　● Get Stuffed

Crow and Skull ▲

- **20th century**
Crow picking at an eyeball of a
human skull decorated with fake
blood, on a metal base.
- *height 59cm*
- £395　　　● Get Stuffed

European Red Fox ▼

- **20th century**
Adult European red fox shown
reclining.
- *length 38cm*
- £275　　　● Get Stuffed

Egyptian Bat ▲

- **20th century**
Egyptian bat with extended wings
on a circular wood base.
- *width 80cm*
- £145　　　● Get Stuffed

Expert Tips

*Animal skins should not show
signs of wear. Heads should be
free of damage.*

Blackbird ◀

- **20th century**
Blackbird traditionally perched
upon a branch, with oval wood
base.
- *height 27cm*
- £95　　　● Get Stuffed

Cock Pheasant ➤

- **20th century**

Cock pheasant in a mating pose, standing on a branch mounted on a circular wooden base.

- *height 87cm*
- £195   • Get Stuffed

Barn Owl ▲

- **20th century**

Barn owl with outstretched wings shown posed on a branch on a polished wood base.

- *height 68cm*
- £390   • Get Stuffed

Persian Cat ◀

- **20th century**

Persian cat shown reclining with one paw raised.

- *length 30cm*
- £295   • Get Stuffed

Asian Insects ▲

- **20th century**

Display cabinet showing three Asian insects: a scorpion, horned beetle and ghost beetle.

- *length 40cm*
- £60   • Get Stuffed

Zebra ➤

- **circa 1900**

A mounted zebra head with a fine expression, preserved in England.

- *height 120cm*
- £475   • Tredantiques

Rooster ▲

- **20th century**

Magnificent rooster naturalistically posed in crowing position, without a base.

- *height 57cm*
- £245   • Get Stuffed

Yorkshire Terrier ◄

- *20th century*

Yorkshire terrier shown seated with a red ribbon tied in a bow in its fur.

- *height 27cm*
- £245 • Get Stuffed

Red Parrot ▼

- *20th century*

South American red parrot with indigo and purple colouring on its feathers, perched on a branch, with a circular base.

- *height 43cm*
- £275 • Get Stuffed

Rudd ▲

- *20th century*

A rudd displayed in a bow-fronted case decorated with marine vegetation.

- *length 48cm*
- £475 • Get Stuffed

Rat ▼

- *20th century*

Rat shown on hind legs with forearms raised.

- *length 20cm*
- £95 • Get Stuffed

Gerbil ▼

- *20th century*

Tan and white gerbil shown on all fours.

- *length 15cm*
- £95 • Get Stuffed

Mouse ▲

- *20th century*

Mouse shown on hind legs with forearms raised, posed on a red apple.

- *height 13cm*
- £75 • Get Stuffed

Roach ▼

- *20th century*

Roach surrounded by marine vegetation and displayed within a bow-fronted case.

- *length 48cm*
- £475 • Get Stuffed

Asiatic Jungle Cat ◄

- *20th century*

Asiatic jungle cat shown on a branch set upon a polished wood base.

- *height 105cm*
- £475 • Get Stuffed

Bush Baby ►

- *20th century*

South American thick-tailed bush baby posed within branches, on a polished wood base.

- *height 64cm*
- £275 • Get Stuffed

Capuchin ▼

- *20th century*

A capuchin naturalistically posed on branches, on a circular wood base.

- *height 60cm*
- £250 • Get Stuffed

Bull's Skull ▼

- *20th century*

Finely preserved skull of a bull.

- *length 55cm*
- £225 • Get Stuffed

Hedgehog ▲

- *20th century*

Adult hedgehog on all fours, mounted on oval wooden base.

- *23cm x 15cm*
- £175 • Get Stuffed

Woodcock ►

- *20th century*

Naturalistically posed woodcock, on a branch with an oval wood base.

- *height 28cm*
- £145 • Get Stuffed

Lioness ▲
- *1910*

An Edwardian lioness from Zimbabwe in an exceptional state of preservation.
- *100cm x 160cm*
- **£1,400**   • Tredantiques

Carnelian ➤
- *20th century*

African carnelian shown with its tail coiled around a branch, on an oval wood base.
- *height 33cm*
- **£175**   • Get Stuffed

Ginger Cat ▲
- *20th century*

Naturalistically posed ginger cat shown curled up and asleep.
- *width 33cm*
- **£295**   • Get Stuffed

Doves ➤
- *20th century*

Pair of doves naturalistically posed, surrounded by a mahogany base with foliate decoration. (With glass dome supplied).
- *height 43cm*
- **£350**   • Get Stuffed

Leopard Tortoise ▲
- *20th century*

An adult leopard tortoise with finely preserved shell.
- *25cm x 16cm*
- **£195**   • Get Stuffed

Expert Tips

Taxidermy has become more popular as pet lovers like to keep their favourite pets alive by having them preserved and presented in their favourite pose. This trend started in America and has now crossed the Atlantic into Europe. This has also received a revival as managed game hunting is now condoned; licenses can now be obtained for very large sums of money, for the culling of specific animals.

Owl ▲
- *20th century*

An owl in an alert pose, mounted on a wooden plaque.
- *height 60cm*
- **£195**   • Get Stuffed

Grey Rabbit ◄
- *20th century*

Adult grey rabbit with white tail, shown in an alert pose.
- *height 25cm*
- **£125**   • Get Stuffed

Textiles & Fans

Often no longer used for their original purpose, textiles are frequently hung on the wall, a practice that has maintained their value.

The rise in value of textiles has come about by the fact that textiles in good condition are very rare, as by their nature fabrics are fragile and at the mercy of moth and mice.
Ever since the importation of silk from the Far East during Roman times, the appetite for luxurious fabrics has never diminished. Pre-twentieth century ladies of leisure spent their hours at needlepoint and embroidery, creating cushion covers, bed quilts and clothes,

and even their children were encouraged to make samplers. These hand-made and unique items are

now extremely collectable, and it is the vital work of the collectors and dealers of textiles, which helps to preserve them for future generations. The importance and interest in fashion as a historical record of popular dress and dress codes, along with the details found in the secrets of their manufacture, is of interest to the designer and dressmaker of today. As fashion style becomes international with the influence of the media, and national dress slowly goes into decline, it is increasingly important to collect and record these items in order to preserve humanity's heritage.

French Louis XIV Needlepoint ➤

- *circa 1670*
French Louis XIV needlepoint panel showing a mythological scene with Neptune, romantic figures and animals in an Arcadian setting.
- *32cm x 30cm*
- **£4,000** • Marilyn Garrow

Needlepoint Panel ◄

- *18th century*
French needlepoint panel showing a romantic couple on horseback within a heraldic border of blue, red and cream.
- *50cm x 46cm*
- **£9,500** • Marilyn Garrow

Royal Feather Fan ▼

- *circa 1900*
Feather fan with tortoiseshell sticks applied with the gold Royal cypher of Princess Marie Maximilianova of Lechtenberg (1841–1911).
- **£850** • Zakheim

Feather Fan ◄

- *circa 1900*
Pink ostrich feather fan with tortoiseshell sticks. Provenance: Princess Marie Maximilianova of Lechtenberg (1841–1911).
- **£750** • Zakheim

Hunting Scene Tapestry ▲

- *17th century*
Tapestry portraying a hunting
scene in a wooded landscape,
showing a horseman with
footman and a dog in the
foreground.
- *width 75cm*
- **£3,800** ● Marilyn Garrow

Marriage Seat Cover ▲

- *18th century*
French needlepoint marriage seat
cover depicting a flowering tree
for fertility and the married
couple either side.
- *32cm x 29cm*
- **£3,000** ● Marilyn Garrow

French Wall Hanging ▶

- *circa 1820*
French Second Empire tapestry
depicting a garden setting with
couples in the foreground.
- *244cm x 320cm*
- **£16,000** ● O.F. Wilson

Ostrich Feather Fan ◀

- *circa 1900*
Ostrich feather fan with
tortoiseshell sticks. Provenance:
Princess Marie Maximilianova of
Lechtenberg (1841–1911).
- **£750** ● Zakheim

Textile Block ◀

- *20th century*
A carved wooden textile printing
block in pseudo-Japanese script
pattern design.
- *30cm x 26cm*
- **£250** ● Zakheim

Georgian Silk Purse ▲

- *1740*
Georgian silk purse finely
embroidered with gold silk
ribboning and foliate designs.
- *width 15cm*
- **£450** ● Marilyn Garrow

Pink Ostrich Fan ◀

- *circa 1900*
A bright pink ostrich feather fan
with tortoiseshell sticks.
Provenance: Princess Marie
Maximilianova of Lechtenberg
(1841–1911).
- **£750** ● Zakheim

Classical Needlepoint ▲

- *18th century*

French needlepoint seat cover showing a group of a classical figures surrounded by a vermilion border.

- *50cm x 40cm*
- £2,200 • Marilyn Garrow

Embroidered Purse ▲

- *1740*

Small lady's Georgian silk purse embroidered with red flowers and green foliage.

- *width 12cm*
- £450 • Marilyn Garrow

Expert Tips

An early piece can have great interest historically, but if the condition is very poor it will not fetch a desirable price.

Bird Tapestry ▲

- *16th century*

Fenilles de Choux tapestry panel with a broad design of a bird among foliage.

- *226cm x 35cm*
- £4,800 • Marilyn Garrow

Peacock Fan ▲

- *circa 1900*

A peacock feather fan onto tortoiseshell. Provenance: Princess Marie Maximilianova of Lechtenberg (1841–1911).

- £750 • Zakheim

Asian Tapestry ▲

- *late 17th century*

Tapestry fragment depicting birds with a foliate design on a cream background, made for the European market.

- *50cm x 58cm*
- £3,000 • Marilyn Garrow

Petit-Point Picture ➤

- *circa 1640*

A very fine petit-point picture of Charles I and Henrietta Maria beside a pond with a lion and a deer each side, in a woodland setting with a castle in the background.

- *30cm x 55cm*
- £4,500 • Marilyn Garrow

Georgian Pillow Case ➤

- *circa 1720*

Exquisite Georgian pillow case with foliate design from eighteenth century.

- *60cm x 40cm*
- £9,500 • Marilyn Garrow

Crewel-Work Waistcoat ▲

- *18th century*
Fine crewel-work waistcoat, embroidered with red, yellow and blue flowers with green foliate designs.
- *95cm x 67cm*
- £4,600 • Marilyn Garrow

French Screen ▼

- *18th century*
French nineteenth century giltwood Chasurrables screen, with eighteenth century embroidered panels.
- *168cm x 70cm*
- £4,800 • Marilyn Garrow

Chinese Embroidery ➤

- *18th century*
Chinese silk panel embroidered with birds and foliate design on a cream background.
- *52cm x 45cm*
- £1,800 • Marilyn Garrow

Jacobean Curtains ◄

- *circa 1680*
One of a pair of Jacobean curtains in beautiful condition, with a trailing foliate design of blue and red flowers, on a cream background.
- *200cm x 120cm*
- £14,500 • Marilyn Garrow

Needlework Casket ▼

- *circa 1680*
Superb Restoration period needlework casket worked in colonized silks depicting Paris and Aphrodite, with fitted interior and original glass bottles with pewter lids.
- *22cm x 28cm*
- £10,500 • Midwinter

Velvet Appliqué ◄

- *1680*
French velvet embroidered appliqué wall hanging, with fine silver thread woven throughout.
- *170cm x 65cm*
- £6,800 • Marilyn Garrow

Stump Work ▼

- *circa 1630*
Stump work fragments of a rural scene, with Charles I and Henrietta Maria in the foreground and a figure in a striped tent.
- *35cm x 50cm*
- £4,500 • Marilyn Garrow

Japanese Fan ▲
- *circa 1900*
Japanese ivory fan with a finely
handpainted watercolour of
water and mountains.
- *width 28cm*
- **£555**   • **Japanese Gallery**

Armorial Tapestry ▲
- *17th century*
An Italian bishop's armorial
tapestry, embroidered with gold
on a crimson background.
- *40cm x 42cm*
- **£1,500**   • **Marilyn Garrow**

Fire Screen Tapestry ▲
- *18th century*
Giltwood fire screen, with an
eighteenth century needlework
panel of green foliate and red
flowers on a cream background.
- *124cm x 61.5cm*
- **£2,800**   • **Midwinter**

Beauvais Tapestry ▲
- *17th century*
Beauvais tapestry with a broad
design of white and red flowers,
with green foliage on a cream
background.
- *36cm x 49cm*
- **£2,200**   • **Marilyn Garrow**

Cromwellian
Needlework Panel ▼
- *circa 1650*
Cromwellian period needlework
panel depicting King Solomon
and the Queen of Sheba with
attendants.
- *32cm x 28cm*
- **£8,500**   • **Midwinter**

Embroidered Panel ▲
- *17th century*
A stunning Italian panel,
embroidered in silk with gold
thread, depicting the Sun God.
- *length 300cm*
- **£4,200**   • **Marilyn Garrow**

Tapestry Covers ▲
- *circa 1780*
A pair of French Louis XVI
Beauvais tapestry seat covers
embroidered with red and blue
foliate sprays within swag borders.
- *29cm x 38cm*
- **£2,800**   • **Marilyn Garrow**

Tools

**The only rule in collecting tools is that there are no rules.
This most arcane of all fields baffles the layman.**

A good starting point for those interested in building collections is tools, as their prices are reasonable, and in the future these items will prove to be of great historical importance.

In recent years there has been a marked interest in early blacksmith tools such as hammers and anvils, along with early scientific tools. Increasingly we see lawnmowers, sprayers, garden edgers and agricultural tools coming into this expanding and popular market. Carts, wheelbarrows,

and wheelwright's tools are also finding collectors. The most popular tools tend to be connected with the cabinet-maker or joinery trades, good examples being box planes and chisels. It is the skill of the historical craftsman's hand that makes these simple, yet effective tools so desirable.

In fact, this interest in tools of the past is currently being energised by the onslaught of petrol-powered lawn mowers, electric hedge clippers and other powered gadgets that now cover the shelves in our local DIY stores.

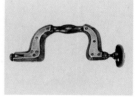

Plated Brace ▲
- *1880*
Victorian Robert Marples beech-registered plated brace in good condition.
- *length 37.5cm*
- **£55** • **Tool Shop Auctions**

Bow Drill ▲
- *circa 1870*
A pianomaker's rosewood and brass bow drill with original bow.
- *length 25cm*
- **£195** • **Tool Shop Auctions**

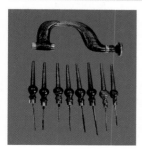

Rosewood Wedge ▲
- *1890*
Victorian gunmetal bullnose rosewood wedge.
- *length 10cm*
- **£100** • **Tool Shop Auctions**

Dutch Pod ◄
- *circa 1850*
A Dutch pod brace made of ash with brass chuck and eight pods.
- *length 37cm*
- **£155** • **Tool Shop Auctions**

Expert Tips

Tools should be stored in a dry and well-ventilated place and kept lightly oiled, and wiped with a soft dry cloth.

Lady's Brace ▲

- *1860*

A beech lady's brace with cocobolo head.
- *length 27.5cm*
- £75   • Tool Shop Auctions

Moulding Plane ▲

- *1880*

A rare, complex two-inch, triple iron moulding plane by Mathieson.
- *length 23.8cm*
- £240   • Tool Shop Auctions

Sheffield Plated Brace ▲

- *1875*

Victorian Sheffield beech-plated brace, unnamed.
- *length 37cm*
- £65   • Tool Shop Auctions

Mitre Plane ▲

- *1870*

An 8-inch dovetailed mitre plane with rosewood infill by Mathieson with super fine mouth.
- *length 21.3cm*
- £510   • Tool Shop Auctions

Shoulder Plane ▼

- *1880*

Victorian one-inch Mathieson dovetailed shoulder plane with rosewood infill and Marples cutter.
- *length 23cm*
- £120   • Tool Shop Auctions

Expert Tips

All brass or metal fittings should be complete and free from severe corrosion. It is not uncommon for box planes, chisels, wooden vices and old hand drills to still be used by the wood worker or cabinet maker today, which is partly due to the high quality and individuality of the design.

Plough Plane ▲

- *1880*

A fine quality rosewood plough plane by Mathieson with rosewood stem wedges and brass fittings and skate front.
- *length 25cm*
- £590   • Tool Shop Auctions

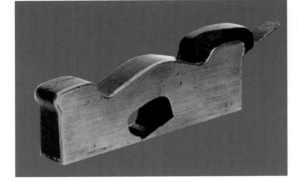

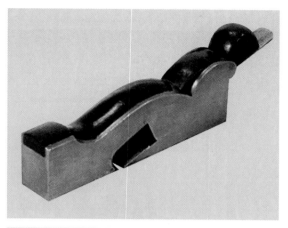

Victorian Shoulder Plane ◄
- *1890*

Victorian steel-soled gunmetal shoulder plane with mahogany infill and wide mouth.
- *length 23cm*
- £55   • Tool Shop Auctions

Scottish Plane ▼
- *1870*

Victorian gunmetal Scottish smoothing plane with overstuffed rosewood infill.
- *length 23cm*
- £220   • Tool Shop Auctions

Boxwood Planes ▼
- *1880*

A pair of rare, miniature boxwood planes by Preston, with a radiussed rebate and a compassed rebate.
- *length 7.5cm*
- £210   • Tool Shop Auctions

Mathieson Plane ▲
- *circa 1920s*

A Mathieson dovetailed parallel-sided smoothing plane with rosewood infill made as a special order for a man with large hands.
- *length 26.3cm*
- £575   • Tool Shop Auctions

Scottish Smoothing Plane ▲
- *1860*

Stylish Scottish iron smoothing plane with walnut overstuffing, cove front and moulded infill at the rear.
- *length 22cm*
- £280   • Tool Shop Auctions

Cutting Gauge ▲
- *1895*

A Victorian fine quality ebony and brass cutting gauge by Frost.
- *length 25cm*
- £110   • Tool Shop Auctions

Expert Tips

Box planes should be avoided if severely damaged, or if they are infested with woodworm.

Plumb Bob ▲
- *1850*

Victorian steel-tipped brass plumb bob with brass reel.
- *length 8.8cm*
- £60 • Tool Shop Auctions

Norris Smoothing Plane ▲
- *1920*

A Norris 20R gunmetal smoothing plane in its original box.
- *length 22cm*
- £700 • Tool Shop Auctions

A1 Panel Plane ▲
- *1930*

A Norris A1 panel plane with dovetailed and rosewood infill.
- *length 44cm*
- £2,050 • Tool Shop Auction

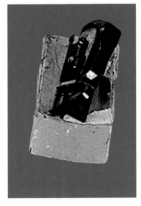

Victorian Plumb and Square ▲
- *1850*

A fine Victorian brass plumb and square with original patina.
- *length 27.5cm*
- £195 • Tool Shop Auctions

Norris A1 Jointer ▲
- *1925*

A Norris A1 jointer with rosewood infill and dovetailed body in excellent condition.
- *length 56cm*
- £4,100 • Tool Shop Auctions

Plumb Board and Bob ▼
- *1830*

George IV decorative mahogany plumb board and bronze plumb bob in classical style with simple carved ornamentation.
- *width 45cm*
- £470 • Tool Shop Auctions

Trimming Plane ▲
- *1880*

Victorian Stanley 95 edge trimming plane in the original box.
- *length 15cm*
- £125 • Tool Shop Auctions

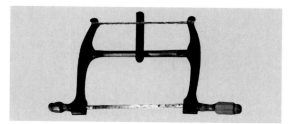

Moulding Plane ▲

- *1880*

A Scottish four-iron gothic sash moulding plane by Wilson, Glasgow.
- *length 24cm*
- **£270** • **Tool Shop Auctions**

Beech Bow Saw ▲

- *1860*

An unusually small beech bow saw with octagonal boxwood handles by Buck, with six-inch blade.
- **£50** • **Tool Shop Auctions**

Victorian Level ▲

- *1860*

Victorian rare waisted rosewood and brass level.
- **£445** • **Tool Shop Auctions**

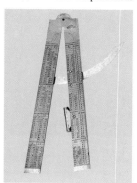

Spirit Level ▲

- *1880*

Victorian Mathieson 14C highly decorative rosewood and brass spirit level.
- **£165** • **Tool Shop Auctions**

Pitchmeter ◄

- *1885*

Rare W. Tates Pitchmeter made by J. Robson of Newcastle upon Tyne. With German silver mounts, graduated protractor arm and adjustable spirit level. Scales calculate diameter in feet versus pitch in feet.
- **£620** • **Tool Shop Auctions**

Rule and Measuring Stick ▲

- *1875*

Rare French Fisheries Officer's boxwood rule and iron measuring stick. The rule measures the denier of the nets to see if they comply with regulations. It has different scales on each face depending on the species being caught. The length of the fish is checked against the fish rule.
- *length 15cm*
- **£200** • **Tool Shop Auctions**

Stanley 45E ◄

- *1923*

An immaculate Stanley 45E, a presentation piece in 1923. Type 15 Sweetheart, in a tin box, complete with instructions and original screwdriver.
- *length 25cm*
- **£130** • **Tool Shop Auctions**

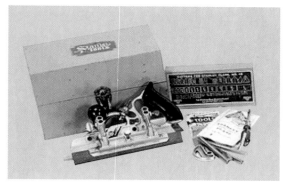

Moving Fillister ▲
- *1870*

A moving fillister plane in solid
Brazilian rosewood with brass
fittings and boxwood stem
wedges.
- *length 25cm*
- £180   • Tool Shop Auctions

Trammels ▼
- *1870*

A rare set of four trammels with
brass and steel tips, seven inch.
- £140   • Tool Shop Auctions

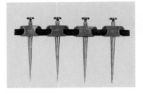

Sash Fillister ▼
- *1870*

Rare Victorian beautifully crafted
sash fillister in solid Brazilian
rosewood with brass fittings and
boxwood stem wedges.
- *length 25cm*
- £400   • Tool Shop Auctions

Oak Router ▼
- *circa 1760*

Oak router with rosewood wedge,
carved in the form of three turrets
with beautiful patina.
- *width 17.5cm*
- £480   • Tool Shop Auctions

Carved Router ▲
- *1780*

European fruitwood carved router
with figured rosewood wedge.
- *width 15cm*
- £50   • Tool Shop Auctions

George II Oak Router ▼
- *1750*

Rare George II carved oak router
with four blades, 12 inches wide.
- £930   • Tool Shop Auctions

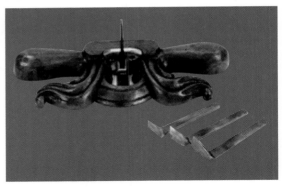

Sliding Bevel ▼
- *1777*

Brass and mahogany sliding bevel
dated 1777.
- *length 17.5cm*
- £160   • Tool Shop Auctions

Toys, Games & Dolls

Toys need to be extremely well cared for to appeal to most collectors.

The well-loved toy, with its scratches and chipped paint is not likely to be the toy with the most value. It is that forgotten and unloved toy, in perfect condition, banished to the attic or stuffed in a box at the bottom of a cupboard, that will fetch the highest value. Toy manufacturing began in the 1890s and the most valuable examples come from the great German workshops of this period. In the late 1950s and '60s there was an increase in toy manufacturing from Japan, with the clockwork and electrically driven, battery operated toy coming to prominence. These toys can be particularly difficult to repair as parts are invariably non-existent and condition appears to be the guiding light as far as the collector is concerned.

The toy collector is not only interested in the period toy, but also the fashionable toys of the recent past, such as the Barbie Doll and the Thunderbirds puppets. Model railways and trains remain popular. Both British and American locomotives and train sets are proving to be very good investments.

Shirley Temple Doll ➤
- **1934**
Shirley Temple porcelain doll with blonde hair, wearing suede dungarees with silver studs and a red check shirt.
- *height 325cm*
- **£325**   • Dolly Land

Hornby Metal Train ▼
- **1958**
Metal train by Hornby in original box.
- *length 28cm*
- **£125**   • Jeff Williams

German-Made Giraffe ➤
- **1950**
German elastoline Giraffe.
- *height 28cm*
- **£75**   • Stephen Naegel

Roman Chariot ▲
- **1960**
Plastic roman chariot by Timber Toys, in the original box.
- *width 42cm*
- **£350**   • Stephen Naegel

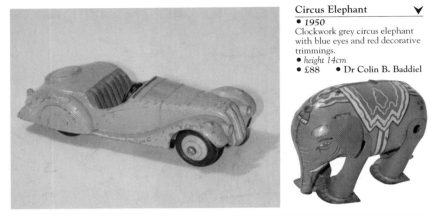

Circus Elephant ▼
- *1950*

Clockwork grey circus elephant with blue eyes and red decorative trimmings.
- *height 14cm*
- £88   • Dr Colin B. Baddiel

Frazer Nash Sports Car ▲
- *1940*

Frazer Nash sports car made by Dinky, with a blue body and wheels, and a grey interior.
- *length 8cm*
- £48   • Dr Colin B. Baddiel

Expert Tips

The 1930s saw the success of Tootsie toys from America.

Rolls Royce ▲
- *1960*

Cream and silver Rolls Royce Phantom V made by Dinky.
- *length 8cm*
- £75   • Dr Colin B. Baddiel

Austin Healey ▲
- *1960*

Cream and silver Austin Healey sports car with red wheels and interior, with driver and the number "23" on the side.
- *length 8cm*
- £113   • Dr Colin B. Baddiel

Blue Mini ▼
- *1966*

Unusual blue Mini in original box, made by Dinky.
- *length 8cm*
- £125   • Dr Colin B. Baddiel

American Ford ▲
- *1920*

Tan American Ford with black wheels and brass radiator, made by Tootsie.
- *length 10cm*
- £27   • Dr Colin B. Baddiel

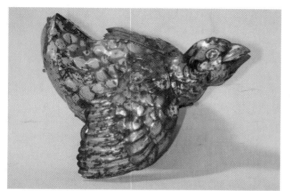

Robot Money Bank ➤
- *1960*

Silver robot with large round eyes, designed with a silver scoop for the money, sitting on a circular brown container.
- *height 14cm*
- £25   • Dr Colin B. Baddiel

Yellow Ferrari ▲
- *1960*

Yellow Ferrari with original box, made by Dinky.
- *length 10cm*
- £40   • Dr Colin B. Baddiel

Expert Tips

In 1934 the British Meccano Company, which was part of the Hornby Empire, pioneered its own range of die-cast model vehicles known as Dinky.

Toy Pheasant ◀
- *1920*

German clockwork toy pheasant.
- *4cm x 6cm*
- £125   • Dr Colin B. Baddiel

Green Racing Car ▲
- *1980*

Green Connaught Dinky racing car with driver, with its original box.
- *length 16cm*
- £80   • Dr Colin B. Baddiel

American Tootsie Car ▲
- *1930*

American brown Tootsie car, by La Salle.
- *length 12 cm*
- £120   • Dr Colin B.

American Fastback ▲
- *1920*

American fastback orange car with black running boards and red enamel wheels, by Mano IL.
- *length 8cm*
- £75   • Dr Colin B. Baddiel

Batmobile Car ◀
- *1960*

American black Batmobile, with red interior.
- *length 10cm*
- £48   • Dr Colin B. Baddiel

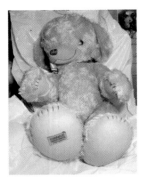

Catterfelda Doll ➤

- *circa 1870*
A German hand-painted porcelain doll made by Catterfelda, wearing the original lace dress.
- *height 66cm*
- £480   • Dolly Land

Expert Tips

The 'teddy' bear originates from 1902, when a cartoon depicting President Theodore 'Teddy' Roosevelt, a keen hunter, showed him refusing to shoot a bear cub. At this time toy bears were being imported from Germany and Roosevelt's followers nicknamed these bears 'teddy'.

Brown Steiff Bear ▼

- *1993*
Brown Steiff bear. Limited edition of 3,000.
- *height 61cm*
- £375   • Dolly Land

Cheeky ◄

- *1995*
'Cheeky', the Merrythought Bear. Limited edition to 250.
- *height 65cm*
- £225   • Dolly Land

Limited Edition Doll ➤

- *1994*
Annabette Himstedt doll, one of a limited edition.
- *height 75cm*
- £750   • Dolly Land

Annabette Himstedt Doll ▲

- *1993–4*
Limited edition of an Annabette Himstedt doll. Hand painted with long blonde hair and original white dress.
- *height 68cm*
- £650   • Dolly Land

Steiff Bear Watches ▲

- *1992*
Steiff bear watch collection.
- *height 51cm*
- £350   • Dolly Land

Porcelain Doll ▼

- *circa 1940*
A Burggrub-Princess Elizabeth Pozellanlabrik porcelain doll with blonde hair and a white organza dress.
- *height 38cm*
- £1,200   • Dolly Land

Steiff Bear and Golly ▲
- *1996*

Jolly Golly and Steiff Bear set,
part of a limited edition of 1,500.
- *height 45cm*
- £295   • Dolly Land

Phantom Brown Bear ➤
- *circa 1910*

Brown Bear made by Phantom,
limited edition of 4,000.
- *height 61cm*
- £380   • Dolly Land

German Doll ▲
- *1930*

Original porcelain and hand-
painted German doll, wearing
original black coat with lace
collar, red dress and hat with lace
trim, and black laced boots.
- *height 37cm*
- £175   • Dolly Land

Merrythought Golly ▼
- *1960*

Merrythought golly, limited
edition of 100.
- *height 32cm*
- £40   • Dolly Land

American School Bus ▼
- *1950*

Yellow American school bus.
- *length 30cm*
- £190   • Dr Colin B. Baddiel

Wellington Bear ▲
- *1992*

Limited edition of Merrythought
Wellington Bear.
- *height 54cm*
- £125   • Dolly Land

Merrythought
Mohair Bear ▼
- *1930s*

Merrythought mohair bear.
A limited edition of 50 was
produced in white brown and
black.
- *height 38cm*
- £55   • Dolly Land

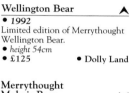

Magic Roundabout ▼

- *1970*

Magic roundabout characters, on a red bicycle with a trailer, made by Corgi Toys.

- *length 8cm*
- £45   • Dr Colin B. Baddiel

American Footballer ▼

- *1950*

American footballer with red and white helmet.

- *height 9cm*
- £85   • Dr Colin B. Baddiel

Red Mercedes Racing Car ▲

- *1930*

Red German Mercedes racing car, by Marklin.

- *length 26cm*
- £750   • Dr Colin B. Baddiel

Black Clockwork Robot ◄

- *1960*

American black clockwork robot with red boots, with original cardboard box.

- *height 125cm*
- £168   • Dr Colin B. Baddiel

Police Van ▼

- *1930s*

Black police van, made by Wells.

- *length 11cm*
- £75   • Dr Colin B. Baddiel

Silver XK120 ▲

- *1950s*

Silver clockwork metal Jaguar XK 120 with original box and key.

- *length 10cm*
- £200   • Dr Colin B. Baddiel

Morris Car ▲

- *1960*

Bull-nosed Morris commemorative toy with a band called The Beat.

- *length 7cm*
- £45   • Dr Colin B. Baddiel

Expert Tips

Pre-war features of Dinky toys included their plain metal wheel hubs, silver plating on their wheels, white tyres and no model numbers on either the base plate or chassis. They were never boxed individually, but always in sets and had wing-mounted wheels.

Blue and Silver Metal Dalek ➤
- *1950s*

Unusual blue and silver metal dalek from the 1950s.
- *height 12cm*
- **£225** • Dr Colin B. Baddiel

French Racing Car ▲
- *1930*

French blue racing car with red decoration, the number "54" on the side and white wheels.
- *length 24cm*
- **£85** • Dr Colin B. Baddiel

Messerschmitt Car ▲
- *1960*

Messerschmitt with red body and a clear cover and three wheels.
- *length 21cm*
- **£360** • Dr Colin B. Baddiel

Red London Bus ◄
- *1950s*

Red London double-decker bus, by Triang toys.
- *length 17cm*
- **£170** • Dr Colin B. Baddiel

Milk Van ▼
- *1950*

English blue and white milk van by Chad Valley toys.
- *length 15cm*
- **£115** • Dr Colin B. Baddiel

Red Fire Engine ▼
- *1960s*

Red fire engine operated by battery with a box snorkel.
- *34cm x 20cm*
- **£85** • Dr Colin B. Baddiel

Clockwork Circus Clown ▼
- *1930*

Clockwork Shiuko circus clown with a drum.
- *height 6cm*
- **£145** • Dr Colin B. Baddiel

Woodbine Dominoes ▶

- *circa 1930*

A box of dominoes in original green box with cream lettering with the words, "Wills Woodbine Dominoes" inscribed on the front of the tin.

- *length 27cm*
- £36   • After Noah (KR)

Black Train ▼

- *1930*

Black metal train with red and gold trim. The maker's name is Maerklin.

- *length 42cm*
- £2,500   • Dolly Land

Hessmobil Car ▲

- *1910*

German blue motor car with yellow wheels and yellow trim around the doors, made by Hessmobil.

- *length 24cm*
- £1,250   • Dolly Land

Curatt Car ▼

- *20th century*

Red motor car with black roof and a brass radiator and side lamp, red running boards, and a man driving, made by Curatt.

- *length 44cm*
- £2,350   • Dolly Land

Steiff Bear ▶

- *circa 1991*

A Steiff bear, one of a limited edition of 300 which were made only for the UK market in 1991. This is a replica of a Steiff bear salvaged from the Titanic and sold for £94,400.

- *height 48cm*
- £450   • Dolly Land

Barbie Doll ▲

- *1960*

Plastic flexible Barbie doll with long blonde hair, a pink hairband and pink pumps, by Matel.

- *height 30cm*
- £75   • Zoom

Expert Tips

Although toy electric locomotives made in the 1960s are currently cheap to buy, their value will increase over the years, making them a good potential purchase for the new collector.

Tudor Doll's House ▼

- *1930s*

Mock Tudor doll's house with white walls and black beams, circa 1930.

- *height 87cm*
- £125   • Dolly Land

Yellow Union Pacific Train ◀
- *1960*
Yellow Union Pacific train by Wese. TT-gauge.
- *length 64cm*
- £225   • Jeff Williams

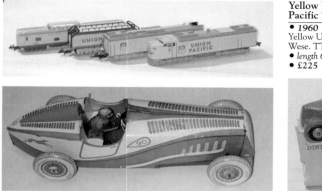

Expert Tips

Most highly-collectable and high-value toys are not particularly old, so it is worth visiting secondhand stores, junk shops, jumble sales and boot fairs to find the best bargains. Often, a very recent example of a popular toy, such as an Action Man, is worth buying now for longterm value.

Bluebird Car ▶
- *1930*
Blue Bluebird racing car, by Kosuge & Co.
- *length 21cm*
- £425   • Lennox Gallery

Racing Car ▲
- *1930*
Clockwork metal, blue and red French racing car with driver, by Charles Rossignol, Paris.
- *length 40cm*
- £485   • Lennox Gallery

Delivery Van ▲
- *1950*
Green delivery van made by Dinky with its original cardboard yellow box.
- *length 8cm*
- £67   • Dr Colin B. Baddiel

Black Fleischmann Train ▼
- *1955*
Black Fleischmann train with red trim and wheels. O-gauge.
- *length 23cm*
- £135   • Jeff Williams

Hornby Train ▲
- *circa 1930*
Brown Hornby train with yellow trim around the windows and black wheels. O-gauge.
- *length 32cm*
- £120   • Jeff Williams

Green Flying Scotsman ◀
- *1950*
Green Flying Scotsman by Bassett, coke O-gauge.
- *length 28cm*
- £1,950   • Jeff Williams

Dumper Truck ▲
- *1950s*

Yellow and red dumper truck, made in Japan by Haji for the American market.
- *length 23cm*
- £60   • Dr Colin B. Baddiel

Mickey Mouse Driving a Car ▲
- *1961*

Mickey Mouse driving a blue open car, with yellow spoked wheels.
- *length 12cm*
- £60   • Dr Colin B. Baddiel

Clockwork Windmill ▼
- *1900*

English clockwork metal windmill with orange sails.
- *height 4cm*
- £90   • Dr Colin B. Baddiel

Horse Box ▲
- *1950*

Yellow and orange horse box, with original packaging.
- *length 21cm*
- £69   • Dr Colin B. Baddiel

Clockwork Clown ▲
- *1950*

Clockwork clown with red jacket and yellow and black hat, riding a bike, with original key.
- *height 7cm*
- £155   • Dr Colin B. Baddiel

Clown on Stilts ▶
- *circa 1950s*

Clown on stilts with red and white striped trousers, red top and green hat, playing a violin, with original box and key.
- *height 20cm*
- £100   • Dr Colin B. Baddiel

Clockwork Steamboat ▶
- *circa 1925*

Clockwork white steamboat boat with yellow funnels and red wheels and trim.
- *length 12cm*
- £238   • Dr Colin B. Baddiel

Metal Soldiers ▲
- *1950*

Set of lead, hand-painted, model British soldiers and horses.
- *height 4cm/soldier*
- £1,500   • Stephen Naegel

German Crocodile Train ▶
- *circa 1960*

Green German crocodile train by Marklin. HO-gauge.
- *length 23cm*
- £445   • Jeff Williams

Rocking Horse ▶
- *circa 1890*

Carved wood and painted dapple grey rocking horse. With leather saddle and bridle, on wooden rockers.
- *120cm x 122cm*
- £3,500   • Midwinter

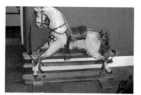

Union Pacific Train by Lionel & Co. ◀
- *1957*

Plastic orange Union Pacific train with black wheels by Lionel & Co.
- *length 28cm*
- £85   • Jeff Williams

German Doll ▼
- *1930*

German doll with hand painted porcelain face, blue eyes and blonde hair, wearing a red hat jacket and dress, with white lace trim and black leather boots.
- *height 57cm*
- £325   • Dolly Land

Tin-Head Doll ▶
- *1930*

Tin-head hand-painted china doll, with long blonde hair, wearing a white silk dress.
- *height 34cm*
- £195   • Dolly Land

Expert Tips

Model soldiers have a long history stretching back to Ancient Egypt, where they were used to represent armies in the Pharaohs' tombs. Roman children are known to have played with figures of soldiers.

Oriental Doll Family ◀
- *20th century*

Japanese family of dolls wearing traditional costumes, the girls having black wigs and hand painted faces.
- *height 36cm/girl*
- £250   • Dolly Land

Fleischmann Train ▲
- *1955*

Fleischmann train with rails, in original box. HO-gauge.
- *width 38cm/box*
- £85   ● Jeff Williams

Armand Marceau Porcelain Doll ▶
- *circa 1890*

Porcelain hand-painted Armand Marceau doll with original blue dress and black lace-up boots.
- *height 59cm*
- £250   ● Dolly Land

Porcelain Doll ▲
- *circa 1894*

Porcelain hand-painted German doll, wearing a red and blue tartan dress with lace pantaloons and black boots.
- *height 57cm*
- £450   ● Dolly Land

Royal Scot Train ▲
- *1935*

Red English Royal Scot metal train with black trim and wheels.
- *length 26cm*
- £425   ● Jeff Williams

Chad Valley Train ▼
- *1950*

An English brown bakelite toy train with two carriages with black wheels on the train, and ivory on the carriages. Maker's name: Chad Valley.
- *length 58cm*
- £700   ● Decodence

Welsh Doll ▲
- *circa 1930*

A Welsh Moa 200 porcelain hand-painted doll, wearing an emerald green velvet dress with a large ribboned belt with diamante clasp, bonnet and black shoes.
- *height 61cm*
- £395   ● Dolly Land

Wax Doll ▲
- *1870*

Victorian hand-painted wax doll with blue eyes and blonde hair, wearing cape embroidered with pink roses and a blue and white dress and bonnet.
- *height 65cm*
- £150   ● Dolly Land

Green Centurion Tank ◀
- *1954–60*

English green centurion tank.
- *length 12cm*
- £50   • Dr Colin B. Baddiel

Figure with Drum ➤
- *1940*

German clockwork figure with drum and cymbal.
- *height 10cm*
- £130   • Dr Colin B. Baddiel

Green MG ▼
- *1950*

Green MG TF sports car made by Band Japan for the USA market.
- *length 22cm*
- £60   • Dr Colin B. Baddiel

Royal Mail Van ▼
- *1950*

Red Royal Mail van made by Dinky, with the original yellow box and picture.
- *height 9cm*
- 120   • Dr Colin B. Baddiel

Tin Motorcyclist ▼
- *1950*

German tin model of a clockwork motorcyclist with an expression of speed.
- *length 16cm*
- £225   • Dr Colin B. Baddiel

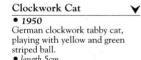

Clockwork Cat ▼
- *1950*

German clockwork tabby cat, playing with yellow and green striped ball.
- *length 5cm*
- £45   • Dr Colin B. Baddiel

Alfa Romeo ▼
- *1978*

Red Alfa Romeo Dinky racing car with red wheels and a figure of a racing driver at the wheel in white, with original box.
- *length 14cm*
- £78   • Dr Colin B. Baddiel

Treen

Treen means "made from trees", and anything wooden qualifies. Artefacts vary from the highly decorated to the basically carved, and all have their own charm.

Treen is a word used to describe objects made from tree wood. The most popular woods for carving are apple or pear, although most fruitwoods can be used, as their straight grain and softness makes them easier to carve. Although oak and walnut are hardwoods, it is not uncommon to find them being utilised for the more expensive commissions.

Carved wood figures and objects are becoming increasingly rare as time and volatile history have not been kind to their preservation; they were often thrown on the fire to give warmth, or burnt in the looting of churches during wars.

Tea caddies and boxes are among the highest valued items of treen. If they resemble a fruit such as a pear, apple or orange they tend to fetch very high prices. Some of the finest religious carvings do not command the prices that one would expect considering their quality and age while, in contrast, an exquisite small Japanese carving of, for example, a toad or a grotesque, can be expected to fetch up to three-figure sums.

Coat of Arms ➤
- *late 16th century*
Carved oak coat of arms, depicting royal crest showing three coronets, surrounded by heavily stylised acanthus leaf carving.
- *height 35cm*
- £6,200 ● Dial Post House

Napkin Rings ▼
- *circa 1900*
Three sycamore Mauchlin ware napkin rings showing various British scenes.
- *height 2cm*
- £18 ● John Clay

Gilt Wall Sconces ▼
- *late 17th century*
One of a pair of gilt wall sconces with candlesticks.
- £6,000 ● Dial Post House

Decorative Wing Tips ▼
- 1920
Pair of wooden aeroplane wing tips, converted to photo frames.
- *height 18cm*
- £350 ● Langfords Marine

Oak Carvings ▲
- *1600*

Pair of oak carvings showing winged mythical creatures, possibly from an overmantle.
- *height 55cm*
- £1,780 • Dial Post House

Beaker and Cover ▲
- *circa 1900s*

An English sycamore cup with a turned lid, with a view of Margate Sands and jetty.
- *height 7.5cm*
- £50 • John Clay

Carving of Bacchus ▲
- *17th century*

A rare English seventeenth century limewood carved figure of the Greek god Bacchus seated on a barrel pouring wine into a goblet.
- *height 25cm*
- £1,600 • Dial Post House

Oak Plaque ▼
- *17th century*

A heavily carved oak seventeenth century plaque showing scrolling geometric patterns around a central rose motif.
- *height 20cm*
- £1,150 • Dial Post House

Amboyna and Maplewood Dish ▲
- *circa 1910*

Dish fashioned from amboyna and maplewood with turned decoration. The dish rests on four maple balls.
- *diameter 32cm*
- £145 • John Clay

Dutch Carved Vases ▲
- *1920*

A pair of Dutch carved vases with the figures of two women in a forest setting.
- *height 38cm*
- £375 • John Clay

Expert Tips

Good patina is very important when considering carvings. Any cracks will greatly reduce the value of items as they cannot be repaired satisfactorily.

Sycamore Beaker ▼
- *circa 1900*

A sycamore beaker with a view of the Lin of Dee.
- *height 7cm*
- £48 • John Clay

Expert Tips

Gold leaf or silver leaf applied to carved items should be of original patina, and when the item has been re-gilded it is important that this has been done with sensitivity, and not overdone, as this can cause a garish or metallic look.

Sycamore Container ➤
- **1900**
A sycamore cylindrical container with a view of the Windsor Castle round tower.
- *height 9cm*
- £45   ● John Clay

Figure of a Friar ▼
- **1860**
A figure of a friar with a beard and habit, standing with clasped hands.
- *height 10cm*
- £725   ● Bill Chapman

Money Box ◀
- *circa 1900*
Sycamore money box with a castellated edge, showing a view of Eastbourne on the front.
- *10cm x 7cm*
- £48   ● John Clay

Ethiopian Cross ▼
- *17th century*
Wooden Ethiopian hand blessing cross.
- *length 16cm*
- £350   ● Iconastas

Shoe Lasts ▲
- *19th century*
Pair of English wooden shoe lasts.
- *length 28cm*
- £75   ● John Clay

Pill Box ▼
- *circa 1900s*
Austrian bullet-shaped pill box inscribed with the words: "Apotheke Zum Heil Agidius. J. Brady Wien VL, Gumpendorferst 105".
- *height 7cm*
- £38   ● John Clay

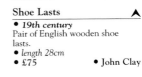

Mask Swags ▲
- *1820*
A pair of carved white and
giltwood swags with masks.
- *26cm x 6cm*
- £7,000   • O.F. Wilson

Walnut Carving ▲
- *18th century*
A fine eighteenth century
Venetian carving in walnut
showing the bust of a young boy
in a scallop shell border with a
hunting motif at the base.
- *height 15cm*
- £895   • Dial Post House

Pair of Swags ➤
- *18th century*
Pair of painted swags with fruit.
- *40cm x 88cm x 14cm*
- £3,250   • O.F. Wilson

Phoenixes ➤
- *1830*
A pair of giltwood phoenix.
- £2,600   • O.F. Wilson

Carved Eagles ▲
- *1810*
Pair of French First Empire
carved giltwood eagles.
- *height 25cm*
- £2,200   • O.F. Wilson

Fruitwood Match Holder ▲
- *1870*
Fruitwood match holder in the
shape of a boot.
- *height 6cm*
- £170   • Bill Chapman

Wall Appliqués ▼
- *1760*
A pair of silvered wall appliqués.
- £1,950   • O.F. Wilson

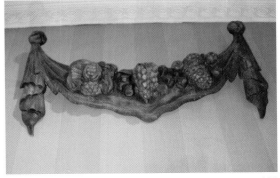

Tribal Art

The proliferation of fakes from Africa and the Far East makes Tribal Art a perilous, but nonetheless rewarding, area for the collector.

The increase in travel to distant shores, which not long ago was the domain of the explorer, has seen a sharp rise in interest in the arts and customs of ancient and tribal people.

With the early documentaries of the 1950s, and magazines such as *National Geographic*, images of unknown tribes, with their alternative religions and customs, were projected into the living rooms of the Western world. This media attention helped to further our knowledge of these peoples, which, in turn, led to the creation of a market for their artefacts and wares.

Museums throughout the world have built up large collections of ethnic and tribal art, further stimulating the interest in this growing market. Works of art come from a diverse range of countries and continents, including South America, the Far East, Australasia and the South Pacific.

There is now a great demand for the genuine piece. A new market for current creative works has also been established, as new artists carry on the traditions of their forefathers in an effort to maintain the skills that may otherwise perish amid the advances of modern industrial life.

Zuni Pot ▲
- *circa 2000*
Zuni ceramic seed pot with two painted frogs, by A. Peynetsa.
- *height 6cm*
- **£89.99**   • Wilde Ones

Garuda Mask ▶
- *19th century*
Deeply carved mask of Garuda Bhutan (code HYM9233).
- *26cm x 32cm*
- **£495**   • Gordon Reece

African Wall Hanging ▶
- *early 20th century*
An unusual ceremonial dance skirt with black abstract patterns on a light brown background, from the Neongo tribe, Zaire.
- *76cm x 40cm*
- **£2,800**   • Gordon Reece

Native American Pot ◀
- *circa 2000*
Native American ceramic pot with a painted black and red geometric pattern, signed "P Beneto".
- *height 24cm*
- **£129**   • Wilde Ones

Expert Tips

When considering purchasing tribal masks or shields, the natural patina is of the utmost importance. These may have been used in fetishism, which can involve the sprinkling of blood, used for exercising their religious rituals.

African Mask ▲
- *circa 1900*
A Songye Kifwebe mask from Zaire.
- *30cm x 29cm*
- £450   • Gooday Gallery

African Stool ▲
- *19th century*
An African stool, made of bush wood.
- *27cm x 46cm*
- £225   • Tredantiques

Zuni Fetish Pot ▲
- *circa 2000*
Zuni fetish pot shaped as an owl with its owlet.
- *height 8cm*
- £89.99   • Wilde Ones

Native American Pot ➤
- *circa 1999*
Native American pot and lid with a rust, white and black geometric design painted with porcupine quills, inscribed "ACOMA".
- *height 6cm*
- £49.99   • Wilde Ones

Dan Mask ▼
- *early 20th century*
Dan mask from Liberia.
- *25cm x 16cm*
- £400   • Gooday Gallery

Yoruban Iron Staff ▼
- *early 1900s*
Ancient ceremonial wrought-iron staff, from Yoruba, Nigeria.
- *64cm x 24cm*
- £720   • Gordon Reece

Expert Tips

Large wooden figures, which are carved out of pieces of very hard wood such as rosewood or ebony, are prone to splitting and cracking, and should be kept in a controlled temperature to stop this damage occurring. A controlled climate also helps to preserve raffia, grasses and natural fibres.

Bakot Figure ▲
- *circa 1900*
Bakot reliquary figure.
- *40cm x 15cm*
- £480   • Gooday Gallery

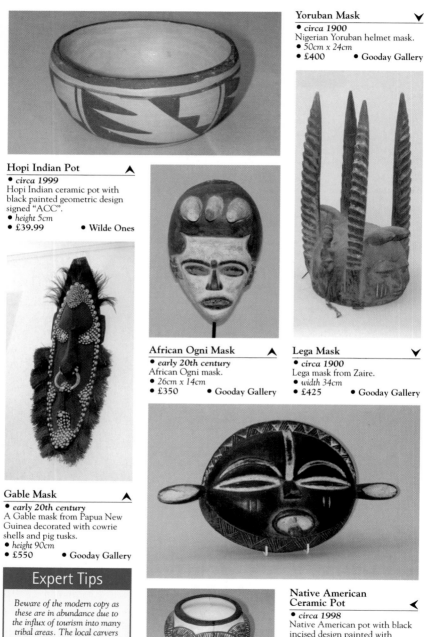

Hopi Indian Pot ▲
- *circa 1999*
Hopi Indian ceramic pot with black painted geometric design signed "ACC".
- *height 5cm*
- **£39.99**   • Wilde Ones

Gable Mask ▲
- *early 20th century*
A Gable mask from Papua New Guinea decorated with cowrie shells and pig tusks.
- *height 90cm*
- **£550**   • Gooday Gallery

Expert Tips

Beware of the modern copy as these are in abundance due to the influx of tourism into many tribal areas. The local carvers often produce much cruder and simpler objects for the mass market.

African Ogni Mask ▲
- *early 20th century*
African Ogni mask.
- *26cm x 14cm*
- **£350**   • Gooday Gallery

Yoruban Mask ▼
- *circa 1900*
Nigerian Yoruban helmet mask.
- *50cm x 24cm*
- **£400**   • Gooday Gallery

Lega Mask ▼
- *circa 1900*
Lega mask from Zaire.
- *width 34cm*
- **£425**   • Gooday Gallery

Native American Ceramic Pot ◄
- *circa 1998*
Native American pot with black incised design painted with porcupine quills, inscribed, "ACOCMA NM KSC".
- *height 7cm*
- **£149.99**   • Wilde Ones

Javanese Mask ▲

- *early 1900s*
Javanese mask of a Mahabarata/
Ramayana character.
- *19cm x 14cm*
- £550   ● Gordon Reece

Grassland Cameroon Stool ▲

- *1890*
An African grassland Cameroon
stool in anthropomorphic form.
- *height 35cm*
- £340   ● Gordon Reece

Naga Mask ▼

- *20th century*
Naga wooden mask.
- *30cm x 18cm*
- £550   ● Zakheim

Kota Figure ▼

- *early 20th century*
Kota wooden figure decorated
with brass and copper plaques.
- *71cm x 33cm*
- £850   ● Zakheim

Carved African Stools ▼

- *early 19th century*
Three unusual carved African
stools with handles.
- *4cm x 12cm x 13cm*
- £360   ● Gordon Reece

Bapende Mask ▲

- *20th century*
Bapende tribal mask decorated
with shells and coconut hair.
- *40cm x 17cm*
- £490   ● Zakheim

Fang Wooden Pulley ▲

- *20th century*
An African Fang wooden pulley
with carved and turned
decoration.
- *height 39cm*
- £390   ● Zakheim

Yoruba Crown ◄

- *20th century*
Yoruban crown decorated with
coconut hair and a face created
from cowrie shells.
- *height 35cm*
- £650 • **Zakheim**

Indian Naga Mask ►

- *19th century*
Naga wooden mask from India
carved with good plains and
fields.
- *30cm x 18cm*
- £550 • **Zakheim**

Tshokwe-Mbuna Mask ▲

- *early 1900s*
A striking mask with natural
patination fibre additions, from
Tshokwe-Mbuna.
- *28cm x 40cm*
- £400 • **Gordon Reece**

Kongo Figure ▲

- *early 20th century*
Kongo wooden fetish with snake
skin strands and monkey hair,
with traces of gesso decoration.
- *height 35cm*
- £650 • **Zakheim**

Expert Tips

*Bronze masks and figures and
ceremonial pots are becoming
much harder to acquire, and
patina is very important, along
with style and design. Iron
masks and cooking vessels are
also of great interest, but
beware of fakes, as this market
has grown considerably over the
last decade and has attracted
unscrupulous sellers.*

African Tribal Masks ◄

- *circa 1900*
Two African tribal masks.
- *16cm x 25cm*
- £3,600 • **Gordon Reece**

Himachal Pradesh Mask ►

- *early 1900s*
A most unusual form with the
upper features on a dome-like
area, with exaggerated slit eyes
and a stylised mouth, with signs
of applied silver and other
applications. From the Himachal
Pradesh region.
- *26cm x 40cm*
- £1,300 • **Gordon Reece**

Tamil Nadu Wall Carvings ▲

- *mid 18th century*
Erotic carvings from a temple
cart.
- *71cm x 26cm*
- £1,800 • **Gordon Reece**

Himalayan Mask ➤

- *circa 1700*

An ancient Himalayan mask in the form of a snow lion. A most unusual broad form by Nepalese standards. Possibly 200–300 years old. Much valued and cared for judging from sympathetic repairs (code HYM96100).
- *24cm x 28cm*
- £795 • Gordon Reece

Pair of Naga Sculptures ▲

- *late 1800s*

Pair of standing Naga figures.
- *64cm x 14cm*
- £1,900 • Gordon Reece

Yarli Lions ▼

- *1700s*

Pair of mythical beasts called Yarli Lions from Kanataka province in South Western India. Originally they were brackets which featured on a chariot or juggernaut.
- *46cm x 18cm*
- £1,420 • Gordon Reece

Iron Lamp ▲

- *early 1900s*

Ancient wrought-iron lamp decorated with birds.
- £820 • Gordon Reece

Wrought-Iron Sculpture ▼

- *early 1900s*

Three wrought-iron currency forms.
- *18cm x 48cm*
- £380 • Gordon Reece

Bambra Mask ▼

- *early 1900s*

Mask from the Bambara tribe but with a strong influence from the Dogon.
- *66cm x 18cm*
- £3,400 • Gordon Reece

Kulia Valley Mask ▲

- *circa 1900*
Very old mask from the Kulia valley area. The heavy wear and patination suggests a very early date or continued heavy usage (code PR9822).
- *26cm x 38cm*
- **£1,450** • Gordon Reece

African Mask ▼

- *early 1900s*
A finely drawn mask with a good patination from the Incangala Tshokwe.
- **£800** • Gordon Reece

African Wooden Sculptures ➤

- *early 1900s*
Three African tribal carved wood sculptures.
- *11cm x 70cm*
- **£360** • Gordon Reece

Kuba Dance Skirt ▲

- *mid 20th century*
Zairean Neongo tribe Kuba dance skirt. Dyed raffia appliquéd.
- *76cm x 400cm*
- **£1,900** • Gordon Reece

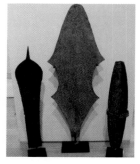

Gable Mask ▼

- *early 20th century*
A gable mask from Papua New Guinea with cowrie shells.
- *height 90cm*
- **£550** • Gooday Gallery

Tribal Mask ▼

- *early 1900s*
Heavily patinated tribal mask (code 9427).
- *22cm x 15cm*
- **£740** • Gordon Reece

Twentieth-Century Design

The twentieth century was rich in innovatory design and revolutionary manufacture. What were 'the antiques of tomorrow' are rapidly becoming the antiques of today.

Twentieth-century furniture and objects must be one of the fastest growing sections of the collectors market. From the Dalton and the Moorcroft vase, to Art Deco chairs and glass and light fittings, all these exciting products and objects make for a vibrant new area for collecting. This is borne out by the resurgence of interest in retro design, which is reflected by items on the market today, especially electronic goods and new motorcars by makers such as Audi or Renault.

One reason for the excellent quality of modern design is the tremendous energy and expertise that abounds in the art schools and colleges throughout the world. The popularity of art, both as a discipline and a consumer product, has inspired new ways of thinking about design. There is a movement today towards the use of good quality traditional materials such as marble, bronze and stainless steel, which is a breath of fresh air after the designs from the 1950s to the1980s, where man-made materials, such as plastic and bakelite, were all the rage.

Ceramics

Porcelain Teapot ◄
- *circa 1990s*
English porcelain teapot, with hand-painted ribbon decoration, by Graham Clarke.
- *height 27.5cm*
- £75 • R. Dennis

Glass Jug ►
- *20th century*
Finely crafted glass gourd-shaped jug with abstract designs, made by Muller Croismare.
- *height 15cm*
- £2,200 • Bizarre

Bee Vase ◄
- *late 1990s*
Dennis China Works ceramic vase of baluster form, decorated with a repeated honeycomb pattern with bees in the foreground.
- *height 11.25cm*
- £300 • R. Dennis

Toucan Vase ▲
- *late 20th century*
English vase decorated with a toucan on a black ground, by Dennis China Works.
- *height 30cm*
- £470 • R. Dennis

Dennis Jar and Cover ▲

- *late 1990s*
Jar painted with a polar bear and
cub in an arctic setting, with a
polar bear finial, by Dennis
China Works.
- *height 10cm*
- £305 • R. Dennis

Poole Ceramic Plate ▲

- *20th century*
Poole pottery plate with a one-off
abstract pattern, designed by
Tony Morris.
- *diameter 40cm*
- £450 • R. Dennis

Expert Tips

*Pottery is prone to chipping and
in some cases the glaze can
flake. Pottery can be a good
starting point for a collection as
many pieces can still be bought
at reasonable prices.*

Kaffe Fasset Vase ➤

- *late 20th century*
Scottish Highland stoneware
baluster vase, hand painted with
leaf and fruit designs by Kaffe
Fasset.
- *height 36.25cm*
- £600 • R. Dennis

Highland Stoneware Bowl ➤

- *1990–9*
Highland stoneware bowl
decorated with a repeated scene
of gold fish within blue borders,
with ear-shape handles.
- *diameter 16.25cm*
- £95 • R. Dennis

English Abstract Dish ▲

- *circa 1950s*
An English ovoid dish with an
abstract geometric pattern on a
black ground with a white rim.
- *32cm x 23cm*
- £75 • Vincenzo

Lawrence McGowan Vase ◄

- *late 20th century*
Lawrence McGowan vase
decorated with a foliate design,
with scrolled handles.
- *height 28.75cm*
- £140 • R. Dennis

Poole Owl Plate ▼

- *late 1990s*
Poole pottery plate painted with
an black owl, with a sunset in the
background, by Tony Morris.
- *diameter 40cm*
- £450 • R. Dennis

Porcelain Bowl ▼
- *1999*
British porcelain bowl with a
hand painted scene of Felbrigg
Hall, Norfolk, by Graham Clarke.
- *diameter 35cm*
- £450   • R. Dennis

Dinonderie Tray ▲
- *20th century*
A rectangular Dinonderie tray
with a red glaze and gilded
decoration, signed by Linossier.
- *21cm x 12cm*
- £1,200   • Bizarre

Dinonderie Plate ▲
- *20th century*
Red and black glazed Dinonderie
dish signed by Linossier.
- *diameter 19cm*
- £2,400   • Bizarre

Signed Dinonderie Saucer ◄
- *20th century*
A red and black glazed
Dinonderie saucer signed by
Linossier.
- *diameter 10cm*
- £550   • Bizarre

Dennis Iris Vase ►
- *late 1990s*
English ceramic vase decorated
with irises by Dennis China
Works.
- *height 36.25cm*
- £940   • R. Dennis

Water Jug ▲
- *1990–9*
Ceramic water jug decorated with
a rooster by Maureen Minchin.
- *height 27.5cm*
- £95   • R. Dennis

Dinonderie Saucer ►
- *20th century*
Fine French Dinonderie saucer,
signed by Linossier.
- *diameter 13cm*
- £950   • Bizarre

Carlton Ware Service ▲
- **1960–70**
Orange Carlton Ware ceramic
table service consisting of salt and
pepper shakers and sugar holder.
- *height 16.25cm*
- **£75** • Zoom

French Ceramic Lamp ▲
- **20th century**
French amber-coloured ceramic
lamp which also can be a perfume
burner, with a turned wooden
cover and base.
- *height 28cm*
- **£200** • Bizarre

Royal Doulton Service ◄
- **20th century**
Royal Doulton teaset of six cups
and saucers, with sugar bowl,
decorated with an orange pattern
with gold borders.
- *height 8cm/cup*
- **£450** • Bizarre

Ceramic Monkeys ▼
- **20th century**
Italian ceramic group of two
monkeys preening each other,
with a rusticated green and blue
glaze.
- *height 19cm*
- **£550** • Bizarre

Expert Tips

*Hand-thrown pieces have
irregular ribbing on the inside
and a less perfect appearance
than moulded wares.*

Ceramic Jar and Cover ▲
- **20th century**
A cylinder-shaped ceramic jar
and cover with an orange glaze,
gilded handles and finial, made
by Hutschenreuther.
- *height 22cm*
- **£200** • Bizarre

Salt and Pepper Shakers ▲
- **1960–70**
English Carlton Ware red salt and
pepper shakers.
- *height 11.25cm*
- **£35** • Zoom

Porcelain Plate ◄

- *late 1990s*
Porcelain plate hand painted with a Norfolk scene in a blue glaze, by Graham Clarke.
- *diameter 40cm*
- £450 • R. Dennis

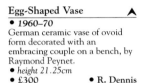

Egg-Shaped Vase ▲

- *1960–70*
German ceramic vase of ovoid form decorated with an embracing couple on a bench, by Raymond Peynet.
- *height 21.25cm*
- £300 • R. Dennis

Balinese Dancer ►

- *20th century*
A ceramic figure of a Balinese dancer by Royal Copenhagen.
- *height 14cm*
- £120 • Bizarre

Poole Pottery Pot ►

- *1970*
Green Poole Pottery pot decorated with large lime green and darker green scrolls, by Caroge Holdan.
- *height 45cm*
- £580 • Gooday Gallery

Ceramic Cat ▼

- *20th century*
Cat in red living glaze, a type of glaze pioneered by Poole Pottery.
- *height 28.75cm*
- £27.50 • R. Dennis

German Ceramic Vase ▲

- *1960*
A German ceramic vase decorated with a romantic scene, with a chinoiserie influence, from the Lover's collection by Raymond Peynet.
- *height 20cm*
- £700 • R. Dennis

Italian Ceramic Vase ►

- *circa 1950s*
Italian three-sided bottle-shaped vase with abstract cartouches on a green ground, by Cossa.
- *height 12cm*
- £150 • Vincenzo Caffarella

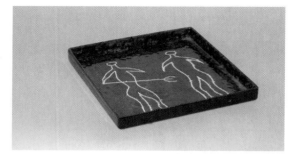

Enamel Ashtray ◀

- *1960*

Square enamel ashtray with two figures outlined in white on a purple base with a raised black rim.
- *16cm square*
- £120 • Vincenzo Caffarella

Ceramic Painted Figure ▲

- *1925*

French ceramic painted figure modelled as a female reclining on a plain base, by Parvillee.
- *24cm x 60cm*
- £1,800 • Gooday Gallery

Danish Ceramic Vase ▶

- *1950s*

Danish ceramic vase of asymmetric form with a white elongated diamond-shaped pattern on a black ground, by Soholm Bornholm.
- *height 57cm*
- £400 • Vincenzo Caffarella

Bosch Frères Vase ▼

- *1920*

Bosch Frères vase of oval form with splayed lip incorporating a geometric design in orange, black and cochineal glaze on a white ground.
- *height 26cm*
- £280 • Gooday Gallery

Italian Ceramic Dish ▼

- *1950s*

Italian black and white ceramic dish of ovoid form on three conical feet by Antonia Campi.
- *8cm x 29cm x 9cm*
- £200 • Vincenzo Caffarella

Italian Ceramic Vase ▲

- *1950s*

Italian bottle-shaped ceramic vase by GTA, decorated with stylised faces.
- *height 48cm*
- £250 • Vincenzo Caffarella

Expert Tips

The Italian ceramic designs from the 1950s are elegant and highly decorative. Look for a clear elegant shape with uncluttered strong lines.

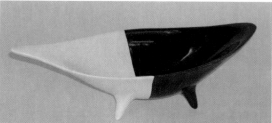

Foxglove Bottle ▼

- *late 1990s*

Foxglove ceramic bottle-shaped vase painted with foxgloves on a blue ground, by Dennis China Works.
- *height 37.5cm*
- £517
- R. Dennis

Cockran Bowl ▲

- *1990–9*

British ceramic deep bowl decorated with a blue octopus, by Roger Cockran.
- *15cm x 21.25cm*
- £130
- R. Dennis

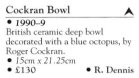

Bisque Rabbit ▲

- *20th century*

Bisque porcelain model of a rabbit with ears erect and head turned to the side.
- *height 30cm*
- £340
- North West 8

Cream-Glazed Vase ▲

- *circa 1930*

French ceramic vase of ovoid proportions with a cream glaze and a rusticated finish.
- *height 20cm*
- £150
- Bizarre

Sicart Ashtray ▼

- *circa 1970s*

Italian circular ceramic ashtray with metal insert by Sicart.
- *6cm x 21cm*
- £185
- Paolo Bonino

Highland Dish ▲

- *late 1990s*

Octagonal Highland stoneware dish, hand painted with a floral design of lillies on a lustre ground.
- *46.25cm x 40cm*
- £189
- R. Dennis

Asymmetric Vase ▲

- *1950s*

Italian ceramic vase of asymmetric form with a green and white design on a black ground.
- *height 30cm*
- £40
- Goya

Cockran Plate ▲
- *late 1990s*

British ceramic plate showing a fish leaping out of the foaming sea, on a blue ground, by Roger Cockran.
- *diameter 26.25cm*
- £125　　　• R. Dennis

Bonzo the Dog Mugs ▲
- *1998*

Pair of mugs decorated with Bonzo the dog, with a gold band around the rim by Richard Dennis Publications.
- *height 8.75cm*
- £11　　　• R. Dennis

Bonzo the Dog Plate ➤
- *1998*

Ceramic plate decorated with a repeated pattern of Bonzo the dog, by Richard Dennis Publications.
- *diameter 21.25cm*
- £155　　　• R. Dennis

Yellow Bonzo Mug ▲
- *late 1990s*

Yellow mug with a Bonzo the dog handle by Dennis China Works.
- *height 12.5cm*
- £165　　　• R. Dennis

English Ceramic Bowl ◄
- *1990–9*

English bowl of deep proportions painted with three hares in a woodland setting by Maureen Michin.
- *diameter 42.5cm*
- £300　　　• R. Dennis

Bonzo Plate ▲
- *1998*

Ceramic plate showing Bonzo the dog with the words "Pot Luck" on the rim, by Richard Dennis Publications.
- *diameter 15cm*
- £12　　　• R. Dennis

Highland Stoneware Vase ▼
- *late 20th century*

Scottish Highland stoneware vase painted with a seascape. Limited edition of 250.
- *height 23.75cm*
- £150　　　• R. Dennis

Expert Tips

Novelty ceramics with depictions of nursery rhymes or cartoon characters are collectable, whether painted on a cup or plate.

Mowart Vase ▼

- *1930*

Unusual vase of bulbous proportions with bubble inclusions within a deep red glaze, by Mowart.
- *height 22cm*
- £595 • A.D. Antiques

Flambé Vase ▲

- *1905–15*

Flambé vase of bottle shape form with a deep red glaze, made by Bernard Moore.
- height 15cm
- £195 • A.D. Antiques

Enamelled Daum Vase ◄

- *1900*

Daum vase of rectangular form, showing a winter scene with an enamelled silver birch and orange sunset.
- *height 9cm*
- £1,500 • French Glasshouse

McGowan Plate ▼

- *late 20th century*

Lawrence McGowan plate, with a central panel of a tree with robins and a poem on the rim.
- *diameter 36.25cm*
- £250 • R. Dennis

Dunmore Vase ▲

- *early 20th century*

Scottish Dunmore ovoid vase in a turquoise glaze with a splayed neck with moulded rim.
- *height 29cm*
- £80 • A.D. Antiques

Art Deco Figure ◄

- *1926*

Art Deco ceramic figure by Stanley Nicholson Babb showing a romantic figure.
- *height 25cm*
- £600 • Gooday Gallery

Expert Tips

Brightly decorated comic characters of the twentieth century are popular items.

Glazed Candlesticks ➤
- *1917–34*

Pair of candlesticks by Minton Hollins Astraware, with a distinct variegated blue green glaze.
- *height 21cm*
- £200   • A.D. Antiques

French Vase ▲
- *20th century*

French green vase, on a bronze tripod base by Daum Majorelle.
- *height 15cm*
- £1,200   • Bizarre

Read Water Jug ◄
- *circa 1920*

Blue water jug with a floral trellis pattern by Frederick Read.
- *height 17.5cm*
- £295   • A.D. Antiques

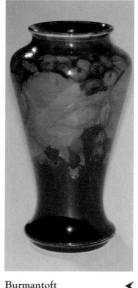

Burmantoft ◄
- *early 20th century*

An amber glazed Burmantoft of amphori form with two elongated handles.
- *height 20cm*
- £235   • A.D. Antiques

Royal Lancastrian Vase ▲
- *circa 1920*

Green Royal Lancastrian vase of organic form in matt green glaze.
- *height 18cm*
- £195   • A.D. Antiques

Expert Tips

There are many different types of glazes for ceramics, and certain potters become renowned for the types of glazes that they favour.

Moorcroft Vase ◄
- *1913–7*

Early Moorcroft pomegranate vase by William Moorcroft.
- *height 19cm*
- £575   • A.D. Antiques

Holyrood Pottery Vase ▼
- *1917–27*

Holyrood pottery bulbous vase with crazing to base.
- *height 34cm*
- £95   • A.D. Antiques

Morris Ware Vases ▲
- *circa 1910*

Pair of Morris ware vases in thistle pattern by George Cartridge.
- *height 32cm*
- **£1,360** • A.D. Antiques

Lustre Vase ▼
- *1910*

Pilkington Royal Lancaster lustre vase with floral decoration on a rich flambé ground by Annie Burton.
- *height 20cm*
- **£665** • A.D. Antiques

Ceramic Group ▲
- *20th century*

Fine ceramic group depicting Diana the huntress after the hunt, by Giovanni Grande for the Lenci Factory, Italy.
- *height 39cm*
- **£4,300** • Bizarre

Art Nouveau Set ▲
- *1920*

Art Nouveau-style jug and bowl set, comprising five pieces.
- **£195** • A.D. Antiques

Flambé Pot ▲
- *1912*

Red and bronze flambé glazed pot of conical form, tapering to the foot with a small finial lid, by Howsons.
- *height 22cm*
- **£265** • A.D. Antiques

Carlton Ware Service ◄
- *20th century*

Carlton Ware five-piece teaset consisting of two cups and saucers, a sugar pot and teapot, milk jug and two saucers with a pistachio glaze and gilded decoration.
- **£450** • Bizarre

Furniture

Cone Chair ▼
- *1958*

A Danish Verner Panton cone chair, with red wool upholstery and cushioned seat and backrest.
- *height 84.5cm*
- £850 • Zoom

French Occasional Table ▼
- *circa 1950*

A French occasional table, with painted pierced metal apron on a tripod base.
- *70cm x 55cm*
- £680 • Myriad

Italian Sofa ▲
- *circa 1950s*

Italian sofa with shaped back and buttoned upholstery, by Gio Ponti.
- *100cm x 192.5cm*
- £5,500 • Themes

Scandinavian Art Deco Hall Stand ▲
- *circa 1928*

Scandinavian Art Deco hall stand, with large oval central mirror and stainless steel and light elmwood side panels, with three central drawers with large stainless steel and plastic handles.
- *184cm x 139cm x 28cm*
- £1,700 • J. Fox

Steamer Chair ▶
- *circa 1900*

Aesthetic Movement ebonized steamer chair, with folding mechanism and cane seat with bobbin turned uprights, after designs by E.W. Godwin.
- *67.5cm x 37.5cm*
- £1,200 • Liberty plc

Egg Chair ▲
- *1958*

Egg chair in black leather on a metal base, by Arne Jacobsen, Denmark.
- *105cm x 85cm*
- £4,000 • Themes

English Oak Stools ▲
- *1910–15*
One of a pair of Art Nouveau oak English stools on tapered square legs, with metal ringed stretcher.
- *height 82cm*
- £500   • Solaris

French Mirror ◄
- *20th century*
French wrought-iron mirror designed by Raymond Subes.
- *120cm x 95cm*
- £2,800   • Bizarre

French Art Deco Stools ▲
- *1820–30*
One of a pair of French Art Deco metal and upholstered stools on scrolled cabriole legs.
- *height 40cm*
- £1,400   • Solaris

Charles Eames Chair ◄
- *1960*
Charles Eames swivel office chair with a chrome tripod stand.
- *height 91cm*
- £1,960   • Zoom

Finnish Leather Armchairs ▲
- *1970*
One of a pair of tan leather moulded armchairs with a metal circular base, by Wryo Kukkapuro, Finland.
- *height 80cm*
- £1,500   • Themes

Leopard Chest ◄
- *circa 1990s*
A chest of drawers decorated with leopards in a jungle setting, by Formasetti, Italy.
- *82.5cm x 100cm*
- £6,400   • Themes

Swivel Office Chair ▼
- 1970

Charles Eames, high-back office swivel and tilt chair, with black wool upholstery and aluminium stand on castors.
- *height 82cm*
- £600 • Zoom

Italian Dining Table ▼
- *circa 1950s*

Italian interlocking sycamore dining table by Ico Parisi.
- *252.5cm x 77.5cm*
- £8,500 • Themes

Spiral Umbrella Stands ▲
- 1960

Italian Pluvium interlocking spiral umbrella stands in red and white plastic, designed by Giancarle Piretti for Castelli.
- *height 62.5cm*
- £125 • Zoom

Mirrored Dressing Table ▶
- 1920

An Art Deco dressing table, the whole being made of mirrors with elegant sabred legs and a fixed mirror with glass handle to drawer.
- *70cm x 86cm x 45cm*
- £800 • Myriad

Mahogany Desk ◀
- 1925

Fine mahogany partner's desk with embossed and gilded leather top. Two cupboards at front and rear, standing on bun feet.
- *79cm x 175cm x 84cm*
- £12,500 • Simon Hatchwell

Parisian Café Table ▲
- *circa 1920*

A small Parisian wrought-iron café table, on a heavy moulded cast iron tripod base.
- *height 70cm*
- £320 • Myriad

Expert Tips

Plastic as a material for furniture and objects has proved to be a very successful medium, but is prone to fading, discoloration and scratches. In some cases the plastic in chairs can crack. This also applies to vinyls, which suffer from fading and tears. All these can be repaired but the cost must be taken into account.

Seagull Chairs ▲

- *circa 1990s*

A pair of seagull chairs by Arne
Jacobsen of Denmark, for Fritz
Hansen.
- *height 75cm*
- £980 • **Themes**

X-Chair ▲

- *1958*

An X-chair in wood and cane, by
Huidt and Nielson, Denmark.
- *height 82cm*
- £1,600 • **Themes**

Dressing Chest ▲

- *circa 1910*

An Arts and Crafts dressing chest
with two large and three smaller
drawers, original brass handles,
and a swing mirror.
- *167cm x 107cm x 53cm*
- £600 • **Old Cinema**

Sacco Beanbag ▼

- *1960*

Red leather and vinyl beanbag of
teardrop shape, by Gatti-Paolini-
Teodori of Italy.
- *height 82.5cm*
- £800 • **Zoom**

Orkney Chair ▼

- *circa 1905*

Child's stained oak Orkney chair
with carved arms and legs.
Original Liberty & Co London
enamel label on underside of
chair.
- *height 82.5cm*
- £475 • **Liberty plc**

Storm Oak Chairs ◄

- *1987–88*

One of a pair of oak chairs, part
of a set which includes a sofa.
The oak is a relic of the great
storm in 1987.
- *106cm x 94cm*
- £2,750 • **Zakheim**

French Art Deco Brown Leather Chairs ▼

- *1925*

One of a pair of brown leather French Art Deco chairs with a curved padded back, scrolled arms and turned feet.
- *height 120cm*
- £3,500 • Bizarre

Occasional Tables ▼

- *1950*

German wood occasional tables inlaid with gilt porcelain plaques, by Rosenthal.
- *42.5cm x 42.5cm x 60cm/largest*
- £1,400 • Themes

Rosewood Chair ▲

- *circa 1904*

Rare Art Nouveau rosewood chair raised on turned legs with pad feet. Designed by Walter Cave for Liberty & Co.
- *92.5cm x 62.5cm*
- £3,500 • Liberty plc

Swedish Art Deco Rosewood Table ▼

- *20th century*

Swedish Art Deco rosewood table, with a flat top, lyre-shaped support on a splayed base.
- *73cm x 150cm x 100cm*
- £3,200 • Bizarre

Swedish Art Deco Birch Desk ◀

- *circa 1920*

A rare example of a Swedish Art Deco desk. It is unique and is veneered in a particularly beautiful masur birch.
- *76cm x 120cm x 60cm*
- £4,500 • R. Cavendish

Oak Bureau ▲

- *circa 1900*

Arts and Crafts fumed oak bureau with shaped bookshelves and cupboard above fall, and drawers and panel doors below fitted with iron mounts.
- *135cm x 80cm*
- £2,450 • Liberty plc

Expert Tips

A label or mark by the artist, design studio, or retailer makes identification of the individual piece more precise and exciting. These individual pieces will prove to be good investments.

Art Nouveau Settee ▼

- *circa 1900*

Art Nouveau two-seater walnut settee. The curved upper rail with scrolled terminals above a turned back rail, with shaped arms above turned legs and square legs at back.
- *120cm x 120cm*
- **£1,995** • Liberty plc

Victorian Stick Stand ▼

- *1900*

Victorian stick stand with pierced back rail with a repeated heart motif, and ebony and boxwood inlay.
- *70cm x 85cm*
- **£475** • Liberty plc

Oak Sideboard ▲

- *circa 1910*

Medium oak Arts and Crafts sideboard, with mushroom bracket supports on upper shelf, above an arched recess between two panelled doors.
- *127.5cm x 147.5cm*
- **£2,250** • Liberty plc

Anglo-Japanese Walnut Fire Screen ▼

- *circa 1900*

Highly unusual Anglo-Japanese walnut fire screen with yellow glass panels enclosed within flat banding, with an ebonized button at the intersection of each. The whole supported on tapered legs.
- *height 82.5cm*
- **£1,950** • Liberty plc

Child's Chair ◄

- *circa 1990s*

Swedish child's chair in shaped wood with black and white cowhide upholstery, by Caroline Schlyter.
- *height 57.5cm*
- **£980** • Themes

Sofa Table ▲

- *circa 1900*

Arts and Crafts oak sofa table in the manner of C.F.A. Voysey. The plank top supported on tapered legs, with an underiler with a storage area for papers, with stylised heart motifs either side.
- *47.5cm x 72.5cm*
- **£1,250** • Liberty plc

Limed Oak Desk with Art Deco Chairs ▲

- *20th century*

A limed oak partner's desk with drinks bar concealed behind curved panel doors, with two Art Deco chairs.
- *77cm x 140cm x 80cm*
- **£4,500** • Bizarre

Hathaway Table ◀
- *circa 1905*

Extendable medium oak draw table with panelled top, X-shaped cross stretcher and tapered legs, by Liberty & Co.
- *height 137.5cm*
- **£2,350**
- Liberty plc

Rocking Chair ▼
- *circa 1900*

Rocking chair with rush seat and slat back on turned legs with a rocker base, by Liberty & Co.
- *height 87.5cm*
- **£495**
- Liberty plc

Umbrella Stand ▲
- *circa 1900*

Oak umbrella stand with tapered plank ends with a pierced inverted heart motif, above three zinc trays within the base, by Liberty & Co.
- *72.5cm x 82.75cm*
- **£695**
- Liberty plc

Art Nouveau Music Cabinet ▲
- *circa 1910*

Mahogany Art Nouveau music cabinet with boxwood and ebony inlays, lined shelves and a leaded glass door decorated with floral motifs. With carved top and side columns, by Liberty & Co.
- *height 120cm*
- **£4,500**
- Liberty plc

Ebonized Music Stool ▼
- *circa 1900*

Ebonized Arts and Crafts music stool with curved seat with scrolled terminals, on a shaped stretcher with turned legs, by Liberty & Co.
- *57.5cm x 32.5cm*
- **£750**
- Liberty plc

Revolving Bookcase ▲
- *circa 1900*

Rare Art Nouveau revolving mahogany bookcase, with fruitwood inlays on each of the four panelled doors, on swept legs.
- *192.5cm x 60cm*
- **£2,500**
- Liberty plc

French Cast-Iron Chairs ▲
- *1940*

One of a pair of French cast-iron chairs with intertwined lattice back and yellow leather seats, on cabriole legs.
- *height 95cm*
- **£1,400**
- Solaris

Glass

Little Empress ▼
- *circa 1990s*

"Little Empress", a twisted glass and steel sculpture by Danny Lane.
- *height 207.5cm*
- £19,000 • Themes

Murano Glass Ashtray ◄
- *1950*

Fish-shaped Venetian Murano glass ashtray decorated with gold medallion splashes.
- *2cm x 8.5cm*
- £45 • Paolo Bonino

Jug and Glass Set ▲
- *circa 1950s*

Rare French glass water jug with two glasses from a set of eight, with gold banding and black geometric patterns.
- £165 • Goya

Italian Glass Sculpture ▲
- *1970*

Glass sculpture with red, yellow, green and turquoise freeform shapes within the glass, by Livio Seguso.
- *height 25cm*
- £4,000 • Themes

Patterned Glass Bowl ▲
- *early 1970s*

Italian glass bowl with a blue and yellow swirling pattern within the glass.
- *9cm x 11.5cm*
- £58 • Paolo Bonino

Venetian Glass Vase ▲
- *circa 1950s*

Venetian glass vase with applied white, green and black spun and dripped decoration.
- *50cm x 28cm*
- £3,750 • Zakheim

Venetian Plate ◄
- *circa 1958*

A circular Venetian plate with white abstract design on a scarlet ground.
- *diameter 18cm*
- £235 • Paolo Bonino

Danish Indigo Vase ▼
- *early 1970s*
Danish indigo blue glass vase of
bottle shape form with splayed lip
by Holmegaard.
- *14.5cm x 7cm*
- £125   • Paolo Bonino

Murano Glass Ashtray ▼
- *1950s*
Italian, Murano glass basket-
shaped ashtray, with sea green
and black design within the glass.
- *diameter 13cm*
- £35   • Goya

French Vase ➤
- *1950*
A French pink and clear vase of
ovoid form.
- *35cm x 25cm*
- £65   • Goya

Venetian Vase ▲
- *circa 1950s*
Italian vase with air bubbles and
aquatic scenes of fish and organic
forms.
- *38cm x 18cm*
- £1,250   • Zakheim

Art Deco Glass Bowl ▲
- *1920*
Art Deco French aubergine glass
bowl, decorated with silver
plated bands, signed "Fains".
- *28cm x 30cm*
- £350   • Gooday Gallery

Circular Bowl ▼
- *1969*
Round glass bowl with orange
design by Tagliapietra.
- *diameter 21cm*
- £450   • Vincenzo Caffarella

English Vase ▼
- *1960*
Indigo and turquoise blue English
vase with pinched lip by
Whitefriars.
- *24cm x 9cm*
- £45   • Paolo Bonino

Italian Murano Glasses ▶

- *circa 1960s*

A pair of Murano glasses of
globular form on a circular base,
by Barovier & Toso.
- *height 13.5cm*
- £200   • Vincenzo Caffarella

The Wave ▲

- *circa 1980s*

"The Wave", a clear glass
sculpture by Colin Reid with
internal colouring of blues, grey
and rust.
- *42cm x 39cm*
- £5,750   • Zakheim

French Crystal Vase ◀

- *circa 1950s*

French crystal vase styled as
water with a fluted body and gobs
of glass around the rim.
- *height 45cm*
- £125   • Goya

Daum Vase ▲

- *1900*

Daum vase with pink poppies
and green foliage with
dragonflies.
- *height 12cm*
- £2,400   • French Glasshouse

Veart Glass Vase ◀

- *1969*

An Italian glass vase with an
avocado green wave pattern
within the glass, by Veart.
- *height 25cm*
- £450   • Vincenzo Caffarella

Italian Glass Decanter ▼

- *20th century*

Italian red glass decanter with an
exceptionally tall glass stopper,
designed by Cenodese.
- *height 50cm*
- £550   • Bizarre

Cenede Vase ▲

- *circa 1980s*

Glass vase of ovoid form with red and blue spiral design and tears, by Cenede.

- *height 28cm*
- **£850** • Vincenzo Caffarella

Signed Lalique Cat ▲

- *1970*

Lalique cat shown sitting with tail curled, with signature etched on the base.

- *height 21cm*
- **£750** • Jasmin Cameron

René Lalique Bowl ▲

- *1920*

René Lalique bowl, with four clam shells at the base.

- *diameter 18.2cm*
- **£600** • Jasmin Cameron

Crouching Lalique Cat ▲

- *1970*

Lalique cat in a crouching position.

- *length 23cm*
- **£750** • Jasmin Cameron

Gallé Vase with Bluebells ▲

- *1900*

Gallé vase, with bluebells and a variegated translucent blue and white background, signed.

- *height 32cm*
- **£2,800** • French Glasshouse

Expert Tips

When choosing Lalique pieces, especially the frosted ware, inspect it very carefully, as re-grinding and re-application of the frosted effect by acid is often used in the case of damaged pieces.

Ice Relief Vase ▲

- *circa 1960s*

An amorphous glass vase with moulded ice relief by Mazzuccato.

- *height 41cm*
- **£400** • Vincenzo Caffarella

René Lalique Ash Tray ▲

- *1920*

Cendrier ashtray incorporating a celtic design on the border, signed "Gao' René Lalique".

- *diameter 9cm*
- **£450** • Jasmin Cameron

Daum Vase ▼
- *1900*

A slightly waisted green Daum vase with a forest pattern, on a moulded foot.
- *height 16cm*
- £2,600 • French Glasshouse

Maltese Medina Glass ▼
- *1978*

Maltese Medina glass with an abstract marine design on an aqua green ground.
- *height 7.5cm, width 5cm*
- £65 • Paolo Bonino

Italian Teardrop Vase ▼
- *circa 1950s*

A glass vase of teardrop form with gold leaf set within the glass, by Seguso.
- *height 30cm*
- £400 • Vincenzo Caffarella

Cenedese Glass Vase ◄
- *circa 1980s*

An amorphous Cenedese glass vase sculpture, with blue and amber designs within the glass.
- *height 31cm*
- £850 • Vincenzo Caffarella

Gallé Vase with Prunus Design ◄
- *1900*

Gallé vase with a prunus design on an amber ground with black rim and base.
- *height 30cm*
- £2,400 • French Glasshouse

Cherry Blossom Vase ▲
- *1900*

Signed Galle vase of oval form with trailing red cherry blossom.
- *height 21cm*
- £2,400 • French Glasshouse

Gallé Cameo Vase ▲
- *1900*

Gallé cameo glass vase with white and orange floral design.
- *height 31cm*
- £900 • French Glasshouse

Cenedese Glass Vase ▼
- *circa 1980s*
Italian amorphous glass vase with orange Murrina design by Cenedese.
- *height 38cm*
- **£950** • Vincenzo Caffarella

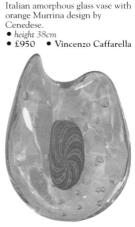

Purple Perfume Bottle ▼
- *circa 1960s*
Purple glass perfume bottle of bulbous form, with an oversized stopper by Cenedese, Italy.
- *height 45cm*
- **£650** • Vincenzo Caffarella

Italian Ashtray ▲
- *circa 1950s*
Italian amber coloured, shell-shaped, glass ashtray with Venturina design by Barovier.
- *21cm x 16cm*
- **£200** • Vincenzo Caffarella

Italian Oval Dish ▲
- *circa 1970s*
Italian emerald glass oval dish, by Cenedese.
- *34cm x 15cm*
- **£250** • Vincenzo Caffarella

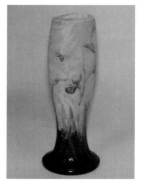

Daum Art Nouveau Vase ▲
- *1900*
Daum Art Nouveau vase with translucent blue and white ground, decorated with flowers, butterflies and insects.
- *height 27cm*
- **£2,500** • French Glasshouse

Bottle-Shaped Vase ▲
- *1900*
Galle bottle-shaped vase with a long tapering neck, decorated with a pastoral scene with purple trees on a soft green background.
- *height 18cm*
- **£1,500** • French Glasshouse

French Gallé Vase ▲
- *1900*
A red and yellow Gallé vase decorated with pink apple blossom.
- *height 14cm*
- **£2,000** • French Glasshouse

Expert Tips

Fore-shortening in vases indicates that the original rim has beed damaged, and in severe cases has been cut down and re-ground. Often, inspecting the balance of the design is the only way to assess this.

Small Gallé Vase ▼
- *1900*

A small Gallé vase with purple
foliate design on a graduated blue
and yellow ground.
- *height 15cm*
- £1,900 • French Glasshouse

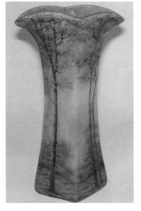

Tinted Cameo Vase ▲
- *1900*

French Gallé tinted cameo glass
vase, decorated with purple
flowers around the base and neck.
- *height 22cm*
- £950 • French Glasshouse

Chrysanthemum Bowl ▼
- *1910*

A green bowl with domed lid by
Gallé, decorated with
chrysanthemums.
- *height 14cm*
- £2,400 • French Glasshouse

Daum Enamelled Vase ▲
- *1900*

French Daum vase with splayed
lip, showing a summer scene with
enamelled trees.
- *height 21cm*
- £3,500 • French Glasshouse

Venetian Glass Bowl ▼
- *circa 1960s*

Venetian glass bowl with a red
spiral design within the glass,
with white enamel on the
reverse.
- *9cm x 16cm*
- £58 • Paolo Bonino

Murano Shell Ashtray ▲
- *circa 1960s*

Murano glass shell-shaped
ashtray with gold leaf flakes
within the glass.
- *14cm x 16cm*
- £100 • Vincenzo Caffarella

Overlay Cameo Vase ▲
- *circa 1900*

Gallé Art Nouveau overlay
cameo glass vase, decorated with
pink orchids and foliate design.
- *height 17cm*
- £600 • French Glasshouse

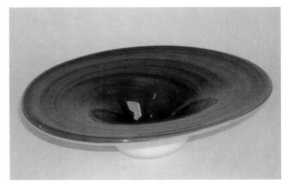

Lighting

Ceiling Lamps ▲
- *circa 1950s*

Three perspex and metal ceiling lamps in aqua green, red and white.
- *diameter 45cm*
- £800 • Zoom

Italian Chrome Lamp ▲
- *1970*

Italian heavy chrome lamp of oval form with brass fittings.
- *diameter 35cm*
- £350 • Zoom

Table Lamp ▲
- *1968*

English table lamp designed for British Home Stores, with a green glass base, chrome neck and pale green perspex shade.
- *height 40cm*
- £150 • Zoom

Glass Table Lamp ◄
- *circa 1970*

Plum and black glass table lamp.
- *height 38cm*
- £30 • Retro Home

Italian Desk Lamp ▼
- *circa 1970s*

Fully adjustable desk lamp with variable strength switch by Arteluce of Italy.
- *height 37.5cm*
- £175 • Zoom

Cloth Lamp Covers ▼
- *1952*

Pair of English, moulded and stretched cloth wall lamp covers by George Nelson.
- *length 30cm*
- £100 • Zoom

Expert Tips

It may seem obvious, but always inspect the wiring and the light fittings themselves, as faulty connections and fittings can create fires and be a hazard to small children.

Chrome Ceiling Lamp ▲
- *circa 1960s*
Chrome ceiling lamp with a series
of interlocking metal tubes.
- *diameter 60cm*
- £750 • Zoom

Metal and Chrome Lamp ▲
- *1970*
Italian table lamp with painted
black metal shade and chrome
base.
- *height 56cm*
- £350 • Zoom

English Ceiling Lamp ▼
- *1952*
Lantern-style ceiling lamp
designed by George Nelson for
Howard Miller.
- *width 46cm*
- £350 • Zoom

Italian Angled Lamp ▲
- *1970s*
Italian fully adjustable angled
lamp.
- *height 37.5cm*
- £175 • Zoom

Fruit-Shaped Lamp ▼
- *circa 1970s*
Italian plastic ceiling lamp in the
shape of a peeled orange.
- *diameter 32.5cm*
- £60 • Zoom

Dome-Shaped Lamp ▼
- *circa 1970s*
Italian dome-shaped glass lamp,
with the light lit from within the
glass base, by Mazzega.
- *height 52.5cm*
- £650 • Themes & Variations

Colomba Lamp ▲
- *1960*
Italian metal and glass, four
globe, white Colomba lamp.
- *height 60cm*
- £350 • Zoom

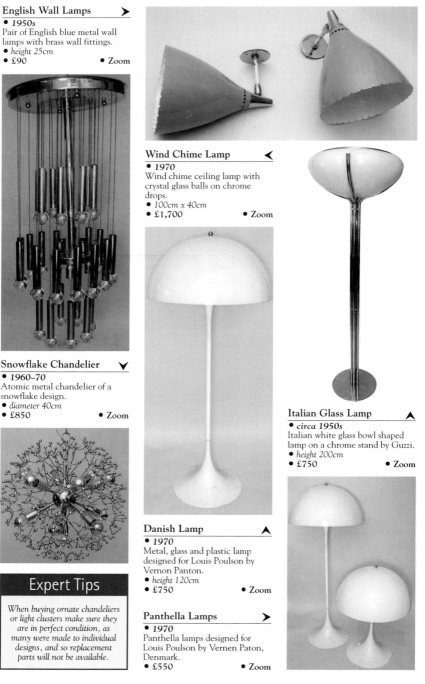

English Wall Lamps ➤
- *1950s*
Pair of English blue metal wall
lamps with brass wall fittings.
- *height 25cm*
- £90 • Zoom

Snowflake Chandelier ∨
- *1960–70*
Atomic metal chandelier of a
snowflake design.
- *diameter 40cm*
- £850 • Zoom

Expert Tips

*When buying ornate chandeliers
or light clusters make sure they
are in perfect condition, as
many were made to individual
designs, and so replacement
parts will not be available.*

Wind Chime Lamp ◄
- *1970*
Wind chime ceiling lamp with
crystal glass balls on chrome
drops.
- *100cm x 40cm*
- £1,700 • Zoom

Danish Lamp ▲
- *1970*
Metal, glass and plastic lamp
designed for Louis Poulson by
Vernon Panton.
- *height 120cm*
- £750 • Zoom

Panthella Lamps ➤
- *1970*
Panthella lamps designed for
Louis Poulson by Vernen Paton,
Denmark.
- £550 • Zoom

Italian Glass Lamp ▲
- *circa 1950s*
Italian white glass bowl shaped
lamp on a chrome stand by Guzzi.
- *height 200cm*
- £750 • Zoom

White Chrome Lamp ▲
- *1950s*

Italian white chrome and plastic ceiling lamp by Harvey Guzzi.
- *diameter 57.5cm*
- £450 • Zoom

Fibre-Optic Lamp ▲
- *1950*

Plastic fibre-optic lamp with plastic flowers within the base.
- *height 75cm*
- £200 • Zoom

Amber Glass Lamp ➤
- *1960*

Amber glass ceiling lamp with a metal top to flex.
- *height 26cm*
- £55 • Retro Home

Pistillo Wall Lamp ▲
- *1970*

Italian silverised wall lamp in a Pistillo design by Studio Tetrarch.
- *diameter 60cm*
- £250 • Zoom

Etling Lamp ▲
- *1930*

French black lamp with red chinoisiere influence, designed by Etling.
- *47cm x 30cm*
- £1,200 • Bizarre

Plastic Ceiling Lamp ◄
- *1960*

Italian oval-shaped ceiling lamp in amber and yellow plastic.
- *diameter 42.5cm*
- £350 • Zoom

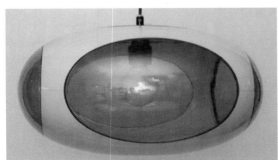

Free-Standing Lamp ▲
- *1960*

Large orange and brown free-standing lamp, with double handles.
- *height 60cm*
- £80 • Retro Home

Desk Lamp ▲
- *circa 1960*

Table or desk lamp with white circular shade and metal base and stand.
- *height 37cm*
- £35 • Retro Home

Adjustable Lamp ▼
- *circa 1970s*

Italian adjustable chrome lamp with marble base.
- *height 56cm*
- £1,200 • Zoom

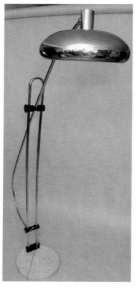

Metal Table Lamp ▼
- *circa 1960*

Metal table lamp with black lamp shade and circular base.
- *height 41cm*
- £85 • Retro Home

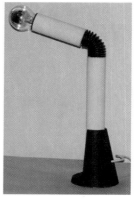

Italian Table Lamp ▲
- *1960*

Italian white table lamp with black base and rubber mobile arm.
- *height 40cm*
- £45 • Retro Home

Louis XVI-Style Chandelier ▲
- *circa 1920*

Two-tiered Louis XVI-style, fine quality cut-crystal chandelier, with four light sconces at the top, and eight below.
- *height 120cm*
- £6,000 • Simon Hatchwell

Expert Tips

Make sure that cut-glass chandeliers and drops are intact, although there are suppliers who make drops for many chandeliers, and in some cases they can be repaired with great success.

American Plaster Lamp ▲
- *circa 1950*
American plaster lamp with lady dancer, with a yellow lampshade with black tassels.
- *height 92cm*
- £175　　　● Radio Days

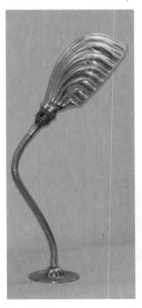

Reading Lamp ▲
- *1970*
Brass reading lamp on a flexible stand and circular base.
- *height 52cm*
- £55　　　● Radio Days

Italian Chandelier ▼
- *1900*
Italian brass chandelier with splayed leaves and blue drop crystals.
- *width 45cm*
- £175　　　● Rainbow

Hour-Glass Candelabra ▼
- *1920*
Italian candelabra with a metal hour-glass base and wire and green glass flower decoration.
- *60cm x 40cm*
- £475　　　● Rainbow

Perspex Lamp ➤
- *1960*
Free-standing lamp with an amber perspex base and fine raffia shade.
- *height 36cm*
- £40　　　● Retro Home

Brass Desk Lamp ▲
- *circa 1930s*
Brass cylinder-shape lamp on a stand with circular base.
- *height 32cm*
- £250　　　● North West Eight

Crystal Chandelier ▲
- *1920s*
Italian chandelier with a gilt metal foliate designed base, and crystal and red glass pendants.
- *65cm x 60cm*
- £395　　　● Rainbow

White Lamp ▼
- *1960*

White ceiling lamp, with rubber flex and stainless steel collar.
- *height 35cm*
- £50   • Retro Home

Ceiling Star Light ▼
- *1900*

Moroccan star ceiling light of mirrored glass.
- *diameter 62cm*
- £240   • Myriad

Adam-Style Chandelier ▼
- *circa 1920*

Fine twelve sconce Adam-style chandelier with pink glass bowl.
- *height 85cm*
- £1,450   • Simon Hatchwell

Oak Candelabras ▲
- *1920*

Pair of German, carved black, forest oak candelabra with a castelated influence.
- *height 48cm*
- £1,950   • Lacquer Chest

Painted Lamp Stand ▲
- *1920*

Naturalistically modelled and painted metal lamp stand showing a floral arrangement of daisies, poppies and wheatsheafs.
- *height 110cm*
- £420   • Myriad

British Spiral Lamp ▼
- *early 1990s*

Gold-coloured leaf spiral lamp on a circular base by Tom Dixon.
- *height 150cm*
- £980 • Themes & Variations

Giltwood Chandeliers ▼
- *20th century*

One of a pair of giltwood, double-tier chandeliers.
- *70cm x 73cm*
- £1,150   • Simon Hatchwell

Expert Tips

When choosing lighting, consider the style and the individuality of a piece as many famous designers have excelled at making fine interior light fixtures. In the future these will be considered to be important works of art in their own right.

Brass Chandelier ▲

- *1930s*
Italian brass chandelier of foliate design, with turquoise teardrop glass pendants.
- *50cm x 40cm*
- £375 • Rainbow

Alabaster Lamps ▲

- *20th century*
One of a pair of alabaster lamps with gilt wrought-iron appliqués.
- *width 45cm*
- £1,200 • Bizarre

French Empire Chandelier ▼

- *circa 1920*
Fine French Empire-style crystal and ormolu chandelier, with anthemion decoration to the rim and crystal tiers below.
- *30cm x 55cm*
- £4,850 • Simon Hatchwell

Lalique Lamp ▼

- *20th century*
Lalique "Thais" lamp of a veiled naked lady dancer, on a bronze base.
- *24cm x 22cm*
- N/A • Bizarre

Brass and Crystal Chandelier ▲

- *1930s*
Italian brass chandelier with crystals swags and turquoise pendants.
- *height 80cm*
- £795 • Rainbow

American Silver Candlesticks ▲

- *1930s*
Unusual American horseshoe-shaped candelabra and two small circular candleholders on clear glass, designed by Chase.
- *height 25cm*
- £270 • Bizarre

Hutschenreuther Candelabra ◄

- *20th century*
Candelabra with two branches of leaves supporting candleholders, with a central cherub standing on a gold circular ball, with a round white base, by Hutschenreuther.
- *height 22cm*
- £1,400 • Bizarre

Beaded Chandelier ▲

- *1900*

Small chandelier with beaded frame and faceted pendant drops.
- *height 38cm*
- £275   • R. Conquest

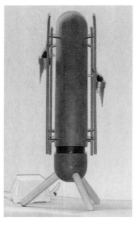

Cylindrical Steel Lamp ▲

- *2000*

Martin Herrick's BA cylinder-shaped steel lamp with an aluminum stand.
- *height 60cm*
- £200   • Retro Home

Expert Tips

There are many reproductions and fakes of Art Nouveau lamps on the market. To check the authenticity of the lamp, look out for numbers, stamps or engraved signatures on these works.

Silver-Plated Candlesticks ▼

- *circa 1900*

Pair of silver-plated five branch candlesticks.
- *height 47cm*
- £590   • Simon Hatchwell

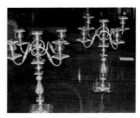

French Table Lamp ▼

- *1930*

French Art Deco table lamp with sandblasted glass shade and silvered bronze stand, signed by Sabino.
- *height 64cm*
- £2,200   • Succession

Art Nouveau Lamp ➤

- *1910*

American Art Nouveau lamp with green shade on a metal stand.
- *height 45cm*
- £600   • Succession

Daum Lamp and Shade ▲

- *1902*

French Art Nouveau lamp with glass lamp and shade, signed by Daum.
- *height 36cm*
- £6,000   • Succession

Hanging Lamp ▲

- *1900*

French hanging lamp with bronze horse chestnut leaf mount signed by Muller Frères.
- *height 68cm*
- £700   • Succession

Art Deco Lamp ▼

- *20th century*
Art Deco white ceramic vase-shaped lamp, with elongated slats for effective lighting.
- *height 32cm*
- £350 • Bizarre

Lamp on Cast-Iron Base ▼

- *1925*
Art Deco lamp with white glass lamp shade, on a tapered cast-iron base, signed Deguy.
- *height 39cm*
- £500 • Succession

Folded Paper Lamp ▶

- *2000*
Folded paper lamp, or dabadul, with a metal stand, by Ingo Maurer of Germany.
- *height 135cm*
- £550 • Themes & Variations

Purzel Lamp ▲

- *circa 1925*
Very rare Art Deco lamp with an anodized bronze stand giving the appearance of copper, with sandblasted glass shade. Signed by Purzel.
- *height 64cm*
- £2,400 • Succession

English Oil Lamps ▶

- *19th century*
Two English oil lamps in moulded light blue glass, with original fluted glass cover and polished brass respectively.
- *height 36cm*
- £70 • Old School

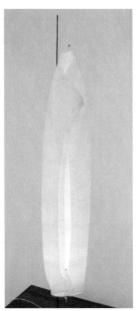

Pewter Candlestick ▼

- *circa 1900*
French pewter Art Nouveau candlestick with a moulded figure within the base, signed "H Siburd".
- *length 15cm*
- £340 • Succession

Austrian Lamp ▼

- *circa 1900*
Austrian hanging lamp, with a moss green shade with gilt thread decoration, designed by by Loetz.
- *height 25cm*
- £850 • Succession

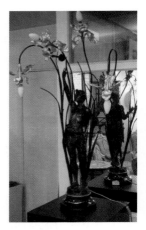

Figured Lamp ▲

- *circa 1910*
Art Nouveau bronzed and gilded figural lamp in the form of a man standing among flowering lilies forming the four lights, on a black marble socle.
- *height 125cm*
- £5,500 • Emanouel

Giltwood Chandeliers ▲

- *early 20th century*
One of a pair of giltwood seven-branch chandeliers after an eighteenth century style.
- *70cm x 69cm*
- £2,800 • M. Luther

Expert Tips

When considering large chandeliers or lanterns, take into account the weight and make sure the ceiling or wall fitting is durable enough and has been fitted correctly. Check whether the lamp or fixture uses a specialised bulb as part of its illumination, as some of these bulbs are unavailable in the shops today, and note the original wattage of the lamp.

Birdcage Frame Chandelier ▼

- *circa 1930*
French silvered bronze birdcage-frame chandelier with plaquette glass drops.
- *130cm x 85cm*
- £6,000 • Guinevere

Austrian Loetz Lamp ▼

- *1900*
Austrian Art Nouveau Loetz lamp with iridescent lampshade, the base by Gerchner.
- *height 46cm*
- £7,500 • Succession

Glass and Bronze Lamp ▶

- *circa 1900*
French bronze horse chestnut Art Nouveau lamp, with an Austrian made glass shade by Loetz.
- *height 64cm*
- £2,200 • Succession

Art Nouveau Wall Lights ▲

- *circa 1920s*
One of a pair of bronze Art Nouveau wall lights with leaf design.
- *height 30cm*
- £380 • Solaris Antiques

Bronze Hanging Lantern ▲

- *circa 1920s*
Cylindrical bronze hanging lantern in the style of Lutvens.
- *80cm x 38cm*
- £4,900 • M. Luther

Third Republic Chandelier ▲
- *1920*
Delicate French Third Republic chandelier with a metal hourglass base, with wire and coloured drops.
- *height 66cm*
- £325   • R. Conquest

Venetian Chandelier ▼
- *1940*
Art-Deco Venetian glass chandelier with glass tendrils flowing from its base.
- *diameter 110cm*
- £4,200   • Solaris

Hand-Painted Chandelier ▼
- *1920*
Green toile chandelier with hand-painted porcelain roses.
- *height 54cm*
- £320   • R. Conquest

Toile Chandelier ◄
- *1920*
French toile chandelier with painted flowers.
- *height 50cm*
- £200   • R. Conquest

French Chandelier ▲
- *1920*
Chandelier on decorative iron frame with faceted crystal drops.
- *height 65cm*
- £500   • R. Conquest

Cherub Wall Sconce ▲
- *1900*
Two-branch gilded wall sconce with scrolling leaves and carved wooden cherub.
- *height 72 cm*
- £550   • R. Conquest

Decorative Chandelier ◄
- *1920*
Toile chandelier with scrolling ormolu pink flowers and green foliage.
- *length 35cm*
- £435   • R. Conquest

English Lamp ▼
- *1960*

English lamp with wood base and plastic shade in brown and white checkered pattern.
- *height 52cm*
- £10 • Retro Home

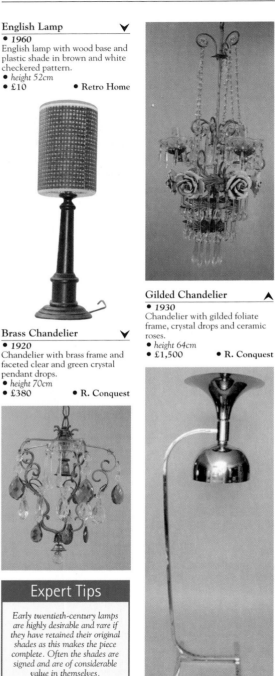

Brass Chandelier ▼
- *1920*

Chandelier with brass frame and faceted clear and green crystal pendant drops.
- *height 70cm*
- £380 • R. Conquest

Gilded Chandelier ▲
- *1930*

Chandelier with gilded foliate frame, crystal drops and ceramic roses.
- *height 64cm*
- £1,500 • R. Conquest

Cherub Chandelier ▼
- *1920*

French gilded figure of a cherub holding two crystal chandeliers.
- *length 39cm/cherub*
- £450 • R. Conquest

Hanging Lamp ▼
- *1900*

Unusual gilded bronze lamp with an abundance of hanging mistletoe.
- *width 65cm*
- £3,200 • Gooday Gallery

Star Light ▼
- *circa 1990s*

Star-shaped light made from paper and reinforced with metal, by Tom Dixon.
- *height 47.5cm*
- £280 • Themes & Variations

Italian Chrome Lamp ◄
- *circa 1960s*

Italian chrome lamp with two shades on an arched chrome base, by Franco Albini.
- *height 50cm*
- £1,400 • Zoom

Expert Tips

Early twentieth-century lamps are highly desirable and rare if they have retained their original shades as this makes the piece complete. Often the shades are signed and are of considerable value in themselves.

Bronze Table Lamp ▲
* *1905*
Very rare bronze table lamp by
Pete Tereszczuk in cire peroue,
with an owl at the base. The
turquoise and indigo shade is by
Loetz.
* *height 38cm*
* £7,000   • Succession

Adjustable Lamp ▼
* *circa 1950s*
Metal, brass and aluminium
adjustable lamp by Gino Safatti
for Arteluce, Italy.
* *height 187.5cm*
* £1,600   • Zoom

Gilded Foliage Chandelier ▼
* *1920*
French chandelier with gilded
frame of flowing leaves, each
bearing a blue opaline glass
pendant drop.
* *height 65*
* £1,100   • R. Conquest

Italian Tube Lamp ◄
* *circa 1970s*
Murano glass lamp with tubes
carrying a white abstract design
within the glass, on a chrome
cylindrical base.
* *height 40cm*
* £1,200   • Zoom

Albini Chrome Lamp ▲
* *1969*
Italian chrome ceiling lamp by
Franco Albini
* *height 45cm*
* £350   • Zoom

Safatti Fan Lamp ▲
* *1950s*
Aluminium and glass fan-shaped
lamp by Gino Safatti, Italy.
* *height 160cm*
* £900   • Zoom

Three-Branched
Chandelier ▲
* *1920*
Chandelier with three branches,
with rose opaline glass drip-pans
and clear faceted crystals.
* *height 75cm*
* £420   • R. Conquest

Metalware

Bronze Figure ▼
● **1921**
Bronze figure entitled "Wind",
signed and dated 1921. Exhibited
by the Royal Academy.
● *height 24cm*
● **£1,100**   ● Succession

Chrome Lighter ▼
● **1970**
Chrome globe lighter raised on a
circular base.
● *height 10cm*
● **£35**   ● Zoom

Bronze Ibex ▲
● **1925**
Fine bronze of a leaping Ibex on a
pink marble plinth, by Fayral.
● *21cm x 28cm*
● **£750**   ● Succession

Metal Lighter ▶
● **1970**
Metal lighter with clear piezo
perspex fluid container by Kogen-
Kingsway.
● *height 15cm*
● **£70**   ● Zoom

Spelter Figure ▲
● **20th century**
Bronze spelter bust of the dancer
Isadora Duncan, of a
phantasmagorical theme.
● *height 42cm*
● **£4,500**   ● Bizarre

Wall Sconces ▶
● **1940**
One of a pair of French metal
wall sconces with enamelled leaf
and flower design.
● *height 40cm*
● **£480**   ● Solaris

Bronze Vase ▲

- *1930s*
Dinoderie bronze vase designed by Grange.
- *height 27cm*
- £1,500   • Bizarre

Art Deco Figure ▲

- *1930*
French Art Deco silvered bronze figure of a dancer, by Henri Molins.
- *height 47cm*
- £1,400   • Succession

Dalou Bronze ▲

- *circa 1905*
Bronze figure of a man digging, by Aime Joule Dalou. Pupil of Carpeaux and Duret his debut was at the Salon in Paris in 1867, signed with the Swiss French Foundry mark.
- *height 9cm*
- £1,650   • Gavin Douglas

Hussman Bronze Figure ▲

- *circa 1920*
Erotic bronze of a nude man on horseback, Signed on the base "Hussman".
- *height 35.5cm*
- £2,750   • Gavin Douglas

Bronze Dancer ▲

- *20th century*
Bronze figure of a female dancer by Rena Rosenthal.
- *height 20cm*
- £300   • Bizarre

German Silver Tray ◄

- *1905*
German silver Art Nouveau tray decorated with red poppies and head of a girl with long red hair.
- *32cm x 40cm*
- £7,000   • Succession

Ivory Figure ▼
- *1925*

Very fine painted bronze and
ivory and gold figure, by F. Preiss.
- *height 18cm*
- **£3,950** • Gavin Douglas

Classical Figure ▼
- *20th century*

Bronze and ivory figure from a
model by Varnier, showing a
classical maiden holding a flower
aloft. On an onyx and marble
base.
- *height 26.7cm*
- **£785** • London Antique

American Chrome Lighter ▲
- *1960*

Ball-shaped chrome lighter by
Ronson of Newark, New Jersey,
USA.
- *height 7.5cm*
- **£45** • Zoom

Art Deco Figure ▲
- *circa 1925*

Art Deco bronze of a young man
holding a lariat, on a marble
plinth.
- *height 30cm*
- **£1,275** • Gavin Douglas

Tudric Jug ▼
- *1930*

Tudric jug of ovoid proportions
made for Liberty of London
- *height 25cm*
- **£85** • Jane Stewart

Chrome Syphon ▼
- *1960*

British-made chrome siphon and
ice bucket.
- *height 40cm*
- **£240** • Zoom

Expert Tips

*When considering purchasing
cigarette lighters or soda siphons
it is important to make sure that
these can contain their fuel and
charges without leakage, and in
the case of coffee percolators
and expresso machines, that
they have been tested before
they are used.*

Bronze Figurine ▲

- *20th century*

Bronze figure of a female dancer by Haggenauer for Wiener Werkstatte.
- *height 24cm*
- £1,500   • Bizarre

Warrior Figure in Bronze ▲

- *20th century*

Bronze figure of an African warrior holding a gilt shield and throwing a spear, by Rena Rosenthal.
- *height 20cm*
- £300   • Bizarre

Rosenthal Bronze ▲

- *20th century*

Bronze figure of a dancer in a straw skirt in a stylised form, by Rena Rosenthal.
- *height 20cm*
- £300   • Bizarre

Signed Bronze Plate ◄

- *20th century*

Bronze plate signed "Tiffany Studios, New York".
- *diameter 23cm*
- £350   • Bizarre

Lenoir Bronze ▲

- *20th century*

Patinated French bronze figurine of a nude lady with an outstretched cloak, standing on a pink marble plinth, by Pierre Lenoir.
- *height 32cm*
- £950   • Bizarre

Chrome Clocks ◄

- *1970*

Scottish-made chrome clocks with red, purple and blue dials, by Westclox.
- *height 18.75cm*
- £50   • Zoom

Wine-Related Items

From corkscrews to taste vins, labels to wine coolers, coasters to trolleys, funnels to claret jugs, wine antiques are not just a good investment, but great to use.

Drinking wine has grown up in a short time, from its relative exclusivity in the late 1960s, to its current position as an everyday tipple; it has now become the nation's favourite drink, pushing beer into a secondary position.

The collecting of wine and the laying down of a cellar as an investment have a long history, and many fortunes have been made by the selling of a fine cellar. This is an excellent way of passing on your wealth to future generations, as it is not only a good investment, but also a joy to own. It is therefore somewhat surprising that the laying

down of cellars and the investment in wine as a very profitable endeavour is not more widespread.

With the growth in the collection and drinking of wine, many collectors are beginning to focus on all of the surrounding paraphernalia associated with it. This is reflected in the amount of effort devoted by inventors into making new designs for cork screws, which are so numerous as to almost be worth a book in itself. The humble corkscrew has now been elevated to a work of art and there are a wide variety of designs and shapes, many of them quite intriguing and ingenious, on the market.

Decanter Labels ▼
- *1798*
Thread design silver labels with the pierced letters "Sherry", and "W Wine", by Joseph Taylor of Birmingham.
- *7cm x 4cm*
- £250   • Linden & Co.

Silver Wine Goblet ▼
- *1870*
Silver wine goblet made by Cooke & Kelvey of Calcutta, India.
- *height 16cm*
- £275   • Linden & Co.

Silver Champagne Flute ◀
- *1910*
Silver champagne flute made by Aspreys of London, dated 1910.
- *height 15cm*
- £300   • Linden & Co.

Silver Decanter Labels ▼
- *19th century*
Silver George IV claret label made in London by Charles Rawlings, and a Silver George IV Madeira label by John Robins in 1804.
- *7cm x 4 cm*
- £120   • Linden & Co.

Silver Wine Funnel ▲
- *1785*
George III silver and glass wine funnel with beaded edging, by Robert Hennell. Assayed in London.
- *height 13cm*
- £850   • Linden & Co.

French Wine Taster ▲
- *circa 1880*
Parisian silver wine taster with circular body with domed centre, with embossed design.
- *diameter 5cm*
- £350   • Linden & Co.

Chinese Wine Cooler ▲
- *circa 1770*
Chinese export wine cooler with applied handles of European silver form, decorated with flowers within elaborate borders.
- *height 29cm*
- £3,100   • Cohen & Cohen

Silver Wine Coaster ▲
- *1811*
George III silver wine coaster with gadroon edge, on a wooden base by Rebecca Eames and Edward Barnard of London, England.
- *diameter 9cm*
- £900   • Linden & Co.

George III Cellaret ▲
- *1800*
George III mahogany hexagonal brass-bound cellaret, with carrying handles on the sides.
- *67cm x 49cm*
- £2,750   • Great Grooms

Brass Bar Corkscrew ▶
- *circa 1900*
Rapid brass bar corkscrew with steel clamp, made in England.
- *57cm x 29cm x 6cm*
- £400   • Henry Gregory

Wine Bottle Pourer ▲
- *1880*
Silver wine bottle holder and pourer made by William Hutton & Sons of Sheffield, England.
- *height 24cm*
- £195   • Linden & Co.

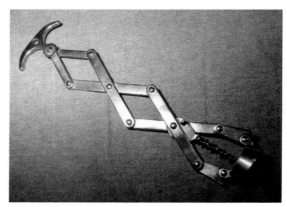

Expanding Corkscrew ▼
- *circa 1902*

English expanding corkscrew by Armstrong.
- *27cm x 16cm*
- £120   • Henry Gregory

Italian Corkscrew ▼
- *1880*

Italian boxwood and steel club corkscrew.
- *height 22cm*
- £325   • Emerson

Dachshund Corkscrew ▲
- *1930*

Dachshund novelty corkscrew, with brass corkscrew tail.
- *length 8cm*
- £45   • Emerson

Punch Ladle ▲
- *1820*

Regency glass punch ladle.
- *length 22cm*
- £220   • Jasmin Cameron

Metal Corkscrew ◄
- *circa 1910*

Expanding polished metal corkscrew.
- *length 14cm*
- £50   • Henry Gregory

Champagne Corkscrew ▲
- *1880*

Holborn champagne nickel plated corkscrew with wood handle.
- *height 17cm*
- £260   • Emerson

Corkscrew with Blade ▲
- *1870*

Simple corkscrew with blade with brass and rosewood handle with a brush.
- *height 13cm*
- £180   • Emerson

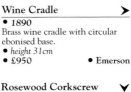

Wine Cradle ➤
- *1890*

Brass wine cradle with circular ebonised base.
- *height 31cm*
- £950   • Emerson

Rosewood Corkscrew ▼
- *1870*

Corkscrew with rosewood handle, and steel corkscrew, by W. Higgs & Son.
- *height 13cm*
- £120   • Emerson

Thomson Corkscrew ▼
- *circa 1850*

Thomson brass corkscrew, with brush and a patent badge.
- *height 17.5cm*
- £490   • Emerson

Victorian Corkscrews ➤
- *1890*

Selection of Victorian corkscrews with mahogany handles and steel screws. Two have brushes.
- *length 10cm*
- £60   • Henry Gregory

Brass Bar Screw ▼
- *1890*

Brass bar screw made by Merritt.
- *length 46cm*
- £450   • Emerson

German Corkscrew ▼
- *circa 1900*

German pillared corkscrew with brass base and ivory handled brush.
- *length 7cm*
- £320   • Emerson

Four-Pillar Corkscrew ▼
- *1850*

Four-pillar English corkscrew, made by Thomson, with a brass base and bone-handled brush.
- *height 18cm*
- £450   • Emerson

Oak Ice Bucket ▼

- *1880–1900*

Oak barrel ice bucket with silver plate banding and lid.
- *15cm x 13cm x 16cm*
- £75 • Henry Gregory

Three Barrel Cask ▶

- *circa 1880*

Unusual English oak three-barrel spirit cask with ivory stoppers.
- *35cm x 40cm x 20cm*
- £1,300 • Henry Gregory

Expert Tips

Hand-made decanters always have a number scratched into the stopper with a corresponding number scratched into the rim. This was to ensure that perfect pairings did not become separated.

Mahogany Wine Cooler ▲

- *1815*

Superb Regency mahogany and ebony inlaid wine cooler of sarcophagus form with canted corners. The wine cooler retains its original finely cast brass lion mask handles. Raised on swept sabre legs.
- £1,100 • Freshfords

King Screw ▶

- *1870*

Four-pillar king screw with bone handled brush and nickel base.
- *height 19cm*
- £600 • Emerson

Beer Tankards ◀

- *circa 1880*

Pair of English beer tankards made of oak, with silver banding and shields.
- *height 18cm*
- £280 • Henry Gregory

Horn Beakers ▲

- *circa 1906*

Pair of English horn beakers with a silver rim and shield cartouche.
- *12cm x 8cm x 7cm*
- £150 • Henry Gregory

Grape Hod ▼

- *1890*

Grape harvesting container with
leather straps for carrying bearing
the Saint-Emilish Chateau
Gironde emblem.
- *height 65cm*
- £420   • R. Conquest

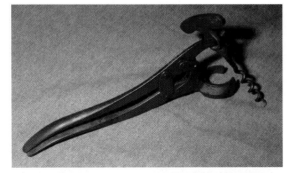

Metal Corkscrew ▲

- *circa 1890*

Victorian metal corkscrew.
- *20cm x 9cm*
- £160   • Henry Gregory

Silver Hip Flask ▼

- *1904*

Edwardian silver hip flask in
excellent condition with silver
hinged lid made in London.
- *height 16cm*
- £550   • Stephen Kalms

Leather Vessel ▲

- *circa 1800*

Small leather hand-cut and
stretched drinking vessel.
- *height 18cm*
- £250   • Holland & Holland

Mahogany Tantalus ▲

- *circa 1880*

Mahogany tantalus with pierced
silver mounts and three cut
crystal spirit decanters.
- *length 38cm*
- £680   • Henry Gregory

Crocodile Hip Flask ➤

- *1920*

Glass hip flask with crocodile
skin cover, silver mounts and
silver cup, made by J. Dixon of
Sheffield.
- *height 18cm*
- £595   • Stephen Kalms

Drinking Vessel ▲

- *circa 1880*

English drinking vessel hand
stretched and stitched with a
silver rim, manufactured by Ross
of Winchester.
- *height 7cm*
- £430   • Holland & Holland

Works of Art & Sculpture

Collecting ancient sculptures and work of art presents the most compelling insight into early civilisations, but is not without its difficulties.

For the purposes of this book, this section incorporates Asian and Oriental, Islamic, Russian and European works of art and sculpture. Each section covers a wide range of periods with emphasis being placed on the figurative and unusual items.

There has always been a lucrative market for pre-revolutionary Russian works of art, and now, with the collapse of the Soviet Union we have witnessed an influx of communist art onto the European and American markets. Particular favourites include portraits of Lenin and other powerful Russian icons which, ironically, are finding their way into the boardrooms of the capitalist world.

When purchasing early Asian works of art, particularly pottery, beware of fakes, and look for a piece that has been tested for authenticity.

Another factor to consider when purchasing overseas is making sure that you have the correct exportation and importation documentation in place as, particularly with expensive items, dealing with customs authorities can be an exasperating and lengthy procedure.

Asian/Oriental

Chinese Kendi ▼
- *18th century*
Chinese kendi and cover with Chinese silver mounts.
- *height 28cm*
- £1,650 • Nicholas S. Pitcher

Chinese Glass Painting ➤
- *early 19th century*
Chinese reverse glass painting, of a river landscape view, with hardwood frame.
- £4,200   • Brandt

Bronze Wine Vessel ▼
- *circa 1100–771 BC*
Western Zhou Dynasty bronze wine vessel with a "hu" lid.
- *height 18cm*
- £2,800 • Malcolm Rushton

Bronze Vessel ➤
- *1027–256 BC*
Bronze wine vessel "hu" with lid. Tiger handles.
- *height 18cm*
- £2,000   • Malcolm Rushton

Pottery Court Ladies ▲
- **618–907 AD**
Pair of painted pottery court
ladies, one with painted leaves in
her hair. Both have Oxford TL
certificates.
- *height 48cm*
- **£20,000** • Malcolm Rushton

Set of Eight Jun Ware Bowls ▲
- **1279–1368 AD**
A set of eight jun ware bowls
with white glaze.
- *diameter15.5cm*
- **£3,800** • Malcolm Rushton

Neolithic Jar ▲
- **4th–2nd Millennium BC**
A painted pottery jar from Gansu
province, with red and black
pigment.
- *height 30cm*
- **£1,200** • Little River

White Marble Buddha ➤
- **circa 549–577 AD**
Finely carved white marble
Buddha, from the Northern Qi
Dynasty.
- *height 49cm*
- **£10,000** • Malcolm Rushton

Food Vessel ▲
- **1650–1027 BC**
Bronze Chinese food vessel
"ding" with "thread relief" frieze
of animal masks to the body and
similar decoration to the legs,
from the Shang Dynasty.
- *46cm x 34cm*
- **£9,000** • Malcolm Rushton

Lacquer Case ▼
- **circa 1850**
Japanese lacquer case in three
parts on Kingi ground and
elaborately decorated in gold
Takamakie Hirigane and
Togideshi style, and inlaid in
Shiboyama style with butterflies
and birds.
- *length 12cm*
- **£5,550** • Japanese Gallery

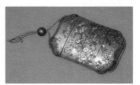

Sumo Wrestlers ➤
- **1868–1912**
A carved wood and dry lacquered
model of two fighting Sumo
wrestlers.
- **£10,000** • Brandt

Wine Jar ▼

- **206 BC–220 AD**
Large Chinese pottery wine jar
with cover after a bronze original.
The jar and cover are from the
Han Dynasty.
- *45cm x 32cm*
- **£2,200** • **Nicholas S. Pitcher**

Chinese Stoneware Jar ▼

- **618–906 AD**
Chinese cream-glazed stoneware
jar from the Tang Dynasty.
- *19cm x 22cm*
- **£1,500** • **Nicholas S. Pitcher**

Chinese Henan Jar ▲

- **12th–13th century**
Chinese Henan glazed pottery jar
from the Jin Dynasty with an oval
form with a splayed lip.
- *18cm x 19cm*
- **£1,350** • **Nicholas S. Pitcher**

Chinese Ming Ewer ▶

- **14th–17th century**
Chinese Ming ewer made for
export to Iran, featuring an
allegorical figure to the neck and
with green and blue openwork to
the body.
- *height 30cm*
- **£6,000** • **Yazdani**

Bronze Vase ◀

- **1868–1912**
A Bronze Japanese vase of the
Meiji period, of ovoid form with a
silver overlaid crane and stylised
clouds.
- *height 39cm*
- **£2,200** • **Brandt**

Pottery Horse ▼

- **18–907 AD**
Tang Dynasty glazed equestrienne
of an unusual apple green colour.
Provenance: Eskenazis inaugural
exhibition in London 1972.
- *49cm x 35cm*
- **£5,500** • **Malcolm Rushton**

Chinese Patinated Bottle ◀

- **206 BC–220 AD**
Chinese green patinated bronze
bottle of bulbous form with garlic
neck from the Han Dynasty.
- *30cm x 21cm*
- **£1,200** • **Nicholas S. Pitcher**

Expert Tips

*Wine jars from China are very
desirable and the condition is
important, but if the glaze is
slightly chipped this will not
detract from the value.*

Mongolian Pottery Figure ▲
- *550–581*

Painted pottery figure in animal skin cloak with elaborate head dress, from the Mongolian border, with traces of red and white paint.
- *31cm x 20cm*
- **£2,000** • Malcolm Rushton

Bronze Food Vessel ▲
- *circa 1100–771BC*

A bronze food vessel "ding" from the Western Zhou Dynasty, with a frieze of confronting bird-like mythical beasts and cicada, interesting green and blue patina.
- *24cm x 18cm*
- **£8,500** • Malcolm Rushton

Model of a Pheasant ➤
- *1868–1912*

Japanese silver and mixed metal model of a pheasant, standing on a rock modelled out of wood.
- *height 29cm*
- **£5,500** • Brandt

Painted Snake ▼
- *36–581 AD*

Painted Chinese pottery snake with a human head at each end "fuxi and Nuwa" with traces of red and white pigment remaining. Has been Oxford TL tested.
- *length 30cm*
- **£900** • Malcolm Rushton

Pair of Ynrli Lions ▼
- *18th century*

One of a pair of mythical Ynrli lions with elephants trunks and heads of human beings to show their supreme power. This pair would be guarding the Gods of a juggernaut or cart, and carrying an idol of Krishna.
- *165cm x 55cm*
- **£7,800** • Gordon Reece

Sealed Pottery Vessel ▲
- *960–1279*

Sealed brown glazed pottery vessel containing remains of original wine used for ritual purposes.
- *19cm x 15cm*
- **£2,500** • Malcolm Rushton

Bronze Casket ▲
- *16th century*

A beautiful bronze casket, with panels of engraved deer and geometric borders. Excellent provenance as it once belonged to the Sultan of Delhi.
- *14cm x 20cm x 14cm*
- **£5,000** • Ghaznavid

Chinese Painted Figure ▲
- *circa 618–906 AD*

Chinese painted figure of a groom from the Tang dynasty. The figure is rare due to the gilding.
- *height 35cm*
- **£3,300** • **Nicholas S. Pitcher**

Japanese Dog ▲
- *circa 1880*

A study of a small Japanese long-haired dog lying on a fan on a padook wood stand.
- *11cm x 7cm*
- **£985** • **Japanese Gallery**

Japanese Water Dropper ▲
- *19th century*

Japanese bronze and silver artist's water dropper in the form of a lotus leaf.
- *diameter 20cm*
- **£2,500** • **Brandt**

Japanese Plaque ▲
- *circa 1880*

A Japanese circular hardwood plaque pierced with interlaced foliate designs.
- *diameter 67cm*
- **£980** • **Westland & Co.**

Ivory Figure ▲
- *late 18th century*

Chinese carved ivory and bone figure of a young boy standing on a rock with a seal.
- *height 9cm*
- **£80** • **John Clay**

Netsuki of Two Rats ▲
- *circa 1880*

Japanese carved wood Okimono-style netsuki of two rats, signed "Ittantu".
- *height 3cm*
- **£1,950** • **Japanese Gallery**

Chinese Amphora ▲
- *618–907 AD*

Green glazed dragon handled pottery amphora – inscription reads "Li Man Shu" – almost certainly belonged to a minor member of the Tang royal family.
- *55cm x 28cm*
- **£3,500** • **Malcolm Rushton**

Expert Tips

Netsuki, the Japanese carved toggles made to secure a sagamono (hanging robe) to an obi (waist belt), are usually made of ivory, lacquer, silver or wood and originate from the sixteenth century.

Pottery Horsemen ▼
- **534–549 AD**
Pair of Chinese painted pottery
horsemen. The figures retain
much of their original pigment
with horses leather armour clearly
delineated, from the Eastern Wei
Dynasty.
- *36cm x 29cm*
- **£8,000** • **Malcolm Rushton**

Mughal Glass ▼
- *18th century*
Mughal glass from India with
moulded reticulated decoration
around the sides.
- *19cm x 18cm*
- **£350** • **Arthur Millner**

Chinese Buddha ▼
- *circa 11th–13th century*
Large painted stucco Buddha
from the Song/Yuan Dynasty,
flanked by a pair of attendants.
- *67cm x 27cm*
- **£4,600** • **Nicholas S. Pitcher**

Chinese Cloisonné Box ▲
- **1736–95**
Small Chinese cloisonné and gilt
metal incense box.
- *diameter 11cm*
- **£2,500** • **Brandt**

Glazed Pottery Vase ▲
- **983 AD**
A glazed pottery vase with four
handles with the inscription
"made in the 8th year of the
Emperor Tai Ping Hing Ko".
- *24cm x 19cm*
- **£7,000** • **Malcolm Rushton**

Hoshiarpur Tray ▶
- *circa 1900*
Hoshiarpur tray with carved rim
and foliate designs in ivory and
ebony inlay.
- *51cm x 31cm*
- **£350** • **Arthur Millner**

Bishop's Staff ▲
- *circa 1800*
An Indian bishop's staff in iron in
the Byzantine style.
- *length 59cm*
- **£1,250** • **Iconastas**

Bronze Figure ▼

- *18th century*
Indian bronze six-armed deity
with three heads, on a figured
marble plinth base.
- *19cm x 24cm*
- **£4,000** • Arthur Millner

Bidri Huqqa ▼

- *circa 1800*
Silver Bidri huqqa inlaid alloy
huqqa with engraved floral
decoration.
- *18cm x 17cm*
- **£800** • Arthur Millner

Brass Ewer ▲

- *18th century*
Brass Indian ewer with bulbous
form with incised floral
decoration with scrolled handle
and finial.
- *28cm x 36cm*
- **£1,500** • Arthur Millner

Sri Lankan Figure ▲

- *circa 1800*
Female ivory figure from Sri
Lanka, standing wearing pleated
costume and necklace, with arms
by her side.
- *10.7cm x 4cm*
- **£200** • Arthur Millner

Portrait of a Raja ▲

- *circa 1770*
Portrait of Raja Surimal of
Nurpur dressed in a white turban
and an orange tunic holding a
falcon in right hand.
- *19cm x 13cm*
- **£1,500** • Arthur Millner

Figure of a Female ▼

- *circa 1850*
Carved and painted alabaster
figure in front of an orange
shrine.
- *31cm x 14cm*
- **£350** • Arthur Millner

Ivory Figure ▼

- *circa 1880*
Carved ivory Indian woman
holding a water jug.
- *22cm x 6cm*
- **£600** • Arthur Millner

Three-Tiered Chinese Box➤
- *18th century*
A three-tiered box, inlaid with
mother of pearl and hard stones.
- *11cm x 21cm x 13cm*
- **£2,750** • **Gerard Hawthorn**

Brass Surahi ▲
- *18th century*
Brass Indian bottle-shaped surahi
with an inscised spiral decoration
around body.
- *24cm x 18cm*
- **£325** • **Arthur Millner**

Chinese Enamel Censer ▲
- *17th century*
A cloisonné enamel censer of
archaic Fang Ding form,
supported on four curved legs of
monster mask and bird design.
The underside decorated with
four flowers amid scrolling
foliage, the body divided by
vertical gilded flanges
- *height 35cm*
- **£14,000** • **Gerard Hawthorn**

Figure of Vishnu ➤
- *17th century*
The four-armed Indian figure of
Vishnu holding attributes in each
hand, standing on a lotus base.
- *47cm x 19cm*
- **£6,000** • **Arthur Millner**

Amida Buddha ▲
- *circa 1600*
A giltwood figure depicting
Amida Buddha on a lotus base.
- *height 58cm*
- **£6,500** • **Brandt**

Chinese Box ▼
- *17th century*
A Chinese intricately carved box
with black, red and dark green
lacquer,with designs of peaches
and blossom, from the Ming
Dynasty.
- *8.5cm x 12cm x 12cm*
- **£1,800** • **Gerard Hawthorn**

Hand Warmer ▼
- *18th century*
Chinese Canton enamel hand
warmer, from the Quing Dynasty,
decorated with a scrolling floral
design with brass handle.
- *9cm x 18cm x 13cm*
- **£4,500** • **Gerard Hawthorn**

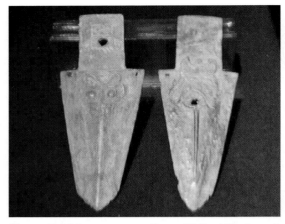

Sichuan Pottery Boar ▲
- *206–220 AD*
A Sichuan pottery boar
naturalistically poised on all four
legs from the Han Dynasty.
- *length 57cm*
- £4,800 • Nicholas S. Pitcher

Chinese Fish Man ▼
- *280–589*
Two very different pottery fish
man images. This combination of
images seems to have denoted
protection for deceased scholars.
- *28cm x 19cm*
- £600 • Malcolm Rushton

Bronze Halberd Heads ▲
- *1650–1027 BC*
Two bronze halberd heads "ge"
with tiger and mostor head
decoration.
- *length 20cm*
- £1,100 • Malcolm Rushton

Pair of Fu Dogs ▲
- *1644–1912*
Fine Chinese stone carving of
pair of Fu dogs with boys riding
on their backs, from the early
Qing Dynasty, with traces of
pigment.
- *height 25cm*
- £1,800 • Little River

Giltwood Buddha ▼
- *18th century*
Giltwood figure showing a seated
Buddha with resplendant copper
headress, on a hexagonal base.
- *height 34cm*
- £4,000 • Brandt

Chinese Pottery Duck ▲
- *206 BC–220 AD*
Chinese slipware, white pottery
duck of good form from the Han
Dynasty. Includes test certificate.
- *length 35cm*
- £4,200 • Nicholas S. Pitcher

Balinese Figure ▲
- *20th century*
Balinese carved wooden prayer
figure with traces of gilding.
- *height 171cm*
- £2,250 • Zakheim

Expert Tips

*The insured value of a statue
or work of art should include the
cost of packaging and shipping.
Always use a reputable
transporter and packager.*

Japanese Bronze Hare ▲
- *1868–1912*
Japanese bronze model of a
crouching hare, from the meiji
period.
- *height 25cm*
- £3,800   • Brandt

Brass Finial ▲
- *18th century*
Brass palanquin finial in the form
of a stylised leopard head.
- *26cm x 14cm*
- £750   • Arthur Millner

Lifan Amphora ▲
- *481–221 BC*
A Lifan culture burnished black
pottery amphora, from the
Sichuan Province.
- *33cm x 32cm*
- £2,500   • Little River

Pair of Gu Vases ▼
- *circa 1750s*
Pair of Gu vases in elephant form
made of fine Chinese bronze from
the Qianlong period, set with
ruby, garnets and turquoise stones.
- *30cm x 25cm*
- £7,000 • Nicholas S. Pitcher

Tang Dynasty ▼
- *618–907 AD*
Red Chinese pottery horse
painted with red and black
pigment, from the Tang Dynasty
in the Henaw Province.
- *33cm x 32cm*
- £1,500   • Little River

Pottery Horse ◄
- *Tang Dynasty 618–907 AD*
Small red Chinese pottery horse
decorated with black, yellow and
white pigments, from the Tang
Dynasty in the Henan Province.
- *20cm x 18cm*
- £450   • Little River

Bronze Sword ◄
- *481–221 BC*
Bronze sword with blade coated
in silver, with the silver showing
through heavy green patination
in some areas.
- *length 48cm*
- £1,400 • Malcolm Rushton

European

Classical Relief of a Centaur ▲
- *circa 1820*
A plaster relief showing the classical scene of the centaur Nessus carrying off Delamra.
- *134cm x 133cm*
- £5,500   • Westland & Co.

Bronze Gymnast ▲
- *1976*
English bronze of a female gymnast on the vault, with a marble plinth, signed by Kelsey.
- *height 35cm*
- £1,850   • Zakheim

Bronze Sculpture ▼
- *20th century*
Amorphous French polished bronze sculpture after Jean Arp.
- *width 23cm*
- £4,450   • Zakheim

Figure of a Knight ▲
- *late 18th century*
French knight carved from pine in a gothic revival manner showing the period armour of the time.
- *183cm x 64cm*
- £4,500   • Westland & Co.

Bronze Gymnast ▶
- *1979*
English bronze of a female gymnast on the bar, with a rectangular marble plinth, signed "K.Carter 1979 2/4".
- *height 42cm*
- £1,850   • Zakheim

Limestone Head ▲
- *circa 1970*
English head of a girl carved from limestone, on a square wooden base, by Mike Grevatte.
- *height 70cm*
- £2,850   • Zakheim

Royal Vienna Vase ▼
- *circa 1870*
A Royal Vienna vase and cover with gold relief, featuring six Greek mythical scenes from the Palace of Athena.
- *140cm x 50cm*
- £25,000   • Emanouel

Italian Marble Figure ▼
- *circa 1890*
An Italian marble figure of Virtue after Tino Camaino. Showing a crowned lady with a posy of flowers in her right hand, possibly by Alceo Dossena.
- *105cm x 32cm x 20cm*
- £4,488   • Westland & Co

Molière Head ◀

- **early 18th century**
An Louis XIV carved stone head of the French dramatist Molière looking to dexter.
- *63.5cm x 55cm*
- **£3,500** • Westland & Co.

Pair of Sèvres Vases ▼

- **19th century**
A pair of Sèvres gilt metal mounted fuchsia vases and covers, with an inner design depicting Romantic couples in a pastoral setting.
- *height 98cm*
- **£22,000** • Emanouel

Bronze Group ▼

- **circa 1930s**
Bronze group of a mother clutching her child astride a horse, executed in a richly patinated bronze. Signed by E. de Valeriola.
- *56cm x 23cm*
- **£4,250** • Zakheim

Danish Sculpture ◀

- **1960**
An abstract wooden sculpture designed by Simon of Denmark.
- *height 37.5cm*
- **£800** • Zoom

Limestone Maquette ▶

- **circa 1930**
Limestone maquette of two seated and embracing figures, after Henry Moore.
- *23cm x 24cm*
- **£12,500** • Zakheim

Bronze Plaque ▲

- **circa 1930**
Bronze Art-Deco plaque depicting Hermes, the Greek messenger of the gods shown in his winged sandals carrying a twin snaked staff.
- *26cm x 28cm*
- **£750** • Zakheim

Sculpted Head ▲

- **1970**
English carved limestone head of a female with her hair in a chignon, on a square wooden base, by Mike Grevatte.
- *height 70cm*
- **£2,850** • Zakheim

Dresden Schneeballen Vase ◀

- **circa 1870**
Dresden schneeballen vase and cover after the Meissen original, applied all over with blue mayflowers and songbirds perched among white snowballs and other encrusted flowers growing from rustic twig handles, the finial in the form of a parrot on a fruiting branch.
- *height 79cm*
- **£3,500** • Emanouel

Islamic

Glass Bowl ▲
- *13th century*

Small translucent turquoise Islamic glass bowl with good iridescence.
- *diameter 9cm*
- £2,000 • **Ghaznavid**

Ink Holder ▲
- *circa 1870*

Persian ink holder decorated with bronze medallions along the shaft, from the Quarshar Dynasty.
- *height 25cm*
- £120 • **Sharif**

Bronze Dish ▲
- *2nd–3rd century AD*

A Sassanian broad shallow bronze dish with a lamb's head design to the handle and good patina.
- *length 45cm*
- £1,200 • **Yazdani**

Terracotta Cover ▲
- *12th century*

A light coloured terracotta cover for a jar showing a carved central panel with phoenix and deer. Excellent condition.
- *diameter 12cm*
- £300 • **Ghaznavid**

Persian Beaker ▲
- *circa 1910*

Persian silver beaker with embossed foliate designs within shaped borders.
- *height 11.25cm*
- £50 • **Sharif**

Syrian Box ▼
- *1910*

Wooden box with mother-of-pearl inlay and red satin interior from Damascus.
- *25cm x 16.25cm*
- £120 • **Sharif**

Islamic Tray ▲
- *circa 1920*

Persian circular brass tray with engraved Islamic lettering and geometric patterns to centre.
- *diameter 58.75cm*
- £110 • **Sharif**

Fish Incense Burner ◄
- *17th century*
A bronze incense burner in the
form of a fish with stylised fins
and inlaid with gold scales
- *length 30cm*
- £950 • Yazdani

Persian Box ▲
- *19th century*
A Persian painted box with bone
and ivory inlay in geometric
patterns on moulded bracket feet.
- *14cm x 35cm x 28cm*
- £850 • John Clay

Persian Glass Bottle ►
- *11th century*
A fire-blown cobalt blue glass
bottle with a fluted body and a
long tapered neck with splayed
lip with iridescence. The bottle is
in excellent condition.
- *height 25cm*
- £800 • Pars

Koran Stand ►
- *circa 1800*
Ottoman Koran stand composed
of two folding panels, with a
geometrical design and inlaid
with mother of pearl.
- *43cm x 63cm*
- £1,750 • Arthur Millner

Bronze Ewer ◄
- *13th century*
A bronze water ewer with copper
inlay, with a bird head lip. There
are fioriated Kufic inscriptions to
the body, base and neck.
- *height 25cm*
- £6,000 • Yazdani

Seljuq Door Fitting ►
- *13th century*
An ornamental bronze door
fitting comprising three circular
bands decorated with gold and
copper inlay with inscriptions.
- *diameter 35cm*
- £950 • Yazdani

Incense Burner ▼
- *2nd–3rd century AD*
Bronze tripod incense burner
decorated with three gazelle head
terminals
- *height 11cm*
- £1,400 • Yazdani

Qajar Gold Pendant ▼
- *19th century*
A Qajar gold pendant incised with a gazelle and wolf motif surrounded with prolific foliate decoration.
- *diameter 7cm*
- £1,250 • Yazdani

Inlaid Wooden Box ▼
- *circa 1915*
Turkish wooden box with mother-of-pearl inlay to the front panel and rim of the lid.
- *height 50cm*
- £400 • Sharif

Islamic Chandelier ◄
- *circa 1870*
An Islamic bronze chandelier of bulbous form with pierced foliate decoration, and blue enamel design.
- *height 77cm*
- £1,200 • Emanouel

Egyptian Brass Kursi ▲
- *19th century*
An Egyptian brass kursi in the Mamluk style with extensive silver inlay, the hexagonal top with a radiating part open-work design involving panels of inscriptions and knot work roundels around a central kufic roundel with gilt centre inscribed Muhammed. The six sides divided into panels, with arches below rising from turned feet.
- *height 81cm*
- £22,000 • Emanouel

Syrian Damascus Table ▲
- *circa 1915*
Damascus table with geometric bone and ivory inlay and architecturally carved legs.
- *62.5cm x 42.5cm*
- £400 • Sharif

Turkish Mosaic Table ▲
- *circa 1870*
A mosaic wood table with applied mother-of-pearl, tortoiseshell and bone inlay, alternating geometric radiating bands surrounded by a raised border, the base decorated with chequered square design raised on ten chamfered legs separated by scrolling brackets.
- *height 70cm*
- £5,000 • Emanouel

Moroccan Chair ◄
- *1910*
A Moroccan cedar chair inlaid with a floral and star pattern, in bone and boxwood. With a moulded seat and shaped legs.
- *height 103cm*
- £350 • John Clay

Russian

Cigarette Case

▲
- *circa 1900*
Russian cigarette champlevé case with a repeating floral pattern in blue, red and white enamel.
- *10cm x 6cm*
- £890 • Iconastas

Virgin of Kazan

▲
- *circa 1895*
Virgin of Kazan covered with an engine-turned silver riza.
- *15cm x 11.5cm*
- £1,250 • Iconastas

Painted Lacquer Box ➤

- *1947*
Rare wartime allegorical lacquered painted box showing the invasion of Russia by Germany, and the eventual defeat of the German army. The box is painted in icon form with the moon on the left hidden by the burning buildings, by F. Kolosov.
- *21cm x 17cm*
- £1,650 • Iconastas

Quadratych ▼

- *circa 1840*
A brass and enamel folding quadratych depicting festivals and venerations of icons of the Virgin and Child.
- *17cm x 40cm*
- £290 • Iconastas

Black Lacquer Box ▼

- *circa 1870*
Circular Russian black lacquer box with a painting of a landscape in a Dutch style by Lukutin.
- *diameter 9cm*
- £1,350 • Iconastas

St Sergei Pendant ➤

- *circa 1840*
Enamel painted pendant of St Sergei set in an oval frame with paste diamonds, on a silver chain.
- *6cm x 4cm*
- £690 • Iconastas

Fedoskino Box ▲

- *1951*
Black lacquer box with a painting of playful couples shown on a bridge over a stream, by the Fedoskino factory.
- *14cm x 7cm*
- £590 • Iconastas

Brass Cross with Enamel Inlay ▲
• *circa 1830*
An unusually large brass Russian cross showing Christ on the crucifix, with enamel inlay.
• *41cm x 20.5cm*
• £390 • Iconastas

Silver Cigarette Case ▲
• *circa 1900*
Russian silver cigarette case decorated in en-plein enamel, with a girl on a swing being pushed by a boy, from a painting by Serge Solamko. It comes with a postcard showing the identical image.
• *9cm x 5cm*
• £2,250 • Iconastas

Drinking Goblet ▼
• *19th century*
Russian drinking goblet with a geometric and swirling design enamelled in blue, turquoise and white gold. Made for Tiffany.
• *height 12cm*
• £1,450 • Iconastas

St George and the Dragon ➤
• *circa 1880*
Balkan icon of St George on horseback slaying the dragon with enamelled face and hands, covered with a silver riza.
• *10cm x 12cm*
• £690 • Iconastas

Brass Cigarette Box ▲
• *circa 1970*
Musical cigarette box in brass, depicting the first Russian space flight.
• *10cm x 8cm*
• £250 • Iconastas

Brass and Blue Enamel Cross ▲
• *circa 1800*
Brass and blue enamel cross with Christ on the crucifix at the centre, surrounded by depictions of festivals surmounted by seraphim.
• *height 28cm*
• £750 • Iconastas

Georgian Cigarette Box ▼
• *circa 1900s*
Georgian cigarette box in silver and niello, depicting two men fighting a lion, with a secret communist interior showing plaques of Lenin and the Hammer and Sickle.
• *10cm x 8cm*
• £1,250 • Iconastas

Cloisonné Cigarette Case ➤

- *circa 1900s*

Russian cloisonné cigarette case with blue, red, white and turquoise floral decoration.
- *height 9cm*
- **£1,350**
- Iconastas

Russian Pendant ▲

- *18th century*

Russian bronze cross inlaid with turquoise and blue enamel.
- *3cm x 3cm*
- **£220**
- Iconastas

Russian Icon ◀

- *18th century*

Russian enamel on copper icon depicting the Saints Zossima, Savarti, Phillip and Roman.
- *height 21cm*
- **£1,350**
- Iconastas

Imperial Cigarette Case ◀

- *circa 1900s*

Silver Russian cigarette case repoussed with Adam and Eve, with a dedication to Tsar Nicholas II on the reverse, and a gold coin, Imperial flags, crown and coat of arms.
- *10cm x 8cm*
- **£1,950**
- Iconastas

Russian Tray ▼

- *circa 1900*

Russian silver tray with blue, turquoise and gold enamel floral decoration. Engraved cypher on reverse, by Gustav Klingert.
- *length 25cm*
- **£2,450**
- Iconastas

Enamelled Case ◀

- *circa 1900s*

Russian cigarette case with an enamelled geometric and foliate design.
- *10cm x 8cm*
- **£1,250**
- Iconastas

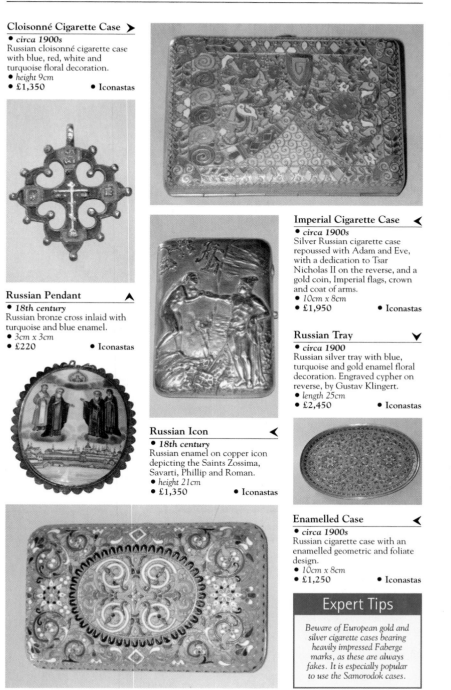

Expert Tips

Beware of European gold and silver cigarette cases bearing heavily impressed Faberge marks, as these are always fakes. It is especially popular to use the Samorodok cases.

Bishop's Cross ▲
- *1854*
Russian silver-gilt bishop's cross
with Christ at the centre,
decorated in garnets, inscribed by
Vilno.
- *height 23cm*
- £1,650 • Iconastas

Bishop's Silver Gilt Cross ▲
- *1890*
Bishop's silver gilt and blue
enamel cross depicting the head
of Christ surrounded by paste
diamonds and rubies. The clasp is
shaped as an Imperial crown,
with a linked silver chain.
- *17cm x 10cm*
- £1,450 • Iconastas

Lenin Figure ➤
- *circa 1925*
Porcelain figure of Lenin shown
standing on a circular base.
- *height 66cm*
- £1,250 • Zakheim

Meerschaum Pipe ◄
- *1801*
Russian Meerschaum pipe in the
shape of a hand, inscribed "Maria
Peodoronna Imperatrioc".
- *20cm x 10cm*
- £1,650 • Iconastas

Bronze Partisan ➤
- *circa 1940*
Revolutionary bronze Russian
partisan shown holding a gun
above his head, on a rectangular
plinth.
- *height 100cm*
- £3,750 • Zakheim

Football Trophy ◄
- *1960*
Russian football trophy painted
under glass, decorated with a
cartouche showing footballers.
- *height 38cm*
- £250 • Zakheim

Commemorative Vase ◄
- *circa 1950s*
Russian commemorative vase
showing Stalin in military
costume on a red glazed ground.
- *height 49cm*
- £1,250 • Zakheim

Bronze Sculpture ➤

- *circa 1920*

Bronze sculpture depicting Lenin in discussion.
- *height 16cm*
- £2,650   • Zakheim

Blue Russian Vases ▼

- *1855–81*

A pair of amphora-shaped Alexander II porcelain vases, with ormolu mounts from the Imperial porcelain factory, profusely moulded with scrolling strawberries, wild flowers, birds and butterflies against a pale lilac ground, enclosing two painted reserves of varying spring bouquets, resting on an elaborate gilt foliate base, by M. Morozov.
- *height 107cm*
- £65,000   • Emanouel

Ceramic Urn ▼

- *circa 1950*

Russian ceramic urn with a sepia portrait of Lenin surrounded by floral decoration, with two scrolled and gilded handles, and gilded banding to the neck and base.
- *49cm x 32cm*
- £750   • Zakheim

Russian Soldier ▲

- *circa 1950*

Ceramic figure of a Russian soldier shown seated playing the accordion.
- *height 42cm*
- £850   • Zakheim

Expert Tips

Look for pre-1940s Soviet political figures as these are becoming scarce, especially busts of Stalin. Soviet cigarette cases with inscriptions by famous leaders are incredibly rare.

Porcelain Dessert Plate ◄

- *1825–55*

A rare St Petersburg porcelain dessert plate from the coronation service of Tzar Nicolas I 1825 ex. Romanoff Collection, Winter Palace.
- *diameter 22cm*
- £1,200   • Boyd-Carpenter

Russian Radio ▲

- *circa 1950s*

A Soviet radio in bakelite, made in the style of an American 1950s car dashboard.
- *35cm x 54cm*
- £750   • Zakheim

Bronze Figures ▲
- *circa 1950s*
Bronze of a man teaching his young son archery, on a triangular base.
- *height 48cm*
- £1,450   • Zakheim

Icon of St John, Nicholas and Ulita ▲
- *18th century*
Octagonal icon depicting the Saints John, Nicholas and Ulita, with her son Kyric, covered with a silver gilt riza.
- *9.5cm x 10.5cm*
- £1,850   • Iconastas

Revolutionary Plaque ▼
- *1917–20*
Russian revolutionary monumental cast bronze plaque, with a rusticated finish, showing a gun, helmet and cartridges and the date "1917–1920".
- *190cm x 105cm*
- £7,500   • Zakheim

Floral Cup and Saucer ◄
- *1825–55*
A Russian cup and saucer, with gilded floral decoration on a pink ground with scattered painted flowers.
- *height 8cm*
- £350   • London Antique

Painted Laquered Box ▲
- *circa 1890s*
Russian painted lacquered box depicting a courting couple in a countryside setting, by the Vishniakov factory.
- *12cm x 8cm*
- £590   • Iconastas

Expert Tips

Old lacquer boxes should never be cleaned with chemicals or varnished. Brasso is the safest cleaning agent for lacquer.

Wooden Toboggan ▼
- *1901*
Russian painted red wooden toboggan from the Volodga region.
- *length 65cm*
- £120   • Zakheim

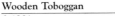

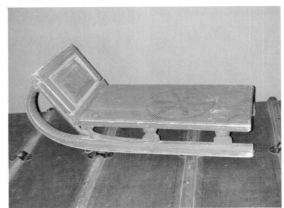

Oval Lacquer Box ▲
- *1870*

Oval red lacquer painted box showing a Russian peasant girl wearing a Kokoshnik, by the Lukitin factory.
- *length 7cm*
- £1,250 • Iconastas

Dancing Scene ▲
- *1860*

Russian painted lacquer box depicting dancers in colourful costumes linking hands in a woodland setting.
- *15cm x 8cm*
- £1,250 • Iconastas

Icon of St. Samon, Gury and Aviv ▲
- *1900*

Russian icon showing the Saints Samon, Gury and Aviv, covered with a silver and turquoise blue enamel riza, by Michelson, Moscow, 1900.
- *7cm x 6cm*
- £1,250 • Iconastas

Portrait of Pushkin ▼
- *1951*

Russian painted lacquer box with a portrait of Pushkin on the front by the Fedoskino factory.
- *height 8cm*
- £750 • Iconastas

Stalin in Uniform ▼
- *1945*

Black painted lacquer box showing Stalin in uniform standing by a railtrack. Made by the Fedoskino factory.
- *height 8cm*
- £890 • Iconastas

Christ Pantocrator ▲
- *circa 1900*

Russian icon depicting Christ Pantrocrator painted on a wooden panel shown holding a bible, covered with a silver riza with an enamel halo and enamel letters on the bible.
- *34cm x 28cm*
- £1,250 • Iconastas

Marshall Voroshilov on Skis ▼
- *1929*

Russian lacquer box depicting the Marshall Voroshilov skiing.
- *18cm x 7cm*
- £1,300 • Iconastas

Icon of Jesus ▲
- *17th century*

Russian icon showing Jesus entering a temple in Jerusalem on a donkey.
- *77cm x 59cm*
- £7,500   • Iconastas

Icon of Virgin and Child ▲
- *17th century*

Icon depicting the Virgin and Child, entitled "Hodegetria", (Pointer of the Way).
- *31cm x 20cm*
- £5,950   • Iconastas

Russian Icon ▲
- *17th century*

Russian icon depicting a saint painted on a wood panel.
- *31cm x 26cm*
- £2,950   • Iconastas

Bronze Ballerina ▼
- *circa 1950s*

Russian bronze Ballerina shown standing on a stone base.
- *height 61cm*
- £5,250   • Zakheim

Iron Statue ▲
- *circa 1950*

Iron statue of Ivan the Terrible in armour on horseback.
- *height 15cm*
- £50   • Zakheim

Bronze Seated Ballerina ▶
- *circa 1950s*

Bronze showing a ballerina seated on a stool, on a square base.
- *height 29cm*
- £3,950   • Zakheim

Writing Equipment

Pens, pencils, portable desks and all the paraphernalia of handwritten communication are the most personal of collectables.

Although inkwells and writing slopes are highly collectable, pens continue to be the mainstay of this market because they make excellent gifts and have an addictive quality that makes them so collectable. Condition is paramount when buying a pen, with strong colour and original fittings being a must. Pens were originally made from hardened rubber and manufacture was expensive. Individual pen makers gave their own names, for example Vulcanite and Raclite, to their rubber compositions, and these are worth looking out for, as they are highly collectable.

By the 1920s however, production had turned to plastic casings. Prominent makers of pens to look out for include Parker, Waterman, Conway Stewart, Mont Blanc and the lesser-known makers, such as Burnham.

Until comparatively recently pens were generally bought from jewellers and may have initials engraved on them. This unfortunately lessens their value, unless the provenance is important. Writing boxes or lap desks are really a portable version of a Davenport and are keenly sought after by the avid collector.

Glass Ink Pot ▼
- 1870

Victorian glass ink pot with faceted glass stopper and brass collar.
- *height 9cm*
- £135   • Jasmin Cameron

Brass Blotter ▲
- 1880–1912

Arts and Crafts brass blotter, stamped "Gesci 9121.2463/10%", from estate of the late Alison Gibbons.
- *length 15cm*
- £275   • Jasmin Cameron

Gold Waterman Pen ▲
- 1920

Gold Waterman fountain pen with basketweave pattern, No.55521/2, with original glass ink dropper.
- *length 14cm*
- £600   • Jasmin Cameron

Pen Wipe and Pen ▶
- 1911

Silver pen wipe with plain oval dip pen, made in London by S. Mordan.
- *height 7cm*
- £165   • Jasmin Cameron

Vesta Box ▲
- *1820*

English bronze vesta box with greyhound on the top, from the late Edward and Alison Gibbons collection, Elm Hill, Worcestershire.
- *height 7cm*
- £320 • Jasmin Cameron

Brass Pen Rack ▲
- *1880*

Victorian six-tier brass pen rack on a square base with pierced foliate design.
- *height 13cm*
- £165 • Jasmin Cameron

Telescopic Pencil ➤
- *1902*

Silver telescopic pencil in sheaf with stirrup loop by Alfred Deeley, Birmingham, 1902.
- *length 3.75cm*
- £220 • Jasmin Cameron

Waterman Pen ▲
- *1920*

American Waterman fountain pen with gold basketweave pattern, No.5552.11/2.
- *length 10cm*
- £600 • Jasmin Cameron

American Fountain Pen ▼
- *1920*

Gold-plated American fountain pen with a gothic design by Maybie Todd & Co.
- *length 13cm*
- £800 • Jasmin Cameron

Pewter Ink Pot ▼
- *1850*

English Court House pewter ink pot inscribed "Stationery Office" on the base.
- *height 10cm*
- £155 • Jasmin Cameron

Expert Tips

Writing boxes are often known as lap desks, and open to provide a sloping leather or velvet-lined writing surface with compartments for pens, pencils and inks, and space for stationery below. They are the equivalent of a portable Davenport desk. Most are pre-Victorian or William IV. They can be highly decorated with some being inlaid with mother of pearl or exotic woods such as macassar ebony, while others are carved in ivory.

Travelling Writing Box ▼

- *1850*
Wood and brass engraved
travelling writing box. Includes
inkwell, quill box, pen, pencil
and rolling blotter.
- *13cm x 8cm*
- £485   • Jasmin Cameron

Mr Punch Paperweight ▼

- *19th century*
English silver-plated Mr Punch
globe paperweight inscribed
"The Punch always on top",
by J. R. Gaunt.
- *height 12cm*
- £430   • Jasmin Cameron

Pencil and Paper Knife ▲

- *1903*
Edwardian combination pencil
and silver paper knife, made
in Birmingham by Perry &
Company.
- *length 15cm*
- £185   • Jasmin Cameron

French Writing Box ▲

- *1860*
French writing slope and
stationery box of outstanding
quality and design. Extensively
decorated with boulle style brass,
ivory and silver on a rosewood
base. Original matching inkwells
and recovered purple velvet
writing tablet. Original key.
- *40cm x 27cm*
- £3,950   • J. & T. Stone

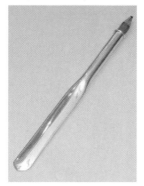

Silver Paper Knife ▲

- *1923*
English rat-tail silver paper knife
with cedar pencil, by Sampson
Mordan.
- *length 18cm*
- £220   • Jasmin Cameron

Ink Blotter ◄

- *circa 1880*
English Victorian brass ink
blotter with brass foliate
decoration.
- *height 23cm*
- £485   • Barham

Lady's Writing Box ▲

• *1875*
Victorian papier mâché lady's
writing slope with extensive
gilded mother-of-pearl
decoration. Original silver topped
inkwells and new internal gilded
navy velvet covering.
• *10cm x 40cm x 29cm*
• £1,575   • J. & T. Stone

Inkwell and Bottles ▲

• *circa 1900*
Adrian Dalpayraat green and
brown leaf design inkstand, with
two glass ink bottles designed for
La Maison Moderne.
• *22cm x 25cm*
• £1,600   • Succession

Parker Pen ▲

• *1942*
Parker Victory fountain pen in
black and green laminated
plastic.
• *length 12.5cm*
• £380   • Jasmin Cameron

Edwardian Ink Stand ▲

• *1904*
Highly decorative ink tray with
pierced gallery, two crystal glass
reservoirs, and moulded apron
raised on shaped feet. Made in
London.
• *26cm x 15cm*
• £2,350   • Stephen Kalms

Glass Ink Stand ▲

• *circa 1925*
Art Nouveau green glass ink
bottle resting on a brass stand.
• *height 8cm*
• £180   • Barham

Stationery Box ▲

• *circa 1840*
Shaped papier mâché stationery
box, the decoration depicting
buildings in a landscape
highlighted with mother of pearl.
• *width 22cm*
• £450   • Hygra

Letter Scale ▼

• *circa 1870*
Victorian letter weighing brass
scales for a post office, standing
on a mahogany base.
• *height 8cm*
• £285   • Barham

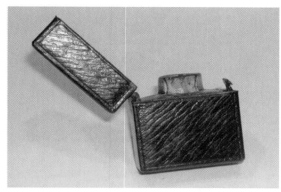

Travelling Inkwell ◄

- *circa 1860s*
Victorian travelling inkwell in original leather case.
- *height 6cm*
- £45   • Barham

Gold-Plated Fountain Pen ▼

- *1920*
Maybie Todd & Co gold-plated fountain pen with a rosette design.
- *length 13cm*
- £800   • Jasmin Cameron

Letter Rack ▲

- *circa 1880*
Victorian pierced brass foliate designed letter rack, with a porcelain ink stand and a dark blue glass ink bottle, resting on a brass shield base with bracket feet.
- *25cm x 20cm*
- £295   • Barham

Writing Slope ▲

- *circa 1880*
Attractive camperwood writing slope with brass banding, possibly made in India.
- *25cm x 52cm x 40cm*
- £750   • Rod Wilson

Writing Box ▼

- *1860*
Victorian coromandel stationery/ writing box with clear glass bottles.
- *28cm x 34cm*
- £580   • Barham

Inlaid Stationery Box ▲

- *1900*
Edwardian mahogany inlaid stationery box with satinwood fan-shaped inlay.
- *height 28cm*
- £375   • Barham

Expert Tips

Pens by makers such as Parker and the gold-plated pens of Todd & Co are highly sought after. Silver pens with nibs are collectable and look most attractive in an elegant art nouveau ink stand, or resting on a highly decorative brass ink stand.

Writing Box ▼

- *circa 1860*

Indian brass inlaid writing box with folding writing slope and compartments inside, the exterior profusely decorated with scrolling foliage.
- *19cm x 30cm x 45cm*
- **£800** • **Arthur Millner**

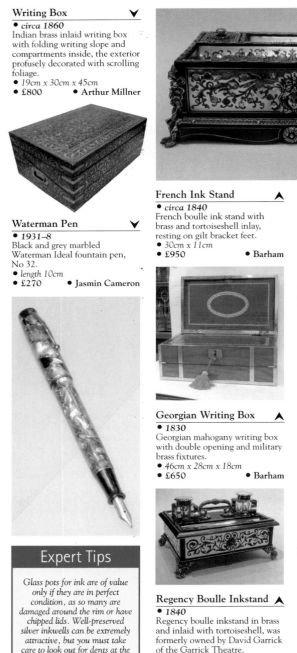

Waterman Pen ▼

- *1931–8*

Black and grey marbled Waterman Ideal fountain pen, No 32.
- *length 10cm*
- **£270** • **Jasmin Cameron**

French Ink Stand ▲

- *circa 1840*

French boulle ink stand with brass and tortoiseshell inlay, resting on gilt bracket feet.
- *30cm x 11cm*
- **£950** • **Barham**

Georgian Writing Box ▲

- *1830*

Georgian mahogany writing box with double opening and military brass fixtures.
- *46cm x 28cm x 18cm*
- **£650** • **Barham**

Regency Boulle Inkstand ▲

- *1840*

Regency boulle inkstand in brass and inlaid with tortoiseshell, was formerly owned by David Garrick of the Garrick Theatre.
- *30cm x 14cm*
- **£750** • **Barham**

Propelling Pencil ▲

- *1900s*

Ivory propelling pencil, decorated with painted enamel flowers, and silver mounts.
- *length 9cm*
- **£79** • **Langfords Marine**

American Eversharp Pen ▲

- *1930*

American Eversharp black and red desk pen with gold banding, with a penholder on a square base.
- *length 22cm*
- **£320** • **Jasmin Cameron**

Expert Tips

Glass pots for ink are of value only if they are in perfect condition, as so many are damaged around the rim or have chipped lids. Well-preserved silver inkwells can be extremely attractive, but you must take care to look out for dents at the base and neck.

Silver Ink Stand ▼

- *1857*

Silver ink stand depicting a desert scene incorporating two glass ink bottles, hand crafted by Hayne & Cater of London.

- *25cm x 35cm*
- £5,250   • Stephen Kalms

Rosewood Writing Slope ▼

- *circa 1835*

Fine inlaid Rosewood and Bird's eye maple writing slope/lap desk with fine mother-of-pearl inlay.

- *width 26cm*
- £750   • Hygra

Rifle Pencil ▶

- *1890*

Fruitwood bolt action rifle pencil with tin barrel and brass banding.

- *length 6cm*
- £165   • Jasmin Cameron

Victorian Inkstand ▲

- *1840*

Victorian electroplate inkstand with glass inkwell, pounce pot, and holder for candle in centre. The whole on a silver stand with foliate design on the feet and rim.

- *length 25cm*
- £575   • Jasmin Cameron

Fountain Pen ▲

- *1951*

English fountain pen with green herringbone design and wide gilt band, by Conway Stewart Duro, No.60, 1951.

- *length 12.5cm*
- £380   • Jasmin Cameron

Ormolu Inkstand ◀

- *circa 1901*

Elkington ormolu inkstand decorated with blue and turquoise enamel, with two cherubs holding a monogrammed plaque, standing on bracket feet, with two clear cut glass bottles with brass and enamelled lids.

- *length 32cm*
- £850   • Barham

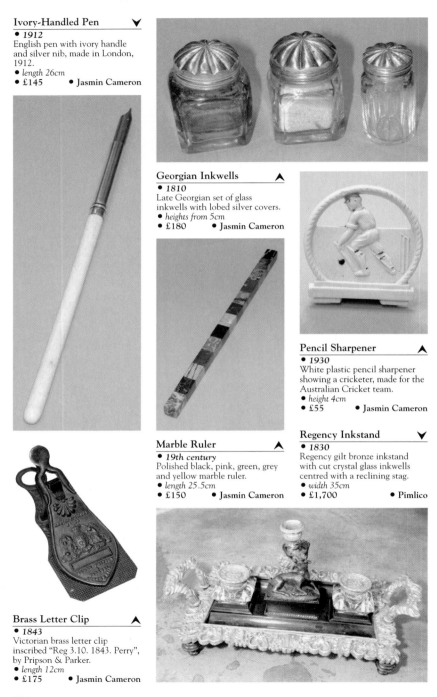

Ivory-Handled Pen ▼
- *1912*

English pen with ivory handle and silver nib, made in London, 1912.
- *length 26cm*
- £145
- Jasmin Cameron

Georgian Inkwells ▲
- *1810*

Late Georgian set of glass inkwells with lobed silver covers.
- *heights from 5cm*
- £180
- Jasmin Cameron

Pencil Sharpener ▲
- *1930*

White plastic pencil sharpener showing a cricketer, made for the Australian Cricket team.
- *height 4cm*
- £55
- Jasmin Cameron

Marble Ruler ▲
- *19th century*

Polished black, pink, green, grey and yellow marble ruler.
- *length 25.5cm*
- £150
- Jasmin Cameron

Regency Inkstand ▼
- *1830*

Regency gilt bronze inkstand with cut crystal glass inkwells centred with a reclining stag.
- *width 35cm*
- £1,700
- Pimlico

Brass Letter Clip ▲
- *1843*

Victorian brass letter clip inscribed "Reg 3.10. 1843. Perry", by Pripson & Parker.
- *length 12cm*
- £175
- Jasmin Cameron

Travelling Inkwell ▼
- *circa 1830*
Travelling carved wood inkwell, painted with castellated screw top, with original glass liner.
- *height 8cm*
- £375   • Bill Chapman

Writing Slope ▲
- *circa 1760*
Extremely rare writing slope with English raised and coloured chinoiserie decoration.
- *width 41cm*
- £1,300   • Hygra

Tunbridge Ware Writing Slope ▲
- *circa 1800*
Very rare, early Tunbridge Ware parquetry writing box/slope/lap desk.
- *width 42cm*
- £950   • Hygra

Rococo Ink Stand ◄
- *1860*
Silver-bronze rococo inkstand in chinoiserie style.
- *28cm x 48cm*
- £1,200   • Sign of the Times

Novelty Pencil ▲
- *1870*
Victorian walnut and silver novelty pencil.
- *height 2cm*
- £225   • Jasmin Cameron

Ink Tray and Bottles ▲
- *1877*
Fine silver ink tray comprising two cut glass ink bottles on a shaped base with leafy shell and scroll border, made in Sheffield.
- *width 33cm*
- £2,900   • Stephen Kalms

Expert Tips

Elegant pens with matching bases from the 1920s' period have increased in value. Do check for damage to the base before you make your purchase as this can devalue the item.

Papier Mâché Inkstand ►
- *circa 1850*
Papier mâché inkstand with original inkwells and pen-trays, mother-of-pearl decoration stamped on underside "Jennens & Bettridge Makers to the Queen 97".
- *width 31cm*
- £340   • Hygra

Main Chinese Periods

SHANG DYNASTY	C. 1523 – 1027 BC
CHOW DYNASTY	1027 – 221 BC
WARRING STATES PERIOD	481 – 221 BC
CH'IN DYNASTY	221 – 206 BC
HAN DYNASTY	206 BC – 220 AD
THREE KINGDOMS	220 – 280
SIX DYNASTIES	280 – 589
NORTHERN WEI	385 – 535
EASTERN WEI	535 – 550
WESTERN WEI	535 – 557
NORTHERN CH'I	550 – 577
NORTHERN CHOW	557 – 581
LIU SUNG (SOUTH)	420 – 478
SOUTHERN CH'I	479 – 501
LIANG	502 – 557
CH'EN	557 – 588
SUI DYNASTY	589 – 618
T'ANG	618 – 906
FIVE DYNASTIES	907 – 959
SUNG DYNASTIES	960 – 1280
YUAN DYNASTIES	1280 – 1368
MING DYNASTIES	1368 – 1643
CH'ING DYNASTIES	1644 – 1912

Ming Period

HUNG WY	1368 – 1398
CHIEN WIEN	1399 – 1402
YUNG LO	1403 – 1424
HUNG HSI	1425 – 1425
HSUAN TE	1426 – 1435
CHENG T'UNG	1436 – 1449
CHING T'AI	1450 – 1457
T'IEN SHUN	1457 – 1464
CH'ENG HUA	1465 – 1487
HUNG-CHIH	1488 – 1505
CHENG TE	1506 – 1521
CHIA CHING	1522 – 1566
LUNG CH'ING	1567 – 1572
WAN LI	1573 – 1619

Ch'ing Period

SHUNG CHIH	1644 – 1661
K'ANG HSI	1662 – 1722
YUNG CHENG	1723 – 1735
CH'IENG LUNG	1736 – 1795
CHIA CH'ING	1796 – 1820
TAO KUANG	1821 – 1850
HSIEN FENG	1851 – 1861
T'UNG CHIH	1862 – 1873
KUANG HSU	1874 – 1908
HSUAN T'UNG	1909 – 1912

Korean Periods

LO LANG	106 BC – 313 AD
PAEKCHE	18 BC – 663 AD
KOGURYO	37 BC – 668 AD
SILLA	57 BC – 668 AD
GREAT SILLA	668 – 936
KORYO	918 – 1392
YI	1392 – 1910

Japanese Periods

JOMON PERIOD	1000 BC – 200 BC
YAYOI PERIOD	200 BC – 500 AD
TUMULUS PERIOD	300 – 700
ASUKA PERIOD	552 – 645
EARLY NARA PERIOD	645 – 710
NARA PERIOD	710 – 794
EARLY HEIAN PERIOD	794 – 897
HEIAN OR FUJIWARA PERIOD	897 – 1185
KAMAKURA PERIOD	1185 – 1392
ASHIKAGA PERIOD	1392 – 1573
MOMOYAMA PERIOD	1573 – 1615
TOKUGAWA PERIOD	1615 – 1868

French General Periods

FRANÇOIS-PREMIER	1515 – 1547	Reign of Francis I
HENRI-DEUX	1547 – 1559	Reign of Henri II
	1559 – 1560	Reign of Francis II
	1560 – 1574	Reign of Charles IX
	1574 – 1589	Reign of Henri III
HENRI-QUATRE	1589 – 1610	Reign of Henri IV
LOUIS-TREIZE	1610 – 1643	Reign of Louis XIII
LOUIS-QUATORZE	1643 – 1715	Reign of Louis XIV
LOUIS-QUINZE	1715 – 1774	Reign of Louis XV
LOUIS-SEIZE	1774 – 1793	Reign of Louis XVI
EMPIRE	1799 – 1814	Reign of Napoleon

English General Periods

TUDOR	1485 – 1558	Reigns of Henry VII Henry VIII Edward VI Mary
ELIZABETHAN	1558 – 1603	Reign of Elizabeth I
JACOBEAN	1603 – 1649	Reigns of James I Charles I
COMMONWEALTH	1649 – 1660	Protectorship of Cromwell
CAROLEAN / LATE STUART	1660 – 1689	Reigns of Charles II James II
WILLIAM AND MARY	1689 – 1702	Reign of William and Mary
QUEEN ANNE	1702 – 1727	Reigns of Anne George I
GEORGIAN	1727 – 1820	Reigns of George II George III
REGENCY	1800 – 1830	Reigns of George III George IV
WILLIAM IV	1830 – 1837	Reign of William IV
VICTORIAN	1837 – 1901	Reign of Victoria
EDWARDIAN	1901 – 1910	Reign of Edward VII

English Monarchs since 1066

WILLIAM I	1066 – 1087
WILLIAM II	1087 – 1100
HENRY I	1100 – 1135
STEPHEN	1135 – 1154
HENRY II	1154 – 1189
RICHARD I	1189 – 1199
JOHN	1199 – 1216
HENRY III	1216 – 1272
EDWARD I	1272 – 1307
EDWARD II	1307 – 1327
EDWARD III	1327 – 1377
RICHARD II	1377 – 1399
HENRY IV	1399 – 1413
HENRY V	1413 – 1422
HENRY VI	1422 – 1461
EDWARD IV	1461 – 1470
HENRY VI	1470 – 1471
EDWARD I	1471 – 1483
EDWARD	1483 – 1483
RICHARD III	1484 – 1485
HENRY VI	1485 – 1509
HENRY VIII	1509 – 1547
EDWARD VI	1547 – 1553
MARY	1553 – 1558
ELIZABETH	1558 – 1603
JAMES I	1603 – 1625
CHARLES I	1625 – 1649
COMMONWEALTH	1649 – 1660
CHARLES II	1660 – 1685
JAMES II	1685 – 1688
WILLIAM AND MARY	1688 – 1694
WILLIAM III	1694 – 1702
ANNE	1702 – 1714
GEORGE I	1714 – 1727
GEORGE II	1727 – 1760
GEORGE III	1760 – 1820
GEORGE IV	1820 – 1830
WILLIAM IV	1830 – 1837
VICTORIA	1837 – 1901
EDWARD VII	1901 – 1910
GEORGE V	1910 – 1936
EDWARD VIII	1936 – 1936
GEORGE VI	1936 – 1952
ELIZABETH II	1952 –

Not all of the terms that follow appear in this volume, but they may all prove useful in the future.

abadeh Highly-coloured Persian rug.

acacia Dull yellow hardwood with darker markings used for inlay and bandings towards the end of the eighteenth century.

acanthus A leaf motif used in carved and inlaid decoration.

Act of Parliament clock Eighteenth-century English clock, wall mounted and driven by weights, with a large, unglazed dial and a trunk for weights. These clocks often hung in taverns and public places and were relied on by the populace after the Act of Parliament of 1797, which introduced taxation on timepieces.

air-beaded Glass with air bubbles resembling beads.

air-twist Spiral pattern enclosed in a glass stem with air bubbles.

albarello Waisted ceramic drug jar.

alder Wood used for country-style furniture in the eighteenth century.

ale glass Eighteenth-century glass drinking vessel with long stem and tall, thin bowl.

amboyna West Indian wood used for veneers, marquetry and inlays. Light brown with speckled grain.

anchor escapement Late seventeenth-century English invented clock movement, named after the anchor shape of the linkage which moves the escape wheel.

angle barometer Also known as signpost barometers. Barometers where the movement of mercury is shown almost on the horizontal.

andiron Iron support for burning logs.

annulated Ringed (of glass).

apostle spoon Spoon with the figure of an apostle as the finial.

applied Attached or added, rather than modelled or carved as part of the body.

apron The decorative panel of wood between the front legs of a chair or cabinet.

arbor The axle on which the wheel of a clock's mechanism is mounted.

arch (clockmaking) The arch above the dial of a post-1700 longcase clock.

argyle Double-skinned metal pouring jugs and tea and coffee pots.

armoire French wardrobe, linen press or large cupboard.

ash Hardwood used for making country furniture and for its white veneer.

astragal Small semi-circular moulding, particularly used as glazing bar in furniture.

automaton clock A clock where the strike is performed by mechanically operated figures.

backboard The unseen back of wall furniture.

backplate The rear plate supporting the movement of a clock, often the repository of engraved information relating to its manufacture.

baff Knot in rug-making.

balance Device counteracting the force of the mainspring in a clock's movement.

balloon-back chair Popular, rounded-backed Victorian dining or salon chair.

baluster (adj.) Having a dominant convex swell at the base, culminating in a smaller, concave one at the neck. (noun) One of a set of upright posts supporting a balustrade.

banjo barometer Wheel barometer dating from circa 1775-1900, with shape resembling a banjo.

barley-sugar twist Spiral-turned legs and rails popular in the seventeenth century. Colloquial.

bat printed Transfer printed (of ceramics).

beech Hardwood used in the manufacture of country furniture and, when stained, as a substitute for mahogany.

bellarmine Stoneware flagon made in Germany from the sixteenth century.

bergère French for an armchair, used in English to describe a chair with caned back and sides.

bevel Decorative, shaved edge of glass, particularly mirror.

bezel The metal rim of a glass cover or jewel.

bird-cage Support mechanism at the top of the pedestal of some eighteenth-century tilt-top tables.

birch Hardwood used principally for carcassing; occasionally for low-quality veneer.

bird's eye maple Wood of the sugar maple with distinctive figure caused by aborted buds. Used in veneering.

biscuit (bisque) Ceramics fired but unglazed, originating in France in the eighteenth century.

blind fretwork Fretwork carving on a solid background.

block front Front shaped from thick boards allowing for a recessed centre section.

blue-dash Blue dabs around the rim of a delftware plate.

bob The weight at the bottom of a pendulum.

bobbin Turned furniture element, resembling a row of connected spheres.

bocage Foliage, bushes and shrubs supporting, surrounding or standing behind porcelain or pottery figures.

bombé Having an outswelling front.

bone china Clay with bone ash in the formula, almost entirely porcellanous. First produced at the end of the eighteenth century.

bonheur du jour Small, lady's writing desk with a cabinet and drawers above. Originally French, from the mid eighteenth century.

bottle glass Low quality coloured glass for bottles, jars etc.

boulle An eighteenth-century marquetry style employing brass and tortoiseshell.

boxlock Flintlock gun with the mechanism enclosed in the breach.

boxwood Pale yellow, close-grained hardwood used for carving and turning and for inlay and pattern veneers.

bow front Convex curve on the front of chests of drawers.

bracket clock Domestic clock so called because of the necessity of standing it on a bracket to allow its weights to hang down, the term later applied to domestic clocks of the eighteenth and nineteenth centuries regardless of their motive force.

bracket foot Plain foot carved into the rail or stretcher to form an ornamental bracket.

brandy saucepan Miniature, bulbous or baluster shaped saucepan with long handle at right angles to the spout.

breakfront Describing a piece of furniture with a central section which projects forward.

breech Rear end of the barrel of a gun.

breech-loading Gun loaded through an opening in the breech.

bright cut Late eighteenth-century silver engraving technique, making the design brilliant in relief.

Bristol glass Eighteenth century coloured (often blue) glass produced in Bristol.

Britannia metal Form of refined pewter used as a silver substitute in the early nineteenth century.

British plate Silver substitute from the nineteenth century, immediately preceding the introduction of EPNS.

broken arch Arch above the dial of a long-case clock which is less than a semi-circle, indicating an early Georgian date.

broken pediment Pediment with a symmetrical break in the centre, often accommodating an urn or some such motif.

bun foot Flattened spherical foot often found on later seventeenth-century furniture.

bureau Desk with a fall front enclosing a fitted interior, with drawers below.

bureau bookcase Bureau with glazed bookcase above.

burr Veneer used in furniture making, with a decorative pattern caused by some abnormality of growth or knotting in the tree. Usually taken from the base of the tree.

cabriole leg Leg of a piece of furniture that curves out at the foot and in at the top.

Introduced in the seventeenth century.

caddy Tea caddy.

caddy spoon Short-handled, large bowled spoon for extracting tea from the caddy.

calendar / date aperture Window in the dial of a clock displaying day, month or date.

canted corner Decoratively angled corner.

canterbury An eighteenth-century container for sheet music.

carcase/carcass The inner frame of a piece of furniture, usually made of inferior wood for veneering.

card case Case for visiting cards, usually silver, nineteenth century.

carriage clock Portable timepiece, invented in nineteenth-century France, with handle above.

cartel clock Eighteenth-century French wall clock with profusely decorated case.

case furniture Furniture intended as a receptical, e.g. chest of drawers.

caster / castor 1. Sprinkling vessel for e.g. sugar. 2. Pivoted wheel attached to foot.

Castleford ware Shiny white stoneware made in Castleford and elsewhere from circa 1790.

caudle cup Covered cup, often in silver.

cellaret A wine cooler or container, usually eighteenth century.

centrepiece Ornament designed to sit in the centre of a dining table. Often in silver.

chafing dish Serving dish, often in silver, with stand incorporating a spirit lamp to retain heat.

chain fusée The fusée of a clock from which a chain unwinds on to the barrel of the mainspring.

chamfer A flattened angle; a corner that has been bevelled or planed.

chapter ring The ring on a clock dial on which the numbers of the hours are inscribed.

Chesterfield Deep-buttoned, upholstered settee from the nineteenth century.

chest on chest Tallboy having two chests fitting together, the lower with bracket feet, the upper with pediment. From the seventeenth and eighteenth centuries.

chest on stand Known as a tallboy or highboy, a chest of drawers on a stand.

cheval mirror Tall mirror supported by two uprights on swivels.

chiffonnier Side cupboard, originally, in the eighteenth century, with solid doors, but latterly with latticed or glazed doors.

chinoiserie Oriental-style decoration on lacquered furniture or artefacts.

chronometer Precision timepiece, often for navigation.

circular movement Clock movement of circular plates.

cistern Chamber containing mercury at the base of the tube of a barometer.

claw-and-ball foot Foot modelled as a ball clutched in a claw, frequently used to terminate a cabriole leg.

clock garniture Mantelpiece ornamentation with a clock as centrepiece.

close helmet Helmet covering the whole head and neck.

coaster Small, circular tray, often in silver, for holding a bottle.

cockbeading Bead moulding applied to the edges of drawers.

cock bracket Bracket supporting a watch mainspring.

coin glass Early eighteenth-century English drinking glass with a coin moulded into the knop of the stem.

commode High quality, highly decorated chest of drawers or cabinet, with applied mounts.

compensated pendulum Pendulum with mercury reservoir, the mercury rising and falling to compensate for the effects on the pendulum of changes of temperature.

composition Putty-like substance for moulding and applying to e.g. mirror frames, for gilding.

console table Often semi-circular table intended to stand against a wall on the pier between two windows (hence also pier table). Usually with matching mirror above.

cordial glass Glass originating in the seventeenth century, with a small bowl for strong drinks.

corner chair Chair with back splats on two sides and a bowed top rail, designed to fit into a corner.

cornice Horizontal top part of a piece of furniture; a decorative band of metal or wood used to conceal curtain fixtures.

coromandel Wood from India's Coromandel coast, used for banding and inlay.

counter-well The small oval wooden dishes inset into early Georgian card tables for holding chips or cash, hence also guinea-well.

country furniture Functional furniture made outside the principal cities. Also provincial furniture.

countwheel strike Clock mechanism determining the number of strikes per hour.

cow creamer Silver or china cream jug modelled as a cow.

crazing Fine cracks in glaze.

creamware Earthenware glazed in a cream colour giving a porcelain effect, in a widely used technique originally devised by Wedgwood in the 1760s.

credence table Late seventeenth-century oak or walnut table with folding top.

credenza Long Victorian side cabinet with glazed or solid doors.

crenellated Crinkly, wavy.

crested china Ware decorated with heraldic crests; originally by Goss, but subsequently by many Staffordshire and German potteries.

crinoline stretcher Crescent-shaped stretcher supporting the legs of some Windsor chairs.

cross-banding Decorative edging with cross-grained veneer.

cruet Frame for holding condiment containers.

crutch The arm connecting a clock's pendulum to the pallet arbor.

cuirass Breastplate (of armour).

cup and cover Round turning with a distinctly separate top, common on legs until circa 1650.

damascene Inlay of precious metal onto a body of other metal for decorative purposes.

davenport Small English desk, reputedly originally produced by Gillow for a Captain Davenport in 1834. A day-bed or sofa in the USA.

deadbeat escapement Version of the anchor escapement that eliminates recoil and improves accuracy.

deal Sawn pine wood.

delftware Seventeenth- and eighteenth-century tin-glazed earthenware, often decorated in the style of Chinese blue and white porcelain or after Dutch seventeenth-century painting, after the style pioneered by the Delft pottery.

Delft ware Items of delftware which actually emanate from Delft.

dentil Small, block-shaped moulding found under a furniture cornice.

dialplate Frontplate of a clock.

diamond cut (of glass) Cut in diamond shape.

dinanderie Fifteenth-century brass artefact from the factories of Dinant, Belgium.

dished table top Hollowed-out, solid top, particularly of a pie-crust, tripod table.

distressed Artificially aged.

dovetails Interlocking joints used in drawers.

double-action A gun which may be cocked or self-cocking.

douter Scissor-like implement for extinguishing a candle.

dowel Peg holding together wooden joint.

dram glass Small, short-stemmed glass with rounded bowl.

drop-in seat Framed, upholstered seat which sits in the framework of a chair.

drop handle Pear-shaped brass furniture handle of the late seventeenth and early eighteenth centuries.

drop-leaf table Table with a fixed central section and hinged flaps.

drum table Circular writing table on a central pedestal with frieze drawers.

dry-edge With unglazed edges.

dummy drawer False drawer with handle.

Dutch strike Clock chime which strikes the next hour on the half hour.

ebonize To stain a wood to the dark colour of ebony.

ebony Much imitated exotic black hardwood, used as veneer in Europe from the seventeenth century, generally for very high quality pieces.

écuelle Two-handled French soup bowl with cover and stand, often Sèvres.

electroplate The technique of covering one metal with the thin layer of another.

elm Hardwood used in the manufacture of chair seats, country furniture and coffins.

embossing Relief decoration.

enamel Second, coloured glaze fired over first glaze.

endstone In a clock mechanism, jewel on which an arbor pivots.

English dial Nineteenth-century English wall clock with large painted dial, previously a fixture in railway stations.

Engshalskrüge Large German tin-glaze jug with cylindrical neck.

épergne Centrepiece of one central bowl surrounded by smaller ones.

escritoire Cabinet with a fall-front which forms a writing surface. With a fitted interior.

escutcheon Brass plate surrounding the edges of a keyhole.

étuis Small, metal oddments box.

everted Outward turned, flaring (e.g. of a lip).

facet-cut (of glass) Cut criss-cross into straight-edged planes.

faience Tin-glazed earthenware.

fairings Porcelain figures, especially German, made in the nineteenth and twentieth centuries in the mould. Usually comical and carrying descriptive captions.

fall front Flap of a bureau or secretaire that pulls out to provide a writing surface.

famille rose Predominantly pink-coloured Oriental porcelain.

famille verte Predominantly green-coloured Oriental porcelain.

fauteuil Open-sided, upholstered armchair with padded elbows.

feather banding Two bands of veneer laid at opposite diagonals.

field Area of a carpet within its decorated borders.

fielded panel Raised panel with chamfered edge fitting into a framework.

figure Natural pattern created by the grain through the wood.

finial Decorative, turned knob.

flamed veneer Veneer cut at an angle to enhance the figuring.

flatware Plates, knives and forks.

flintlock Gun mechanism whereby the priming in the pan is ignited by a spark created by a flint.

flute glass Glass with tall, slender bowl.

fluting Decorative parallel grooving.

foliate carving Carved flower and leaf motifs.

foliot Primitive form of balance for clock mechanisms.

fretwork Fine pierced decoration.

frieze Long ornamental strip.

frit The flux from which glass is made. An ingredient of soft-paste porcelain.

frizzen The metal which a flint strikes to create a spark in a flintlock mechanism.

fruitwood Generally the wood of apple, cherry and pear trees, used for ebonising and gilding, commonly in picture frames.

fusee The conical, grooved spool from which a line or chain unwinds as it is pulled by the mainspring of a clock movement.

gadroon Carved edge or moulded decoration consisting of a series of grooves, ending in a curved lip, with ridges between them.

Gainsborough chair Deep, upholstered armchair with padded, open arms and carved decoration.

galleried Having a wood or metal border around the top edge.

garniture Set of ornamental pieces of porcelain.

gateleg Leg that pivots to support a drop leaf.

gesso Plaster-like substance applied to carved furniture before gilding or moulded and applied as a substitute for carving.

gilt-tooled decoration Gold leaf impressed into the edges of leather on desk-tops.

gimbal Mounting which keeps a ship's barometer level at all times.

girandole Wall-mounted candle holder with a mirrored back.

gorget Item of armour for protecting the throat.

Goss china Range of porcelain, particularly heraldic, produced in Stoke-on-Trent from 1858.

greave Armour protecting lower leg.

Greek key Ancient key-shaped decoration often repeated in fretwork on furniture.

gridiron pendulum Clock pendulum consisting of rods of a mix of metals positioned in such a way that the dynamics of their behaviour when subjected to heat or cold keep the pendulum swing uniform.

halberd Double-headed axe weapon with projecting spike.

half hunter Watch with an opening front cover with glass to the centre and a chapter ring, giving protection to the glass over the dial.

hallmark The mark by which silver can be identified by standard, place of assay and date.

hard-paste porcelain Porcelain made with kaolin and petuntse in the Chinese fashion, pioneered in Europe at Meissen in the early eighteenth century.

hunter Watch with a hinged, opening front cover in solid metal.

husk Formalised leaf motif.

ice glass Glass with uneven, rippling surface.

Imari Japanese porcelain made in and around Arita from the early eighteenth century and shipped to Europe from the port of Imari. Blue, red and gold coloured.

improved A pejorative term implying that a piece has been altered in order dishonestly to enhance its value.

inlay The decorative setting of one material into a contrasting one.

intaglio Incised design.

ironstone Stoneware patented by Mason in 1813, in which slag from iron furnaces was mixed with the clay to toughen the ware.

istoriato Of some Italian majolica, meaning 'with a story on it'.

japanned Painted and varnished in imitation of Oriental style lacquer work.

jardinière An ornamental pot or vase for plants.

jasper ware Variety of coloured stoneware developed by the Wedgwood factory.

joined Manufactured with the use of mortice and tenon joints and dowels, but without glue.

kabuto Japanese Samurai helmet.

kingwood Exotic, purplish hardwood used in veneer.

kneehole desk Desk with a recessed cupboard beneath the frieze drawer.

knop Rounded projection or bulge in the stem of a glass.

lacquer Resinous substance which, when coloured, provides a ground for chinoiserie and gilding.

ladder-back Chair with a series of horizontal back rails.

lantern clock Clocks made in England from the sixteenth century, driven entirely by weights and marking only the hours. Similar in appearance to a lantern.

lappit Carved flap at the top of a leg with a pad foot.

latten Archaic term for brass.

lead crystal Particularly clear, brilliant glass including lead in the process.

lead-glazed the earliest glaze for Western pottery, derived from glass making.

lever escapement Modification of the anchor escapement for carriage clocks and, particularly, watches.

lion's paw foot Foot carved as a lion's paw. Commonly eighteenth century and Regency.

lock Firing mechanism of a gun.

lockplate Base holding firing mechanism on a gun barrel.

loo table Large Victorian card or games table.

longcase clock The 'grandfather' clock, housed in a tall wooden case containing the weights and pendulum.

loper Pull-out arm that supports the hinged fall of a bureau.

lowboy Small side table with cabriole legs, from

the seventeenth century.

lustre ware Ceramic ware decorated with a metallic coating which changes colour when fired.

mahogany The hardwood most used in the production of furniture in England in the eighteenth and nineteenth centuries. Used as a solid wood until the nineteenth century, when its rarity led to its being used for veneer.

majolica Originally tin-glazed earthenware produced in Renaissance Italy, subsequently all nineteenth century wares using the same technique.

mantel clock Clock with feet designed to stand on a mantelpiece.

maple North American hardwood used for its variety of veneers.

marine chronometer Precision clock for use in navigation at sea.

marquetry The use of wooden and other inlays to form decorative patterns.

married Pejorative term applied to a piece of furniture which is made up of more than one piece of the same period.

matchlock Firing mechanism of a gun achieved by lowering a slow match into the priming pan.

mazarine Metal strainer fitting over a dish.

mercury twist Air-twist in glass of a silver colour.

millefiori Multi-coloured or mosaic glass.

moonwork Clock mechanism which computes and displays the phases of the moon.

moquette Heavy imitation velvet used for upholstery.

morion Helmet with upturned front peak.

mortice Slot element of a mortice and tenon joint.

moulding decorative, shaped band around an object or a panel.

mount Invariably metal mounting fitted to a piece of furniture.

mule chest Coffer with a single row of drawers to the base.

musical clock Clock with a cylinder which strikes bells to play a tune.

Nailsea Late eighteenth-century, boldly coloured, opaque glass from Nailsea, near Bristol.

nest of tables Set of three or four occasional tables which slot into each other when not in use.

oak Hardwood which darkens with age, predominant in English furniture manufacture until the middle of the seventeenth century.

obverse The front side of a coin or medal.

ogee An S-shaped curve.

ogee arch Two S-shaped curves coming together to form an arch.

oignon Onion-shaped French watch of the eighteenth century.

ormolu From French *dorure d'or moulu*: 'gilding with gold paste', gold-coloured alloy of copper, zinc, and sometimes tin, in various proportions but usually containing at least 50% copper. Ormolu is used in mounts (ornaments on borders, edges, and as angle guards) for furniture, especially eighteenth-century furniture.

orrery Astronomical clock which shows the position of heavenly bodies. Named after Charles Boyle, fourth Earl of Orrery.

overglaze See enamel.

overmantel mirror Mirror designed to hang over a mantelpiece.

ovolo A rounded, convex moulding, making an outward curve across a right angle.

oyster veneer Veneer resembling an open oyster shell, an effect achieved by slanting the cut across the grain of a branch.

pad foot Rounded foot on a circular base, used as termination for cabriole legs.

pair-case A double case for a watch, the inner for protection of the movement, the outer for decoration.

pallet Lever that engages in a clock's escapement wheel in orderb to arrest it.

papier mâché Moulded and lacquered pulped paper used to make small items of furniture and other artefacts.

parian Typically uncoloured, biscuit-style porcelain developed in the nineteenth century by Copeland and named after Parian white marble.

parquetry Veneered pattern using small pieces of veneer, often from different woods, in a geometrical design.

patera Circular ornament made of wood, metal or composition.

patina The layers of polish, dirt, grease and general handling marks that build up on a wooden piece of furniture over the years and give it its individual signs of age, varying from wood to wood.

pearlware White, shiny earthenware, often print decorated.

pedestal desk A flat desk with a leathered top standing on two banks of drawers.

pediment Architectural, triangular gable crowning a piece of furniture or a classical building.

pegged furniture Early furniture constructed with the use of mortice and tenon joints and pegged together with dowels.

pembroke table Small, two-flapped table standing on four legs or a pedestal.

pepperette Vessel, often in silver, for sprinkling pepper.

petuntse Chinese name for the feldspathic rock, an essential element of porcelain, which produces a glaze.

pewter Alloy of tin, lead and often various other metals.

pie-crust Expression used to describe the decorative edge of a dished-top tripod table.

pier glass Tall mirror for hanging on a pier between windows.

pietra dura Composition of semi-precious stones applied to panels of – usually Italian – furniture.

pillar (watchmaking) A rod connecting the dial-plate and backplate of a movement.

pillar rug Chinese rug made to be arranged around a pillar.

pine Softwood used for carcassing furniture.

platform base Flat base supporting a central pedestal and table-top above and standing on three or four scrolled or paw feet.

plinth base Solid base not raised on feet.

pole screen Adjustable fire screen.

pommel Knob at the end of the handle of a dagger.

pontil mark Mark made by the pontil, or blowpipe, on the base of hand-blown glass.

porcellanous Having most of the ingredients or characteristics of porcelain.

porringer Large, two-handled cup with cover.

potboard Bottom shelf of a dresser, often just above the floor.

pounce box A sprinkler for pounce, a powder for drying ink.

Prattware Staffordshire earthenware of the late eighteenth and early nineteenth centuries, decorated in distinctive colours on a buff ground.

print decoration Mass-produced decoration. Not hand painting.

provincial furniture See **country furniture**.

punch bowl Large bowl for the retention and dispensation of punch.

quartered top Flat surface covered with four pieces of matching veneer.

quartetto tables Nest of four occasional tables.

quillon Cross-piece of a sword.

rail A horizontal member running between the outer uprights of a piece of furniture.

rating nut Nut under the bob of a clock's pendulum by which the rate of swing may be adjusted.

redware Primitive eighteenth-century American ware made from a clay which turns red when fired.

reeding Parallel strips of convex fluting.

re-entrant corner Shaped indentation at each corner of a table.

register plate Plate on a barometer with inscriptions to be read against the level of mercury.

regulator Precision timepiece of the eighteenth century.

relief Proud of the surface.

repeating work Mechanism by which the pull of a cord or the press of a button operates the striking mechanism of a clock or watch to the last hour.

repoussé An embossed design which has been refined by chasing.

rosewood Named after its smell when newly cut, rather than its flower or colour, a dark-brown hardwood with an attractive stripe or ripple, used for veneering.

rule joint Hinge on furniture which fits so well that, when open, no join can be detected between two hinged parts.

runners Strips of wood, fitted to furniture, on which drawers slide.

sabre leg Chair leg in the shape of a sabre, typical of the Regency period.

saltglaze Stoneware in which salt is added to the recipe creating a porcellanous, glassy surface. Dates back to the early eighteenth century.

salver A large metal dish or tray for transporting smaller dishes.

satinwood A light golden-coloured, close-grained hardwood used for veneer, panelling and turning from the mid-eighteenth century onwards.

scagiola Composite material resembling marble.

scalloped Having a series of circular edges in the shape of a scallop shell.

scalloped leaf Serpentine flap on some pembroke tables.

sconce 1. Cup-shaped candle holder. 2. Metal plate fixed to the wall, supporting candle holder or light.

scratch blue Eighteenth-century saltglaze decoration where the body is incised and the incisions painted blue.

scroll, scrolling Carving or moulding of a curled design.

seat rail Horizontal framework below the chair seat uniting the legs.

secretaire Writing desk with false drawer front which lets down to reveal a writing surface and fitted interior.

secretaire bookcase Secretaire with bookcase fitted above.

serpent The arm holding the match or flint by which the priming of a gun was ignited.

serpentine Of undulating shape.

settee Upholstered settle.

settle Hard bench seat with back. The earliest form of seating for two or more people.

Sheffield plate Rolled sheet silver placed either side of a layer of copper and fused. Recognised by the Sheffield assay office in 1784, but made elsewhere, notably Birmingham, as well.

shoe piece Projection on the back rail of a chair into which the splat fits.

side chair Chair without arms designed to stand against the wall.

side table Any table designed to stand against the wall.

skeleton clock Clock with the workings exposed.

slipware Earthenware to which mixed clay and water has been added as decoration.

sofa Well-upholstered chair providing seating for two or more people.

sofa table Rectangular table with hinged flaps designed to stand behind a sofa.

soft-paste porcelain Porcelain using frit or soapstone instead of the petuntse of hard-paste porcelain. English, from the eighteenth century.

spade foot Square, tapered foot.

spandrel Pierced, decorative corner bracket found at the tops of legs.

sparrow-beak jug Jug with a triangular spout.

spill vase Container for lighting-tapers.

spindle Thoroughly turned piece of wood. The upright bars of a spindle-back chair.

splat The central upright of a chair back.

sprig Applied or relief ornamentation of any kind on a ceramic artefact.

squab Detachable cushion or upholstered seat of a chair or bench.

standish Inkstand, often in silver.

stick barometer Barometer with a straight, vertical register plate running alongside the mercury tube.

stiles Archaic term for the vertical parts of the framework of a piece of furniture.

stoneware Earthenware that is not porous after firing.

stretcher Rail joining the legs of a table or chair.

strike / silent ring Dial to disengage or re-engage the striking of a clock.

stringing Fine inlaid lines around a piece of furniture.

stirrup cup Cup used for alcoholic refreshment prior to hunting, usually shaped in the head of a fox or, less usually, a hound.

stuff-over seat Chair that is upholstered over the seat rail.

subsidiary dial Small dial, usually showing seconds, within the main dial of a clock or watch. Hence **subsidiary seconds**.

swagged With applied strips formed in a mould (of metal).

swan-neck pediment Pediment with two broken curves.

swan-neck handle Curved handle typical of the eighteenth century.

sycamore Hardwood of the maple family, light yellow in colour, used for veneering.

tang The end of the blade of a sword, covered by the hilt.

tankard Large beer-mug with a hinged lid and thumb-piece.

tazza Italian plate, cup, basin or wide-bowled glass.

teapoy Small piece of furniture designed for holding tea leaves. Usually Anglo-Indian.

tenons The tongues in mortice and tenon joints.

thumb moulding Decorative concave moulding.

thumb-piece Projection attached to a hinged lid which will open the lid when pressure is applied by the thumb.

tine Prong of a fork.

tin-glazed Lead-glazed earthenware to which tin is added, e.g. majolica.

toilet mirror Small dressing mirror with a box base and drawers.

touch mark Individual mark of the maker of a piece of early English pewter.

transfer Ceramic print decoration using colours held in oil.

trefid spoon A seventeenth-century spoon with the handle terminating in the shape of a bud, usually cleft or grooved into two lobes.

trefoil Having three lobes.

trembleuse Cup-stand with feet.

tripod table Small, round-topped table on three-legged base.

tulipwood Pinkish, naturally patterned hardwood used in veneer.

turnery Any wood turned on a lathe.

tureen Large bowl in porcelain or metal, usually with a lid and two handles.

turret clock Clock of any size driven by a weight suspended by a rope wrapped round a drum.

underglaze Colour or design painted below the glaze of a ceramic artefact.

uniface Medal or coin with modelling on one side only.

urn table Eighteenth-century table designed to hold an urn.

veneer A thin sheet of wood laid across a cheaper carcase or used as inlay decoration.

verge escapement Mechanism for regulating a clock movement before the anchor escapement.

Vesta case Match box for Vesta matches, often in silver, from circa 1850.

vinaigrette Small, eighteenth-century box, often silver, to hold a sponge soaked in vinegar to ward off germs and the unpleasant odours of the day.

wainscot chair Joined chair with open arms and a panelled back.

walnut The hardwood used in England for the manufacture of furniture from the Restoration, originally in solid form but mostly as veneer, particularly burr walnut, after the beginning of the eighteenth century.

well Interior of a plate or bowl.

Wemyss ware Late nineteenth-century lead-glazed earthenware originally from Fife, Scotland.

whatnot Mobile stand with open shelves.

wheel-back chair Originally late eighteenth-century chair with circular back with radiating spokes.

windsor chair Wooden chair with spindle back.

yew Tough, close-grained hardwood used for turning, particularly in chair legs, and in veneer.

Directory of Dealers

There follows a list of antique dealers, many of whom have provided items in the main body of the book and all of whom will be happy to assist within their areas of expertise.

Aaron Gallery
(ref: Aaron)
34 Bruton Street,
London W1X 7DD
Tel: 020 7499 9434
Fax: 020 7499 0072
www.AaronGallery.com

Islamic and ancient art; New Eastern, Greek, Roman and Egyptian antiquities.

Abacus Antiques
(ref: Abacus)
Grays Antiques Market,
58 Davies Street, London W1Y 2LP
Tel: 020 7629 9681

Antiques.

Abbey Green Antiques
(ref: Abbey Green)
Mariaplatts 45,
Utrecht 3511 LL
The Netherlands
Tel: 030 232 8065

Emmy Abe
Stand 33, Bond Street Antiques Centre,
124 New Bond Street,
London W1X 9AE
Tel: 020 7629 1826
Fax: 020 7491 9400

Exclusively selected antique and modern jewellery.

Aberg Antiques
(ref: Aberg)
42 The Little Boltons,
London SW10 9LN
Tel: 020 7370 7253
Fax: 020 7370 7253

Furniture.

A. D. Antiques
The Swan at Tetsworth, High Street,
Tetsworth, Thame,
Oxfordshire, OX9 7AB
Tel: 07939 508171
www.adantiques.com

Decorative arts.

Norman Adams Ltd
8–10 Hans Road,
London SW3 1RX
Tel: 020 7589 5266
Fax: 020 7589 1968
www.normanadams.com

Eighteenth-century fine English furniture, works of art, mirrors, paintings and chandeliers.

After Noah
121 Upper Street,
London N1 8ED
Tel: 020 7359 4281
Fax: 020 7359 4281
www.afternoah.com

Antique furniture, linen and postcards.

After Noah (Kings Road)
(ref: After Noah (KR))
261 Kings Road,
London SW3 5EL
Tel: 020 7351 2610
Fax: 020 7351 2610
www.afternoah.com

Antique furniture, linen and postcards.

Albany Antiques
(ref: Albany)
8–10 London Road, Hindhead,
Surrey GU26 6AF
Tel: 01428 605 528
Fax: 01428 605 528

Georgian furniture, eighteenth-century brass, Victorian antiques, porcelain and statuary.

AM-PM
V35 Antiquarias Antiques Market,
135 Kings Road,
London SW3
Tel: 020 7351 5654

Antique and modern watches.

Paul Andrews Antiques
The Furniture Court,
553 Kings Road,
London SW10 0TZ
Tel: 020 7352 4584
Fax: 020 7351 7815
www.paulandrewsantiques.co.uk

Eclectic furniture, sculpture, tapestries, paintings and works of art.

Angel Antiques
Church Street, Petworth,
West Sussex GU28 0AD
Tel: 01798 343 306
Fax: 01798 342 665

Oak, country furniture.

Antique Warehouse
9–14 Dentford Broadway,
London SE8 4PA
Tel: 020 8691 3062
Fax: 020 8691 3062
www.antiquewarehouse.co.uk

Decorative antiques.

Antiques Pavilion
175 Bermondsey Street,
London SE1 3LW
Tel: 020 7394 7856

Furniture from the Georgian period to the 1930s; also restorations.

Armoury of St James, The
(ref: The Armoury)
17 Piccadilly Arcade,
London SW1Y 6NH
Tel: 020 7493 5083
Fax: 020 7499 4422
www.armoury.co.uk/home

Royal memorabilia and model soldiers.

Sean Arnold Sporting Antiques
(ref: Sean Arnold)
1 Pembridge Villas,
London W2 4XE
Tel: 020 7221 2267
Fax: 020 7221 5464

Sporting antiques.

Victor Arwas Gallery
(ref: Arwas)
3 Clifford Street,
London W1X 1RA
Tel: 020 7734 3944
Fax: 020 7437 1859
www.victorarwas.com

Art Nouveau and Art Deco, glass, ceramics, bronzes, sculpture, furniture, jewellery, silver, pewter, books and posters, from 1880–1940. Paintings, watercolours and drawings, 1880 to date. Original graphics, lithographs, etchings and woodcuts from 1890 to date.

Ash Rare Books
(ref: Ash Books)
153 Fenchurch Street,
London EC3M 6BB
Tel: 020 7626 2665
Fax: 020 7626 2665
www.ashrare.com

Books, maps and prints.

Ashcombe House
(ref: Ashcombe)
Ashcombe Coach House,
Brighton Road, Lewes,
East Sussex BN7 3JR
Tel: 01273 474794
Fax: 01273 705959

Eighteenth and nineteenth-century furniture and decorative objects.

Garry Atkins
107 Kensington Church Street,
London W8 7LN
Tel: 020 7727 8737
Fax: 020 7792 9010
www.englishpottery.com

English and continental pottery from the eighteenth century and earlier.

Aurum
Grays Antiques Market,
58 Davies Street,
London W1K 5LP
Tel: 020 7409 0215
www.aurum.uk.com

Antique and period jewellery, and Shelly china.

**Axia Art Consultants Ltd
(ref: Axia)**
21 Ledbury Road,
London W11 2AQ
Tel: 020 7727 9724
Fax: 020 7229 1272

*Islamic and Byzantine works of art, textiles,
metalwork, woodwork, ceramics and icons.*

B. and T. Antiques
79–81 Ledbury Road,
London W11 2AG
Tel: 020 7229 7001
Fax: 020 7229 2033

*Eighteenth-century Art Deco English and continental
furniture, and objets d'art.*

Dr Colin B. Baddiel
B24 Grays Antiques Market,
Davies Mews,
London W1
Tel: 020 7408 1239
Fax: 020 74939344

Die-cast and tin toys.

David Baker
Grays Mews Antique Market,
1–7 Davies Mews,
London W1Y 2LP
Tel: 020 8346 1387
Fax: 020 8346 1387

Oriental art.

**Barham Antiques
(ref: Barham)**
83 Portobello Road,
London W11 2QB
Tel: 020 7727 3845
Fax: 020 7727 3845

*Victorian walnut and inlaid continental furniture,
writing boxes, tea caddies, inkwells and inkstands,
glass épergnes, silver plate, clocks and paintings.*

**R. A. Barnes Antiques
(ref: R. A. Barnes)**
26 Lower Richmond Road,
London SW15 1JP
Tel: 020 8789 3371
Fax: 020 8780 3195

*Continental glass, English and continental porcelain,
Art Nouveau, small furniture, paintings, English
metalware, eighteenth and nineteenth-century brass,
Belleed and Wedgwood.*

Don Bayney
Grays Mews Antiques Market,
1–7 Davies Mews,
London W1Y 2LP
Tel: 020 7629 3644
Fax: 020 8578 4701

Japanese works of art.

**Bazaart 51 Antiques
(ref: Bazaart)**
51 Ledbury Road,
London W11 2AA
Tel: 020 7615 3472
Fax: 020 7615 472

*Italian ceramics and Venetian glass from
1500–1900.*

**Frederick Beck Ltd.
(ref: F. Beck)**
22–26 Camden Passage,
Islington, London N1 8ED
Tel: 020 7226 3403
Fax: 020 7288 1305

General antiques.

Linda Bee
Grays in the Mews Antiques Market,
1–7 Davies Mews,
London W1Y 1AR
Tel: 020 7629 5921
Fax: 020 7629 5921

Vintage costume jewellery and fashion accessories.

Julia Bennet (Antiques)
Flemings Hill Farm,
Great Easton, Dunmow,
Essex CM6 2ER
Tel: 01279 850279

Eighteenth and early nineteenth-century furniture.

Beverley
30 Church Street,
Marylebone,
London NW8 8EP
Tel: 020 7262 1576
Fax: 020 7262 1576

*English ceramics, glass, metal, wood, pottery,
collectables and decorative items from 1850–1950.*

Andrew Bewick Antiques
287 Lillie Road,
London SW6 7LL
Tel: 020 7385 9025
Fax: 020 7385 9025

Decorative antiques.

Big Baby & Little Baby Antiques
(ref: Big Baby Little Baby)
Grays Antiques Market,
Davies Mews,
London W1
Tel: 020 8367 2441
Fax: 020 8366 5811

Dolls, teddies, prams and related collectables.

Bike Park
63 New Kings Road,
London SW3
Tel: 020 7565 0777

Bikes, rentals, repairs and clothing.

Bizarre
24 Church Street,
London NW8 8EP
Tel: 020 7724 1305
Fax: 020 7724 1316
www.antiques-uk/bazarre

Art Deco, continental furniture, wrought iron, glass, and ceramics.

Oonagh Black Antiques
(ref: Oonagh Black)
Lower Farm House, Coln Rogers,
Gloucestershire GL54 3LA
Tel: 01285 720717
Fax: 01285 720910

French and English country furniture, decorative accessories, and French science and textiles.

John Bly
27 Bury Street,
London SW1Y 6AL
Tel: 020 7930 1292
Fax: 020 7839 4775
www.johnbly.com

Eighteenth and nineteenth-century English furniture, works of art, objets d'art, paintings, silver, glass, porcelain and tapestries.

Paolo Bonino
Stand S001, Alfie's Antique Market,
13–25 Church Street,
London NW8 8DT
Tel: 020 7723 6066

European twentieth-century glass and ceramics.

Book and Comic Exchange
(ref: Book & Comic)
14 Pembridge Road,
London W11 3HL
Tel: 020 7229 8420
www.buy-sell-trade.co.uk

Modern first editions, cult books and comics.

Malcolm Bord Gold Coin Exchange
(ref: Malcolm Bord)
16 Charing Cross Road,
London WC2 0HR
Tel: 020 7836 0631/020 7240 0479/
020 7240 1920

Dealing in all types of coin, medal and bank note.

Julia Boston
2 Michael Road,
London SW6 2AD
Tel: 020 7610 6783
Fax: 020 7610 6784
www.juliaboston.co.uk

Tapestry cartoons, engravings and eighteenth and nineteenth-century decorative antiques.

M. J. Bowdery
12 London Road, Hindhead,
Surrey, GU26 6AF
Tel: 01428 606376

Eighteenth and nineteenth-century furniture.

Patrick Boyd-Carpenter
(ref: P. Boyd-Carpenter)
Unit 331–332 Grays Antiques Market,
58 Davies Street, London W1Y 2LP
Tel: 020 7491 7623
Fax: 020 7491 7623

Wide range of antiques, sixteenth and eighteenth-century sculpture, paintings and prints.

Elizabeth Bradwin
75 Portobello Road,
London W11 2QB
Tel: 020 7221 1121
Fax: 020 8947 2629
www.elizabethbradwin.com

Animal subjects.

Lesley Bragge
Fairfield House, High Street,
Petworth, West Sussex
Tel: 01798 342324

Wine-related items.

**Brandt Oriental Art
(ref: Brandt)**
First Floor, 29 New Bond Street,
London W1Y 9HD
Tel: 020 7499 8835
Fax: 020 7409 1882

Chinese and Japanese works of art.

Bridge Bikes
137 Putney Bridge,
London SW15 2PA
Tel: 020 8870 3934

Bikes.

F. E. A. Briggs Ltd
5 Plaza Parade, Winchester Road,
Romsey, Hampshire SO51 8JA
Tel: 01794 510061

Victorian and Edwardian furniture and textiles.

Aubrey Brocklehurst
124 Cromwell Road,
London SW7 4ET
Tel: 020 7373 0319
Fax: 020 73737612

English clocks and barometers.

**David Brower Antiques
(ref: David Brower)**
113 Kensington Church Street,
London W8 7LN
Tel: 020 7221 4155
Fax: 020 7721 6211
www.davidbrower-antique.com

Porcelain, European bronzes, and Japanese works of art.

Brown
First Floor, 533 Kings Road,
London SW10 0TZ
Tel: 020 7352 2046

Furniture.

**I. and J. L. Brown Ltd
(ref: I. & J. L. Brown)**
632–636 Kings Road,
London SW6 2DU
Tel: 020 7736 4141
Fax: 020 7736 9164
www.brownantiques.com

English country and French provincial antique and reproduction furniture.

**Brown's Antique Furniture
(ref: Browns)**
First Floor, The Furniture Cave,
533 Kings Road,
London SW10 0TZ
Tel: 020 7352 2046
Fax: 020 7352 6354
www.thecave.co.uk

Library and dining, and decorative objects from the early eighteenth century.

S. Brunswick
Alfie's Antiques Market,
13–25 Church Street,
London NW8 8DT
Tel: 020 7724 9097
Fax: 020 8902 5656

Functional and decorative furnishings for house, garden and conservatory.

**Peter Bunting Antiques
(ref: Peter Bunting)**
Harthill Hall, Alport, Bakewell,
Derbyshire DE45 1LH
Tel: 01629 636203
Fax: 01629 636190

Early oak and country furniture, portraits and tapestries.

**Butchoff Antiques
(ref: Butchoff)**
220 Westbourne Grove,
London W11 2RH
Tel: 020 7221 8174
Fax: 020 7792 8923

English and continental furniture, decorative items, porcelain and mirrors.

Butchoff Interiors
229 Westbourne Grove,
London W11 2SE
Tel: 020 7221 8163
Fax: 020 7792 8923

One-off items, textiles, collectables, dining tables, chairs, consoles and accessories.

Vincenzo Caffarella
Alfie's Antique Market,
13–25 Church Street,
London NW8 8DT
Tel: 020 7723 1513
Fax: 020 8731 8615
www.vinca.co.uk

Twentieth-century decorative arts and antiques.

Cameo Gallery
151 Sydney Street,
London SW3 6NT
Tel: 020 7352 0909
Fax: 020 735 20066

Art Nouveau to Art Deco.

Jasmin Cameron
Antiquarias Antiques Market,
135 Kings Road,
London SW3 4PW
Tel: 020 7351 4154
Fax: 020 7351 4154

Drinking glasses and decanters 1750–1910, vintage fountain pens and writing materials.

Canonbury Antiques Ltd
(ref: Canonbury)
174 Westbourne Grove,
London W11 2RW
Tel: 020 7229 2786
Fax: 020 7229 5840
www.canonbury-antiques.co.uk

Eighteenth and nineteenth-century furniture, reproduction furniture and accessories.

Vivienne Carroll
Stand N1, Antiquarius
135–141 Kings Road,
London SW3 4PW
Tel: 020 7352 8882
Fax: 020 7352 8734

Silver, jewellery, porcelain and ivory.

C. A. R. S. of Brighton
(ref: C. A. R. S.)
4–4a Chapel Terrace Mews,
Kemp Town, Brighton BN2 1HU
Tel: 01273 622 722
Fax: 01273 601 960
www.carsofbrighton.co.uk

Classic automobilia and regalia specialists, and children's pedal cars.

Cartoon Gallery, The
(ref: Cartoon Gallery)
39 Great Russell Street,
London WC1 3PH
Tel: 020 7636 1011
Fax: 020 7436 5053

Comics.

Mia Cartwright Antiques
(ref: Mia Cartwright)
20th C. Theatre Arcade,
291 Westbourne Grove (Sats),
London W11
Tel: 01273 579700

Rupert Cavendish Antiques
(ref: R. Cavendish)
610 Kings Road,
London SW6 2DX
Tel: 020 7731 7041
Fax: 020 7731 8302
www.rupertcavendish.co.uk

European twentieth-century paintings.

Cekay
Stand 172, Grays Antique Market,
58 Davies Street,
London W1Y 2LP
Tel: 020 7629 5130
Fax: 020 7730 3014

Antiques.

Ronald G. Chambers Fine Antiques
(ref: Ronald G. Chambers)
Market Square, Petworth,
West Sussex GU28 0AH
Tel: 01798 342305
Fax: 01798 342724
www.ronaldchambers.com

Eighteenth and nineteenth-century furniture, paintings, objets d'art, clocks and jewellery.

Bill Chapman
Shop No. 11, Bourbon/
Hanby Antique Centre,
151 Sydney Street,
London SW3 6NT
Tel: 020 7351 5387

Collectables.

**Chelsea Gallery and Il Libro
(ref: Chelsea Gallery)**
The Plaza, 535 Kings Road,
London SW10 0SZ
Tel: 020 7823 3248
Fax: 020 7352 1579

*Antique illustrated books, literature, prints, maps,
specialising in natural history, travel, architecture
and history.*

**Chelsea Military Antiques
(ref: Chelsea (OMRS))**
Stands N13–14, Antiquarius,
131–141 Kings Road,
London SW3 4PW
Tel: 020 7352 0308
Fax: 020 7352 0308
www.chelseamilitaria.co.uk

*Pre-1945 militaria, edge weapons, medals including
British and foreign campaign/gallantry medals.*

Circa
L43, Grays Mews Antique Market,
1–7 Davies Mews,
London W1Y 2LP
Tel: 01279 466260
Fax: 01279 466 260

Decorative and collectable glass.

**John Clay Antiques
(ref: John Clay)**
263 New Kings Road,
London SW6 4RB
Tel: 020 7731 5677

*Furniture, objets d'art, silver and clocks from the
eighteenth and nineteenth century.*

**Clock Clinic Ltd, The
(ref: Clock Clinic)**
85 Lower Richmond Road, Putney,
London SW15 1EW
Tel: 020 8788 1407
Fax: 020 8780 2838
www.clockclinic.co.uk

*Antique clocks and barometers, all overhauled and
guaranteed.*

Clock Workshop, The
17 Prospect Street, Caversham,
Reading, Berkshire RG4 8JB
Tel: 0118 947 0741
www.lapada.co.uk

English clocks and French carriage clocks.

Cobwebs
73 Avery Hill Road, New Eltham,
London SE9 2BJ
Tel: 020 8850 5611

Furniture, general antiques and collectables.

Cohen & Cohen
101b Kensington Church Street,
London W8 7LN
Tel: 020 7727 7677
Fax: 020 7229 9653
www.artnet.com

Chinese export porcelain works of art.

**Garrick D. Coleman
(ref: G. D. Coleman)**
75 Portobello Road,
London W11 2QB
Tel: 020 7937 5524
Fax: 020 7937 5530
www.antiquechess.co.uk

Antiques, fine chess sets and glass paperweights.

J. Collins & Son
28 High Street, Bideford,
Devon EX39 2AN
Tel: 01237 473103
Fax: 01237 475658

*Georgian and Regency furniture, Victorian oil
paintings and watercolours.*

**Rosemary Conquest
(ref: R. Conquest)**
4 Charlton Place,
London N1 8AJ
Tel: 020 7359 0616

*Continental and Dutch lighting, copper, brass and
decorative items.*

Hilary Conqy
Antiquarias Antiques Market,
135 Kings Road,
London SW3 4PW
Tel: 020 7352 2099

Jewellery.

Marc Constantini Antiques
(ref: M. Constantini)
313 Lillie Road,
London SW6 7LL

Sheila Cook Textiles
184 Westbourne Grove,
London W11 2RH
Tel: 020 7792 8001
Fax: 020 7229 3855
www.sheilacook.co.uk

European costume, textiles from the mid eighteenth century to the 1970s.

Country Seat
Huntercombe Manor Barn,
Henley on Thames,
Oxfordshire RG9 5RY
Tel: 01491 641349
Fax: 01491 641533

Seventeenth to twentieth-century furniture designed by architects, post-war furniture, art, pottery and metalwork.

Sandra Cronan Ltd
18 Burlington Arcade,
London W1V 9AB
Tel: 020 7491 4851
Fax: 020 7493 2758

Art Deco jewellery.

Curios Gardens & Interiors
(ref: Curios)
130c Junction Road,
Tufnell Park,
London N19 5LB
Tel: 020 7272 5603
Fax: 020 7272 5603

Garden furniture, statuary, reclaimed pine furniture and antique furniture.

Ronan Daly Antiques
Alfie's Antiques Market,
13–25 Church Street,
London NW8 8DT
Tel: 020 7723 0429

Michael Davidson
54 Ledbury Road,
London W11 2AJ
Tel: 020 7229 6088
Fax: 020 7792 0450

Eighteenth-century furniture, regency furniture, objects and objets d'art.

Jesse Davis Antiques
(ref: Jesse Davis)
Stands A9–11 Antiquarius,
131–141 Kings Road,
London SW3 4PW
Tel: 020 7352 4314

Nineteenth-century pottery, majolica, Staffordshire and other collectable factories, and decorative objects.

Decodence
21 The Mall,
359 Upper Street,
London N1 0PD
Tel: 020 7354 4473
Fax: 020 7689 0680

Classic plastics such as bakelite, celluloid and catalin; vintage radios, lighting, telephones and toys.

Deep, The
The Plaza, 535 Kings Road,
London SW10 0SZ
Tel: 020 7351 4881
Fax: 020 7352 0763

Recovered shipwrecked items.

Richard Dennis Gallery
(ref: Richard Dennis)
144 Kensington Church Street,
London W8 4BH
Tel: 020 7727 2061
Fax: 020 7221 1283

Antique and modern studio ceramics.

Dial Post House
Dial Post, Near Horsham,
West Sussex RH13 8NQ
Tel: 01403 713388
Fax: 01403 713388

Furniture.

Dodo
Stand Fo73, Alfie's Antiques Market,
13–25 Church Street,
London NW8 8DT
Tel: 020 7706 1545
Fax: 020 7724 0999

Posters, tins and advertising signs, 1890–1940.

Dolly Land
864 Green Lanes,
Winchmore Hill,
London N21 2RS
Tel: 020 8360 1053
Fax: 020 8364 1370
www.dollyland.com

Dolls.

Dolly Land (Steiff Club)
864 Green Lanes,
Winchmore Hill,
London N21 2RS
Tel: 020 8360 1053
Fax: 020 8364 1370
www.dollyland.com

Dolls, Steiff bears, Scalextric, trains and die-cast toys.

Gavin Douglas
75 Portobello Road,
London W11 2QB
Tel: 020 7221 1121
www.antique-clocks.co.uk

Clocks, bronzes, sculpture and porcelain.

**Drummonds Architectural Antiques Ltd
(ref: Drummonds)**
The Kirkpatrick Buildings,
25 London Road, Hindhead,
Surrey GU26 6AB
Tel: 01428 609444
Fax: 01428 609445
www.drummonds-arch.co.uk

Restored original and new bathrooms, reclaimed wood and stone flooring, fireplaces, statues, garden features, lighting, gates and railings, doors and door furniture, radiators, antique furniture, windows and large architectural features.

S. Duggan
First Floor, 533 Kings Road,
London SW10 0TZ
Tel: 020 7352 2046

Antiques.

**Emanouel Corporation U.K. Ltd.
(ref: Emanouel)**
64 South Audley Street,
London W1Y 5FD
Tel: 020 7493 4350
Fax: 020 7499 0996

Important antiques and fine works of art from the eighteenth and nineteenth century, and Islamic works of art.

Emerson
Bourbon & Hanby Antiques Centre,
Shop No. 2, 151 Sydney Street,
London SW3 6NT
Tel: 020 7351 1807
Fax: 020 7351 1807

Corkscrews and collectables.

Penny Fawcett at Tilings
High Street, Brasted,
Kent TN16 1JA
Tel: 01959 564735
Fax: 01959 565795

**Finchley Fine Art Galleries
(ref: Finchley)**
983 High Road, North Finchley,
London N12 8QR
Tel: 020 8446 4848

Watercolours, paintings, fine eighteenth and nineteenth-century furniture, pottery and porcelain.

J. First Antiques
Stand 310, 58 Davies Street,
London W1Y 1LB
Tel: 020 7409 2722
Fax: 020 7409 2722
www.firstsilver18@hotmail.com

Antique English silver collectables.

David Ford
2 Queenstown Road, Battersea,
London SW8
Tel: 020 7622 7547

A. & E. Foster
Little Heysham, Forge Road, Naphill,
Buckinghamshire HP14 4SU
Tel: 01494 562024
Fax: 01494 562024

Antique treen works of art and early treen.

**Judy Fox Antiques
(ref: J. Fox)**
81 Portobello Road/
176 Westbourne Grove,
London W11
Tel: 020 7229 8130/8488
Fax: 020 7229 6998

Furniture.

Lynda Franklin
25 Charnham Street, Hungerford,
Berkshire, RG17 0EJ
Tel: 01488 682404
Fax: 01488 626089

*Antiques and interior design, french furniture
from the seventeenth and eighteenth centuries.*

**French Country Living
(ref: French Country)**
Rue des Remparts,
Mougins, France
Tel: 00 33 4 93 75 53 03
Fax: 00 33 4 93 75 63 03

Antiquities and decoration.

**French Glasshouse, The
(ref: French Glasshouse)**
P14–P16 Antiquarias Antiques Market,
135 Kings Road,
London SW3 4PW
Tel: 020 7376 5394
Fax: 020 7376 5394

*Gallé and Daum glassware, and Japanese works
of art.*

French Room, The
5 High Street, Petworth,
West Sussex GU28 0AU
Tel: 01798 344454
Fax: 01403 269880

French period furniture and decorative wares.

Freshfords
High Street, Freshford,
Bath BA3 6EF
Tel: 01225 722111
Fax: 01225 722991
www.freshfords.com

*Fine antique furniture and works of art, specialising
in dining and library furniture.*

**Charles Frodsham & Co. Ltd
(ref: C. Frodsham)**
32 Bury Street,
London SW1Y 6AU
Tel: 020 7839 1234
Fax: 020 7839 2000

*Clocks, watches, marines chronometers and other
horological items.*

**Fulham Antiques
(ref: Fulham)**
320 Munster Road,
London SW6 6BH
Tel: 020 7610 3644
Fax: 020 7610 3644

*Antique and decorative furniture, lighting and
mirrors.*

**Furniture Vault, The
(ref: Furniture Vault)**
50 Camden Passage,
London N1 8AE
Tel: 020 7354 1047
Fax: 020 7354 1047

Eighteenth and nineteenth-century furniture.

G Whizz
17 Jerdan Place,
London SW6 1BE
Tel: 020 7386 5020
Fax: 020 8741 0062
www.metrocycle.co.uk

Bikes.

Marilyn Garrow
The Farmhouse, Letheringham,
Woodbridge,
Suffolk IP13 7RA
Tel: 01728 746215

Fine and rare textiles.

**Michael German Antiques
(ref: Michael German)**
38b Kensington Church Street,
London W8 4BX
Tel: 020 7937 2771
Fax: 020 7937 8566
www.antiquecanes.com
www.antiqueweapons.com

Antique walking canes, antique arms and armour.

Get Stuffed
105 Essex Road,
London N1 2SL
Tel: 020 7226 1364
Fax: 020 7359 8253
www.thegetstuffed.co.uk

Taxidermy and natural history artefacts.

Ghaznavid
A30 Grays Antiques Market,
1–7 Davies Mews,
London W1Y 2LP
Tel: 020 7629 2813
Fax: 020 8896 2114

Roman.

Gabrielle de Giles
The Barn at Bilsington,
Swanton Lane, Bilsington,
Ashford, Kent TN25 7JR
Tel: 01233 720917
Fax: 01233 720156

*Antique and country furniture, home interiors,
designer for curtains and screens.*

Gooday Gallery, The
(ref: Gooday Gallery)
14 Richmond Hill, Richmond,
Surrey TW10 6QX
Tel: 020 8940 8652

*Arts and Crafts, Art Nouveau, Art Deco, post
modernism, tribal art, and African and Oceanic
masks.*

Gordon's Medals
Stand 14–15 Grays Antiques Market,
Davies Mews,
London W1Y 1AR
Tel: 020 7495 0900
Fax: 020 7495 0115
www.gordonsmedals.co.uk

*Militaria, uniforms, headgear, badges, medals and
documents.*

Gosh
39 Great Russell Street,
London WC1B 3PH
Tel: 020 7436 5053
Fax: 020 7436 5053

Goya
Stand S002, Alfie's Market,
13–25 Church Street,
London NW8 8DT
Tel: 020 7723 6066

Twentieth-century glass.

Anita & Solveig Gray
58 Davies Street,
London W1Y 2LP
Tel: 020 7408 1638
Fax: 020 7495 0707
www.chinese-porcelain.com

*Oriental and European porcelain works of art from
the sixteenth to the eighteenth century.*

Great Grooms Antique Centre
(ref: Great Grooms)
Great Grooms, Parbrook,
Billinghurst, West Sussex RH14 9EU
Tel: 01403 786202
Fax: 01403 786224
www.great-grooms.co.uk

*Furniture, porcelain, jewellery, silver, glass and
pictures.*

Anthony Green Antiques
(ref: Anthony Green)
Unit 39, Bond Street Antiques Centre,
124 New Bond Street,
London W1S 1DX
Tel: 020 7409 2854
Fax: 020 7409 2854
www.anthonygreen.com

Vintage wristwatches and antique pocket watches.

Gregg Baker Oriental Art
(ref: Gregg Baker)
132 Kensington Church Street,
London W8 4BH
Tel: 020 7221 3533
Fax: 020 7221 4410
www.greggbaker.com

Japanese and Chinese works of art.

Henry Gregory
82 Portobello Road,
London W11 2QD
Tel: 020 7792 9221
Fax: 020 7792 9221

*Silver-plate, silver, sporting goods and decorative
antiques.*

Guest & Gray
Grays Mews Antique Market,
1–7 Davies Mews,
London W1Y 2LP
Tel: 020 7408 1252
Fax: 020 7499 1445
www.guest-gray.demon.co.uk

Oriental and European ceramics and works of art, and reference books.

**Guinevere Antiques Limited
(ref: Guinevere)**
574–580 Kings Road,
London SW6 2DY
Tel: 020 7736 2917
Fax: 020 7736 8267

Mirrors, cabinets, lights and chandeliers.

**Gurr and Sprake Antiques
(ref: Gurr & Sprake)**
283 Lillie Road,
London SW6 7LL
Tel: 020 7381 3209
Fax: 020 7381 9502

Eighteenth and nineteenth-century English and French furniture, lighting and unusual architectural pieces.

**Gutlin Clocks and Antiques
(ref: Gutlin)**
616 Kings Road,
London SW6
Tel: 020 7384 2439
Fax: 020 7384 2439
www.gutlin.com

Longcase clocks, mantle clocks, furniture and lighting, all eighteenth and nineteenth century.

**J. de Haan & Son
(ref: J. de Haan)**
PO Box 95, Newmarket,
Suffolk CB8 8ZG
Tel: 01440 821388
Fax: 01440 820410

Old English furniture, barometers, gilt mirrors and fine tea caddies.

**Hadji Baba Ancient Art
(ref: Hadji Baba)**
34a Davies Street,
London W1Y 1LG
Tel: 020 7499 9363
Fax: 020 7493 5504

Near and Middle East antiquities.

**Robert Hales Antiques
(ref: Robert Hales)**
131 Kensington Church Street,
London W8 7LP
Tel: 020 7229 3887
Fax: 020 7229 3887

Oriental and Islamic arms, armour, from medieval to nineteenth century.

Ross Hamilton Antiques Ltd
95 Pimlico Road,
London SW1W 8PH
Tel: 020 7730 3015
Fax: 020 7730 3015
www.lapada.uk/rosshamilton/

Seventeenth to nineteenth-century fine English and continental furniture, sixteenth to twentieth-century paintings, oriental porcelain, objets d'art and bronzes.

Jim Hanson & Argyll Etkin Ltd
18 Claremont Field,
Ottery St Mary,
Devon EX11 1NP
Tel: 01404 815010
Fax: 01404 815224

Philatelist and postal historian.

**Keith Harding's World of Mechanical Music
(ref: Keith Harding)**
The Oak House,
High Street, Northleach,
Gloucestershire GL54 3ET
Tel: 01451 860181
Fax: 01451 861133
www.mechanicalmusic.co.uk

Harpur Deardren
First Floor, 533 Kings Road,
London SW10 0TZ
Tel: 020 7352 2046

Furniture.

**Adrian Harrington Antiquarian Bookseller
(ref: Adrian Harrington)**
64a Kensington Church Street,
London W8 4DB
Tel: 020 7937 1465
Fax: 020 7368 0912
www.harringtonbooks.co.uk

Antiquarian, rare and secondhand books on literature, children's illustrated and travel.

Kenneth Harvey Antiques
(ref: Kenneth Harvey)
Furniture Cave,
533 Kings Road,
London SW10 0TZ
Tel: 020 7352 8645
Fax: 020 7352 3759
www.kennethharvey.com

*English and French furniture, chandeliers and
mirrors from the late seventeenth to twentieth
century, and leather armchairs.*

Victoria Harvey at Deuxieme
(ref: Victoria Harvey)
44 Church Street,
London NW8 8EP
Tel: 020 7724 0738
Fax: 020 7724 0738

General decorative antiques.

W. R. Harvey & Co. Ltd
86 Corn Street, Witney,
Oxfordshire OX8 7BU
Tel: 01993 706501
Fax: 01993 706601
www.wrharvey.co.uk

*Important stock of English furniture, clocks,
pictures, mirrors and works of art from 1680–1830.*

Simon Hatchwell Antiques
(ref: S. Hatchwell)
533 Kings Road,
London SW10 0TZ
Tel: 020 7351 2344
Fax: 020 7351 3520

*English and continental furniture, early nineteenth
and twentieth-century chandeliers, lighting, bronzes,
barometers and clocks, including grandfather clocks.*

Gerard Hawthorn Ltd
(ref: Gerard Hawthorn)
104 Mount Street,
London W1Y 5HE
Tel: 020 7409 2888
Fax: 020 7409 2777

*Chinese, Japanese and Korean ceramics and works
of art.*

Henry Hay
Unit 5054, 2nd floor,
Alfie's Market, 13–25 Church Street,
London NW8
Tel: 020 7723 2548

*Art Deco and twentieth-century chrome and brass
lamps and bakelite telephones.*

Heytesbury Antiques
(ref: Heytesbury)
PO Box 222, Farnham,
Surrey GU10 5HN
Tel: 01252 850893

Antiques.

Holland & Holland
31–33 Bruton Street,
London W1X 8JS
Tel: 020 7499 4411
Fax: 020 7409 3283

Guns.

Hope & Glory
131a Kensington Church Street
(entrance in Peel Street),
London W8 7LP
Tel: 020 7727 8424

*Commemorative ceramics including royal and
political subjects.*

Paul Hopwell
(ref: Paul Hopwell)
30 High Street, West Haddon,
Northampton,
Northamptonshire NN6 7AP
Tel: 01788 510636
Fax: 01788 510044
www.antiqueoak.co.uk

*Seventeenth and eighteenth-century English oak
furniture.*

Jonathan Horne
66c Kensington Church Street,
London W8 4BY
Tel: 020 7221 5658
Fax: 020 7792 3090
www.jonathanhorne.co.uk

Early English pottery, medieval to 1820.

**Howard & Hamilton
(ref: H. & H.)**
151 Sydney Street,
London SW3 6NT
Tel: 020 7352 0909
Fax: 020 7352 0066

Scientific instruments.

**Huxtable's Old Advertising
(ref: Huxtable's)**
Alfie's Market,
13–25 Church Street,
London NW8 8DT
Tel: 020 7724 2200

*Advertising, collectables, tins, signs, bottles,
commemoratives and old packaging from late
Victorian.*

Iconastas
5 Piccadilly Arcade,
London SW1
Tel: 020 7629 1433
Fax: 020 7408 2015

Russian fine art.

J. A. N. Fine Art
134 Kensington Church Street,
London W8 4BH
Tel: 020 7792 0736
Fax: 020 7221 1380

*Japanese, Chinese and Korean ceramics,
bronzes and works of art.*

P. L. James
590 Fulham Road,
London SW6 5NT
Tel: 020 7736 0183

*Gilded mirrors, English and oriental lacquer,
period objects and furniture.*

**Japanese Gallery Ltd
(ref: Japanese Gallery)**
66d Kensington Church Street,
London W8 4BY
Tel: 020 7729 2934
Fax: 020 7229 2934

*Japanese woodcut prints, Japanese ceramics, swords,
armour and Japanese dolls.*

**Jessop Classic Photographica
(ref: Jessop Classic)**
67 Great Russell Street,
London WC1
Tel: 020 7831 3640
Fax: 020 7831 3956

*Classic photographic equipment, cameras
and optical toys.*

Juke Box Services
15 Lion Road,
Twickenham TW1 4JH
Tel: 020 8288 1700
www.jbs-ltd.co.uk

Juke boxes.

**Stephen Kalms Antiques
(ref: Stephen Kalms)**
The London Silver Vaults,
Chancery Lane,
London WC2A 1QS
Tel: 020 7430 1254
Fax: 020 7405 6206

*Victorian and Edwardian silver, silver plate and
decorative items.*

Kieron
K6 Antiquarias Antiques Market,
135 Kings Rd,
London SW3 4PW
Tel: 020 7352 2099

Decorative arts.

Kitchen Bygones
13–15 Church Street,
Marylebone,
London NW8 8DT
Tel: 020 7258 3405
Fax: 020 7724 0999

Kitchenalia.

L. & E. Kreckovic
559 Kings Road,
London SW6 2EB
Tel: 020 7736 0753
Fax: 020 7731 5904

Early eighteenth to nineteenth-century furniture.

La Boheme
c21 Grays Mews,
1–7 Davies Mews,
London W1Y 2LP
Tel: 020 7493 0675

Glass.

Lacquer Chest, The
(ref: Lacquer Chest)
75 Kensington Church Street,
London W8 4BG
Tel: 020 7937 1306
Fax: 020 7376 0223

Military chests, china, clocks, samplers and lamps.

Lamberty
The Furniture Cave,
533 Kings Road,
London SW10 0TZ
Tel: 020 7352 3775
Fax: 020 7352 3759
www.lamberty.co.uk

Langfords
Vault 8–10, London Silver Vaults,
Chancery Lane,
London WC2A 1QS
Tel: 020 7242 5506
Fax: 020 7405 0431
www.langfords.com

Antique and modern silver and silver plate.

Langfords Marine Antiques
(ref: Langfords Marine)
The Plaza, 535 Kings Road,
London SW10 0SZ
Tel: 020 7351 4881
Fax: 020 7352 0763
www.langfords.co.uk

Nautical artefacts.

Judith Lassalle
7 Pierrepont Arcade,
Camden Passage,
London N1 8EF
Tel: 020 7607 7121

Optical toys, books and games.

Lennox Gallery Ltd
(ref: Lennox Gallery)
4 Davies Mews,
London W1Y 1LP
Tel: 020 7491 0091
Fax: 020 7491 0657

Antiquities and numismatics.

Liberty plc
210–220 Regent Street,
London W1R 6AH
Tel: 020 7734 1234
Fax: 020 7578 9876
www.liberty.co.uk

*Twentieth-century furniture, jewellery, ceramics,
clothes and kitchenware.*

Libra Designs
34 Church Street,
London NW8 8EP
Tel: 020 7723 0542
Fax: 020 7286 8518
www.libradeco.com

Linden & Co. (Antiques) Ltd
(ref: Linden & Co.)
Vault 7, London Silver Vaults,
Chancery Lane,
London WC2A 1QS
Tel: 020 7242 4863
Fax: 020 7405 9946

Silver plate and works of art.

P. Lipitch
120 and 124 Fulham Road,
London SW3 6HU
Tel: 020 7373 3328
Fax: 020 7373 8888

General antiques.

Little River Oriental Antiques
(ref: Little River)
135 Kings Road,
London SW3 4PW
Tel: 020 7349 9080

Chinese antiquities and domestic ceramics.

London Antique Gallery
(ref: London Antique)
66e Kensington Church Street,
London W8 4BY
Tel: 020 7229 2934
Fax: 020 7229 2934

Meissen, Dresden, Worcester, Minton, Shelley, Sèvrea, Lalique and bisque dolls.

Stephen Long
348 Fulham Road,
London SW10 9UH
Tel: 020 7352 8226

Painted furniture, small decorative items and English pottery, from 1780–1850.

M. Luther Antiques
(ref: M. Luther)
590 Kings Road, Chelsea,
London SW6 2DX
Tel: 020 7371 8492
Fax: 020 7371 8492

Eighteenth and nineteenth-century English and continental furniture, tables, chairs, mirrors and lighting.

Mac Humble Antiques
(ref: Mac Humble)
7–9 Woolley Street, Bradford on Avon,
Wiltshire BA15 1AD
Tel: 01225 866329
Fax: 01225 866329
www.machumbleantiques.co.uk

Eighteenth and nineteenth-century furniture, needlework, samplers, metalware and decorative items.

Mac's Cameras
(ref: Mac's)
262 King Street, Hammersmith,
London W6 0SJ
Tel: 020 8846 9853

Antique camera equipment.

Magpies
152 Wandsworth Bridge Road,
London SW6 2UH
Tel: 020 7736 3738

Small furniture, kitchenware, door furniture, cutlery, lighting, silver and silver-plate.

C. H. Major
154 Kensington Church Street,
London W8 4BH
Tel: 020 7229 1162
Fax: 020 7221 9676

Eighteenth and nineteenth-century English furniture.

E. & H. Manners
66a Kensington Church Street,
London W8 4BY
Tel: 020 7229 5516
Fax: 020 7229 5516
www.europeanporcelain.com

Eighteenth-century European porcelain and pottery.

Map House, The
54 Beauchamp Place,
London SW3 1NY
Tel: 020 7584 8559
Fax: 020 7589 1041
www.themaphouse.com

Antique maps from fifteenth to nineteenth century, decorative engravings from sixteenth to nineteenth century.

Marks Antiques
49 Curzon Street,
London W1Y 7RE
Tel: 020 7499 1788
Fax: 020 7409 3183
www.marksantiques.com

Antique silver.

David Martin-Taylor Antiques
(ref: D. Martin-Taylor)
558 Kings Road,
London SW6 2DZ
Tel: 020 7731 4135
Fax: 020 7371 0029
www.davidmartintaylor.com

Eighteenth and nineteenth-century continental and English furniture, objets d'art, decorative art, from the eccentric to the unusual.

Megan Mathers Antiques
(ref: M. Mathers)
571 Kings Road,
London SW6 2EB
Tel: 020 7371 7837
Fax: 020 7371 7895

Nineteenth-century continental and English furniture, porcelain, lighting and objets d'art.

A. P. Mathews
283 Westbourne Grove,
London W11
Tel: 01622 812590

Antique luggage.

Gerald Mathias
Stands 3–6, Antiquarius,
131–141 Kings Road,
London SW3 4PW
Tel: 020 7351 1484
Fax: 020 7351 0484
www.geraldmathias.com

*Antique wooden boxes, tea caddies and stationery
cabinets.*

**Sue Mautner Costume Jewellery
(ref: Sue Mautner)**
Stand P13, Antiquarius,
131–141 Kings Road,
London SW3 4PW
Tel: 020 7376 4419

*Costume jewellery from the 1940s and 1950s,
including Christian Dior, Miriam Haskell,
Schiaparelli, Coppolo Toppo, Har and Schreiner.*

Pete McAskie Toys
Stand A12–13, Basement,
1–7 Davies Mews,
London W1Y 2LP
Tel: 020 7629 2813
Fax: 020 7493 9344

*Tin toys from 1895–1980, die-cast toys, robots,
battery operated toys and lead figures.*

**Nicholas E. McAuliffe
(ref: N. E. McAuliffe)**
First Floor, 533 Kings Road,
London SW10 0TZ
Tel: 020 7352 2046

Furniture.

Fiona McDonald
57 Galveston Road,
London SW15 2RZ
Tel: 020 2270 5559

Mirrors, decorative furniture and lighting.

Metro Retro
1 White Conduit Street,
London N1 9EL
Tel: 020 7278 4884/
01245 442047
www.metroretro.co.uk

*Industrial-style and stripped steel furniture, lighting
and home accessories.*

**Midwinter Antiques
(ref: Midwinter)**
31 Bridge Street,
Newcastle under Lyme,
Staffordshire ST5 2RY
Tel: 01782 712483
Fax: 01630 672289

*Seventeenth and eighteenth-century town and
country furniture, clocks and textiles.*

Arthur Millner
180 New Bond Street,
London W1S 4RL
Tel: 020 7499 4484
www.arthurmillner.com

*Indian and Islamic art and related European
material.*

Mora & Upham Antiques
584 Kings Road, London SW6 2DX
Tel: 020 7731 4444
Fax: 020 7736 0440

*Gilded French chairs, antique chandeliers, eighteenth
and nineteenth-century English and continental
furniture and mirrors.*

**More Than Music Collectables
(ref: More Than Music)**
C24–25 Grays Mews Antiques Market,
1–7 Davies Mews,
London W1Y 2LP
Tel: 020 7629 7703
Fax: 01519 565510
www.mtmglobal.com

*Rock and popular music memorabilia, specialising in
The Beatles.*

**Clive Morley Harps Ltd
(ref: Clive Morley)**
Unit 121, Grays Antiques Market,
58 Davies Street,
London W1 5LP
Tel: 020 7495 4495
Fax: 01367 860 659
www.morleyharps.com

Harps.

Robert Morley and Company Limited
(ref: Robert Morley)
34 Engate Street, Lewisham,
London SE13 7HA
Tel: 020 8318 5838
Fax: 020 8297 0720

Pianoforte and harpsichord workshop.

Terence Morse & Son
(ref: T. Morse & Son)
237 Westbourne Gove,
London W11 2SE
Tel: 020 7229 4059
Fax: 020 7792 3284

Eighteenth and nineteenth-century fine English and continental furniture, linen presses and library furniture.

Motor Books
33 St Martin's Court,
London WC2N 4AN
Tel: 020 7836 3800
Fax: 020 7497 2539

Motoring books.

Mousa Antiques
(ref: Mousa)
B20 Grays Mews Antiques Market,
1–7 Davies Mews,
London W1Y 1AR
Tel: 020 7499 8273
Fax: 020 7629 2526

Bohemian glass specialists.

Murray Cards (International) Ltd
(ref: Murray Cards)
51 Watford Way,
London NW4 3JH
Tel: 020 8202 5688
Fax: 020 8203 7878
www.murraycards.com

Cigarette and trade cards.

Music & Video Exchange
(ref: Music & Video)
38 Notting Hill Gate,
London W11 3HX
Tel: 020 7243 8574
www.mveshops.co.uk

CDs, memorabilia, vinyl – deletions and rarities.

Myriad Antiques
(ref: Myriad)
131 Portland Road,
London W11 4LW
Tel: 020 7229 1709
Fax: 020 7221 3882

French painted furniture, garden furniture, bamboo, Victorian and Edwardian upholstered chairs, mirrors and objets d'art.

Stephen Naegel
Grays Antiques Market,
1–7 Davies Mews,
London W1Y 2LP
Tel: 020 7491 3066
Fax: 01737 845147
www.btinternet.com/~naegel

Toys.

Colin Narbeth and Son
(ref: C. Narbeth)
20 Cecil Court,
London WC2N 4HE
Tel: 020 7379 6975
Fax: 0172 811244
www.colin-narbeth.com

Banknotes, bonds and shares of all countries and periods.

New Century
69 Kensington Church Street,
London W8 8BG
Tel: 020 7937 2410
Fax: 020 7937 2410

Design from 1860–1910.

New Kings Road Vintage Guitar Emporium
(ref: Vintage Guitar)
65a New Kings Road,
London SW6 4SG
Tel: 020 7371 0100
Fax: 020 7371 0460
www.newkingsroadguitars.co.uk

Vintage guitars.

Chris Newland Antiques
(ref: C. Newland)
30–31 Islington Green,
Lower Level, Georgian Village,
London N1 8DU
Tel: 020 7359 9805
Fax: 020 7359 9805

Furniture.

John Nicholas Antiques
First Floor, 533 Kings Road,
London SW10 0TZ
Tel: 020 7352 2046
www.thecave.co.uk

*Eighteenth to twentieth-century furniture,
accessories, chandeliers, lighting and tapestries.*

**North West Eight
(ref: North West 8)**
36 Church Street,
London NW8 8EP
Tel: 020 7723 9337

Decorative antiques.

**Oasis Ancient and Islamic Arts
(ref: Oasis)**
Stand E14, Grays Mews Antiques Market,
1–7 Davies Mews,
London W1Y 1AR
Tel: 020 7493 1202
Fax: 020 8551 4487

*Ancient and Islamic art from 2000BC to eighteenth
century.*

Ocean Leisure
11–14 Northumberland Avenue,
London WC2N 5AQ
Tel: 020 7930 5050
Fax: 020 7930 3032
www.oceanleisure.co.uk

**Old Cinema Antiques Warehouse, The
(ref: Old Cinema)**
160 Chiswick High Road,
London W4 1PR
Tel: 020 8895 4166
Fax: 020 8995 4167
www.antiques-uk.co.uk/theoldcinema

*Georgian to Art Deco furniture, large items of
furniture, clocks and silver.*

**Old Cinema Antiques Warehouse, The
(ref: Old Cinema)**
157 Tower Bridge Road,
London SE1 3LW
Tel: 020 7407 5371
Fax: 020 7403 0359
www.antiques-uk.co.uk

*Victorian, Edwardian, reproduction furniture,
babies' chairs, telephone boxes, and reproduction
leather Chesterfields.*

Old Father Time Clock Centre
101 Portobello Road,
London W11 2QB
Tel: 020 8546 6299
Fax: 020 8546 6299
www.oldfathertime.net

Unusual and quirky clocks.

Old School
130c Junction Road,
Tufnell Park,
London N19
Tel: 020 7272 5603

Gardens and interiors.

**Old Telephone Company, The
(ref: Old Telephone Co.)**
The Battlesbridge Antiques Centre,
The Old Granary, Battlesbridge,
Essex SS11 7RE
Tel: 01245 400 601
www.theoldtelephone.co.uk

Antique and collectable telephones.

**Old Tool Chest, The
(ref: Old Tool Chest)**
41 Cross Street,
London N1 0PG
Tel: 020 7359 9313

*Ancient and modern tools of all trades,
woodworking, dentistry, veterinary, mason's, and
books.*

Old World Trading Co
565 Kings Road,
London SW6 2EB
Tel: 020 7731 4708
Fax: 020 7731 1291

*Eighteenth and nineteenth-century English and
French chimney places, fire dogs and grates.*

**Oola Boola Antiques London
(ref: Oola Boola)**
166 Tower Bridge Road,
London SE1 3LS
Tel: 020 7403 0794
Fax: 020 7403 8405

*Victorian, Edwardian, Art Nouveau, Art Deco, and
Arts and Crafts furniture.*

Jacqueline Oosthuizen Antiques
23 Cale Street, Chelsea,
London SW3 3QR
Tel: 020 7352 6071
Fax: 020 7376 3852

Staffordshire pottery and jewellery.

Pieter Oosthuizen
(ref: P. Oosthuizen)
Unit 4, Bourbon Hanby Antiques Centre,
151 Sydney Street,
London SW3
Tel: 020 7460 3078
Fax: 020 7376 3852

Dutch and European Art Nouveau pottery and Boer War memorabilia.

Oriental Rug Gallery
(ref: Oriental)
230 Upper High Street,
London W1Y 5HF
Tel: 020 7493 0309
Fax: 020 7629 2665
www.orientalruggallery.com

Russian, Afghan, Turkish and Persian carpets, rugs, kelims and oriental objets d'art.

Paul Orssich
2 St Stephens Terrace,
London SW8 1DH
Tel: 020 7787 0030
Fax: 020 7735 9612
www.orssich.com

Maps and 20,000 rare secondhand books.

Fay Orton Antiques
(ref: Fay Orton)
First Floor, 533 Kings Road,
London SW10 0TZ
Tel: 020 7352 2046

Furniture.

Pacifica
Block 7, 479 Park West Place,
Edgware Road, London W2
Tel: 020 7402 6717

Tribal art.

Pars Antiques
(ref: Pars)
35 St George Street,
London W1R 9FA
Tel: 020 7491 9889
Fax: 020 7493 9344

Antiquities.

Pendulum of Mayfair
King House, 51 Maddox Street,
London W1R 9LA
Tel: 020 7629 6606
Fax: 020 7629 6616

Clocks: including longcase, bracket and wall, and Georgian period furniture.

Percy's Ltd
16 The London Silver Vaults,
Chancery Lane,
London WC2A 1QS
Tel: 020 7242 3618
Fax: 020 7831 6541

Eighteenth and nineteenth-century decorative silver and plate.

Trevor Philip & Son Ltd
75a Jermyn Street,
London SW1Y 6NP
Tel: 020 7930 2954
Fax: 020 7321 0212
www.trevorphilip.demon.co.uk

Early scientific instruments, and seventeenth to nineteenth-century globes.

Photographer's Gallery, The
(ref: Photo. Gallery)
5 Great Newport Street,
London WC2H 7HY
Tel: 020 7831 1772
Fax: 020 7836 9704
www.photonet.org.uk

David Pickup Antiques
(ref: David Pickup)
115 High Street, Burford,
Oxfordshire OX18 4RG
Tel: 01993 822555

Fine English furniture, emphasis on the Cotswold Arts and Crafts movement and early twentieth century.

Pillows of Bond Street
(ref: Pillows)
Bond Street,
London W11
Tel: 0468 947265

Pillows.

Pimlico Antiques
(ref: Pimlico)
Moreton Street,
London SW1
Tel: 020 7821 8448

Furniture, works of art and paintings.

Nicholas S. Pitcher Oriental Art
(ref: Nicholas S. Pitcher)
1st Floor, 29 New Bond Street,
London W1Y 9HD
Tel: 020 7499 6621
Fax: 020 7499 6621

Early Chinese ceramics and works of art.

Planet Bazaar
151 Drummond Street,
London NW1 2PB
Tel: 020 7387 8326
Fax: 020 7387 8326
www.planetbazaar.co.uk

Designer furniture, art, glass, lighting, ceramics, books and eccentricities from the 1950s to 1980s.

Christopher Preston Ltd
(ref: C. Preston)
The Furniture Cave,
533 Kings Road,
London SW10 0TZ
Tel: 020 7352 4229

Antique furniture and decorative objects.

Annette Puttnam
Norton House,
Nr. Lewes, Iford,
Sussex BN7 3EJ
Tel: 01273 483366
Fax: 01273 483366

Radio Days
87 Lower Marsh,
London SE1 7AB
Tel: 020 7928 0800
Fax: 020 7928 0800

Lighting, telephones, radios, clothing, magazines and cocktail bars from the 1930s–1970s.

Raffety Walwyn
79 Kensington Church Street,
London W8 4BG
Tel: 020 7938 1100
Fax: 020 7938 2519
www.raffetyantiqueclocks.com

Fine antique clocks.

Rainbow Antiques
(ref: Rainbow)
329 Lillie Road,
London SW6 7NR
Tel: 020 7385 1323
Fax: 0870 052 1693

Italian and French period lighting from 1880–1940, chandeliers, lamps and lanterns.

Ranby Hall Antiques
(ref: Ranby Hall)
Barnby Moor, Retford,
Nottingham DN22 8JQ
Tel: 01777 860696
Fax: 01777 701317
www.ranbyhall.antiques-gb.com

Antiques, decorative items and contemporary objects.

Mark Ransom Ltd
(ref: Mark Ransom)
62 and 105 Pimlico Road,
London SW1W 8LS
Tel: 020 7259 0220
Fax: 020 7259 0323

Decorative Empire and French furniture.

RBR Group at Grays
(ref: RBR Group)
Stand 175, Grays Antiques Market,
58 Davies Street,
London W1Y 2LP
Tel: 020 7629 4769

Jewellery and objects.

Red Lion Antiques
(ref: Red Lion)
New Street, Petworth,
West Sussex GU28 0AS
Tel: 01798 344485
Fax: 01798 342367
www.redlion-antiques.com

Seventeenth to nineteenth-century furniture.

Gordon Reece Gallery
(ref: Gordon Reece)
16 Clifford Street,
London W1X 1RG
Tel: 020 7439 0007
Fax: 020 7437 5715
www.gordonreecegalleries.com

*Flat woven rugs and nomadic carpets, tribal
sculpture, jewellery, furniture, decorative and
non-European folk art especially ethnic and
oriental ceramics.*

Reel Poster Gallery
(ref: Reel Poster)
72 Westbourne Grove,
London W2 5SH
Tel: 020 7727 4488
Fax: 020 7727 4499
www.reelposter.com

Original vintage film posters.

Reel Thing, The
(ref: Reel Thing)
17 Royal Opera Arcade, Pall Mall,
London SW1Y 4UY
Tel: 020 7976 1830
Fax: 020 7976 1850
www.reelthing.co.uk

Purveyors of vintage sporting memorabilia.

Retro Exchange
20 Pembridge Road,
London W11
Tel: 020 7221 2055
Fax: 020 7727 4185
www.I/fel.trade.co.uk

Space age-style furniture and 1950's kitsch.

Retro Home
20 Pembridge Road,
London W11
Tel: 020 7221 2055
Fax: 020 7727 4185
www.I/fel.trade.co.uk

Bric-a-brac, antique furniture and objects of desire.

A. Rezai Persian Carpets
123 Portobello Road,
London W11 2DY
Tel: 020 7221 5012
Fax: 020 7229 6690

*Antique oriental carpets, kilims, tribal rugs
and silk embroideries.*

Riverbank Gallery Ltd
(ref: Riverbank)
High Street, Petworth,
West Sussex GU28 0AU
Tel: 01798 344401
Fax: 01798 343135

*Large English eighteenth and nineteenth-century
furniture, decorative items, garden furniture and
decorative paintings.*

Michele Rowan
V38 Antiquarias Antiques Market,
135 Kings Road,
London SW3 4PW
Tel: 020 7352 8744
Fax: 020 7352 8744

Antique jewellery.

Malcolm Rushton
Studio 3, 13 Belsize Grove,
London NW3 4UX
Tel: 020 7722 1989

Early oriental art.

Russell Rare Books
81 Grosvenor Street,
London W1X 9DE
Tel: 020 7629 0532
Fax: 020 7499 2983
www.folios.co.uk

Rare books.

Samiramis
M14–16 Grays Mews Antiques Market,
1–7 Davies Mews,
London W1Y 1FJ
Tel: 020 7629 1161
Fax: 020 7493 5106

Islamic pottery, silver, Eastern items and calligraphy.

Christopher F. Seidler
G13 Grays Mews Antiques Market,
1–7 Davies Mews,
London W1Y 2LP
Tel: 020 7629 2851

Medals, arms and militaria.

Shahdad Antiques
(ref: Shahdad)
A16–17 Grays-in-Mews,
1–7 Davies Mews,
London W1Y 2LP
Tel: 020 7499 0572
Fax: 020 7629 2176

Islamic and ancient works of art.

Bernard J. Shapero Rare Books
(ref: Bernard Shapero)
32 George Street,
London W1R 0EA
Tel: 020 7493 0876
Fax: 020 7229 7860
www.shapero.com

Guide books from the sixteenth to the twentieth century, antiquarian and rare books, English and continental literature, specialising in travel, natural history and colour plate.

Sharif
27 Chepstow Corner,
London W2 4XE
Tel: 020 7792 1861
Fax: 020 7792 1861

Oriental rugs, kilims, textiles and furniture.

Nicholas Shaw Antiques
(ref: N. Shaw)
Great Grooms Antique Centre,
Parbrook, Billinghurst,
West Sussex RH14 9EU
Tel: 01403 786 656
Fax: 01403 786 656
www.nicholas-shaw.com

Scottish and Irish fine silver, small silver and collector's items.

Shiraz Antiques
(ref: Shiraz)
1 Davies Mews,
London W1Y 1AR
Tel: 020 7495 0635
Fax: 020 7495 0635

Asian art, antiquities, glass, marble and pottery.

Sieff
49 Long Street, Tetbury,
Gloucestershire, GL8 8AA
Tel: 01666 504477
Fax: 01666 504478

Eighteenth and nineteenth-century French provincial fruitwood, and some twentieth-century furniture.

Sign of the Hygra
(ref: Hygra)
2 Middleton Road,
London E8 4BL
Tel: 020 7254 7074
Fax: 0870 125669
www.hygra.com

Boxes.

Sign of the Times
St Oswalds Mews,
London N6 2UT
Tel: 020 7584 3842
www.antiquesline.com

Furniture, decorative metalware and glass.

B. Silverman
26 London Silver Vaults,
Chancery Lane,
London WC2A 1QS
Tel: 020 7242 3269
Fax: 020 7430 7949
www.silverman-london.com

Seventeenth to nineteenth-century fine English silverware and silver flatware.

Jack Simons Antiques Ltd
(ref: Jack Simons)
37 The London Silver Vaults,
Chancery Lane,
London WC2A 1QS
Tel: 020 7242 3221
Fax: 020 7831 6541

Fine antique English and continental silver and objets d'art.

Sinai Antiques
219–221 Kensington Church Street,
London W8 7LX
Tel: 020 7229 6190

Antiques and works of art.

Sleeping Beauty
579–581 Kings Road,
London SW6 2DY
Tel: 020 7471 4711
Fax: 020 7471 4795
www.antiquebeds.com

Antique beds.

Solaris Antiques
(ref: Solaris)
170 Westbourne Grove,
London W11 2RW
Tel: 020 7229 8100
Fax: 020 7229 8300

Decorative antiques from France and Sweden, from
all periods up to 1970s

Something Different
254 Holloway Road,
London N7 6NE
Tel: 020 7697 8538
Fax: 020 7697 8538

Individually made African wood and stone sculptures

Somlo Antiques Ltd
7 Piccadilly Arcade,
London SW1Y 6NH
Tel: 020 7499 6526
Fax: 020 7499 0603
www.somloantiques.com

Vintage wristwatches and antique pocket watches.

Ian Spencer
17 Godfrey Street,
London SW3 3TA

Large desks, sets of chairs and dining tables.

Star Signings
Unit A18–A19 Grays Mews Antiques Market,
1–7 Davies Mews
London W1Y 2LP
Tel: 020 7491 1010
Fax: 020 7491 1070

Sporting autographs and memorabilia.

Steinway & Sons
44 Marylebone Lane,
London W1M 6EN
Tel: 020 7487 3391
Fax: 020 7935 0466

New and refurbished pianos.

Jane Stewart
C 26–27, Grays Mews Antiques Market,
1–7 Davies Mews,
London W1Y 2LP

Early seventeenth to nineteenth-century pewter,
oak and writing slopes.

Constance Stobo
31 Holland Street,
London W8 4HA
Tel: 020 7937 6282

Eighteenth and nineteenth-century pottery, English
lustre ware, and Staffordshire animals.

June & Tony Stone
(ref: J. & T. Stone)
75 Portobello Road,
London W11 2QB
Tel: 020 7221 1121

Fine antique boxes.

Succession
18 Richmond Hill, Richmond,
Surrey TW10 6QX
Tel: 020 8940 6774

Art Nouveau, Art Deco, furniture, bronzes, glass
and pictures.

Sugar Antiques
(ref: Sugar)
8–9 Pierrepont Arcade,
Camden Passage,
London N1 8EF
Tel: 020 7354 9896
Fax: 020 8931 5642
www.sugarantiques.com

Wristwatches, pocketwatches, costume jewellery,
lighters, fountain pens and small collectables.

Mark Sullivan
14 Cecil Court,
London WC2N 4EZ
Tel: 020 7836 7056
Fax: 020 8287 8492

Antiques and decorative items.

Swan at Tetsworth, The
(ref: The Swan)
High Street, Tetsworth, Thame,
Oxfordshire OX9 7AB
Tel: 01844 281777
Fax: 01844 281770
www.theswan.co.uk

Seventy dealers in historic Elizabethan coaching inn.

Talbot
65 Portobello Road,
London W11 2QB
Tel: 020 8969 7011

Fine scientific instruments.

Talking Machine, The
30 Watford Way,
London NW4 3AL
Tel: 020 8202 3473
www.gramophones.endirect.co.uk

Mechanical antiques typewriters, radios, music boxes, photographs, sewing machines, juke boxes, calculators and televisions.

Telephone Lines Ltd
(ref: Telephone Lines)
304 High Street, Cheltenham,
Gloucestershire GL50 3JF
Tel: 01242 583699
Fax: 01242 690033

Telephones.

Templar Antiques
(ref: Templar)
28 The Hall Antiques Centre,
359 Upper Street,
London N1 0PD
Tel: 020 7704 9448
Fax: 01621 819737
www.templar-antiques.co.uk

Eighteenth and nineteenth-century glass, English, Irish and Bohemian.

Temple Gallery
6 Clarendon Cross,
Holland Park,
London W11 4AP
Tel: 020 7727 3809
Fax: 020 7727 1546
www.templegallery.com

Russian and Greek icons, from twelfth to sixteenth century.

Themes & Variations
231 Westbourne Grove,
London W11 2SE
Tel: 020 7727 5531

Post-War design.

Thimble Society, The
(ref: Thimble Society)
Geoffrey van Arcade, 107 Portobello Road,
London W11 2QB
Tel: 020 7419 9562

Thimbles, sewing items, snuff boxes and lady's accessories.

Sue & Alan Thompson
(ref: S. & A. Thompson)
Highland Cottage, Broomne Hall Road,
Cold Harbout RH5 6HH
Tel: 01306 711970
Fax: 01306 711970

Objects of vertu, antique tortoiseshell items, period furniture and unusual collector's items.

Through the Looking Glass
(ref: Looking Glass)
563 Kings Road,
London SW6 2EB
Tel: 020 7736 7799
Fax: 020 7602 3678

Nineteenth-century mirrors.

Through the Looking Glass
(ref: Looking Glass)
137 Kensington Church Street,
London W8 7LP
Tel: 020 7221 4026
Fax: 020 7602 3678

Nineteenth-century mirrors.

Tin Tin Collectables
(ref: Tin Tin)
Ground Units 38–42, Antiques Market,
13–25 Church Street,
London NW8 8DT
Tel: 020 7258 1305
www.tintincollectables.com

Handbags, from Victorian to present day, decorative evening bags and luggage.

Tool Shop Auctions
78 High Street,
Needham Market,
Suffolk IP6 8AW
Tel: 01449 722992
www.uktoolshop.com

Auctioneers and dealers of antique woodworking tools and new Japanese, French and American tools.

Tool Shop, The
(ref: Tool Shop)
High Street, Needham Market,
Suffolk IP6 8AW
Tel: 01449 722992
Fax: 01449 722683
www.toolshop.demon.co.uk

Antique and usable carpenter's and joiner's tools.

Tower Bridge Antiques
(ref: Tower Bridge)
159–161 Tower Bridge Road,
London SE1 3LW
Tel: 020 7403 3660
Fax: 020 7403 6058

Town & Country Antiques
(ref: Town & Country)
88 Fulham Road,
London SW3 1HR
Tel: 020 7589 0660
Fax: 020 7823 7618
www.anthony-james.com

English furniture.

Travers Antiques
71 Bell Street,
London NW1 6SX
Tel: 020 7723 4376

Furniture and decorative items from 1820–1920.

Tredantiques
77 Hill Barton Road, Whipton,
Exeter EX1 3PW
Tel: 01392 447082
Fax: 01392 462200

Furniture.

Trio/Teresa Clayton
(ref: TRIO)
L24 Grays Mews Antiques Market,
1–7 Davies Mews,
London W1Y 2LP
Tel: 020 7493 2736
Fax: 020 7493 9344

Perfume bottles and Bohemian glass.

Turn on Lighting
116–118 Islington High Street,
Camden Passage,
London N1 8EG
Tel: 020 7359 7616
Fax: 020 7359 7616

Antique lighting specialists.

Vintage & Rare Guitars
(ref: V&R Guitars)
6 Denmark Street,
London WC2H 8LP
Tel: 020 7240 7500
Fax: 020 7373 0441
www.vintageandrareguitars.com

Guitars.

Vintage Wireless Shop
(ref: Vintage Wireless)
The Hewarths Sandiacre,
Nottingham NG10 5NQ
Tel: 0115 939 3139

Radios.

Michael Wakelin & Helen Linfield
(ref: M.W. & H.L.)
PO Box 48, Billingshurst,
West Sussex RH14 0YZ
Tel: 01403 700004
Fax: 01403 700004

*Metalware, pottery, treen, lighting, textiles and
mirrors.*

Graham Walpole
The Coach House,
189 Westbourne Grove,
London W11 2SB
Tel: 020 7229 0267
Fax: 020 7727 7584

*Small furniture, eighteenth and nineteenth-century
dolls' houses, equestrian items, bronzes, pictures and
decorative items.*

Westland & Company
(ref: Westland & Co.)
St. Michael's Church,
The Clergy House,
Mark Street,
London EC2A 4ER
Tel: 020 7739 8094
Fax: 020 7729 3620
www.westland.co.uk

*Period fireplaces, architectural elements and
panelling.*

**Westminster Group Antique Jewellery
(ref: Westminster)**
Stand 150, Grays Antiques Market,
58 Davies Street,
London W1Y 2LP
Tel: 020 7493 8672
Fax: 020 7493 8672

*Victorian and Edwardian secondhand jewellery and
watches.*

Wheels of Steel
B10–11 Grays Mews Antiques Market,
1–7 Davies Mews,
London W1Y 2LP
Tel: 020 8505 0450
Fax: 020 7629 2813

Trains and toys.

**Whitford Fine Art
(ref: Whitford)**
6 Duke Street, St. James',
London SW1Y 6BN
Tel: 020 7930 9332
Fax: 020 7930 5577

*Oil paintings and sculpture, from late nineteenth
century to twentieth century; post-War abstract and
pop art.*

Wilde Ones
283 Kings Road, Chelsea,
London SW3 5EW
Tel: 020 7352 9531
Fax: 020 7349 0828

Jewellery.

Jeff Williams
Grays Antiques Market,
58 Davies Street,
London W1K 5LP
Tel: 020 7629 7034

Toy trains.

**O. F. Wilson Ltd
(ref: O. F. Wilson)**
Queen's Elm Parade, Old Church Street,
London SW3 6EJ
Tel: 020 7352 9554
Fax: 020 7351 0765

*Continental furniture, French chimney pieces,
English painted decorative furniture and mirrors.*

Rod Wilson
Red Lion, New Street, Petworth,
West Sussex, GU28 0AS
Tel: 01798 344485
Fax: 01798 342367

Furniture.

Yacobs
Grays Mews Antiques Market,
1–7 Davies Mews,
London W1Y 2LP
Tel: 020 7629 7034
Fax: 020 7493 9344

Islamic art.

**Yazdani Mayfair Gallery
(ref: Yazdani)**
128 Mount Street, Mayfair,
London W1Y 5HA
Tel: 020 7491 2789
Fax: 020 7491 3437

*Ancient and Islamic art, Islamic ceramics, sculpture
and antiquities.*

Youll's Antiques
27–28 Charnham Street, Hungerford,
Berkshire RG17 0EJ
Tel: 01488 682046
Fax: 01488 684335
www.youll.com

*English/French furniture from seventeenth to
twentieth century, porcelain, silver and decorative
items.*

Zakheim
52 Ledbury Road,
London W11
Tel: 020 7221 4977

*Russian art from icons to Soviet, architectural,
and decorator's items.*

Zoom
Arch 65, Cambridge Grove,
Hammersmith,
London W6 OLD
Tel: 0958 372 975
Tel: 07000 966620
Fax: 020 8846 9779
www.retrozoom.com

*Twentieth-century furniture, lighting, telephones and
works of art.*

There follows our selection of the best antiques centres and markets in the country. These present the best of both worlds, with several dealers showing their particular specialities at the fair prices we expect from the reputable retailer.

BEDFORDSHIRE, BUCKINGHAMSHIRE, HERTFORDSHIRE
Antiques at Wendover Antiques Centre
The Old Post Office, 25 High Street,
Wendover HP22 6DU
Tel: 01296 625335
Dealers: 30

Barkham Antiques Centre
Barkham Street, Barkham RG40 4PJ
Tel: 0118 9761 355   Fax: 0118 9764 355

Buck House Antiques Centre
47 Wycombe End, Old Town,
Beaconsfield HP9 1LZ
Tel: 01494 670714

Luton Antiques Centre
Auction House, Crescent Road,
Luton LU1 2NA
Tel: 01582 405281   Fax: 01582 454080

Woburn Abbey Antiques Centre
Woburn Abbey, Bedfordshire MK17 9WA
Tel: 01525 290350   Fax: 01525 290271
Dealers: 50

BRISTOL, BATH, SOMERSET
Bartlett Street Antiques Centre
5-10 Bartlett Street, Bath BA1 2QZ
Tel: 01225 466689   Fax: 01225 444146
Dealers: 50+

Bath Saturday Antiques Market
Walcot Street, Bath BA1 5BD
Tel: 01225 448263   Fax: 01225.317154
Mobile: 083653 4893
Dealers: 70+

CAMBRIDGESHIRE
Fitzwilliam Antique Centre
Fitzwilliam Street, Peterborough PE1 2RX
Tel: 01733 565415

Hive Antiques Market, The
Unit 3, Dales Brewery, Gwydir St,
Cambridge CB1 2LG
Tel: 01223 300269

Gwydir Street Antiques Centre
Untis 1&2 Dales Brewery, Gwydir St,
Cambridge CB1 2LJ
Tel: 01223 356391

Old Bishop's, The Palace Antique Centre
Tower Road, Little Downham, Nr Ely
Cambridgeshire CB6 2TD
Tel: 01353 699177

CHESHIRE AND STRAFFORDSHIRE
Antique Furniture Warehouse
Unit 3-4 , Royal Oak Buildings, Cooper Street,
Stockport, Cheshire SK1 3QJ
Tel: 0161 429 8590   Fax: 0161 480 5375

Knutsford Antiques Centre
113 King Street, Knutsford, WA16 6EH
Tel: 01565 654092

CORNWALL
Chapel Street Antiques Market
61/62 Chapel Street, Penzance TR18 4AE
Tel: 01736 363267
Dealers: 30-40

Waterfront Antiques Complex
4 Quay Street, Falmouth, Cornwall TR11 3HH
Tel: 01326 311491
Dealers: 20-25

THE COTSWOLDS
The Antique and Interior Centre
51A Long Street GL8 8AA
Tel: 01666 505083
Dealers: 10

CUMBRIA AND LANCASHIRE
Carlisle Antiques Centre
Cecil Hall, 46A Cecil Street,
Carlisle CA1 1NT
Tel: 0122 8536 910   Fax: 0122 8536 910
carlsle-antiques.co.uk

Cockermouth Antiques Market
Courthouse, Main Street,
Cockermouth CA15 5XM
Tel: 01900 826746

DERBYSHIRE AND NOTTINGHAMSHIRE
Alfreton Antiques Centre
11 King Street, Alfreton DE55 7AF
Tel: 01773 520781
alfretonantiques@supanet.com

Castle Gate Antiques Centre
55 Castle Gate, Newark NG24 1BE
Tel: 01636 700076   Fax: 01636 700144
Dealers: 10

Chappells and the Antiques Centre Bakewell
King Street DE45 1DZ
Tel: 01629 812 496   Fax: 01629 814 531
bacc@chappells-antiques.co.uk
Dealers: 30

Memory Lane Antiques Centre
Nottingham Road, Ripley DE5 3AS
Tel: 01773 570184
Dealers: 40-50

Portland Street Antiques Centre
Portland Street, Newark NG24 4XF
Tel: 01636 674397   Fax: 01636 674397

Top Hat Antiques Centre
70-72 Derby Road, Nottingham NG1 5DF
Tel: 0115 9419 143
sylvia@artdeco-fairs.co.uk

DEVONSHIRE
Abingdon House
136 High Street, Honiton EX14 8JP
Tel: 01404 42108
Dealers: 20

Antique Centre on the Quay, The
The Quay, Exeter EX2 4AP
Tel: 01392 493501
home free.emailamail.co.uk

Barbican Antiques Centre
82-84 Vauxhall Street, Barbican PL4 0EX
Tel: 01752 201752
Dealers: 40+

Honiton Antique Centre McBains Antiques
Exeter Airport, Industrial Est., Exeter EX5 2BA
Tel: 01392 366261   Fax: 01392 365572
mcbains@netcomuk.co.uk
Dealers:10

Newton Abbot Antiques Centre
55 East Street, Newton Abbot TQ12 2JP
Tel: 01626 354074
Dealers:40

Sidmouth Antiques and Collectors Centre
All Saints Road, Sidmouth EX10 8ES
Tel: 01395 512 588

DORSET
Bridport Antique Centre
5 West Allington, Bridport DT6 5BJ
Tel: 01308 425885

Colliton Antique Centre
Colliton Street, Dorchester DT1 1XH
Tel: 01305 269398 / 01305 260115

Emporium Antiques Centre
908 Christchurch Road, Boscombe,
Bournemouth, Dorset BH7 6DL
Tel: 01202 422380   Fax: 01202 433348
Dealers: 8

Mattar Antique Centre
Mattar Arcade, 17 Newlands DT9 3JG
Tel: 01935 813464   Fax: 01935 813464

ESSEX
Baddow Antique Centre
The Bringey, Church Street, Great Baddow,
Chelmsford, Essex CM2 7JW
Tel: 01245 476159

Finchingfield Antiques Centre
The Green, Finchingfield, Braintree,
Essex CM7 4JX
Tel: 01371 810258   Fax: 01371 810258
Dealers: 45

Harwich Antique Centre
19 King's Quay Street, Harwich, Essex
Tel: 01255 554719   Fax: 01255 554719
Dealers: 50
harwich@worldwideantiques.co.uk

Saffron Walden Antiques Centre
1 Market Row, Saffron Walden,
Essex CB10 1HA
Tel: 01799 524534   Fax: 01799 524703

HAMPSHIRE AND ISLE OF WIGHT
Dolphin Quay Antique Centre
Queen Street, Emsworth,
Hampshire PO10 7BU
Tel: 01243 379994   Fax: 01243 379251
enquiriesnancy@netscapeonline.co.uk

Eversley Antique Centre Ltd
Church Lane, Eversley, Hook,
Hampshire RG27 0PX
Tel: 0118 932 8518
Dealers: 11

Lyndhurst Antique Centre
19-21 High Street, Lyndhurst,
Hampshire SO43 7BB
Tel: 0238 0284 000
Dealers: 50

The Antique Centre
Britannia Road, Southampton,
Hampshire SO14 0QL
Tel: 0238 0221 022
Dealers: 46

The Antique Quarter
'Old' Northam Road, Southampton,
Hampshire SO14 0QL
Tel: 0238 0233 393
Dealers: 15

GLOUCESTERSHIRE
Struwwelpeter
The Old School House,
175 London Road, Charlton Kings,
Cheltenham Gloucester GL52 6HN
Tel: 01242 230088
Dealers: 7

HEREFORD AND WORCESTERSHIRE
Antique Centre, The
5-8 Lion Street, Kidderminster,
Worcestershire DY10 1PT
Tel: 01562 740389   Fax: 01562 740389
Dealers: 12

Hereford Antique Centre
128 Widemarsh Street, Hereford HR4 9HN
Tel: 01432 266242
Dealers: 35

Leominster Antique Centre
34 Broad Street, Leominster HR6 8BS
Tel: 01568 615505
Dealers: 22

Leominster Antique Market
14 Broad Street, Leominster HR6 8BS
Tel: 01568 612 189
Dealers: 15+

Linden House Antiques
3 Silver Street, Stansted CM24 8HA
Tel: 01279 812 373

Malvern Link Antique Centre
154 Worcester Road, Malvern Link,
Worcestershire WR14 1AA
Tel: 01684 575750
Dealers: 10

Ross on Wye Antique Gallery
Gloucester Road, Ross on Wye,
Herefordshire HR9 5BU
Tel: 01989 762290   Fax: 01989 762291
Dealers: 91

Worcester Antiques Centre
15 Reindeer Court, Mealcheapen Street,
Worcester WR1 4DF
Tel: 01905 610680/1   Fax: 01905 610681
Dealers: 45

KENT
Antiques Centre, The
120 London Road, Tubs Hill TN13 1BA
Tel: 01732 452104

Coach House Antique Centre
2a Duck Lane, Northgate, Canterbury,
Kent CT1 2AE
Tel: 01227 463117
Dealers: 7

Copperfield Antique & Craft Centre
Unit 4, Copperfield's Walkway, Spital Street,
Dartford, Kent DA1 2DE
Tel: 01322 281445
Dealer: 35

Corn Exchange Antiques Centre
64 The Pantiles, Tunbridge Wells, Kent TN2 5TN
Tel: 01892 539652   Fax: 01892 538454
Dealers: 11

Tenterden Antiques Centre
66 High Street TN30 6AU
Tel: 01580 765885   Fax: 01580 765655
Dealers: 20+

Tunbridge Wells Antique Centre
12 Union Square, The Pantiles,
Tunbridge Wells TN4 8HE
Tel: 01892 533708
twantique@aol.com

Village Antique Centre
4 High Street, Brasted, Kent TN16 1RF
Tel: 01959 564545
Dealers: 15

LEICESTERSHIRE, RUTLAND AND NORTHAMPTONESHIRE
Finedon Antique (Centre)
11-25 Bell Hill, Finedon NN9 5NB
Tel: 01933 681260   Fax: 01933 681779
sales@finedonantiques.com

The Village Antique Market
62 High Street, Weedon NN7 4QD
Tel: 01327 342 015
Dealers: 40

LINCOLNSHIRE
Astra House Antique Centre
Old RAF Helswell, Nr Caenby Corner,
Gainsborough, Lincolnshire DN21 5TL
Tel: 01427 668312
Dealers: 50

Guardroom Antiques
RAF Station Henswell,
Gainsborough DN21 5TL
Tel: 01427 667113
Dealers: 50

Henswell Antiques Centre
Caenby Corner Estate, Henswell Cliff
Gainsborough DN21 5TL
Tel: 01427 668 389   Fax: 01427 668 935
info@Hemswell-antiques.com
Dealers:270

St. Martin's Antique Centre
23a High Street, St Martin's, Stamford PE9 2LF
Tel: 01780 481158   Fax: 01780 766598

Stamford Antiques Centre
The Exchange Hall, Broad Street,
Stamford PE1 9PX
Tel: 01780 762 605   Fax: 01733 244 717
anoc1900@compuserve.com
Dealers: 40

LONDON
Alfie's Antique Market
13-25 Church Street NW8 8DT
Tel: 020 7723 6066   Fax: 020 7724 0999
alfies@clara.net

Antiquarius
131-41 King's Road SW3 4PW
Tel: 020 7351 5353   Fax: 020 7351 5350
antique@dial.pipex.com

Bermondsey
corner of Long Lane & Bermondsey Street
SE1 3UN
Tel: 020 7351 5353

Camden Passage
Upper Street, Islington N1
Tel: 020 7359 9969
www.camdenpassage.com

Grays Mews Antique Markets
58 Davis Street, and 1-7 Davis Mews WIY 2LP
Tel: 020 7629 7034
Dearlers: 300

Hampstead Antique and Craft Market
12 Heath Street, London NW3 6TE
Tel: 020 7431 0240   Fax: 020 7794 4620
Dealers: 20

Jubilee Market Hall
1 Tavistock Court, The Piazza
Covent Garden WC2 E8BD
Tel: 020 7836 2139

Lillie Road
237 Lillie Road, SW6
Tel: 020 7381 2500   Fax: 020 7381 8320

Portobello Road
In Notting Hill Gate W10 and W11
Tel: 020 7727 7684   Fax: 020 7727 7684
Dealers: 280

Spitalfields,
65 Brushfield Street E1 6AA
Tel: 020 8983 3779   Fax: 020 7377 1783

NORFOLK
Fakenham Antique Centre,
The Old Congregational Church, 14 Norwich
Road, Fakenham, Norfolk NR21 8AZ
Tel: 01328 862941
Dealers: 20

NORTHUMBERLAND AND DURHAM
The Village Antique Market
62 High Street, Weedon NN7 4QD
Tel: 01327 342015
Dealers: 40

OXFORDSHIRE
Antique on High Ltd
85 High Street, Oxford OX1 4BG
Tel: 01865 251075   Fax: 0129 665 5580
Dealers: 38

Country Markets Antiques and Collectables
Country Garden Centre, Newbury Road,
Chilton, nr. Didcot OX11 0QN
Tel: 01235 835125   Fax: 01235 833068
countrymarketsantiquesandcollectables
@breathnet.com
Dealers: 35

Old George Inn Antique Galleries
104 High Street, Burford, Oxfordshire OX18 4QJ
Tel: 01993 823319
Dealers: 22

Station Mill Antique Centre
Station Yard Industrial Estate, Chipping Norton,
Oxfordshire OX7 5HX
Tel: 01608 644563   Fax: 01608 644563
Dealers: 73

Swan at Tetsworth
High Street, Tetsworth, Oxfordshire OX9 7AB,
Tel: 01844 281777   Fax: 01844 281770
antiques@theswan.co.uk
Dealers: 80

SHROPSHIRE
Bridgnorth Antique Centre
Whitburn Street, Bridgnorth,
Shropshire WV16 4QP
Tel: 01746 768055
Dealers: 19

K. W. Swift
56 Mill Street, Ludlow SY8 1BB
Tel: 01584 878571   Fax: 01746 714407
Dealers: 20, book market.

Old Mill Antique Centre
Mill Street, Shropshire WV15 5AG
Tel: 01746 768778   Fax: 01746 768944
Dealers: 90

Princess Antique Centre
14a The Square, Shrewsbury SY1 1LH
Tel: 01743 343701
Dealers: 100 stallholders

Shrewsbury Antique Centre
15 Princess House, The Square,
Shrewsbury SY1 1UT
Tel: 01743 247 704

Shrewsbury Antique Market
Frankwell Quay Warehouse,
Shrewsbury SY3 8LG
Tel: 01743 350619
Dealers: 30

Stretton Antiques Market
36 Sandford Avenue, Stretton SY6 6BH
Tel: 01694 723718   Fax: 01694 723718
Dealers: 60

STAFFORDSHIRE

Lion Antique Centre
8 Market Place, Uttoxeter, Staffordshire ST14 8HP
Tel: 01889 567717
Dealers: 28

SUFFOLK

Church Street Centre
6e Church Street, Woodbridge, Suffolk IP12 1DH
Tel: 01394 388887
Dealers: 10

Long Melford Antiques Centre
Chapel Maltings, CO10 9HX
Tel: 01787 379287   Fax: 01787 379287
Dealers: 40

Woodbridge Gallery
23 Market Hill, Woodbridge, Suffolk IP12 4OX
Tel: 01394 386500   Fax: 01394 386500
Dealers: 35

SURREY

The Antiques Centre
22 Haydon Place, Corner of Martyr Road,
Guildford GU1 4LL
Tel: 01483 567817
Dealers: 6

The Antiques Warehouse
Badshot Farm, St George's Road,
Runfold GU9 9HY
Tel: 01252 317590   Fax: 01252 879751
Dealers: 40

Enterprise Collectors Market
Station Parade, Eastbourne, East Sussex BN21 1BD
Tel: 01323 732690
Dealers: 15

The Hampton Court Emporium
52-54 Bridge Road, East Molesey,
Surrey KT8 9HA
Tel: 020 8941 8876
Dealers: 16

The Kingston Antiques Market
29-31 London Road, Kingston-upon-Thames,
Surrey KT2 6ND
Tel: 020 8549 2004   Fax: 020 8549 3839
webmaster@antiquesmarket.co.uk
Dealers: 90

Packhouse Antique Centre
Hewetts Kilns, Tongham Road, Runfold,
Farnham, Surrey GU10 1PQ
Tel: 01252 781010   Fax: 01252 783876
hewett@cix.co.uk
Dealers: 80

Victoria and Edward Antique Centre
61 West Street, Dorking, Surrey RH4 1BS
Tel: 01306 889645
Dealers: 26

SUSSEX

Almshouses Arcade
19 The Hornet PO19 4JL
Tel: 01243 771994

Brighton Flea Market
31A Upper Street, James's Street BN2 1JN
Tel: 01273 624006   Fax: 01273 328665
arwilkinson@aol.com

Eastbourne Antiques Market
80 Seaside, Eastbourne BN22 7QP
Tel: 01323 642233
Dealers: 25

Lewes Antique Centre
20 Cliff High Street, Lewes BN7 2AH
Tel: 01273 476 148 / 01273 472 173
Dealers: 60

The Old Town Antiques Centre
52 Ocklynge Road, Eastbourne, East Sussex
BN21 1PR
Tel: 01323 416016
Dealers: 16

Olinda House Antiques
South Street, Rotherfield, Crowborough,
East Sussex TN6 3LL,
Tel: 01892 852609

Petworth Antiques Market
East Street, Petworth, GU28 0AB
Tel: 01798 342073   Fax: 01798 344566

WARWICKSHIRE

Barn Antique Centre
Long Marston Ground, Station Road, Long
Marsdon, Stratford-upon-Avon CV37 8RB
Tel: 01789 721399   Fax: 01789 721390
barnantiques@aol.com
Dealers: 50

Bridford Antique Centre
Warwick House, 94-96 High Street, Bidford on
Avon, Alcester, Warwickshire B50 4AF
Tel: 01789 773680
Dealers: 7

Dunchurch Antique Centre
16a Daventry Road, Dunchurch, Rugby,
CV22 6NS
Tel: 01788 522450
Dealers: 10

Malthouse Antique Centre
4 Market Place, Alcester, Warwickshire B49 5AE
Tel: 01789 764032
Dealers: 20

Stables Antique Centre, The
Hatton Country World, Dark Lane CV35 8XA
Tel: 01926 842405
Dealers: 25

Stratford Antiques and Interiors Centre Ltd
Dodwell Trading Estate, Evesham Road
CV37 9SY
Tel: 01789 297729 Fax: 01789 297710
info@stratfordantiques.co.uk
Dealers: 20

Vintage Antiques Centre
36 Market Place, Warwick CV34 4SH
Tel: 01926 491527
vintage@globalnet.co.uk
Dealers: 20

Warwick Antiques Centre
22 High Street, Warwick CV34 4AP
Tel: 01926 491382 / 01926 495704
Dealers: 32

WILTSHIRE
Brocante Antiques Centre
6 London Road, Marlborough SN8 1PH
Tel: 01672 516512 Fax: 01672 516512
brocante@brocanteantiquescentre.co.uk
Dealers: 20

Marlborough Parade Antique Centre, The
The Parade, Marlborough SN8 1NE
Tel: 01672 515331
Dealers: 70

YORKSHIRE
Arcadia Antiques Centre
12-14 The Arcade, Goole,
East Yorkshire DN14 5PY
Tel: 01405 720549
Dealers: 20

Banners Collectables
Banners Business Centre, Attercliffe Road,
Sheffield, South Yorkshire S9 3QS
Tel: 0114 244 0742
Dealers: 50

Barmouth Road Antique Centre
Barmouth Court
off Abbeydale, Sheffield, South Yorkshire S7 2DH
Tel: 0114 255 2711 Fax: 0114 258 2672
Dealers: 60

Cavendish Antique & Collectors Centre
44 Stonegate, York YO1 8AS
Tel: 01904 621666 Fax: 01904 644400
Dealers: 60

The Harrogate Antiques Centre
The Ginnel, off Parliament Street HG1 2RB
Tel: 01423 508857 Fax: 01423 508857
Dealers: 50

Halifax Antique Centre
Queens Road, Halifax,
West Yorkshire HX1 4OR
Tel: 01422 366 657 Fax: 01422 369 293
antiques@halifaxac.u-net.com
Dealers: 30

Malton Antique Market
2 Old Maltongate, Malton YO17 0EG
Tel: 01653 692 732

Pickering Antique Centre
Southgate, Pickering,
North Yorkshire YO18 8BN
Tel: 01751 477210 Fax: 01751 477210
Dealers: 35

Stonegate Antique Centre
41 Stonegate, York, North Yorkshire YO1 8AW
Tel: 01904 613888 Fax: 01904 644400
Dealers: 120

York Antiques Centre
2a Lendal, York YO1 8AA
Tel: 01904 641445 / 641582
Dealers: 16+

SCOTLAND
Clola Antiques Centre
Shannas School House,
Clola by Mintlaw AB42 8AE
Tel: 01771 624584 Fax: 01771 624584
Dealers: 10

Scottish Antique & Arts Centre
Abernyte PH14 9SJ
Tel: 01828 686401 Fax: 01828 686199

WALES
Antique Market
6 Market Street, Hay-on-Wye HR3 5AD
Tel: 01497 820175

Cardiff Antiques Centre
10-12 Royal Arcade CF10 2AE
Tel: 01222 398891
Dealers: 13

Chapel Antiques
Methodist Chapel, Holyhead Road, Froncysyllte,
Denbighshire, Llangollen LL20 7RA
Tel: 01691 777624 Fax: 01691 777624
Dealers: 20

Jacobs Antique Centre
West Canal Wharf, Cardiff C51 5DB
Tel: 01222 390939
Dealers: 50

Index